"Say Can You Deny Me"

A GUIDE TO SURVIVING MUSIC
BY WOMEN
FROM THE 16TH
THROUGH THE 18TH CENTURIES

"Say Can You Deny Me"

A GUIDE TO SURVIVING MUSIC
BY WOMEN
FROM THE 16TH
THROUGH THE 18TH CENTURIES

Barbara Garvey Jackson

THE UNIVERSITY OF ARKANSAS PRESS

FAYETTEVILLE • 1994

98 97 96 95 94   5 4 3 2 1

Designed by Ellen Beeler

The paper used in this publication meets the minimum requirements of the American
National Standard for Permanence of Paper for Printed Library Materials
Z39.48-1984. ⊗

Library of Congress Cataloging-in-Publication Data

Jackson, Barbara Garvey.
    Say can you deny me: a guide to surviving music by women from the 16th through
  the 18th centuries / Barbara Garvey Jackson.
        p.   cm.
    Includes bibliographical references and index.
    ISBN 1-55728-303-6
    1. Women composers' music—Bibliography—Union lists.   2. Catalogs. Union.
  I. Title.
    ML128.W7J3   1994
    016.78'082—dc20   94-6332
                                                  CIP
                                                   MN

To Kern Jackson

A partner in the search for music by women composers
as in all else

Acknowledgments

The author deeply appreciates the help and cooperation of many libraries, publishers, and individuals. In the list that follows, all names of libraries are the names of the libraries as they were at the date of our correspondence; some have changed in the interim. In Austria: Rosemarie Gruber, Librarian, Salzburger Museum Carolino Augusteum (Salzburg); Dr. Otto Biba, Gesellschaft der Musikfreunden (Vienna); Hofrat Dr. Günter Brosche, Direktor, Musiksammlung, Österreichesches Nationalbibliothek (Vienna). In Belgium: Dr. Paul Raspé, bibliothécaire, Conservatoire Royal de Musique de Bruxelles (Brussels); the publishing company Alamire (Peer). In Denmark: Susanne Thorbek, Musikafdelingen, Det Kongelige Bibliothek (Copenhagen). In France: Departement de la musique, Bibliothéque Nationale (Paris). In Germany: A. Winter, Bibliothekarin, Sektion Ästhetik und Kunstwissenschaften, Der Humboldt-Universität (Berlin); Wolfgang Goldhan, Direktor der Musikabteilung, Deutsche Staatsbibliothek (Berlin); Helmut Hell, Musikabteilung, Staatsbibliothek Preußischer Kulturbesitz (Berlin); I. Kräupl-Mohamed, Bibliothekarin, Anton-und-Katharina-Kippenberg-Stiftung, Goethe-Museum (Düsseldorf); Dr. Wolfgang Reich, Direktor, and Marina Lang, Fachreferentin, Sächsische Landesbibliothek (Dresden); Robert Münster, Bayerische Staatsbibliothek (Munich); Dr. Gisela Urbanek, Bibliotheksoberrätin, Staatliche Bibliothek Regensburg (Regensburg); Hùgo Angerer, Furst Thurn und Taxis Zentralarchiv-Hofbibliothek (Regensburg); Dr. Rafael Köhler, Bischöfliche Zentralbibliothek (Regensburg). In Great Britain: Nicholas Chadwick, Music Librarian, The British Library (London); The Fitzwilliam Museum, University of Cambridge (Cambridge). In Italy: Giorgio Piobini, Il bibliotecario, Civico Museo Bibliografico Musicale (Bologna); Agostina Zecca Laterza, Conservatorio di Musica "Giuseppe Verdi" (Milan); Biblioteca Ambrosiana (Milan); P. Gioacchino d'Andrea, direttore, Biblioteca Provinciale Francescana

"P. Ludovico da Casoria"; Convento S. Chiara (Naples); Biblioteca Casanatense (Rome). In the Netherlands: Dr. W. H. J. Dekkar, Librarian, Stichting Toonkunst-Bibliotheek (Amsterdam). In Poland: Dr. Stefan Kubów, director of the University Library, Biblioteka Uniwersytecka (Wroclaw, Poland); Prof. Irena Poniatowska, University of Warsaw Institute of Musicology (Warsaw). In Russia: G. A. Timoshchenkova, Department of Published and Recorded Music, Gosudarsstvennaya Ordena Lenina Biblioteka SSSR imeni V. I. Lenina (Moscow). In the U.S.: Bart Smith, The Newberry Library (Chicago); Mrs. Nym Cooke, Library Assistant, Isham Memorial Library, Harvard University (Cambridge, Mass.); Music Division, The Library of Congress (Washington D.C.); Music Library, University of Illinois (Urbana); Music Library, University of North Carolina (Chapel Hill); Yale University (New Haven, Conn.); Werner Josten Library, Smith College (Northhampton, Mass.); Forbes Library (Northhampton, Mass.); North Texas State University Library (Denton); Joel Silver, Librarian, The Lilly Library, Bloomington (Bloomington, Ind.); Sylvia Glickman, president, Hildegard Publishing Company; Alan Pedigo (Booneville, Ark.), who located the violin sonata of Helene Liebmann in Leipzig; Prof. Marjorie Rudolph, now Emerita, University of Arkansas Department of Foreign Languages, for her translation of Russian correspondence (Fayetteville); and Dr. Jean Woods, Professor Emerita of the University of Oregon, for information on learned German women (Portland).

Very heartfelt thanks go to Christine Martin, Stellvertretende Leitung, RISM-A/II (Frankfurt) for providing a listing of composers and works in the processed files of RISM Series A/II: Music Manuscripts 1600–1800 elec-tronic database (status as of March 26, 1992), and for a listing of the new library sigla for German libraries. A separate publication on the women composers in RISM A/II is planned by RISM Central Editorial Office in Frankfurt in collaboration with the Arbeitskreis "Frau und Musik" in Kassel at some time in the future.

Special thanks go to two specialized libraries and study centers in Germany that are especially devoted to research and the fostering of perfor-mance of works by women composers. Both libraries have especially rich collections of nineteenth- and twentieth-century works, but each holds some earlier original prints and manuscripts, as well as a valuable large collection of microform, photographic, and handwritten copies of prints and manu-scripts from earlier periods. They are also actively working to acquire modern editions of earlier music as they become available. Frau und Musik Internationaler Arbeitskreis/Archiv in Kassel, affiliated with the Gesamthochschule Kassel, contains several thousand compositions, manu-scripts, autographs, theses, books, iconography, and sound documents and has published a catalogue of their scores. They also publish a journal, *INFO: Archivnachrichten*, and provide various research services to their members. The Internationale Komponistinnen-Bibliothek der Stadt Unna, affiliated with the Hochschule Detmold, is a merger of the large collection of the Europäisches Frauenmusik Archiv, formerly in Düsseldorf, and the private collection of Elke Mascha Blankenburg (Cologne). The curator of the Unna collection, Antje Olivier, has previously published catalogues of the books, scores, and recordings in the Düsseldorf collection, and Elke Blankenburg has recently published a catalogue of the new Unna collection.

There are many private working collections, primarily of microfilms and photocopies, in the United States, Canada, and Europe, but I have had especially invaluable help from Dr. Calvert Johnson, Agnes Scott College (Decatur, Ga.); William Bauer, Ars Femina Ensemble (Louisville, Ky.); Annie Janiero Randall, graduate student at University of Cincinnati College-Conservatory of Music; and Ursula Rempel, University of Manitoba (Winnipeg, Canada). I am very grateful to them for their generous contribution of time and information and for allowing me to examine private collections not open to the public.

Research time and a grant from the Fulbright College of Arts and Sciences of the University of Arkansas, Fayetteville, facilitated the beginning of this project, and the research time made available to me through early retirement from teaching made its completion possible. I am very grateful to the College and the University for both. In the nearly forty years I have been at the University, the library and its staff have been extremely helpful. No part of the entire institution has been more unfailingly helpful and efficient in helping my research over the years than the Interlibrary Loan Division of the library, which has brought the world to my office in Fayetteville. For many projects, the Special Collections Division in Mullins Library has been of great help, first under Curator Samuel Sizer, and currently under Curator Michael Dabrishus. The Jackson collection (my own working collection of microfilms, photocopies, books, and other materials on women's music) will eventually go to that collection. I have also had wonderful help from the Reference Division of Mullins Library, especially in my OCLC search, and from Music Cataloguer Jennifer Kolmes, Fine Arts Librarian Norma Mosby, and Director John Harrison.

It has been a great pleasure to work with the University of Arkansas Press and with my editor, Scot Danforth, and I gratefully acknowledge his guidance and assistance with this project—including his inspired suggestion for the title.

In the preparation of this book, my husband, Dr. Kern C. Jackson (Professor Emeritus of Geology, University of Arkansas), has traveled with

me to several libraries and worked tirelessly in the search for women composers in printed catalogues. We thank the Leslie Sims family (then in
Raleigh, N.C.) for hospitality when we were working at the music library at
the University of North Carolina at Chapel Hill; the Paul Jacksons, whose
home has always been our headquarters when working at the Library of
Congress or the University of Maryland; and members of the Garvey family
in Champaign-Urbana, where we have spent many hours at the University
of Illinois Library.

Finally, this book could not have been written without the encouragement and hours of hard work contributed by my husband, Kern. His interest
in the project helped it to be launched, his hours of library work contributed
countless entries to the book, and in our hours of discussion about the project, he made many excellent suggestions for organization and solutions for
other problems in the project. And, finally, his encouragement to stick to the
job and finish it and his proofreading of the entire manuscript have made
the completion of the work possible.

As this volume goes to press, word has been received of the untimely
death of Jane L. Baldauf Berdes in August 1993. Her extensive library and
archives on music in Venice and on the role of women in music history will
become the Dr. Jane L. Berdes Archive for Women in Music at the Duke
University Music Library and will be a new and valuable resource in the
United States for the time period covered in this *Guide*.

Contents

Preface

With the current great interest in studying, performing, editing, and publishing the heritage of music from the past by women composers, there is need for a convenient guide to those works that are known to survive in European and American libraries. I became particularly aware of this need when writing a chapter on seventeenth- and eighteenth-century women in music for a recent music history text. It was quickly apparent that everyone working in this field must do certain basic bibliographic work all over again before it is possible to start any particular project, and that if a more comprehensive *Guide* existed, much duplication of effort could be avoided. By bringing scattered information together in one reference work on surviving music by women of the renaissance, baroque, and classic periods of music, it will also be easier to identify some of the areas in which further search or clarification is needed. Moreover, the *Guide* will make known materials more accessible and searches much more efficient. For performers and publishers who are primarily interested in going "beyond biography"[1] to bring the music itself to life it is hoped that this *Guide* will make access to the music easier. Those works known to have been extant until recent loss or destruction are also listed, together with what is known of their loss. The phrase "Say Can You Deny Me" in the title of the *Guide* is the first line of a song by Gertrud Elisabeth Mara, one of the greatest singers of the eighteenth century who was also a composer.

Although original copies have survived for many works listed in this *Guide,* for a distressingly large number only single copies survive, even of published works. While our century is one of rediscovery of the heritage of women in the arts, it has at the same time been a century of large-scale

---

1. "Beyond Biography" was the title of the Seventh International Congress on Women in Music, Utrecht, the Netherlands, May 29–June 2, 1991.

destruction. Books and music become fragile with age and will not last forever, even without the aid of the wars and natural disasters that have taken their toll. Music by women was probably among the music lost in the Lisbon earthquake of the eighteenth century; it was undoubtedly lost in Warsaw in1939 and in World War II air raids in Dresden and Milan; and it is certainly in peril today in the Balkans. Music can get lost in libraries even in peacetime when it is misshelved or stolen (for example, a work of Anna Bon that is supposed to be in a Moscow library cannot now be found, as is also the case for some Badalla motets catalogued in Brussels). Current wars and civil unrest certainly will lead to permanent losses. However, nowadays almost every scholar who is studying particular works has assembled some sort of microfilm collection, and there are several working collections of microfilms, photocopies, and manuscript copies that have been developed by scholars, performers, and publishers. Thus, for some of the repertory, the music has been disseminated, and many formerly sole copies have been filmed and now exist in more than one copy. The publication of modern editions of previously rare works also provides protection for their survival. For these reasons, I have shown copies of library originals in institutional or private collections in individual entries. I am hopeful that more such copies will come to light in the future.

Much valuable bibliographic work has been done on women composers in recent years, culminating in Aaron Cohen's massive *International Encyclopedia of Women Composers* (2 vols., 2d edition, 1987) and the forthcoming *New Grove Dictionary of Women Composers*. There are now several dissertations on women composers, such as Isabella Leonarda (Stewart Carter, 1987), Antonia Bembo (Marinella Laini, 1990, and Claire Fontjein, ongoing), and Elisabeth-Claude Jacquet de la Guerre (Carol Bates, 1975), that provide works lists for their subjects, and most (but not all) give the locations of individual works that are not found in modern editions. Many, but by no means all, of the entries on women composers in the *New Grove Dictionary of Music and Musicians* (1980) and *Die Musik in Geschichte und Gegenwart* (completed 1986) give works lists; some also give the locations of manuscripts. Bibliographies for some specific instrument repertories also give locations of works, among them Joan M. Meggett, *Keyboard Music by Women Composers: A Catalog and Bibliography* (1981), Heidi M. Boenke, *Flute Music by Women Composers: An Annotated Catalogue* (1988), Rose-Marie Johnson, *Violin Music by Women Composers: A Bio-Bibliographical Guide* (1989), and Adel Heinrich, *Organ and Harpsichord Music by Women Composers: An Annotated Catalog* (1991). But a unified list of surviving music specifically by women composers, with locations, has not previously existed.

Cohen's *Encyclopedia* provides lists of works known (or thought) to have been composed by women, but only occasionally gives locations of sources. He does not indicate which works exist in modern editions or in recent facsimiles. Especially for the time period covered by this *Guide*, his works lists contain various errors and ambiguities, such as listing the titles of items within a volume together with the title of larger works without clarifying the relationship of the titles in the list, or listing the same work more than once on the basis of varying forms of the title (including translations) in secondary reference material. Another serious problem is that no distinction is made between extant music and works known or thought to have existed but now destroyed or otherwise lost.

My search for the composers in the *Guide* began with listings of sixteenth-, seventeenth-, and eighteenth-century women from Cohen's *Encyclopedia*, from Eitner's early twentieth-century *Quellenlexikon*, and from the various RISM listings of printed music. Much published early music by women is listed in the *Répertoire International des Sources Musicales* (RISM) series of printed works by a single composer printed before 1800 (A/I), volumes of collections of works printed in the sixteenth and seventeenth centuries (B/I), and collections from the eighteenth century (B/II). These listings are, of course, confined to printed works. A lot of music by women, however, even by major figures like Marianne von Martinez (classic era, Vienna), survives only in manuscripts. RISM is currently processing files on about one million five hundred thousand manuscripts that will form the RISM Series A/II: *Music Manuscripts 1600–1800* worldwide. This will take many decades to complete and will be in an electronic database that is not yet fully accessible. Microfiche publication of the data so far includes only one hundred thousand titles. The Frankfurt RISM office provided me with all RISM Series A/II material on women composers that had been processed by March 1992.[2]

A systematic search of a large number of printed catalogues of individual libraries was also made for composers and their works. For example, the page-by-page search of the many volumes of the *Catalogue of Printed Music of the British Library* (CPM) turned up many composers and works that had not been located by any other means. When a listing of about 815 names had been assembled, a further search was made in the *National Union Catalogue of Pre-1956 Imprints,* and an OCLC computer search was run. Correspondence with many libraries was also helpful. For many composers, not all the works

---

2. A partial listing of women in RISM Series A/II (not yet all processed) is available in the article by Ulrike B. Keil, "Quellendokumentation—eine Perspektive?" *INFO Archivnachrichten, Frau und Musik Internationaler Arbeitskreis* 22 (1991): 19–20. This listing includes a few names not covered in the *Guide*.

they are known to have composed have survived. These works may be found listed in various reference works, but they have not been included in this *Guide*. See appendix 1 for a list of abbreviations to the references cited in the *Guide*. For many composers, no works at all could be located. Appendix 2 lists composers for whom no surviving music has yet been found.

Time Period Covered

The time covered by this *Guide* is from the sixteenth century to the end of the eighteenth century. If a composer is known to have been born before 1800, she is included and her works after 1800 are given. If a birthdate is not known but the composer was active into the 1830s, her works are also included.

Information in Individual Entries

The *Guide* is organized alphabetically by composer, with an entry for each work. Composers known only by initials are listed at the beginning of each letter of the alphabet in the same form as they are found in the original catalogue. Thus some are alphabetized by the first initial and some by the initial of the presumed surname.

Names

Whenever possible, the composer's name is given in the form she used most commonly for her works. Each listing includes the composer's usual designation, her birth name (indicated by the French *née* for all nationalities), married name or names, pseudonyms, religious name (for nuns), and variant spellings or other variant forms. Cross-references for all difficult cases are given, particularly for aristocratic names, common errors (e.g., *Isabella Leonarda* as a religious name instead of the correct order *Leonarda*—family name, *Isabella* —given name), or composers who published under several names.

For titled composers, the English form of the title is normally used, as in *Anna Amalia, Princess of Prussia*. For minor nobility or in cases in which a specific rank is not given, the form in the language of the composer will be used, as in *Marianne von Martinez* or *Maria Theresia von Paradis*.

There are actually three categories of composers for whom no name is known in the *Guide*: those who are known only by pseudonym, those who are described as anonymous with some gender identification such as "a Lady" or "Anonymous nun of S. Clare," and those who use initials or other partial name forms. Of course, there are probably many anonymous composers whose gender cannot be identified.

For composers known only by incomplete forms of their names, all available information is given, as in *La Pierre, Mme.* or *A. v. K., geb. v. S.* (geb. or geboren indicates the birth name initials and identifies the composer as female, even though no other information is known about her). If the title follows the given name, in the order *Millard, Virtue, Mrs.* the name preceding the title is the composer's given name. If she is listed only under her husband's name, the title precedes his given name, as in *Cumberland, Mrs. William.*

For some composers there is a real identity problem. Scholars are not agreed as to whether Vittoria Aleotti and Raffaella Aleotti are different names for the same composer or whether they were sisters and thus two different individuals. Library cataloguers and scholars are not agreed as to whether the three names Maria Hester Park(e) (later Beardmore), Miss M. F. Park or Parke, and Maria Hester Reynolds (later Parke) belong to one, two, or three individuals. As much information as possible has been given with each entry. In doubtful cases, generally the name used in the composer's own work has been the basis for the form used for entries in the *Guide*. Sometimes very similar names may belong to the same person (for example, Catherine de Licoschin and Katherina Likoschin), but unless there is specific evidence for that interpretation, they are treated as separate individuals in this listing.

The husband's name (or names if the composer was married more than once) is given in the entry even if it is not the surname under which works are known to have appeared. It may well happen that subsequent research will uncover music which does use the married surname or surnames, so the most complete name information possible is given.

Dates of Birth and Death, Places of Origin and of Death

Years and places of birth and death are given following the name. For composers for whom this information is not available, the places in which they published or flourished and approximate years of composing activity are given instead. If no dates are given, entries are from such sources as RISM for which the cut-off date is within the period covered by the *Guide*.

Title and Publication or Manuscript Information

Titles are given in the form and language of the publication or manuscript. They are alphabetized using all words of the title, including articles and numbers, in the title page order. Where exact titles of individual pieces are not available, square brackets enclose descriptive generic titles, as in:

[4 Lieder] in: *Blumenlesen*. There may not be information on the specific category of work for all the items published in the monthly, weekly, or annual periodicals so popular in eighteenth-century France, Germany, and England. For such cases the form is: [Work(s)], showing in square brackets that a work or works by the composer is in the collection or periodical.

Square brackets are used to identify the category of the works [Singspiel], [opera in 3 acts], [song], and the like. Categories will use normal technical terms like *Singspiel*, but will use English where a general description is involved (opera in 3 acts).

Publication information includes the city, publisher (and in some cases also the printer or engraver), and date of publication. Manuscripts are identified as Ms., with a date or approximate date if available. Score and/or partbook format, including the number of partbooks, is indicated wherever possible.

If the composer had a co-composer for a work (as in the case of quartet by Maddalena Lombardini Sirmen and her husband, Ludovico Sirmen) both names will appear in the entry. For some works, the melody was the only thing written by the person listed as composer, and the title page usually indicates who arranged, harmonized, or made an acompaniment for it. In these entries the phrase "Melody only by . . ." appears at the end of the title section of the entry in italics.

When possible, authors of song texts or libretti are given as part of the title information or at the end of the entry.

A list of abbreviations used in the entries can be found in Appendix 1.

Arrangements

Arrangements, whether by the composer herself or by other composers, are listed under the name of the composer, with the name of the arranger also given if known. Arrangements ranging from added optional flute and guitar parts to variations and fantasies on the composer's theme were very common in the eighteenth century. They give evidence of the composer's popularity and are an indication of the regions in which her work was known. In the days before recordings, the innumerable periodicals with "Collections of the Best Compositions from the Operas, etc." in England, France, and German-speaking lands gave currency to a composer's work with every sort of combination of instruments, so that work might be heard arranged for two violins or any other two treble instruments, for the harp, or for many instrumentations or voices which the composer might never have considered. A performer wishing to perform such a work in modern times would be perfectly justified in using an arrangement from the period, for it would be a valid historical representation of the way in which a composer's music might have been heard in her own time.

Medium of Performance

Instruments required (with choices given by the composer, as in *harpsichord or piano)*, number and (where possible) range of voices, and indication of ensemble group (such as orchestra or wind band) are given for all nondramatic works for which the information is available. For vocal pieces for one singer for which the accompaniment instrument is not specified, the term "song" is used. Some songs (especially in some of the periodical publications) are actually unaccompanied melodies; if this information is available they are so identified. In many cases medium of performance is based on title page or catalogue information. In some cases the contents indicate additional options.

Operas and other dramatic works do not show a list of voice requirements of roles or instrumentation, but are simply labeled "stage works." Specific instrumentation is given for some but not all orchestral or wind band pieces. Abbreviations of performance media are listed in Appendix 1.

Libraries

Each entry for a particular work includes a listing of the known library holdings, using the standard RISM Library Sigla. In a few cases, a siglum has been devised using the RISM principles for a particular library or collection that is not listed in RISM. All known library holdings, including incomplete or defective copies, are included except for items in periodical collections or similar sets for which only complete runs will be listed. In cases in which a very large number of incomplete runs exist, scattered through many libraries, the user should check RISM B/II. A list of collection sigla is in Appendix 1.

Microfilm and Other Modern Copies

Holdings in a few private collections as well as microfilms and other copies in numerous libraries are indicated at the end of the library listing. It should be remembered that private collections are not staffed or available for public use.

References

References that have provided locations for the music are given in abbreviated form at the end of each entry. Each reference is to information about the individual work and its location, except for entries in *Cohen*, *New Grove*, and *MGG*, which are principal references for biographical information. Appendix 1 contains a list of reference abbreviations.

Appendices

Key to Collections Sigla, Terms, and Abbreviations

This appendix is divided into three parts. The first part is a list of Library Sigla based on, but not limited to, the standard RISM Library Sigla. The second part consists of reference abbreviations for the sources of information about individual works and their locations. The third part is a list of terms, abbreviations, and performance medium designations.

Composers for Whom No Surviving Music Has Been Located

Composers for whom no surviving music has been found are listed in Appendix 2. Dates for each are given if known, and some other brief information.

Male Composers Who Have Been Misidentified as Female

Some male composers are misidentified as female in Cohen and elsewhere. A listing of these (with their correct male names) is given in Appendix 3 for the period covered by this *Guide*.

Family Relationships between Composers within the Guide

When working with male composers, identical surnames tend to group many relatives together automatically. With females, however, the normal changes of name at marriage or in religious life may make noting family relationships more difficult. All composers for whom both a birth name and another adult name exist are given all their names in each entry. In the course of the study, it was interesting to note that many of the composers within the *Guide* were related. I believe that some way of showing this relationship would be helpful for users of the book for many reasons (including facilitating further searches for surviving materials not yet found). At first, I hoped that cross-references at each entry could be used to show composers who were related to one another. This proved to be very cumbersome, so I have given a list of family relationships between the composers in the *Guide* in Appendix 4.

Modern Editions, Arrangements, and Facsimile Reprints

Appendix 5 is a list of modern editions. Modern is defined as after 1850, and some of these items are now also rare materials. Locations have therefore been given for many older modern editions.

Index by Medium of Peformance

An index by medium of performance is provided at the end of the *Guide*. A slash (/) between instrument or voice abbreviations indicates "and" or "with"; thus *vin/pf* would indicate *violin and piano*. A semicolon is used to separate groupings for different works in a category; thus *SATB/bc; SAATB/bc* would mean that the composer had one or more examples of each combination of voices with basso continuo.

In the period covered in the *Guide* instrumentation is sometimes not specified by the composer, as in the works which call for an *unspecified* treble instrument. In the cases of the items in periodicals, it has not always been possible to determine from catalogue information what the medium of performance is. When this is the case, the terms *undetermined* or *instrument undetermined* are used.

Barbara Garvey Jackson
Fayetteville, Arkansas

Guide to Surviving Works

A. v[on] K., geb. v[on] S.

pub. 1808, Berlin

Wiegenlied für die am lsten Februar geborne Königlich-Preußische Prinzessin. Ihr Majestät der Königin von Preußen . . . überreicht . . . Königsberg: den 19ten February 1808. Berlin: Rudolph Werckmeister, 1808.

song

A: Wn.

RISM A/I (IN 15).

Abrams, Harriett (Harriet, Henriette)

c. 1758, London?–c. 1822 London? (Jewish)

"All Nature mourns" . . . Duett. London: [1805?].

2 voices/pf

GB: Lbl [G.805.m.(1.)].

CPM.

"And must we part?" 1. Duet. [From: *A second sett of Italian and English canzonets,* #1]. In: *The Harmonist,* vol. 2, No. 3, pp. 8–10 [179–?]. 2. In: Bland, *The Ladies' Collection,* Vol. 2, #243, pp. 220–21. London [182–?] 3. Duett . . . with an Accompaniment for the Piano Forte or Harp. London: L. Lavenu [1800?]. 4. W. Mitchell, [c. 1820]. 5. Reissue, London: [1825] 6. "And must we part for ever," A favorite duett for two voices [London]: s. n., [c. 1800]. 3 pp.

1–5. AT/pf; 6. 2 voices/pf or harp

1–2. US: Bp (**M.218.8), (**M.235.17). 3–5. GB: Lbl [E.270.e.(1.)], [809.yy.(4.)], [G.809.(1.)]. 6. GB: Gu.

1–2. NUC (NA 0028922). 3–5. CPM. 6. RISM A/I (A 189), BUC.

The Ballad of William and Nancy . . . on the embarkation of the 85th Regt. August 10th, 1799 at Ramsgate . . . composed and arranged for the harp or piano forte. London: Lewis Lavenu [1799]. 4 pp.
voice/harp or pf
GB: Lbl [H.2832.l.(1.)]. US: NYp, Wc.
RISM A/I (A 216), BUC, CPM, NUC (NA 0028923), Cohen.

The birks of Aberfeldy . . . a favorite Scotch air, to which is added a movement harmonized & composed by Miss Abrams ("And are ye sure the news is true." Trio). 1. London: Lewis Lavenu [1799?]. 2. London: Lewis Lavenu [1801?]. Nos. 3 and 14 of her *Collection of Scotch songs.* Ed. with Evans, C. *6 glees . . .* pp. 8–10, 32–35. 3. Glasgow: Steven [181–?]. 2 pp. Ed. with Stevenson, J. "Oh! never shall my soul forget."
1. SAB/pf; 2–3. 3 voices unacc.
1. GB: Gu, Lbl [E.318.(11.)]. US: CA, Wc. 2. US: CA. 3. US: CA.
1. RISM A/I (A 192), BUC, CPM, NUC (NA 0028924), OCLC (20166334). 2. NUC (Sup. NSA 0006631), OCLC (20166334). 3. NUC Sup. (NSA 0006632), OCLC (20166335).

[A Book of Songs, with frontispiece by Gilbray; dedicated] to the Queen. London: 1803.
voice/pf
GB: Lbl [D.392.(1.)].
CPM.

A collection of Scotch songs harmonized for 2 & 3 voices with an accompaniment for the piano forte or harp. 1. London: J. Dale. 2. Lewis Lavenu, 1800. 3. Lavenu & Mitchell [1790 or 180?]. 39 pp.
2 voices/pf or harp; 3 voices unacc.
1. GB: En, Gu. 2. GB: DU. 3. US: CA, Wc.
1–3. RISM A/I (A 183, 184, 185). 1-2. BUC. 3. NUC (NA 0028925) & OCLC (2016636). Cohen, NG.

Crazy Jane ("Why fair maid in ev'ry feature"). A favorite song . . . with an accompaniment for the harp or piano forte. 1. London: Lewis Lavenu [179–? or c. 1800]. 4 pp. 2. London: G. Walker. 3. Dublin: Hime. 4. Philadelphia: G. Willig [1801]. 5. Boston: Von Hagen [1799–1802]. 6. London: Lavenu & Mitchell [1804?]. 7. London?: Pirated edition?, c. 1805. 8. Lavenu [c.1805]. 9. [London]: Printed for H. Andrews [c. 1810]. 10. S.l.: s.n. [c. 1800]. 11. London: L. Lavenu [c. 1800]. 12. London:

G. Shade [1818?, 1821]. 13. London, #136 in: *Cyclopoedia of Music*. Misc. series of songs [1856]. 14. In: *The Lady's Magazine and Musical Repository*, I, #2, p. 106. New York: Nathaniel Bell, Feb. 1801. 15. In: *The Songster's Museum*, pp. 50–51. [*Melody and text only*]. Northampton, Mass., 1803. 16. In: *The Baltimore Musical Miscellany*, I, p. 42–43. [*Melody and text only*]. Followed by *The Death of Crazy Jane* ("O'er the gloomy woods resounding") to the foregoing tune, p. 44. Baltimore, 1804. 17. Crazy Jane a favorite Ballad. In Ms. collection, p. 31. Ms. 18/19th century.
voice/harp or pf; 17. voice/hpsch
1. D: B. GB: AB, Cfm, Clp, Lbl [H.1652.cc.(8.) & G.426.pp. (9)]. P: Ln.
2. US: CA (*fEC8 L5875 Gz800m), Wc. 3. GB: Lbl [H.1653.j.(53.)]. US:
Wc. 4. US: AA, AUS, NH, NYp, NYsha, PIlevy, R, PHf, PHlc, Wc, WOa.
5. US: NYp. 6. GB: Lbl [G.798.(1.)]. 6–8. US: CA(*fEC8 L5875
Gz800m). 6–7. GB: Lbl [G.798.(1.)] & [G.809.kk.(8.)]. 9. GB: Lbl
[G.809.kk.(8.)]. 10. US: BE. 11. US: NH, Su. 12. GB: Lbl
[H.3690.ww.(29.)]. US: CA (*fEC8 L5875 Gz800m). 13. GB: Lbl
[H.2342]. 14. See *Union List of Serials* for U.S. locations. 15. US: Bp, BUg,
CA, NYcuh, NYfuld, NYhs, PIlevy, PROu, WOa. 16. US: PROu, Wc,
WOA. 17. US: PHf (Carr Collection 1).
1–4. RISM A/I (A 193, 194, 195, 196). 1. BUC, CPM. 1–3. NUC (NA0028926, '28, '29), NUC Sup. (NSA 0006634, '36, '38, '40), OCLC (5418823), Wolfe (6), Tick. 4. Sonneck. 5–8. NUC Sup. (NSA 0006641–44). 6–7., 9. CPM. 10. OCLC (19011138). 11. OCLC (19726430). 12. CPM. 12. NUC Sup. (NSA 0006645). 13. CPM. 14. Wolfe (8, 5201). 15–16. Wolfe (8451, 9, 10, 433). 15., 17. RISM A/II (#114824). Cohen.

Crazy Jane, composed by Miss Abrams and danced in the ballet of Barbara and Allen as a pas de trois. Arr. with variations for the Pianoforte by J. B. Cramer.
1. London: L. Lavenu [179–?]. 2. London: [1801?]. 3. *The popular air of Crazy Jane*, arr. with variations for the pianoforte, by T. Haigh. # 52 of *Le Melange*. London: Lewis Lavenu [c. 1800].
pf
1. US: NYp, Wc. 2. GB: Lbl [g.272.g.(14.)]. 3. GB: Lbl [g.270.e.(13.)].
1. NUC (under Cramer, Johann Baptiste, NC 0772352). 2. CPM. 3. BUC, CPM.

"Dite che peno ma dite ancor." Duettino with a pianoforte accompaniment. London: Monzani & Hill, No. 286.
2 voices/pf
I: BAn.
RISM A/I (A 197).

Eight Italian and English canzonets for one or two voices, with an accompanyment for the harpsichord or piano forte. London: Author [1780?]. 31 pp.
1–2 voices/hpsch or pf
GB: CDp, Lbl [B. 699.b.(1.)].
RISM A/I (A 186), BUC, CPM, Cohen, Eitner.

The Emigrant, a favorite song. London: Lewis Lavenu [c.1800]. 5 pp.
voice/pf
GB: Lbl [H.1652.g.(17.)]. US: NYp.
RISM A/I (A 198), BUC, CPM, NUC (NA 0028930), Cohen.

Female Hardship . . . with an accompaniment for the harp or piano forte. London: Lewis Lavenu [c. 1800]. 4 pp.
voice/harp or pf
GB: Lbl [G.805.m.(2.)].
RISM A/I (A 199), BUC, CPM, Cohen.

The Friend of my Heart . . . set to music with an accompaniment for the harp or piano forte. London: Lewis Lavenu [1799]. 3 pp.
voice/harp or pf
GB: Lbl (2 ex.) [G.805.j.(1.) & G.806.(1.)].
RISM A/I (A 200), BUC, CPM, Cohen.

"Friend of my soul, when far away." London: [1814].
voice/harp or pf
GB: Lbl [H.1660.(5.)].
CPM.

The Gamester ("Dark was the night, and dreary was the scene"). Favorite song. Words by M. P. Andrews. New York: John Paff, [1798 or 1812].
voice/pf
US: CA, NYcuh, PROu, PROub.
RISM A/I (A 201), Wolfe (11), NUC (NA 0029831).

"Gniancora non se stuffa." A Venetian melody. Trio with accompaniment for pianoforte. London: Monzani & Co., No. 261., n.d.
3 voices/pf
I: BAn.
RISM A/I (A 202).

The Gaoler, a favorite ballad, the words by M. G. Lewis . . . London:
Lavenu & Mitchell [1804]. 4 pp., followed by an accompaniment for the
flute.
voice/pf, with acc. for flute
GB: Lbl (G.809.p.(12.)].
CPM.

"If silent oft you see me pine" . . . with accompaniment for the harp or
piano forte. 1. London: Robert Birchall [c. 1795]. 2. [on later paper]
London: Birchall [c. 1800]. 4 pp. 3. with violin & unfigured bass. London:
L. Lavenu [18–?]. 4 pp.
voice/harp or pf (treble staff of piano/harp part also labeled "violino")
1. GB: Lbl [G.806.j.(1.)]. 2. GB: Lbl [H.1652.g.(16.)]. 3. US: Wc
(M1621.3.A).
1. RISM A/I (A 203). 1–2. BUC, CPM. 3. NUC (NA 0028932). Cohen.

The last time I came o'er the moor. A favorite duett . . . with an accompaniment
for the harp or piano forte. London: Lewis Lavenu [c. 1800]. 3 pp.
2 voices/harp or pf
GB: Cfm.
RISM A/I (A 204), BUC.

Little Boy Blue . . . glee, for three voices. London: Lewis Lavenu [1799]. 3 pp.
3 male voices
GB: Lbl [G.808.g.(1.)], Lcm. US: NYfuld, NYp.
RISM A/I (A 205), BUC, CPM, NUC (NA 0028933), Eitner.

O memory thou fond deceiver. A favorite song, with an accompaniment for the
piano forte or harp. London: Longman & Broderip [1790 or 1794]. 4 pp.
Words by O. Goldsmith.
voice/pf or harp
GB: Gu, Lbl (2 ex.) [G.361.(4.) & H.2821.(24.)], Ob.
RISM A/I (A 206), BUC, CPM, Cohen, Eitner.

The Orphan's Prayer. ("The frozen streets in moonshine glitter") . . . ballad
. . . words by M. G. Lewis. 1. London: Lewis Lavenu [c.1800]. 6 pp.
2. New York: I. & M. Paff. 3. Anon. in: *Musical Journal,* II, #29, Baltimore:
J. Carr, 1800. 4. *Boston Musical Miscellany,* II, 1815, pp. 167–73. [*Melody and
text only*].
voice/harp or pf
1. GB: Bp, Gu, Ckc, Lbl [G.805.j.(3.)]. US: PHf, PHu, Wc (M1624.4A),

CA (1812) [*fEC8, L5875, Gz800a]. 2. US: NYp [Am1–V], PHfk, PHu, Wc. 3. US: NYp [Am1–V]. 4. US: Ba, Bhs, Bp, CA, ECstarr.
1–2. RISM A/I (A 207, A 208). 1. BUC, CPM. 2. NUC (NA0028934), Sonneck. 3. NUC sup. (NSA 0006647). 2–3. US: NYp Shelf List. 4. Wolfe (12, 994). Cohen.

A second sett of Italian and English canzonets, for one, two, or three voices, with a accompanyment [*sic*] for the piano forte or harp. 1. London: Longman & Broderip, for the author [1785?]. 2. Lewis Lavenu, for the author [1800?].
1–3 voices/pf or harp
1. GB: Lbl [R.M.8.b.6.], Mp. US: NYp. 2. GB: Lbl [E.600.z.(1.)].
1. RISM A/I (A 187), NUC (NA 0028935). 1–2. BUC, CPM. Cohen, Eitner.

A second set of Italian canzonets. London: Lavenu [1789?].
songs
US: NYp.
RISM A/II (A 188), NUC (NA 0028936).

The shade of Henry ("Stranger do you ask me why"). Words by M. P. Andrews. 1. With an accompaniment for the harp or piano forte. London: Lewis Lavenu [c.1800]. 5 pp. 2. Acc. for pf. Philadelphia: G. Willig [1801].
voice/harp or pf
1. GB: AB, Cu, Lbl [G.805.h.(2.)]. 2. US: BUg, PHfk.
1. RISM A/I (A 190, 191), BUC, CPM. 2. Wolfe (13), Sonneck. Cohen.

A smile and a tear ("You own I'm Complacent")
1. London: Lewis Lavenu [1799]. 2. Dublin: M. Hime [1800]. 3. New York: J. & M. Paff [c. 1800–03]. 4. [Reissue] [1800]. 5. London: L. Lavenu [1808]. 6. In: *The Lady's Magazine and Musical Repository,* I, #4, p. 232, April 1801, New York. 7. Philadelphia, Willig [1810–1812]. 8. Ms. in: Songs with pianoforte accompaniment in score. 9. Ms. [together with a song by William Shield. Probably copied by Eliza E. Jacobs] [c. 1800]. 4 pp.
voice/pf
1. GB: Lbl [G.805.j.(2.)]. US: Bp. 2. GB: Lbl [H.1653.j.(9.)]. 3. US: NYp [Am1–V], Wc (M1.411, vol. 14, #29), WOa. 4–5. GB: Lbl [H.1860.ww.(37.)], [G.805.b.(1.)]. 6. See *Union List of Serials* for locations of *Lady's Magazine* in U.S. . . . . 7. US: PHf, PROu, WOa. 8. GB: Lbl (Add. ms. 25075, no. 15, f. 22). 9. US: NYp
1–2. RISM A/I (A 211, 212). 1., 2., 4., 5., 8. CPM. 1–3. NUC

(NA 0028937–8). 3., 6–7. Wolfe (14, 15, 16). 3. US: NYp Shelf List, Sonneck, Tick. 7. Sonneck. 9. OCLC (24087781). Cohen.

The Soldier's grave ("The wind it blows cold"), the words by M. G. Lewis . . . with an accompaniment for the harp or piano forte. 1. London: Lewis Lavenu [c.1800]. 4 pp. 2. London: [1805?].
voice/harp or pf
1. GB: Lbl [H.1652.cc.(9.)]. US: AA (bound in Musical Miscellany).
2. GB: Lbl [G.805.j.(4.)].
1. RISM A/I (A 213), CPM. 2. NUC Sup. (NSA 0006648). Cohen.

The three sighs: Sorrow, Hope & Bliss. A favorite song. The words by a gentle-man . . . with an accompaniment for the harp or piano forte. 1. London: L. Lavenu [180–?]. 2. Lavenu & Mitchell [1806?]. 3. Dublin: Hime [c.1810].
high voice/pf or harp
1. US: Wc (M1624.4.A). 2. GB: Lbl [G.805.b.(2.)]. 3. GB: Lbl [H.1653.j.(10.)].
1. NUC (0028939). 2–3. CPM.

Tom Halliard . . . song . . . with an accompaniment for the harp or piano forte. London: Lewis Lavenu [c.1800]. 4 pp.
voice/harp or pf
GB: Lbl [G.805.h.(4.)].
RISM A/I (A 214), BUC, CPM, Cohen.

Twelve songs with piano accompaniment. [London: Printed for the author by Lavenu & Mitchell, 1803]. [4 of the 12 songs are by M. G. Lewis].
voice/pf
US: PHtu.
OCLC (5380046).

The White Man. A favorite ballad with an accompaniment for the piano forte or harp. The words taken from Mr. Park's *Travels.* Dublin: M. Hime, [c.1800].
voice/pf or harp
GB: Lbl [H.1653.j.(11.)].
RISM A/I (A 215), BUC, CPM, Cohen.

[Work(s)] in: *The Flowers of harmony, being a collection of the most celebrated catches, glees & duets . . . selected from the most eminent composers . . .* London:

G. Walker, [c. 1800]. 4 vol.
voices
DK: Kk. GB: Lbl. US: Bp (3 vols), U.
RISM B/II (p. 182).

Ye Silvan Pow'rs that rule the Plain . . . Duett for two voices, with an accompaniment for the harp or piano forte. 1. London: Lewis Lavenu, 1800. 2. Philadelphia: G. Willig, n.d.
2 voices/harp or pf
1. GB: Lbl [G.805.h.(3.)]. 2. US: PHu.
1. BUC, CPM. 1–2. RISM A/I (A 209, 210). Cohen.

Ager, Mrs.
pub. c. 1750, Dublin
[Work(s)] in: *Select minuets.* Collected from castle balls, and the publick assemblies in Dublin. Composed by the best masters for the harpsichord, violin, or german flute . . . Dublin: W. Mainwaring, [c. 1750].
hpsch, and/or vln, or flute
GB: En (inc.), Lbl.
RISM B/II (p. 352).

Agnesi, Maria Teresa d' (married Pinottini, also as Agnesi-Pinottini; pseud. Francesco Mainini)
1720–1795, Milan
[Airs divers for voice/harp]. Ms.
voice/harp
Formerly A: Wn. Apparently now lost.
NG, Eitner, Cohen, MGG, Olivier.

Allegretto Authore Illma Sigra Dona Theresa Agnesi [in G, for organ]. Ms., c. 1770. 6 ff.
organ
YU: KLf (C–94).
RISM A/II (#78084).

Allegro Della S.a Teresa Agnesi [A]. Ms., c. 1800. 2 ff.
pf
D: B (Mus. Ms. 339).
RISM A/II (#150078), Meggett, Cohen, MGG, Olivier, De Jong. (Some listings as "Allegro ou Presto," hpsch).

Ciro in Armenia (dramma serio, 3 acts). Milan: 1753. Ms. Libretto by composer, after U. Manferrari v. G. Manfredi.
stage work
I: Mc (acts 2–3 only). Formerly also in D: Dlb (lost in WWII).
NG, Eitner, Mellen, Cohen, MGG, Olivier, De Jong.

[Ciro riconosciuto, excerpt from?]. "Non piangeti amati rai." Aria Della Sig. Agnesi. Ms. score, 18th century. 6 pp. Text by Pietro Metastasio.
S/strings
F: Pn (Mus. D. 14413 (4)).
RISM A/II (#93085).

[Concerto for Klavier in F Major, with 2 vln and b]. Ms.
kbd/2 vlns/b
A: Wgm (VII 2314).
NG, Eitner, Cohen, MGG, Olivier, De Jong.

[Concerto in F (1740) for keyboard (cembalo or pf) with strings.] Ms. partbooks.
hpsch or pf/2 vlns/bass or 2 vlns/vla/vlc
B: Bc (5859). Copy in Ars Fem coll.
NG, Eitner, Cohen, MGG, Olivier, De Jong, letter (Ars Fem).

Concerto per il Cembalo del Sig.ra Agnesi (F). Ms., 18th c. 4 ff.
hpsch/orch
D: Dl (Mus 3275 T 1) (cembalo part only, other parts missing).
RISM A/II (#17566). May be the same as concerto in B: Bc.

"Fra l'orror di mille affanni." Aria Della Sig.a.D. a Teresa Agnesi. Ms. score, 18th century. 10 ff.
S/strings/brasses
F: Pn (Mus. D. 14413 (2)).
RISM A/II (#93086).

Il re pastore (dramma serio, 3 acts), 1756. Ms. Score. 179 pp. Libretto by Metastasio.
stage work
A: Wn (Ms. 19211).
NG, Eitner, Mellen, MGG, Olivier, De Jong.

Insubria consolata (componimento drammatico, 2 acts). Naples, 1766.
Ms. Libretto also attributed to composer.
stage work
F: Pc (as Pinottini).
Eitner (under Pinottina), NG, Cohen, Mellen, MGG (reported music lost), Olivier.

L'Olimpiade (?), [excerpts] Dalla Sig. Agnesi. Ms. score, 18th century. 5 pp.
S/strings
F: Pn (Mus. D. 14413 (3)).
RISM A/II (#93087).

La Sofonisba (drama erocio per musica, 3 acts). Naples [1765, NG &
MGG; 1771, Mellen]. 3 vols. Ms. score. Libretto by A. & G. F. Zanetti.
(A: Wgm copy has dedication to Franz I of Austria.)
stage work
A: Wn (Ms. 19230), Wgm (Q1127 [IV 2821]).
NG, Eitner, Cohen, Mellen, MGG, Olivier, De Jong.

Minuetto [in F Major for Clavier]. In: D. Schiebeler & J. J. Eschenburg
(editors), *Unterhaltungen.* Hamburg: M. Chr. Bock. Vol. 2, 1766.
kbd
D: DÜk (cat.# 5).
NG, Cohen, Olivier (as "diverse works for piano or harpsichord").

[Siroe re di Persia, excerpt from?] "Ch' io mai vi possa lasciar d' amare."
Della Sig.ra D.na Tere Agnesi. Ms. 18th century. 4 ff. Text by Pietro
Metastasio.
S/strings
F: Pn (Mus. D. 14413 (1)).
RISM A/II (#93088).

[Sonata for keyboard]. Ms. Milan, 1767. [May be from the 2 keyboard
sonatas (1767) cited in Breitkopf catalogues].
kbd (pf or hpsch?)
B: Bc. (Ms. 17490). Copy in Ars Fem coll.
Eitner (as Pinottina), letter (Ars Fem).

Sonata [G, for harpsichord]. Ms. n.d.
hpsch
D: UNikb, KA (#Hs. 5, formerly Mus. Ms. 339).
NG, Eitner, Cohen, Meggett, MGG, Olivier, De Jong.

Sonate Agnesa [6 Sonatas for organ: G, D, G, D, F, D]. Ms. 18th century.
6 ff.
organ
I: Mdemicheli (MSS. Mus 121).
RISM A/II (#96665).

[12 arias with instruments.] Ms. score, partbooks.
voice/various instruments
D: Dlb (3275/I/1, formerly Ms. 88).
NG, MGG, Eitner, Cohen, Olivier, De Jong.

[2 Arias]. "Sospender le mie pene" & "Al selva, al prato, al fonte." Ms.
score (name as Pinottini).
voice/orch
D: DS (Eitner, modern location not confirmed).
Eitner (as Pinottina).

[2 fantasias, Marche and Aria]. Ms.
kbd
D: Bds (Ms. 30106).
De Jong.

[2 fantasies, 1 allegro]. Ms.
kbd
D: B. (Ms. 137, pp. 37, 58, 128 [beginning page nos.])
NG, Eitner, Cohen (allegro ou presto), Meggett (with allegro ou presto), Olivier.

Ulisse in Campania [serenata (in 2 parts) with sinfonia]. Ms. score.
Libretto attributed to composer.
stage work for 4 voices/orch.
I: Nc (21.2.22).
NG, Cohen, Mellen, MGG, Olivier, De Jong.

Agostino, Corona
pub. 1592, Venice
"Beati omnes." With: G. M. Asola, et al. *Sacra omnium solemnitatum psalmodia*
vespertina cum cantio beatae virginis. Venice: Amadino, 1592. 5 partbooks.
5 voices
I: Bc, CE (A, B, 5 only), Ls, Mc, PC.
RISM B/I (1592 [3]) (does not specify which library in Cesena, I: CE, or Piacenza,
I: PC), Eitner (in Asola and Amadino entries), Cohen, NG (Asola entry).

Ahlefeldt, Maria Theresia, Countess of, née Princess of Thurn und Taxis

1755, Regensburg–1823, Prague
[2 dances from *Telemak*]. In: *Musikaliskt tidsfördrif,* 1799, pp. 94–96 and 1800, p. 56. Stockholm: Kongl. Privilegierade Not Trycheriet. 1799, 1800.
undetermined instruments
S: L, LI (1799 inc., 1800), Sdt, Sk, Skma, Sm, SKa (1799, inc.), ST (1799), Uu. SF: T. US: NYp.
RISM B/II (p. 252), MGG.

Balletten Telemaque. [Opera ballet] 1805. Overført fra Det kgl. Teater. Ms. score, 160 pp., voice parts included.
stage work
B: Bc. DK: Kk (C II, 105d. Mu 6306.0632).
Letter (DK: Kk), Cohen, Mellen, MGG.

Klage in: *Vermischte Gedichte* von I. F. Zehelein. Bayreuth: in Verlag der Zeitungsdruckerei [c. 1788].
voice/fl/kbd
CH: L. D: Mbs.
RISM B/II (p. 396. Does not specify which library in CH: L), Cohen, NG, MGG.

L'harmonie. Cantata à Sopr. Imo, IIdo et Basso, 2 Violons, Altes, Flûtes, Clairons, Oboi, Bassons, Cors, Violoncello et Basse. 1792. Piano-vocal score, ms., 18th century.
SSB/orch (only p-v score survives)
D: Dlb (Mus. 3703/G/1).
RISM A/II (#17587), NG, Cohen, Eitner, MGG.

Romance de Nina. Ms. score.
S/2 vlns/2 hns/b
D: Dlb (Mus. 1/F/82.2).
Cohen, Eitner, MGG.

Sinfonia [D major]. Ms. (c.1770) score and parts. Score inscribed Ahlefeld. [Rtt notes same as autograph score (Pokorny 46) by Pokorny; attributed to Pokorny (NG), authorship doubtful according to MGG].
orch
D: Rtt (Rtt Ahlefeldt 2).
NG, MGG and NG consider authorship doubtful, letter (D: Rtt).

Sinfonia [F major]. Ms., c. 1780. (11 partbooks, with 2 each of violin parts and of basso).
orch (2 vlns/vla/basso, 2 obs/2 hns)
D: Rtt (Rtt Ahlefeldt l).
RISM A/II (#60010), letter (D: Rtt), NG. NG & MGG considers authorship doubtful.

Telemak på Calypsos Øe. [Opera-ballet, 4 acts, 1792]. Balletmaster, Galeotti. 1. Copenhagen: S. Sønnichesen, 1794 [or 1795?]. Piano-vocal score [arranged by composer]. 70 pp. 2. Ms. orch parts, c. 1782. (43 vols.: vln 1 & 2, vla, b, fl picc, fl 1 & 2, ob 1 & 2, bsn 1 & 2, hn 1&2, tr 1 & 2, trb 1 & 2, timp. Multiple copies). 3. *Telemak auf der Insel Calypso.* Ein Opern Ballet in IV Acten vom Ballet Meister Galeotti in Music gesetzt und zum Klaviereingerichtet von Gräfin M. T. von Ahlefeldt geborene Princess von Thurn und Taxis. Ms. score, c. 1800. 51 pp.
stage work
1. B: Bc. CH: Bu (Ed. w/Ger. title). D: KIl, Sl (Ger. title). DK: Kc, Kk (305.0930.D.6.), Ou. GB: Lbl (Ger. title [F. 703]). N: Ou (Ger. title). Copy of N: Ou in Ars Fem coll. 2. DK: Kk (mu7406.2731). 3. D: Dl Mus.3703 F 1).
1. RISM A/I (A 502), BUC, CPM, NG, MGG, letter (DK: Kk), Mellen, Cohen, Eitner, letter (Ars Fem). 2. RISMdan (supplies date of c. 1782). 3. RISM A/II (#17588).

Veddemaalet af Grevinde Ahlefelt. Ms. copy, c. 1793. Souffleur partie. l bind. (S.P. 64). Setting of P. H. Haste, *Vaeddemalet.*
stage work
DK: Kk (KTA 64.mu 7302.0633).
RISMdan, letter (DK: Kk), Cohen, MGG (believed it lost).

Ahlström, Carolina
late 18th century, Sweden
[Work(s)] in: *Skaldestycken satte i musik.* [ed. O. Ahlström]. I [–XVII] Delen. Stockholm: Kongl. Privilegerade Not Tryckeriet, Johan Lindh, 1794–1823. 36 vol.
undetermined instruments
D: B–MG, LEu. S: LI, L, N, Sk, Sdt, Skma, Sm, Uu. Other library holdings are incomplete runs.
RISM B/II (p. 357).

Alderson, Amelia. See **Opie, Mrs. Amelia,** née **Alderson**

Aleotti, Raffaela (Raffaella). (Raffaela and Vittoria listed as two individuals; see literature for discussion.)

c. 1570, Ferrara–after 1646, probably Ferrara

"Angelus ad pastores ait" and "Facta est cum Angelo" from: *Sacrae cantiones quinque, septem, octo, et plurium vocibus.* Ms. copies of two of the motets from the published collection.

5 voices (SSATB, SATTB)

D: Nla (Ms. Fenitzer IV, 2o 226)

RISM A/I (A 821), Bowers & Tick, Cohen, NG (bio), MGG, Carruthers-Clement.

Sacrae cantiones quinque, septem, octo, & decem vocibus decantande. Liber primus. Venice: Ricciardo Amadino, 1593. Partbooks.

5, 7, 8, 10 voices.

D: Kl (complete: SATB5). I: Vnm (T).

RISM A/I (A 821), Bowers & Tick, Cohen, NG (bio), MGG, Carruthers-Clement.

Aleotti, Vittoria

c. 1573, Ferrara—after 1620, probably Ferrara

"Di pallide viole" In: *Giardino de musici ferraresi madrigali à cinque voci . . .* Venice: Giacomo Vincenti, 1591. 5 partbooks.

5 voices

I: MOe (A [incomplete] TB) (Mus. F. 1348).

RISM B/I (1591 [9]), Bowers & Tick, NG (bio), Eitner, Cohen, MGG, Caruthers-Clement.

Ghirlanda de madrigali a quatro voci. Venice: Giacomo Vincenti, 1593. 4 partbooks. [21 madrigals].

SATB

D: WRtl. I: Bc (R. 2), Nc. Copy of I: Bc in Ars Fem coll.

RISM A/I (A 822), Bowers & Tick, NG (bio), Cohen, MGG, Carruthers-Clement, letter (Ars Fem).

Alessandra, Caterina

pub. 1772, Paris

"Se viver non posso" and "L'amour jeune Bergère" [aria and air] in: *Recueil lyric.* Paris, 1772. vol. 2, p. 59 and following.

voice/vln /bc

I: MOe (Mus. F 1524).

Estense.

Alexandre, Claire

pub. 1777, Paris

"Jeune Flore à l'amour." Air in: *Mercure de France*, May 1777. [Paris]: s.n., 1777.

voice/kbd

GB: Lbl (297. f. 14). Copy in Ars Fem coll.

RISM A/I (AA 850 I, 1), BUC, Cohen, CPM, letter (Ars Fem).

Alsop, Frances, Mrs.

d. 1821, New York

Collection of [6] melodies, the gift of Mrs. Alsop to Mr. Clifton, shortly before her death. Baltimore: G. Willig [1824]. Issued in series, with piano accompaniments arranged by A. Clifton. Three melodies are by Mrs. Alsop and 2 by Mr. Clifton. #2 is lost.

voice/pf

See individual songs for locations.

Wolfe (84).

Last New Year's Day ("Last new year's day as I've heard say"). Melody and words by Mrs. Alsop and sung by her, at the theatres. #6 in the series: *Collection of melodies.* Baltimore: G. Willig [1824].

voice/pf

US: Cn (Case 8A 2289), PIlevy, Wc.

NUC Sup. (NSA 0040169), Wolfe (85).

The poor Hindoo ("'Tis thy will and I must leave thee"). Words by Mrs. Opie. #1 in the series: *Collection of melodies.* Baltimore: G. Willig [1824].

voice/pf

US: BAhs, CHAhughes, ECstarr, NYp, PIlevy, PROu.

Wolfe (86).

William and Mary ("William in accents of love would complain"). Melody and words by Mrs. Alsop. #4 in the series: Collection of [6] melodies. Baltimore: G. Willig [1824].

voice/pf

US: PIlevy.

Wolfe (87).

Amalia (Amalie), Marie Friederike Auguste, Princess of Saxony
(pseud. **A. Heiter, A. Serena**)

1794, Dresden–1870, Dresden

Die Siegesfahne. 1. ["Musikalische Passe" in 1 act]. Ms. autogr. Score. 1834. 2. Opera [1 act]. Ms. Score and parts. [1834].
stage work
1. D: Dlb (Mus. 4822–F–27). 2. (Mus. 4822–F–29).
Letter (D: Dlb, as Marie Amalia), Cohen, Olivier.

Elisa ed Ernesto. Opera [2 acts]. Ms. Score and parts [1823].
stage work
D: Dlb (Mus. 4822–F–10).
Letter from D: Dlb (as Marie Amalia), Cohen, Olivier.

Elvira, Duet from. "Per esempio." Ms. Score.
2 voices / orch
D: Dlb (Mus. 4822–F–9).
Letter (D: Dlb, as Marie Amalia).

Elvira. Opera [2 acts]. Ms. Score and parts [1821].
stage work
D: Dlb (Mus. 4822–F–8).
Letter from D: Dlb (as Marie Amalia), Cohen, Olivier.

[Entwürfe und Studien] Ms. autogr.
studies or sketches, instruments unspecified
D: Dlb (Mus. 4822–B–1).
Letter (D: Dlb, as Marie Amalia).

[Il figlio pentito]. Drama [3 acts]. Ms. Score and parts 1831.
stage work
D: Dlb (Mus. 4822–F–22).
Letter (D: Dlb, as Marie Amalia), Cohen (as Il Figlio perduto or pentito), Olivier.

Il Marchesino. Drama giocoso [2 acts]. Ms. Parts. 1833 or 1834.
stage work
D: Dlb (Mus. 4822–F–26 [Mus. Q 5309]).
Letter (D: Dlb, as Marie Amalia), Cohen, Olivier.

Il prigionere. Drama [2 acts]. Ms. [1817 or 1825].
stage work
D: Dlb (Mus. 4822–F–6).
Letter (D: Dlb, as Marie Amalia), Cohen, Olivier.

La casa disabitata. Cavatina from. "Oh luce del giorno . . . " Arr. by
F. Baumfelder. Ms. Parts.
stage work (excerpt)
D: Dlb (Mus. 4822–F–500).
Letter (D: Dlb, as Marie Amalia), Cohen.

La casa disabitata. Farce [1 act]. Ms. Parts [1835].
stage work
D: Dlb (Mus. 4822–F–32).
Letter (D: Dlb, as Marie Amalia), Cohen, Olivier.

La fedeltà alla prova. Drama giocoso [2 acts]. 1. Ms. autogr. Score [1826].
2. Ms. score and parts.
stage work
D: Dlb 1. (Mus. 4822–F–12), 2. (Mus. 4822–F–15).
Letter (D: Dlb, as Marie Amalia), Cohen, Olivier.

Le nozze funeste. Ms. Score and parts [1816].
stage work
D: Dlb (Mus. 4822–F–5).
Letter (D: Dlb, as Marie Amalia), Cohen, Olivier.

Le tre cinture. Drama giocoso [2 acts]. Ms. Score (2 vol.) [1817].
stage work
D: Dlb (Mus. 4822–F–4).
Letter (D: Dlb, as Marie Amalia), Cohen, Olivier.

Stabat Mater [Conclusion]. "Quando corpus orietur." Ms.
Kbd, with text underlaid (sketch for choir?)
D: Dlb (Mus. 4822–D–500).
Letter (D: Dlb, as Marie Amalia), Cohen, Olivier.

Una donna. Dramma Giocoso [2 acts]. Ms. parts [1816].
stage work (4 orch parts, 4 voice parts)
D: Dlb (Mus. 4822–F–2).
Letter (D: Dlb, as Marie Amalia), Cohen, Olivier.

Vecchiezza e gioventù. Drama giocoso [2 acts]. Ms. Score and parts [1826].
stage work
D: Dlb (Mus. 4822–F–17).
Letter (D: Dlb, as Marie Amalia), Cohen, Olivier.

Amalia Catharina (Katharina), Duchess of Erbach (Erpach), née von Waldeck zu Eisenberg

1640, Arolsen–1697, Cuylenburg (Netherlands)
*Andächtige Sing-Lust, Das ist: I. Morgen- II. Abend- III. Tage- IV. Beth- V. Buß-
VI. Klag- u. Trost- VII. Lob- u. Danck- VIII. Lehr- Lieder* . . . Hildburghausen:
Samuel Wentzel, 1692.
voice/bc
D: Bds, Cl, GOl, WE. DK: Ku. Copy of DK: Ku in Ars Fem coll.
*RISM A/I (AA 898 I, 1), RISM–DKL, Cohen (Erpach, Amalia Katharina, von),
NG, Eitner, MGG, letter (Ars Fem).*

Anastasia von Schwartzburg Arnstad und Sundershausen

pub. 1555, Frankfurt
[Lied] in Anhang to: *Ein hübsch vnnd Christlich Spiel des gantzen Buchs Esther*
. . . folget das lied Welches der Wolgebornene Gråuin vnd frawen Frawen
Anastasia . . . zun ehrn gemacht ist. Frankfurt am Mainz: Jost Kran, 1555.
song
D: Mbs.
RISM–DKL.

Anley, C[harlotte], Miss

1796?–1893, British
"God is light." Hymn. London: [1824?].
song
GB: Lbl [E.1660.(18.)].
CPM. Composer is principally known for her many hymn texts.

The harp of Bendemeer ("Why is that harp now so silently thrown"), a ballad
sung by Mrs. French, written and composed by Miss C. Anley . . .
1. London: [1824]. 2. Baltimore: John Cole [1825?]. 3 pp.
voice/pf
1. GB: Lbl [H.1660.(17.)]. 2. US: Cn (Case 8A 1590), CHAhughes,
PIlevy, BAhs, NYp, Wc.
1. CPM. 2. NUC Sup. (NSA 0063768), Wolfe (139). Cohen.

"O think not that this heart is gay." A song. 1. London: [1825]. 2. . . . written and composed by M. C. Anley. London: [1856]. 3. London: [1825].
song
GB: Lbl: 1. [G.807.C.(3.)], 2. [H.1771.(42.)], 3. [G.807.C.(3.)].
CPM.

"Rest warrior . . . " Song. London: [1825?].
song
GB: Lbl [G.807.c.(2.)].
CPM.

Anna Amalia (Amalie), Duchess of Saxe-Weimar, née von Braunschweig
1739, Wolfenbüttel–1807, Weimar
Adolar und Hilaria. Ms. score.
See: Die Zigeuner, by Anna Amalia of Saxe-Weimar.

Allegro [D major, pianoforte] comp. von der Prinzessin Amalia. Ms.
pf
CH: Zz [Ms.Car.XV 243 (23.) (Ms. 1073)].
RISM A/II (#7852).

Alma Redemptoris. Ms. score.
4 voices / orch
A: Wgm (as Amalie).
Cohen, Eitner, NG (considers attribution doubtful), Olivier.

Bänkelsängerlied ("Ihr lieben Christen allgemein"). Text by Goethe.
voice / pf
D: DÜk (#40).
Düsseldorf-Goethe.

Concerto für 12 Instrumente und obl. Cembalo.
See: Sonatina [G major] per il Cembalo obligato, Corno 1, 2, Oboe 1, 2,
Flauto l, 2, Fagotto, Violino 1, 2, Viola e Basso di Amalia.

Das Jahrmarktsfest zu Plundersweilern, eine Operette in einem Aufzuge
in Musick gesetzt von Sr. Hochfürstl. Durchl. Amalia Herzogin z. S. w.
Weimar, 20 Oct. 1778. Ms. piano score. 31 ff., 17 ms. part books. Text by
Goethe.
stage work
D: WRl, WRtl (Mus II a:2, Mus II c:3). Microfilm of ms. piano score from
D: WRtl in Randall coll.
RISM A/II (#17676), NG, Cohen, MGG, Olivier, letter (Randall).

Die Zigeuner, ein Walddrama nach K. S. von Einsiedel [also known as
Adolar und Hilaria]. Ms. piano score. 55 leaves. 25 ms. partbooks.

stage work (4 voices / orch / bc)
D: WRtl (Mus II a:ll; Mus II c:2). Microfilm of ms. piano score in Randall coll.
RISM A / II (#17677), MGG, Olivier, letter (Randall).

Divertimento [B-flat] *per il piano-forte, clarinetto, viola e violoncello* [adagio and allegro]. Weimar: Ambrosius & Zahn [c. 1780]. Parts.
pf / cl / vla / vlc
D: WRgs, WRtl. GB: Lbl (Hirsch III. 13). Copies in D: UNikb, D: KAf&m, Jackson coll., Ars Fem coll., and Randall coll. (D: WRtl).
RISM A / I (A 1246), Cohen, NG (wks list), MGG, CPM, Frauenmusik, Olivier, Frau & Musica, letters (Ars Fem, Randall).

Divertimento for Piano and Strings.
See: Sonatina [G major] per il Cembalo obligato, Corno 1, 2, Oboe 1, 2, Flauto 1, 2, Fagotto, Violino 1, 2, Viola e Basso di Amalia.
[Recorded by Rosario Marciano as *Divertimento for Piano and Strings* (TV 34754, Vox / Turnabout, 1980).]

Erwin und Elmire [Singspiel] 1776. 1. Ms. score. 184 pp. 2. Ms. score, 130 pp. & 15 partbooks. Play by Goethe.
stage work
1. A: Wn (Eitner, Ms. 16740). 2. D: WRl, WRtl (Mus II a:98. Mus II c:l).
1. Eitner. 2. RISM A / II (#17675). Cohen, NG, Mellen, MGG, Friedländer-Goethe, Olivier.

Erwin und Elmire [Singspiel], excerpts. [3 arias].
voice / acc.
D: WRtl, copies in D: KAf&m, UNikb.
Frau & Musik, Olivier.

La Forza Del Fraterno Amore. Opera Buffa in trè Atti. Ms. score. 3 vol. (142 pp, 189 pp, 49 pp).
stage work
D: B (Mus. ms. 567).
RISM A / II (#150388, attribution questioned).

Partita [per] Corno Primo, . . . Secondo, Oboe Primo, . . . Secondo, Flauto Trav: Primo, . . . Secondo, Fagotto, Violino Primo, . . . Secondo, II Viole e Basso de la Composition de S.A.S. Madame la Duchesse de Saxe Weimar. Ms., 12 parts (some missing).

orch (vlns 1 & 2/vlas 1 & 2/ b/hns 1 & 2)
D: Dl [in Dlb] (Mus. 3410 P 1).
RISM A/II (#17678, as Suite; attribution doubtful).

Regina coeli. Ms. score.
4 voices/orch
A: Wgm (as Amalie).
Cohen, Eitner, NG (considers attribution doubtful), Olivier.

Salve regina. Ms. score.
4 voices/orch
A: Wgm (as Amalie).
Cohen, Eitner, NG (considers attribution doubtful), Olivier.

"Se perdesti la Germania." Cavatina. Ms. score, 1823. Composed for Sig.
Costanza Tibaldi (all'attual Servizio di S. M. il Re di Saßonia)
mezzo-S/orch
I: Bc (Eitner, Kat. 3,264).
Letter (I: Bc), Cohen, Eitner, NG (considers attribution doubtful), Olivier.

Sinfonia [G major] a due Oboi, due Flauti, due Violini, Viola, e Basso di
AMALJA [Andante con Sordini, Allegro un poco, Presto]. 12 ms. part-
books [1765 acc. to RISM, c. 1780 acc. to Randall].
orch (2 obs/2 fls/2 vlns/vla/basso)
D: WRtl (Mus III c:110). Microfilm copy in Randall coll.
RISM A/II (#17679), MGG, Olivier, letter (Randall).

Sonatina in G di Amalia Cembalo obligato [title on inside cover, Clavier
Sonata in G] c. 1780. Autograph ms., 12 ms. partbooks (Corno 1, 2,
Oboe 1, 2, Flauto 1, 2, Fagotto, Violino 1, 2, Viola e Basso di Amalia).
hpsch/2 hns/2 obs/2 fls/bsn/2 vlns/vla/basso
D: WRtl (Mus II f:1). Copies in D: KAf&m and UNikb as Concerto für
12 Instrumente . . . , xerox copy of ms. parts in Randall coll.
*RISM A/II (#17680, listed as Concerto), MGG (considers attribution doubtful),
Olivier, D: UNikb, Frau & Music, letter (Randall).*

[2] Duetti: di Azima e Diamantina, di Rosalba e Ubaldo. Ms.
2 voices/accompaniment
A: Wgm.
Cohen, Eitner, NG (considers attribution doubtful), Olivier.

[Work(s)] in: *Notenbuch zu des akademischen Liederbuchs* erstem Bändchen . . .
Erster [-zweyter] Theil. Altona: J. D. A. Eckhardt. 1783–1796. 2 vol.
song(s)
B: Bc (2). D: F(1), DÜk (2), Mbs (1), HVl. DK: Kk. GB: Lbl. US: Wc (2).
RISM B/II (p. 260).

Anna Amalia, Princess of Prussia
1723, Berlin–1787, Berlin
Allegro für 2 Viol. u. 1 Grundstimme. In: Kirnberger, *Die Kunst des reinen
Satzes*, I, p. 226 and II, p. 75. I: Berlin: Christian Fr. Voss, 1771. II:
Berlin/Königsberg: G. J. Decker & G. L. Hartung, 1776–1779 (and later
editions).
2 vln/bc
Locations for first edition of both parts of Kirnberger only. For others see
RISM.
B: Br. D: Bds, Lr, MÜm, W, WE. F: Sim. GB: Cu, Er, Ge, Lbl. NL: At.
S: Skma. US: Cn, Cu, CA, I, IO, NYu, SLb, Wcm.
RISM–EICM, letter (D: Bds).

An den Schöpfer ("Dich soll mein Lied erheben"). Autograph ms. score,
July 14, 1780. 1 p.
voice/bc
D: Bds (Mus. ms. autogr., Friedrich d. Grosse). Facsimile in *Hohenzollern
Jahrbuch*, 1910.
Letter (D: Bds), Komponistinnen.

"Bringt Gott, ihr Christen" [chorale]. Autograph ms., 1779.
SATB/org
D: Bds (Mus. ms. autogr., Amalia 1 [5]).
Letter (D: Bds).

[Chorale] in: Kollmann, A. F. C. *An essay on musical harmony, according to the
nature of that science and the principles of the greatest musical authors.* London:
J. Dale, 1796.
SATB
B: Br. D: Bds, G. F: Pc. GB: Ckc, Cpl, Cu, Cus, Er, Ge, Lam, Lbl (3 ex.),
LEp. US: BA, BE, BER, NH, U, Wc (musical examples missing).
RISM B/II (p. 89), RISM-EICM.

[Contrapuntal exercises]. Autograph mss.
Tonarten (4 pp.), Imitationen (14 pp.), Erste Studien zur Fuge (3 pp.), &
Varia (3 pp.).

sketches (unspecified instruments)
D: Bds (Am.B. 604/9a-d).
RISM A/II (#17671, 17672, 17673, 17674), letter (D: Bds), Blechschmidt.

"Das Jahr geht still zu Ende," set to the melody of "Christ alles was dich kränket." In: *Missionsharfe,* Gr. (Bertelsm.) 2. (53).
SATB
D: Bds (Mus. 0.14466, but lost since 1945).
Letter (D: Bds).

Der Bruder und die Schwester ("Ich will mit Chloris mich vermahlen"). Duetto. Autograph ms. score, 1776.
2 voices/bc
D: Bds (Mus. Ms. autogr., Friedrich d. Grosse)
Letter (D: Bds).

Der Tod Jesu [cantata], excerpts [original never completed]. Text by Ramler. In: Kirnberger, *Die Kunst des reinen Satzes,* I, p. 226 and II, p. 75. I: Berlin: Christian Fr. Voss, 1771. II: Berlin/Königsberg: G. J. Decker & G. L. Hartung, 1776–1779 (and later editions).
choir/orch
Locations for first edition of both parts of Kirnberger only. For others see RISM.
B: Br. D: Bds, Lr, MÜm, W, WE. F: Sim. GB: Cu, Er, Ge, Lbl. NL: At. S: Skma. US: Cn, Cu, CA, I, IO, NYu, SLb, Wcm.
RISM–EICM, NG, Cohen, MGG, Komponistinnen, letter (D: Bds).

"Dir folgen meine Tränen" [text from the Roman, *Miss Fanny Wilkes*]. Autograph ms., October 31, 1777.
voice/bc
D: Bds (Mus. ms. autogr., Amalia 1 [1]).
Letter (D: Bds), Komponistinnen.

"Du, dessen Augen flossen." 1. Chorale for 4 voices, in score, the bass being figured for organ by La Princesse Amelie de Prusse. 2. In: Christmann, J. F., *Vollständige Sammlung theils ganz neu componirter, theils verbesserter, vierstimmiger Choralmelodien . . .* , p. 72. Stuttgart: Mäntler, 1799.
1. SATB/org; 2. SATB
1. GB: Lbl (Printed Book, 557, d. 34, f. 1b). 2. D: Bds (O.58903).
1. Brit. Cat. Ms. 2. Letter (D: Bds), Komponistinnen.
"Ermuntere dich mein schwacher Geist." Vier-Stimmiger Choral mit

gantzen #Accords. Consonirenden#. Autograph ms. score, 1 p.
SATB
D: Bds (Mus. ms. autogr. Amalia 1 [6]).
Letter (D: Bds).

[5 Lieder] "Rosen glücke, Rosen blühe," "Seufzer eines Ehemanns" (texts
by Gleim, composed 1776), & "Ihr Götter macht auch jünst die Müh,"
"Auf Tapfre Krieger, auf ins Feld," "Wenn ich einsam zärtlich weine."
Autograph ms., 1778.
S/bc
D: Bds (Am.B. 604/5).
RISM A/II (#17666, poet's name as Glaim), letter (D: Bds), Blechschmidt, Cohen,
Komponistinnen.

"Freu dich sehr, o meine Seele" [chorale]. Autograph ms. score, 1778. 1 p.
2 voices
D: Bds (Mus. ms. autogr.).
Letter (D: Bds).

Fünfstimmiger Zirkel-Canon in der Ober-Quinta nebst dem Contrapunct
der Octava [C major]. Autograph ms.,1779. 2 pp.
5 instruments (unspecified)
D: Bds (Am.B. 604/8 & Mus. ms. autogr. Amalia 1 [5]).
RISM A/II (#17670), letter (D: Bds), Blechschmidt, Komponistinnen.

"Gelobt, gelobt seÿst du mit Freuden" [chorale]. Autograph ms., 1779.
SATB/org
D: Bds (Mus. ms. autogr., Amalia 1 [5]).
Letter (D: Bds).

["Hiskias according to Jesaias," 2 sketches for an Oratorio]. Autograph
ms. (In Salomon: Hiskias Mus. ms. 19390).
unspecified instruments
D: Bds (Am.B. 604/12 [Mus. ms. autogr.]).
Letter (D: Bds), Blechschmidt.

"Ich hab mein Sach Gott heimgestellt" [elaborated chorale for 1 keyboard
instrument]. Autograph ms. score, 1777. 1 p.
kbd
D: Bds (Mus. ms. autogr. Amalia 1 [2]).
Letter (D: Bds).

"Io morro spietato amante." Duetto per un Alto è Soprano, from Act II, Scene IV of Metastasio's *Dido,* comp. 1780. Text edited by Sanseverino, in German and Italian. Autograph score, ms. copy of score & set of parts.
SA/strings/bc
D: Bds (Am.B. 604/4).
RISM A/II (#17664, #17665), letter (D: Bds), Blechschmidt, Komponistinnen.

"Jesu meine Freude" [elaborated chorale]. Autograph ms., 1778. 5 ff.
4 voices/orch.
D: B (Am.B. 604/3).
RISM A/II (#17669), letter (D: B), Blechschmidt, Komponistinnen.

Kleinigkeiten [sketches & beginnings]. "Gottes Allgegenwart," "Nie bist du, Höchster, von uns fern," Choral "O Ewigkeit! du Donnerwort," "Harre des Herrn," "Mache dich selbst nicht traurig" [2-voice canon?]. Autograph ms.
unspecified instruments
D: Bds (Am.B. 604/10, 11).
RISM A/II (#17663), letter (D: Bds), Blechschmidt.

Kriegslied. "Auf! tapfre Krieger" (Schlachtgesang, text by T. W. Ramler).
voices
D: Bds (modern editions only; see modern editions).
Letter (D: Bds).

"Man lobt dich in der Stille." 1. Chorale. In : Rellstab, *Melodie und Harmonie,* 1788. 2. See: *Vierstimmige Choräle für das neue Gesangbuch . . .* [see also 10 Chorales].
SATB/org
1. D: Bds (Am.B. 604/2 & Mus. 9533, lost since 1945). 2. D: Bds (Mus. ms. 568).
1. RISM A/II (#17662). 2. RISM A/II (#150390).

Marche [B-flat]. Pour le Régiment du Comte Lottum. Berlin, March 29, 1767. Autograph ms. score.
wind band (tr in B-flat/2 obs/bsn)
D: Bds (Mus. ms. autogr. Amalie 2).
Letter (D: Bds), NG, Cohen, MGG, Haynes, Komponistinnen.

Marche [B-flat]. Pour le Régiment du L. Géneral Saldern. May 16, 1768. Autograph ms. score.

wind band (tr in B-flat / 2 obs / bsn)
D: Bds (Mus. ms. autogr. Amalie 2).
Letter (D: Bds), NG, Cohen, MGG, Haynes, Komponistinnen.

Marche [E major]. First of the two marches in: Ms, c. 1790. 9 partbooks.
wind band (4 cls / 2 hns / 2 trs / bsn)
D: DS (Mus. ms 1223/21).
RISM A / II (#30617).

Marche [E-flat]. Pour le Régiment du L. Géneral Bülow. Berlin, August
14, 1767. Autograph ms. score.
wind band (tr in E-flat / 2 obs / bsn)
D: Bds (Mus. ms. autogr. Amalie 2).
Letter (D: Bds), NG, Cohen, MGG, Haynes, Komponistinnen.

March. Pour le Régiment du General F. de Möllendorff, 1777. Ms. score.
wind band (tr / 2 clarini / 2 obs / basso [bsn?])
D: Bds (Mus. ms. autogr. Friedrich d. Grosse).
*Letter (D: Bds), NG, Cohen, Komponistinnen, MGG (for arr. by Lenzewski for string
orch).*

Mess-Choräle [to the words of the German Mass]. Composed Nov. 22,
1778. Autograph ms., 4 fol. Kyrie "Hier liegt vor deiner Majestät," Zum
Gloria "Gott soll gepriesen werden," Offertorium "Nimm an, O Herr! die
Gaben," Zum Sanctus "Singt heilig, heilig, heilig" Nach der Wandlung
"Sieh, Vater! sieh vom Höchsten Thron," Zum Agnus Dei "Betrachtet ihn
in Schmerzen," Die geistliche Communion "O Herr! ich bin nicht
würdig," Zum Beschluß der Heiligen Messe "Nun ist das Lamm
geschlachtet."
4 voices / org
D: Bds (Am.B.1. 604/1).
RISM A / II (#17661), Blechschmidt, letter (D: Bds), NG (bio), Komponistinnen.

"Nun freut euch lieben Christ'n gemein" [elaborated 3-voiced chorale for
1 keyboard instrument]. Autograph ms. score, April 19, 1778. 1 p.
kbd
D: Bds (Mus. ms. autogr. Amalia 1 [3]).
Letter (D: Bds).

"O Ewigkeit! du Donnerwort." Text zu einer Kirchenmusik über Tod und
Ewigkeit verfert. v. d. Prinz. Amalie d. 28 Jun 1785. Autograph ms. score,

1785. [See also Kleinigkeiten.]
choir/orch
D: Bds (Am.B. 604/11).
RISM A/II (#17660).

Sein Odem ist schwach. [Cantata for choir and strings]. Ms., 8 pp.
voices/strings
Location of original not known. Photocopy in D: UNikb.
D: UNikb.

6 Märche [C major]. Ms, c. 1800. 8 partbooks.
Wind Band (obs/2 cls/bsn/2 hns/2 trs)
D:DS (Mus. ms. 1223/19).
RISM A/II (#30611)

Sonata per il Flauto traverso e Basso [F major]. Composed 1771.
1. Autograph ms., score. 2. Copy.
fl/bc
1. D: Bds (Am.B. 604/7). 2. US: Wc. (M242.A).
*Blechschmidt. NG, Cohen, Boenke, MGG, Komponistinnen. 1. RISM A/II
(#17667), letter (D: Bds). 2. US: Wc card cat.*

[10 Chorales]. "Auf schicke dich," "Aus deiner milden Segenshand,"
"Christ alles was dich kränket," "Der Todes Graun," "Du! daß sich alle
Himmel," "Freu dich sehr o meine Seele," "Gott dessen Hand die Welt
ernährt," "Gott ist mein Lied," "Gott sorgt für uns," "Man lobt dich in
der Stille." Autograph ms., most composed 1780.
SATB/org
D: Bds (Am.B. 604/2).
RISM A/II (#17662), Blechschmidt, Komponistinnen.

Trio [D major] für 2 Viol. u. Baß.
2 vlns/bc
D: Bds.
NG, Cohen, MGG, Komponistinnen, letter (D: Bds).

Trio for organ. In: Becker, *Cecilia.* Leipzig Bd. II, No. 8. (Kahnt)
(Stadbibliothek).
org
D: LEm.
Cohen, Pazdírek.

Vierstimmige Choräle für das neue Gesangbuch. Verfertiget von Amélie Prinzessin von Prussen, 1780. Contents: "Christ alles was dich kränket," "Gott ist mein Lied, er ist der Gott der Stärke," "Auf schicke dich recht feierlich," "Man lobt dich in der Stille." Ms. score, copied by F. A. Grasnirk, c. 1830. [See also 10 chorales.]
SATB/org
D: Bds (Mus. ms. 568).
Letter (D: Bds).

"Zion klagt mit Angst und Schmertzen" [elaborated 3-voice chorale for 1 keyboard instrument]. Autograph ms. score, 1778. 1 pp.
kbd
D: Bds (Mus. ms. autogr. Amalia 1 [4]).
Letter (D: Bds).

Zweistimmige Fuge für Violine und Viola. Composed May 5, 1776. Autograph ms., score and parts.
vln/vla
D: Bds (Am.B. 604/6).
RISM A/II (#17668), letter (D: Bds), Blechschmidt, Komponistinnen.

Anna Maria, Duchess of Prussia, née **Duchess of Braunschweig-Lüneburg** (married **Duke Albert Friedrich of Prussia**)
1532–1568, lived in Neuhausen bei Königsberg
[Psalms]. 2 mss., apparently autograph. Score.
5 voices
B: Br (#1433). PL: WRu (not confirmed if it survived the war).
Eitner, Cohen (as Braunschweig, Anna Maria von), letter (Woods).

Anna Maria von Sachsen-Jülich-Cleve, née **Mecklenburg-Schwerin** (married **August, Duke of Sachsen-Weissenfels**)
1627–1669
"Allein nach dir mein Herr und Gott." In: *Monumentum.* Halle: Christoph Salfelden, 1669. Score.
5 voices
D: WGp. Copy in Ars Fem coll.
RISM A/I (AA 1246 I, 1), letters (Ars Fem, Woods).

Anna Sophie, Landgravine of Hesse-Darmstadt and Abbess of Quedlinburg
1638, Marburg–1683, Quedlinburg

Der treue Seelen Freund Christus Jesus mit nachdencklichen Sinn Gemählden anmuthi-
gen Lehr-Gedichten und neuen geistrichen Gesangen . . . 1. Jena: Löfler, 1658. 2.
[new ed. with Neuer Anhang]. Frankfurt/Leipzig: Henning Grossens . . . ,
1675. 3. Leipzig, 1689.
songs
1. D: W. GB: Lbl. 2. D: MGu, US: CAa (770 A614tr 1675). 3. Location
unknown.
1–3. Letter (Woods) 2. NUC (NA 0331551).

Anna von Köln
fl. 1525
Liederbuch der Anna von Köln. Ms.
monophonic songs
D: B (germ.oct.280). Photocopy (14 pp.) in: D: UNikb.
MGG (entry on Lied), NG (entry on Sources), D: UNikb.

Anonymous (Governess of the Female Orphan School of Limerick)
pub. c. 1820, Dublin
A Sonata for the Piano Forte, published for the benefit of the Female Orphan
School of Limerick, composed by one of the governesses . . . Dublin:
W. Power's [c. 1820]. 5 pp.
pf
GB: Lbl [g.352.w.(8.)].
CPM.

Anonymous (Nun of the order of S. Clare)
pub. 1688, Venice. Convent in Rome.
Philomela Angelica Cantionum Sacrarum, quas Romæ Virgo quædam DEO
dicata Ordinis S. Claræ. Venice: Daniel Speer, 1688. 6 partbooks (C & B,
A instr. & voce, T instr. & voce, Vln I, Vln II, Continuus). [5 motets for
C + 5 str; 1 for 2 A + 4 str; 1 for A + 5 str; 12 for ATB + 2 str]. S/5 str;
A/5 str; AA/4 str; ATB/2 str; all with org bc.
1–3 voices; 2–5 strings/bc
D: F (complete: SATB/2 vlns/bc, 2 ex.). F: Pn. Microfilm copy in Jackson
coll.
RISM A/I (S 4073), Eitner (under Speer), Brenet, Cohen (under Clarisse de Roma).

Anonymous. See also **Lady (anonymous).** Composers who published
with initials only are listed by initials

Anspach (Ansbach), Elizabeth, Margravine of. See Craven, Elizabeth, née Berkeley

Argenville, Mme. d'

pub. 1783, Paris

Menuet de 1 Acte du Feu de Mr. Edelmann [arr. by Mme. d'Argenville]. In: *Journal de clavecin par les meilleurs maîtres*, 2me Année #5. Paris: LeDuc, May 1783 [with violin part].

hpsch/vln

F: Pn.

RISM B/II (pp. 206–207), letter (C. Johnson).

Arkwright, Mrs. Robert, née Kemble

d. 1849, England

The Greek Exile. A ballad by Mrs. Hemans, the music by Mrs. R. Arkwright. Boston: C. Bradlee [1830–58?]. 4 pp.

voice/pf

US: Cn (Case sheet music oM 1 .A13 No. 455)

NUC Sup. (NSA 0080245).

One struggle more, ballad. [Words] by Lord Byron; music by Mrs. Robert Arkwright. Boston: Oliver Ditson [c. 1840]. 4 pp.

voice/pf

US: HA.

OCLC (17697948).

A set of six ancient Spanish ballads, historical and romantic. The words by John Lockhart, . . . music by Mrs. Robert Arkwright. London: J. Power [c. 1832]. 63 pp.

voice/pf

US: NH.

OCLC (20911884).

Treasures of the deep, a ballad. [Words] by Mrs. Hemans, the music by Mrs. Robt. Arkwright. 1. New York: Dubois & Stodart, [between 1827 and 1834]. 4 pp. 2. New York: Dubois & Stodart [183–?].

voice/pf

US: 1. US: DM (W.C.L. M780.88 R58VD no. 14), 2. HA.

1. NUC Sup. (NSA 0080246), OCLC (9511266), 2. OCLC (17698612). Cohen.

Xarifa, or, *The bridal of Andalla.* Written by John Lockhart; music by Mrs. Robt. Arkwright. 1. Boston: C. Bradlee [1834–40]. 2. Baltimore: G. Willig [18—]. 3 pp.

voice/pf

1. US: Cn (Case sheet music oM1 .A13 No. 396). 2. Pu.
1. NUC Sup (NSA 0080247). 2. OCLC (24526672).

Arnim, Bettina (Elisabeth) von, née Brentano (Pseud. Beans van Bor)

1785, Frankfurt–1859, Berlin

7 Gesangstücke mit Pianoforte dedié à Spontini. Leipzig: En Commission chez Breitkopf & Härtel [1843]. Contents: "Mondenschein schlafert ein," "O schaudre nicht," "Wintergarten," "Ein Stern der Lieb," "Herbstgefühl," "Abendstille" (duet), "Vom Nachten getragen" (duet).

1 or 2 voices/pf

D: DÜk (Nr. 51). Copy in D: UNikb.

NG (as Brentano), Cohen, Friedlander-Goethe, Frauenmusik, letter (D: DÜk).

Aus *Faust.* Autograph ms.
voice/pf
D: DÜk. Copy in D: UNikb.
Frauenmusik, letter (D: DÜk).

"Ein Stern der Lieb." Autograph ms.
voice/pf
D: DÜk. Copy in D: UNikb.
Frauenmusik, letter (D: DÜk).

Hafis. Autograph ms.
voice/pf
D: DÜk. Copy in D: UNikb.
Frauenmusik, letter (D: DÜk).

Lied beim Scharpiezupfen für Gesang und Klavier.
voice/pf
Original source not known. Copies in D: Kf&m, UNikb.
Frau & Musik, Frauenmusik.

Lied des Schülers aus *Isabella von Ägypten, Kaiser Karls des Fünften erste Jugendliebe.* Text by Achim von Arnim, melody by Bettina von Arnim.
1. Berlin: 1812. 2. In *Novellen von Ludwig* Achim von Arnim. Ed. Wilhelm Grimm. Berlin: 1839. 3. Autograph ms.
voice/pf
1–3. D: DÜk. Copies in D: Kf&m, UNikb.
Frau & Musik, Frauenmusik, letter (D: DÜk).

"Mondenschein schläfert ein." Autograph ms.
voice/pf
D: DÜk. Copy in D: UNikb.
Frauenmusik, letter (D: DÜk).

"O schaudre nicht" from Goethe's *Faust*. Melody by Bettina von Arnim,
accompaniment by Joseph Joachim. In: *Armut, Reichthum, Schuld und Buße
der Gräfin Dolores* . . . vol. 2. Berlin: Realschule Buchhandlung, 1810. [See
also *7 Gesangstücke mit Pianoforte . . . Spontini.*]
voice/pf
D: DÜk (Nr. 52). Copy in: D: UNikb.
NG (as Brentano), letter (D: DÜk), Cohen, Frauenmusik, Friedlander-Goethe.

Romanze. Autograph ms.
voice/pf
D: DÜk. Copy in D: D: UNikb.
Frauenmusik, letter (D: DÜk).

Romanze ("Der Kaiser flieht vertrieben") from: Achim von Arnim, *Armut,
Reichtum, Schuld und Buße der Gräfin Dolores.* 1. Written, 1839. Weimar: 1842.
2. Under the Pseud. Beans van Bor, in *Ludwig Achims v. Arnim Sämtliche
Werke,* Berlin: 1853, 1840.
voice/pf
D: Kf&m, UNikb.
Frau & Musik, Frauenmusik.

Suleika. Autograph ms.
voice/pf
D: DÜk. Copy in D: UNikb.
Frauenmusik, letter (D: DÜk).

Vision des Heiligen Johannes. Autograph ms.
voice/pf
D: DÜk. Copy in D: UNikb.
Frauenmusik, letter (D: DÜk).

Vom Nachten getragen. [Duet]. Autograph ms.
2 voices/pf
D: DÜk. Copy in D: UNikb.
Frauenmusik, letter (D: DÜk).

Wanderers Nachtlied. Autograph ms.
voice/pf
D: DÜk. Copy in D: UNikb.
Frauenmusik, letter (D: DÜk)

Assandra, Caterina (Catherina, Catharina)

c. 1580, fl. 1609, Italian, worked in Pavia
"Ego flos campi" & "Ave verum corpus." In organ tablature ms.
org
D: Rtt (Musikhandschrift F.K.mus.II.Abt. 22). Copy in Jackson coll.
Cohen, letter (D: Rtt).

"Impetum fecerunt in Stephanum" & "O dulcis amor, Jesu." 1. In:
Promptuarii Musici, Concentus Ecclesiasticos II. III. et IV. vocum æ Coll. by
Joanne Donfrido . . . Strasbourg: P. Ledertz, 1622. 5 partbooks. 2. In: *Siren
coelestis duarum, trium et quatuor vocum.* Munich: A. de Berg, 1616. 2a.
Reprint, 1622. 4 partbooks.
SSB; SAT; SSA/all with org bc
1. A: K. B: Br. CH: Fcl (v 1). D: HR (bc), Kl (v 1), LEm (v.1 & 2), Mbs, Rp
(v. 2–4), Rs (bc), Sl (v. 1 & 3). F: Pn. GB: Lbm (v. 2–4). PL: Wu (v. 1 & 2,
bc), S (lost in WW II). 2. D: Rp, SAh (T inc.). 2a. D: F, Mbs (bc inc.). GB:
Lbl (S missing).
*1. RISM B/I (1622 [2]), Bohn, Eitner. 2–2a. RISM B/I (1616 [2], reprint
1622 [3]). Bowers & Tick, NG, Cohen, MGG.*

"Salve Regina." In: Benedetto Rè, *Integra Psalmodia.* Venice: A. Vincenti,
1611.
8 voices
I: Bc.
MGG, Eitner, Cohen.

[17] *Motetti à due & trè voci, per cantar nell'Organo con il Basso continuo* . . .
opera seconda. . . . Milano: heredi di Simon Tini & Filippo Lomazzo,
1609. 4 partbooks (C I, C II with violin and violone, B and A, bc,
unfigured).
SB; SSB; SAT; SAA; all with org bc; SB/vln/violone/org bc
D: Rp (B only). I: Bc (V.III). Microfilms in US: CAi (3167.768.58.1),
Jackson coll. and Ars Fem coll.
*RISM A/I (A 2637), RISM B/I (1609 [3]), Bowers & Tick, NG, Cohen, Eitner,
MGG, letters (US: CAi, Ars Fem).*

Atkinson, Miss

fl. 1785. Pub. London
How sleep the brave. An ode by Collins. [London]: G. S[mart] [c.1785]
voice/kbd
GB: Lbl [G. 308. (119)]. Copy in Ars Fem coll.
RISM A/I (AA 2655 I, 1), BUC, CPM, letter (Ars Fem).

The shepherd's complaint. [London]: G. S[mart] [c. 1785].
voice/kbd
GB: Lbl [G. 306.(146.)]. Copy in Ars Fem coll.
RISM A/I (AA 2655 I, 2), BUC, CPM, letter (Ars Fem).

Aubert, Mrs.

pub. 1719, London
Harlequin-Hydaspes, or *The Greshamite.* Burletta, 3 acts. A mock-opera. As it
is performed at the theatre in Lincoln's Inn Fields. [A parody of Francesco
Mancini's *Idaspe fedele*]. Perf. London. Lincoln's Inn Fields, May 27, 1719.
stage work
US: AA, CA, Cu, NH, PHu.
NUC (NA 0487150), Mellen.

Aubigny von Engelbrunner (Engelbronner), Nina d'. (Jana Synandina Gertrut d'Aubigny von)

Kassel, 1787–?, Bombay
*Briefe an Natalie über den Gesang, als Beförderung der häuslichen Glückseligkeit und
des geselligen Vergnügens.* Ein Handbuch für Freunde des Gesanges. [8 music
ex.] 1. Leipzig, 1803. 2. 2d enlarged edition, 1824.
instruction book (voice)
1. D: Mbs. CH: E. US: Wc (MT820.E56). 2. A: Wgm. B: Br. D: HVs,
LEm. GB: Lbl. US: BE, NH, NYp, PHu, U, Wc (MT820.E562).
1. Eitner, 1–2. NUC (NE 0124641–2), OCLC (16827358 & 2229575). Cohen.

Deutsche, italienische und französiche Gesänge mit Begleitung des Pianoforte.
Augsburg: Gondhardtsche Musikhandlung, #351 [1797].
voice/pf
A: Wgm. D: Kf&m. GB: Lbl (E. 118.). Copy of A: Wgm in Ars Fem coll.
RISM A/I (AA 2840 I, 1), Cohen, Eitner, CPM, Frau & Music, letter (Ars Fem).

Drei hindostanisch-persishe Lieder für Singstimme und Klavier. Offenbach am
Main: [André], #2280, n.d.
voice/pf

Copy in D: Kf&m. Location of original unknown.
Frau & Musik.

Margretens Romanze für Singstimme und Klavier. Offenbach am Main: [André], #2280, n.d.
voice/pf
Copy in D: Kf&m. Location of original unknown.
Frau & Musik.

Six songs with original English and translated German text. Work 8th. Collection lst (& 2d). Offenbach: Johann André, # 2279, 2280, n.d.
voice/pf
D: GOl, Kf&m, OF.
RISM A/I (AA 2840 I, 2), Frau & Musik, Cohen.

Weep no more, a song. London: s.n. [1806?].
voice/pf
GB: Lbl [H. 1668. (18.)].
RISM A/I (AA 2840 I, 3), Cohen, Eitner, CPM.

The woodland hallò [song]. London: G. J. Vollweiler [1806?].
voice/pf
GB: Lbl [H. 1668. (19.)].
RISM A/I (AA 2840 I, 4), Cohen, Eitner, CPM.

Audini, Mlle
pub. late 18th century, Paris
[Work(s)] in: *Etrennes lyriques anacréontiques* . . . [ed. Cholet de Jetphort]. Paris: l'auteur, 1784–89, 1793–94, 1803, 1808–22.
undetermined
B: Bc (1786), Lc (1788). E: Mn (1786), F: CF (1784, 89), Pc (1784–89, 93), Pn, RS (1789), VN (1790). US: Cn (1786), R (1785).
RISM B/II (p. 169).

Auenbrugg, Marianna d' (von) (Auenbrugger, Auenbrügger)
d. 1786, Vienna
Sonata per il clavicembalo o forte piano . . . con ode d'un amico & ammiratore delle di lei rare virtudi, messa in musica dal . . . Anton Salieri. Vienna: Artaria & Co., #14 [c. 1787].
hpsch or pf
A: Wgm (2 ex.), Wst. B: Gc. DK: Kk. I: TLP. US: Wc (M23 A92 Case &

Microfilm). Copy of B: Gc in Ars Fem coll. and of US: Wc in Jackson coll.
RISM A/I (A 2851, AA2851), RISM B/II, Eitner, Cohen, Meggett, NUC (micro. NA 0493261), letter (Ars Fem).

Auernhammer, Josepha Barbara von. See **Aurnhammer, Josephine**

Augusta Sophia, Princess of Great Britain and Ireland
Six Canzonets . . . Dedicated to . . . the Queen . . . The Copyright . . . presented to M. A. C. Welsh. London: [1810?].
songs
GB: Lbl [H.1213.].
CPM.

Aurelia, Schwester (Sister)
pub. 1782, Leipzig
Wie's hergieng bey der höchst schauervollen Exekution, welche im Monath Hornung dieses Jahrs an einigen Hundert eingesperrten Schwestern, und . . . an der ehrsürdigen Mutter Anastase . . . (Lied) mit musik fürs Klavier. Leipzig: s.n., 1782.
voice/kbd
A: Wn (2 ex.), Wst. H: Ba. Copy in Ars Fem coll.
RISM A/I (A 2872, AA 2872), Cohen, letter (Ars Fem).

Aurnhammer, Josephine von (Auernhammer, Aurenhammer, Josepha Barbara von). Married **Bösenhönig (Bessenig)**
1758, Vienna–1820, Vienna
Dix Variations dediées à Madame la Baronne de Braun . . . [on Salieri's "La Stessa, la stessima"]. Vienna, *Magazin de Musique des Théâtres* "op. 63," [1799] (Cohen & MGG), [1803] (NG)
hpsch or pf
CS: K. D: BNba, Mbs.
RISM A/I (A 2877, AA 2877), Eitner (B.B.), Cohen, NG, Meggett (given as two works), MGG .

VIII. Variazione per il clavicembalo o piano forte sopra la contradanza del ballo intitolato "La Figlia mal Custodita." Vienna: Artaria & Co., No. 507, [1794].
hpsch or pf
A: Wgm (as *La Figlia mal Garde*), Wst. D: DEl, DO. I: BGi. Copy of A: Wgm in Ars Fem coll.
RISM A/I (A 2875, AA 28875), Eitner (B.B.), Cohen, NG, Meggett (as D:ddr: Deutsche [sic for Dessau]), MGG.

"Pace caro io sposo." Duo varié pour le Clavecin ou Pfte. par Madame Josephe Aurnhammer. In Ms. collection, with: 2 Sonatas [for piano] by Sigra. Giuseppa d'Aurnhammer.
hpsch or pf
Formerly D: Bds (Eitner, Ms. 901). Now lost (NG).
Cohen (as Duo varié, 4 hand), NG, MGG, Meggett, Eitner.

VI. Variazione per il clavicembalo della opera Molinara, "Nel cor piu non mi Sento."
Leipzig: Breitkopf & Härtel/Speyer: Bossler, # 226, 1791.
hpsch
A: Wgm. Copy in Ars Fem coll.
RISM A/I (A 2876), Cohen, NG, Meggett, Eitner (B.B.), MGG (dated 1790), letter (Ars Fem).

VI Variazione per il forte piano (dedicated to Countess Rumbeke). Vienna: Tranquillo Mollo & Co., #160, 1801.
pf
A: Wst.
RISM A/I (A 2878), Eitner (B.B.), Cohen, NG, Meggett, MGG.

Sechs Variationen über ein ungarisches Thema
See: *6 variations sur un thême hongrois pour le piano-forte.*

VI. Variazioni dell' aria "Der Vogelfänger bin ich ja" . . . del Sig.r Mozart, . . .
clavicembalo or piano forte. 1. Vienna: Artaria, 1792. 2. As: *Six Variations de l'air: "Der Vogelfänger bin ich ja"* . . . (*Journal de musique pour les dames,* #49). Offenbach: Johann André, 1793.
hpsch or pf
1. A: M (this copy now lost). CS: Pnm. D: DO, HAu. I: Nc. YU: Zha.
2. CS: Pu. DK:Kk. S: Sm.
1–2. RISM A/I (A 2873, A 2874). NG, MGG, Cohen, Meggett.

6 variations sur un thême hongrois pour le piano-forte. Vienna: Chemische Druckerey, #1409 [c. 1810].
pf
A: Wn. Copy in Ars Fem coll.
RISM A/I (A 2880), Cohen, NG, Meggett, letter (Ars Fem).

[Sonata in C for cembalo and violin]. 2 Ms. partbooks.
hpsch/vln
D: Bds (Eitner, Ms. 900 in K.). Lost (according to NG).
Cohen (kbd as piano), NG (kbd as piano), Eitner, MGG.

[10 Variations on the theme of the ballet *Les folies amoureuses.* Vienna: Cappi]. [May be the same as *Dix Variations* . . . , which see.] Paris: *Magazin de Musique des Theätres,* # 63.
pf
D: BNba, Mbs (Meggett).
Meggett, Cohen, NG (believes lost), MGG (as Auernhammer).

2 Sonatas [for piano] by Sigra. Giuseppa d'Aurnhammer. In same ms. vol. as "Pace caro io sposo."
hpsch or pf
Formerly D: Bds (Eitner, Ms. 901). Now lost (NG).
NG, MGG, Meggett, Eitner.

Variations pour le piano-forte . . . dediées a Madame la Comtesse de Migazzi née Comtesse de Thürheim. Vienna: Ludwig Maisch # 386, [1810].
pf
A: Wgm.
RISM A/I (A 2879), Cohen, NG, Meggett, Eitner (as an untitled vol. of variations in A: Wgm).

[Work(s)] in: *Notenblätter zur musikalischen Korrespondenz der teutschen Filarmonischen Gesellschaft.* Speir: Bossler, 1790–92. 3 vol.
undetermined
A: Wgm, Wn (1–2), Wst (1–2). D: LEm, Mbs, MÜs (3), Rp, Rs, SP, WRm (2), WÜu. F: Po (2–3).
RISM B/II (p. 260).

Aurore, Mlle

late 18th cent., French
[Work(s)] in: *Etrennes de Polymnie. Recueil de chansons, romances, vaudevilles* . . . Paris: au bureau de la petite bibliothèque des théatres, Belin, 1785–89. 5 vol.
song(s)
D: LEm. F: Ma, Pcf, Pn, V. US: Wc. Other library holdings are incomplete runs.
RISM B/II (p. 168).

B

B., C., Miss
pub. c. 1795, Edinburgh
Earl St. Vincent's Strathspey by Miss C. B. Edinburgh: N. Stewart [c. 1795].
kbd
GB: Lbl [G.426.xx.(13.)].
CPM.

B., Countess of (Countess of Balcarres?)
pub. between 1813 and 1816, Albany, NY
Lady Eliza Lindsays [*sic*] *hornpipe.* By the Countess of B. Albany: I. C.
Goldberg [1813-16]. 1 p.
pf
US: NYmc.
Wolfe (Addenda, 10120).

B., Dem[oiselle]s. v[on].
published c. 1800, Hamburg, etc.
[Work(s)] in: *Auswahl der besten Compositionen für das Clavier oder Pianoforte von
dem berühmtesten Componisten . . .* [ed. by Johann Heinrich Olbers].
Hamburg: Meyn, Hanover: J. T. Lamminger [c. 1800]. 4 vol.
clavichord or pf
D: Lr.
RISM B/II (p. 110).

B., Madame Elise
n.d.
Douze Alemands pour le Piano Forte composées par Madame Elise B. S.l., s.n.
[Vienna: Kozeluch?].
pf
A: Wst.
RISM A/I (IN 26).

B., Mlle de [compositions listed may be by different composers using the same initial]
pub. 1696, Paris
[Air] in: *Recueil d'airs sérieux et à boire de différents auteurs pour l'année 1696.*
Paris: C. Ballard, 1696.

song
D: Mbs. F: Pc, Pn. GB: Lbl. Other library holdings incomplete runs.
RISM B/II (1696 [2]).

pub. 1714, Paris
[Work(s)] in: *Recueil d'airs sérieux et à boire de différents auteurs pour l'année 1714.*
Paris: C. Ballard, 1714.
song(s)
F: Pn. US: NYp. Other library holdings incomplete for this year.
RISM B/II (p. 314).

B., Mme de
n.d.
Raccolta di Romances per Canto e Pianoforte o Arpa su testo francese . . . ("O sou-
venir a mon cœur," "La comparaison de l'amour et de l'amitié,"
"Romance" (Paroles de Mr le Comte de Taxis), "Le Temps et l'Amour"
(Paroles de Mr le Baron de Munkhausen). S.l., s.n., n.d.
voice/pf or harp
I: Mc.
RISM A/II (IN 24).

B******, Mrs.
pub. c. 1811, London
My Life, I love you! Set to music with an accompaniment for the piano forte,
by Mrs. B******. London: Printed by J. Monro [1811]. Text by Lord
Byron.
voice/pf
GB: Lbl [G.425.ss.(2.)].
CPM.

B., Pauline von
pub. 1805, Leipzig
Frage und Antwort ("Wie des Bächleins leises Stöhnen"). [Lied] in: *Journal für
deutsche Frauen von deutsche Frauen geschrieben*, Leipzig: G. J. Göschen, 1805.
voice/pf
D: DÜk (#56).
Düsseldorf-Goethe.

B . . . d . . . , Mlle de
pub. 1716, Paris

[Work(s)] in: *Recueil d'airs sérieux et à boire de différents auteurs pour l'année 1716.* Paris: C. Ballard, 1716.
song(s)
F: Pn. Complete run only listed.
RISM B/II (p. 314).

Bachmann, Charlotte Caroline Wilhelmine, née Stowe
1757, Berlin–1817, Berlin
"Mädchen, wenn dein Lächeln winket." Lied in: Rellstab, J. C. Fr., *Clavier-Magazin für Kenner und Liebhaber.* Quarterly vol. #19. Berlin: Verlag der Rellstabschen Musikhandlung, 1787.
voice/kbd
D: Dl, MB. US: AA (lacks vol. 3).
RISM B/II (p. 131), Cohen, Eitner, NG, MGG.

[Work(s)] in: *Sammlung kleiner Clavier Stücke von verschiedenen Meistern.* 1tes Heft. Vienna: F. A. Hoffmeister [c. 1787].
kbd (probably pf)
A: Wn. D: Mbs.
RISM B/II (p. 131, as S[towe?] Bachmann).

Badalla (Badalli), Rosa Giacinta (Hiacinta)
pub. 1684, Venice
Camillio Tellier. [cantata] Ms., 1697.
voice (baritone)/2 trs/org bc
F: Pn (spelled Badalli).
Letter (Ars Fem), NG, Eitner (as Italian ariettes).

"Vuo [*sic*] cercando quella speme" [song or cantata]. In: Cantatas, arias, etc. with figured bass harpsichord score. Ms., after 1699.
voice/bc
GB: Lbl (Harley 1273, #62, f. 44–56. Spelled Badalli).
Eitner, CPM.

[12] Motetti a voce sola. Venice: Giuseppe Sala, 1684.
voice/bc
B: Bc (as of 1992 cannot be located in collection), Br.
RISM A/I (B 624 , BB 624), Cohen, Eitner, Bowers & Tick, NG, letter (Ars Fem).

Baird, Henrietta, of Saughton-Hall

pub. [1801], Edinburgh/London
[Two tunes] in: M., Miss, of O. *Lady Maria Parker's . . . Strathspey . . . To which is added four tunes,* two of which are composed by Miss H. Baird of Saughton-Hall. Edinburgh: Gow & Shepherd; London: John Gow, [1801].
instrument undetermined
GB: Lbl [g.352.jj.(5.)].
CPM.

Balcarres, Countess of (Barnard, Lady Anne, née Lindsay)

1750–1825, pub. Edinburgh
Work(s) in: *A collection of celebrated marches & quick steps for the piano forte, flute, violin, &c . . .* composed by . . . Countess of Blacarras [*sic*], Mrs. Major Tytler, Meschett, Watlen, &c. Edinburgh: J. Watlen [c.1796].
pf/vln/fl/etc. (specific instrumentation undetermined)
GB: Gu.
BUC.

[Work(s)] in: *A selection of Scotch, English, Irish and foreign airs, adapted for the fife, violin or german flute . . .* Volume the first [fifth]. Glasgow: J. Aird. [1782–97]
fife, vln, or fl/kbd
EIR: Dn (1–3). F: Pc (2). GB: En (inc.), Gm (inc.), Lbl (2–5). US: Nf (1–2).
RISM B/II (p. 106), Northampton.

Bamberger, Regina

pub. 1830s, Frankfurt, Leipzig.
Fantasiestück für das Pianoforte. Leipzig: Breitkopf & Härtel (#6473), n.d.
pf
D: Kf&m.
Frau & Musik.

La Perte, Andante pour Pianoforte, op. 2. Th. Henkel, n.d.
pf
D: Kf&m.
Frau & Musik.

Sechs Walzer für das Piano-Forte. Frankfurt: Bei A. Fischer [c. 1835]. 9 pp.
pf
GB: Lbl [e.283.f.(1.)].
CPM.

Souvenir de Frankfort, op. 4. Th. Henkel, n.d.
pf
D: Kf&m.
Frau & Musik.

Wasserfahrt, Fantasiestück für das Pianoforte, op. 3. Th. Henkel (#6473), n.d.
pf
D: Kf&m.
Frau & Musik.

Bannister (Banister), Miss
pub. 1790s, London, Philadelphia
"When we sailors, lad, first put to sea." A favorite song, sung by Mr.
Bannister. 1. London: Longman & Broderip. 2. As "When we sailor lads
first put to sea." Philadelphia: G. Willig [1799?]. 3. In: Collection of early
American Music, published or manuscript, v. 3, #36 [179–?–182–?].
voice/pf
1. GB: KNt, Obharding. 2. US: Wc. 3. US: Wc (M 1.A11). Copy in Ars
Fem coll.
*1–2. RISM A/I (BB 851 III, 1 & 2). 2. Sonneck (In Thomas Attwood's "The
mariners" as "Compos'd by Miss Bannister"). 3. NUC (NB 0097947). Letter
(Ars Fem).*

Banti, Brigitta, née Giorgi
Monticelli d'Ongina, c. 1756–Bologna, 1806
"God save Great George our King" . . . God save the King as sung by
Sig[no]ra Banti . . . publish'd with her graces & ornaments [c. 1800].
Embellishments and Graces only by Banti
voice/pf
GB: Lbl [H.1652.w.(3.)].
CPM.

"When Britain first at Heav'ns command" . . . *Rule Britannia* [song from
T. A. Arne's *Alfred*] as sung by Sig[no]ra Banti . . . publish'd with her
graces & ornaments [c. 1800].
Embellishments and Graces only by Banti
voice/pf
GB: Lbl [fol.H.1652.vv.(4.)].
CPM, NG (bio only; biography by her son Giuseppe Banti, SJ (1869) in I: Bc).

Baptista, Gracia. An incorrect form of the name. See **Gracia Baptista (nun).**

Barnard, Lady Anne, née **Lindsay.** See **Balcarras, Countess of**

Barthélemon, Cecilia Maria (Mrs. Henslowe)
1770, London?–c. 1827, London?
The Capture of the Cape of Good Hope, for the pianoforte or harpsichord, concluding with a song & chorus. [London]: Lewis Lavenu [1795].
voices / pf or hpsch
GB: Lbl [g.272.t.(5.)]. Microfilm in C. Johnson coll.
RISM A/I (B 1076), BUC, CPM, Cohen, Eitner, Meggett, Olivier, letter (C. Johnson).

Six sonatas for the harpsichord or pianoforte or with an accompanyment for a violin.
London: Printed for the author by E. Riley [c. 1800].
pf or hpsch / vln
US: PHu.
OCLC (21940292).

Sonata [G] for the piano-forte or harpsichord . . . dedicated to J. Haydn . . . op. 3. London: John Bland, 1794. 9 pp.
pf or hpsch
GB: Gu, Lbl [g. 143.(1.)], Ob. H: Bn. Microfilm of Lbl copy in C. Johnson coll.
RISM A/I (B 1074, BB 1074), BUC, CPM, Cohen, Meggett, Olivier, Eitner, letter (C. Johnson).

A sonata for the piano-forte or harpsichord, with an accompaniment for a violin . . . op. IV. London: Longman & Broderip, for the Authoress [c. 1795]. Parts.
pf or hpsch / vln
GB: Gu (incomplete), Lbl (2 ex.) [g.188.(2.) & R.M.17.f.14.(7.)], Ob. Microfilm of Lbl copy in C. Johnson coll.
RISM A/I (B 1075), BUC, CPM, Cohen, Meggett, Olivier, letter (C. Johnson).

Three sonatas for the piano-forte, or harpsichord, the second with an accompaniment for the violin . . . opera prima. Vauxhall: The Author,1786. Score, 22 pp. Dedicated to Princess Sophia Matilda [NYp copy with composer's autograph].
pf or hpsch / vln

GB: Gu, Lbl (2 ex.) [g.147.(1.) & R.M.16.b.22.] (date [1791]), Ob. H: Bn.
US: NYp. Copies in C. Johnson coll., Ars Fem coll., and D: Kf&m.
*RISM B 1072, BUC (date 1791), CPM, NUC (NB 0156333), Frau & Musik,
Cohen, Eitner, Meggett, Olivier, MGG (bio), letters (C. Johnson, Ars Fem).*

*Two sonatas for the piano-forte, or harpsichord, with accompaniments for the violin,
german flute & violoncello* . . . opera seconda. 1. [London, 1792]. Parts.
2. London: for the author by E. Riley . . . [1803?]. [Composer's presenta-
tion copy to Henslowe, with autograph]. 3. London: Vauxhall, 1792.
pf or hpsch / vln or flute / vlc
1. GB: Gu, Lbl [g.192.(2.)], Ob. 2. US: NYp. 3. D: UNikb [cat. date as
1729]. Copies of GB: Lbl copy in C. Johnson coll. and D: Kf&m
*RISM A/I (B 1073), BUC, CPM, Cohen, Eitner, Boenke, Meggett, letter
(C. Johnson), Frau & Musik. 2. NUC (NA 056335). 3. Olivier.*

Barthélemon, Maria (Mary, Polly), née **Young**
1749, London–1799, London.
An ode on the late providential preservation of our . . . *Gracious Sovereign* . . . op.
5. London: Culliford, Rolf & Barrow [c.1795]. 7 pp.
Text by Baroness Nolcken.
voice / kbd
GB: Lbl [C.368.(4.)], Ob.
RISM A/I (B 1134 [2 ex.]), CPM, Cohen, Eitner (dated 1800), BUC, MGG.

Six English and Italian songs . . . opera 2da. Vauxhall [London]: author;
Harrison & Co., Longman & Broderip, Thompson, Napier, Holland
[c. 1790]. 25 pp.
S or T / violins and pf or string quartet
F: Pc [Fol.Y.370]. GB: Bu, Gu, Lbl, Obharding. US: Bp. Copy in Ars Fem
coll.
*RISM A/I (B 1132, BB 1132), CPM (date as 1786), BUC, NG (under Young
family), Cohen, Eitner, MGG, letter (Ars Fem).*

Six sonatas for the harpsichord or piano forte with an accompanyment for a violin.
1. London: William Napier, for the authoress [1776]. 26 pp. 2. London:
E. Riley, c. 1780. 26 pp.
hpsch or pf / vln
GB: Lbl (2 ex.) [h.40. & R.M.16.b.24]. US: PHu (lacks vln), R, Wc.
Copies of GB: Lbl copy in C. Johnson coll. and Ars Fem coll.
*RISM A/I (B 1136, BB 1136a), CPM, BUC, Cohen, Eitner, Meggett, MGG,
NUC Sup. (NSB 0025279), letters (C. Johnson, Ars Fem).*

Three hymns, and three anthems . . . composed for the Asylum and Magdalen Chapels
. . . op. 3. London: John Bland, for the authoress [c. 1794]. 21 pp.
2 solo treble voices/treble unison choir/SAB choir/org
GB: En, Lbl (2 ex.) [G.503.(1.) & R.M.14.f.4.(2.)] (date [1795]), Ob.
H: Bn. US: Wc (M20458 .B Case). Microfilm of US: Wc in Jackson coll.
RISM A/I (B 1133), CPM, BUC, Cohen, Eitner, MGG.

The Weavers' Prayer [song]. London: Preston & son, [c. 1790?]. 4 pp.
voice/kbd
GB: Lbl (2 ex.) [H.28322.g.(7.) & R.M.8.b.11.].
RISM A/I (B 1135), BUC, CPM, Cohen, Eitner, MGG.

Bartolozzi, Theresa (Mrs.)

pub. 1814–20?, London
Dussek's Minuet, with five brilliant Variations for the Piano Forte. London: Printed
by G. Walker [1814]. 16 pp.
pf
GB: Lbl [h.3870.s.(15.)].
CPM.

Four quadrilles and one waltz. London: s.n. [1820].
pf
GB: Lbl [h.103.(4.)].
CPM.

Rosy Ann, a favourite song with an accompaniment for the piano forte. The
Melody . . . by Mrs. Bartolozzi. [London:] Printed for G. Shade [1815?].
Melody only by Bartolozzi
voice/pf
GB: Lbl [G.424.a.(5.)].
CPM.

Bataille, Mlle

pub. 1699–1704, Paris
[Work] in: *Recueil d'airs sérieux et à boire de différents auteurs pour l'année 1699.*
Paris, C. Ballard, 1699.
song
F: Pc, Pn.
RISM B/I (1699 [2]).

[Work(s)] in: *Recueil d'airs sérieux et à boire de différents auteurs pour l'année 1704.*
Paris: C. Ballard, 1704.
song(s)
CH: MO. F: Pc (2 ex.), Pn.
RISM B/II (p. 312).

Bauer, Catherine

b. c. 1800, United States
A favorite waltz. With 12 variations for the piano forte composed at the age
of thirteen by Miss Catherine Bauer, pupil of Mr. Sterkel. Philadelphia,
G. E. Blake [1814–17].
pf
US: BUg, PHfk, NYp, Wc.
Wolfe (466).

Bauer, Katharine (Catharina)

1785, Würzburg–after 1798
Douze variations de l'air . . . Schüßerl und . . . Reind'l composées pour le piano-forte
. . . Offenbach: Johann André (#1395), n.d.
pf
CS: Bm, K. D: DEsa. DK: Kk. Copy of DK: Kk in Ars Fem coll.
RISM A/I (BB 1337 I, 1), Eitner, Cohen, Meggett, MGG, letter (Ars Fem).

Douze variations pour le piano-forte. Offenbach: Johann André (#1193), 1798.
pf
D: DEsa.
RISM A/I (BB 1337 I, 1), Eitner, Cohen, Meggett, MGG.

Baur, Marie-Marguerite

1748–? fl. Paris.
[Work(s)] in: *Premier Recueil d'airs, ariettes, menuets et gavottes, variées et arrangées*
en pièces de harpe . . . Paris: Bordet, n.d.
harp
F: Pa, Pc (2 ex.), Pn (3 ex.).
RISM B/II (as Mme Baur, p. 301), NG (bio mention only as daughter of Jean
Baur).

Bawr, Alexandrine Sophie, née Goury de Champgrand (Baronne de) (Saint-Simon, Mme or Comtesse de Baur, Mme de)

1773, Paris–1860, Paris
Après une coupable. Le retour. Romance indienne. Paris: Sieber (#97), n.d.

voice/pf or harp
S: Skma.
RISM A/I (S 384, as Saint Simon, Mme), Eitner.

"Dis moi ce que j'éprouve en approchant de toi." La déclaration.
Romance . . . avec accompagnement de forte-piano ou harpe. Hamburg:
Johann August Böhme, n.d.
voice/pf or harp
S: Skma.
RISM A/I (S 385, as Saint-Simon, Mme), Eitner.

Léon, ou le château de Montaldi [melodrama in 3 acts, text by composer].
Paris: Barba, 1811. 44 pp.
stage work
US: AA, PHu (libretto only).
NUC (NB 0204643), Cohen, Eitner (without title), MGG.

1. Histoire de la musique. In: *Encyclopédie des Dames,* Paris: Audot,1823. 279 pp.
2. Also in German translation, freely adapted by Lewald, Aug. *Geschichte
der Musik für Freunde und Verehrer dieser Kunst.* Nürnberg:
Haubenstricker,1826. 192 pp.
instruction
1. US: CLp, SY, Wc (ML 160. B36). 2. US: Chs.
1. NUC (NB 0204640). 2. NUC Sup. (NSB 0031849). Eitner, MGG.

Bayon-Louis, Mme. See **Louis, Marie Emmanuelle,** née **Bayon
(Bajon)**

Bazin, Mlle
pub. 1788, France
*Premier recueil de romances et d'ariettes avec accompagnement de clavecin ou piano-forté
. . .* deuxième édition. Paris: Guenin (#9),1788.
voice/hpsch or pf
F: Pn [4o Y.847], Pc.
RISM A/I (B 1435), Cohen, Paris Lib. Cat.

Beaucé, Mme. Anne-Augustine-Sophie, née **Porro**
pub. c. 1817–34, Paris
La Berceuse: Fantaisie et Variations pour le Piano Forte [op. 1]. Paris: Chez Beaucé
et chez P. Porro [1817].
pf

F: Pn (Vm12 2500). Photocopy in C. Johnson coll.
Letter (C. Johnson).

Mimi ou *La Mort du petit chat,* parodie du *Bibi* de Mr. Bérat, Paroles
arrangées par Mr. Bxxx. Paris: a la Bibliothèque de Musique [1834].
voice/pf
F: Pn.
Letter (C. Johnson).

Trois Nouveaux Quadrilles, Suivis de Walses Allemandes & Sauteuses. Pour le
Piano-Forte, op. 2. Paris: Chez Joubert/Chez P. Porro/Chez Beaucé
[1817].
pf
F: Pn (Vm12 e467). Photocopy in C. Johnson coll.
Letter (C. Johnson).

Beaucourt, Louise de
pub. c. 1820–30, Paris
La Mélancolie. Romance ("Quand vous riez"). Paris: [1825?]. Words by
Dumoustier.
voice/pf
GB: Lbl [G.807.c.(11.)].
CPM.

Le Jeune Hirman. Romance. Paris: [1830?].
Words by Mr. Fromen.
voice/pf
GB: Lbl [G.807.c.(7.)].
CPM.

Le Sourire. Romance ("Charmant sourire"). Paris: [1830?].
voice/pf
GB: Lbl [G.807.c.(8.)].
CPM.

[3 Romances]. "Preux Chevalier veut mourir pour son Roi" (Le
Troubadour Français); "O Dieu de paix, j'implore ta puissance" (Prière à
deux voix); & "Vive le Roi" (Romance en chœur). Paris: [1820?].
1–2 voices/pf
GB: Lbl [G.807.c.(10.)].
CPM.

Vive le roi quand même. Cri de guerre des Vendéens. [Song, "Je vais chanter"]. Paris: [1830?].
voice/pf
GB: Lbl [G.807.c.(9.)].
CPM.

Beaumesnil, Henriette-Adélaïde Villard de

1758, Paris–1813, Paris
"Chaque jour avec plus de zèle" [Air à vln]. S.l., s.n.
voice/vln/pf
S: Sm.
RISM A/I (B 1453a), Cohen.

"Je méprisais l'amour." [Air à 1]. S.l., s.n., n.d.
song
S: Sm
RISM A/I (BB 1455a).

Tibule et Délie, air from. "Dans ces boccages." S.l.: s.n. [1784].
song
F: Pn [4o Vm7 1731 (96)].
RISM A/I (B1454), Paris Lib. Cat.

Tibule et Délie, air from. "Dans ces jardins charmans." [Air à 1] s.l., s.n.
song
F: Pn [4o Vm7 1731 (95)].
RISM A/I (B1455), Paris Lib. Cat.

Tibule et Délie, air from. "Vainement je voudrois feindre." S.l.: s.n. [1784].
voice/kbd
F: Pn [4o Vm7 1731 (94)]. US: PHu.
RISM A/I (B1456), Paris Lib. Cat.

Tibule et Délie, Airs détachés de [excerpts from]. Paris: aux adresses ordinaires de musique, n.d. Score.
voice/vln/pf
F: V. Copy in Ars Fem coll.
RISM A/I (B 1453), letter (Ars Fem), Cohen.

Tibule et Délie, ou *les Saturnales.* Opéra en un act . . . le 16 févier 1784 et par l'Académie Royale de Musique le lundy 15 mars suivant. 1. Paris,

Deslauriers (gravé par Le Roy l'ainé). Printed score [c. 1784 or 1785].
2. Ms. score.
stage work
1. D: Bds, HR. F: Pn–Pc (2 ex.) [L. 11066 & D. 3096]. S: Skma. US: Bp,
Wc (**M. 22). 2. D: DS (may have been lost in WW II). F: Po.
1. RISM A/I (B 1452), NUC (NB 02271154), Cohen, Eitner (under Villard de Beaumesnil), Paris Lib. Cat.

[Work] in: *Choix de musique,* dédié à S.A.S. Monseigneur de duc regnant
des Deux-Ponts [bi-monthly]. Paris: Sanson et Comp., 15 July 1783 [–84].
instrument undetermined
B: Bc. D: B–MG, DS, HR, Mb (1784), ZW (1784). F: Pc, Pn. GB: Lbl.
RISM B/II (as de Beaumesnil, p. 130), Eitner (under Choix de musique & Villard de Beaumesnil).

[Work(s)] in: *Journal de violon dédié aux amateurs.* Ce journal est composé
d'airs d'opéras sérieux et comiques, airs de ballets, arietes italienes, rondeaux, vaudevilles et chansonettes . . . Paris: Bornet l'ainé, monthly from
1784–89.
2 vlns or 2 vlcs
F: Pc (inc.), Pn (inc.). US: NYp (1784 only).
RISM B/II (as Mlle Bauménil, p. 211).

[Work(s)] in: *Recueil d'ariettes choisies des meilleurs auteurs et de divers opéras
comiques, arrangées pour deux clarinettes* par Mr. Abraham . . . Paris: Frère
[1779–85]. 15 vol.
2 cls
F: Pc (inc.).
RISM B/II (as Mlle de Beaumesnil, p. 319).

Bembo, Antonia, née Padoani
Padua or Venice, c. 1640–Paris, c. 1715
L'Ercole amante, tragedia nuovamente posta in musica . . . , 1707. Ms.
score, 2 vol. 508 pp.
stage work
F: Pn (Rés. Vm4 9, Rés. Vm4 10). Microfilm copies in US: DM, WSwf.
Laini, Cohen, Rokseth, Olivier, Fontijn, OCLC (micro. 11461032), letter (Fontijn).

Les sept psaumes de David . . . [170–?] Ms. score. 285 pp. [texts in
French].
voices/orch

F: Pn (Ms. Vm1 116). Microfilm in US: DM.
Eitner, Laini, Cohen, Rokseth, Olivier, Fontaijn, OCLC (micro. 22516927), letter (Fontijn).

Produzioni armoniche della Dama Bembo nobile Veneta, consacrate al nome immortale di Luigi XIIII . . . [1, 2, 3, voices/cto]. [170–?] Ms. score. 268 pp. [Sacred and secular, with French, Italian and Latin texts.]
1–3 voices/some with bc
F: Pn (Rés. Vm1 117). Microfilm in US: DM.
Eitner, Laini, Cohen, Rokseth, Olivier, Fontijn, OCLC (micro. 22516922), letter (Fontijn).

Te Deum [#1] pour . . . la conservation d'un monarcha così Grande come Luigi XIV . . . accompagnato da un Exaudiat [#2] [170–]. Ms. score. 65 pp.
SSB solo/choir/strings
F: Pn (Ms. Vm1 114–115). Microfilm in US: DM. Copy in Ars Fem coll. and D: Kf&m.
Eitner, Laini, Cohen, Rokseth, Olivier, Fontijn, OCLC (micro. 22516939), letter (Fontijn) Frau & Musik, letter (Ars Fem).

Te Deum per render grazie a Sua Divina Maestà [#1] . . . che a dato al mondo un Principe . . . con l'aggionta d'un piccolo divertimento per la nascita del medisimo Principe [#2] [1705]. Ms. score. 75 pp.
#1, SSB/2 vlns/bc; #2, SSATB/2 vlns/bc
F: Pn (Ms. Vm1 112–113). Microfilm in US: DM.
Eitner, Laini, Cohen, Rokseth, Olivier, Fontijn, OCLC (micro. 22516932), letter (Fontijn).

Benaut (Benault), Mademoiselle
c.1776–?, Paris
Premier livre des pieces de clavecin ou le piano forte. Paris: Chez l'Auteur, [17—].
hpsch or pf
F: Pc. Microfilm in US: CA, as Benaut, __.
Cohen, Eitner, NUC Sup. (NSB 0046555).

Recueil d'airs avec variations arrangés pour le clavecin ou forte piano . . . agée de dix ans. Œuvre troisième. Paris: Mme Mercier [c. 1786 or 1788].
hpsch or pf
F: Pn [Vm7 5954(3)]. Photocopy in C. Johnson coll.
RISM A/I (BB 1841 I, 3), Cohen, Eitner, Paris Lib. Cat., letter (C. Johnson).

Recueil d'airs avec variations arrangés pour le clavecin ou forte piano . . . œuvre second. Paris: chez l'auteur/Chez Mlle Castagnerie et aux Addresses Ordinaires de Musique (gravé par James) [c. 1787].
hpsch or pf
F: Pn [Bm7 5954(2)]. Copies in C. Johnson coll. and Ars Fem coll.
RISM A/I (BB 1841 I, 2), Cohen, Eitner, Paris Lib. Cat., letters (C. Johnson, Ars Fem).

Recueil d'airs avec variations arrangés pour le clavecin ou forte piano . . . œuvre quatrième. Paris: Mme Mercier [1788].
hpsch or pf
F: Pn (4 ex.) [Vm7 5954(4), Vm7 8255, Vm7 3086, & A. 1217].
Photocopy of Vm7 5954(4) in C. Johnson coll.
RISM A/I (BB 1841 I, 4), Cohen, Eitner, Paris Lib. Cat., letter (C. Johnson).

Recueil d'airs avec variations arrangés pour le clavecin ou forte piano par Melle. Benaut agée de neuf ans. Œuvre premier. Paris: auteur/Chez Mle Castagnerie et aux Addresses Ordinaires de Musique, (gravé par James) [c. 1787].
hpsch or pf
F: Pn [Vm7 5954(1)]. Photocopy in C. Johnson coll.
RISM A/I (BB 1841 I, 1), Cohen, Eitner, Paris Lib. Cat., letter (C. Johnson).

Benda, Juliane. See Reichardt, Bernadine Juliane, née Benda.

Berthe, Mme
n.d.
Les Plaisirs de l'Hotel Royal [dance].
kbd
F: Pn. Copy in Ars Fem coll.
Letter (Ars Fem).

Bertrand, Aline
1798, Paris–1835, Paris
Fantasie on the favorite romance from Joseph [by Méhul] *for the Harp.* London: [1835?].
Italian edition as op. 3, Milan: Ricordi.
harp
GB: Lbl [h.184.d.(4.)]. Location and date of Italian edition not known.
CPM, Cohen.

The favorite air "Nel cor più non mi sento" [by Paisiello] arranged with variations for the harp. London [1835?]. Italian edition as op. 1, Milan: Ricordi.
harp
GB: Lbl [h.184.d.(5.)]. Location and date of Italian edition not known.
CPM, Cohen.

Beydale, Cécile, Mlle (I. Pany Cecylii Beydale)

d. 1854, Paris
Leszek Biały [Spiew o Leszku Białym] ("Od dworaków opuszczona"),
Bolesław Chrobry [Spiew o Bolesławie Chrobrym] ("Ten co najpiérwszy ujrzał światlo wiary"). In: Julian Ursyn Niemcewics, *Śpiewy historycznye* [Historic songs]. Warsaw: 1816. Texts by Niemcewicz.
voice/pf
F: Pn. PL: Kc, Wn, Wmickiewicz. Copies of PL: Kc in Jackson coll.
Sowinski, Cohen, letter (Poniatowska).

Bianchi, Lady

n.d.
[2 songs]. "Sweetest floeret, the hearts-ease," "Tis love that murmurs."
songs
S: S (library not specified). US: LAu. Copy in Ars Fem coll.
Letter (Ars Fem).

Biber, Maria Anna Magdalena von (wife [geb. **Weissin**] or daughter of **Heinrich von Biber**)

17th cent., Salzburg
Gesangsheft der M. A. M. de Bibern [textless]. Ms., 1694.
songs
A: Sn.
Cohen, Eitner, Kassel Archiv, DTÖ Jg. 5/2, p. x.

[Mass in C]. Ms.
voices (SSATTB)
A: Sn. Copy in Ars Fem coll.
Letter (Ars Fem).

Bigot de Morogues, Marie-Catherine-Salomé, née **Kiéné**

1786, Kolmar–1820, Paris. Lived in Vienna, 1804–09
Andante variè [Andante avec variations], op. 2. Vienna: Artaria, n.d.
[c. 1805?].
pf

F: Pn (Cons. Ac. p. 1931). Photocopy in C. Johnson coll.
NG (Bio), Cohen, MGG, letter (C. Johnson).

Rondo pour le Piano Forte [last movement of Sonata, op. 1.]. Paris: chez
Melles Erard [1818].
pf
F: Pn (Vm12 3274, 2 ex.). Photocopy in C. Johnson coll.
Cohen, MGG, letter (C. Johnson).

Sonate pour le pianoforte [B flat major], op. 1. Vienna: Artaria, [c.1806].
Dedicated to the Queen of Prussia.
pf
F: Pn (Cons. Ac. p. 1964). Photocopy in C. Johnson coll.
MGG, letter (C. Johnson).

Suite d'Études pour le Piano-Forte, Livre 1. Paris: chez Melles Erard [1817 or
1818].
pf
F: Pn (2 ex., Vm12 56). Photocopy in C. Johnson coll.
Cohen, MGG, letter (C. Johnson).

Billeh, Mlle
18th cent., French?
[Work(s)] in: *Meslanges de musique latine, françoise et italienne, divisez par saisons*
. . . Paris: J. B. C. Ballard, 1728.
song(s)
F: Pn.
RISM B/II (p. 233).

Billington, Elizabeth, née Weichsell (later married Felissent [Felican])
1765 or 1768, London–1818, near Treviso
Six progressive lessons for the harpsichord or piano forte composed by Mrs.
Billington, late Miss E. Weichsell, op. 2. London: John Bland [c.1793].
hpsch or pf
US: Wc. Microfilm copy in Rempel coll.
RISM A/I (B 2659), letter (Rempel), Cohen.

Six sonatas [G, A, B-flat, E-flat, F, G] *for the piano forte or harpsichord . . .*
composed . . . in the eleventh year of her age, opera 2da. London: author
[c. 1776/1769?]. 35 pp.

pf or hpsch
GB: Lbl [h.726.1.(8.)], Lcm. Microfilm of GB: Lbl copy in C. Johnson coll.
RISM A/I (B 2658), BUC (Weichsell), Eitner, MGG (Weichsell), CPM, letter (C. Johnson).

Three lessons [D, E-flat, A] *for the harpsichord or piano forte* . . . by Elizabeth Weichsell, a child eight years of age. London: Welcker [c.1773 or 1775].
19 pp.
hpsch or pf
GB: Lbl [e.5.b.(5.)]. US: Cn (VM 23 B598t), Wc. Microfilm of GB: Lbl copy in C. Johnson coll.
RISM A/I (B 2657), BUC (Weichsell), NUC (NB 0487714), Cohen, NG (bio), MGG (Weichsell), CPM, letter (C. Johnson).

Biro, Françoise de
n.d.
IX Variations pour le forte-piano, et violon . . . œuvre II. Vienna: Franz Anton Hoffmeister. Parts.
pf/vln
A: Wst. I: Raf (pf, lacks vl). Copy of A: Wst in Ars Fem coll.
RISM A/I (B 2736), letter (Ars Fem).

Blackwood, Helen Selina, Baroness Dufferin (later Hay, Countess of Gifford, née Price Blackwood)
before 1834
By-Gone Hours ("'Tis sad to think upon the joyous days of old"). In:
Collection of Songs and Piano forte Compositions in Fair-copy, ff. 21b–22.
Ms. owned by Fanny Griffith, March 11, 1834, Bombay, India.
voice/pf
GB: BA (BRm 189.D.).
Bath.

Bland, Dorothea (Dora). See Jordan, Dorothea (Dorothy), Mrs.
(pseud.)

Bland, Maria Theresa, née Romanzi (called by the diminutive Romanzini during her early career)
1769, Italy–1838, London (Jewish Italian)
The banks of Allenwater . . . the melody by Mrs. Bland, newly arranged with an accompaniment for the pianoforte by T. B. Phipps. London: s.n.
[1856].

Melody only by Bland.
voice/pf
GB: Lbl [H.1771.b.(12.)].
CPM.

The favorite March now performing by the Duke of York's band [pianoforte arr.].
London: s.n. [1805?].
pf
GB: Lbl [g.272.t.(7.)].
CPM.

The river queen ("The water rush'd, the water swell'd"). Composed and sung by Mrs. Bland. 1. London: Preston, n.d. 2. In: *A selection of the most admired ballads,* pp. 21–23, Philadelphia: John Morgan, 1801.
voice/pf
US: 1. CA. 2. CHAhughes, NYp, PIlevy.
1–2. Wolfe (872, 7885).

The rose of Aberdeen ("Frae Barra vale i'v ta'en my way"). A Scotch ballad sung by Mrs. Bland. 1. London: Preston, n.d. 2. [Words] written by Rannie; compos'd by Mrs. Bland. New York: J. & M. Paff [1807].
voice/pf
1. US: NYcu. 2. US: Cn, CAdriscoll, NYp [Am1–V], PROu,Wc (M1.A1B [M16211, M1747]).
1. RISM A/I (BB 2841b). 2. NYp Spec. Coll. Shelf List, NUC Sup. (NSB 00744021). NG (bio).

Six ballads, composed and inscribed by permission to Mrs. Sheridan by Mrs. Bland. London: Goulding, Phipps & d'Almaine [c. 1806].
voice/pf
US: CA.
NUC (NB 0539650).

"Stay dear Youth" [song]. Composed and sung by Mrs. Bland. London: Preston [c.1815]. 3 pp.
voice/pf
GB: Lbl [G.295.xx.(34.)].
CPM.

To Delia ("To other shades my Delia flies"). A ballad. The music by Mrs. Bland. New York: E. Riley [1812–14]. 3 pp.

voice/pf
US: CA, NYp, NYcuh, PROu, R.
Wolfe (874).

"'Twas in the solemn midnight hour." A favorite ballad with an accompaniment for the piano forte in the new comedy of *Sighs,* or *The Daughter.*
1. London: Theodor Monzani [1799]. 2. Dublin: Hime [1800]. 3. In: *A Selection of the Most Admired Ballads,* pp. 24–25, Philadelphia: John Morgan 1801. 4. Dublin: Rhames [1800]. 5. London: Caulfield [1802].
voice/pf
1. GB: Lbl [H.1652.cc.(14.)]. US: Cn, CHua (*ML .8444 vol. 137, #12)
2. GB: Lbl [H.1653.n.(5.)]. 3. US: CA, CHAhughes, NYp, PIlevy, Wc.
4. GB: Lbl (2 ex.) [1654.n.(22.) & H.1860.xx.(3.)]. 5. GB: Lbl [G.7996.(6.)].
1–3. RISM A/I (B 2840, 2841, BB 2841a). 2. CPM. 3. NUC (NB 0539651), Wolfe (870, 7885). 4–5. CPM. Cohen, NG (bio only).

Blangini, Therese
b. 1780, Turin
Tre canzonette italiane. Vienna: Thadé Weigl, n.d.
songs
A: Wn. Copy in Ars Fem coll.
RISM A/I (BB 2844 I, 1), Cohen (Mlle Blangini), letter (Ars Fem).

Trio [A] *à violon principal, second violon et basse* . . . œuvre 1er. Paris: Benoit Pollet [c. 18—?]. 4 parts.
2 vlns/bc
A: L. D: WINtj. US: R (M351. B642). Copy in Ars Fem coll.
RISM A/I (BB 2844 I, 2), OCLC (18206249), letter (Ars Fem), Cohen.

Blondel, Mlle
pub. c. 1760, Paris
Menuets nouveaux pour le violon, flûte, hautbois, pardessus de viole, violoncelle et basson avec la basse-continue . . . aussi . . . sur le clavecin et sur la harpe. Paris: auteur, aux adresses ordinaires, n.d. [1760, RISM; 1768, Paris cat.]. Score 9 pp.
vln, fl, ob, pardessus, vlc, bsn, bc (hpsch or harp)
F: Pc (Bn. D. 11355).
RISM A/I (B 2983), Boenke, Paris Lib. Cat., Haynes.

Bocquet, Anne (or Marguerite)
fl. 2d part of 17th cent., France

Allemande. In: late 17th century ms. ff. 10–11.
lute
B: Br (Brux. II 276)
Rollin.

Courante. In: Compositions for Lute, ms. collection, #6, ff. 101b–103.
Ms., c. 1683. No first name given, may be Anne or Marguerite Bocquet.
lute
GB: Lbl (Sloan 2923).
Rollin, CPM.

Gigue. In: late 17th century ms. pp. 28–29.
lute
GB: Ob (Oxf. G. 618).
Rollin.

La Polonaise Allemande. Sarabande. Chaconne. Late 17th century ms.
"Ex-libris J. B. Barbe, conseiller de la Cour des Aydes."
lute
F: Pn
Rollin.

Praeludia, Sarabande. In: Stamm- und Lautenbuch des Johann David
Keller von Schleittheim (1663). Ms.
lute
F: Pn
Rollin.

[17] Préludes marquant les cadences.
Prélude sur tous les tons. [3 Préludes, 3 Allemandes, 2 Courantes,
5 Sarabands, Sérénade]. Ms.
lute
F: Pn (Vm7 6214).
NG, Cohen, Rollin.

**Boetzelaer, Josina Anna Petronella, Baroness. (Boetselaer,
Giustina)**
n.d.
Arie sciolte, e coro con sinfonie . . . opera quarta. Den Haag, s.n. Parts.

voices / orch.?
YU: NM.
RISM A / I (B 3299), Cohen.

Raccolta d'arie sciolte con sinfonie . . . opera II. S.l., s.n. Parts.
voice / orch.?
US: AA.
RISM A / I (B 3298), Cohen.

Boleyn, Anne
c.1507–1536, English
"O Deathe, rock me asleepe" (attributed to Anne Boleyn, 1536). See
modern editions.

Bon, Anna (di Venezia)
Venice, 1738–?
Sei divertimenti a tre. Nürnberg: Bathasar Schmidts Witwe [c. 1760]. Parts.
2 fls / bc
B: Bc. Copy in Ars Fem coll.
RISM A / I (B 3426), Vester, Cohen, Boenke, letter (Ars Fem).

Sei Sonate per il Cembalo, Opera seconda. Nürnberg: Balthazar Schmidts
Witwe, #49 [RISM has #34], 1757.
hpsch
D: Rtt (Bon 2). Copy in Jackson coll. and in D: UNikb.
RISM A / I (B 3425), Cohen, Frauenmusik.

VI Sonate da camera [C, F, B-flat, D, g, C] *per il flauto traversiere e violoncello o
cembalo . . .* opera prima. 1. Nürnberg: Balthasar Schmidts Witwe (#46),
1756. Score. 2. [Egtved, Denmark] Ms. copy.
flute / vlc or hpsch bc
1. D: BE, GO1, Rtt (Bon 1). USSR: Ml (Library does not confirm as
extant). Copy of D: Rtt in Ars Fem coll. 2. DK: Kk. 1–2. Copies in
Jackson coll. and in D: UNikb.
*1. RISM A / I (B 3424, BB 3424). 2? Eitner (B. B., Berlin Th., Berlin K. H. l
son. in ms.) 1–2. Vester, Boenke, Frauenmusik. Cohen. 2? Eitner (B. B., Berlin Th.,
Berlin K. H. l son. in ms.). 1–2. Vester, Boenke, Frauenmusik. Cohen.*

Bonaparte, Julie, née Clary (Madame Joseph Bonaparte)
?, Marseilles–after 1820?
"Ne m'oubliez pas." Ballad. London: s.n. [1820?].

voice/pf
GB: Lbl [G.809.(31.)].
CPM.

Bonito, Delia, Domina (Bonita, S. Delia)
fl. 1723, Naples
Missae 2 vocibus quas domina S . . . , chori praefecta, tempore vicariatus
S. D. Beatricis de Franchis componebat. Ms. 1723.
SA/bc
I: N-Biblioteca Provinciale Francescana, Convento S. Chiara. (Microfilm
or Xerox not possible)
*Eitner (Bonita), Cohen (Bonita, lists additional works), letter (I: N-Biblioteca
Provinciale Francescana).*

Bonnay, Mlle
pub. c. 1798, Paris
Ier Recueil de XII Romances ou airs avec accompagnement de piano-forte ou harpe.
Paris: auteur [1798]. Score, 17 pp.
pf or harp
F: Pn (2 ex., Vm7 7602, Vm7 8293).
RISM A/I (B 3510), Paris Lib. Cat., Cohen.

Bonneuil, Mme de
pub. c. 1789, Paris
[Work(s)] in: *Journal d'airs italiens et français avec accompagnement de guitarre.*
[No. 1–180. daily.] Paris: Le Duc [c. 1789].
voice/guit
B: Bc. F: Pc. Neither is a complete run.
RISM B/II (p. 203).

Bonwick, Miss
pub. c. 1790, London
Sophia. A new song, the words and music by Miss Bonwick, fourteen years
of age. London: Longman & Broderip [c. 1790]. Followed by accompaniments for guitar or German flute.
voice/pf/opt. guit or fl
GB: Lbl [H. 1653.b.911.0]. Copy in Ars Fem coll.
RISM A/I (BB 3667 I, 1), CPM, letter (Ars Fem).

Borghese, Agathe-Elisabeth-Henriette, née Larrivée
1764 or 1765, Paris–1839, Paris

[Piano reduction of] Rossini, G. A., *Torwaldo e Dorliska*. S.l.: s.n. [1820?].
pf
GB: Lbl [h.625.c.].
CPM.

Bouchardy, Caroline
pub. c. 1830, Paris
Picciola, valse brillante . . . pour le Piano. Op. 5. Paris: s.n. [1830?].
pf
GB: Lbl [g.270.a.(10.)].
CPM.

Bourges, Clementine de
?, Lyon–1561, Lyon
"Da bei rami" [4 voice setting, based on Arcadelt]. In: J. Paix, *Ein schön
nutz und gebreüchlich Orgel Tabulaturbuch . . . der schönsten Lieder, Pass'è mezzo, und
Täntz, alle mit grossem Fleiss coloriert*. Laugingen: L. Reinmichel, 1583.
org
A: Wgm. B: Bc. D: HEu, Mbs, ROu, W.
RISM B/I (1583 [23]), Cohen, Eitner [as Clementine (f.) or Clement (m.)?].

Bouvardinska, Mme
pub. c. 1740, Paris
Les rigueurs de Climene. Chansonette. In: *Mercure de France*, June, 1740. Paris:
1740.
song
GB: Lbl [298.b.6].
CPM, Cohen.

Boyd, Elisabeth
fl. London, 1739–44
Altamira's ghost, or, Justice triumphant. A new ballad. Occasion'd by a certain
nobleman's cruel usage of his nephew. Done extempore. By E. B. London:
Charles Corbett, 1744.
May be text only
song
US: AUS.
OCLC (12128884).

Don Sancho, or The Student's Whim, a ballad opera in 2 acts, with *Minerva's
triumph*, a masque. London: 1739. Libretto by composer.

stage work
Music lost. Text only, US: Cu, NH, SM, Wc, Ws. Micro-opaque and
microfiche in many locations: see OCLC.
*NUC (NB 0716806), OCLC (12128884, micro. 9825658, 23587234), Cohen,
Mellen.*

Brandenstein, Karoline von (Caroline)
1754, Schordorf, Württemberg–1813, Berlin
Clavier Sonate [D] *einer Voglerischen Schülerin* [with violin]. 1. In: Vogler's
Betrachtungen der Mannheimer Tonschule, Jg. 3, Lfg. 7–9. S.l., s.n. Parts. 2. Also
in: [*Mannheimer Monatschrift*] Jg. 3, Lfg. 7–9 [1781]. 3? As *Sonate für Klavier u.
Violon.* Speyer: Bossler, 1780. May be the same as RISM (B 4220).
hpsch/vln
1. D: HR. 2. GB: Lbl (H. 3311.c.). 3. Copy in D: UNikb. Copies of other
eds. in D: Kf&m, UNikb & in Ars Fem coll.
*1–2. RISM A/I (B 4220, BB 4220). 2. CPM, BUC. 3. Frauenmusik. Frau &
Musik. Eitner, Cohen, letter (Ars Fem).*

[Work(s)] in: *Gesänge für Clavier.* Zweiter Heft. Wüstenstein: in dem
Brandensteinische Verlag, 1791.
voice/kbd
D: Mbs.
RISM B/II (p. 190).

Brandes, Minne (Charlotte Franzizka Wilhelmine)
1765, Berlin–1788, Hamburg
Allegro [in d minor, pf]. In: *Musikalisches Nachlass von Minne Brandes* . . . ed.
by Friedrich Hoenicke. Hamburg: Johann Heinrich Herold (Gottlieb
Friedrich Schniebes), 1788. Score.
pf
A: Wn (2 ex.). B: Bc. D: Bds, HAu, LEm. H: Bn. USSR: KA (formerly
B. Kgsbg 24747, location not confirmed). Copy in Ars Fem coll.
RISM A/II (B 4221), RISM–DKL, Eitner, Cohen, letter (Ars Fem).

[8] Lieder, in: *Musikalisches Nachlass von Minne Brandes* . . . ed. by Friedrich
Hoenicke. Hamburg: Johann Heinrich Herold (Gottlieb Friedrich
Schniebes), 1788. Score.
voice/pf
A: Wn (2 ex.). B: Bc. D: Bds, HAu, LEm. H: Bn. USSR: KA (formerly
B. Kgsbg 24747, location not confirmed). Copy in Ars Fem coll.
RISM A/I (B 4221), RISM–DKL, Eitner, Cohen, Boenke, letter (Ars Fem).

Largo. In: *Musikalisches Nachlass von Minne Brandes* . . . ed. by Friedrich
Hoenicke. Hamburg: Johann Heinrich Herold (Gottlieb Friedrich
Schniebes), 1788. Score.
strings and winds (orch)
A: Wn (2 ex.). B: Bc. D: Bds, HAu, LEm. H: Bn. USSR: KA (formerly
B. Kgsbg 24747, location not confirmed). Copy in Ars Fem coll.
RISM A/I (B 4221), RISM–DKL, Eitner, Cohen, letter (Ars Fem).

"Parnel sono." Duetto. In: *Musikalisches Nachlass von Minne Brandes* . . . ed.
by Friedrich Hoenicke. Hamburg: Johann Heinrich Herold (Gottlieb
Friedrich Schniebes), 1788. Score.
SS/2 vlns/vla/b
A: Wn (2 ex.). B: Bc. D: Bds, HAu, LEm. H: Bn. USSR: KA (formerly
B. Kgsbg 24747, location not confirmed). Copy in Ars Fem coll.
RISM A/I (B 4221), RISM–DKL, Eitner, Cohen, Boenke, letter (Ars Fem).

"Tacite ombrose piano" [Cavatina]. In: *Musikalisches Nachlass von Minne
Brandes* . . . ed. by Friedrich Hoenicke. Hamburg: Johann Heinrich Herold
(Gottlieb Friedrich Schniebes), 1788. Score.
S/hns/fls/bsns/vlns/vla/b/hpsch
A: Wn (2 ex.). B: Bc. D: Bds, HAu, LEm. H: Bn. USSR: KA (formerly
B. Kgsbg 24747, this location not confirmed). Copy in Ars Fem coll.
RISM A/I (B 4221), RISM–DKL, Eitner, Cohen, Boenke, letter (Ars Fem).

Braunschweig, Anna Maria von. See **Anna Maria, Duchess of
Braunschweig**

Braunschweig, Sophie Elisabeth von. See **Sophie Elisabeth,
Duchess of Braunschweig-Wölfenbüttel,** née **Mecklenburg-
Güstrow**

Breitenbauch, Antoinette von
pub. 1780s, Rinteln
"Offender, non so offender." S.l., s.n., n.d.
voice/pf
D: LCH. Copy in Ars Fem coll.
RISM A/I (BB 4308 I, 1), letter (Ars Fem), Cohen.

[Work(s)] in: *Musikalische Nebenstunden*. Rinteln: A. H. Bösendahl, 1787.
4 vols.
instruments undetermined

A: Wgm (3 only), Wn (1 only). D: Bds (1–2), RH (2–4)
RISM B/II (p. 249).

Brentano, Josepha
1770–1806
[2 Lieder]. "Zieh nicht in den dunklen Wald" [Ballade] & "Sei getrost"
[geistliches Lied]. Offenbach: André (#10960–64), n.d.
voice/pf
D: Kf&m, UNikb.
Frau & Musik, Frauenmusik, letter (D: UNikb).

[2 Lieder für eine Alt-Stimme u. Klavier]. "Stummer Schmerz, lautes
Glück" & "O träume nur."
voice/pf
D: UNikb.
Frauenmusik, letter (D: UNikb).

Bresson, Mlle (Brisson)
Paris, 1785–?
Au Rossignol ("Amiable oiseau"). Romance. Paris: s.n. [1805?].
voice/pf
GB: Lbl [G. 548.(34.)].
CPM, Cohen, Eitner.

Breynton, Augusta
pub. c. 1830, London
"A Fair good night to thee, love." London: s.n. [1830?].
voice/pf
GB: Lbl [H.1772.d.(28.)].
CPM.

Briggs, Miss
pub. c. 1822, London
"The Night is dark upon the Water." London: Birchall & Co. [1822?]. 3
pp.
voice/pf
GB: Lbl [H. 1663.(37.)].
CPM.

"See how beneath the Moonbeam's Smile." London: Birchall & Co.
[1822?].

voice/pf
GB: Lbl [H. 1663.(36.)].
CPM.

Brillon de Jouy (Juvi), Anne-Louise Boyvin, née d'Hardancourt, Mme

1744, Paris–1824, Paris
Duetto [B-flat major, for 2 harpsichords]. Ms. c. 1775–85.
2 hpschs
US: PHps (Cembalo I missing) (781.508 B762, #23; Microfilm copy Film
1353). Microfilm copy in Jackson coll.
Gustafson, Johnson.

Duetto en sol a deux clavecin [title page]. Copyist's ms. 2 partbooks, one
labeled (in copyist's hand) "pianoforte" and the other "clavecin," c. 1775–83?
pf/hpsch
US: PHps (781.508 B762, #11; Microfilm copy Film 1353). Microfilm
copy in Jackson coll.
NUC (NB 0801772), Gustafson, Johnson.

1er duetto en ut mineur [pour piano-forte et clavecin]. Parts. Copyist's
ms., c. 1779–85?
pf/hpsch
US: PHps (781.508 B762, #7 [2 ex. of part I, 1 of part 2]; Microfilm copy
Film 1353). Microfilm copy in Jackson coll.
NUC (NB 0801777), Gustafson, Johnson.

La fauvette [Milon and Chloé] [cantata for 2 violins, viola, and bass,
soprano and tenor (or alto)]. Autograph ms., c. 1775–83?
ST(or A)/2 vlns/vla/b
US: PHps (781.508 B762, #15; Microfilm copy Film 1353). Microfilm
copy in Jackson coll.
NUC (NB 0801773), Gustafson, Johnson.

Marche [Marche des Insurgents] pour 2 violons, 2 flutes et hautbois [dou-
bled], 2 clarinettes, 2 cors, 1 basson, 1 alto, 1 basse et des timballes. Ms.,
Dec. 1777?.
(2 vlns/vla/b/2 fls/2 obs/2 cls/2 hns/bsn/perc)
US: PHps (percussion part missing) (781.508 B762, #1; Microfilm copy
Film 1353). Microfilm copy in Jackson coll.
NUC (NB 0801774), Gustafson, Johnson.

Quartetto di cembalo, due violini e basso [E-flat Major] da Madama
Brillon di Jouy. Parts. Copyist's ms., c. 1775–85?
hpsch / 2 vln / b (vlc)
US: PHps (Violin I part missing) (781.508 B762, #4; Microfilm copy Film
1353). Microfilm copy in Jackson coll.
NUC (NB 0801778), Gustafson, Johnson.

Romances et recueil de cansonettes. Musique d' Madame Brillon. Œuvre
1 [6 romances], œuvre 2 [6 romances], 4me & 5me œuvre [15 songs, of
which #13 has music by J. J. Rousseau?]. Copyist's ms., 4 vols. in 2.
C. 1775–85?
voice / pf (#3 of œ. 2 also with horn part)
US: PHps (781.508 B762, #17; Microfilm copy Film 1353). Microfilm
copy in Jackson coll.
NUC (NB 0801780), Gustafson, Johnson.

2d duo de harp et piano, sol mineur.
Autograph ms, c. 1775–83?
harp / pf
US: PHps (781.508 B762, #3; Microfilm copy Film 1353). Microfilm copy
in Jackson coll.
NUC (NB 0801771), Johnson, Gustafson, Cohen (bio).

Sonatas [*sic*] po[u]r forte Piano [avec accompagnement d'un Violon]
[G major]. Ms., c. 1775–85.
pf / vln
US: PHps (781.508 B762, #24; Microfilm copy Film 1353). Microfilm
copy in Jackson coll.
Gustafson, Johnson.

Sonate en trio pour le forte piano, un violon et un violoncelle obligè
[G major]. Parts. Copyist's ms., 1775–85?
pf / vln / vlc
US: PHps (781.508 B762, #9; Microfilm copy Film 1353). Microfilm copy
in Jackson coll.
NUC (NB 0801781), Gustafson, Johnson.

Sonatta [sic] [G Major] pour le forté piano et accompagnement de flute.
No. 3. Parts, copyist's ms., c. 1775–85?
pf / fl
US: PHps (fl part missing) (781.508 B762,#12; Microfilm copy Film

1353). Microfilm copy in Jackson coll.
NUC (NB 0801775), Gustafson, Johnson.

Sonnatta [*sic*] en la mineur [for harpsichord]. Autograph ms., c. 1775–85?
hpsch
US: PHps (781.508 B762, #2; Microfilm copy Film 1353). Microfilm copy in Jackson coll.
NUC (NB 0801782), Gustafson, Johnson.

3e cahier cansonnétta ("Des que Robin eut vû partir Toinette," "Tu parois distraite quand je suit des pas" & "Un beau berger sur sa muzétte chantoit toujours"). Autograph ms., c. 1775–85? [copies also found in #17, op. 5, #1, #5, #8].
voice/pf
US: PHps (781.508 B762, #16; Microfilm copy Film 1353). Microfilm copy in Jackson coll.
Gustafson, Johnson.

3e duo en ut mineur [for two harpsichords]. Parts. Copyist's ms., 1775–85? [rewritten as: Trio a trois Clavecin en ut Mineur (#6), q. v.].
2 hpschs
US: PHps (781.508 B762, #25; Microfilm copy Film 1353). Microfilm copy in Jackson coll.
NUC (NB 0801787), Gustafson, Johnson.

Trio a trois clavecin en ut mineur. 3 partbooks (labeled "piano anglois," "clavecin," and "piano allemand") Copyist's ms., c. 1775–85?
2 pfs / 1 hpsch
US: PHps (781.508 B762, #6; Microfilm copy Film 1353). Microfilm copy in Jackson coll.
NUC (NB 0801783), Gustafson, Johnson.

Trio en la min. per il forte piano, violino, basso composte da Madama Brillon. 3 partbooks. Copyist's ms., c. 1775–85?
pf/vln/b (vlc)
US: PHps (781.508 B762, #5; Microfilm copy Film 1353). Microfilm copy in Jackson coll.
NUC (NB 0801786), Gustafson, Johnson.

Trio en sol min. per il forte piano, violino, violoncello. Parts. Copyist's ms., c. 1775–85?

pf/vln/vlc
US: PHps (violin part missing) (781.508 B762, #10, cello part is ms.#22; Microfilm copy Film 1353). Microfilm copy in Jackson coll.
NUC (NB 0801784), Gustafson, Johnson.

Trio en ut majeur pour trois clavecin [*sic*]. 3 partbooks (labeled "clavecin," "piano forte allemand," & piano forte anglais"). Copyist's ms., c. 1775–85?
2 pfs/hpsch
US: PHps (781.508 B762, #8; Microfilm copy Film 1353). Microfilm copy in Jackson coll.
NUC (NB 0801785), Gustafson, Johnson.

[2 songs] Pour Madame de la Saumés. Romance de trois notes ("La jeune et tendre Calliméne") & Marche for voice and piano ("Le son revenoit du village"). Autograph ms., c. 1775–85?
voice/pf
US: PHps (781.508 B762, #22, see also #10; Microfilm copy Film 1353). Microfilm copy in Jackson coll.
NUC (NB 0801779), Gustafson, Johnson.

In 1993 Bruce Gustafson located many previously unknown works by Mme Brillon de Jouy in France. His publication describing this music will be forthcoming.

Browne, Harriet Mary. See **Owen, Harriet Mary,** née **Browne**

Brühl (Bruehl), Countess. (Married to **Hans Moritz [Mauriçe] von Brühl,** d. 1811)
late 18th cent.
9 chansons pour le clavecin. Contents: "Chloris an die Nachtigall," "Chloe," "Die Erinnerung," "Lied aus der Ferne," "Todes Stille deckt das Thal," "Ich denke dein," "Ich singe nicht Reiche nicht Helden," "Winterfrost und lange Nächte," "Am Fenster stand ich diesen Morgen." Ms., 18th cent. 10 pp.
voice (S)/hpsch
D: Dlb (Mus. 3720–K–1).
RISM A/II (#21594), Letter (D: Dlb), Eitner.

Chanson de Rousseau avec accompagnement d'une Flute, Guitarre, Piano-Forte e Violoncello composé per . . . Bruehl et varié par Himmel. Zerbst: Menzel, n. d.

voice/fl/guit/pf/vlc
USSR: KA (formerly Königsberg [14212(16)] (present status unconfirmed).
Königsberg

Bryan, Mrs. M. A.
pub. c. 1800–10, London
The Bilberry Lass. A pathetic ballad [words] written by Miss Wilkinson. Composed by Mrs. M. A. Bryan. 1. London: F. Bryan, [c. 1800]. 2. New York: G. Gilfert [1804–06]. 2 pp.

A Divertimento for PianoForte or Pedal Harp (Op. 1st). Bloomsbury: Music Warehouse/ London: Music Warehouse, Bland & Weller's [c.1800].
pf or harp
GB: Lbl [h. 721.r.20.)].
CPM.

The lute of Lisette. An elegiac Canzonet for the Piano Forte, Harp, or Lute . . . . London: F. Bryan [c. 1800].
harp or lute or pf
GB: Lbl [G.798.(14.)].
CPM, Cohen, Eitner.

The maid of Herts; Poor Ellen, a descriptive ballad. The sufferings of a beautiful insane of the county of Herts is the subject of this ballad. London: Printed by Clementi, Banger, Hyde, Collard & Davis, [180–]. 3 pp.
voice/pf
US: Wc (Collection of Early American music, Ml.All, vol. 7, no. 26).
NUC (NB 0902134).

The Maid of Wooburn. A pathetic ballad . . . for the piano forte or pedal harp . . . London: F. Bryan, [17—? or c. 1805]. 3 pp.
pf or pedal harp
GB: Lbl [H.2831.(21.)]. US: Wc (M 1621 .B Case).
CPM, NUC (NB 0902135), Cohen, Eitner.

The Peasant's Prayer. An elegiac canzonet. London: L. Lavenu [c. 1800].
pf or pedal harp
GB: Lbl [G.793.(11.)].
CPM, Cohen, Eitner.

The Splendid Penny. A Ballad. London: [F. Bryan, c. 1810].
voice/pf
GB: Lbl [G.809.(35.)].
CPM, Eitner.

The Sylvan Scene of Love. Ariette a la turca. [Words] written by F. Bryan.
London: L. Lavenu [c. 1800].
voice/pf
GB: Lbl (2 ex.) [H.2830.f.(24.) & H.2831.(22.)]
CPM, Cohen, Eitner.

"A Village Boy in Lowly State." The Boy and the Flag'let. Ballad . . .
Music by the composer of *The Maid of Wooburn.* S.l., s.n. [1805?].
voice/pf
GB: Lbl [G.798.(6.)].
CPM.

Bühler, Dorothée de (Daria von), Baroness
n.d.
Six romances, allemandes et française s.l.: P. v. Phillisdorf, n.d.
voice/pf
A: Wgm. D: B.
RISM A/I (BB 4883 II, 1), Eitner.

Bürde, Jeanette Antonie, née Milder
1799, Huttleindorf (near Vienna)—Berlin?
Das Mädchen und der Todtenkopf, Das Heiden-Röslein. [2 poems of Houwald &
Goethe set to music and dedicated to her sister Anna Milder.] Berlin:
Verlag und Eigenthum von T. Trautwein, 1825.
voice/pf
D: DÜk (#177).
Düsseldorf-Goethe, Cohen (as Buerde).

Burney, Cecilia
1789, London–1821, London
Lady Avondel's song ("Oh! tell me have I lost"). The words from *The Refusal*
by Mrs. West. London: [Chappell, 1817].
voice/pf
GB: Lbl [H.1663.(50.)], Ob [in an album with Charles Burney, *Courtenay's
Four Patriotic Songs,* London: Broderip & Wilkinson].
CPM, Scholes.

Le Séjour agréable. A sonata, for the piano forte . . . Op. 2. London:
G. Walkar [*sic*] [1810?]. 8 pp.
pf
GB: Lbl [Hirsch M.1287.(6.)].
CPM.

Bury, Mrs.
pub. c. 1815, London
Erin go Bragh [song, "There came to the beach"]. Arranged for the Harp.
London: s.n. [1815?].
harp
GB: Lbl [G.805.d.(4.)].
CPM.

Bussi, Countess of (Bussy. La Comtesse de Bussi)
pub. 1780s, Paris
[Work(s)] in: *Recueil de romances, chansons et vaudevilles arrangés pour la harpe,*
dédiés à la Reine . . . Paris: Benaut [1781].
harp
F: Pc.
RISM B/II (p. 333).

[Work(s)] in: *Recueil de romances, chansons et vaudevilles arrangés pour le clavecin ou*
le forte-piano avec accompagnement de deux violons et la basse chifrée par M. Benaut
. . . Paris: Benaut [c. 1780].
hpsch or pf/2 vlns
GB: Lbl [F.678].
CPM, RISM B/II (p. 333).

Butler, Miss
pub. 1820, Edinburgh
The ivy branch, composed by Miss Butler, and arranged with variations for
the Piano Forte by T. H. Butler. Edinburgh: T. H. Butler, 1820.
Melody only by Miss Butler.
pf
GB: Lbl [h.280.(5.)].
CPM.

Buttier, Mlle
pub. 1727–32, Paris
"Moments delicieux les plus chers." In: *Meslanges de musique*, Paris: J. B. C.

Ballard, 1727.
S/bc
F: Pn. I: MOe (Mus. F. 1378).
RISM B/II (p. 233), Estense, Cohen.

"Vole, amour, dieu vanquer" [air]. 1. In: *Mercure de France,* Feb. 1729. 2. In: *Nouveau recueil de chanson choisies,* vol. 5. Paris: La Haye, P. Gosse & J. Neaulme, 1732.
song
1. GB: Lbl [298.a. 3]. 2. A: Wgm, Wn. B: Lc. C: Qul. CH: N. CS: Pu. D: AAst, Bhm, BIR, CO, HEu, Mbs, Rtt, WI. E: Mn. F: AM, B, CF, D, DO, Pa, Pc (2 ex.), Pn (3 ex.), R, Sim, Sn, T, TLc. GB: Lbl. NL: DHk. S: L, Sk, Uu. US: NHf, NYp, PHf, R, Wc. YU: Lu.
1. CPM, BUC, Northampton. 2. RISM B/II (p. 262), Cohen.

C., Elisabeth

pub. 1814, London
Twelve original waltzes for the Piano Forte. London: s.n. [1814].
pf
GB: Lbl [h.106.(1.)].
CPM.

C . . . , Mlle de [compositions listed may be by different composers using the same initial]

pub. 1763, Paris
Par un charme invincible et doux. In: *Mercure de France,* October, 1763.
song
GB: Lbl [298.d.13.].
CPM.

pub. 1775, Paris
Une rose vient d'éclore. [Song. Words and music by Mlle C. aged 14 years.] In:
Mercure de France, September, 1775.
song
GB: Lbl [298.e.39.].
CPM.

pub. 1709, Paris and Amsterdam
[Work(s)] in: *Recueil d'airs sérieux et à boire de différents auteurs* . . . Paris: Ch.
Ballard, [1709].
song(s)
F: Pc, Pn. GB: Lbl.
RISM B/II (p. 313).

[Work(s)] in: *Recueil d'airs sérieux et à boire de différents auteurs* . . . Augmenté
considérablement de différents airs manuscrits des plus habiles maîtres &
des plus beaux airs des opéra. Amsterdam: E. Roger, monthly, 1709.
song(s)
NL: DHk.
RISM B/II (p. 316).

C. B., Miss

pub. c.1797, Edinburgh

Lord Jervis, or *the 14th of February 1797,* by Miss C. B. Edinburgh:
N. Stewart, c. 1797.
pf
US: Cn.
RISM A/I (IN 41).

C . . . t, Mme de
pub. 1806, Paris
[Romances and Chansons by Mme de la Fer], Musique de Mme de
C . . . t. Paris: s.n.,1806.
song(s)
GB: Lbl [637.e.32.].
CPM.

Cabanes, A., Madame
pub. c. 1830, Paris
Le temps deviendra beau. Chansonette. 1. Paris: Chez A. Petit [c. 1830].
2. Another ed. Paris: s.n. [1835].
song
1–2. GB: Lbl [G.554.(21.)].
CPM.

Caccini, Francesca (married **Signorini**)
1587, Florence–c. 1640
"Ch'io sia fedele." In: *Le risonanti sfere da velocissimi ingegni armonicamente raggirate; e non solo per se stessa ciascuna, ma anco in oppositione, et aspetto di Trino tra di
loro corrispondenti.* Con il primo mobile del basso continuo. Rome: G. B.
Robletti, 1629.
voice/bc
I: Rvat.
RISM B/I (1629 [9]), Cohen, NG, Eitner.

"Dov'io credea le mie speranze vere." In: *Ghirlandetta amorosa, arie, madrigali,
e sonetti . . . a uno, à due, à tre, & à quattro . . .* da Fabio Costantini . . . Op.
7. Libro primo. Orvieto: M. A. Rei et R. Ruuli, 1621. 4 partbooks (S, S, B,
Bc).
voice/bc
GB: Lbl (SI, SII, B only). I: Bc. Copy in D: Kf&m.
RISM B/I (1621 [14], as F. Cecchina), Cohen, NG, Eitner, Olivier, Frau & Musik.

Il primo libro delle musiche a una, e due voci. Firenze: Zanobi Pignoni, 1618.
Score. 98 pp.
[32 for S/bc, 4 for SB/bc; 7 sacred Latin texts]
1–2 voices/bc (some for chitarra or lute)
F: Pn [B.N. [Rés.F.24]. I: FN, MOe [Mus.D.39]
Microfilm copy US: LAu [Film M 20]. Copy in Ars Fem coll.
RISM A/I (C 2), Cohen, NG, Eitner, Olivier, Paris Lib. Cat., NUC (micro. NC
0007410), letter (Ars Fem).

La liberazione di Ruggiero dall'isola d'Alcina. Balletto . . . rappresentata nel
Poggio imperiale, villa della Sernissima Arciducess ad'Austria Gran
Ducessa di Toscana. 1. Florence: Pietro Cecconcelli,1625. Score. 74 pp.
2. [a 2d edition, n.d.] Libretto by Ferdinando Saracincelli.
stage work
F: Pn [B.N. [Rés.F.25]. GB: Lbl [K.8.g.17]. I: Ma, Rc, Rsc, Vnm
(Microfilm in US: I [Film 903]). US: NYp [libretto only]. Copies in D:
Kf&m, UNikb; copy of 2 versions in Ars Fem coll.
1. RISM A/I (C 3), Cohen, NG, Eitner, Olivier, Paris Lib. Cat., NUC (micro.
C 000748), NUC (libretto only, NC 0007406), D: Uikb cat. 1–2. letter (Ars Fem),
Frau & Musik [dates 1624, 1625].

Caccini, Settimia (married A. Ghivizzani)

1590, Florence–c. 1638, Florence
"Ave luci ridenti." In: untitled ms. dedicated to "Sig. Filippo Del Nero,"
including works with works by Signora Settimia and Signor Alessandro
Ghivizzani, f. 25v–26r.
(S) voice/bc (unfigured)
I: Bc (Q49). Microfilm in Jackson coll.
NG, Cohen (as Caccini-Ghivizzani).

"Lanta gl'augel l'innamorati." In: untitled ms. dedicated to "Sig. Filippo
Del Nero," including works by Signora Settimia and Alessandro
Ghivizzani, f. 27.
(S) voice/bc (unfigured)
I: Bc (Q49). Microfilm in Jackson coll.
NG, Cohen (as Caccini-Ghivizzani).

"Lasterò di sequir' l'empia." In: untitled ms. dedicated to "Sig. Filippo Del
Nero," including works by Signora Settimia and Signor Alessandro
Ghivizzani, f. 25r.
(S) voice/bc (unfigured)

I: Bc (Q49). Microfilm in Jackson coll.
NG, Cohen (as Caccini-Ghivizzani).

"Si miei tormenti con dolci accenti." In: untitled ms. dedicated to "Sig.
Filippo Del Nero," including works by Signora Settimia and Signor
Alessandro Ghivizzani, f. 31.
(S) voice/bc (unfigured)
I: Bc (Q49). Microfilm in Jackson coll.
NG, Cohen (as Caccini-Ghivizzani).

[Songs.] In ms. including works by Signora Settimia and Alessandro
Ghivizzani.
voice/bc
CS: Pnm (II La 2).
NG, Cohen (as Caccini-Ghivizzani).

Calegari, Maria Caterina (Cattarina) (secular name, **Cornelia**)
c. 1644, Bergamo–1664, Milan
Madrigali a due voci
2 voices/bc
I: Bc. Copy in Ars Fem coll.
NG (compositions thought to be lost), letter (Ars Fem), Cohen.

Messe a sei con stromenti
6 voices/instruments
I: Bc. Copy in Ars Fem coll.
NG (compositions thought to be lost), letter (Ars Fem), Cohen.

Troviamo un magnifico elogia.
voices (unacc?)
I: Bc. Copy in Ars Fem coll.
NG (compositions thought to be lost), letter (Ars Fem), Cohen.

Campana, Francesca (Romana) (married **Giovan Carlo Rossi,**
brother of **Luigi Rossi**)
?, Rome–1665, Rome?
Arie a una, due, a tre voci . . . opera prima. Rome: Giovanni Battista Robletti,
1629. Score, 23 pp. Contents: "Semplicetto augellin," sonnet for solo
voice/bc, "Occhi belli," madrigal for 3 unaccompanied voices, and several
strophic songs.
voice/bc & 3 voices,a cappella

F: Pn [B.N. [Rés.F.37]. I: Rvat-sistina. Copy of F: Pn in Ars Fem coll.
RISM A/I (C 612), Bowers & Tick, NG, Cohen, letter (Ars Fem).

"Pargoletta vezzosetta" & "Donna se l'mio servir." In: Robletti, *Le risonanti sfere da velocissimi ingegni armonicamente raggirate . . .* Con il primo mobile del basso continuo. Rome: Robletti, 1629
aria for voice/bc; madrigal for 2 voices/bc
I: Rvat.
RISM B/I (1629[9]), NG, Cohen, Eitner, Bowers & Tick.

Campanile, Madame (pseud.). See Cianchettini, Clelia

Campbell, Agnes M.
pub. c. 1803, London
Four Canzonettas with accompaniment for Harp or Pianoforte. London: s.n., [1803?].
voice/harp or pf
GB: Lbl [G.805.j.(18.)].
CPM.

A second sett of two Canzonets with accompaniment for Harp or Pianoforte. London: s.n. [1805?].
voice/harp or pf
GB: Lbl.
CPM.

"Spring returns." From: *Four Canzonettas with accompaniment for Harp or Pianoforte* (#3). London: L. Lavenu [1816].
voice/harp or pf
GB: Lbl [G.805.o.(35.)].
CPM.

Campbell, Caroline
pub. c. 1787–88, London
Two sonatas and three English airs with variations, for the harp or harpsichord. London: Longman & Broderip [c. 1787].
harp or hpsch
GB: Gu, Lbl [h.106.(5.)]. Copy of GB: Lbl in Ars Fem coll.
RISM A/I (C 617), CPM, Cohen, letter (Ars Fem).

Two sonatas, six songs and some English airs with variations and an accompaniment for the harp . . . op. II. London: Longman & Broderip [c. 1788].
harp; voice/harp
GB: Gu, Lbl [h.106.(6.)], Ob, Obharding. Copy of GB: Lbl in Ars Fem coll.
RISM A/I (C 618, CC618), CPM, Cohen, letter (Ars Fem).

Campbell, Mary
pub. c. 1830, London?
A Waltz Movement and a A Bolero . . . by M. C. S.l.: s.n. [c. 1830]. 5 pp.
pf
GB: Lbl [h.16.zz.(6.)].
CPM.

Campet de Saujon, Mme (or **Mlle**)
fl. 1811–27
Chansonnette italienne avec traduction française . . . *avec accompaniment de Piano et Harpe.* Paris: chez Pacini [1810? or after 1815?].
voice/pf and/or harp
GB: Lbl [G.424.u.(5.)].
CPM, letter (C. Johnson).

Deux Airs Variés Pour le Piano Forte, op. 5. Paris: Chez Mr Pacini/chez Mr Ch[ar]les Bochsa [1813].
pf
F: Pn (Vm12 4590, 2 ex.). Photocopy in C. Johnson coll.
Letter (C. Johnson).

Deux Divertissements Pour le Piano Forte, op. 13. Paris: Mlles Erard [1819].
pf
F: Pn (Vm12 4591, 2 ex.). Photocopy in C. Johnson coll.
Letter (C. Johnson).

Fantasie avec variations Pour le Piano Forte, sur la Romance de Joseph, Musique de Méhul, op. 4. Paris: chez Mr. Pacini [1812].
pf
F: Pn (Vma 113(1), Vm12 4592). Photocopy in C. Johnson coll.
Letter (C. Johnson).

Fantasie sur la Romance "Bon Menestrel" [de Méreaux] *Mise en Duo avec variations pour Harpe et Piano,* op. 12. Paris: chez Melles Erard, [1818].

pf / harp
F: Pn [Vm9 3984, 2 ex.].
Letter (C. Johnson).

Souvenir Mélancolique Pour le Piano Forte, op. post. Paris: Au Magasin de
Musique de Pacini, n.d.
pf
F: Pn (Vm12 4594, 2 ex.). Photocopy in C. Johnson coll.
Letter (C. Johnson).

Vive Henry Quatre Pour le Piano Forte, op. post. Paris: Chez Mr Pacini/Chez
Mr Bochsa Père [1815].
pf
F: Pn (Vm12 4593, 2 ex.). Photocopy in C. Johnson coll.
Letter (C. Johnson).

Candeille, Emilie (Amélie) Julie, same as **Mme Delaroche,** later
Mme Simons, later **Mme Pérlé.** (Professional name often
F. Simons-Candeille)
1767, Paris–1834, Paris
*Cantique des Parisiens à une, deux, ou trois voix ad libitum, avec accompagnement de
Piano ou Harpe* [for the] Duchesse d'Angoulême. Paris: chez l'auteur
[1814].
1, 2, or 3 voices / pf or harp
B: Bc.
RISM A / I (C 795a), NG, letter (C. Johnson).

Catherine, ou *La belle fermière.* Comédie en trois actes en prose, mêlée de
chant . . . [given as] *La belle fermière.* Paroles et musique de Julie Candeille.
1. Paris: Maradan, 1793. 2. Toulouse: Broulhiet, 1793. 3. Paris: Barba,
1797. 4. Barba, 1805. Only text survives.
stage work
1. US: Wc. 2. US: Cu. 3. US: Ca, Cu. 4. Wc. Only libretto survives.
Selected locations given.
NUC (NC 0103333–9).

Catherine, ou *La belle fermière,* Partition de l'ouverture et des airs [excerpts
from]: *Catherine* . . . comédie en trois actes en prose, mêlée de chant. Paris:
Auteur (gravée Huguet), 1792. 36 pp. Score [with 7 parts in ms]. Text by
composer.
stage work (excerpts)

US: AA ("Le Duc" pasted over publisher and composer's autograph), Wc.
RISM A/I (C 788), NUC (NC 0103346), NG, Cohen.

Catherine, ou *La belle fermière*, Romance from ("Au temps orageux de folie")
. . . avec accompagnement de clavecin, ou harp. 1. Paris: Imbault (#155),
s.d. 2. Frére (#137) [c. 1793]. 3. . . . avec guittare. Imbault
[c. 1797]. 4. Lebeau, s.d.
stage work (excerpt), voice/pf, harp, or guit
1. S: Skma. 2 & 3. F: Pn [B.N. [Fol. Vm 229 (60) & B.N. [Vmd. 237 (21)].
2 & 4. US: PHu.
*1–4. RISM A/I (C 789, 790, 791, CC 791a & b), 2–3. Paris Lib. Cat., letter
(C. Johnson). NG.*

Catherine, ou *La belle fermière*, Rondeau from ("Lise avec ses quinze ans").
Paris: Lebeau [c. 1792]. 2 pp.
stage work (excerpt), voice/kbd
F: Pn [B.N. [Fol. Vm 229 (58)]. US: PHu.
RISM A/I (C 791c), NG, Paris Lib. Cat., letter (C. Johnson).

Catherine, ou *La belle fermière*, Vaudeville from ("O mon dieu du'es' qu'on
dira") . . . avec accompagnement de guittare. 1. Paris: Imbault [c. 1793].
2. Lebeau [c. 1793]. 3. Frère [c. 1793]. 4. Ms. copy, c. 1800–1810. 5. In:
Journal d'Apollon pour le forte piano, 1ere année, #2. Paris: H. Naderman [1793].
stage work (excerpt), voice/guit, 4 voices/pf
1–3. F: Pn. 2. US: PHu. 4. DK: Tv (R138). 5. Location not given.
*1–3. RISM A/I (C 792, CC 792a & b). NG. 4. RISMdan. 5. Letter
(C. Johnson). NG.*

[Chanson] in: Recueil des chansons. Ms. collection. [Text attributed to
King Henry IV, music by Mme. Simons-Candeille.]
song
F: Pa.
Letter (C. Johnson).

Concerto [D] *pour le forte piano ou clavecin à grand orchestre qui peut s'exécuter avec
un premier violon, 2e violon, alto et basse . . . œuvre IIe. Paris: auteur (gravées
par Dessaux) [1787]. 7 partbooks.*
pf or hpsch/2 vlns/vla/b/ob/fl/2 bsns/2 hns
F: Pn [B.N. [Vm7 5971]. Photocopy in C. Johnson coll.
*RISM A/I (C 797), Paris Lib. Cat., Cohen (as concerto #2), NG, Eitner (as
Simons, Mme), letter (C. Johnson).*

Deux grandes sonates [D, g] *pour clavecin ou forté-piano* . . . œuvre 8e. Paris:
Jean-Henri Naderman/Chez Lobry (#543) [1798].
hpsch or pf
F: Pn (2 ex) [Vm7 5626 & Vm12 26522]. Photocopy in C. Johnson coll.
RISM A/I (C 799, CC 799), NG, Paris Lib. Cat., Eitner (as Simons, Mme),
Cohen, letter (C. Johnson).

Duo [A] *pour deux piano-forte* executé par l'auteur et le citoyen Baptiste ainé
au Theâtre de la République, 1793 . . . œuvre 3e. Paris: Boyer [179–?]. In:
Journal de pièces de clavecin par differens auteurs (#123) [1794]. 2 partbooks.
2 pfs
B: Bc. US: Bp (primo only, lacks secondo) Microfilm copies in US: Bp &
C. Johnson coll.
RISM A/I (C 798, CC 798), NUC (NC 0103343), OCLC (micro. 23894181),
Cohen, NG (listed as lost), Eitner (as Simons, Mme), letter (C. Johnson).

L'Aile du Temps ("Du sein ma solitude"). Romance avec accompagnement
de Piano. Paris: chez B. Viguerie [1810]. [#2 of *Arsenne ou l'Eptire*
Dédicatoire, Trois Romances et une Chansonette . . . , published separately.]
voice/pf
GB: Lbl [G.548.(48.)].
CPM, letter (C. Johnson).

La jeune hôtesse, Chanson from ("Lisi avait de la jeunesse"). 1. Paris:
Imbault, s.d. 2. Frère, s.d. 3. . . . avec piano forte. Paris: Mlle Lebeau, s.d.
4 . . . avec guitare. Paris: Mlle Lebeau, n.d. 5. Ms. copy, c. 1800–10.
stage work (excerpt), voice/pf or guit
1. GB: Lbl (many anony. eds. of "Lisi avait de la jeunesse"; see under
"Jeune" in CPM). US: CA. 2 & 3–4. F: Pn [4o Vm7 1957 (10) &
B.N. [Fol. Vm 229 (58)]. 5. DK: Tv (R135).
1–3. RISM A/I (C 794, CC 794 a, b, c), CPM. 1. OCLC (21273460), 2–4.
Paris Lib. Cat. 5. RISMdan. Letter (C. Johnson).

La jeune hôtesse. Comédie en trois actes, en vers; par le Citoyen Carbon-
Flins. Paris: Barba, 1794. Score.
stage work
GB: Lbl (according to CPM, only the many anonymous editions of the
excerpt "Lisi avait de la jeunesse" are in Lbl; see the listing "Jeune" in
CPM).
RISM A/I (C 793), CPM, Cohen.

La jeune hôtesse, excerpt from, arr. for piano. ("Lisi avait de la jeunesse.") In: J. A. Gaultier, *Les Plaisirs de l'Enfance ou Choix de Petits Airs d'Une Difficulté Graduelle Pour le Forte-Piano Formant trois Suites*. Paris: chez Boyer/Lyon, Garnier [c.1792].
pf
F: Pn [Vma 2414].
Letter (C. Johnson).

La Montagnarde du Tyrol ("Or écoutez"). Romance. Paris: au Magasin de Musique de Meissonnier [1835?].
voice/pf
GB: Lbl [G.553.(41.)].
CPM, letter (C. Johnson).

Le Bain. Romance. Paroles de M. de Murville. In: *Almanach des muses*, p. 261–64. Paris: Delalain, 1786.
song
D: Ngm. F: CN, Pi, Pn (2 ex). GB: Lbl. US: R.
RISM B/II (Melle de Candeille, p. 83), letter (C. Johnson).

Le Choix de Lucas. In: *Courier lyrique et amusant ou Passe-temps des toilettes par Mme. Dufrenoy*, vol. I/5, pp. 33–34. Paris: Knapen et fils, August 1, 1785. [Also a work by Emilie C. in Jan. 1789, may be by same person.]
song
F: Pn. Holdings in other libraries incomplete runs.
RISM B/II (Melle de Candeille, Emilie C., p. 147), letter (C. Johnson).

L'embarras du Choix. Romance Pastorale. In: *Courier lyrique et amusant ou Passe-temps des toilettes par Mme. Dufrenoy*, pp. 1–6. Paris: Knapen et fils, March 16, 1788.
[Also work by Emilie C., Jan. 1789, may be same person.]
song
F: Pn. Holdings in other libraries incomplete runs.
RISM B/II (Melle de Candeille, Emilie C., p. 147), letter (C. Johnson).

Le sentiment discret. Ariette avec accompagnement de 1r & 2e violons ou flûtes et basse. Paris: auteur, aux addresses ordinaires (gravée par Mlle Aubert) [after 1795]. Score and parts.
voice/2 vlns or fls/b(c)
F: PA [Ars.[M.314].
RISM A/I (C 795), Paris Lib. Cat., letter (C. Johnson).

"Nos plaisirs sont legers" [song from M. Saujon's comédie, *Le Couvent]* arr. for piano. In: J. A. Gaultier, *Les Plaisirs de l'Enfance* ou *Choix de Petits Airs . . . Pour le Forte-Piano Formant Trois Suites.* Paris: chez Boyer/Lyon: Garnier [c.1792].
pf
F: Pn [Vma 2414].
Letter (C. Johnson).

Nouvelle Fantaisie Facile et Brillante Pour le Piano (sur une jolie Romance de Messrs Hoffmann et feû Solié) [g /G], op. 13. Paris: Chez Naderman/LeDuc/ Paccini/et aux Adresses ordinaires, n.d.
pf or hpsch/2 vlns/vla/b; also ob/fl/2 bsns/2 hns
F: Pn (2 ex., Vm12 26523). Photocopy in C. Johnson coll.
Letter (C. Johnson).

Sept variations sur l'hymne de la Nativité. Théme Portugais. Paris: Momigny/Paccini [c. 1808?].
kbd
CS: K.
RISM A/I (C 799a), NG, Cohen, letter (C. Johnson).

Trio ou nocturne pour piano, violon, et violoncelle obligés . . . Fantasie no 5 . . . Opera 11. Paris: chez Mme Duhan [1815?].
pf/vln/vlc
GB: Lbl [g.271.q.(12.)].
CPM, letter (C. Johnson).

Trois sonates [G, C, E-flat] *pour le forte piano ou clavecin avec accompagnement de violon (à volonté) . . .* œuvre premier. Paris: auteur (gravées par Dessaux) [1786]. Parts.
pf or hpsch/ vln ad lib
F: Pn [B.N. [Vm7 5370]. Photocopy in C. Johnson coll.
RISM A/I (C 796), Paris Lib. Cat., Cohen (date as 1796), NG, Eitner (acc. de violon e vclle, Leduc, 1788), letter (C. Johnson).

Une grande sonate pour le piano-forte [E-flat] *. . .* œuvre 5e. Paris: Chez Momigny/Imbault/Naderman/Pleyel/et Adresses ordinaires [1798].
pf
F: Pn [B.N.[L.14.835]. Photocopy in C. Johnson coll.
RISM A/I (C 798a), Paris Lib. Cat., NG (lists as lost), letter (C. Johnson).

[Work(s)] in: *Musikaliskt tidsfördrif.* Stockholm: Kongl. Privilegierade Not Tryckeriet [1789–1834].
instruments undetermined
S: L, Sk, Skma, Sm, Uu. SF: T. US: NYp (incomplete run). Holdings in other libraries also incomplete runs.
RISM B/II (J. Candeille, p. 252). RISM does not specify which library in Turku (SF: T).

Cantelo, Anne (Mrs. Harrison after 1790. May have been student of J. C. Bach)

c. 1760, ?–1831, London
Werter's Sonnet ("Make thou my tomb") . . . 1. [London]: Longman & Broderip [1786 or 1788]. 4 pp. 2. In: *The Philadelphia Repository and Weekly Register,* II, #21, p. 164. Philadelphia, 1801. 3. [New York, Paff?, c. 1801].
1. voice/pf, harp or hpsch 2–3. voice/pf
1. GB: Lbl [G. 377.(9.)], Ob. US: NH (Music C22 W788). 2. US: For many locations of this journal see *Union List of Serials.* 3. US: CAdriscoll, NYp, Wc. Copy in Ars Fem coll.
1. RISM A/I (C 881, dated 1790), CPM. 2–3. Wolfe (1499, 1500, 6976). 3. NUC (NC 0111172). NG (bio, Miss Cantelo), Cohen. Letter (Ars Fem).

[Work(s)] in: *Hime's pocket book for the german flute or violin.* Containing a variety of the newest & favorite airs, duets, marches, songs &c . . . Vol. I–VI. Dublin: Hime [c. 1800].
flute or vln/kbd?
EIR: Dn.
RISM B/II (Miss Cantelo, p. 200), NG (bio, Miss Cantelo), Cohen.

Caroline de Saxe (possibly Caroline, Duchess of Saxony-Coburg, Deaconess of Gandersheim)

1753–1829
[Work(s)] in: *Blumenlese für Klavierliebhaber, eine musikalische Wochenschrift.* [Ed. by H. P. Bossler.] Speier: 1783. 2 vols.
kbd
D: Bds, Mbs. F: Pc. NL: DHgm. US: Bp (2), Wc (2). Holdings in other libraries incomplete.
RISM B/II (p. 115), letter (Woods).

Caroline, of Litchfield

pub. 1804, Portsmouth NH
"The village hind with toil had done" In: *The Nightingale,* Portsmouth NH, 1804, pp. 51–53.

Melody and text only.
song (unacc.)
US: AA, Ba, Bp, BUg, CA, NYcuh, NYfuld, NYp, PIlevy, PROu, SM, Wc, WOa.
Wolfe (1531, 6534).

Caron, Mme
pub. c. 1790, Paris
La petite curieuse, ou *papa vous fera pendre.* [Paris]: frères Savigny [c. 1790].
song
GB: Lbl [B.362.n.(8.)].
RISM A/I (CC 1232 1, 1), CPM.

Carr, Mrs.
pub. 1799, London
"I hate that drum's discordant sound." Air. [London: J. Johnson, 1799.]
Bound up at the end of "Biographiana."
song
GB: Lbl [980.1.6].
RISM A/I (CC 1236 II, 1), CPM.

Carter, Elizabeth
1717–1806, England
1. *Ode to wisdom* ("The solitary bird of night"). In: Richardson, Samuel, *Clarissa: Or, the history of a young lady,* vol. 2 [1st & 3d eds.], pp. 48–51, music between pp. 50 and 51, part of Letter IX, as if by "Clarissa Harlowe." London: published by the editor of *Pamela,* for the author Samuel Richardson, 1748. 2. *Ode an die Weisheit. Aus dem englischen er Clarissa.* Übersezt von J. P. Uz. Nebst dem englischen Grundtext und der Musik. Berlin [actually Ansbach]: 1757. 16 pp. [Translation of "Ode to Wisdom."]
song (unacc. melody)
1. The first edition of the novel is in: US: FA. Other copies of the novel may be found in many libraries. 2. US: CA (*GC7 Uz105 757o).
1. Cohen (as Harlow, Clarissa [sic, the fictional character!]), US: FA Special Collections. 2. NUC Sup. (NSC 0025368).

Carver, Miss
pub. c.1787–90, Liverpool
Free from bustle, noise & strife. A favorite cantata. Liverpool: J. B. Pye [1789].
song

GB: Lbl [G. 377.(11.)]. Copy in Ars Fem coll.
RISM A/I (C 1399), CPM, Cohen, letter (Ars Fem).

Patty the milk maid. A favorite ballad. Liverpool: J. B. Pye [1787].
song
GB: Lbl [H.1653.(26.)], Ob.
RISM A/I (C 1400, dated 1790), CPM, Cohen.

The Queen of flowers. A favorite song. Liverpool: J. B. Pye [1789].
song
GB: Lbl [G.377.(12.)]. Copy in Ars Fem coll.
RISM A/I (C 1401, dated 1790), CPM, Cohen, letter (Ars Fem).

Casson, E., Miss
pub. c. 1795, London
The Pearl. A favorite glee [3 voices]. London: author [1795?].
3 voices
GB: Lbl [G. 809.(46.)]. Copy in Ars Fem coll.
RISM A/I (C 1444), CPM, Cohen (as Margaret Casson), letter (Ars Fem).

Casson, Margaret [may be more than one composer by this name]
?, c. 1775–?
Attend ye nymphs whilst I impart. A favorite song . . . composed by M. Casson
in the seventh year of her age. London: Longman & Broderip [c. 1795].
song
GB: Lbl [G.809.(45.)]. Copy in Ars Fem coll.
RISM A/I (C 1449), CPM, Cohen, letter (Ars Fem).

The Cuckoo ("Now the sun is in the west"). A favorite song with an accompanyment for the piano forte or pedal harp. 1. Parts printed for the guitar
and flute on p. 4. London: G. Goulding [c. 1790]. 2. W. Wybrow [1820?].
3. Diether [1822].
voice/pf or harp (1. or guit/fl)
1. GB: Ckc, Gu, Lbl, Obharding. US: Nyfuld, NYp, Pu, Wc. 2. GB: Lbl
[G.383.h.(23.)]. 3. GB: Lbl [H.3690.ww.(1.)]. Copy in Ars Fem coll.
*1–2. RISM A/I (C 1451, CC 1451). 1. NUC (0190529). 2–3. CPM. Cohen.
Letter (Ars Fem).*

The Cuckoo. [Song by M. Casson.] Arranged as a rondo for the piano forte,
by George F. Harris . . . [1830?].
pf

GB: Lbl[G.798.(15.)]. Copy in Ars Fem coll.
CPM, letter (Ars Fem).

Noon. A Favorite Rondo. The Words by Mrs. Cobbold . . . London:
[Cobbold, c. 1800].
song
GB: Lbl [G.798.(15.)]. Copy in Ars Fem coll.
RISM A/I (C 1450), CPM, Cohen, letter (Ars Fem).

Casulana de Mezari, Maddalena (Casolana, Madalena. La Casulana)

c. 1540, Casule d'Elsa, Siena–c. 1583
"Amorosetto fiore." In: *Terzo libro del Desiderio. Madrigali a quattro voci de Orlando Lasso et d'altri eccel. Musici* . . . per Giulio Bonagionta . . . Venice:
Girolamo Scotto, 1567. 4 partbooks.
4 voices (SATB)
I: Bc.
RISM B/I (1567 [16]), Bowers & Tick, NG, Pescerelli, Eitner (as Mezari), Frau & Musik (lists copies of 25 Madrigals from I: Tci).

Di Madalena Casulana il secondo libro de madrigali à quattro voci . . . Venice:
Girolamo Scotto, 1570. 4 partbooks. Dedicated to D. Antonio Londonio,
Milan. [15 madrigals by Casulana, 1 by L. Mira.]
4 voices (SATB)
D: Bds, W.
RISM A/I (C 1518), RISM B/I (1570 [24]), Bowers & Tick, NG, Pescerelli, Cohen, Olivier, Frau & Musik (lists copies of 25 Madrigals from I: Tci).

Il primo libro de madrigali a cinque voci. Ferrara: Angelo Gardano, 1583. 5
partbooks. Dedicated to Count Mario Bevilacqua, Verona. [as: Madalena
Mezari detta Casulana]
5 voices (SA5[A]TB)
A: Wn (S, T, 5 only). I: VEaf (5 only). PL: GD (T, B, 5 only).
RISM A/I (C 1519), Bowers & Tick, NG, Pescerelli, Cohen, Olivier, Frau & Musik (lists copies of 25 Madrigals from I: Tci).

Il primo libro de madrigali a quattro voci. 1. Venice: Girolamo Scotto, 1568.
2. Milan: Tini & Brescia: Vincenzo Sabbio, 1583. 4 partbooks. [Includes
the 5 madrigals of *Il Desiderio* from 1566–67.] Dedicated to Isabella de'
Medici.
4 voices (SATB)

1. I: Bc (T only). 2. D: AN (S only), I: Moe (S, T only, Mus.G.45).
*1–2. RISM A/I (C 1516, 1517), Bowers & Tick, NG, Pescerelli. Cohen, Olivier,
Frau & Musik (lists copies of 25 Madrigals from I: Tci).*

"Stavasi il mio bel sol." In: Il *Gaudio primo libro de madrigali de diversi eccellen.
musici à tre voci* . . . Venice: L'herede di Girolamo Scotto, 1586. 3 partbooks.
3 voices
D: Bds, Tü. I: Bc (B only).
*RISM B/I (1586 [12]), Bowers & Tick, NG, Pescerelli, Cohen, Frau & Musica
(lists copies of 25 Madrigals from I: Tci).*

"Vedesti Amor giamai," "Sculpio ne l'am'Amore," "Morir no può il mio
cuore," & "Se scior si ve'il laccio." In: *Primo libro de diversi eccellent mi auttori à
quattro voci* . . . *Il Desiderio* . . . per Giulio Bonagionta. Venice: Girolamo
Scotto, 1566. 4 partbooks.
4 voices (SATB)
D: Mbs, W. I: Bc (SAB only).
*RISM B/I (1566 [2]), Bowers & Tick, NG, Pescerelli, Cohen, Frau & Musik (lists
copies of 25 Madrigals from I: Tci).*

Catalani, Angelica (married **Valabrègue**)
1780, Sinigaglia–1849, Paris
Airs favorits, nr. 1, avec accompagnement de piano–forte, chantés et variés
par Madame Catalani. Vienna: Artaria [1817]. 21 pp.
voice (S)/pf
US: DM.
OCLC (23744198).

"Cease your funning." 1. As sung by Madame Catalani, Ms., n.d. 2 pp.
2. With Madame Catalani's variations as sung by Mrs. French. Philadelphia:
G. E. Blake [1825?]. Flute pt. on p. 3. 3. In: G. S. Thornton, *The Melodist,*
I, p. 64. NY: G. Singleton, 1820 [melody only].
voice (S)/pf (2. with fl)
1. US: NYp. 2. US: CHAhughes, HA, NYcuh, NYp, PROu, R, WOa.
3. US: Cn, CA, NH, NYp, Wc.
*1–2. NUC (NC 0204174, NC 0204175). 3. OCLC (18663427). 1–3. Wolfe
(1738, 1739).*

[4] Airs favorits variés. Ms.
songs
A: Wgm.
Eitner, Cohen.

A Favorite Cavatina ["Lungi dal caro bene," from *Giulio Sabino,* by G. Sarti.] Sung . . . by Madame Catalani . . . with Madame Catalani's own graces [c. 1805].
voice/pf
GB: Lbl [H.1652.rr.(49.)].
CPM.

Four Italian Ariettes and a Duetto, for soprano & tenor . . . 1. London: The Author; Chappell & Co [1813]. 2. [1815?].
voices (ST)/pf
GB: Lbl 1. [F.1256.vv.(8.)], 2. [E.601.e.(1.)].
1–2. CPM. Eitner, NG (bio), Cohen.

Madam Catalani's favourite German waltz for the Pianoforte. Edinburgh: [1815?]. [Arr. from melody by Catalani?]
pf
GB: Lbl [h.1480.k.(11.)].
CPM, Eitner, NG (bio), Cohen.

"Nel cor più non mi sento" [from *La Molinara* by G. Paisiello] . . . 1. As sung in the opera of *Il Fanatico per la musica,* by Made Catalani with her own variations [c. 1810]. 2. As . . . sung by Madame Catalani, with her own Variations [1824].
voice (S)/pf
GB: Lbl 1. [H. 1980.n.(4.)]. 2. [G.811.a.(32.)].
1–2. CPM.

"O dolce concento" ["Das klinget so herrlich"] from *Die Zauberflöte* by W. A. Mozart] . . . The variations by Madm Catalani. 1. [1805?]. 2. Sung by Madme Catalani in the opera of *Le Virtuose in puntiglio* . . . the variations by Madme Catalani [1810]. 3. Sung by Madme Catalani in the opera of *Le Virtuose in puntiglio* . . . the variations by Madme Catalani; arr. for harp or piano forte by G. G. Ferrari. Philadelphia: G. E. Blake [183–?].
4. Edinburgh: Corri, [180–?]. 5. London: Birchall, [1819?].
1–2., 5. voice (S)/pf, 3–4. voice (S)/harp or pf
GB: Lbl 1. [H. 1652.y.(6.)]. 2. [H.1980.n.(5.)]. 3. US: DM. 4. US: CA. 5. US: CA.
1–2. CPM. 3–4. OCLC (18663456, 20164143). 5. OCLC (20164074).

"Olà t'arresta." Grand aria by Pio Cianchettini, with ornaments as sung by Madame Catalani. London: Willis [182–?].

voice (S)/pf
US: CA.
OCLC (21666264).

"Papa non dite." Canzonetta sung . . . by Madame Catalani in the opera of *Il Furbo contro il furbo* [by Valentino Fioravanti] . . . the melody by Mme. Catalani, the accompaniments by G. G. Ferrari . . . 1. London: L. Lavenu [1808?]. 4 pp. 2. Adolfo Ferrari [c. 1810]. 3. London: Clementi & Comp [1820?]. 4. Leipzig: Kühnel. 5. Arr. for the harp or piano forte by J. Elouis, London: J. Elouis [1809]. 2 pp. 6. London: L. Lavenu [1827]. 4 pp.
voice/pf or harp (editions vary)
1. GB: Lbl [G.794.(2.)]. US: CA (bound with Begres, Amplessi soavi, et al.) (date 181–?). 2. GB: Lbl [G.426.cc.(13.)]. 3. GB: Lbl [Hirsch M. 1274.(19.)]. 4. USSR: KA (B. Kgsb in Eitner, modern location not confirmed). 5. GB: Lbl [h.109.(17.)]. 6. US: NYp.
1–2. CPM 2. OCLC (#1. 21457042). 3, 5. CPM. 4. Eitner. 6. NUC (NC 0204177). NG (bio), Cohen.

"Pietosá á miei lamenti." The much admired cavatina by William Clements of Vienna. Arr. by permission, . . . with Madame Catalani's alterations and embellishments by Pio Cianchettini. London: Willis [182–?]. 5 pp.
voice (S)/pf
US: CA.
OCLC (21666310).

"Questo palpito soave" . . . Cavatina . . . [from *La Morte di Cleopatra*] . . . arr. by G. G. Ferrari. London: [1806].
voice/pf
GB: Lbl [G.809.(47.)].
CPM, Eitner, NG (bio), Cohen.

Rode's celebrated Air [Air varié, op. 10, by J. P. Rode]. 1. . . . for the piano forte . . . with Madame Catalani's variations [1822]. 2. *Variationen über ein Thema von Rode von Mme Catalani.* Mit Begleitung des Piano-Forte [1828]. 3. sung by Made. Catalani, arr. for the harp with addition of new variations . . . by N. C. Bochsa. London: Chappell [between 1819 & 1826]. 9 pp. 4. [arr.] for the piano forte . . . with Madame Catalani's Variations by Pio Cianchettini. "The only Genuine Copy of [my] Variations. . . . sanctioned, Angelica Catalani." Liverpool: Yaniewicz & Weiss [182–]. 7 pp.
1–2. voice/pf 3. harp 4. pf

GB: Lbl 1. [H. 1980.s.(37.)]. 2. [E.1050.v.(5.)]. 3. US: BE, R. 4. US: R. *1–2. CPM. 3. OCLC (16449235). 4. OCLC (24934014).*

Rule Britannia [from *Alfred,* by T. A. Arne]. With Madame Catalani's variations [arr. by Cianchettini]. [1820?].
voice (S)/pf
GB: Lbl [H.1653.h.(9.)].
CPM.

"Sul margine d'un rio," air varié per il Sopr. Ms.
song
A: Wgm.
Eitner, Cohen.

[2] Airs favorits variés. Ms.
songs
A: Wgm.
Eitner, Cohen.

Catley, Anne
1745, London–1789, near Brentford
"Cease gay seducers." A favorite air in *Love in a Village.* [London: L[ongman], L[ukey & co], J. J[ohnston], 1775.
voice/pf
GB: Lbl [H.1944.(9.) & H.1980.yy.(12.)] (also in many anonymous editions and arrangements in GB: Lbl. See CPM under title), Obharding. US: U.
RISM A/I (CC 1523 1, 1), CPM, NG (bio), Cohen.

Cavendish, Georgiana Spencer, Duchess of Devonshire. See Devonshire, Duchess of, Georgiana Cavendish (Cavendish, Georgiana, née Spencer)

Cazati, Maria
18th century
Nisi Domino aedificav. Ms.
3 voices/2 vlns/bc
D: B (Ms. 3102).
Eitner, Cohen, letter (D: B).

Cécile, Jeanne, Mlle
b. 1762?, fl. Paris
Concerto [C] *Per Forte Piano* con due violini, due oboe, due corni, violetta et basso . . . exécuté . . . au concert spirituel le 29 mai 1783. Paris: auteur [1783]. 7 partbooks.
pf/2 vlns/vla/b/2 obs/2 hns
F: Pn [B.N. (Ac. e9 6)]. Copies in C. Johnson coll., Jackson coll., & Ars Fem coll.
RISM A/I (C 1680), Paris Lib. Cat., Cohen, letters (C. Johnson, Ars Fem).

Cesis, Sulpiza (Sulpitia)
pub. 1619, Modena
Motetti spirituali. Modena: Cassiani, 1619. [Contains 15 motets à 8, 1 à 12, 2 à 6, 1 à 5, 2 à 4, & 2 à 2 voices.]
2 to 12 voices
GB: Lbl [F.6.] (AI, BI only), I: MOe (complete. Choir I: SATB; Choir II: SATB.)
RISM A/I (C 1764), NG (bio), Bowers & Tick, Eitner, Estense, CPM, Cohen, Brenet.

Chaistaignerais, Mme de la
pub. 1699, Paris
[Work] in: *Suite de danses pour les violons et haut-bois,* quise joüent . . . aux bals chaz le Roy . . . la plus grande partie par Philidor l'aîné . . . Livre premier. Paris: C. Ballard, 1699.
vlns/obs/bc?
F: Pn.
RISM B/I (1699 [7]).

Chamberger, Mme du
n.d., France?
Jamais adieu ("Ne t'en va pas"). Paroles de M.me Desbordes Valmore, Musique de M.me Du Chambger. Ms. 9 pp.
voice/pf
CH: AR [Mus Ms A28 (Ms 7514)].
RISM A/II (#11210). Chamberger is name supplied by RISM.

La Séparation ("l le faut je renounce à toi"). Paroles de M.me Desbordes Valmore, Musique de M.me Du Chambger. Ms.
voice/pf
CH: AR [Mus Ms A32 (Ms 7487)].
RISM A/II (#10870). Chamberger is name supplied by RISM.

Chambers, Miss
pub. c. 183–?
Simple ballads. London: Boosey, [183–?]. 33 pp.
voice/pf
US: CA.
OCLC (21457285).

Charlotte August, consort of **Leopold, Prince of Saxe-Coburg.** See
modern editions for facsimile

Charriére, Isabella Agneta Elisabeth de, née **van Tuyll (Sophie de
Charriére,** also known as **Belle van Zuylen)**
1740, Zuylen, near Utrecht–1805, Neuchâtel
Airs et romances avec accompagnement de clavecin. Paris: Bonjour [1789]. Score,
17 pp.
S/hpsch; S/2 vlns/hpsch; S/fl/vln/hpsch
CH: N. F: Pn [Vm7 7604]. Copy of F: Pn in Ars Fem coll. and Jackson
coll.
RISM A/I (C 1920), Paris Lib. Cat., Cohen, letter (Ars Fem).

Arbre charmant qui me rapelle. Romance avec accompagnement de clavecin
(et de violon ad libitum). S.l., s.n. (gravé par Dessaux) [1788]. 3 pp.
voice/hpsch/vln ad lib.
F: Pn [Vm7 40347]. Copy in Ars Fem coll.
RISM A/I (C 1921), Paris Lib. Cat., letter (Ars Fem).

Chant guerrier. Adressè aux Prussiens en May 1813. (Zuruf an Prussens
Freywillige. Das Vaterland ist in Gefahr.) Deux romances et deux airs
allemands. Zürich: Orel, Füssli & Co., 1814.
voice/pf
CH: N. D: UNikb.
RISM A/I (CC 1921a), Frauenmusik.

Julien et Juliette [opèra buffon]. Ms. score.
stage work
D: D (Eitner, Ms. 125). Modern location not confirmed.
Eitner, Cohen.

Tout cède à la beauté d'Elise. Air avec accompagnement de clavecin (et de
violon ad libitum). Paris: (gravé par Dessaux) [1788]. 3 pp.
voice/hpscd/vln ad lib.

F: Pn [Vm7 40346]. Copy in Ars Fem coll.
RISM A/I (C 1922), Paris Lib. Cat., letter (Ars Fem).

Trois sonates pour le clavecin ou pianoforte . . . œuvre I. Paris: Ches le Sr. le
Duc/au bureau d'abonnement musical/et aux adresses ordinaires
[c.1783].
hpsch or pf
F: Pn [Vm7 5375]. Copies in C. Johnson coll. & Ars Fem coll.
*RISM A/I (C 1923), Paris Lib. Cat., Cohen (as 6 piano sonatas), letters
(C. Johnson, Ars Fem).*

Trois sonates pour le clavecin ou pianoforte . . . œuvre II. Paris: au bureau
d'abonnement musical et aux adresses ordinaires [c. 1783]. 9 pp.
hpsch or pf
F: Pn [Vm7 5376]. Copies in C. Johnson coll. & Ars Fem coll.
RISM A/I (C 1924), Paris Lib. Cat., Cohen, letters (C. Johnson, Ars Fem).

Trois sonates pour le clavecin ou pianoforte . . . œuvre III. Paris: au bureau
d'abonnement musical et aux adresses ordinaires [c. 1783]. 9 pp.
hpsch or pf
F: Pn [Vm7 5377]. Copies in C. Johnson coll. & Ars Fem coll.
RISM A/I (C 1925), Paris Lib. Cat., Cohen, letters (C. Johnson, Ars Fem).

Chazal, Elisabetta. See **Gambarini, Elisabetta de**

Cherbourg, Mlle
pub. c. 1765, Paris
*Premier recueil de chansons avec accompagnement de guitarre et six menuets en duo pour
deux guitarres.* Paris: Bailleux [c. 1765]. Score, 15 pp.
voice/ guit; 2 guits
F: Pn [Vmg. 7998].
RISM A/I (C 2016), Paris Lib. Cat., Cohen.

**Chodkiewicz (Chodkiewiozowey, Chodkiewiezowej), W. Hrabiny,
Countess**
pub. 1816
Karol Chodkiewicz [or Chodkiewiczu] ("Kiedy Batory na Moskalów godzi").
In: Julian Ursyn Niemcewicz, *Śpiewy historycznye* [Historic songs]. Warsaw:
1816. Text by Niemcewicz.
voice/pf
F: Pn. PL: Kc, Wn, Wmickiewicz. Copies of 2 editions in PL: Kc in

Jackson coll.
Cohen, Sowinsky.

Christie, A., Miss
pub. 1820, London
Les quadrilles du Parterre . . . for the Piano Forte. London: Printed for the
Regent's Harmonic Institution [1820]. 8 pp.
pf
GB: Lbl [h.104.(6.)].
CPM.

Cianchettini, Clelia (Veronica Elizabeth?) (pseud. Madame Campanile)
pub. 1829, London
L'Emulazione ("Fra i sassi"). Arietta. London: Lonsdale & Bills [1829]. 5 pp.
voice/pf
GB: Lbl [H.1665.(40.)].
CPM.

Cianchettini, Veronica Rosalie, née Dussek. See Dussek (Dusikova), Katerina Veronika Anna Rosalia Elisabeta

Cibbini, Katherina, née Kozeluch (Koželuh) (pub. as Cibbini-Kozeluch)
1790, Vienna–1858, Vienna
Deux divertissements brillants et d'un style élegant pour le PF . . . sur motifs favoris,
œuvre 3. Vienna: A. Diabelli, n.d.
pf
I: MOe (Mus. E. 270).
MGG (under Koželuch), Estense, Cohen.

Divertissement [piano]. Ms.
pf
A: Wmg (VII 31225).
MGG (under Koželuch).

Impromptu in Es [E-flat, piano]. Vienna: P. Mechetti, n.d.
pf
CS: Bu.
MGG (under Koželuch), Cohen.

Impromptu pour le PF. sur un Thême de Mad. Clary di Zentner, op. 7. Vienna: Tobias Haslinger, n.d.
pf
I: MOe (Mus. E. 169).
Estense, Cohen.

Introduction et Polonaise pour le PF, œuvre 8. Vienna: P. Mechetti (pl.#2376), 1833.
pf
I: MOe (Mus. D. 567). D: Kf&m.
MGG (Koželuch), Estense, Cohen (as op. 9), Frau & Musik.

Introduction et Variations brillantes sur un Thème de Caraffa pour le PF., op. 2. 1. Vienna: Diabelli [1828]. 2. Ms.
pf
1. A: Sca (10478). I: MOe (Mus. E. 28). 2. A: Wgm (VII 31226).
1. Estense, Salzburg, Cohen. 2. MGG.

Introduction et Variations in Es, œuvre 5. Vienna: Haslinger, c. 1830.
pf
I: MOe (Mus. E.29).
MGG (Koželuch), Estense, Cohen.

La Rimembranza: Grand Trio Concertante, op. 10. 1. Vienna: A. Diabelli, n.d. 2. Vienna: Artaria, 1834.
2 pfs/vlc
1. A: Wgm. I: Moe (Mus. D. 566). 2. CS: Bu.
1. MGG (Koželuch), Eitner, Estense. 2. Cohen.

March et trio [piano]. Vienna: P. Mechetti, n.d.
pf
CS: Bu.
MGG (Koželuch), Cohen.

Polonaise [piano]. Ms.
pf
A: Wgm (WII 31223, 31227).
MGG (Koželuch).

Première Fantaisie [piano]. Ms., 1825.
pf

A: Wgm (WII 31228).
MGG (Koželuch).

Seize Valses op. 9. Vienna: P. Mechetti, 1833.
pf
A: Wgm.
MGG (Koželuch).

6 Valses für Klavier, op. 6. Vienna: T. Haslinger (pl.# 6040), c. 1830.
pf
CS: Bu. D: Kf&m.
MGG (Koželuch), Cohen, Frau & Musik.

Variations [piano]. Ms.
pf
A: Wgm (WII 31224).
MGG (Koželuch).

Clarisse de Rome. See **Anonymous** (Nun of the order of St. Clare)

Clark, Caroline
pub. 1824, Boston
Lafayette's March composed by Miss Caroline Clark for the Boston
Independent Cadets and performed by their band at the review in honour
of Genl. La Fayette. Boston: Author [1824?].
pf (arr.)
US: AAclements, Bp, HA, NYp, WGw.
Tick, NUC (NC 0451210), OCLC (18853540).

Clark of Tetbury, Mrs.
pub. 1790, London
[Work(s)] in: *Parsley's lyric repository for 1790* . . . all the favorite songs, duets,
trios &c. now singing at the theatres-royal, the Anacreontic society, and
every polite assembly of wit and harmony in the metropolis . . . London:
R. Parsley [1790].
song(s)
US: NYp.
RISM B/II (p. 282).

Clarke, Elizabeth
pub. 1822, Edinburgh

The Blue Bell [song]. Words by Edward Nairne Boyce. Edinburgh: Published and to be had at the Music Shops [1822].
song
GB: Lbl [H.1653.r.(5.)].
CPM.

Clarke, Jane
pub. c.1795–1810, London
Select Portions of Psalms & Hymns Set to music with Thorough Basses . . . arr. for the Organ or Piano Forte as sung at Oxford, Wilbeck & Portland Chapels, St. Mary-le-Bone. The second edition. 1. London: R. Birchall, [1795?]. 2. 2d ed. [c. 1800 or 1810].
voice(s) / organ or pf
1. GB: Lbl [F.550.d.]. 2. GB: Lbl [E.1373.], Lgc.
1–2. CPM. 2. OCLC (24239901). Cohen.

Clarkson, Jane [may be more than one composer by this name]
pub. c. 1795–1851, London
The electric quadrilles. London: s.n. [1851].
pf
GB: Lbl [h.954.(53.)].
CPM.

The Fond Hope ("I do not ask"). Ballad. The poetry by the Lady F. Hastings. London: s.n. [1850?].
voice / pf
GB: Lbl [H.2832.i.(20.)].
CPM.

Le délice dela jeuness, valse Cellarius. London: s.n. [1847].
pf
GB: Lbl [h.936.(19.)].
CPM.

Le Jasmin, rondeau à la valse. London: s.n. [1835?].
pf
GB: Lbl [g.270.i.(11.)].
CPM.

Les fleurs d'hiver, valses. 1. London: [1843]. 2. In: *The Musical Bijou for 1844,* pp. 90–92.

pf
GB: Lbl 1. [h.930.(43.)], 2. [H.2330].
1–2. CPM.

Lieder ohne Worte. 2 books. London: s.n. [1851].
pf
GB: Lbl [h.723.c.(15.)].
CPM.

The Sikh Polka. London: s.n. [1850].
pf
GB: Lbl [h.944.(10.)].
CPM.

The Turkish Polka. London: s.n. [1850].
pf
GB: Lbl [h.947.(21.)].
CPM.

Two Marches composed for the Right Honorable Lord Napier and George Baillie, Esp.
London: Corri, Dussek & Co. [c. 1795]. 2 pp.
pf
GB: Lbl [g.352.e.(10.)].
RISM A/I (C 2629), CPM, Cohen.

The Woodhill Polka. London: s.n. [1852].
pf
GB: Lbl [h.945.(54.)].
CPM.

Cléry, Mme, née **Duvergé** (**Duverger**)
1759, Paris?–1809, Paris
"Chacun, dans ce monde." Chanson patriotique. Air du vaudeville de la
Piété filiae. Paris: Frère [1793].
song
F: Pn (2 ex.) [Vm7 16400–16401].
RISM A/I (C 3199a), Paris Lib. Cat., letter (C. Johnson).

*Cinq romances composées en 1793 et 1795 pour les illustres prisonniers du Temple
avec accompagnement de fortepiano ou de harpe.* Paris: Sieber [1814]. Score.
voice/pf or harp

F: Pc (Pn).
RISM A/I (C 3198), letter (C. Johnson).

Le Soldat patriote au champ de Mars à la confédération nationale, avec accompagnement de harpe ou forte-piano. Paris: Frère (#82). Score, 3 pp.
voice/pf or harp
F: Pn [B.N. [H2 166].
RISM A/I (C 3199), Paris Lib. Cat.

Potpourri [c] *pour la harpe* (1. année, 17. livraison). [Paris]: Mme Duhan & Cie., (#33), n.d.
harp
S: Skma (without title page).
RISM A/I (C 3201).

Recueil d'airs arrangés pour la harpe avec accompagnement de flûte et violon contenant l'ouverture de Dardanus, un air de danse, l'ouverture de la Caravanne, une sonate et un pot-pourri pour la harpe seule . . . œuvre II. Versailles: l'auteur, Blaizot [1785?].
harp
F: Pn [X.642].
RISM A/I (CC 3200a), Paris Lib. Cat.

[Sonates pour la harpe avec accompagnement de violon]. Ms.
harp/vln
F: Pn
Letter (C. Johnson).

Trois sonates [C, E-flat, B-flat] *pour la harpe ou piano-forte avec accompagnement de violon . . .* œuvre 1er. Versailles: auteur; Paris: Bailleux (gravé par Mlle Fleury).
harp or pf/vln
F: Pn [B.N.A.33601]. Photocopy in C. Johnson coll., microfilm in Jackson coll.
RISM A/I (C 3200), Paris Lib. Cat., letter (C. Johnson).

[Work(s)] in: *Etrennes lyriques anacréontiques . . .* [ed. Cholet de Jetphort]. Paris: l'auteur, 1784–89, 1793–94, 1797, 1803, 1807–22 (only years with music listed).
song(s)
Complete holdings in F: Pn only. Partial in B: Bc (1786), Lc (1788). E: Mn

(1786). F: CF (1784, 1789), Pc (1784–89, 1793), RS (1789). US: Cn (1786), R (1785).
RISM B/II (Mme Duverger-Cléry, p. 169).

Coccia, Maria Rosa [1 of 3 female members of the Accademica della Filarmonica of Bologna in the 18th century]
Rome, 1759–Rome, 1833
Arsinoe. Cantata Per Musica a quattro Voci. Dedicata a Maria Amalia Augusta Principessa di due Ponti ed Elettrice di Sassonia & composta da Maria Rosa Coccia, Maestra di Capella Romana ed Accademica Filarmonica di Bologna. Ms. score, 1783. 2 vol. (132 pp., 88 pp.).
4 voices/orch
D: Dl (Mus. 3995 L1).
RISM A/II (#21877), Eitner (as Dresden, Mus. Nr. 884, cantata without title), NG, Cohen.

Confitebor a Quattro Concertato da due Canti Con R. R. E. Organo Della Sig.r Maria Rosa Coccia Maestra di Cappella Romana. Ms. score. 40 pp.
2 voices (S)/choir/bc (org)
D: MÜs (SANT Hs 1146).
RISM A/II (#69200).

Dixit dominus, 1775. 1. Ms. autograph score. 2. Ms. score. Dixit A otto pieno Composto Dalla Sig.ra M.a Rosa Coccia Romana Mra di Cappella. 20 pp.
8 voice choir/org (or bc)
1. GB: Cfm (dated 1793. Mu. Ms. 15). 2. D: MÜs (SANT Hs 1145). Microfilm of GB: Cfm in Jackson coll.
1. Eitner, NG. 2. RISM A/II (#69199). Cohen (as "with instruments").

Hic vir despiciens mundum (Comm. Conf. non Pont. Ad mag. antiph.). [Rome: 1774]. Score. Ms. copy at Cambridge. Same as composition for the Accademia di St. Cecilia (Rome, 11/28/74), Bologna Ms.
4 voices (SATB)
GB: Lbl [printed. Hirsch iv. 736.], Cfw (ms). I: Bc (ms., Kat. 1, 342).
RISM A/I (CC 32511, 1), CPM, NG, Cohen, Eitner.

Il trionfo d'Enea. Cantata in musica. Dedicata alle Reali Maestà di Ferdinardo IVᵉ Maria Carolina d'Austria . . . Ms. score with printed title page. 205 pp.

SSAT solo/orch
I: Rc (Ms. 2504). Microfilm in Jackson coll.
RISM A/I (CC 32511, 2), Cohen.

Magnificat, October 2, 1774. 1. Ms. score. 2. Magnificat [D major] a 4.
voci concertato Della Sig.ra Maria Rosa Coccia Maestra di Cappella. Ms.
score, 14 pp.
SATB/org bc; S/org bc; A/org bc
1. GB: Cfm (Ms. 16). 2. D: MÜs (SANT Hs 1148).
1. NG. 2. RISM A/II (#69202). Cohen.

Qualche lagrime spargete (Semiramide). Ms.
voices
B: Bc (2.1065, Eitner). Modern location not confirmed.
Eitner, Cohen.

Salve Regina [G major] a due Voci, Canto, ed Alto, della Sig.r Maria
Rosa Coccia. Ms. score. 6 pp.
2 voices (SA)/org
D: MÜs (SANT Hs 1147).
RISM A/II (#69201).

Veni Creator Spiritus a Quattro Concertato e Organo Obbligato di Maria
Rosa Coccia Romana Maestra di Cap. Ms. score.
4 voices (SATB)/org
D: MÜs (SANT Hs 1144).
RISM A/II (#69198).

Coco, Mlle
pub. 1709, Paris
[Work(s)] in: *Recueil d'airs sérieux et à boire de différents auteurs pour l'année 1709.*
Paris: C. Ballard, 1709.
song(s)
F: Mc (July, Dec), Pa (July, Dec), Pc, Pn. GB: Lbl.
RISM B/II (p. 313).

Colbran, Isabella Angela (married **Gioacchino Rossini**)
1785, Madrid–1845, Bologna
Six petits aires italiene avec paroles françaises et accompaniment de piano ou harp . . .
3eme recueil. Paris: Au magasin de musique dirigé par M. M. Cherubini
[c. 1810].

voice/pf or harp
GB: Lbl [H.1653.o.(6.) (imperfect copy)].
CPM, NG, Cohen, Eitner.

Six petits airs italiens des differens caracters avec accompnt. de piano ou harp. "Placido
zeffiretto," "Amo te solo," "Vanne felice rio," "Vanne al mio sene,"
"Sempre piu t'amo," "Voi siete a luci belle." Paris: De Momigny
[c. 1815?]. 13 pp.
voice/pf or harp
US: NYp.
NUC (NC 0525094).

Collier, Susannah
pub. 1829–31, London
[3 songs] The Pole's Adieu ("Star of my Soul, Farewell") In: *The
Harmonicon,* vol. 9, pt. 2, pp. 117–18, 1831. *The Swiss Cowherd's Song.* In: *The
Harmonicon,* vol. 8, pt. 1, pp. 231–33, 1830. "When Eyes are Beaming." In:
The Harmonicon, vol. 7, pt. 2, pp. 81–84, 1829.
songs
Catalogued together in GB: Lbl [P.P.1947].
CPM.

Corri-Dussek, Sophie. See Dussek, Sophie Giustana, née Corri

Cosway, Maria Cecilia Catherine Louise, née Hadfield
1759, Florence–1838, Lodi, Italy
*Deux sonates pour le clavecin, avec un violon, arrangées pour deux. Harpe et clavecin,
Piano-Forte ou l'Orgue par P. J. Meyer.* London: Birchall & Andrews, 1787.
Parts.
hpsch/vln, arr. harp, hpsch, pf, or org
GB: Gu (incomplete), Lbl (complete: hp/pf, vln) [h.64.(3.)]. Copies of GB:
Lbl in Ars Fem coll. and Jackson coll.
RISM A/I (C 4251), CPM, Eitner, Cohen, letter (Ars Fem), Bullock.

Songs and duets [for harp and voice]. 1. [London: c. 1787?]. 2. Ms., 8 pp.
1–2 voice(s)/harp
1. US: NYp. 2. CHum (at Monticello). Box 1, folder 5, Monticello Music
Collection, Ms., Dept. Copy of US: NYp in Ars Fem coll., copy CHum in
Jackson coll.
1. RISM A/I (C 4250, CC 4250), Cohen, letter (Ars Fem). 2. Cripe, Bullock.

Coultart, Mary Jane

pub. c. 1827, London

"Ah! Why from that bosom of feeling." A favourite Ballad. Words and music by M. J. C. London: Wm. Card [1827]. 5 pp.

song

GB: Lbl [H.1654.hh.(9.)].

CPM.

Coventry, Mrs.

pub. c. 1810, London

Lord Collingwood's Waltz . . . harmonized by Augustus Voigt. London: Purday & Button, [1810?].

Only melody is by Coventry.

pf

GB: Lbl [g.443.q.(17.)].

CPM.

Cozzolani, Chiara Margarita (Clara Margarita, Chiara Margaretha, Monaca S. Radegonda di Milano)

?–1653, Milan?

Concerti sacri à une, due, et quattro voci con una messa à quattro . . . Opera seconda. Venice: Alessandro Vincenti, 1642. 5 partbooks.

1, 2, and 4 voices (SATB)/bc

PL: WRu (50369 Muz.UNIKAT). Microfilm in US: CAi (3302.899.65.1). Copy in Ars Fem coll.

RISM A/I (C 4360), Eitner, Bowers & Tick, Bohn, NG, Cohen, letter (CAi), letter (Ars Fem).

Nò, nò, nò che mare [arie col basso].

voice/bc

Formerly in Berliner Singakademie. Lost in World War II, apparently in Krakow.

Eitner, letter (D: B).

"O dulcis Jesu" [motet] In: *Corollarium geistlicher collectaneorum,* . . . von Ambrosio Profio Organ. bey der Kirchen zu S. Elisabeth in Breslau. Leipzig: T. Ritzsch,1649. 7 partbooks. [Composer as Chiara Margaretha.]

2 voices/bc

D: Dl (T, B, 5, 6, Bc only), FRl (S56), Kl, KMr (SAT only), SAh (A, 5, Bc only), Z (T, 5 only). F: Pn. S. Uu. Copy in D: Uikb.

RISM B/I (1649 [6]), Bowers & Tick, Eitner (B.B.), NG, Cohen, D: Uikb (as madrigal).

Primavera di fiori musicali concertati nell' organo à 1, 2, 3, e 4 voci. Op. 1. Milan: 1640.
1–4 voices/bc (org)
PL: Wroclaw. Lost in WW II (NG).
Bowers & Tick, Eitner, NG, Cohen.

Salmi a otto voci concertati et due Magificat à otto con un Laudate Pueri à 4 voci, & doi violini, & un Laudate Dominum . . . à voce solo, & doi violini, motetti, et dialoghi à due, tre, quattro, e cinque voci. Opera terza. Venice: Alessandro Vincenti, 1650. 9 partbooks.
SS/bc; SSB/bc; SSAT/bc; SAAT/bc; SSSTT/bc; S/2 vlns/bc; SS/TT/2 vlns/bc; SSAATTBB/bc
I: Bc [Z.32]. PL: WRu (A I & II, T II, B I & II, bc only). Microfilm of Bologna copy in US: CAi (3302.899.65.2); copies in Jackson coll. and Ars Fem coll.
RISM A/I (C 4362), Bowers & Tick, Eitner (B. Br.), Bohn, letter (US: CAi), letter (Ars Fem).

Scherzi di sacra melodia a voce sola . . . Opera terza. Venice: Alessandro Vicenti, 1648.
voice/bc
B. Br. I: Bc (S only, lacks bc). PL: WRu (50370 Muz.) (S only, lacks bc). Copy in Ars Fem coll.
RISM A/I (C 4361), Bowers & Tick, Eitner, Bohn, letter (Ars Fem).

Venite gentes. In: a manuscript collection (only basso continuo).
voice (lost)/bc
USSR: KA (Kat. S. 19). Location not confirmed.
Eitner.

Cramer, Miss
pub. c. 1810, Dublin
A Farewell Promise to Mary [song]. A national air for the harp. Words by a gentleman of the city. Dublin: Paul Alday's [1820].
voice/harp
GB: Lbl [G.196.b.(2.)].
CPM.

Mr. Jeremy Pickle, a ballad. Arr. with entire new symphonies & accompaniments for the piano forte by Miss Cramer. New York: Firth & Hall [c.1829]. [#45 in a volume bound by the collector, Mary J. Shorter.]

voice/pf
US: DM (W.C.L. A780.88 A51200).
NUC (0771683).

Craven, Elizabeth, née **Berkeley.** Later **Margravine of Anbach (Anspach).** [also a writer of literary works]
1750, London–1828, Naples
Airs and chorusses [*sic*] from *The Princess of Georgia,* an opera. Perf. April 19, 1794, and at Brandenburg, 1798.
Only text survives
stage work
US: Cn (texts only).
NUC (NC 0778143), NG, Cohen.

"O Mistress mine." A favorite madrigal, the words from Shakespear [*sic*] . . . adapted for two voices by Joseph Major. 1. London: Preston & Son, 1795. Score. 2. In: *Cyclopedia of Music.* Miscel. Series of Songs (#356). London: [c. 1856]. 3. In: Collection of early American music, published or manuscript. 4. In: *Musical Journal for the Pianoforte.* Philadelphia: Benjamin Carr, # 69 (vocal section) [1801–02].
1–2. 2 voices/kbd 3–4. voice/pf
GB: Lbl 1. [G.360.(58.)] 2. [H.2342]. 3. US: Wc (M1. A11. Vol. 14, no. 51). 4. US: Wc. PHf (reissue from same plates, 1806–07), WGc (reissue from same plates, 1803–05).
1–2. RISM A/I (C 4403), CPM, NG (Anspach, Elizabeth), Cohen (Anspach).
1–4. Wolfe (as Anspach, Elizabeth, Margravine of: 140, 140a, 140b, 6377).
4. NUC (NC 0778158).

The Silver Tankard, or *The Point at Portsmouth;* Songs, duets, trios, &c from. Perf. July 18, 1781. London: Printed for T. Cadell, in the Strand, 1781. 23 pp.
Only text survives.
stage work
US: CA, NH (also on microfilm).
NUC (NC 00778169), OCLC (micro. 23795402) NG, Cohen.

Crouch, Anna Maria, née **Phillips**
1763, London–1805, Brighton
"Go, you may call it madness, folly." Adapted for the harp or piano forte. 1. [London]: Kelly [c.1802]. Keyboard arrangement. 2. [Song]. London, [1802]. 3. with accompaniment for the harp & pianoforte by Madame Dusseck. London: [1805?].

1. harp or pf. 2. voice/bbd. 3. voice/harp & pf
1. DK: Kv. GB: Lbl [H.1654.g.(11.)]. 2. GB: Lbl [G.361.(48.)]. 3. GB: Lbl
[G.798.(17.)]. Copy in Ars Fem coll.
1–3. RISM A/I (C 4554, 1–3), CPM. NG (bio), Cohen, Eitner.

"Say, was it love." [c. 1800].
song
GB: Lbl. Copy in Ars Fem coll.
Cohen, Eitner, letter (Ars Fem).

*Mrs. Crouch's Favorite pocket companion; being a select assemblage of the most elegant
and wittiest songs.* Now in vogue, at Drury-lane, Covent-Garden, Haymarket
. . . &c. London: Printed for J. Rosch . . . , 1789.
Texts only, compiled by Crouch
song
US: NH. (texts only).
NUC (NC 0807691).

Cuboni, Maria Teresa
pub. in Milan, perhaps from Modena
*Introduzione e Variazioni per PF. sopra un tema "'Si, si, verrò, ma paventato"
dell'Opera L'Orfanello di Ginevra.* [Written at the age of 12.] Milan: Preso
Francesco Lucca, n.d.
pf
I: MOe (Mus.73).
Cohen, Estense.

Cumberland, Mrs. William
pub. c. 1797, England
Ten canzonets for a single voice with an accompaniment for the harp or piano forte.
Dedicated by Permission to Her Majesty. S.l., s.n. [1797].
voice/harp or pf
GB: Lbl [G.295.p.(28.)]. I: Nc. US: CHu (in sheet music collection, *ML
.S444, v. 137, #2). Copy of GB: Lbl in Ars Fem coll.
RISM A/I (C 4580), CPM, NUC (NC 0830564), Cohen, letter (Ars Fem).

Czartoryska (Czartorkska, Cazartorkska), Izabela de Princess of Poland née Countess Elizabeth Fleming
b. England, d. Poland
Romance de Roland ("Roland étant petit garçon"). Paris: s.n. [1780?].

[Words by Mr. le Marquis de Paulcuy.]
song
CH: BEl. GB: Lbl [B.362.a.(3.)]. Copy of CH: BEl in Ars Fem coll.
RISM A/I (C 4618), CPM, Cohen, letter (Ars Fem).

Czartoryska, Zophie, Princess of Poland. See **Zamoyska, Countess Sophia (Zofia),** née **Princess Czartoryska (Z. z X. C. Zamojskiej, Zamoyskiey)**

D

D., Madame [compositions under this initial may not be by same composer]
n.d.
*Airs composés pour le clavecin ou piano-forte et arrangés pour deux clarinettes, deux cors
de chasse et deux bassons* . . . s.l., s.n., n.d. Parts.
2 cls / 2 hns / 2bsns
F: Pn.
RISM A / I (IN 55).

pub. c. 1802?
Andante [Pleyel] . . . *The variations by Madame D.* [Madame de Ronssecy?].
S. l., s.n. [1802?].
harp
GB: Lbl [H.2819.(40.)].
CPM.

D***, Madame. A pseudonym of **Maria Antonia Walpurgis.** See
Maria Antonia Walpurgis

D . . . , Mlle
pub. 1758, Paris
"Lorsque sur ta musette." Musette. [Paris]: Gravée par Mlle Labassée,
Imprimée par Tournell, 1758. (Also in: *Mercure de France*, October, 1758.)
song
GB: Lbl [297.d.15.].
BUC, CPM.

D. C., Mme
pub. 1780s, Paris
[Work(s)] in: *IIème Suite des plaisirs de la société. Vè* [-*VIè*] *recueil* . . . *d'ariettes
. . . opéra, opéra-comiques et autres, arrangées pour le forte-piano ou le clavecin, avec un
accompagnement de violon ad libitum* . . . par Mr. Foignet. Paris: Le Duc [1785].
pf / vln ad lib.
F: Pc, Pn (lacks vln).
RISM B / II (p. 376).

[Work(s)] in: *Les Plaisirs de la société. Recueil d'ariettes* . . . *opéra, opéra-comiques et
autres, arrangées pour le forte-piano ou le clavecin, avec* . . . *accompagnement de violon
ad libitum* . . . par Mr. Foignet. Paris: Le Menu . . . [1781]. 3 vol.

pf or hpsch/vln ad lib.
D: Bds (vol. 2), Bhm (vol. 2), F: Pc, Pn. GB: Lbl (vols. 1–2).
RISM B/II (p. 288).

Dahmen, Miss
pub. 1823, London
A Second Air, with Variations for the piano forte. London: Goulding, D'Almaine
& Co. [1823].
pf
GB: Lbl [h.61.m.(4.)].
CPM.

Three original Airs, with variations for the pianoforte. No. 1 [lacking 2 & 3].
London: Goulding, D'Almaine & Co. [1823].
pf
GB: Lbl [h.61.m.(5.)].
CPM.

Dall, Miss
1776, London–1794, London
"A linnet, just fledg'd" [song]. Composed and Sung by Miss Dall. London:
Longman & Broderip [1792]. Text by T. Hurlstone.
song
GB: Lbl. Copy in Ars Femina coll.
RISM A/I (DD 7931 I, 1), BUC, Cohen, letter (Ars Fem).

Danzi, Franziska Dorothea. See Le Brun (Lebrun), Franziska Dorothea, née Danzi

Danzi, Maria Margarete, née Marchand ("Gretl"—nickname in L. Mozart's letters)
1768, Frankfurt am Main?–1800, Munich
Trois sonates [E-flat, B-flat, E] *pour le piano forte avec violon obligé . . .* œuvre
I. Munich: Macario Falter, No. 77, 1799. 2 parts.
pf/vln
D: Mbs. Copies in D: UNikb, US: R, Ars Fem coll., and D: Kf&M.
*RISM A/I (D 1045), OCLC (micro. 11827577), Frauenmusik (dated 1800), NG,
Cohen, Eitner, letter (Ars Fem).*

Darion, Mlle
pub. c. 1800, Paris

Douze airs avec accompagnement de forte piano, ou de harpe . . . premier œuvre.
Paris: auteur (gravés par Van Jæm), [c. 1800]. 21 pp.
voice/pf or harp
GB: Lbl [E.1717.i.]. Copy in Ars Fem coll.
RISM A/I (D 1072), CPM, BUC, letter (Ars Fem).

**Dashkova (Daschkow, Daschkaw), Ekaterina Romanovna,
Princesse de,** née **Vorontsova**
1743, St. Petersburg–1810, near Moscow
Recueil des airs. Edinburgh: s.n. (gravés par Jaques Johnson) [c.1777].
21 pp.
songs
GB: DU, En, Gu, Lbl [H.1652.k.(1.)].
RISM A/I (D 1079), CPM, BUC, Cohen.

Dauphine, Mme la. See **Marie Adélaïde of Savoy, Duchess of
Burgundy** and **Dauphine of France**

Dauvergne de Beauvais, Mlle
fl. 1760, Paris
Les songes heureux et malheureux, song from. "Quand Neptune après un
orage." Cantatille avec accompagnement. Paris: Bayard, Le Clerc, Mlle
Castagnery (gravée par Mlle Vendôme). Score.
voice/kbd
F: Pn.
RISM A/I (D 1111).

Le Réveil heureux. "Par les plus agréables songes." Cantatille avec accompagnement. Paris: aux adresses ordinaires (gravée par Mlle Vendôme),
n.d. Score, 3 pp.
voice/kbd
F: Pn (2 ex.) (Vm7 475).
RISM A/I (D 1111, DD 1112), Paris Lib. Cat.

Les songes heureux et malheureux. Cantatille avec accompagnement. Paris:
Bayard, Le Clerc, Mlle Castagnery (gravée par Mlle Vendôme) [1760].
[as d'A . . . , Mlle. Believed to be Dauvergne de Beaurvais]
voice/kbd
F: Pc (B.N. [Vm7 476 & L. 379(1)].
RISM A/I (D 1), Paris Lib. Cat.

Davis, Eliza

pub. before 1832, London/New York

The better land ("I hear thee speak of a better land"). 1. The words by Mrs. Hemans. The music by Eliza Davis. 4th ed. London: Willis [1832]. 7 pp. 2. The words by Mrs. Hemans. The music by her sister . . . arr. by Robert G. Paige. New York: James Hewitt [1836?]. 3 pp.

voice/pf

US: 1. DM (W.C.L. M780.88 E58VD, no. 15). 2. DM.

1. NUC Sup. (NSD 0010773). 2. OCLC (10077747).

Dawson, Nancy

pub. 1760

"Of all the girls in our town." S.l.: s.n., 1760.

song

US: SM.

Cohen, Huntington.

De Gambarini, Elisabetta. See Gambarini, Elisabeth de (Elisabetta, Elizabeth. Married Chazal)

Del Caro, Madame. See Dilcaro, Mrs. (Signora)

Delaval, Camille, Mlle

c. 1794–?, pub. Paris & Netherlands

Les Six Amies, Contre-danses pour le Piano Forte. Paris: Mlles Erard/Den Haag: F. J. Weygand/[Amsterdam]: á la Bibliothèque, n.d.

pf

F: Pn (2 ex, Vm12 e1251). Photocopy in C. Johnson coll.

Letter (C. Johnson).

Delaval, Mme

pub. 1790s, London & Paris

Air russe: varié pour la harp. Paris: Mlles Erard/Den Haag: chez F. J. Wegand/[Amsterdam]: à la Bibliothèque Royale [180–?]. 7 pp.

harp

Paris imprint: US: BE, R.

OCLC (16456194), letter (C. Johnson).

A Grand Sonata for the harp, with accompaniments for a violin, tenor [i.e., viola] & violoncello, ad libitum. Op. 4. London: Printed for Rt. Birchall, 1801. 4 part-books.

harp / vln / vla / vlc ad lib.
GB: Lbl [h.2604.b.(3.)].
CPM, letter (C. Johnson).

*Prelude and Divertimento for the Harp and Pianoforte, with accompaniment for 2
French horns, ad libitum,* op. 3. London: Rt Birchall [c.1795 or 1801]. 3 part-
books.
harp & pf / 2 hns ad lib.
F: Pn (B.N. Vm9 4043). GB: Lbl [g.271.q.(2.)] (lacks piano part). Copies of
GB: Lbl in C. Johnson coll. and Ars Fem coll.
*RISM A / I (D 1383), CPM, Paris Lib. Cat., BUC, Cohen, letter (C. Johnson), letter
(Ars Fem).*

Three sonatas for the harp or piano forte, with an accompaniment for the violin . . . op.
Ima. 1. London: Rt Birchall [c.1790]. Parts. 2. London: Author . . . at
J. Dale's shop [c. 1795]. 31 pp.
harp or pf / vln
1. GB: Lbl [h.3200.(8.)] (lacks vln). Microfilm in C. Johnson coll. 2. US:
Cn (8A 1118) (lacks vln). Copy in Ars Fem coll.
*1. RISM A / I (D 1381), CPM, BUC, Eitner. 2. NUC (ND 0137825). Letter
(C. Johnson), letter (Ars Fem).*

[Work] in: *Longman and Broderip's selection of music for the pedal harp intended for
the use of performers in general including . . . preludes and the compositions of . . . much
admired authors . . .* London: Longman and Broderip [c. 1795]. 11 vol.
harp
D: Bds (vol. 11). EIR: Dn (vols. 2–7, 9). GB: Lbl (vol. 1).
RISM B / II (p. 225), letter (C. Johnson).

Delieu, Mlle
fl. 1815–1820
"Ni jamais ni toujours." Nocturne, arrangé à deux voix avec accompagne-
ment de guitare par Gatayes. 1. Paris: Frere fils [c. 1815]. 3 pp. 2. London:
G. Walker [1815?]. No arranger indicated. 3. Arrangé par Made Gail.
Paris: Ph. Petit [c. 1820].
2 voices / guit
GB: Lbl 1. [E.1717.p.(24.)]. 2. [G.424.u.(6.)]. 3. [G.555.(2.)].
CPM.

Delorme, Mlle
pub. between 1777 and 1789, Paris

[Work(s)] in: *La muse lyrique dédiée à la Reine*. Recueil d'airs avec accompagnement de guitarre . . . Paris: Baillon, 1777–1789.
voice/guit
F: D (1776–1777, 1786), Pn (1778, 1780–83, 1785–86, 1789). GB: Lbl (1781). US: U (1779), Wc (1783).
RISM B/II (p. 243). Does not specify which Dijon library (F: D).

Demar (Demars?), Theresia
1801–?, France
Le mariage de la Tubéreuse et du Lis ("Un jour la fière Tubéreuse"). Romance. Paris: s.n. [1810?]. Text by Mr. Desquiron de St. Agnan.
song
GB: Lbl [G.548.(28.)].
CPM.

L'absence, au Rendezvous. ("Olivier, je t'áttends") Paris: s.n. [1815?].
song
GB: Lbl [G.546.(59.)].
CPM.

Demars, Hélène-Louise (Henrietta-Louise, according to Fétis)
c. 1736–?, Paris?
"Il est parti." Romance . . . avec accompagnement de harpe ou piano. Paris: auteur, No. 112, n.d.
voice/harp or pf
CH: Gpu. Copy in Ars Femina coll. (as Terese Demars).
RISM A/I (D 1600). Cohen (as work for harp, by Theresa Demar), letter (Ars Fem).

Deux airs variée pour harpe et violon. Contents: "Soyez sensible" par Mozart, "Je ne vous dirai pas" par Haydn. Paris: Benoît Pollet, n.d.; Orléans, auteur (écrit par Joannès) (#42), n.d. Parts.
harp/vln
CH: AR (vln only).
RISM A/I (DD 1599a).

Fami et Betzi ("Betzi toi douce amie"). Paris: Pleyel, n.d.
voice/harp
S: Skma.
RISM A/I (DD 1599b).

Hercule et Omphale. Ire Cantatille à voix seule et simphonie. Paris: auteur, Le Clerc, Mme Boivin (gravée par Joseph Renou) [c. 1751 or 1752]. Score.
voice/instrument[s]
B: Bc. F: Pn, Pc (B.N.[Vm7395]), [D. 2781 (2)]. Copy in Ars Fem coll. (as Terese Demars).
RISM A/I (D 1598), Paris Lib. Cat. Cohen (as Theresa Demar), Eitner, NG, letter (Ars Fem).

Les avantages du buveur. Seconde Cantatille à voix seule et simphonie. Paris: auteur, Le Clerc, Mme Boivin (gravée par Charpentier) [c. 1751–52]. Score, 10 pp.
voice/instrument[s]
F: Pn (2 ex.) [Vm7 3996] & [D. 2781(1)]. Copy in Ars Fem coll. (as Terese Demars).
RISM A/I (D 1599), Paris Lib. Cat., NG, Cohen (as Theresa Demar), letter (Ars Fem).

Pot-pourri d'airs connus pour la harpe ou le forté-piano. Paris: Benoît Pollet, n.d.; Orléans, Demar, n.d.; Würzburg, Demar (#20), n.d.
harp or pf
A: Wst.
RISM A/I (D 1601), Cohen (as Therese Demar).

Six nouvelles romances pour harpe ou forte-piano . . . œuvre 2eme. Paris: Benoît Pollet, n.d.; Orléans, Demar (#38), n.d.
harp or pf
A: Wgm.
RISM A/I (D 1602), Cohen (as Therese Demar).

Thème favori de Mysta tagoju uk raschennyil, varié pour la harpe. Paris: Orléans, Demar (#49), n.d.
harp
A: Wgm.
RISM A/I (D 1603), Cohen (as Therese Demar).

Demilliere, Marthesie
fl. 1812–1818, New York
Malbrook, with four variations. New York: Mr. Demilliere, engraved by E. Riley [1812–18]. 3 pp.
pf
US: NYp, Wc (M1. A1D).
Wolfe (2383), NUC (ND 0159092), Cohen.

Denis, Mlle

pub. 1711, Paris

[Work(s)] in: *Recueil d'airs sérieux et à boire de différents auteurs* . . . Augmenté considérablement . . . des plus habiles maistres . . . airs italiens et de cantates françoises. Amsterdam, E. Roger 1711.

song(s)

B: Bc, Lc. GB: Lbl (inc.), Lcm.

RISM B/II (Melle Denis, p. 316).

[Work(s)] in: *Recueil d'airs sérieux et à boire de différents auteurs pour l'année 1711.* Paris: C. Ballard, 1711.

song(s)

B: Br (inc.). F: Pn.

RISM B/II (Melle. Denis, p. 313).

Dennett, H. M., Miss

pub. c. 1830, Dublin

Six waltzes . . . for the Pianoforte. Dublin: s.n. [1830?].

pf

GB: Lbl [g.271.c.(38.)].

CPM.

Dering, Lady Mary, née Harvey (married to Sir Edward Dering. Sometimes spelled as Deering)

1629, Folkestone, Kent–1704, Pluckley, Kent

"And this is all? What, one poor kiss." Mss. [1659]. [Originally printed in Lawes, *Select ayres & Dialogues* . . . , 1655.]

voice/kbd

GB: Lbl (Add. Ms. 11608), Ob (MS Don. c57). US: SM. Copy of GB: Lbl in Ars Fem coll.

NG, Cohen, Huntington, letter (Ars Fem).

"A False designe to be cruel." Ms.?, n.d.

voice/kbd

F: Bn. Copy in Ars Fem coll.

Letter (Ars Fem).

[3 songs] "When first I saw fair Doris's eyes," "And is this all? What one poor kiss?" & "In vain fair Chloris, you designe." [Texts by Edward Dering.] 1. In: Lawes, *Select ayres & dialogues* . . . The second book. London: John Playford, 1655, pp. 24, 25. 2. In: *Select ayres & dialogues* . . . The second

book. London: W. Godbid for J. Playford, 1659, p. 25 [was one of 3 songs in: Lawes, *Select ayres & dialogues* . . . , 1655]. 3. In: *The treasury of Musick:* . . . to sing to the theorbo-lute or basse-viol . . . Composed by Mr. Henry Lawes . . . and other excellent masters. London: W. Godbid for J. Playford, 1669, p. 9 [was one of 3 songs in: Lawes, *Select ayres & dialogues* . . . , 1655].
voice / lute or viol
1. GB: Ckc, Cu, HAdolmetsch (lacking title page), Lbl (incomplete), Lcm. US: Bp, CA, NYp, PRu, R, SM, Wc, Ws. 2. D: Hs. GB: Cu, Ccc, Cfm, DRc, Ge, Lbl, Lcm, Lcs. US: Cn, NYp, R, SM, Wc, Ws. 3. GB: Ctc, CDp, Er, Ge, Lbl, Lcm. US: AA, LAuc, NYp, R, Wc, Ws.
1. RISM A/I (L 1168—Lawes), NG (entries on Mary Harvey & Henry Lawes), Kerr, Cohen. 2. RISM B/I (1659 [5]). NG (entries on Mary Harvey & Henry Lawes), Kerr, Cohen. 3. RISM B/I (1669 [5]). NG (entries on Mary Harvey & Henry Lawes), Kerr, Cohen.

Desfossez (Desfossés, Desfosses), Françoise Elizabeth (later **Mme Caraque, Countess**) (initials sometimes as E. C. or F. E.)
fl. 1789–1820
[1re] Sonate pour le piano-forte [E-flat]. Paris: Prader, [c. 1789 or 1790]. 11 pp.
pf
F: Pn (2 ex.) (B.N.[Vm7 5417 & A.33738). Microfilm in US: CA. Copies in C. Johnson coll. and Ars Fem coll.
RISM A/I (D 1744), Paris Lib. Cat., NUC Sup. (micro., NSD 002832), letters (C. Johnson, Ars Fem).

[2e] Sonate pour le piano-forte [B-flat]. Paris: aux adresses ordinaires de Musique, Gravé par Mme Oger [c. 1790]. 11 pp.
pf
F: Pn (B.N.[Vm7 5417b). Microfilm in US: CA; Copies in C. Johnson coll. and Ars Fem coll.
RISM A/I (D 1746), Paris Lib. Cat., NUC Sup. (micro., NSD 002832), letters (C. Johnson, Ars Fem).

[3me] Sonate pour le piano-forte [b]. Paris: aux adresses ordinaires de Musique, Gravé par Mme Oger [c. 1790]. 11 pp.
pf
F: Pn (B.N.[Vm7 5417c). Microfilm in US: CA. Copies in C. Johnson coll. and Ars Fem coll.
RISM A/I (D 1745), Paris Lib. Cat., NUC Sup. (micro., NSD 002832), letters (C. Johnson, Ars Fem)

Trois sonates [C, c#, G] *pour le pianoforte avec accompagnement de violon obligé et de violoncelle ad libitum.* Œuvre III. Paris: chez l'auteur/Pleyel [1798]. 3 partbooks.
pf/vln/vlc ad lib.
D: Kf&m. F: Pn (Vm7 5418 & A.33735–33737). Microfilm of F: Pn in US: CA. Copies of F: Pn in C. Johnson coll. and Ars Fem coll.
RISM A/I (D 1743), Paris Lib. Cat., NUC Sup. (micro., NSD 002833), Frau & Musik, Eitner (as piano sonatas), Cohen, letters (C. Johnson, Ars Fem).

Desmaisons, Madame
pub. 1786
Rondeau pour le Forte-Piano. In: *Mercure de France*, Paris, February 1786.
pf
F: Pn.
Letter (C. Johnson).

D . . . et, Mlle
pub. 1758, Paris
"Tircis voyant que sa Lisette." Chanson Nouvelle. In: *Mercure de France*, July 1755.
song
GB: Lbl [298.c.24.].
BUC, CPM.

Devisme (Devismes), Jeanne-Hippolite, née Moyroud
1765, Lyon–1808, Paris
La Double Recompense [opera, prod. Paris, 1805].
stage work
F: Po.
Cohen.

Praxitèles, ou la Ceinture [opera in 1 act]. Prod. Paris, 1800. Ms. Libretto by Milcent. [Devismes spelling of name for this item.]
stage work
F: Po.
Mellon, Eitner, Cohen.

Devonshire, Duchess of, Georgiana Cavendish (Cavendish, Georgiana, née Spencer)
1757–1806, London
"I have a silent sorrow here." The favorite song . . . in *The stranger,* the

words by R. B. Sheridan. 1. London: Longman & Broderip [1798]. 4 pp.
2. Longman, Clementi & Co.[1800?]. 3. London: Clementi [1801]. 4.
New York: G. Gilfert [1798–1801]. 5. In: G. S. Thornton, *The Melodist*, I,
p. 87–88. New York: Singleton, 1820. [Melody only.] 6. In: *The Musical
Magazine*, #3. With part for German flute. New York: G Gilfert/Boston,
P. A. von Hagen [1799?]. 7. Philadelphia: J. Hewitt/Baltimore: J. Carr.
8. Dublin: Rhames. 9. Followed by an accompaniment for flute or flageolet.
London: W. & S. Wybrow [1825]. 10. In: *A Collection of favourite Glees.* . . . ,
London: C. Knyvett, 1800 [flyleaf dated 1796]. 11. . . . sung by Mrs.
Bland . . . s.l., s.n., [18–]. 12. Incomplete setting, ms. [180–?]. 13. Sung
with great applause by Mrs. Merry. The words by R. Sheridan . . . the air
by A. Reinagle [*sic*]. Acc. arr. for flute and for guitar. Philadelphia,
J. Carr/New York, J. Hewitt [ca. 1799]. 2 pp. 14. [Instrumental arrange-
ment] London: Longman & Broderip. Score. 15. [arranged as duet] Sung
. . . in *The stranger* . . . the air by Her Grace the Dutchess [*sic*] of
Devonshire. [Arr. by T. Shaw as "To welcome Mirth & harmless Glee."]
Duet. Composed by Thos. Shaw. London: Clementi, Banger, Collard,
Davis & Collard [c. 1815]. Score. 9 pp.
*1. voice/orch (vln 1 & 2/vla/2 obs/2 fls/2 hns/pf) 3, 7, 9–12, voices/kbd, 4–6,
8. with part for fl. 13. voice/kbd (optional fl or guit) 14. hns/flutes/obs/2
vlns/vla/pf 15. 2 voices/kbd*
1. GB: Cpl, Lbl (2 ex.) [G.249.(39.) & G.425. ff. (20.)], Ob. US: NH, NYp.
2. GB: Cu, CDp, Gu, Lbl [H.1601.e.(17.)]. 3. GB: Lbl [H.1652. kk.(16.)].
4. NYp, Wc, WOa. 5. US: Cn, CA, NH, NYp, Wc. 6. US: Wc. 7. US:
PHf, Wc (3 ex.). 8. US: Lu. 9. GB: Lbl [H.3690.ww.(24.)]. 10. GB: Lbl
[Printed Book, E.18]. 11. US: HA. 12. US: DM. 13. US: Cn, NH,
NYlevy, NYp, NYshap, PHfk, PHhs, PHlc, R, Wc, Wmcdevitt, WOa.
14. GB: Ckc. US: NYp. Copy in Ars Fem coll. 15. GB: Lbl [H.1652.kk.(15.)].
*Cohen. 1–2. RISM A/I (D 2116, 2118), 1–3. CPM, BUC (Cavendish), 1.
OCLC (19726353). 4. NUC (ND 0228566–70), Sonneck, Wolfe (1723, 9367).
5. OCLC (18853300). 6–8. Sonneck. 9. CPM. 11. Brit. Cat. Ms. (1965). 10,
12. OCLC (19007775, 7017286). 13. OCLC (20911629), Sonneck (as
Reinagle). 14. RISM A/I (D 2117), letter (Ars Fem). 15. CPM.*

"Sweet is the vale." A favorite Duo. 1. Baltimore: J. Carr [1807 or 1808].
2. Boston: Graymer [1808?]. 3. Philadelphia: G. Willig [1808?]. 4. 2 print-
ings/Philadelphia: John Aitken [1808–11?]. 5. 2 printings/Philadelphia:
A. Bacon [1816]. 6. G. Woodham, G. Graymer [1818?]. 7. Baltimore:
Carr [1805–06]. 8. Arr. by Woodham. 2 printings/Boston: Graupner
[1805–06]. 8a. Reissue as Boston: Bradlee [c. 1836]. 9. 3 printings/New
York: E. Riley [1809–10, 1811?, 1812–18]. 10. Philadelphia: Blake

[c. 1807]. 11. [1803–14?]. 12. Boston: [1816–25?]. 13. Duetto IV ("Sweet is the vale, where innocence resides"). Acc. arr. for piano or harp. s.l., [18–]. 14. In: *The Vocal Companion*, I, p. 34. Boston: Buckingham, 1815. 2 voices, open score. 15. In David Vinton: *The masonick minstrel*, pp. 145–47. Dedham, Mass., 1816. 16. In: Luke Eastman, *Masonick melodies*, pp. 93–95. 2 voices, open score. Boston: 1818 & 1825.

1–12. 2 voices/pf. 13. 2 voices/pf (or harp). 14–15. 2 voices

1–6. US: Wc (Ml. A1D Case and Ml. A11, vol. 1, #22). 1. US: BAhs, Cn, CA, CHAhughes, NYp, PHf, PIlevy, PROu, WOa. 3. US: AA, Cn, CAdriscoll, CHAhughes, NYp, PHf, PROu, WOa. 4. US: BE, CA, NYp, PHlc, WOa. 5. US: BUg, CA, ECstarr, Wc, WOa. 7. US: CAdriscoll, PIlevy, BAhs, CA, WOa, NYp, PHhs, PHf, PHlc, PROu. 8. US: AA, Bp, Bhs (2), BUg, Cn, CAdriscoll, CA, NYp (2), Wc, WOa. 8a. US: CA. 9. US: AA, BUg, CA, CAdriscoll, Cn, NYcuh, NYp (2), PROu (2), WOa. 10. US: Cn, CA, CAdriscoll, NYp, PHf, PHfk, PHlc, PIlevy, PROu, Wc (Ml. A1D Case and Ml. A11, vol. 1, #22), WOa. 11. US: AA. 12. US: CA, Bp, PHlc. 13. US: NH. 14. US: Bp, CA, NYp, PROu, Wc. 15. US: AA, Bp, BUg, CA, NH, NYhs, PHlc, PROu, Wsc, WOa. 16. US: Ba, Bp, BUg, ECstarr, NH, NYfm, PROu, Wc.

Cohen (as Cavendish). 1–5. RISM A/I (D 2116, 2118, 2119, 2120, 2121). 3. NYp Spec. Col. Shelf List. 1–4. Wolfe (1724, 1728, 1729, 1729A). 5–6. Wolfe (1734, 1734A). 8–9. Wolfe (1730, 1730A, 1730B). 10–11. NUC & Sup. (ND 0228579–90, NSD 0031058–63). 13. OCLC (197228163). 10–12. Wolfe (1726,1732, 9516, 7133, 9493). 14. OCLC (2114457285). 15–16.Wolfe (2646, 2647).

Dezéde, Florine (D. Z., Mlle)

1765?, Paris–c. 1792, Paris

Lucette et Lucas. Comédie en un acte en prose . . . représentée pour la première fois par les comédiens italiens le 8 novembre 1781. Paris: Des Lauriers, 1786. Score, 89 pp. Libretto by Forgeot.

stage work (opéra-bouffe)

F: Pn-Pc [B.N.[Vm5 176) & [D.3383], R (Sc), Lm (Sc & 10 pts, 2 ex. each). GB: Lbl [H.455]. NL: DHgm (Sc & pts). US: Bp, Cn. PL: LZu. Copy in Ars Fem coll.

RISM A/I (D 2125, DD 2125). Paris Lib. Cat. MGG, Eitner, Mellon, CPM ([1781], as Z., D. Mademoiselle), letter (Ars Fem), Cohen (other works he lists are by her father Nicholas).

Dibdin, Mary Anne

1799–1886, London

Fantasia for the harp, on the favorite air "I give thee all, I can no more." [Air by Sir Henry R. Bishop.] London: Goulding & D'Almaine [c. 1830]. 11 pp.
harp
GB: Lbl [h.2605.n.(3.)].
CPM.

Fantasia on the favorite air, "O' twine a wreath of evergreen." London: Goulding & d'Almaine [183–?]. 11 pp.
harp
US: CA.
OCLC (22280095).

A Favorite Sauteuse, arranged for the Harp. [London:] Whitaker & Co, [1821?].
harp
GB: Lbl [h.2605.k.(2.)].
CPM.

Fleurs choisies, Petit Mélange sur trois Thèmes favoris de Donizetti, pour la Harpe. London: R. Mills [1840].
harp
GB: Lbl [h.108.(17.)].
CPM.

Grand Fantasia, for the harp, on the Chorus of Greeks, from Rossin[i]'s opera L'Assedio di Corinto . . . London, Dublin: Willis & Co. [1835].
harp
GB: Lbl [h.2605.v.(17.)].
CPM.

Hymns and Spiritual songs. London: [1848].
songs
GB: Lbl [H.1181.(14.)].
CPM.

Introduction and Rondo for the Harp Composed and Dedicated to Miss Jane Long by Miss M. A. Dibdin. London: s.n. [1828].
harp
GB: Lbl [h.108.(14.)]. Microfilm copy in Rempel coll.
CPM, letter (Rempel).

Introduction and Rondoletto upon a favorite Tyrolean Air, for the Harp. Composed and Dedicated to The Honble. Mrs. Cavendish by Miss M. A. Dibdin. London: S. Chappell [1828].
harp
GB: Lbl [h.108.(15.)]. Microfilm copy in the Rempel coll.
CPM, letter (Rempel).

Introduction & Variations on an admired French Waltz, for the Harp Composed and dedicated to Miss Knight, by Miss M. A. Dibdin. London & Dublin: Willis & Co [c. 1825 or 183–?]. 7 pp.
harp
GB: Lbl [h.184.i.(9.)]. US: CA. In bound collection of 19th century harp music in Rempel coll.
CPM, OCLC (22280097), letter (Rempel).

"La Pensée du moment," for the harp. London: Chappell's Musical Circulating Library [1835].
harp
GB: Lbl [h.2605.v.(18.)].
CPM.

Marche à la Grecque, for the Harp, Introducing some of the new Effects, composed by M. A. Dibdin. London: S. Chappell [1834]. 5 pp.
harp
GB: Lbl [h.108.(16.)], US: CA. Microfilm copy of GB: Lbl in Rempel coll.
CPM, OCLC (22280099), letter (Rempel).

Moorish March . . . for the Harp. London: Willis & Co. [1833]. 7 pp.
harp
GB: Lbl [g.661.(18.)].
CPM.

The Savoyard boy [The Boarding School Miss]. [Song, "I come from a land far away."] London: [1825?]. Text by C[harles] Dibdin.
voice/pf
GB: Lbl [H.2826.c.(13.)].
CPM.

The Scotch ballad "John Anderson my Joe," with variations for the harp by M. A. Dibdin. London: [1840].
harp

GB: Lbl [h.108.(18.)].
CPM.

Six Waltzes, for the harp . . . London, Dublin: [1833]. 5 pp.
harp
GB: Lbl [h.2605.v.(16.)].
CPM.

Sweet Rose come away. A ballad written by Chas Dibdin Esq., composed &
Inscribed to Miss Frances Cockburn Sims by Miss M. A. Dibdin. London:
J. Power [c. 1820]. 4 pp.
voice/pf
GB: Lbl [H.1652.II.(5.)]. US: NYp.
*CPM, NUC (ND 0243133). [Penciled note on title of NY copy gives birth and death
dates of 1808 and 1834.]*

Variations for the Harp on A. Lee's Ballad, Poor Prince Charlie . . . London:
Mori & Lavenu [1835?].
harp
GB: Lbl [h.173.d.(8.)].
CPM.

The White Cockade, with variations for the Harp. 1. London: [1825?]. 2. London:
[1830?].
harp
1.& 2. GB: Lbl [h.184.c.(8.)], [h.184.d.(18.)].
CPM.

Dibdin, Mrs. Charles (may be **Harriet Pitt,** or **Isabelle Dibdin,** née
Perkins; source does not specify which of the two **Mrs. C. Dibdins**)
pub. c. 1800
"Sweetly the birds were singing, O!" A favorite song [with words] written
by C. Dibdin, Junr., composed by Mrs. C. Dibdin. London: Goulding
[c. 1800]. 2 pp.
voice/pf
US: Wc (M 1621.D).
RISM A/I (D 2984), NUC (ND 0243135), Cohen (as Isabelle Perkins Dibdin).

Tamborines. A favorite comic song. London: J. Longman, Clementi & Co.
[c. 1800].
voice/pf

GB: Lbl [H.2830.f.(47.], Obharding.
RISM A/I (D 2985, DD 2985), CPM, BUC, Cohen (as Isabelle Perkins Dibdin).

Dickons, Mrs. See **Poole, Maria**

Diede, Ursula Margarethe de (?), née **Gräfin von Callenburg**
(Married **Christoph Wilhelm von Diede zum Fürstenstein,** 1772)
1752–1803, Germany
Sonate [D Major] pour le Clavecin ou Pianoforte. Composees par
Madamme la Baronne de Diede. Ms., c. 1800. 6 pp. (Allegro, Menuett,
Rondo) Contained in a ms. package: Sonates pour le Clavecin Seul.
hpsch or pf
D: Rtt (Sammelband 1/1).
RISM A/II (#60350), letter (D: Rtt).

Dilcaro, Mrs. (Signora)
pub. c. 1800, Dublin
Sigra Dilcaro's Favorite Hornpipe ("O! Had I been by fate decreed") 1. [Arr.
for pianoforte.] A favorite song [by S. Howard in: *Love in a Village*]. Dublin:
Hime, [1800?]. 2. [Various instrumental versions, arr. for various combinations of instruments: vln/pf; 2 clarinets; 2 horns and timpani; 2 vlns,
vlc, and organ.]
1. pf 2. various instruments
1. GB: Lbl [H.1601.g.(33.)]. 2. GB: En. US: IO. Copies of GB: En and
US: IO in Ars Fem coll. (as Madame Del Caro).
1. CPM, BUC. 2. Letter (Ars Fem). Cohen (describes as 17th century Irish).

Droste-Hülshoff, Annette Elisabeth von, Baroness
1797, Münster–1848, Meersburg am Bodensee
All meine Gedanken.
voice/pf
D: UNikb.
Olivier.

Ich reise übers grüne Land.
voice/pf
D: UNikb.
Olivier.

Lieder mit Pianoforte-Begleitung. Münster: Russells, 1877
voice/pf

D: UNikb. US: CA, BLu.
Frauenmusik, Olivier, NUC Sup. (NSD 0052551), Cohen.

Mich brennt's an meinen Reiseschuhen.
voice/pf
D: UNikb.
Olivier.

Wach auf mein Hort
voice/pf
D: UNikb.
Olivier.

Dubois, Dorothea Annesley, Lady [attributed to]
1728, Dublin–1774
The Magnet. A musical entertainment as sung at Marybone Gardens.
London: T. Becket, 1771.
[Bound with Rolt, R. *Almena.* London, 1764. Binder's title: Musical
dramas, vol. 25.] Does not contain music. Dubois may be librettist only.
stage work
US: CHAu (Rare PR 1268 M8 vol. 25). Text only.
NUC Sup. (NSD 0053867).

Dubonnet, Mlle
pub. c. 1772, Paris
[Work(s)] in: *Abeille lyrique ou recueil périodique de petits airs arrangés pour la harpe
et le forte-piano avec ou sans accompagnement de violon* . . . Paris: Cousineau
[1772].
harp or pf/with or without vln
F: Pc.
RISM B/II (p. 57).

Duchambge, Pauline, née Charlotte-Antoinette-Pauline de Montet
1778, Martinique–1858, Paris
À demain. ("Quittons la solitaire allée.") Song. Paris: s.n. [1835?]. Words by
A. van Hasselt.
voice/pf
GB: Lbl [H.2831.e.(53.)].
CPM.

A mon ange gardien. Song. Brussels: H. Messemaeckers [c.1825].
voice/pf
GB: Lbl [G.561.c.(15.)].
CPM, NG, MGG, Cohen, Frauenmusik.

[About 400 Romanzes in autograph ms.]
voice/pf
F: Pc.
NG, MGG, Eitner, Cohen.

Adieu donc mon pays, or Le Suisse au regiment. S.l., s.n. [182–?]. Ms.
copy (incomplete). 1 pp. Text by E. Scribe.
voice/pf
US: Pu.
OCLC (16105277).

Albert de Novalaise. Romance. Paris: s.n. [1835?]. Words by E. Géraud.
voice/pf
GB: Lbl [G.545.(6.)].
CPM.

Album musicale. Paris: Catelin & Co., n.d.
voice/pf
D: Bds (Eitner, modern location not confirmed).
NG, MGG, Eitner, Cohen.

Chanson de l'hirondelle. Autograph ms.
voice/pf
D: UNikb.
Frauenmusik.

Die fromme Himmelsbraut. Mayence: Schott, n.d.
voice/pf
D: Bds (Eitner, modern location not confirmed).
MGG, NG, Eitner

Francine. Ballade. Paris: s.n. [1835?] Words by E. Barateau.
voice/pf
GB: Lbl [G.552.(60.)].
CPM.

Je suis seul. ("Je vois le clocher") song. Paris: s.n. [1835?]. Words by le
Marquis de Custine.
voice/pf
GB: Lbl [G.545.(59.)].
CPM.

Jeannette. ("Quand la violette") song. Paris: s.n. [1830?]. Words by E.
Barateau.
voice/pf
GB: Lbl [G.551.(56.)].
CPM.

La Blanche Maison. ("Je sais sur la colline") song. Paris: s.n. [1830?]. Words
by A. de Lamartine.
voice/pf
GB: Lbl [G.543.(71.)].
CPM.

La Brigantine ou *le Départ.* Romance. 1. Ms., c. 1830. 2. Berlin: Schlesinger,
n.d. Words by Jean François Casimir Delavigne.
voice/pf
1. D: DO (Mus. Ms. 2417). 2. D: Bds (Eitner).
1. RISM A/II (#88362). 2. Eitner. NG, MGG, Cohen.

La Fiancée del Marin. ("Tristess amère") romance. Paris: s.n. [1830?]. Words
by Madame Desbordes-Valmore.
voice/pf
GB: Lbl [G.545.(58.)].
CPM.

La Jeune Châtelaine. ("Je vous defends") song. Paris: s.n. [1835?]. Words by
Madame Desbordes-Valmore.
voice/pf
GB: Lbl [G.551.(52.)].
CPM.

La Pauvre vieille pleura . . . Song. Paris: Chez Ph: Petit [1830?]. Words by
Emile Barateau.
voice/pf
GB: Lbl [G.561.c.(17.)].
CPM.

La Paysanne & le Soldat. ("Du canton une paysanne") song. Paris: s.n., [1820?]. Words by J. de Rességuier.
voice/pf
GB: Lbl [H.2831.e.(52.)].
CPM.

La Pêcheur de Sorrente. ("Sorrente, doux rivage") song. Paris: s.n. [1835?]. Words by Mlle D. Gay.
voice/pf
GB: Lbl [G.542.(47.)].
CPM.

La Pêcheur. ("Quand vient la nuit") song. Barcarolle. Paris: s.n. [1830?]. Words by J. de Rességuier.
voice/pf
GB: Lbl [E.1717.(52.)].
CPM.

La Retour en Bretagne. Song. Paris: Chez Ph: Petit [c. 1830]. Words by E. Souvestre. 3 pp.
voice/pf
GB: Lbl [G.561.c.(18.)].
CPM.

La Soeur de Charité. ("Voici la paisible demeure") romance. Paris: s.n. [1835?]. Words by A. Bétourné.
voice/pf
GB: Lbl [H.2830.d.(38.)].
CPM.

La Valse et l'aumone. ("L'harmonie et les fleurs") song. Paris: s.n. [1835?]. Words by Madame Desbordes–Valmore.
voice/pf
GB: Lbl [G.553.(5.)].
CPM.

Le Béarnais. Romance. Paris: Pleyel et fils aîné, n.d.
voice/pf
D: Bds (Eitner, modern location not confirmed).
NG, MGG, Eitner, Cohen.

Le Bouquet de Bal. ("Vous partez") song. Words by Scribe. 1. Paris: s.n. [1830?]. 2. Paris: s.n. [1830?]. 3. Ms.
voice/pf
GB: Lbl 1. [G.543.(69.)]. 2. [E.1717.(50.)]. 3. D: DO (Mus. Ms. 2753). *1–2. CPM. 3. RISM A/II (#93830).*

Le Couvre-feu. Ballade. Brussels: H. Messmaeckers [c. 1825]. Words by F. de Courcy.
voice/pf
GB: Lbl [G.561.c.(16.)].
CPM.

Le Rêve du Mousse. ("L'air était froid") barcarolle. Paris: s.n. [1835?]. Words by Madame Desbordes-Valmore.
voice/pf
GB: Lbl [H.2830.d.(37.)].
CPM.

Le temps heureux. Romance. Paris: Bolle, n.d.
Words by Corradi.
voice/pf
D: UNikb.
Frauenmusik.

Le Venitien. ("Rame, rame") song. Paris: s.n. [1830?]. Words by Mazères.
voice/pf
GB: Lbl [E.1717.(57.)].
CPM.

Le village de Marie. Romance. Paris: Bolle, n.d. Words by Briseux.
voice/pf
D:UNikb.
Frauenmusik.

Les Chanteurs Italiens. ("C'est la Toscane") duet. Paris: s.n. [1840?]. Words by E. Deschamps.
2 voices/pf
GB: Lbl [G.544.(26.)].
CPM.

Les cloches du couvent. Die fromme Himmelsbraut. Mayence: Schott, n.d.
voice/pf
D: Bds (Eitner, modern location not confirmed).
MGG, NG, Eitner, Frauenmusik.

Malheur a mois. Paris: Hanry #2765, n.d. Words by Mme Valmore.
voice/pf
D: Kf&m.
Frau & Musik.

Penses tu que ce soit de t'aimer. ("Trouver dans mes songes") romance. Paris:
s.n. [1835?]. Words by M. E. Souvestre.
voice/pf
GB: Lbl [G.556.(44.)].
CPM.

Prenez bien garde. ("Sous l'ombrage du Retiro") cantatille. Paris: s.n. [1835?].
Words by E. Barateau.
voice/pf
GB: Lbl [G.548.(24.)].
CPM.

Qu'elle est jolie. ("Grands Dieux") cantatille. Paris: s.n. [1830?]. Words by
P. J. de Béranger.
voice/pf
GB: Lbl [G.559.(53.)].
CPM.

Qu'elle est triste. ("Voyez la jeune fille") cantatille. Paris: s.n. [1835?]. Words
by Barateau.
voice/pf
GB: Lbl [H.2831.e.(54.)].
CPM.

Sur la montagne. Romance. Paris: Hanry #2300, n.d.
voice/pf
D: Kf&m.
Frau & Musik.

Duchange, Mme
pub. c. 1830, Paris

Le chien du Voyageur. ("Felix, éveille-toi") romance. Paris: s.n. [1830?]. Words by Mr. Duchange.
voice/pf
GB: Lbl [G.552.(56.)].
CPM.

Dufresne, Fidèle (?)
pub. c. 1800, Paris
Deuxième Pot-Pourri d'Airs Variés pour Violon, avec accompagnement de Violon et Basse. Paris: Pleyel [1800?]. Partbooks.
2 vlns/b (vlc)
GB: Lbl [g.409.a.(3.)].
CPM.

Dufresnoy, Mme
pub. c. 1800, London. French?
A favorite sonata . . . for the harp or piano forte, arranged with accompaniments for two french horns, ad libitum . . . by H. Leander. London: Robert Birchall [c. 1800]. Parts.
harp or pf/2 hns ad lib (added by Leander)
GB: Lbl [h.14800.h.(7.)] (lacking Leander's horn parts).
RISM A/I (D 3671), CPM, BUC, Cohen, Eitner (as hpsch only).

Sonata per Arpa.
harp
US: LOu (Ricasoli collection). Copy in Ars Fem coll.
Letter (Ars Fem).

Two sonatas for the french pedal harp, with an accompaniment for a violin ad libitum . . . op. 1st. London: author [c. 1800]. Parts.
harp/vln ad lib
GB: Lbl [h.3200.(10.)] (incomplete, lacking violin part).
RISM A/I (D 3670), CPM, Cohen.

Dumur, Anne Constance, Madame
18th century, French, fl. St. Petersburg
Air russe varié [c] *pour la harpe ou le forte piano,* œuvre 6. St. Petersburg: F. A. Dittmar, No. 940.
harp or pf
CH: Gpu. Copy in Ars Fem coll.
RISM A/I (DD 3712 II, 1), Cohen, letters (C. Johnson, Ars Fem).

Dupré, Mme

fl. 1750, France

La toilette de Venus. Cantate pour un dessus avec simphonie. Paris: auteur, Le Clerc, Mme Boivin (gravée par Mme Charpentier), 1750. Score, 12 pp.

S/treble instrument unspecified/bc

F: Pn [Vm7 277]. Microfilm in Jackson coll.

RISM A/I (D 3888), Paris Lib. Cat.

Dussek (Dusíkova), Kateřina Veronika Anna Rosalia Elisabeta (married Francesco Cianchettini)

1769, Čáslav–1833, London

A Duet for two Performers on one Piano-Forte . . . In which is introduced the favorite air of "L'Hymen" from the opera of Blaise et Babet [by N. Dezède] . . . Op. 9. London: R. Birchall [c. 1810]. 11 pp.

pf (4 hand)

GB: Lbl [g.545.y.(2.)].

CPM, MGG (bio).

Délassement Champêtre d'une Allemande en Ecosse, pour le Piano Forte. London: s.n. [1804].

pf

GB: Lbl [h.324.(10.)].

CPM, MGG (bio).

A favorite la Chasse Russe for the Piano-Forte and an accompaniment for the Flute . . . Op. 10. for the piano forte . . . London: s.n. [1805?].

pf/fl

GB: Lbl [g.272.w.(2.)].

CPM, MGG (bio).

A Grand Divertimento pastorale, with a pollacca for the piano forte . . . Op. 11. London: s.n. [c. 1815].

pf

GB: Lbl [h.1203.w.(8.)].

CPM, MGG (bio).

Hungarian Quick Step. A military rondo, for the piano forte . . . London: Goulding, Phipps & D'Almaine [1805?]. 6 pp. [Also identified on each page as "Cianchettini's Military Rondo."]

pf

GB: Lbl [g.443.t.(9.)].

CPM, MGG (bio).

Madame Cianchettini's Return to England. A characteristic Fantasia for the Pianoforte. London: s.n. [1809?].

pf

GB: Lbl [g.271.c.(29.)].

CPM, MGG (bio).

A Military Overture for the Piano Forte, in which is introduced a new German Quick step . . . London: s.n. [1810?].

pf

GB: Lbl [g.272.a.(6.)].

CPM, MGG (bio).

New Rondo for the Pianoforte on . . . "*Kommt ein schlanker Bursch" from Der Freischütz,* by C. M. von Weber. London: s.n. [1825?].

pf

GB: Lbl [g.272.m.(32.)].

CPM, MGG (bio).

Overture to the Favorite Opera La Bell'Arsene [by P. A. Monsigny]. Adapted as a duetto, for two performers on one piano forte by Sigra Cianchettini. London: Printed by Goulding, Phips, & D'Almaine [1802].

pf (4 hand)

GB: Lbl [h.3290.z.(1.)].

CPM, MGG (bio).

A Second Sett of favorite Airs, and a March, arranged as rondos: for the piano forte . . . 1. London: Goulding, Phipps & D'Almaine [1802]. 11 pp. 2. London: Goulding, Phipps & D'Almaine [1803].

pf

GB: Lbl 1. [Hirsch M. 1279.(5.)]. 2. [g.272.a.(5.)].

CPM, MGG (bio).

Six Variations for the Piano Forte, on a favorite Roman air . . . London: Printed for Cianchettini & Sperati [1808]. 7 pp.

pf

GB: Lbl [h.61.c.(5.)].

CPM, MGG (bio).

Six Waltzes and a Sauteuse for the Piano Forte. 2d. Set. London: s.n. [1825?].

pf

GB: Lbl [h.324.(9.)].

CPM, MGG (bio).

Six Waltzes for the Piano Forte, composed after the German Style for Dancing.
London: Mitchell's Musical Library [1811?]. 5 pp.
pf
GB: Lbl [g.443.m.(17.)].
CPM, MGG (bio).

Six Waltzes for the Piano Forte with an accompaniment for the flute. London: s.n. [1809].
pf/fl
GB: Lbl (2 ex.) [h.324.(8.) & H.2819.(24.)].
CPM, MGG (bio).

A Sonata, for the Piano-Forte . . . in which is introduced a favourite Scotch air and a new polacca, with an accompaniment for a flute, (ad libitum) . . . Op. 6. London:
Printed by Goulding, Phipps & D'Almaine [1802].
pf/fl ad lib
GB: Lbl [g.271.dd.(4.)] (flute part missing).
CPM, MGG (bio).

A sonata [F] *for the piano-forte, with or without additional keys, in which is introduced the . . . Portuguese hymn, "Adeste fideles"* . . . op. 2. London: Goulding, Phipps
& D'Almaine [c.1800]. 15 pp.
pf
GB: Lbl [g.543.u.(4.)].
RISM A/I (D 4656), BUC, CPM, Cohen, NG (bio), MGG.

Third grand divertimento for the Pianoforte. Op. 14. 1. London: [1815?]. 2. . . . *in which is introduced the favorite air of Durandarte & Belerma.* London: Mitchell's
Musical Library [1822]. 12 pp.
pf
1. & 2. GB: Lbl [g.272.m.(33.)], [h.61.c.(8.)].
CPM, MGG (bio).

Three favorite national airs arranged as rondos for the Piano Forte . . . London: s.n.
[1803?].
pf
GB: Lbl [g.272.a.(4.)].
CPM, MGG (bio).

Three original Waltzes. Arranged as duettinos for two performers on one
piano-forte, or harp, and piano forte . . . Op. 3. London: Goulding, Phipps
& D'Almaine [1801].

pf (4 hands) or harp / pf
GB: Lbl [h.925.aa.(7.)].
CPM, MGG (bio).

Three Sonatas for the Piano-Forte . . . in which are introduced . . . Favorite Airs as Adagios & Rondos . . . Op. 6. London: Goulding, Phipps & D'Almaine [1803?].
pf
GB: Lbl [h.1568.d.(2.)].
CPM, MGG (bio).

Two sonatas for the piano forte with an accompaniment for a violin & violoncello, op. 4, by Sigra. Cianchettini. London: Goulding, Phipps & D'Almaine [c.1800]. 3 partbooks in portfolio.
pf / vln / vlc
US: BE.
MGG (bio), OCLC (21850963).

A Trip to Paris. A favorite reel arranged as a rondo for the piano-forte, with or without additional keys by V:C: [*sic*] Cianchettini. London: Printed by Goulding, Phipps & D'Almaine [c. 1800].
pf
GB: Lbl [h.724.p.(5.)].
CPM, MGG (bio).

Variations on the favorite Portuguese Hymn "Adeste fidelis" [sic] *with additional passages for piano fortes up to F by . . .* Pio Cianchettini. (New edition). London: D'Almaine & Co. [c. 1840]. [Pio Cianchettini was the son of Sigra. Cianchettini.]
pf
GB: Lbl [h.1203.s.(12.)].
CPM, MGG (bio).

Vicountess Sudley's favorite Waltz, with Variations for the Piano Forte. London: Corri, Dussek & Co. [1797?].
pf
GB: Lbl [g.272.t.(19.)].
CPM, MGG (bio), Cohen.

The Victory at Talavera, a characteristic fantasia, for the piano forte . . . London: Cianchettini & Sperati [1811].
pf

GB: Lbl [g.352.m.(5)] (incomplete, lacking all pages after p.6).
CPM, MGG (bio).

Dussek, Olivia (married **Buckley** or **Bulkley**)

pub. c. 1827–29, London & Dublin

"Day is Departing," an Air on Three Notes composed by I. Willis, Arranged with Variations for the Harp and Dedicated to Miss Susanna Ellis by Olivia Dussek Bulkley. London & Dublin: I. Willis [1827–29].

pf

In bound collection of 19th-century harp music in Rempel coll.
Letter (Rempel).

Fantasia for the Piano Forte Composed & Dedicated to Miss Bogle by Olivia Dussek. London: S. Chappell, n.d.

pf

GB: Lbl. Microfilm copy in Rempel coll.
NG (bio in article on Sophia Dussek), letter (Rempel).

"Rule Britannia." Arranged as a Duet for the Harp and Piano Forte and Dedicated to Miss Marianmé & Miss Harriet Benham by Olivia Dussek. London: Clementi, n.d.

harp/pf

GB: Lbl. Microfilm copy in Rempel coll.
Letter (Rempel).

Dussek, Sophia Giustina, née **Corri** (later married **Moralt**)

1775, Edinburgh–1847, London

Adeste fideles. With variations for the harp. 1. London: Chappell & Co. [1821] 6 pp. 2. London: F. T. Latour [1827]. 3. With variations for the harp or piano forte. Philadelphia: C. E. Blake, [182–?]. 5 pp.

harp. 3. harp or pf

1. GB: Lbl [h.307.(23.). In bound collection of 19th-century harp music in Rempel coll. 2. GB: Lbl [g.452.p.(5.)]. 3. US: Cn, CAdriscoll, Wc.
1. CPM, letter (Rempel). 2. CPM. 3. NUC Sup. (NSD 0061295), Wolfe (2639). MGG (bio).

"Ah! que l'amour," a favorite French air, arranged for the harp. London: Chapell [1820].

harp

GB: Lbl [h.2605.ii.(7.)].
CPM, MGG (bio).

The air "Scots wha hae," arranged for the harp. London: s.n. [1826].
harp
GB: Lbl [h.307.(32.)].
CPM, MGG (bio).

The air "We're a'noddin" with an introduction and variations for the harp. London:
s.n. [1823].
harp
GB: Lbl [h.307.(18–?)].
CPM, MGG (bio).

"The boatie rows," a Scotch air, with variations for the Harp. London: s.n.
[1810?].
harp
GB: Lbl [h.307.(11.)].
CPM, MGG (bio).

"The Campbells are coming," a Scotch air arranged for the harp. London: s.n.
[1822].
harp
GB: Lbl [h.307.(25.)].
CPM, MGG (bio).

The celebrated overture to Lodoiska [by R. Kreutzer] *arranged for the harp, with an
accompaniment for the piano forte ad libitum.* [London]: author [1811].
harp / pf ad lib.
CH: AR. GB: Lbl [h.307.(43.)].
RISM A/I (DD 4655d), CPM, MGG (bio).

"C'est l'amour," a French air, with variations for the harp. London: s.n., [1825].
harp
GB: Lbl [h.307.(10.)].
CPM, MGG (bio).

"Charmant ruisseau," a third French air arranged for the harp. London: s.n.
[1823].
harp
GB: Lbl [h.307.(14.)].
CPM, MGG (bio).

Chorus of Virgins [from P. von Winter's *Das unterbrochene Opferfest*] *arranged with variations for the harp.* S.l.: s.n. [1827].
harp
GB: Lbl [h.307.(29.)].
CPM, MGG (bio).

"The Deserter's meditations," a favorite Irish air, arranged for the harp. London: s.n. [1813].
harp
GB: Lbl [h.307.(5.)].
CPM, MGG (bio).

A duett for the harp and pianoforte, dedicated to Mrs. Colebrooke. London: s.n. [1812?].
harp/pf
GB: Lbl [h.307.(44.)].
CPM, MGG (bio).

Duett for the harp and pianoforte, in which is introduced a favorite air ["Ah vous dirai-je"] *with variations and an introduction.* London: s.n. [1823].
harp/pf
GB: Lbl [h.307.(41.)].
CPM, MGG (bio).

The Favourite Air of "O cara armonia" [by Mozart], *& an Introduction & Spanish Military Air, for the Harp.* London: Monzani & Hill [1815?].
harp
GB: Lbl [h.3200.d.(5.)].
CPM, MGG (bio).

The favourite Air of "O! Nanny wilt thou gang with me" [by T. Carter] . . . *arranged for the Harp.* London: [1807]. 2. . . . *and a original rondo composed and arranged for the harp.* London: s.n. [1812].
harp
1. GB: Lbl [g.661.(26.)]. 2. GB: Lbl [h.307.(8.)].
CPM, MGG (bio).

The Favorite Airs, of "Drink to me only," "La Mia crudel tiranna" & "My ain kind Deary O!" with variations for the harp, and flute or violin accomp. ad libitum. Set 7. London: Monzani & Hill [c.1815].
harp/fl or vln ad lib.

GB: Lbl [h.2605.kk.(2.)]. US: NYp (harp part only).
CPM, NUC (ND 0459770), MGG (bio).

The favorite chorus in "La Dame blanche" [by Boieldieu], arranged for the harp.
London: s.n. [1827].
harp
GB: Lbl [h.307.(16.)].
CPM, MGG (bio).

The favorite march [from P. von Winter's *Das unterbrochene Opferfest*], arranged
by S. Dussek. S.l.: s.n. [1826].
harp
GB: Lbl [h.307.(28.)].
CPM, MGG (bio).

A favorite waltz with variations for the harp. London: Chappell & Co., No. 784,
n.d.
harp
AUS: Sma.
RISM A/I (DD 4655a), MGG (bio).

A favorite waltz, with variations for the harp. London: s.n. [1816].
harp
GB: Lbl [h.307.(37.)].
CPM, MGG (bio).

The favorite Welsh air of "Beauty in Tears" with variations for the Harp. London:
s.n. [1810?].
harp
GB: Lbl [h.184.a.(19.)].
CPM, MGG (bio).

Four favorite airs arranged for the harp, book 4th. London: Robert Birchall, n.d.
harp
DK: Kk.
RISM A/I (D 4652), MGG (bio).

A French air, with variations for the harp. London: s.n. [1820].
harp
GB: Lbl [h.307.(34.)].
CPM, MGG (bio).

"The Garland of Love," a favorite air with variations and an introduction for the harp.
1. London: Chappell & Co. [1813]. 2. A reissue. London: s.n. [1824].
harp
1. & 2. GB: Lbl [h.307.(36.)], [h.184.i.(7.)].
CPM, MGG (bio).

"Gentile Annette," a French air [from *Le Petit chaperon rouge* by Boieldieu]
arranged for the pianoforte. 1. London: s.n. [1824]. 2. London: S. Chappell
[1827?]. 7 pp.
pf
1. & 2. GB: Lbl [h.307.(2.)], [g.443.u.(16.).
CPM, MGG (bio).

*Giornovichi's Celebrated Concerto arranged for the Piano Forte or Harp with an accom-
paniment for the Violin and Violoncello* by S. Dussek. 1. S.l.: s.n. [1808?]. 2. *The
Celebrated Concerto* [Giornovichi] *arr. for Piano Forte, with an Accompaniment for
Violin and Bass* . . . by S. Dussek. S.l.: s.n. [1815].
pf or harp/vln/vlc
1. & 2. GB: Lbl [h.1568.h.(2.)], [g.661.b.(54.)].
CPM, MGG (bio).

"Go, you may call it madness, folly" by Anna Maria Crouch, née Phillips,
with accompaniment for the harp & pianoforte by Madame Dusseck [*sic*].
London: s.n. [1805].
voice/harp/pf
GB: Lbl [G.798.(17.)].
CPM, MGG (bio).

"God save the King," with variations for the harp. London: Chappell & Co.
(#1968), [1822].
harp
AUS: Sma. GB: Lbl [h.307.(20.)].
RISM A/I (DD 4655b), CPM, MGG (bio).

A Grand March by Mozart [*sic*, actually "Dieu d'amour" from Grétry's *Les
Mariages samnites*] *arranged* [with variations] *for the harp.* London: Chappell &
Co. [1822?].
harp
GB: Lbl [h.307.(18.)].
CPM, MGG (bio).

"In my cottage," with variations for the harp. London: s.n. [1816].
harp
GB: Lbl [h.307.(38.)].
CPM, MGG (bio).

Introduction and march for the harp. London: s.n. [1822].
harp
GB: Lbl [h.307.(21.)].
CPM, MGG (bio).

Introduction and waltz for the harp and pianoforte. London: s.n. [1822].
harp/pf
GB: Lbl [h.307.(45.)].
CPM, MGG (bio).

Introduction and waltz, with variations for the harp. London: s.n. [1818].
harp
GB: Lbl [h.307.(35.)].
CPM, MGG (bio).

Italian Air in Nina, Welsh Air (Wyres Megen) *& Spanish Boleros* [sic], *arranged for the harp, with a flute or violin accomp. ad libitum.* Set 9. London: Monzani & Hill [c.1810]. 12 pp.
harp/fl or vln
GB: Lbl [h.2605.kk.(3.)] (lacking fl or vln).
CPM, MGG (bio).

J. L. Dussek's much admired concerto for the harp . . . arranged by S. Dussek. S.l.: s.n., 1813.
harp
GB: Lbl [h.307.(39.)].
CPM, MGG (bio).

Jäger Chorus [from Weber's *Der Freischutz*], *arranged for the harp.* London: s.n. [1825].
harp
GB: Lbl [h.307.(31.)].
CPM, MGG (bio).

"Kind willst du ruhig schlafen." The favorite quartett [from P. von Winter's *Das unterbrochene Opferfest*], *with variations for the harp* by S. Dussek. S.l.: s.n.

[1827].
harp
GB: Lbl [h.307.(30.)].
CPM, MGG (bio).

La Chasse, rondo for the harp. London: s.n. [1824].
harp
GB: Lbl [h.307.(26.)].
CPM, MGG (bio).

"Le Petit tambour," a French air with variations for the harp. London: s.n. [1828].
harp
GB: Lbl [h.307.(15.)].
CPM, MGG (bio).

"Let us all be merry," a Venetian Air, Arranged as a duett for Harp and Pianoforte and Dedicated to Miss Lockhart and Miss Anne Lockhart, by S. Dussek. London: s.n. [1817].
harp/pf
GB: Lbl [h.307.(40.)]. Copy [with only the harp part] in bound volume of 19th-century harp music in Rempel coll.
CPM, letter (Rempel).MGG (bio).

"Logie o'Buchan," a Scotch air, arranged for the harp. London: s.n. [1824].
harp
GB: Lbl [h.307.(24.)].
CPM, MGG (bio).

"Love thou maddening Power." [Song] arrang'd for the harp, the words by the late Rich. Tickell . . . Sung by Mr. Kelly in *Love in a Village.* [London:] M. Kelly [180l].
voice/harp
GB: Lbl [H.1980.jj.(22.)].
CPM, MGG (bio).

"The maid of Derby," a favorite air, arranged for the harp. London: s.n. [1819].
harp
GB: Lbl [h.307.(22.)].
CPM, MGG (bio).

A march and two waltzes for the pianoforte. London: s.n. [1824].
pf
GB: Lbl [h.307.(1.)].
CPM, MGG (bio).

The much admired Ballad of Robin Adair, sung by Mr. Braham, with new accompaniment for the piano forte or harp. Edinburgh: N. Corri [c.1810].
voice / harp
GB: Lbl [G.426.dd.(42.)].
CPM, MGG (bio).

The new German waltz, adapted as a rondo for the harp or piano forte. 1. London: Corri, Dussek [c.1795 or 1799]. 3 pp. 2. Dublin: Edmund Lee, n.d. 3. London: s.n. [1810?].
harp or pf
1. GB: Cu, Gm. US: Pu. 2. US: NYp, PHu.
3. GB: Lbl [g.272.g.(27.)].
1–2. RISM A / I (D 4654, D 4655). 1. OCLC (21940317). 2. BUC. 3. CPM. Cohen (Corri-Dussek), MGG.

The new Tyrolean waltz, arranged for the harp. London: s.n. [1820].
harp
GB: Lbl [h.307.(4.)].
CPM, MGG (bio).

Notturno russiano [E-flat], *for the harp.* London: Monzani & Hill, n.d.
harp
CH: AR.
RISM A / I (DD 4655c), MGG (bio).

"Nous nous aimions." A favorite French air arranged as a rondo for the harp. In: *Musical Journal* No. 7. [London]: Pleyel, Corri, Dussek, 1797. Parts.
harp
CS: Bm.
RISM A / I (D 4653), Cohen (Corri-Dussek), MGG (bio).

"O thou wert born to please me" [composed by Martini] *arranged with variations for the harp.* London: s.n. [1826].
harp
GB: Lbl [h.307.(33.)].
CPM, MGG (bio).

The Overture to The Deserter [composed by P.A. Monsigny] *arranged as a Rondo for the Piano Forte.* In: Pleyel, Corri & Dussek's *Musical Journal* [no. 2]. London, Edinburgh: Dussek & Co., 1797.
pf
GB: Lbl [g.137.(21.).
RISM B/II (Madame Dussek), BUC, CPM, MGG (bio).

"Partant pour la Syrie," a French air [composed by Hortense, Queen of Holland], *arr. for the harp.* London: s.n. [1822].
harp
GB: Lbl [h.307.(13.)].
CPM, MGG (bio).

Pleyel's German Hymn, arranged by S. Dussek [from Quartett. Op. 7]. S.l.: s.n. [1826].
voice/pf or guit
GB: Lbl [h.307.(27.)].
CPM, MGG (bio).

"Pray Goody," the favorite air from the opera of Midas, arranged for the harp. London: Chappell [1813 or 1815?]. 5 pp.
harp
GB: Lbl [h.307.(6.)]. US: NYp.
CPM, NUC (ND 0459771), MGG (bio).

Rossini's air "Di piacer" [from *La Gazza Ladra*], arranged by S. Dussek. S.l.: s.n. [1823].
harp
GB: Lbl [h.307.(42.)].
CPM, MGG (bio).

"Saint Patrick's day," a favorite Irish air, arranged for the harp. London: s.n. [1813].
harp
GB: Lbl [h.307.(9.)].
CPM, MGG (bio).

"Se il cielo al mio tormento" [composed by Michael Kelly] . . . with . . . an accompaniment for the harp by Madame Dussek. S.l.: s.n. [c.1805].
voice/harp
GB: Lbl (2 ex) [G.809.kk.(4.) & G. 424.kk.(15.)].
CPM, MGG (bio).

Second French air arranged for the harp. London: s.n. [1822].
harp
GB: Lbl [h.307.(12.)].
CPM, MGG (bio).

Sicilian air on which is founded the ballad "Home, sweet home" [by Sir H. R. Bishop] arranged for the harp. London: s.n. [1826].
harp
GB: Lbl [h.307.(17.)].
CPM, MGG (bio).

Six sonatinas for the harp [C, F, G, B-flat, F, E-flat]. 1. London: J. Dale. 2. . . . pour la harpe. Paris: Mlles Erard; Lyon: Garnier #25, n.d. 3. Leipzig: Breitkopf & Härtel, #110, n.d. 4. Offenbach: Johann André, #3566, n.d. 5. . . . pour piano forte ou harpe. Vienna: T. Mollo, #1544, n.d. [Title page reads J. L. Dussek; works considered by Craw to have been written by S. G. Dussek.]
1–4. harp, 5. pf or harp
1. D: LEmi. GB: Lbl, Ob. 2. CH: W. D: B. D: Gol. 3. S: Skma. 4. CS: Bu. D: OF. 5. A: Wst. I: Mc.
RISM A/I (D 4607–4611, as Johann Ludwig Dussek), Craw.

A Sonata, for the Piano Forte. [London]: Theobald Monzani [c. 1805].
pf
GB: Lbl [h.722.oo.(11.)]. Microfilm copy in Rempel coll.
CPM, letter (Rempel), MGG (bio).

A sonata for the piano forte or harpsichord with an accompaniment for a violin or german flute . . . op. 1st. London: Corri, Dussek & Co. [c. 1793]. Parts.
pf or hpsch / vln or fl
GB: Lcm. US: Wc.
RISM A/I (D 4647), BUC, NG (bio), Cohen (Corri-Dussek), MGG (bio).

A Sonata, for the Piano Forte or Harpsichord, With an Accompaniment for a Violin or Ger. Flute Dedicated to Miss Cornella Collins, Composed by Sophia Giustina Dussek. Op. 1st. London: Corri, Dussek & Co., Edinburgh [17–?].
pf or hpsch / vln or fl
US: Wc. Microfilm copy in Rempel coll.
Letter (Rempel).

Three favorite airs ["Lewie Gordon," "Thy Fatal Shafts," "Queen Mary's Lamentation"]. Arranged for the Harp by S. Dussek. Book 5th. London: Rt. Birchall, n.d.
harp
In bound volume of 19th-century harp music in Rempel coll.
Letter (Rempel).

Three favorite airs ["O Mary Turn Awa That Bonnie Face o' Thine," "She Rose and Let me in," "The Rising of the Sun" (a Welsh Air)]. Arranged for the Harp by S. Dussek. Book 6th. London: Rt. Birchall, n.d.
harp
In bound volume of 19th-century harp music in Rempel coll.
Letter (Rempel).

Three favorite airs ["Roy's Wife of Aldevaloch," "Allegretto," "Farewell to Lochaber"]. Arranged for the Harp and Dedicated to Mrs. Lam. Hill by S. Dussek. Book 1st. London: Rt. Birchall, n.d.
harp
In bound volume of 19th-century harp music in Rempel coll.
Letter (Rempel).

Three favorite airs with variations for the harp, book [I]. London: Monzani, n.d.
harp
DK: Kk.
RISM A/I (D 4651), MGG (bio).

Three favorite airs . . . with variations for the harp. 2d set. London: s.n. [1815?].
harp
GB: Lbl [h. 1480.h.(9.)].
CPM, MGG (bio).

Three favorite Canzonetts [by Steffano Mandini], *arranged with an accompaniment for the piano forte or guitar . . .* (The [guitar] accompaniment by Mme Dussek.). S.l.: s.n. [1799].
voice/pf or guit
GB: Lbl [E.1501.pp.(2.)].
CPM, MGG (bio).

Three favorite Pieces for the Harp, with a Flute or Violin accompt. ad libitum. Set #8. Contents: La Biondina, "Adieu my Fears & Sorrows" [comp. by M. Kelly] & A Grand March.

London: Monzani & Hill [1820?].
harp
GB: Lbl [h.173.d.(12.)].
CPM, MGG (bio).

Three Scotch airs arranged for the harp. Book 2. London: s.n [1810].
harp
GB: Lbl [h.307.(7.)].
CPM, MGG (bio).

Three sonatas for the harp, with Scots airs and reels, for the adagios & rondos, . . .
[E-flat, F, C]. London/Edinburgh: Corri, Dussek & Co. [c.1795]. [Not the
same work as [1798] Op. 2, Bk. l, which is also in GB: Lbl].
harp
GB: Lbl [h. 2605.j.(4.)].
RISM A/I (D 4650), CPM, BUC, MGG (bio).

Three sonatas for the harp, with Scots airs and reels, for the adagios & rondos . . . op.
2, Bk. 1 [B–flat, G, c]. London/Edinburgh: Corri, Dussek & Co. [1798].
harp
GB: Lbl [h.2605.s.(3.)].
RISM A/I (D 4649), CPM, Cohen (Corri-Dussek), MGG (bio).

Trois Airs italiens variés pour la Harpe, avec accompagnement de Flûte [ad lib. for
#1 & 3]. Paris: Naderman [1826]. 2 partbooks.
harp/fl
I: OS (Ediz. Musiche A–109l).
Ostiglia, MGG (bio).

Trois sonates [B-flat, C, D] *pour clavecin ou forte-piano avec accompagnement de violon . . .* œuvre Ie. Paris: Sieber (#1013), n.d. Parts.
hpsch or pf/vln
I: Mc (hpsch only).
RISM A/I (D 4648), MGG (bio).

*The Troubadour, and Darmstadt Waltzes, arranged for two performers on the
pianoforte.* London: s.n. [1824].
pf (4 hand)
GB: Lbl [h.307.(3.)].
CPM, MGG (bio).

Two favorite airs, "Lewie Gordon" and "The rising of the sun," adapted for the harp and pianoforte. London: s.n. [1812].
harp and pf
GB: Lbl [h.307.(46.)].
CPM, MGG (bio).

"The white cockade" [a Scotch air] *arranged for the harp.* London: s.n. [1823].
harp
GB: Lbl [h.307.(19.)].
CPM, MGG (bio).

[Work(s)] in: *Pleyel, Corri & Dussek's musical journal for harp.*
London/Edinburgh: Dussek & Co., 1797.
harp
GB: Lbl. Other library holdings incomplete.
RISM B/II (Madame Dussek, p. 290), MGG (bio).

Duv[al], Mlle (not the same as **Mlle Louise Duval**). Could also be completed as **Duv[ergé].** See **Cléry, Mme,** née **Duverger**
1761–?, Paris?
"Tout ce que vois me rappelle." [Air, composed by Mlle Duv . . . aged 15 years]. In: *Mercure de France,* June 1776). [Paris] s.n., 1776.
song
GB: Lbl. Copy in Ars Fem coll.
RISM A/I (D 4696), BUC, Cohen, NG, letter(Ars Fem).

Duval, Louise Mlle
?–1769?
Les Génies, ou *Les Caractères de l'amour.* Ballet . . . représenté par l'Académie royale de musique . . . 18 Octobre 1736. Paris: Mlle Duval, Vve Boivin, Le Clerc (gravé par de Gland) [1736]. Score, 350 pp.
orch (stage work)
F: Pa (M.666), Pc & Pn ([Vm2 412] & [D.3765]), Po (A. 137), TLc, V.
US: BE, Wc. Copy in Ars Fem coll.
RISM A/I (D 4695), Paris Lib. Cat., Eitner, Cohen, NG, Mellon, letter (Ars Fem).

Duverger-Cléry, Mme. See **Cléry, Mme,** née **Duverger**

$\mathcal{E}$

E[bdon], M[ary]
1766–1851, Durham
March in A; Rondo, Allegro in A; Minuetto in A. Ms.
kbd
GB: DRc (D3:10, D3:20–1, D3:21).
Durham.

Single chant in G. Ms., August 2, 1797.
voice (unacc.)
GB: DRc (A22:29).
Durham.

E., M. M., Madlle
pub. c. 181–?, Philadelphia
Fantaisie sur un air ecossais. Pour le piano forte. Op. X. Philadelphia:
G. Willig [181?]. 11 pp.
pf
US: Wc.
Wolfe (2642).

Marche de la Nouvelle Orleans. Pour le piano forte [Philadelphia: G. Willig,
c. 1819?].
pf
US: NYcuh.
Wolfe (2643).

E. T. P. A. (Pseud. for **Maria Antonia Walpurgis.** See **Maria Antonia
Walpurgis, Princess of Bavaria, Electress of Saxony**)

Eberlin, Maria Caecilia Barbara (**"E. Waberl"** in the **Mozart letters**)
1728, Salzburg–1806, Salzburg
"Daß die Welt nit [*sic*] mehr soll büssen." Cantilena de B. V. M. et S. S.
Joanne Evangelista â Canto Solo . . . Della Sigra Caeciliae Eberlinin [D
major]. 7 ms parts [c. 1750–51]. [Title in organ part in the hand of Joh.
Ernst Eberlin.] 2 copies of voice part, the second with the text "Wer gibt
mir heut Taubenflügel."
S/2 vlns/org bc/2 hns in F
D: Mbs (Mus. ms. 1337. Ms. 1751. WZ: Mbs 161). (Formerly owned by
Max Keller, 1770–1855.)
Letter (D: Mbs), MGG, Cohen (death date 1766, says married Meißner), Eitner.

"Undankbahre Salems Söhne." Cantilena de Passione Domini â Canto Solo Della Sigra Caecilia Eberlinin [C minor]. 4 ms. parts [c. 1760].
S/2 vlns/org bc
D: Mbs (Mus. ms. 1339. Ms. 1751. WZ: Mbs 161). (Formerly owned by Max Keller, 1770–1855.)
Letter (D: Mbs), MGG, Cohen (death date 1766, says married Meißner), Eitner.

"Was will meine Stimm beginnen." Cantilena de S. Joanne Baptista â Canto Solo . . . Della Sigra Caeciliae Eberlinin. [Title in organ part in the hand of Joh. Ernst Eberlin] [F major]. 6 ms parts. [c. 1750–51].
S/2 vlns/org bc/2 hns in F
D: Mbs (Mus. ms. 1338. Ms. 1751. WZ: Mbs 161). (Formerly owned by Max Keller, 1770–1855.)
Letter (D: Mbs), MGG, Cohen (death date 1766, says married Meißner), Eitner.

"Wie soll ich dich heut besingen." Cantilena â Canto Solo . . . Della Sigre Caecilia Eberlin. [Title in organ part in the hand of Joh. Ernst Eberlin] [D major]. 7 ms. parts, 2 copies of voice, the second with the text "Augen heftet eure Blicke" [c. 1750–51].
S/2 vlns/org bc/2 hns
D: Mbs (Mus. ms. 1336. Ms. 1751. WZ: Mbs 161). (Formerly owned by Max Keller, 1770–1855.)
Letter (D: Mbs), MGG, Cohen (death date 1766, says married Meisßner), Eitner.

Echenfeld, Katharina
fl. 1521
[Mass—according to Eitner, a Missal]. Parchment codex, 239 pages. Chant book?
voice (unaccompanied)
B.B. (Ms. Z2 of Kloster Tangendorff, Naumburg Diocese. Modern location not confirmed.)
Cohen, Eitner.

Edelman (Edelmann), Mlle (sister of Johann Friedrich Edelman)
pub. 1780s, Paris
Andante. In: *Journal de clavecin par les meilleurs maîtres*, 2eme année, #5/23 (May 1783), 40. Paris: LeDuc, 1783.
hpsch
F: Pn (L. 280).
RISM B/II (pp. 206–207), letter (C. Johnson).

Minuetto et Trio. In: *Choix de musique, dédié à S.A.S. Monseigneur de duc regnant des Deux-Ponts*. [Bi-monthly]. Ded. Deux-Ponts. Paris: Sanson et Comp. (#48), 1784.

kbd

B: Bc. D: B–MG, DS, HR, Mbs, ZW. F: Pc, Pn. GB: Lbl.

RISM B/II (Edelmann, p. 130), Eitner (under the title, Choix de musique), letter (C. Johnson).

Minuetto et Trio. In: *Journal de clavecin par les meilleurs maîtres*, 3eme année, #2 (1784), pp. 10–11. Paris; LeDuc, 1784. [May be same work as preceding entry.]

hpsch

F: Pn (L. 280).

RISM B/II (pp. 206–207), letter (C. Johnson).

Rondeau [for violoncello and hpsch]. 1750.

vlc/hpsch

F: Pn. Copy in Ars Fem coll.

Letter (Ars Fem).

[2d Sonata] in: *Trois Sonates pour le Clavecin, Avec accompagnement d'un Violon ad Libitum*, op. 8 [of Johann Friedrich Edelmann]. 1. Paris: chez l'auteur/chez Mad. Lemarchand/à l'Opéra/Mde le Menu/Mme Berault [1779]. 2. Offenbach/André/aux adresses ordinaires, n.d. 3. London: J. Blundell, n.d. 4. Mannheim: Johann Michael Götz. 5. As: Sonata 2 (Op. 10): Cette sonate est de la composition de Mlle Edelmann, soeur de l'auteur. Ms. copy, c. 1783–86. Parts. 6. In ms. copy of: [20] Sonatas by J. F. Edelmann, c. 1783–86. Parts.

hpsch/vln ad lib

1. F: Pn (Vm7 5455). Photocopy in C. Johnson coll. 2. S: Skma. 3. GB: Lbl, S: Skma. 4. D: Dlb. USSR: Ml. 5. DK: Kk (mu7409.1533). 6. DK: Kk (mu6501.2030).

1–3. RISM A/II (E 413, E 404, E 414), letter (C. Johnson). 4. RISM A/I (E 415), letter (C. Johnson). 5–6. RISMdan (cat. also shows unidentified printed edition from which these copies were made).

[Sonata] in: *3 Sonates pour le Clavecin ou Forte-piano*, composés par Mademoiselle Edelman, Monsieur Darondeau, et Monsieur Pin. Leipzig: C. G. Hilscher, 1787. 24 pp. in volume.

hpsch or pf

B: Bc (WQ 6324).
Wotquenne, Eitner, letter (C. Johnson).

Edwards, Elizabeth
pub. c. 1820, London
A Selection of Favorite Canzonetts and Glees, with an accompaniment for the Piano Forte, and one arranged for a full Military Band. London: Author [1820?].
voice(s)/ pf & one piece for wind band
GB: Lbl [R.M.14.b.8.(3.)].
CPM.

Eichner, Maria Adelheid (Adelheid Marie)
1762, Mannheim–1787, Potsdam
"Ich hatt' ein kleines Lämmchen nur." Romanze. In: *Poetische Blumenlese auf das Jahr 1783.* Göttingen: J. Chr. Dieterich, 1783.
voice/pf
D: DÜk (#266).
Düsseldorf-Goethe.

"Mach mir vom Volk" in: *Lieder, Arien und Duette beym Klavier. . . .* [ed. Johan André]. 2ter Jahrgang. Berlin: C. S. Spener, 1781–82. 2d vol., p. 51.
voice/kbd
A: Wn. CH: Bu (inc.). D: HAu. F: Pc. US: NH. USSR: KA (this location not confirmed).
RISM B/II (M. A. Eichner, p. 218), Eitner, Cohen, Königsberg.

[1 Lied] in: *Musikalischer Blumenstrauß zum neuen Jahr.* [Ed. J. F. Reichardt.] Berlin: Neue Berlinische Musikhandlung, 1792 (in vol. 1).
voice/pf
D: BÜ, DÜk.
RISM B/II (A. Eichner, p. 249), Eitner, Cohen, MGG.

[2 Chansons avec le Pfte.] in: *Choix de musique, dédié à S.A.S. Monseigneur de duc regnant des Deux-Ponts.* [Bi-monthly.] Paris: Sanson et Comp., 1784, issue no. 3.
voice/pf
B: Bc. D: B–MG, DS, HR, Mbs (1784), ZW (1784). F: Pc, Pn. GB: Lbl.
RISM B/II (Mlle. Eichner, p.130) Eitner, Cohen, MGG, Friedländer-Lied.

[Work(s)] in: *Lieder, Arien und Duette beym Klavier*. . . . [ed. Johan André].
Berlin: Haude und Spener (C. S. Spener), 1780–81.
voice/kbd
B: Bc. D: Bds, HAb. F: Pc. US: NH. USSR: KA (this location not
confirmed).
RISM B/II (M. A. Eichner, p. 218), Eitner, Cohen, Königsberg.

Zwölf Lieder mit Melodien für Klavier. Potsdam: Carl Christian Horvath,
1780. Texts by Overbeck, Bürger, Jakobi, Goethe, and others.
voice/kbd
B: Bc. D: BNu, UNikb. Copy in Ars Fem coll.
RISM A/I (E 572), Cohen, Eitner, MGG, Friedländer-Lied, Frauenmusik, letter
(Ars Fem).

Elizabeth, Princess of England (daughter of **King George III,**
married **Friederick V, Landgrave of Hesse-Homburg**)
1770, London–1840, Frankfurt am Main
The Life, Death, and Burial of Cock Robin [cantata]. ("Little Robin Red Breast
sat upon a Pole.")17 pp. S.l.: s.n., n.d.
voice/pf
GB: Lbl [K.9.c.13.].
CPM.

Elizabeth (von Saxe-Weimar?)
before 1800
3 Duetto [*sic*] a Cembalo della Sua fedele Sorella Elisabetha. Contents:
"Ricordati ben mio che mi giurasti amor," "Numi se giusti siete," "Amo te
solo." Ms. score. 4 pp. Texts by Pietro Metastasio.
2 voices/hpsch
D: WRtl (Mus VII a 312).
RISM A/II (#22284).

Ellis, Mrs.
n.d.
Sympathy. Song.
voice/pf
US: NH. Copy in Ars Fem coll.
Letter (Ars Fem).

Erpach, Amalia Katharina von, Countess. See **Amalia Catharina (Katharina), Duchess of Erbach (Erpach),** née **von Waldeck zu Eisenberg**

Esprit, Charlotte. Said by Cohen to be pseud. of **Krumpholtz, Fanny**

Essex, Margaret
pub. 1795–1807, London
Absence. [Song.] London: for the author [c. 1795]. Text by T[imothy?] Essex.
voice/pf
GB: Lbl [G.361.(66.)].
CPM, BUC, Cohen (gives pub. as Birchall).

The Amusement of a Leisure Hour. From: *Easy Airs for the Pianoforte or Harp.* London: Birchall for the author [1807]. 3 pp.
pf or harp
GB: Lbl [h.109.(27.)].
CPM, Cohen.

Beautiful eyes. A canzonet for the harp, or piano forte. London: Robert Birchall, for the composer [c. 1795]. 3 pp.
harp or pf
GB: Lbl [G.361.(68.)], Ob. Copy in Ars Fem coll.
RISM A/I (E 844), BUC, CPM (date as 1801), Eitner, Cohen, letter (Ars Fem).

Good humour's my motto. A favorite canzonet for the piano forte or pedal harp. London: Robert Birchall, for the composer [ca. 1795].
pf or pedal harp
GB: Lbl [G.361.(71.)]. Copy in Ars Fem coll.
RISM A/I (E 845), BUC, CPM (date as 1800), Cohen, Eitner, letter (Ars Fem).

The olive branch. [Song] written and set to music with a harp or piano forte accompaniment. London: Robert Birchall, for the author [1802]. 3 pp.
voice/pf or harp
GB: Lbl [G.361.(67.)], Ob.
RISM A/I (E 842), CPM, BUC, Cohen.

Select songs. Contents: 1. The Silent Admirer. 2. Unfading Beauty. 3. Humid Seal of Soft Affection. 4. The Butterfly. 6. The Lover's Address. 7. Cupid's Dismissal. London: Robert Birchall, for the author [c. 1795–1800].

voice/pf
1–2. GB: Lbl [G.361.(64–5)]. 3., 4., 6., 7. GB: [H.1668.(22–25.)], Ob.
Copy in Ars Fem coll.
RISM A/I (E 841), CPM, BUC, Cohen, Eitner, letter (Ars Fem).

Three sonatas [D, B, B-flat] *for the piano forte . . . with an accompaniment for a violin ad libitum . . .* op. 1st. London: printed for the composer [c. 1795]. 23 pp.
pf/vln ad lib.
GB: Lbl [g.144.(2.)], Ob. Microfilm of GB: Lbl copy in C. Johnson coll.
RISM A/I (E 843), BUC, CPM (date as 1796), Cohen, Eitner, letter (C. Johnson).

Evance, Miss
pub. 1805?, London
'*Tis Wither'd,* a Song, to the memory of Her Royal Highness Princess Charlotte Augusta, of Saxe Coburgh. London: Clementi [1805?].
song
GB: Lbl [H.1652.j.(3.)].
CPM.

Evance, (Miss?)
pub. 1796, London
[Work(s)] In: *Psalms, hymns and anthems, for the Foundling Chapel . . .* London: Skarratt, 1796.
voice(s)
D: Hs. GB: Lbl.
RISM B/II (Sup. p. 408).

F

F., Mlle de
pub. 1700, Paris
[Song] in: *Recueil d'airs sérieux et à boire, de différents auteurs. Pour l'année 1700.*
Paris: C. Ballard, 1700.
song
F: Pc (2ex.), Pn. Other library holdings incomplete.
RISM B/I (1700 [2]).

Fedele, Diacinta, Romana
b. Rome, pub. 1628, Vicenza
Scelta di villanelle napolitane bellissime con alcune ottave sciciliane nove, con le sue intavolature di guitarra alla spagniola. Posta in luce da me Diacinta Fedele, Romana. Vicenza: Francesco Grossi, 1628.
voice/Spanish guit
GB: Lbl [1071.g.16.(8.)]. Copy in Ars Fem coll.
RISM A/I (F 150), CPM, Bowers & Tick, Cohen, letter (Ars Fem).

Fenton, Miss
pub. c. 1817, London
Ten favorite fantasies for the pianoforte. London: Chappell & Co. for the author [1817].
pf
GB: Lbl [h.110.(3.)].
CPM.

Ferrier, Charlotte
pub. 1823, London
Farewell bright illusion [song]. London: [1823]. Text by G. L. Chesterton.
song
GB: Lbl [H. 1669.(5.)].
CPM.

Festetits, Julia
n.d.
Pièces, arr. for pf 4 hands. Ms.
pf (4 hands)
H: KE.
RISM A/II #01644.

Finch, Miss

pub. c. 1800, Edinburgh
Capt Campbell of Shanfield's march. Edinburgh: J. Hamilton [c. 1800].
pf
GB: En.
RISM A/I (FF 804 I, 1), BUC, Cohen.

Fitz-Gerald, Paméla (Mrs. Edward Fitz-Gerald)

d. 1831
"I Remember how my child." Song. Ms. 4 pp.
voice/pf
D: DO (Mus. Ms. 2680). GB: En. Copy of GB: En in Ars Fem coll.
RISM A/II (#87845), letter (Ars Fem).

Flad (Fladt), Josephine von, née Kanzler (Giuseppa di Flad, nata Canzler)

1778, Martk-Tolz, near Munich–1843
[Albumleaf. Emuleation einer Fuge.] 1 p. Autograph, marked at the end
"München, den 17. Fbr. 1838. von Josephine von Flad."
unspecified
D: Mbs (Mus. Mss. 9075).
Letter (D: Mbs).

"Ich denke Dein." 4 voice canon. Text by Goethe. 1 p. Autograph ms.,
Munich, Sept. 7, 1836.
4 voices
D: Mbs (Mus. Mss. 11496).
Letter (D: Mbs).

[Kanon für Klavier, C-Dur]. Autograph ms., c. 1840. 2 pp. [Dedicated to
Rudolf Joseph Schachner (1816–1896), composer and piano virtuoso, who
was a piano student of J. von Flad. See D: Mbs cat.]
pf
D: Mbs (Mus. Mss. 12594, formerly owned by G. L. de Baranyai,
Munich).
Letter (D: Mbs).

Missa [C Major] . . . 6 voci, 4 viole, violoncello, contrabasso con organo
[without Gloria]. 14 partbooks. Ms. copied c. 1836.
6 voices/4 vlas/vlc/db/org

D: Mmk (Mm 369).
Michaelskirche.

Missa [C Major] . . . VI vo[cum] . . . [without Gloria]. Score, 14 pp. Ms.
copied c. 1840.
SATTB
D: Mbs.
Letter (D: Mbs).

Missa [F Major] . . . 4 voci [without Gloria]. 8 partbooks [two copies of
each part].
SATB
D: Mmk (Mm 370).
Michaelskirche.

Missa quadragesimalis [g minor] . . . 6 voci [without Gloria]. 16 partbooks
[some in duplicate]. Ms. copied c. 1840.
SSATTB/3 vlns/2 vlas/vlc/db/org
D: Mmk (Mm 371).
Michaelskirche.

Rondo pour le Pianoforte composé presenté à Mdme la Princesse
Mathilde de Bavière. 7 pp. Ms.
pf
D: Mbs (Mus. Ms. 3519).
Letter (D: Mbs).

Sei canzonette a due Voci con Accompagnamento di Cembalo composte da
Giuseppa di Flad, nata Canzler, Op. III. Monaco: Dalla lithografia di
Giuseppe Sidler, n.d. 23 pp.
2 voices/hpsch (pf)
D: Mbs (4 Mus.pr. 48480).
Letter (D: Mbs).

Fleming, Lady
fl. before 1775, English
Lady Fleming's Favourite Minuet [arr. J. Dietz], *Six Variations on Lady Fleming's
Favourite Minuet.* London: Welcker, c. 1775.
pf
Source of original unknown. Dietz's variations are in GB: Lbl, Ob.
Cohen, BUC.

Flint, Lady

pub. c. 1815?, London

C'est mon ami, rendez-le moi ("Ah! s'il est dans notre village"). Romance. London: [1815?].

song

GB: Lbl [H.2831.(38.)].

CPM.

Foote, Maria, Countess of Harrington (married **Stanhope**)

1797?–1867

The Cypress Wreath ("O Lady twine"). [Song]. London: [1820?]. Text by Sir W. Scott.

song

GB: Lbl [H.2815.b.(15.)].

CPM.

"You ask me to wake the soft strain." Canzonet. London: [1820?].

song

GB: Lbl [H.1669.(15.)].

CPM.

Ford, Ann (married **Thicknesse**)

1737–1824

Instructions for playing on the musical glasses . . . by Miss Ford. London: [c.1761].

20 pp. of music. [first instruction book for the glass harmonica]

musical glasses (instruction book)

GB: Lbl (a photostat facsimile) [b.5.]. US: CA.

CPM, NUC (as Thicknesse, NT 0148722), MGG (entry on "Glasharmonika"), RISM-EICM (as Thicknesse, Ann).

A letter from Miss F—d, addressed to a person of distinction. With a new ballad to an old tune. Sent to the author by an unknown hand [arr. by Miss Ford]. 1. London: 1761. 2. 2d ed. with a postscript. London, 1761.

song

US: NYp, NH (2 eds.), CA, Cn (2 eds.), U, DM (2 eds.).

NUC (NT 0148723–4).

Lessons and Instructions for playing on the Guitar. [London]: Author [c.1761].

9 pp.

guit (instruction book)

GB: Lbl [i.160.c.].
CPM.

Forrest, Margaret

pub. c. 1780, London
*Six sonatas for the harpsichord or piano forte with accompaniments for a violin and bass
. . . op. l.* London: William Napier, for the author [c.1780]. Parts.
hpsch or pf/vln & b (vlc)
GB: Ckc, Lbl [h.70.c.]. US: NYp. All surviving copies lack vln and b parts.
RISM A/I (F 1526, FF 1526), NUC (NF 0247139), CPM, Cohen.

Fowler, Miss

pub. c. 1816, London
My native Land good Night (Version of *My native shore adieu.*) 1. 3d ed. London:
T. Williams [1817?]. 3 pp. 2. 4th ed. (2 versions, in C & B-flat). London:
T. Williams [1827]. 5 pp. 3. New York: W. Dubois [1821?]. 4. Philadelphia:
J. G. Klemm, [1823–24]. 2 pp. 5. As sung by Mrs. French. New York:
Torp & Unger [c. 1839].
voice/pf
1–2. GB: Lbl [H.1653.e.(27.)], [H.1654.z.(33.)]. 3. US: CA, NYcug, NYp,
PHf, PIlevy, PROu, Wc, WOa. 4. US: Cn. 5. US: NYp.
1–2. CPM. 3. NUC Sup. (NSF 0032366). 3–4. Wolfe (2846). 5. Tick.

My native shore adieu ("Adieu! adieu! my native shore") Poem from Lord
Byron's *Childe Harold* sung in the revived comic opera, *Maid of the Mill.*
1. London: T. Williams [1816]. 5 pp. 2. New York: Wm. Dubois [c. 1817].
3. New York: John Paff [1811–17]. 4. In G. S. Thornton: *The Melodist*, I,
pp. 227–230. New York, 1820. Text and melody only. See also *My native
Land good Night.*
voice/pf
1. GB: Lbl [H.1669.(19.)]. 2. US: AB, BAhs, Bp, BUg, CAdriscoll,
ECstarr, NYcuh, NYp, PROu, WOa. 3. US: NYp, PROu, Wc. 4. US: CA,
Cn, NH, NYp, Wc.
*1. CPM. 2. Wolfe (2844A), Tick. [Brown & Stratton (1897) & Tick consider
Fowler erroneous for Eliza Flower (1803–1846), but first publication dates are too
early.] 2–4. Wolfe (2844, 2844A, 2845).*

Fresnoy, du, Madame. See **Dufresnoy, Madame**

Freystaler, Maria (name uncertain)

Sonata per il Clavi-Cempalo [*sic*] e Violino. 2 partbooks.

hpsch/vln
D: Mbs. (modern location not confirmed).
Eitner.

Frotta, Judith
pub. c. 1825, Milan
Fantasie pour la Guitare sur le duo de Mr Paer: Quel sepolocro che racchindo. Milan: [1825?]. Arrangement by Frotta.
guit
GB: Lbl [h.259.c.(11.)].
CPM.

G

G., G., Lady
pub. c. 1800, Edinburgh
A Favorite New March & Quick Step. Edinburgh: Urbani & Lisbon [1800?].
pf
GB: Lbl [h.1568.b.(6.)].
CPM.

G., M. et C. de, Mmes
before 1800
Duo ("M'aimeras-tu toujours Silvie"). Musique et accompagnement par
Mmes M*** et C*** de G***. S.l.: s.n., n.d.
2 voices/pf
CH: LAcu.
RISM A/I (IN 204).

G. C., Miss
pub. late 18th cent., Edinburgh
[Work(s)] in: *The Scots musical museum . . . of six hundred Scots songs with proper
basses for the piano forte &c. . . .* the airs chiefly harmonized by S. Clarke.
Edinburgh: J. Johnson [1787–1803]. 6 vol.
voice/pf
B: Bc. BR: Rn. C: SA. CH: Bu. EIR: Dn. GB: A, Cu, DU, En, Esl, Ge,
Lbl, Lcm, Mp, P, WI. US: Cn, DE, HA, MI, Su, U, Wc, WI. Holdings in
other libraries are incomplete runs.
RISM B/II (p. 350).

G . . . D, Madame
pub. c. 1820, Paris
Romance d'Inès ("Unique objet"). Paris: s.n. [1820?]. Text by Florian.
song
GB: Lbl [H.2831.(42.)].
CPM.

Gail (Gayl), Edmée-Sophie, née Garre (usually found as Sophie Gail)
1775, Paris–1819, Paris
"A mes fleurs." Hymne à 3 voix. 1. Paris: Boboeuf et Die, 1838. 2. Paris:
Ph. Petit successeur, n.d. 3 pp.
3 voices/pf

1. Location not known 2. D: Mbs (2 Mus.pr.3736, Beibd.13).
1. MGG. 2. Letter (D: Mbs). Cohen.

Angela, ou L'atelier de Jean Cousin. [1 act opera, composed together with Boieldieu] Ms. 1814. Libretto by Mr. d'Epinay.
stage work
F: Pn.
Cohen, NG (see Boieldieu), MGG, Olivier.

"Celui qui sut toucher mon cœur." Tyrolienne. [with pf]. 1. Paris: Costallat, n.d. 2. [Song.] London: I. Power [1819?]. 3. [1835?]. 4. [1864].
5. Avec variations pour la voix, suives d'une ritornelle, dediès Mme. Beylard par P[eter] Gilles [arranger]. The voice part may be played with the flute an octave higher or as written. Philadelphia, Author [Giles] 1823.
[Instrumental arrangements]: 6. for the Piano Forte by E. C. Vernet [1832]. 7. with variations for the Piano Forte by J. Calkin [1824].
8. Fantasia on, by Pio Cianchettini [1819]. 9. Tirolienne de Mme Gail, Barcarole . . . Variés pour la Harpe [1820?]. 10. Used as a theme for variations by Farrenc, H. Karr, M. Lupperger, Niedermeyer, Vernier. Ms.
[Many other arrangements and sets of variations by other composers.]
1–4. voice/pf. 5. voice/pf, with optional fl. 6–8. pf. 9 harp. 10. voice/pf
1. Location not known. 2–4. GB: Lbl [G.424.n.(10.)], [G. 545.(48.)], & [H.1772.k.(15.)]. 5. US: PHf. 6–8. GB: Lbl [h.2128.(1.)], [h.292.(6*.)], [h.324.(3.)], [h.173.c.(23.)]. 10. F: Pn (Vma 117[12]).
2–4., 7–9. CPM, S. Wolfe (2891), 2–4., 10. MGG, NG, Cohen.

Cinq Romances Françaises. [contents]: Inès ("Ce soir Inès"), Le Barde, Le Petit Questioneur ("Quelle est cette pastourelle"), Amour de la jeunesse, Je ne veux plus aimer. Paris: s.n. [1820?]. Texts by various authors.
voice/pf
GB: Lbl [G.555.(1.)].
CPM.

Deux nocturnes et une romance avec acc. de forté-piano. Paris: A. Le Duc [180–?].
7 pp.
2 voices/pf (nocturnes); 1 voice/pf (romance)
US: STu (M1 A3 v. 5).
NUC (NG 0011598).

Deux Nocturnes français à deux voix et une Tyrolienne . . . 1er recueil. 1. Paris: Chez l'auteur [1816?]. 2. 5 vol. in 1. Vol. 1, Paris: Chez l'auteur; vol. 2,

Paris: Gaveaux; vols. 3–5, Paris: Petit. 3. Paris: Chez l'auteur et chez Gaveaux. 7 pp.
2 voices/pf
D: UNikb. 1. GB: Lbl [P.P.1947]. 2. US: CA. 3. D: Mbs (2 Mus.pr. 3736, Beibd.8).
Olivier. 1. CPM. 2. OCLC (23148808). 3. Letter (D: Mbs).

Dimanche dans la Plaine. Nocturne à 2 voix. 1. Paris: A la Lyre moderne (#166). 3 pp. 2. . . . avec pfte. ou de harpe. Paris: Nadermann, n.d. 3. La Haye: Lyon (PN 277), n.d. 4. Paris: Mme Benoist, n.d. Poem by S. Gail.
2 voices/pf or harp
1. D: Mbs (2 Mus.pr.3693, Beibd.22). 2. I: Mc. 3. D: Dlb. 4. Location unknown.
1. Letter (D: Mbs). 2. Olivier, Eitner. 3. Letter (D: Dlb). 4. MGG.

Duetto ("Ah come volano"). Musique et accompagnement de piano ou harpe. Paris: Petit successeur, n.d. 7 pp.
2 voices/pf or harp
D: Mbs (2 Mus.pr.3736, Beibd.12).
Letter (D: Mbs).

Duetto L'Eco. Ms., c. 1820. 6 pp. Words by Conta Alfieri.
voice (S)/pf
D: RH (Ms. 923).
RISM A/II (#83063).

"Heure du soir" [with piano or harp]. 1. In: *Journal hebdomadaire, composé d'airs d'opéra comiques . . . avec accompagnement de clavecin . . . .* Paris: Le Duc, May 30, 1808. 2. In: *Le Chansonnier des Grâces avec la musique gravée des airs nouveaux.* Paris: Louis, 1809.
voice/pf or harp
1. S: Skma. US : Wc. 2. F: BO, VN.
1–2. RISM B/II (pp. 126 & 211). Cohen, MGG.

Honneur et patrie (Salut au vaillant).
voice/kbd (pf)
A: Wgm.
Cohen, Eitner.

"Jeune beauté cause de mon martyre." Boleros [d minor]. 1. In: *Tänze und Lieder,* pp. 388–41. Ms. 2. [in b minor] Ms.

voice/pf
1. D: Mbs (Mus. Mss. 16276). 2. CH: AR [Mus. Ms. A 32 (Ms. 7483)].
1. Letter (D: Mbs). 2. RISM A/II (#10966).

La Barcarole: avec paroles italiennes et allemandes . . . a 1 ou à 3 voix avec accompagnement de piano-forte ou guitarre. S.l.: s.n., n.d.
1 or 3 voices/pf or guit
D: Mbs (4 Mus.pr. 9105).
Letter (D: Mbs).

La jeune et sensible Isabelle. Romance à deux voix, chanté par Mlles de Lihu.
1. London: Birchall [1815]. 5 pp. 2. London [1830?] 3. Also arr. by F. J.
Dizi as *Introduction & Air* (by E. S. Garre) *with Variations for the Harp.* S.l.: s.n.
[1827?].
voice/pf; also arr. for harp
GB: Lbl 1. [H.1653.yy.(22.)], 2. [G.809.a.(6.)], 3. h.173.d.(9.)].
CPM, Cohen (as La jeune et charmante Isabelle).

La plus belle. Romance ("J'avais juré"). Paris: s.n. [1820?].
voice/pf
GB: Lbl [H. 2831.(43.)].
CPM.

La Sérénade, excerpt from. *Barcarole venitienne à 3 voix avec acc. de piano.*
1. arrangée par M.me Gail. Autograph (?) ms. 2 pp. 2. Ms. copy. 3. Paris:
Petit. 4. Arrangée à 3 voix par Mde Gail. Avec accompagnement de
pianoforte (ou guitarre) ou à 4 voix sans accompagnement [with Germ.
trans.]. Bonn et Cologne: Simrock (Pl. # 1826). Score (4 pp.) + 4 voice
parts.
1–3. 3 voices (STB)/pf 4. 3 voices/pf or guit; 4 voices unacc.
1–2. D: DO (Mus. Ms. 2430, Mus. Ms. 1238). 3. A: Wgm. I: unacc. Mc.
4. D: Mbs (4 Mus.pr. 1179).
1–2. RISM A/II (#74110,#74551). 3. Cohen, Eitner, Olivier. 4. Letter (D: Mbs).

La Sérènade, excerpt from. "O pescator dell'onda." Chanson Vénitienne.
1. In: 10 Lieder für 1 Singst. mit Klavier . . . Ms.
2. A version for 3 voices and piano. Berlin: Simrock, n.d.
1. voice/pf 2. 3 voices/pf
1. D: Mbs (Mus. Mss. 8049(9)). 2. Location not known.
1. Letter (D: Mbs). 2. Olivier.

La Sérènade, excerpts from. Duo ("Beauté, divine beauté"), Duo ("Que dis-tu?"), Polonaise ("Ah! Croyez moi sa douceur est extrême"), Couplets ("Boire et ne jamais se griser"), Barcarole vénitienne ("O pescator dell' onda fidelin"), Boléro ("Amo te solo") [Paris: Ch. Petit, 1818?].
1–3 voices/pf (optional acc. for harp)
US: NYp.
NUC (NG 0011600).

La Sérènade [opéra-comique in 1 act]. Paris: Ch. Petit [1818?]. Score. 205 pp. Perf. 1818 at Théâtre Feydeau. [Libretto by Sophie Gay (1776–1852), after the comedy by Regnard].
stage work
B: Bc. GB: Lbl [G.129.]. US: NYp.
Cohen, Eitner, NG, Mellon, MGG, Olivier, CPM, OCLC (21527008).

L'Amour et l'amitié. Romance. Accompagnement de lyre ou guitare par Meissonnier jeune. Paris: Ph: Petit [c. 1820].
voice/lyre or guit
GB: Lbl [E.1717.o.(34.)].
CPM.

L'autre Jour. Romance. London: s.n., n.d. [1830?].
voice/pf
GB: Lbl [G. 806.b.(23.)].
CPM.

Le Chateau de Frankenberg [or Frankemberg]. Romance dédiée son Altesse Royale le Prince Charles de Prusse [words and music by Sophie Gail]. 1. Brussels: Messemaeckers (VN 265). 2. Paris: Petit successeur (Pl.#121). 3 pp.
1. ST/hpsch 2. voice/pf
1. D: Dlb (Mus. 4758–L–501). 2. D: Mbs (2 Mus.pr. 3736, Beibd.11).
1. Letter (D: Dlb). 2. Letter (D: Mbs).

"Le Serment." Nocturnes française à 2 voix [with piano]. 1. In: *Echos de France*, vol. I, p. 122. Paris: G. Flaxland, n.d. 2. S.l.: s.n., 1800.
2 voices/pf
1. I: Mc. 2. D: Kf&m
1. Eitner. 2. Frau & Musik. Cohen

Le Vaisseau, ou *le Retour en France.* In: *Journal d'Euterpe,* 5e Année, 12e liv.,
No. 48. 1820, p. 116. Paris.
voice/pf
GB: Lbl [G.547.(15.)].
MGG, CPM.

Les Deux jaloux, excerpt from. Duo. "Parlez, parlez petite amie." Brussels:
Terry (VN 1264. No. 33), n.d.
2 voices/pf (Pf-arr.)
D: Dlb (Mus. 4758–F–501).
Letter (D: Dlb).

Les Deux jaloux, excerpt from. Polonaise. "Monsieur, ce qui se passe ici . . ."
Paris: Gaveaux, n.d.
2 voices/pf
D: Dlb (Mus. 4758–F–500).
Letter (D: Dlb).

Les Deux jaloux, excerpt from. Romance ("Il est vrai que Thibaut mérite").
In: *Chansonnier des Grâces.* Paris: Louis, 1814.
voice/pf, lyre or harp
D: Kf&m, UNikb.
MGG, Frau & Musik, Frauenmusik.

Les Deux jaloux, excerpt from. Trio ("Ma [or Ta] Fanchette est charmante"). 1. Brussels: Terry (VN 1264. #31). 2. Acc. de lyre ou guitare par
Mr. Lami. Paris: P. Gaveaux [c. 1816?]. 3. In: *Echo de France,* vol. I, p. 134.
Paris: Flaxland, 1853. 4. "Ma Fanchette . . . " by G . . . , Sophie, arr. by
R. N. C. Bochsa as *Fantasie et variations . . . pour la harpe.* 5. Arr. by J. B.
Duvernoy, pour Piano [1874].
3 voices/pf (Pf-arr.)
1. & 3. D: Dlb (Mus. 4758–F–502). 2. US: BE. 4., 5. GB: Lbl.
[g.661.b.(38.)], [h.3023.a.(9.)]. Copies in D: Kf&m and UNikb.
*1., 3. Letter (D: Dlb). 2. OCLC (16455798). 4–5. CPM. MGG, Olivier, Frau &
Musik.*

Les Deux jaloux, excerpts from. [Arias from, arranged for 2 violins] in: *Journal
de Violon dédié aux amateurs* [monthly]. Paris: Bornet l'aîné, 1784 (#10).
2 vlns
F: Pc, Tc. US: NYp.
RISM B/II (S. Gail, p. 211), MGG.

Les Deux jaloux, excerpts from. Polonaise ("Monsieur, ce qui se passe"), Duo ("Parlez, petite amie"), Trio ("Je ne me trompe pas"), Trio ("Ta Fanchette est charmante"), Air ("Mon cher Frontin"), Couplets ("Il est vrai"), Duo ("Pour commencer ma chère amie"). Paris: Gaveuax, 1813?, but the Couplets by Petit, c. 1816.
1–3 voices/pf (optional acc. for harp)
US: NYp.
NUC (NG 0011602).

Les Deux jaloux [opéra-comique, in 1 act]. Perf. at Théâtre Feydeau 1813. Paris: Gaveaux, 1813?. Score. 118 pp.
Libretto by Dufresny & J. B. Vial.
stage work
B: Bc. F: Pc. GB: Lbl [(G.129.a.)] (composer's name as Mme Sophie G . . .). US: CA, NYp.
Cohen, Eitner, NG, Mellon, MGG, Olivier, CPM, NUC (NG 0011596), OCLC (23148807).

"Les langueurs." Nocturne française à 2 voix [with piano]. 1. In: *Echos de France*, vol. I, p. 126. Paris: G. Flaxland, n.d. 2. S.l.: s.n., 1803.
2 voices/pf
1. I: Mc. 2. D: Kf&m
1. Eitner. 2. Frau & Musik. Cohen.

Mademoiselle de Launay à la Bastille [1 act opéra-comique], excerpt from. Mlle de Launay . . . , Romance. Musique de Mme Sophie G. Acc. de lyre ou guitare par Mr. Lami. Paris: P. Gaveaux [c. 1815]. [Opera perf. 1813 at Théâtre Feydeau. Libretto by A. F. Creuzé de Lesser, Roger, & Mme. Villiers. Location of complete opera not known.]
voice/lyre or guit
GB: Lbl [E.1717.o.(32.)].
CPM, Cohen, NG, Mellon, MGG, Olivier

Mademoiselle de Launay à la Bastille, excerpts from. Romance ("Ma liberté"), Quatuor ("Madame, madame, madame"), Duo ("L'ordre de la maison"), Polonaise ("Heureux oiseaux") [Paris: Gaveaux, 1813?].
1, 2, or 4 voices & pf or harp
US: NYp.
NUC (NG 0011604), MGG ("Ma liberté").

Medée [opera], [1 scene] from. Ms. score.
stage work (excerpt)
F: Pc.
Eitner, Cohen, NG.

Moeris. Romance [attributed to Sophie Gail, and arr. as Romance variée pour le piano by T. Lecureux, in *Trois morceaux de Salon*, #2. Paris, 1861].
[The original is actually by Sophie Gay, see entry.]
arr. for pf
GB: Lbl [h.849.(3.)].
CPM.

N'est-ce pas elle. Romance. 1. In: *Journal hebdomadaire, composé d'airs d'opéra et opéra comiques, mêlé de vaudevilles . . . avec accompagnement . . . par les meilleurs auteurs . . .* , Paris: Le Duc,1807. 2. Paris: [1820?]. 3. Ms. (on pp. 48–49).
voice/pf
1. GB: Lbl. 2. GB: Lbl [G.547.(37.)]. 3. CH: AR [Mus. Ms. A 30 (Ms. 7528)].
Cohen, MGG. 1–2. CPM. 3. RISM A/II (#11022).

"Ni jamais ni toujours," by Mlle Delieu, arranged by Made. Gail. Paris: Ph. Petit [c. 1820].
voice/pf or harp
D: Mbs, GB: Lbl [G.555.(2.)].
Letter (D: Mbs), CPM. For other versions of this piece see Delieu, Mlle.

"Ni jamais, ni toujours." Nocturn . . . à deux voix . . . avec accompagnement de piano-forte ou harpe. 1. In: *The Harmonicon*, vol. 6, pt. 2, pp. 10–11. 1828. 2. No. 38 in vol. collected by Rosalia Seemuller, detached from: *The Musical Library*, #14, pp. 48–49.
2 voices/pf or harp
1. GB: Lbl [P.P.1947]. 2. US: DM (W.C.L.M780.88 O697E, #38).
CPM, NUC Sup. (NSG 0001781).

"O Pescator dell'onda." Chanson Vénitienne. 1. In: 10 Lieder für 1 Singst. mit Klavier . . . Ms. 2. A version for 3 voices and piano. Berlin: Simrock, n.d.
1. voice/pf 2. 3 voices/pf
1. D: Mbs (Mus. Mss. 8049(9)). 2. Location not known.
1. Letter (D: Mbs). 2. Olivier.

Pigmalione. Duetto ("Evero nò non m'inganuo"), œuvre posthumous.
[Paris]: Petit successeur [after 1819]. 7 pp.
2 voices/pf
D: Mbs (2 Mus.pr.3736,Beibd.14).
Letter (D: Mbs).

Trois Nocturnes français à deux voix . . . 2ème recueil. Paris: P. Gaveaux
[1816?]. 7 pp.
2 voices/pf
D: Mbs (2 Mus.pr. 3736, Beibd.10). GB: Lbl [H. 1797.pp.(8.)].
Letter (D: Mbs), CPM.

Trois Nocturnes français à deux voix . . . 3ème recueil. Paris: P. Petit successeur
(Pl.# 4) [1817?]. 7 pp.
2 voices/pf
D: Mbs. GB: Lbl [H. 1797.pp.(9.)].
Letter (D: Mbs), CPM.

Tyrolienne avec acc. de piano. Paris: Petit, n.d.
2 voices/pf
D: Kf&m. I: Mc.
Eitner, Frau & Musik, Cohen.

Vous qui priez, priez pour moi. Dernière romance de Millevoye ("Dans la
solitaire bourgade"). Paris: s.n. [1820?].
voice/pf
GB: Lbl [G.555.(3.)].
CPM, Olivier, Cohen.

[Work(s)] in: *Feuilles de Terpsichore ou journal composé d'ouvertures, d'airs arrangés
et d'airs avec accompagnement pour le clavecin.* Paris: Cousineau père et fils
(Imbault), 1784–98.
voice/hpsch
A: Wn. D: AD. F: AI, BO, Pa, Pc, Pn, Psg. GB: Ckc, Lbl. All holdings are
incomplete runs.
RISM B/II (Gail, p. 181).

Galli, Caterina (Signora) (may be the **Catterina Gallo** mentioned by Forkel)

c. 1723, Cremona?–1804, Chelsea, England
Conservati fedele [ariette].

S/vln/vla/db
US: SM.
Cohen, NG (bio).

"Se son Lontana." In: *Twelve Duets or canzonets for two german flutes or voices. Composed by sigr. Hasse &c.*, to which is added the favourite song of signra. Galli. London: Walsh [1748]. [See also: "When first I saw thee graceful move," an English version of this song.]
voice/kbd
A: Wgm. CH: LAc. GB: Bu, Ckc (2 ex.), CDp (2 ex.), Er, Lbl [E.525.(4.)], Mp. US: NYp.
RISM B/II (p. 160), CPM, BUC, Cohen (incorrect as 12 duets), NG (bio). This is the earliest version of this song. The title of the volume refers to Hasse's duets only.

"When first I saw thee graceful move" ["Se son lontana"]. A New Song.
1. [London]: Engraved by Sigra Phillips [c.1750]. 2. S.l., s.n., n.d. 3. In: *The Gentleman's Magazine*, vol. 25, p. 515. London, 1755. 4. In: *Chloe, or the Musical Magazine*, #27 [1760?]. 5. In: *The Universal Magazine*, vol. 33, p. 152, London, 1763. 6. Vol. 25, s.l., s.n. 7. [London], 1760, with arrangement for two German flutes. 8. In: A. Aimwell's [pseud.], *The Philadelphia songster*, p. 11. Philadelphia: 1789. Melody and text only. 9. As "The graceful move" in: *The American musical miscellany: a collection of the newest and most approved songs, set to music*, pp. 158–59. Northampton: A. Wright for D. Wright and Co. 1798. [Duet version of the song]: 10. In: *Social Harmony*, London [1818], p. 291. 11. In: *Musical Library*, London [1854], vol. 4, p. 145. 12. Ms., 1773. 13. For two voices, two german flutes, or two guittars. S.l., Sk[illern], n.d. 14. [For two voices]. S.l., s.n., n.d.
1–6., 8–9. voice/kbd. 7. voice/kbd/2 fls. 10–12. 2 voices (TT)/kbd. 13. 2 voices or 2 fls or 2 guits. 14. 2 voices.
1. GB: Obharding. 1–7. GB: Lbl [G.313.(95.)], [250.c.2], [G.425.mm.(8.)], [G.433.], [P.P.5439]. Lbl also has many other editions published as "anonymous." 8. NYp. 9. GB: Ge, Gm, Lbl. US: A, AA, Bp, BU, Cn, CAh, HP, LA, Nf (2 ex.), NH, NYcu, NYh, NYp (2 ex.), NYts, PHf, PHu, PRts, PROub, R (2 ex.), Su, SM, U, Wc, WOh. 10–11. US: Bp (#233 in *M. 215.21, #50 in **M.235.18.40). 12. GB: Ge (R. d. 26). 13. GB: Obharding. 14. US: BAep.
1–7. RISM A/I (GG 167 I, 1–5., 7–8.), CPM, BUC. 8–9. Sonneck, RISM B/II (p. 85). 10–11. NUC (NG 0025229). 12. RISM A/II (#70541). 13–14. RISM A/I (GG167 I, 8, 167 I, 6), Cohen (duet version), NG (bio).

[Work(s)] in: *A choice collection of two, three & four part songs, compos'd by . . . eminent masters.* Book 2nd. London: C. and S. Thompson [c. 1775].

2, 3, and/or 4 voices/kbd
GB: Lbl.
RISM B/II (p. 61).

[Work(s)] in: *Dale's introduction to the piano-forte, harpsichord or organ . . .*
containing . . . a variety of lessons . . . selected, arranged, and composed by
J. Dale. London: for the author [c. 1796]. 2 vol.
pf, hpsch, or org
GB: Ckc, Lbl, Ob.
RISM B/II (p. 148).

[Work(s)] in: *Duets or canzonets for two voices, guitars or two german flutes and a*
bass compos'd by sigr. Jomelli, Hasse and the most eminent Italian masters. [Nos.
I–X.] London: J. Walsh [c. 1755–62]
2 voices, 2 guits or 2 fls/b
B: Bc. GB: Ge, Lam. US: CAh. Other library holdings incomplete runs.
RISM B/II (p. 160).

Gambarini, Elisabeth de (**Elisabetta, Elizabeth.** Married Chazal)
1731–1764, London
"Honors, riches, marriage, blessing." Song.
voice/pf
Original location unknown. Modern edition (OP) in: *A collection of*
Uncommon and Rare Pieces of Shakespeare Music in US: Wc (M 1619.5 .S52Al
Case).
US: Wc card cat.

Lessons for the harpsichord, intermix'd with Italian and English songs, opera 2de.
London: author [1748]. 31 pp. With mezzotint portrait of the composer
by N. Hone.
hpsch; voice/hpsch
GB: Cpl, Lbl (2 ex.) [e.9.] & [R.M.15.hg.18.]. US: BE. Copies of the GB:
Lbl copy in C. Johnson coll. and Ars Fem coll.
RISM A/I (G 311), CPM, BUC, Eitner, NG, Cohen, letters (C. Johnson,
Ars Fem).

Organ concerto. Ms.? c. 1764.
org/orch
GB: Lbl. Copy in Ars Fem coll.
Cohen, NG, letter (Ars Fem).

Pastorella per due Violini e Basso [D Major]. 3 partbooks. Ms. [No first name given in manuscript of this piece.]
2 vlns/bc
I: Gi(l).
Genova.

Six sets of lessons [G, D, F, G, C, d] *for the harpsichord,* op. 1. London: author, 1748.
hpsch
GB: Lbl [R.M.15.h.17]. US: STu (M23 G1856), Wc (M1613 .S24 Case). Copies of GB: Lbl copy in C. Johnson coll. and Ars Fem coll.
RISM A/I (G 310), CPM, BUC, NUC (NG 0033505–6), NG, Cohen, letters (C. Johnson, Ars Fem).

XII English & Italian songs, for a german flute & thorough bass . . . opera III. [London]: authoress [c. 1748–50]. 14 pp.
voice/fl/bc
GB: Cpl, Lbl [H.1398]. US: BE.
RISM A/I (G 312) (shows two ex. in Lbl), CPM (lists only one ex.), BUC, Eitner, NG, Cohen.

[Works] in: *Rutherford's compleat collection of one hundred and twelve of the most celebrated minuets and their basses . . . proper for the german flute, violin or harpsichord.* London: D. (& J.) Rutherford [c. 1775–1780]. 2 vol.
fl or vln/bc (hpsch)
GB: Lbl. US: Wc (vol. 1 only). Microfilm of Lbl copy in C. Johnson coll.
RISM B/II (Miss Gambarini, p. 343), letter (C. Johnson).

Gannal, Therese

n.d.
Di tanti palpiti.
2 harps
F: Pn.
Letter (Ars Fem).

Methode complete pour harpe.
harp instruction
F: Pn
Letter (Ars Fem).

6 romances nouvelles.
harp/pf
F: Pn
Letter (Ars Fem).

Gardel, Amélie, Mlle
pub. c. 1800, Paris
De ce ruisseau. Romance. Air et accompagnement de forte-piano ou harpe.
In: *Journal de la lyre d'Orphée*, année 5., no. 3. [Paris:] Les Frères Gaveaux
[c. 1800].
voice/pf or harp
F: Pc. GB: Lbl 9H.346.d.(11.)]. US: Wc.
RISM A/I (GG 391 I,1), RISM B/II (A. Gardel, p. 208), CPM.

Gatehouse, Lady
Twelve songs composed by Lady Gatehouse, published by her ladyship's permis-
sion. S.l., s.n. [17—?]. 17 pp. [Binder's title marked Dibdin.]
voice/pf
US: Cn (VM 1497, D54t).
RISM A/I (G 567), NUC (NG 0076459).

Gattie, Mrs. John Byng
pub. principally 1824–26, London
"Angels who round Jehovah's throne." A motett [*sic*] [with text] written by
Miss Hamilton. London: n.d. [1846].
voice(s)
GB: Lbl [H.1180.(10.)].
CPM.

The Egean Mariner's Song. A duett. ("Bounding o'er the boundless deep")
London: s.n. [1825?].
2 voices/pf
GB: Lbl [H.2830.f.(62.)].
CPM.

"Gracious Son of Mary hear." A hymn, the poetry by . . . H. H. Millman
. . . London: R. Mills for the Proprietor [1840]. 3 pp.
song
GB: Lbl [H.1847.h.(16.)].
CPM.

"O warbling birds" arranged by Mrs. B. Gattie [from: C.M. von Weber, *Preciosa*]. London: s.n. [1826].
voice/pf
GB: Lbl [H.1670.(7.)].
CPM.

"The rose is my favorite flower." A canzonet, the words from Bowring's *Specimens of the Russian Poets.* London: s.n. [1824].
voice/pf
GB: Lbl [H.1670.(8.)].
CPM.

"There's a Bower of Roses," ballad . . . the words from *Lalla Rookh* by Thomas Moore. London: J. Power [1825]. 7 pp.
voice/pf
GB: Lbl [H.1660.l.(4.)].
CPM.

"Through the forest have I gone." A canzonet. The poetry by Shakspeare. London: s.n. [1825?].
voice/pf
GB: Lbl [H.2630.f.(61.)].
CPM.

Gaudin, Mlle de
pub. 1780s, Paris
[Work(s)] in: *Etrennes de Polymnie.* Recueil de chansons, romances, vaudevilles . . . Paris: au bureau de la petite bibliothèque des théatres, Belin, 1785–89. 5 vol.
song(s)
D: LEm. F: Ma, Pcf, Pn, V. US: Wc. Other library holdings incomplete runs.
RISM B/II (p. 168).

Gautherot, Victoire, Mme
pub. 1780s–1810, Paris & London
A favorite air with variations for the harp. London: Author [1810] 6 pp.
harp
GB: Lbl [h.111.(3.)].
CPM.

[Work(s)] in: *Feuilles de Terpsichore ou journal composé d'ouvertures, . . . pour le clavecin* [fortnighly]. Paris: Cousineau père et fils (Imbault), 1784–98. *hpsch*
A: Wn. D: AD. F: AI, BO, D, Pa, Pc, Pn. GB: Ckc, Lbl, T. All library holdings are incomplete runs.
RISM B/II (p. 181).

Gay, Marie-Françoise-Sophie (Gay, Sofia Maria Francesca.
Literary pseud. **Nichault de Lavalette**)
1776, Paris–1852, Brussels
Moeris. Romance ("Mais d'où me vient"). 1. Paris [1815?]. 2. Paroles et Musique de Mme S. Gay. Ms., c. 1847.
voice/pf
1. GB: Lbl [G.547.(13.)]. 2. D: DO (Mus.Ms. 2759).
1. CPM. 2. RISM A/II (#164106, as Gail, Edmée Sophie?).

Genlis (Genglis), Stéphanie-Félicité, Countess, née Ducrest (Du Crest) de Saint-Aubin. (Later Mme, Marquise de Sillery)
1746, Champcéry (Autun)–1830, Paris
[Air varié]. In: Petrini, Henri, *Recueil de trois airs variées et deux sonates . . .* dédiés à Mlle d'Orléans, œuvre Xe. Paris: Cousineau (gravés par Mme Oger), n.d.
harp
F: Pc (2 ex.), Pn.
RISM A/I (P 1639, Petrini), MGG, NG.

Nouvelle méthode pour apprendre à jouer de la harpe en moins de 6 mois de leçons . . . Paris: Mme Duhan, 1802, 2d ed. 1811. [Reprint 1974.]
instruction book
F: Pn.
Eitner, Cohen, NG (bio), MGG.

[Work(s)] in: *Courier lyrique et amusant ou Passe-temps des toilettes par Mme Dufrenoy* [Bi-monthly]. Paris: Knapen et fils, 1 June 1785–16 Jan. 1789. 5 vol.
instrument not determined
CH: Gpu. NL: DHgm. US: Bp. All library holdings are incomplete runs.
RISM B/II [as Mme de Sillery (Genlis)].

Genty, Mlle (Gentry?)
fl. c. 1760s?, France

IIe Recueil de chansons avec accompagnement de guitarre par musique & par tablature.
Paris: de La Chevardière, aux adresses ordinaires [1761]. 21 pp.
voice/guit
F: Pc [4o Y.111(2)].
RISM A/I (G 1585), Paris Lib. Cat., Cohen.

Recueil de chansons avec un accompagnement de guitarre. Paris: auteur, aux
adresses ordinaires (gravé par Mlle Vendôme). 20 pp.
voice/guit
F: Pc (2 ex.) (B.S.[4o Y.111(1, 3)].
RISM A/I (G 1584), Paris Lib. Cat., Cohen.

Georgeon, Henriette
pub. c. 1800–15, Paris
C'est le caprice [song]. Accompagnement de lyre ou guitarr par de Méliant.
Paris: Omont [c. 1815].
Melody only by Georgeon
voice/lyre or guit
D: Bds. GB: Lbl [E.1717.o.(44.)].
RISM A/I (GG 1593 I, 2), CPM.

L'Adieu. Romance [Paris: Nadermann] 1800. 1 p.
voice/pf
F: Pn [B.N. Vm7 59169].
RISM A/I (GG 1593 I, 1), Paris Lib. Cat.

Le pauvre barde. Romance [words and music by H. Georgeon]. Paris: Le
Duc [1805?].
voice/pf
GB: Lbl [H.346.(5.)].
RISM A/I (GG 1593 I, 3), CPM.

Serment d'amour. No. 4. Paris: Mme Duhan & Cie, #450, n.d.
voice/pf
US: R.
RISM A/I (GG 1593 I, 4).

Unissons nos voix et nos cœurs. Le cri du cœur. Paris: Mme Benoit, n.d.
voice/pf or harp
S: St.
RISM A/I (GG 1593 I, 5).

Georgon, Mlle. May be **Georgeon, Henriette**
pub. 1812, Paris
[Work(s)] in: *La Lyre d'Anacréon, choix de romances, vaudevilles, rondes de table, et ariettes* . . . [ed. Mercier de Compiègne & Chazet]. Paris: Favre, 1812.
song(s)
F: Pn. Holdings in other libraries are incomplete runs.
RISM B/II (p. 227).

Geraldini, Josephine
before 1800
Six romances avec accompagnement de piano ou harpe. Paris: Carli, n.d.
voice/pf or harp
I: Nc.
RISM A/I (GG 1593 IV, 1).

Valses pour le pianoforte. S.l.: s.n., n.d.
pf
A: Wgm.
RISM A/I (GG 1593 IV, 2).

Gibson, Isabella Mary, née **Scott**
1786, Edinburgh–1838, Edinburgh
The Bouquet, a song . . . the words by Mr. Pinchen. London: Preston, for the Composer [1805]. 3 pp.
voice/pf
GB: Lbl [H.1683.(35.)].
CPM.

Come sweet Content, an admired rondo, with an accompaniment for the harp or piano forte . . . London: Preston, for the Composer [1805]. 5 pp.
voice/harp or pf
GB: Lbl [H.1683.(34.)].
CPM.

Kenmure's on and awa. A Scottish ballad arranged with an accompaniment for the harp or piano forte by Miss Scott. 2d ed. . . . . Edinburgh: Robt. Purdie [1820].
voice/harp or pf
GB: Lbl [G.425.ff.(14.)].
CPM.

Loch na Garr [song]. [Text] written by Lord Byron. Arranged with symphonies & accompaniments for the harp or piano forte by Mrs. Gibson. 1. Edinburgh: Robt Purdie [1822]. 3 pp. 2. *Loch-na-gar* [song] In: R. A. Smith, *Scotish [sic] Minstrel.* Edinburgh: s.n., 1825.
voice/harp or pf
1. GB: Lbl [H.16001.dd.(1.)], 2. Location not known.
CPM, Cohen, NG (See Robert Archibald Smith).

Mount and go, a favorite Scottish ballad, with symphonies and accompaniments for the harp or piano forte by Miss Scott. Edinburgh: Robt. Purdie [c. 1815]. 3 pp.
voice/harp or pf
GB: Lbl [h.141.gg.(9.)].
CPM.

O say not that my Heart's too small [song]. [Text] written by a gentleman . . . With an accompaniment for the harp: or piano forte by Miss Scott. Edinburgh: Robt. Purdie [c. 1815]. 3 pp.
voice/harp or pf
GB: Lbl [H.2830.g.(57.)].
CPM.

[Psalm tunes]. In: Stevens, Richard John Samuel [church music]. London: Turnbull, 1833.
song
GB: Cfm.
Cohen, NG (See Stevens, Richard).

Row Gondolier, a Barcarolle . . . London: Willis [1840?].
voice/harp or pf
GB: Lbl [G.383.h.(41.)].
CPM.

Ye Banks & Braes of bonny Doon. Arranged for the harp . . . by Miss Scott. Robt Purdie: Edinburgh [c. 1820]. 4 pp.
voice/harp or pf
GB: Lbl [h.2605.ii.(6.)].
CPM.

Gingant, Mlle
early 18th cent., French

[Work(s)] in: *Recueil d'airs sérieux et à boire de différents auteurs pour l'année 1704*. Paris: C. Ballard,1704.
song(s)
CH: MO. F: Pc (2 ex.), Pn.
RISM B/II (p. 312).

Giusti, Marieta
fl. at the Pietà, Venice, 1612–24.
[Textless solo motet with basso continuo.] Ms.
voice/bc
GB: Lbl (Add. Ms. 31504.f.7.)
Baldauf-Berdes.

Goguo, C., Mlle
pub. 1697, Paris
[Air] in: *Recueil d'airs sérieux et à boire de différents auteurs pour l'année 1697*. Paris: C. Ballard, 1697.
song
F: Pc (2 ex). Holdings in other libraries are incomplete runs.
RISM B/I (1697[2]).

Golovyna, Barbara Nicholaevna, Countess, née Princess Golytsin
1766–1821
Romance de Amadis de Gaulies ("Roses d'amour embellissaient ma vie") & "Al buojo vo cercando Nenella dovesta" [for voice and guitar]. #29 in: *Journal d'airs italiens, français et russes [pour chant] avec accompagnement de guitarre* par I. B. Hainglaise. Année I. St. Petersburg: chez l'auteur, et Gerstenberg et Dittmar [1796], columns 58–59.
voice/guit
USSR: Ml (M3 P–I/271(A–I).
Letter (USSR: Ml).

Gore, Katharina, née Francis (Mrs. Charles). Published as Mrs. Charles Gore
1799, Nottingham–?
"And ye shall walk in silk attire." Song. No. 2 in: *Guitar Songs*. London: [1867]. Text by Robert Burns.
voice/guit
GB: Lbl [H.2330].
CPM, Cohen.

The Earlie's Bride & *The Soldier frae the War returns.* Songs, in: *The Musical Bijou* . . . , 1843. p. 19, p. 23.
voice/pf
GB: Lbl [H.2330].
CPM.

The Song of the Highland Chiefs ("Welcome, welcome"). London [1827].
voice/pf
GB: Lbl [H.1670.(36.)].
CPM.

"'Tis three long years." Ballad. London [1827].
voice/pf
GB: Lbl [H.1670.(36.)].
CPM.

Goubau d'Hovorst, Leopoldine

pub. c. 1813, Vienna
Adagio en forme de fantaisie suivi d'un thême varié pour la harpe ou pianoforte.
Vienna: Chemische Druckerei, #1215, n.d.
pf or harp
A: Wgm. CS: Pm.
RISM A/I (GG 3190 I, 10).

Caprice marche et variations sur l'air "O ma chère Musette" pour le pianoforte.
Vienna: Chemische Druckerei, #714, n.d.
pf
A: Wgm. H: KE.
RISM A/I (GG 3190 I, 11).

Caprice pour le piano forte . . . œuv. 9. Vienna: Ludwig Maisch, #424, [1813].
pf
A: Wgm (2 ex.). CS: K, Pnm.
RISM A/I (GG 3190 I, l), Cohen (as Goubau d'Havorst).

Fantaisie pour le piano-forte . . . œuv. 18. Brussels: H. Messemaeckers, #P. 13, n.d.
pf
A: Wgm.
RISM A/I (GG 3190 I, 9).

Fantasie pour le piano-forte . . . œuv. 11. Vienna: Ludwig Maisch, #476, n.d.
pf
A: Wgm.
RISM A/I (GG 3190 I, 3).

Grande sonate à deux piano-forte . . . œuv. 14. 1. Vienna: S. A. Steiner, #2240, n.d. 2. [may be same work as *Sonata in A-Flat* (2 pf). Vienna: Haslinger, n.d.]
2 pfs
1. A: Wgm, Wn (lacking pf II). D: Bds. 2. Location not known.
1. RISM A/I (GG 3190 I, 6). 2. Cohen (as Goubau d'Havorst).

Polonaise en Rondeau pour le pianoforte sur le thème du rondeau "Oh momento fortunato" de l'opéra Camilla de Ferdinand Paer. Vienna: Johann Cappi, #1375, n.d.
pf
A: Wgm.
RISM A/I (GG 3190 I, 12).

Rondeau pour le pianoforte sur un thème tiré de l'ouverture de l'opéra L'amor conjugale de Ferdinand Paer. Vienna: Chemische Druckerei, #880, n.d.
pf
A: Wgm.
RISM A/I (GG 3190 I, 13).

Sonate [g] *pour le pianoforte.* Vienna: Chemische Druckerei, #497, n.d.
pf
A: Wgm. CS: K.
RISM A/I (GG 3190 I, 14).

Sonate pour le piano-forte . . . op. 13. Vienna: Ludwig Maisch, #490, n.d.
pf
A: Wgm. CS: K.
RISM A/I (GG 3190 I, 5).

Sonate pour le piano-forte . . . œuv. 16. Vienna: Ludwig Maisch, #4, n.d.
pf
CS: K.
RISM A/I (GG 3190 I, 8).

Tre divertimenti [a, A-flat, A] *per canto* [e pf] . . . op. 15. Vienna: Pietro Mechetti qdm. Carlo, #346, n.d.
voice/pf

A: Wgm. D: LCH.
RISM A/I (GG 3190 I, 7).

Variations pour le piano-forte sur le canone "Un geloso acerbo sdeguo" tiré de l'opéra Federica ed Adolfo de Adalbert de Gyrowetz . . . œuv. 12. Vienna: Pietro Mechetti qdm. Carlo, #161, n.d.
pf
A: Wgm, Wst. I: Nc.
RISM A/I (GG 3190 I, 4).

Variations pour le pianoforte sur la cavatine "Il mio Visetto" tirée de l'opéra Le due burle de Joseph de Roesler. Vienna: Chemische Druckerei, #1121, n.d.
pf
A: Wgm. CS: Pnm.
RISM A/I (GG 3190 I, 15).

Variations pour le piano-forte sur la romance "Je suis modete et soumise" de l'opéra Cendrillon . . . œuv. 10. Vienna: Pietro Mechetti, #48, n.d.
pf
A: Wgm.
RISM A/I (GG 3190 I, 2).

Variations sur le trio du ballet d'Iphigenie en Tauride de Gluck pour le pianoforte. Vienna: Chemische Druckerei, #561, n.d.
pf
A: Wgm.
RISM A/I (GG 3190 I, 17).

Variations sur un thème russe pour le pianoforte. Vienna: Chemische Druckerei, #629, n.d.
pf
A: Wgm.
RISM A/I (GG 3190 I, 16).

Gougelet, Pierre-Marie de, Mme (same as **Mlle le Grand**)
Méthode ou abrégé des regels d'accompagnement de clavecin, et Recueil d'airs avec accompagnement d'un nouveau genre . . . Œuvre III. Paris: Cousineau [1771].
hpsch, instruction book; voice/hpsch
B: Bc. GB: Lbl [h.3821.r.(3.)] (lacking *Recueil d'airs*). Copy of B: Bc in Ars Fem coll.
RISM A/I (G 3212), RISM-EICM, CPM, letters (C. Johnson, Ars Fem).

Premier recueil d'airs [voice and guitar]. Paris: s.n., n.d.
voice / guit
B: Bc. Copy in Ars Fem coll.
Letter (Ars Fem).

Recueil d'airs tirés des opéra comiques arrangés pour le clavecin ou le forte piano par
Madame Gougelet, ci-devant Mademoiselle le Grand. Œuvre II. Paris:
Hugard de St.-Guy/le Sr. Borrelly . . . , [c. 1770–72]. [Contains
Gougelet's arrangements of music of Berton, Burri, Duni, Monsigny,
Rebel et Francoeur.]
hpsch or pf
F: Pn (2 ex.) (Vm7 5945 & K. 7452). Photocopy in C. Johnson coll.
RISM A/I (GG 3212a), RISM B/II (p. 317), letter (C. Johnson).

Troisiéme recueil d'airs choisis avec accompagnement de guitarre. Paris: Cousineau,
n.d.
voice / guit
I: Nc.
RISM A/I (GG 3213a).

Gouy, Mlle

pub. 1714, Paris
[Work(s)] in: *Recueil d'airs sérieux et à boire de différents auteurs pour l'année 1714.*
Paris: C. Ballard, 1714.
song(s)
F: Pc, Pn. Holdings in other libraries are incomplete runs.
RISM B/II (p. 314).

Grabowska, Clementine (Kleméntya), Countess

1771, Poznan–1831, Paris
Sonata [B-flat Major], *composée pour le piano-forte* par la Comtesse Clémentine
Grabowska. Œuvre II. Poznan: C. A. Simon [180–?]. 15 pp.
pf
US: Cn (8A 742).
NUC (NG 0365404), Sowinski, Pazdirek, Cohen, Eitner.

Gracia Baptista (nun)

pub. 1557, Spain
Conditor Alme. From: Luis Venegas de Henestrosa, *Libro de cifra nueva para
tecla, harpa y vihuela* . . . Alcalá de Hemares, Joan de Brocar: 1557 [organ
tablature].

org
E: Mn (2 ex.).
RISM A/I (V 1108, in Venegas de Henestrosa, Luys), Cohen (as Baptista, Gracia, incorrect order for religious name), letter (C. Johnson).

Grazianini, Caterina Benedicta (Gratianini, Caterina Benedetta)
early 18th century, Italian
San Gemigniano vescovo e protettore di Modena [oratorio]. 1705. Ms. score.
solo voices (SSAB)/orch
A: Wn (Ms. 18683). Microfilm copy in Jackson coll.
Eitner, Cohen.

Santa Teresa [oratorio]. N.d. Ms. score [second spelling of composer's name is in this manuscript].
solo voices (SATB)/orch
A: Wn (Ms. 18684). Microfilm copy in Jackson coll.
Eitner, Cohen.

Grétry, Angelique-Dorothée-Lucile (Lucille, Lucie. Married du Champcourt)
1770, Paris–1790, Paris
Le mariage d'Antonio. Divertissement en un acte et en prose. Perf. Paris, 1786. 1. Paris: Houbant, Lyon, Castaud [c.1786]. Score, 62 pp. 2. Paris: Houbaut [1786–1800?]. 62 pp. 3. Marseilles: Lippi, n.d. Libretto by Mme de Beaunoir, orchestrated by André Grétry.
stage work (opéra-comique)
1. B: Bc (2 ex.). F: Pn (B.N. [Vm5 238], [D.49454], & [L. 4341]). 1–2. GB: Lbl [H.512], [Hirsch.II.368.]. US: DN. 2. NL: DHgm. 3. US: R. Copy of one version in Ars Fem coll.
1–2. RISM A/I (G 4582, GG4582), CPM, BUC, Paris Lib. Cat., Eitner [as Jenny Grétry], NTSU Lib. Cat. 3. RISM A/I (GG 4582), OCLC (2. 21350406), Cohen, Mellon, letter (Ars Fem).

Le Mariage d'Antonio, excerpt. Air. "Ah, quel plaisir." 1. [for 1 voice] Paris: Frère [c. 1786]. 2 pp. 2. . . . arrangé pour le forté piano par M. Beauvarlet Charpentier fils. Paris: Leduc (#109), n.d. Keyboard arr.
1. song. 2. pf arr.
1. F: Pn [B.N.[4o Vm7 813(32)]. 2. S: Skma. Copy of S: Skma in Ars Fem coll.
RISM A/I (G 4583, GG 4583a), Paris Lib. Cat., letter (Ars Fem).

Le mariage d'Antonio, excerpt. "Dès les premiers jours du printemps."
Vaudeville. [Paris]: Frère [c. 1786].
song
F: Pn [B.N.[Vm7 671]. GB: Lbl [B.362.c.(98.)]. Copy of GB: Lbl copy in
Ars Fem.
*RISM A/I (G 4584, GG 4584), Paris Lib. Cat., CPM, BUC, letter (Ars Fem),
Cohen.*

Le mariage d'Antonio, excerpt. "Je ne croyais pas vous déplaire." Romance,
arr. for harp by M. Javurek. Paris: Mlle Lebeau, [c. 1786]
harp
F: Pn [B.N.[A.34503].
RISM A/I (GG 4584a), Paris Lib. Cat.

"Que ce chapeau dont je pare ta tête" [air]. [Paris]: Frère, n.d.
song
S: Sm.
RISM A/I (GG 4584b).

[Work(s)] in: *Courier lyrique et amusant ou Passe-temps des toilettes par Mme.
Dufrenoy* [bi-monthly]. Paris: Knapen et fils, 1 June 1785–16 Jan. 1789.
5 vols.
instrument not determined
F: Pn. Holdings in other libraries are incomplete runs.
RISM B/II (p. 147).

[Work(s)] in: *Etrennes chantantes ou choix des plus nouvelles ariettes, romances et
vaudevilles avec accompagnement de guitarre* . . . Paris: Goujon fils, 1787.
voice/guit
B: Bc. F: Pn, TLm. NL: DHk. US: CAe.
RISM B/II (p. 167).

[Work(s)] in: *Feuilles de Terpsichore ou journal composé d'ouvertures, d'airs arrangés
. . . pour le clavecin* [fortnightly]. Paris: Cousineau père et fils (Imbault),
1784–98.
hpsch
A: Wn. F: AI, BO, D, Pa, Pc, Pn, Psg. GB: Ckc, Lbl. All holdings are
incomplete runs.
RISM B/II (p. 181).

[Work(s)] in: *Feuilles de Terpsichore ou journal composé d'ouvertures, d'airs arrangés . . . pour le harpe . . . .* [fortnightly]. Paris: Cousineau père et fils, 1784–99.
harp
B: Bc. F: Pa, Pc, Pn. GB: Lbl. S: Skma. US: Bp. All holdings are incomplete runs.
RISM B/II (pp. 181–82).

[Work(s)] in: *Journal de harpe par les meilleurs maîtres* [weekly]. Paris: Le Duc. 1781–95.
harp
B: Bc. F: AG, Pa, Pc, Pn. US: Cn. All holdings are incomplete runs.
RISM B/II (p. 207).

[Work(s)] in: *Journal de violon . . . airs d'opéras . . . arietes italienes, rondeaux, vaudevilles et chansonettes arrangés . . . pour deux violons ou deux violoncelle . . .* [monthly]. Paris: Bornet l'ainé, 1784–89. 6 vol.
2 vlns or 2 vlcs
F: Pc, Pn, Tc, T. US: NYp. All holdings are incomplete runs.
RISM B/II (pp. 210–11).

[Work(s)] in: *Journal hebdomadaire . . . airs d'opéra . . . vaudevilles, rondeaux, ariettes françoises et italiennes, duos, romances . . . avec accompagnement de clavecin, . . .* Paris: Le Duc, 1784–1808.
voice(s)/hpsch
B: Bc. D: B–MG, BNu, RH, SWl. F: Pa, Pc, Pn. GB: Lbl. NL: DHgm. S: Skma. US: Cn, Wc. All holdings are incomplete runs.
RISM B/II (pp. 211–12)

[Work(s)] in: *Le Momus lyrique.* Étrennes chantantes et joyeuses. Pour la présente année . . . Paris: frères Savigny [c. 1785].
song(s)
A: Wn. F: BO.
RISM B/II (pp. 239–40).

[Work(s)] in: *Les Délassemens de Polymnie ou les petits concerts de Paris . . . l'ariette du jour, les romances, et les chansons . . . avec violon et basse chiffrée . . .* [bi-monthly]. Paris: Porro. 1786–89.
voice/vln/bc
A: Wgm. B: Bc. F: Pn. I: Nc. All holdings are incomplete runs.
RISM B/II (p. 149).

[Work(s)] in: *Recueil de musique arrangée pour le cistre ou guitarre allemande contenant les plus jolies ariettes avec accompagnement, et des airs variés* . . . par M. Pollet l'ainé. Paris: l'auteur [1782].
guit or lyre (may be with voice)
F: Pn. NL: DHgm. All holdings are incomplete runs.
RISM B/II (p. 328).

Grimani, Maria Margherita

18th cent., fl. 1715–18, Italian
La decollazione di S. Giovanni Battista [oratorio] 1715. Ms. Score.
solo voices (SSATB)/orch
A: Wn (MS. 17666). Copies in Ars Fem coll. and Jackson coll.
Cohen, Eitner, letter (Ars Fem).

La visitazione di Santa Elizabetta [oratorio] 1713. Ms. Score.
solo voices (SAAB)/orch
A: Wn (Ms. 17668). Copies in Ars Fem coll. and Jackson coll.
Cohen, Eitner, letter (Ars Fem).

Pallade e Marte [dramatic work in music]. Ms. Score. Perf. Vienna, 1713.
[Sinfonie [*sic*], 1713 is not a separate work but is the opening movement of this piece.]
stage work, solo voices/orch
A: Wn. Microfilm at US: CAi; copy in Ars Fem coll.
Cohen, Eitner, Mellon, letter (Ars Fem).

Guedon de Presles, Mlle (Guédon, Guesdon)

?–c. 1754. Lived in Paris
"Autrefois sur ma musette." Musette. In: *Mercure de France,* March 1748, p. 149.
unacc. voice without bc
GB: Lbl.
MGG.

"Ave regina coelorum" [motet]; "J'ay perdu l'aimable Sylvie" [chansonnette]; "Adorable blonde" [chansonnette]. In: *Meslanges de musique latine, françoise et italienne, divisez par saisons.* . . . Paris: J. B. C. Ballard, Summer 1731, p. 127, 177, 181.
voice/bc
F: Pn.
RISM B/II (Mlle Guédon de Presles, p. 234), MGG.

"C'est en vain." 1. [Ariette for voice with or without bc]. In: *Meslanges de musique latine, françoise et italienne, divisez par saisons. . . .* Paris: J. B. C. Ballard, Summer 1730, p. 216. 2. "C'est en vain qu'on veut se défendre." Ariette. In: *Mercure de France,* May 1744, p. 983.
voice/with and without bc
F: Pn.
RISM B/II (Mlle Guédon de Presles, p. 234), MGG.

"C'est trop vous montrer" [Récit de basse bacchique, for bass without bc]; "Le berger que suivoit" [for soprano without bc]; "Lorsqu'une cruelle" [for bass with violin]. In: *Meslanges de musique latine, françoise et italienne, divisez par saisons. . . .* Paris: J. B. C. Ballard, Spring 1729, p. 77, 95, 100.
B or S/one with vln, no bc
1. F: Pn. 2. GB: Lbl [298.b.25].
1. RISM B/II (Mlle Guédon de Presles, p. 233). 2. RISM A/I (G 4816), CPM, BUC. NG, Cohen, MGG.

"Dans le séjour" [ariette-rondeau for sop. & bc]; "Tendres amants dans l'ardeur" [air for sop. & bc]; and "Vole amour viens règner" [musette for voice, traverso & bc]. In: *Meslanges de musique latine, françoise et italienne, divisez par saisons. . . .* Paris: J. B. C. Ballard, winter 1730, p. 42, 46, 52.
voice (2 for S)/bc/(one with fl)
F: Pn.
RISM B/II (Mlle Guédon de Presles, p. 234), MGG.

"Depuis peu, j'aime une brunette" [brunette]; "Amour, viens dans mon coeur" [air sérieux]; and "Raccommodons-nous, ma Lisette" [brunette]. In: *Meslanges de musique latine, françoise et italienne, divisez par saisons. . . .* Paris: J. B. C. Ballard, Spring 1731, p. 104, 112, 118.
voice/bc
F: Pn.
RISM B/II (Mlle Guédon de Presles, p. 234), MGG.

"Des oiseaux amoureux" [air tendre]. In: *Mercure de France,* Dec. 1747, II/174.
unacc. voice without bc
GB: Lbl.
MGG.

"D'un tendre amant, l'objet qui règne." Air sérieux. In: *Mercure de France,* Oct. 1742, p. 2279. Paris: 1742.

unacc. voice without bc
GB: Lbl [G4816].
RISM A/I (G 4814), CPM, BUC, NG, Cohen, MGG.

"Guerre, guerre immortelle," air bacchique, "Bois de l'eau," Rigaudon-chanson bacchique, and "Non, Cimène, ni toute son adress," Gavotte-bacchique. In: *Meslanges de musique latine, françoise et italienne, divisez par saisons. . . .* Paris: J. B. C. Ballard, Summer 1729, p. 142, 162, 217.
voice/bc
F: Pn.
RISM B/II (Mlle Guédon de Presles, p. 233), MGG.

"La Bergère indifférente." Musette. In: *Mercure de France*, Sept. 1742, p. 2069. Paris: s.n. 1742.
voice/bc
GB: Lbl [298.b.17].
RISM A/I (G 4813), CPM, BUC, NG, Cohen, MGG.

"L'Amour, belle Philis" [tendresse bacchique for 2 voices without bc] and "Que j'aime à choquer" [chansonnette bacchique for voice and bc]. In: *Meslanges de musique latine, françoise et italienne, divisez par saisons . . .* Paris: J. B. C. Ballard, Fall 1728, p. 232, 241.
1, 2 voices/with and without bc
F: Pn.
RISM B/II (Mlle Guesdon de Presles, p. 233), NG, MGG.

"L'amour d'un air doux et flatteur" [chansonnette]. 1. In: *Mercure de France*, June 1742, I/1425. Paris: s.n. 1742. 2. "L'amour d'un air doux" In: [Collection of 33 French airs principally for 1 or 2 unacc. voices] Ms.
SS without bc
1. GB: Lbl [298.b.16]. 2. US: BE (Ms 800) (Guidon, Mlle).
1. RISM A/I (G 4812), CPM, BUC, NG, Cohen, MGG. 2. Pre-1900 Vocal Ms.

"Le Dieu de mystère." Rondeau. In: *Mercure de France*, Aug. 1742, p. 1845.
voice without bc
GB: Lbl [298.b.17.].
RISM A/I (G 4815), CPM, BUC, Cohen, MGG.

"Le retour du printemps." Chanson Musette. In: *Mercure de France*, May 1742, p. 1196.
voice without bc

GB: Lbl [298.b.15.].
RISM A/I (G 4818), CPM, BUC, NG, Cohen, MGG.

"Petits oiseaux, qui sous ces verds feuillages." Air sérieux. 1. In: *Mercure de France,* March 1742, Paris, p. 567. 2. In: *Meslanges de musique latine, françoise et italienne, divisez par saisons . . .* Paris: J. B. C. Ballard, Spring 1730, p. 212.
voice/bc
1. GB: Lbl 1. [298.b.15.]. 2. F: Pn.
1. RISM A/I (G 4817), CPM, BUC, NG, Cohen, MGG. 2. RISM B/II (Mlle Guédon de Presles, p. 234).

"Quand je songe," air [tenor and bc], and "Parette, ma chère commère," Chansonette bacchique [voice without bc]. In: *Meslanges de musique latine, françoise et italienne, divisez par saisons. . . .* Paris: J. B. C. Ballard, Fall 1729, p. 209, 227.
voice/with and without bc
F: Pn.
RISM B/II (Mlle Guédon de Presles, p. 233), MGG.

"Qu'un jaloux est incommode." Vaudeville In: *Meslanges de musique latine, françoise et italienne, divisez par saisons . . .* Paris: J. B. C. Ballard, Spring 1730, p.142.
unacc. voice without bc
F: Pn.
RISM B/II (Mlle Guédon de Presles, p. 234), MGG.

"Rassurez-vous, Iris," chansonette [voice/bc], "Rendez-voux, trop aimable bergère," ariette [Sop./bc], and "Solitaires témoins," air sérieux [voice/bc]. In: *Meslanges de musique latine, françoise et italienne, divisez par saisons. . . .* Paris: J. B. C. Ballard, Spring 1730, p. 102, 104, 136.
voice (1 for S)/bc
F: Pn.
RISM B/II (Mlle Guédon de Presles, p. 234), MGG.

"Règne amour," Tendresse champêtre [2 voices, without bc]; "Le vin flate," Menuet bacchique [voice/bc]; and "Chantons la gloire," Duo bacchique [2 voices, without bc]. In: *Meslanges de musique latine, françoise et italienne, divisez par saisons . . .* Paris: J. B. C. Ballard, Fall 1731, p. 196, 198, 212.
1 voice/bc and 2 voices/without bc
F: Pn.
RISM B/II (Mlle Guédon de Presles, p. 234), MGG.

"Reviens, reviens parfure amant," air sérieux; "L'Amour déguisé," vaudeville; "Cher Tircis, seul objet," air sérieux; and "Belle Catin, je vous adore," ariette. In: *Meslanges de musique latine, françoise et italienne, divisez par saisons* . . . Paris: J. B. C. Ballard, Winter 1731, p. 41, 50, 53, 56.
voice/bc
F: Pn.
RISM B/II (Mlle Guédon de Presles, p. 234), MGG.

"Sans une brillante fortune," chansonette & "Quel spectacle enchanteur!" récit. De basse bacchique [without bc]. In: *Meslanges de musique latine, françoise et italienne, divisez par saisons* . . . Paris: J. B. C. Ballard, Summer 1728, p. 172, 175
voice/with and without bc
F: Pn.
RISM B/II (Mlle Guesdon de Presles, p. 233), NG, MGG.

"Tu m'accuses d'être volage," "L'Amour d'un air doux," chansonnettes [voice and bc], and "Quand au Styx arriva," chanson bacchique [Bass without bc]. In: *Meslanges de musique latine, françoise et italienne, divisez par saisons* . . . Paris: J. B. C. Ballard, Winter 1729, p. 15, 27, 41.
voice/with and without bc
F: Pn.
RISM B/II (Mlle Guédon de Presles, p. 233), MGG.

"Veni sancte Spiritus," motet [Sop./bc]; "Philis, la jeunesse," ariette [Sop./bc]; and "Belle Célimène" & "Iris, vos jeux," 2 menuetts [voice without bc]. In: *Meslanges de musique latine, françoise et italienne, divisez par saisons* . . . Paris: J. B. C. Ballard, Spring 1731, p. 64, 94, 98.
S/bc. One for voice without bc
F: Pn.
RISM B/II (Mlle Guédon de Presles, p. 234), MGG.

Guest, Jane Mary (Jeanne Marie. Married **Miles**)
c. 1769, Bath–after 1814
The Bonnie Lassie ("Of a' the airts the wind can blaw'). Song. London: s.n. [1830?]. Text by Robert Burns.
voice/pf
GB: Lbl [H.2831.j.(14.)].
CPM.

The bonnie wee wife. Ballad. 1. London: I. Willis, for the Author [1823]. 7 pp. 2. 2d ed. London: I. Willis [1825]. 6 pp. 3. 3d ed. London: I. Willis [1827?]. 4. 4th ed. London: I. Willis [c.1830]. 8 pp. 5. New ed. London: s.n. [1858]. 6. Philadelphia: G. E. Blake, n.d.
voice/pf
1–5. GB: Lbl [H.2831.j.(14.)], [H.1676.(24.)], [H.1652.d.(43.)], [G.425.cc.(17.)], [H.1771,m.(29)]. 6. US: PHu.
1–5. CPM. 6. RISM A/I (GG 4889a).

"Brignal banks." A Glee for four voices. London: Willis [1825]. 11 pp. Text by Sir Walter Scott, from *Rokeby.*
4 voices
GB: Lbl [H.1676.(25.)].
CPM.

"Come buy my garlands gay." Ballad. London: S. Chappell [1826]. 5 pp. Text by Dr. Sigmond.
voice/pf
GB: Lbl [H.1676.(23.)].
CPM.

Dalton Hall ("O Brignal banks"). Ballad. London: s.n. [1830?].
voice/pf
GB: Lbl [G.806.c.(55.)].
CPM.

"Di te non mi fido." Spanish melody arranged as a duet, with an accompaniment for the pianoforte . . . by Mrs. Miles. London: Birchall [1827]. 5 pp.
2 voices/pf
GB: Lbl [h.62.d.(6.)].
CPM.

Divertimento for the Piano Forte, in which is introduced the Round "Hark the bonny Christchurch bells." London: S. Chappell [1829].
pf
GB: Lbl [h151.(9.)].
CPM.

"Fair one, take this rose." Song. London: s.n. [1830].
voice/pf

GB: Lbl [H.2831.j.(13.)].
CPM.

The Fairies' dance. Duet for two voices. 1. London: Lonsdale & Mills [1829].
2. London: s.n. [1863].
2 voices/pf
1–2. GB: Lbl[H.1676.(26.)], [H.1772.v.(18.)].
CPM.

The field daisy: a song. London: C. Lonsdale [1842]. The words from
"Juvenile Rhymes."
voice/pf
GB: Lbl [H.1676.(27.)].
CPM.

Introduction for the Pianoforte and March from Rossini's opera of Ricciardo e Zoraide
... London: s.n. [1820].
pf
GB: Lbl [h.1480.g.(10.)].
CPM.

Jessica ("My Jessica's false"). A ballad. London: s.n. [1825?]. Text by
J. Laurence.
voice/pf
GB: Lbl (2 ex.) [H.2832.j.(9.)] & [H.2830.g.(8.)].
CPM.

La Georgiana: Introduction and Waltz for the Piano Forte. London: Birchall
[1826].
pf
GB: Lbl [h.151.(11.)].
CPM.

La Jeannette: Introduction and original air for the Piano Forte. London: Birchall
[1828]. 11 pp.
pf
GB: Lbl [h. 151.(10.)].
CPM.

La Jolie Julienne. Polacca for the Piano Forte. London: S. Chappell, [1826].
pf

GB: Lbl [h.151.(12.)].
CPM.

Marion, or *Will ye gang to the burn side.* A ballad. 1. London: s.n. [1820?].
2. London: s.n. [1825?]. 3. As: *Marion* ("Will you gang to the ewe bughts
Marion"). New York: Dubois & Stodart [1823–26].
voice/pf
1–2. GB: Lbl [G.807.(31.)], [G.806.c.(56.)]. 3. US: AB, CHAhughes, NYp,
PHf, WOa.
1–2. CPM. 3. Wolfe (5859).

Quatre sonates [G, A, B-flat, E-flat] *pour la clavecin ou piano forte, accompagée d'un
violon . . .* œuvre premier. 1. Berlin: Johann Julius Hummel/Amsterdam:
grand magazin de musique, aux adresses ordinaires, No. 472 [c. 1783].
2. Sonate pour le Clavecin ou Piano Forte accompagnee d'un violon. Ms.
copy of G Major sonata, c. 1780.
hpsch or pf/vln (or fl)
1. D: Dl. 2. DK: Kk (mu6509.2131, lacks vln part). Copy of D: Dl in Ars
Fem coll.
1. RISM A/I (G 4889), letter (Ars Fem). 2. RISMdan. Eitner, NG, Cohen.

Six sonatas [A, D, B-flat, G, E-flat, B-flat] *for the Harpsichord or Piano Forte,
with an accompanyment for a Violin or German Flute* Composd, and most
humbly dedicated (by permission) to her most Gracious Majesty The
Queen of Great Gritain . . . Opera Prima. [London:] T. Harmar [1783].
Score, 60 pp.
hpsch or pf/vln or fl
D: SWl. F: Pc [B.N.[A.34269]. GB: Ckc, Lam, Lbl (2 ex.) [g. 454] &
[R.M.16.d.10]. US: NYp, Wc. Copies of GB: Lbl copy in C. Johnson coll.
& Ars Fem coll., of US: Wc copy in Rempel coll.
*RISM A/I (G 4887), Paris Lib. Cat., CPM, BUC, NUC (NG 0579597), Eitner,
Cohen, NG (bio), Boenke, letters (C. Johnson, Ars Fem, Rempel).*

Six sonates pour la clavecin ou fortepiano avec accompagnement d'un violon. Paris:
Imbault, Siebert [1784]. Parts.
hpsch or pf/vln
F: Pn [Vmg.12317] (hpsch, vln incomplete). Copy in Ars Fem coll.
RISM A/I (G 4888), Paris Lib. Cat., letter (Ars Fem).

Sonata for the Piano Forte, with an accompaniment for the Violin ad libitum. London:
Clementi & Co., for the author [1807]. Score, 29 pp.

pf/vln ad lib.
GB: Lbl [h.151.(8.)].
RISM A/I (G 4887), Paris Lib. Cat., CPM, Eitner, Cohen, NG (bio), Boenke.

"Yes! I'll gang to the Ewe Bughts," an Answer to the Ballad of *Marion*.
Song. London: Goulding, D'Almaine & Co. [c. 1830].
voice/pf
GB: Lbl [H.1980.p.(16.)].
CPM.

Gunn, Anne, née Young (Mrs. John Gunn)
?–1828, England or Scotland
The Elements of Music and of Fingering the Harpsichord. Edinburgh: Muir
Wood/London: T. Preston, c. 1803, 2d ed. 1820 [according to MGG,
probably the earliest keyboard method book in English].
instruction book
location not known
NG, MGG (for both see John Gunn entry).

Instructions for playing the Musical Games; invented by Anne Young.
Edinburgh: C. Stewart, 1801. 66 pp.
instruction book
US: Cn.
NUC (0602186).

*An introduction to music, in which the elementary parts of the science, & the principles
of the Thor. B. & modulation . . .*
1. Edinburgh: Muir, Woods Co., 1803. 2. 2d ed. Edinburgh: J. Ballantyne,
1820.
instruction book
1. GB: Lbl, Gu. US: STu, Wc (MT6.G94 1803). 2. B: Br (7316). GB: Gu.
US: Cn, Wc (MT6. 094 1820).
1–2. NUC (NG 0602187–8), Eitner. NG (see John Gunn entry).

*An Introduction to Music in which the Elementary Parts of the Science . . . as illus-
trated by the Musical Games . . . are fully . . . explained . . . together with a
Description of the Apparatus of the Games.* c. 1803.
instruction book
EIRE: Dn. (as Dubliner Museum für Kunst und Wissenschaft in MGG).
MGG (see John Gunn entry).

Gyllenhaal, Matilda Valeriana Beatrix, Duchess of Orozco (married **Conami,** then **Montgomery-Cederhjelm,** then **Gyllenhaal**)
1796, Milan–1863, Stora Ekeby, Sweden.
[Songs in]: Esaias Tegner, *Frithiof's saga.* Translated from Swedish . . . with XII musical accompaniments [by B. Crusell, the Countess Mathilde Montgomery-Cederhielm, & G. Stephens]. Stockholm: A. Bonnier, 1839.
voice/pf
US: AUS, BE, BK, BO, CH, COu, I, MOSu, NH, NYp, PHkm, ST.
NUC (NT 0079164), Cohen.

H., L., Miss (L. Hime?). See **Hime, Miss**

H., S. M. I. R. See **Hortense (Sa Majesté la Reine Hortense), Queen of Holland**

Haden, Mrs.
pub. c. 1830, London
The Spanish Maiden's Song ("By a Streamlet"). London: s.n. [1830?].
song
GB: Lbl [H2832.a.(29.)].
CPM.

Thou bid'st me to seek Columbia's shades. Ballad. London: s.n. [1830?].
song
GB: Lbl [H2832.a.(30.)].
CPM.

Hagen, Joannetta Catharine Elizabeth von (van)
d. 1810, Massachusetts
The country maid, or *Amour est un enfant trompeur.* With variations for the piano forte or harpsichord by Mrs. van Hagen. S.l.: s.n. [18–?]. 4 pp.
pf or hpsch
US: CAdriscoll.
Sonneck.

Hague, Harriet
1793–1816, England
Six songs. London: s.n., 1814.
voice/pf
GB: Lbl [G.807.d.(26.)].
CPM, Cohen.

Hardin, Elizabeth (may be the same as **Elizabeth Harding** or **Miss Hardin,** see entries)
pub. 1760s–1770, London
Amintor's choice ("Would kind fate bestow a lover"). 1. (In: *London Magazine,* Oct. 1767), p. 530. 2. *Royal Magazine,* vol. XVI (1767), p. 325. 3. London [1767?].
voice/kbd

1–2. GB: Lbl [158,1.12.], [P.P.5441]. 3. C: Lu. GB: Lbl [G.313.(230.)].
US: SM. Copy in Ars Fem coll.
RISM A/I (H 2012, 2013, 2014), CPM (Miss Harding), BUC (Miss Harding),
Cohen, letter (Ars Fem, as Harding).

Six lessons for the harpsichord. London: for the author [c.1770]. 25 pp.
hpsch
GB: Ckc, DU, Lbl [R..M.16.a.13.(6.)], Ob. Copies of GB: Lbl copy in
C. Johnson coll. and Ars Fem Coll.
RISM A/I (H 2015), CPM (Hardin), BUC (Elizabeth Hardin), Cohen, letters
(C. Johnson, Ars Fem (as Harding)).

Hardin, Miss (same as **Hardin(g), Elizabeth?**)
pub. 1760s–70, London
[Work(s)] in: *The Musical magazine, or compleat pocket companion for the year*
1767[–1772] consisting of songs and airs for the german flute, violin,
guittar [*sic*]and harpsichord . . . London: T. Bennett 1767[–1772]. 6 vols.
fl, vln, and/or guit/hpsch
GB: Lbl. Other library holdings incomplete runs.
RISM B/II (p. 246).

Harley, Lady Jane
pub. c. 1827, London?
Introduzione, etc. by B. Negri sopra un tema di Lady J. Harley. Theme only by
Harley
pf
GB: LBl [h.120.(5.)].
CPM.

Harlow, Clarissa (fictional character who wrote song in Samuel
Richardson's novel, *Clarissa*). See **Carter, Elizabeth** for actual composer.

Harrison, Anna Maria
pub. c. 1813–15, London
The Evening was fair. Ballad. London: s.n. [1815?].
song
GB: Lbl [G.805.b.(55.)].
CPM.

"Fair in the shady sweet retreat." Ballad. London: s.n. [1813].
song

GB: Lbl [H.1671.(28.)].
CPM.

Harrison, Anne, née Cantelo. See Cantelo, Anne

Harrison, Emma
pub. c. 1813, London
"Mai l'amor mio verace." Ariette. Acc. for harp & Piano Forte. London:
s.n. [1813].
voice/harp &(or) pf
GB: Lbl [H.1671.(30.)].
CPM.

"Va! Più non dirmi infida." Ariette. Acc. for harp & Piano Forte. London:
s.n. [1813].
voice/harp &(or) pf
GB: Lbl [H.1671.(29.)].
CPM.

Harvey, Mary. See Dering, Lady Mary

Haulteterre, Elisabeth de (Hauteterre, Hotteterre. Married Lévesque)
fl. 1776
IVe Recueil d'airs choisis avec accompagnement de harpe dédié à la Reine par
Boilly . . . Paris: Cousineau [c. 1776]. [This item as Mlle Levesque.]
voice/harp
F: Pc (4 ex.).
NG, RISM B/II (p. 302, as Melle Levesque).

*Recueil de chansons choisies avec accompagnements de harpe . . . ces accompagnements
font très bien sur le clavecin* [arr. by Mlle de Haulteterre]. Paris: Cousineau
[c. 1768]. 19 pp.
voice/harp or hpsch
F: Pc (B.N.[A.34308]).
RISM A/I (H 2407), RISM B/II (p. 323), Paris Lib. Cat., NG.

Hebenstreit, Sophie
n.d.
Six ecossoises et quatre walzes à quatre mains pour le fortepiano. Leipzig: s.n., n.d.
pf

D: HAu.
RISM A/I (HH 4932 I, 1).

Helv . . . . . ., **Mlle**

early 18th cent., French
[Work(s)] in: *Recueil d'airs sérieux et à boire de différents auteurs pour l'année 1704.*
Paris: C. Ballard, 1704.
song(s)
CH: MO. F: Pc (2 ex.), Pn.
RISM B/II (p. 312).

Hemans, Felicia Dorothea, née **Browne**

1793, Liverpool–1835, Dublin
Tyrolese evening hymn ("Come to the sunset tree"), The Sleeper ("Oh lightly tread"). Songs in: *Lydia Kirkpatrick's Songbook: A collection of 109 English songs and Hymns.* Ms. [Composer principally known for poetry and hymn texts.]
voice/pf
US: BE.
Berkeley.

Hemery, Mde. **Clément**

pub. 1799, Paris
Tu ne connois pas ton amant. Romance [Paris: 1799]. In: *Journal des Dames et des Modes,* #V, Troisième Année, p. 72.
song
GB: Lbl [907.h.1.].
CPM.

Hérault, **Mlle**

fl. 1702–1726?, France
La sage bergere ("Bergères, voulez-vous, m'en croise"). In: *Nouveau recueil de chansons choisies* [Vol. III]. Paris: La Haye: chez Jean Neaulme, 1726.
song
A: Wn. B: Lc. CH: N. D: AAst, Bds, B–MG, Bhm, BIR, ERu, Mbs,
W (639,3).
RISM B/II (p. 261), Wölfenbüttel.

[Work(s)] in: *Recueil d'airs sérieux et à boire de différents auteurs pour l'année 1702.*
Paris: C. Ballard, 1702.
song(s)

D: W. F: Pc (2 ex.), Pn, TLc.
RISM B/II (p. 312).

Herville, Mlle
pub. 1710, Paris
[Work(s)] in: *Recueil d'airs sérieux et à boire de différents auteurs pour l'année* 1710.
Paris: C. Ballard, 1710.
song(s)
F: Pn. Holdings in other libraries are incomplete runs.
RISM B/II (p. 313).

Hime, Miss (L. Hime?, L. H.?)
pub. c. 1805–20, Liverpool
My mother. Song from: *Original Poems for Infant Minds.* Acc. harp or
pianoforte. Liverpool: Hime & Son [1805].
voice/harp or pf
GB: Lbl [G.425.tt.(22.)].
CPM.

Young Lochinvar. Song from *Marmion* by W. Scott. Liverpool: s.n., [1820?].
voice/harp or pf
GB: Lbl [H.2817.a.(63.)].
CPM.

Hinckesman, Maria
pub. 1823–28, London
Andante con variazioni per il Piano Forte e flauto ad libitum. London: s.n. [1824].
pf/fl ad lib
GB: Lbl [h.113.(39.)].
CPM.

The blue eyed lassie. [Song, "I gaed a woeful gate."] London: s.n., [1825].
Text by Robert Burns.
voice/pf
GB: Lbl [H.1672.(11.)].
CPM.

Hosanna to the prince of Light. [Hymn] . . . for four voices, Op. 1. London: s.n.
[1824?]. Text by Isaac Watts.
4 voices (SATB)

GB: Lbl [H.1672.(8.)].
CPM.

The old Celtic march performed by the Highlanders on the landing of George the fourth in Scotland, arranged for the Piano Forte by M. Hinckesman. London: s.n. [1828].
pf
GB: Lbl [H.1672.(15.)].
CPM.

The rose and the thistle, arranged as a duet . . . from the tune to which Prince Charles and Lady Eleanor Wemys danced at the last ball given in Holyrood Palace in the year 1745, by M. Hinckesman. London: s.n. [1828].
2 voices/pf
GB: Lbl [H.1672.(14.)].
CPM.

A rose bud drenched in April's show'r; a song. London: s.n. [1824?]. Text by W. G.
2 voices/pf
GB: Lbl [H.1672.(12.)].
CPM.

The snow drop, a rondo with variations for the sostenente, harp or Piano Forte. London: s.n. [1823].
harp or pf or sostenente (bowed piano)
GB: Lbl [h.113.(40.)].
CPM.

The Zostera ("More near to the orb"), a plaintive song. London: s.n. [1824?].
voice/pf
GB: Lbl [H.1672.(13.)].
CPM.

There is a mystic thread of life [song]. London: s.n. [1825]. Text by Lord Byron.
voice/pf
GB: Lbl [H.1672.(9.)].
CPM.

Ye tell me shepherds, a song. London: s.n. [1824].
voice/pf

GB: Lbl [H.1672.(10.)].
CPM.

Hodges, Ann Mary (Mrs.)
d. before 1798
Songs composed by Mrs. Hodges, harmonized and published by Mr.
Hullmandel for the Benefit of her Orphan Children. [London: G. Nichol]
1798. 31 pp.
Melodies only by Hodges.
voice/pf (1 for 3 voices)
AUS: CAnl. D: W. GB: Lbl (3 ex.) [G. 295.(2.), R.M.13.e.23., G.580.],
Obharding. US: BE, LAu (micro), NYp, R, Wc (M 1621. H). Copy of US:
NYp in Ars Fem coll.
*RISM A/I (H 5680, HH 5680), NUC (NH 0421647), OCLC (22879147,
micro. 24528067), Cohen, BUC, CPM, letter (Ars Fem).*

Hoffman, J. A., Miss. (Probably the same as Hoffmann, J., Miss, see
below)
pub. 1795–96, London
A collection of favorite airs, marches and sonatinas for the harp or piano-forte. Op. 11.
London: author, n.d.
harp or pf
GB: Lbl.
RISM A/I (HH 5761a).

*Fourteen country dances for the year 1796 with their proper figures, for the harp or
piano-forte.* 1st book, London: author [1796]. 24 pp.
harp or pf
GB: Gu, Lbl, Ob.
BUC (as J. A. Hoffmann).

*A Sonata for the harp or Piano Forte with the accompaniment for a violin ad libitum
. . .* Op. 16. London: author [c. 1795 or 1796]. Partbooks.
harp or pf/vln ad lib
AUS: CAnl (lacking violin). GB: Gu, Lbl [g.192.a.(13.)], Ob. US: PHu.
*RISM A/I (H 5759–62, HH 5760a, HH 5761), CPM, BUC (as J. A.
Hoffmann), OCLC (21940278), Eitner (hpsch).*

Three sonatas for the harp or piano forte with an accompaniment for a violin . . . [Op.
8]. London: author [c.1795]. Partbooks.
harp or pf/vln

GB: Cu, Gu (incomplete), Lbl, Ob.
BUC (as J. A. Hoffmann).

Hoffmann (Hoffman), J., Miss
pub. c. 1790s–1803, London
A Duett, for the Harp & Piano Forte, or Two Harps . . . Op. 6. London: author
[1803]. 2 partbooks.
harp & pf or 2 harps
GB: Lbl [g.192.a.(7.)].
RISM A/I (HH 5758a), CPM, Cohen (date 1795).

"In yonder vale." A new song . . . the words by C. Rickman. London:
author, 1795.
voice/pf
GB: Lbl [G.366.(16.)], Ob. Copy of GB: Lbl in Ars Fem coll.
RISM A/I (H 5754), CPM, BUC, Cohen, letter (Ars Fem).

Six duetts for two performers on one piano forte. London: author [c. 1795]. 13 pp.
pf (4 hands)
GB: Lbl [g.131.(7.)], Ob. Copies of GB: Lbl copy in C. Johnson coll. and
Ars Fem coll.
*RISM A/I (H 5757), CPM (dated 1801), BUC (dated 1798), Cohen, letters
(C. Johnson, Ars Fem).*

*Three Duetts, the First for Two harps, or One Harp, and One Piano-forte, the other
Two for Two Performers on one pianoforte.* London: author [1795]. 7 pp.
1.: 2 harps or harp and pf. 2, 3. pf (4 hands)
GB: Gu, Lbl [e.108.(7.)], Ob. Microfilm of Lbl copy in C. Johnson coll.
RISM A/I (H 5758), CMP, BUC, Cohen (as two duets), letter (C. Johnson).

The world. A new song . . . the words by C. Rickman. London: author [c.
1796].
voice/pf
GB: Lbl [G.366.(61.)], Ob. Copy of GB: Lbl copy in Ars Fem coll.
RISM A/I (H 5755), CPM, BUC, Cohen, letter (Ars Fem).

"Ye Britons be bold." A favorite song . . . the words by Mrs. Duckrell.
London: author, 1795.
voice/pf
GB: Lbl [G.366.(15.)], Ob. Copy of GB: Lbl in Ars Fem coll.
RISM A/I (H 5756), CPM, BUC, Cohen, letter (Ars Fem).

Hohenlohe, Sophia von, Princess

late 18th/early 19th cent.
"Auf ihr Schwestern, auf ihr Brüder" (Geschwister Lied). 1. [Without composer]. Ms., c. 1790. 2. [Without title or composer]. Ms. c. 1795. 3. Arie. Auf ihr Schestern von prinzes Sophia de Hohenlohe. Ms., 18th cent.
voice/pf
1. D: DGs (A 202). 2. D: BFb (S–am–66). 3. D: DS (Mus. ms 850).
1–3. RISM A/II (#38738, #2619, #10522).

Hohenzollern, Pauline von, Princess

n.d.
Doux Sentiments pour le Piano Forte mise en Musique par S.A. Madame Princesse Pauline Hohenzollern [c minor]. Ms.
voice/pf
CS: BER (HU 749).
RISM A/II (#31746).

Hoijer, Anna Ovena

pub. 1650, Amsterdam
Annae Ovenae Hoijers Geistliche und weltliche poemata. Amsterdam: Ludwig Elzevieren, 1650. Contains two poems with melodies (pp. 282–93). "Christe Gotts eigner Sohn du bist" & "Kommet her, mit fleiß betrachted" (var. of Hassler, "Mein Gemüth").
songs (unacc.)
GB: Lbl. NL: Au, Lu. PL: WRu (this location not confirmed). Copy in Ars Fem coll.
Bohn, Cohen, Eitner, letter (Ars Fem).

Home, Ann. See Hunter, Ann (Anne), Lady, née Home

Horatio (Orzaio), Susanna

17th cent.
[3 songs]. In an Ms. collection, vol. 2, pp. 276–286 [these songs marked by a later hand, Orazio Susanna], 17th cent.
voice (S)/bc
I: Nc (C.I. 13).
RISM A/II (#58461).

[2 cantatas] Di Horatio Susanna. In Ms. collection, vol. 2, pp. 29–34, 214–224 , 17th cent.

voice (S)/bc
I: Nc (C.I. 13).
RISM A/II (#58457).

Horne, Mrs.
pub. c. 1815, Dublin
Head of the Church [Hymn]. Harmonized by David Weyman. Dublin: Geo.
Allan [c.1815]. 3 pp.
Melody only by Horne.
song
GB: Lbl [H.3690.xx.(40.)].
CPM.

Horsley, F. E. (Mrs.)
pub. c. 1815, London
Six Spanish airs, with English words and two original ballads. London: [1815?].
songs
GB: Lbl (2 ex.) [I.276. & R.M.13.e.27.].
CPM.

**Hortense (Eugénie de Beauharnais), Queen of Holland
(S.M.I.R.H., Sa Majesté la Reine Hortense)**
1783, Paris–1837, Arenenberg
Adieux d'une mère à son fils partant pour la croisade. 13 songs in ms.,
18th–19th cent., pp. 66–67, 98–99, 106–07, 110–15, 120–25, 128–29,
140–41, 144–45, 148–49. Texts by Rousseau, Bastide, Piis, Arnantz,
M. elle, Marmontel, Despré. Contents: "Ami sans toi," "Au bord,"
"Écoutes gente demoiselles," "En soupirant j'ai vu," "Enfin je te revois
paraitre," "J'en vu de notre roi," "Je pense à toi quand l'aube," "Je
possède un réduit," "La triste et plaintive romance," "Le dieu de Cytère
vous prend pour sa mère," "Que fais-tu dans ces heux," "Que l'aime le
prairie," "Viens embrasser la mére." Ms.
voice/pf
CH: AR (Mus. Ms. A 30; Ms. 7534, 7540, 7543, 7546, 7548).
RISM A/II (#11028).

[15] Songs with pianoforte accompaniment. C. 1815, ms.
voice/pf
GB: Lbl [Add. Ms. 30148], pp. 1–17.
Brit. Cat. Ms.

The knight errant [Eng. version of *Partant pour la Syrie,* trans. by Walter Scott].
1. Philadelphia: G. E. Blake [1818–20]. 2. New York: J. A. & W. Gelb
[1818–20]. 3. New York: W. Dubois [1819]. 4. 2 printings/Philadelphia,
G. Willig [1819?]. 5. 4 printings/Charleston SC: P. Muck, printed by
Graupner, Boston [1820?, 182–] 6. Baltimore: T. Carr [1821?]. 7. In: *The
Musical Cabinet,* I, #1, pp. 13–15. Charlestown MA: T. M. Baker,
1822–[1823]. 8. Baltimore: Geo. Willig, [1823]. 9. Baltimore: Geo. Willig,
n.d. [printed with *Tyrolese waltz for pf*]. 10. Baltimore, John Cole [1825?].
Arr. with easy accompaniment by B. Carr. 11. Philadelphia: B. Carr
[1822?]. 12. In: B. Carr, *Musical bagatelles,* I, p. 5. Philadelphia: B. Carr,
n.d. 13. *As Romance of Dunois.* In: E. Guilbert, *Twelve English Songs,* pp. 6–8.
2 printings/ Philadelphia: Klemm, [1823–24]. 14. In: *The Melodist,* pp.
29–30. New York: Smith, 1824 [melody and text only]. 15. Philadelphia:
G. Willig [183–?]. 2 pp.
1–12, 15. voice/pf; 13. voice/guit or lyre; 14. voice (unacc.)
1. US: CAdriscoll, CHAhughes, NYcuh, NYhs, NYp, PHhs, PHf, PHfk,
PIlevy, PROu, R, Wc, WOa. 2. US: AB, CA, ECstarr, NYp, PROu. 3. US:
AB, CA, CAdriscoll, NYp, PHhs, PROu, R, Wc. 4. US: CA, CAdriscoll,
CHAhughes, NYhs, NYp, PIlevy, PROu, WOa. 5. US: Bhs, Bp, BUg (3),
CA (2), CAdriscoll (2), CHAhughes, ECstarr, NYp (3), PHf, PHfk, PIlevy,
PROu (3), R, Wc, WOa. 6. US: PIlevy. 7. US: Bp, PROu. 8. US: CA,
NYcuh, PHf. 9. US: NYp. 10. US: Bhs, Wc. 11. US: CA. 12. US:
CAdriscoll, NYcuh, PHfk. 13. US: CAdriscoll, NYp, WOa. 14. US: BUg,
NYp, PHlc, PROu, WOa. 15. US: HA.
*1–3. Wolfe (4340, 4341, 4342). 4–5. Wolfe (4343, 4345, 4345A, 4346,
4346A, 4346B, 4346C). 6–10. Wolfe (4348, 4351, 6373, 4352, 4352A,
4356). 11–12. Wolfe (4353, 4353A, 3239, 3239A). 13–14. Wolfe (4354,
4355, 5843), 15. OCLC (18553407).*

Partant pour la Syrie. [Believed written at Utrecht, 1807; National air of the
Second Empire of France]. 1. Ms., c. 1825. 2. Ms. c. 1810. 3. Ms. c. 1830.
4. Ms. c. 1876. 5. Romance de la Reine de Hollande. Musique & Paroles.
Ms., 19th cent. 6. [1810?], Avec acc. de guitare. 7. s.l; s.n. [c.1815], avec
acc. de piano forte ou harpe. 8. as: *Le romance. Le beau Dunois* [New York,
Torp & Unger, after 1838?]. 9. Arr. for the flute and pianoforte or harp by
L. Drouet. [With "'Tis the last rose of summer"]. New York: W. Hall
[1854?]. 10. *Drey Romanzen* [with *La Sentinelle, Vous me quittez*] . . . *Piano-Forte
auf 4 Hände mit Hinweglassung der Singstimme.* Vienna: A. Diabelli [1820].
11. with variations for the piano forte . . . by Joseph C. Taws. Philadelphia:
B. Carr [1821?]. 12. with variations for the piano forte . . . P. K. Moran.
New York: W. Dubois [1821?]. 13. variée pour le piano forte . . . par J. L.

Dussek. Philadelphia: G. E. Blake [1822?].
1–5. voice/pf. 6–8. voice/pf (or harp or guit). 9. fl/pf or harp. 10. pf (4 hands).
11–13. pf
1–3. D: BFb (G-es 9; inc. 1 d 19, In: H–Im 56, & A–us 56 hoch a–d). 4–5.
D: DO (Mus. Ms. 2774, Mus. Ms. 2462). 6–7. GB: Lbl [Hirsch M.
660.(6.)], [H.346.e.(12.)]. See CPM for other Lbl. 8. US: CH (*M1 .S444
v. 162, #17). 9. US: Wc (ML30.4c #2777, Miller). 10. US: DM. 11. US:
CAdriscoll, PHfk (2). 12. US: AB, HA, NYp, Wc, WOa. 13. CAdriscoll, Wc.
NG, Cohen. 1–5. RISM A/II (#3342, #3162, #2281, #88560, #88404).
6. CPM. 7. NUC (NH 05331962). 9–10. OCLC (21674959, 24831300).
11–13. Wolfe (4347, 4349, 4350), 12 OCLC (18195490).

Reposez vous bon chevalier. Musique d'Hortense Reine . . . Ms., c. 1876.
voice/pf
D: DO (Mus. Ms. 2774).
RISM A/II (#88561).

Romances mises en Musique par Hortense Duchesse de Saint-Leu, ex-reine de
Hollande. With a preface and biography by A. L. C. de Lagarde. 1. Cox &
Baylis: 1824. Illustrations and portrait engraved, after the original plates,
by W. Read. [Songs have also been attributed to Louis Drouet.] (Part of
Mémoires sur Madame la Duchesse de St.-Leu . . . Londres: chez Colburn et
Bentley). 2. London: Dobbs & Co. [1832?]. 3. [With *Une journee a Augsbourg*
by Comte de La Garde]. London: 1824. 4. London: Dobbs & Co. [1824].
5. [London: Cos et Baylis, 1824?]. 6. [Paris: s.n., 1813]. With aquatint
illustrations from drawing by Queen Hortense and a stippled portrait by
Monsaldi after Isabey [of the Queen]. 7. *Romanzen, Musikbegleitung von*
I[rher] *M*[ajestät] *d*[ie] *K*[önigin] *H*[ortense]. Leipzig: s.n. [1820?].
[Contents may not be identical.]
voice/pf
1. GB: Lbl [K.10.a.6.]. US: CA. 2. GB: Lbl [Hirsch III.847.]. US: NYp.
3. US: CA. 4. US: Bp. 5. US: NYp, Cn. 6. GB: Lbl [K.7.h.2.]. 7. GB: Lbl
[E.870.(14.)].
1. CPM, OCLC (24393207). 2. CPM. 3–5. NUC (NH 0531963–6). 6–7.
CPM (H., S.M.I.R.).

[2 compositions for three voices with pianoforte accompaniment].
c. 1813, ms.
3 voices/pf
GB: Lbl [Add. Ms. 30148], pp.17–22.
Brit. Cat. Ms.

Vient [viens] embrasser ta mère. Musique de la Reine d'Hollande. Ms., c. 1876. [See also Hortense, Queen of Holland, Adieux d'une mère à son fils partant pour la croisade. 13 songs in ms.]
voice/pf
D: DO (Mus.Ms. 2774).
RISM A/II (#88562).

Hübner, Caroline
18th cent., German
Sechs Polonaisen für das Pianoforte. Berlin: "auf Kosten der Komposition," n.d. 2d Printing. Berlin: Rosentrater, n.d.
pf
D: BFb (on loan to MÜu), D: Kf&m (2d printing). Copy of D: BFb in Ars Fem coll.
RISM A/I (H 7766), Cohen, letter (Ars Fem), Frau & Musik.

Hullmandel, (Adelaide Charlotte) Evelina (Evalina) (married Bartholomew)
pub. c. 1825–29, London
Musical Souvenir, or *a New Year's Gift for Children.* London: s.n., 1827.
musical game (instruction)
GB: Lbl [M.M.].
CPM, NG (in entry on Nicolas-Joseph Hüllmandel).

A Set of Quadrilles selected from Der Freischütz [C. M. von Weber] *and arr. for piano.* London: s.n. [1825].
pf
GB: Lbl [h.114.(27.)].
CPM, NG (in entry on Nicolas-Joseph Hüllmandel).

Souvenirs de Malibran. London: s.n., [1829].
pf
GB: Lbl [h.103.(3.)].
CPM, NG (in entry on Nicolas-Joseph Hüllmandel).

Hunter, Ann (Anne), Lady, née Home (also literary works. Wrote song texts for Joseph Haydn)
1742, Greenlaw, Scotland–1821, London
"Ah, could my sorrowful ditty," a favourite song . . . composed by a Lady . . . [in] Sheridan's new play of *The Stranger.* London: W. Rolfe, 1798.
voice/pf

GB: [G.808.e.(29.)].
CPM, Cohen.

"Bless'd those sweetly shining eyes" [song]. Music by a Lady. In: *Lady's Magazine,* June 1797.
voice/pf
Lbl [P.P.5141].
CPM, Cohen.

The celebrated death song of the Cherokee Indians. 1. London: Longman & Broderip, No. 2 (3). 2. "The sun sets in night." *The death song of the Cherokee Indians;* an original air . . . London: Preston, for the author. 3. *Alknomook. The death song of the Cherokee Indians.* New York: G. Gilfert. 4. [Newly arranged] in: *The Musical Library,* vol. II [ca. 1845]. 5. London: W. Boag, n.d. 6. London: G. Walker, n.d.
voice/pf
1. I: Nc. NZ: Ap. US: Phu, SM, Wc, Wsc. 2. US: NYp. 3. US: NYp. [RISM addenda shows "other editions" in GB: BA, CU, Obharding (HH 6428)]. 4. Rempel coll. 5. US: Cn. 6. US: Wc.
1–3. RISM A/I (H 6428, HH6428, H 6429, HH 6429, 6430, as Home). 4. Letter (Rempel). 5–6. RISM A/I (HH 6429a. 6429b). Cohen.

The genie of the mountains of Balagete. An ode composed by a Lady [Ann Home, afterwards Mrs. J. Hunter], Author of the *Death Song of the Cherokee Indians,* and some other poetical and musical attempts. [London]: Longman & Broderip [1784]. 4 pp.
voice/pf
GB: Lbl [G.307.(217.)].
RISM A/I (H 6431, as Home), BUC (as Lady), CPM (Hunter).

The Indian Chief. Song [verses with music by Anne Home Hunter]. New York: G. Gilfert [1800?].
voice/pf
US: NYp.
NUC (NH 0623717).

Mary Macgie's dream [song]. The music by a Lady [Ann Home, afterwards Mrs. J. Hunter], author of *Canzonetts,* etc. [London]: Longman & Broderip, for the author [c.1790].
voice/pf

GB: Lbl [G.311.(162.)].
RISM A/I (H 6432, as Home), CPM (Hunter), BUC (as Lady), Cohen.

Nine canzonetts for two voices; and six airs with an accompanyment for the piano-forte by a Lady, to which is added *The death song of the Cherokee Indian.* London: Longman & Broderip, for the author [1782]. 36 pp. [See also separate listings for *The Death Song of the Cherokee Indians.*]
1–2 voices/pf
GB: BA, Obharding, P. Copy in GB: BA lost and believed destroyed when library was flooded in the 1960s.
RISM A/I (H 6427, HH 6427, as Home), BUC (under Lady), Cohen, Bath Central Library (letter).

Second set of canzonets with an accompaniment for the harp or piano composed by a Lady [Ann Home, afterwards Mrs. J. Hunter?]. London: Preston [c. 1785]. 21 pp.
voice/harp or pf
GB: LEc.
BUC (under Lady), Cohen.

"When merry hearts were gay." Donnel and Flora. A Ballad. Edinburgh: N. Stewart, n.d.
voice/pf
GB: Obharding
RISM A/II (HH 64321).

[Work] in: *Scottish songs in two volumes* . . . London: J. Johnson and Egerton, 1714 [*sic* for 1794]. Vol. 2.
voice/pf
D: Mbs, WÜu. GB: Cu, Ru. NL: DHk. S: Sk. US: AA, BE, CAc, G, Nf, SM, Wc.
RISM B/II (Mrs. A. H. Hunter, p. 350), Northhampton.

Hunter, Henrietta Elizabeth
pub. c. 1795, Edinburgh
The Grenadiers march for the Edinburgh volunteers [for pianoforte and German flute]. Edinburgh & London: Corri, Dussek & Co. [c. 1795]. 2 pp.
pf/fl
GB: En. US: BE. Copy of GB: En in Ars Fem coll.
RISM A/I (H 7942), OCLC (16451655), BUC, Cohen, letter (Ars Fem).

Hutchinson, S. M., Madame
n.d.
Napoleon's glory. La glorie de Napoleon. Chant héroique. Paris: H. J. Godefroy,
n.d.
voice/pf
A: Wgm. D: KA, Mbs.
RISM A/I (HH 8040 I, 1).

Hutton, Agnes S.
pub. c. 1827, London
The Cumberland quadrilles. London [1827?].
pf
GB: Lbl [h.112.(38.)].
CPM.

Hutz, L., Mlle
pub. c. 1830, Paris
O ma mère pardonne moi ("Le jour où ton âme"). Romance. Paris: s.n.
[1830?].
song
GB/ Lbl H. 2831.e.(81.)].
CPM.

J

Isabella di Medici. See **Orsini (Orsina), Isabella de,** née **Medici, Duchess of Bracciano**

Isabella Leonarda. (Incorrect for **Leonarda, Isabella,** see entry)

J

Jackson, E., Miss
pub. c. 1805, London
A pastoral; a rondo, and a march for the harp. London: J. Dale [1805].
harp
GB: Lbl [h.115.(4.)].
CPM.

Jacobson, Henrietta
18th cent., fl. Warsaw 1779–1788
Divertissement. 1778.
hpsch
PL: Wn (lost in World War II).
Cohen.

Polonaises. 1778–79
hpsch
PL: Wn (lost in World War II).
Cohen.

[Various pieces for harpischord.]
hpsch
PL: Wn (lost in World War II).
Cohen.

Jacquet de la Guerre, Elisabeth-Claude (Elizabeth. Married name may be found as Laguerre, De La Guerre, or La Guerre)
1664?, Paris ?–1729, Paris
"Aux vains attraits d'une nouvelle ardeur." [Duet without bc]. In: *Recueil d'airs sérieux et à boire de différents auteurs pour l'année 1710.* Vol. 16, p. 80. Paris: C. Ballard, 1710.
2 voices
F: Pn. USSR: KAu ([13782] Eitner, modern location not confirmed).
RISM B/II (Mlle de Laguerre, p. 313), Eitner, MGG.

Cantates françoises, sur des sujets tirez de l'Écriture, à I. [&] II. voix et basse-continue; partie avec symphonie & partie sans symphonie . . . livre second, con-tenant Adam, Le temple rebasti, Le Déluge, Joseph, Jephté, Samson. Paris: Christophe Ballard, 1711. Score, 70 pp.
1–2 voices/vln/bc

C: Qul. F: Pc–Pn [Rés. Vm7 152] &[D.6534(2)], R, V. GB: Lbl [E.69.].
US: Wc, Pu. Copies in Ars Fem coll. and D: Kf&m.
*RISM A/I (J 239), Paris Lib. Cat., CPM, BUC, OCLC (21933860), Borroff,
Cohen, Frau & Musik, MGG, Olivier, letters (C. Johnson, Ars Fem).*

*Cantates françoises, sur des sujets tirez de l'Écriture, à voix seule et basse continue;
partie avec symphonie & partie sans symphonie* . . . livre premier, contenant
Esther, Le passage de la Mer Rouge, Jacob et Rachel, Jonas, Susanne et
les vieillards, Judith. Paris: Christophe Ballard, 1708. Score, 73 pp.
1 voice/bc/some with instruments
C: Qul. F: Pc–Pn [Rés.Vm7151] & [D.6534 (1)], R, V. GB: Lbl [E.69.].
US: AA, Wc (M2102.L3.C3 Case), Pu. Copies in Ars Fem coll. and D:
Kf&m.
*RISM A/I (J 238), Paris Lib. Cat., CPM, BUC, Cohen, NG, MGG, Olivier, Frau
& Musik, letters (C. Johnson, Ars Fem), NUC (NL 0033356), OCLC
(21933860).*

Céphale et Procris. Tragédie mise en musique [5 acts]. 1. Paris: Christophe
Ballard, 1694. Score. 148 pp. 2. Tragédie. En musique. Representée par
l'Academie royalle de musique. Suivant la copie imprimée a Paris.
Amsterdam: Chez Antoine Schelte . . . , 1695. 56 pp. In: *Recueil des opera.*
Amsterdam: s.n., 1693–1712. Libretto by Joseph-François Duché de
Vancy.
stage work
1. B: Bc, Br. D: AN, Mbs, Sl, Tu. F: Pa [M224–225], Pc–Pn (3 ex.) [Vm2
123–24], [Rés.F.351], & [A.309], Po [A.34], TLc (2 ex.), V. GB: Cfm. US:
BE (M1500.D42C4.Case X). Copies in Ars Fem coll., D: Kf&m and US:
AA [Music FILM 490(2)], CLAc. 2. US: U (782.4 R245 1693 v.5).
*1. RISM A/I (J 237), NUC (NL 0033356, micro. 0033358), OCLC
(21807431, micro. 16158767), Borroff, Cohen, Boenke, MGG, Olivier, letters
(C. Johnson, Ars Fem), Frau & Musik. 2. NUC (NL 00333560).*

Céphale et Procris, excerpt from. Duet. "Les Rossignols dès que le jour com-
mence." 1. In: *Recueil d'airs sérieux et à boire,* Vol. 27, p. 83. Paris: Ballard,
1721. 2. As *Rigaudon: Rossignol.* In: *Nouveau recueil de chansons choisies,* vol. 4,
p. 363, and vol. 4, p. 333, The Hague: Gosse & Neaulme,1729. 3. 2d ed.
H. Scheurleer, 1732 (but without bc).
2 voices/bc
1. F: Pn. 2. A: Wgm, Wn. B: Lc. Ch: N. D: AAst, Bds, Bhm. E: Mn. F: Pc,
Pn. GB: Cu, Ge, Gm, Lbl. NL: DHk. PL: Wn. S: L, Sk. US: NYp. 3. C:
Qlu. D: Bds, HEu, PO. F: AIXc, AM, CF, Pa, Pn, Sim, Sn, TLc. GB: Lbl.

I: Tci. NL: DHk. S: Sk, Skma. US: Cn, NYp, PHf, R.
1–2. RISM B/II (Mlle de Laguerre, p. 262, 315), letter (C. Johnson). 3. RISM B/II (Mlle de Laguerre, p. 262). NG, MGG, Wallon.

Céphale et Procris, excerpt from. *Loure* [for oboe and basso continuo]. Paris: s.n., 1694.
oboe/bc
Copy in D: Kf&m. Original location not known.
Frau & Musik.

Céphale et Procris, excerpt from. Parody of Bourrée "Tant que je verrons ce pol." Air à boire. In: *Recueil d'airs sérieux et à boire*. Vol. 30, p. 18, Paris: Ballard, 1724.
2 voices/bc
F: Pn.
MGG, RISM B/II (as both Mlle de Laguerre & Mme de Laguerre, p. 315), NG, letter (C. Johnson).

Céphale et Procris, Prologue from. Ms. [169–?]. Score (28 pp.) and 9 parts in 1 vol. (116 pp.). (4 vocal and 5 instrumental parts).
stage work, excerpt
F: Pn (MS. Vm2. 125). Microfilm copy in US: AA [FILM M490(1)].
Paris Lib. Cat., NUC (micro., NL 0033357).

"Entre nous, mes chers amis." Air à boire. In: *Recueil d'airs sérieux et à boire*, Vol. 30, p. 23. Paris: Ballard, 1724.
1 voice without bc
F: Pn.
RISM B/II (both as Mlle de Laguerre & Mme de Laguerre, p. 315), Borroff, NG, Cohen, MGG.

[4 sonates en trio, g, B-flat, D, C]. Sonnatta [*sic*] della Signora de la guerre [on title page]. Ms. score [from S. de Brossard but not in his hand].
2 vlns/cello/bc
F: Pn (Vm7 1110). Copies in D: Kf&m and Ars Fem.
Borroff, Bates, NG, Cohen, MGG, Olivier, Frau & Musik, letters (C. Johnson and Ars Fem).

"Heureux l'instant qui vous vit naître," "Pour la gloire des souverains," "Cédons tous aux tendres ardeurs," & "Cher favori de la Victoire." in:
R. Trépagne de Ménerville, *Les amusemens de Monseigneur le Duc de Bretagne,*

Dauphin. Paris: G. Cavelier, 1712.
1 voice/bc
F: Pn (B.N. [Impr.Z 61713).
Paris Lib. Cat., Borroff, NG, MGG, Cohen, Wallon, Olivier.

Les pièces de clavessin [*sic*] . . . [premier livre.] Paris: author, Sr de
Baussen (gravé par H. de Baussen, Liebaux sc.), 1687.
hpsch
I: Vc (Stampe antico 137).[first page of dedication missing]
NG & MGG (then thought to be lost), Bates, Cohen, Olivier, letter (C. Johnson).

[*Les Pièces de clavessin*, 1687, work from]. Gavotte [also in 3d Suite in A
minor of: *Les Pièces de clavessin*]. In: "Cecilia MS." Authorship unascribed
in ms. but piece is variant of the published version.
hpsch
I: Rsc [MS A/400, folio 53v].
Bates.

[*Les Pièces de clavessin*, 1687, work from]. Minuet [also found in 4th Suite in
F Major of: *Les Pièces de clavessin*]. Ms. Authorship unascribed in ms. but it
is a copy of the published piece.
hpsch
GB: Lkc [Dart Collection, MS no. 2, folio 22r].
Bates.

Pièces de clavecin qui peuvent se Jouer sur le Viollon . . . Paris: author (gravées par
H. de Baussen), 1707. 26 pp. Printed together with: *Sonates* [d, D, d, e, a, A]
pour le violon et pour le clavecin. Paris: auteur, Foucault, Ribou (gravées par H.
de Baussen). Could be purchased separately and copies survive separately.
hpsch; vln/bc
F: Pn [Vm7 1860]. Copy in Ars Fem coll.
RISM A/I (J 241), MGG, Bates, Cohen, letters (C. Johnson, Ars Fem).

Raccommodement comique [de Pierrot et Nicole]. Reprinted in: Le Sage, *La
Ceinture de Vénus*, Paris: Le Sage, 1715 and in: *Le théâtre de la Foire ou l'opéra-
comique, contenant les meilleures pièces qui on ét représentées aux foires de St-Germain
et St-Laurent* . . . Paris: E. Ganeau, Vve Pissot et P. Gandouin, 1721. Vol. I,
air #176.
SB/bc
F: Nm, Pcf, Pn (2 ex.), Po. US: NYcu. Other library holdings incomplete runs.
RISM B/II (Mlle de La Guerre, p. 385), MGG, Olivier.

Sémélé, L'île de Delos, Le sommeil d' Ulisse. Cantates françoises aûquelles on a joint le *Raccommodement Comique* [de Pierrot et Nicole]. Paris: Ribou, Foucault, author (gravées par H. de Baussen) [c. 1707 or 1715]. Score, 83 pp.
1 or 2 voices/bc, some with vln
F: B, Pa [M.226], Pc–Pn [Vm7 161] & [D.6609], Po. GB: Lbl [I.298.]. Copies in D: Kf&m and Ars Fem coll.
RISM A/I (J 240), Paris Lib. Cat., CPM, BUC, Cohen, NG, MGG, Olivier, Frau & Musik, letter (C. Johnson).

Sonates [d, D, d, e, a, A] *pour le violon et pour le clavecin.* Paris: auteur, Foucault, Ribou (gravées par H. de Baussen), 1707. Pp. 27–80. Printed together with: *Pièces de clavecin qui peuvent se Jouer sur le Viollon . . .* Paris: author, (gravées par H. de Baussen). Could be purchased separately and copies survive separately.
vln/bc; hpsch
F: Pn [D.6534(3)]. GB: Lbl [f.380.q.]. Copies in D: Kf&m, UNikb, and Ars Fem coll.
RISM A/I (J 242), Bates, NG, Cohen, Borroff, Olivier, Frau & Musik, letters (C. Johnson, Ars Fem).

[2] Suonata [a, a] . . . a violino solo e viol. di gamba obligata . . . con organo. Ms. partbooks, apparently copied by Sebastien de Brossard, c. 1695.
vln/viola da gamba/org bc
F: Pn [Vm7. 1111]. Microfilm, US: AA [Music FILM M493(2)]. Copies in D: Kf&m and Ars Fem coll.
MGG, Borroff, Bates, letters (C. Johnson, Ars Fem), Frau & Musik, NUC Sup. (micro. NSL 0003511).

[Work(s)] in: *Recueil de chansons choisées.* Tome IV. Paris: La Haye, n.d.
song(s)
US: Nf.
Northhampton.

[Work(s)] in: *Théâtre de M. Favart ou recueil des comédies, parodies et opéra comiques qu'il a donnés jusqu'à ce jour, avec les airs, rondes, et vaudevilles notés dans chaque pièce . . .* Paris: Duchesne. 1763[–1772] 10 vol.
song(s)
CH: Gpu. F: B, Pcf, Pi, Pc, Pn. US: Wc.
RISM B/II (Mlle La Guerre, p. 386).

Jervis, Mary Anne (Honorable)

pub. 1830s, London

"Aure amiche." Aria. London: Willis [1836?]. 5 pp.
voice/pf
GB: Lbl [M. 2830.a.(39.)].
CPM.

"Shall this pale cheek." Ballad. London/Dublin: Willis [1831]. 5 pp.
voice/pf
GB: Lbl [M. 2830.a.(39.)].
CPM.

Two Italian Duets and One Song ("Misero in che peccai," "D'ogni amator," "Aure amiche").
London: Willis [1836]. 14 pp. [See also separate printing of "Aure amiche."]
2 voices/pf & 1 voice/pf
GB: Lbl [D.836.ii.(7.)].
CPM.

Johnson, L., Miss

pub. late 18th cent., Edinburgh

[Work(s)] in: *A . . . collection of strathspey reels with a bass for the violoncello or harpsichord . . .* by Niel Gow at Dunkeld. Edinburgh: the author [1785–92]. 3 vol.
unspecified instruments with vlc or hpsch
C: Tp. GB: Ep, Lbl. Other library holdings are incomplete runs.
RISM B/II (p. 76).

[Work(s)] in: *The Scots musical museum . . . of six hundred Scots songs with proper basses for the piano forte &c. . . .* the airs chiefly harmonized by S. Clarke. Edinburgh: J. Johnson [1787–1803], 6 vol.
Probably melody only by Miss Johnson
voice/pf
B: Bc. BR: Rn. C: SA. CH: Bu. EIR: Dn. GB: A, Cu, En, Es, Ge, Lbl, Lcm, Mp, P, WI. US: Cn, DE, HA, MI, S, U, Wc, WI. Other library holdings incomplete runs.
RISM B/II (p. 350).

Jordan, Dorothea (Dorothy), Mrs. (pseud.) (Born Bland, Dorothea (Dora), later Mrs. Ford)

1762, Waterford–1816, St. Cloud, near Paris

The blue bell of Scotland. A favorite ballad. 1. London: J. Longman, Clementi & Co. [c. 1800]. 2. London: Major's Cheap Music Shop, [between 1800 &1818]. 3. Dublin, Rhames [c.1800]. 4. Anon. in: *Musical Journal,* II, #25. Baltimore: Carr, 1800. 5. New York: G. Gilfert [c. 1800]. 6. New York: W. Hall & Son, 1809. 7. London: J. Dale, [c. 1800]. 8. Philadelphia: Willig [c. 1800]. 9. Boston: von Hagen, c. 1800. 10. New York: E. Riley [between 1819–31]. 11. Philadelphia: G. Willig [1801]. 12. London: G. Walker, n.d. 13. a favorite song with an accompaniment for the piano forte, harp, guitar or lute. London: Bland & Weller, n.d. 14. London: J. Buckinger, n.d. 15 . . . for the piano or harp. Edinburgh: N. Stewart, n.d. 16. A favorite Scotch ballad. Philadelphia: G. Willig. 17. New York: G. Gilfert. 18. Boston: P. A. von Hagen, n.d. [Arrangements] 19. Arr. with variations for the piano forte by P. Dale. New York: Firth & Hall [c. 1835]. 20. arr. for piano and harp. n.d.
Innumerable other editions and arrangements, often listed in catalogues only by title.
1–12., 15–18. voice/pf, 13. voice/pf, harp, guit, or lute, 14. voice/pf or harp 19. pf; 20. pf/harp
1. GB: Lbl [G.249.(60.)], Ob. I: Nc. US: NH, HA, Pu. 2. US: BE. 3. GB: Lbl [H.1654.n.(31.). 2., 4–6. US: NYp [Am1–V]. 4. U.S: BAhs (inc.), NYsha, PIlevy, Wc, Wmcdevitt. 5. CAdriscoll, NYsha, Wc. 7. US: NH. 8. U.S.: BUg, PHfk, PHhs, PIlevy, Wc. 9. U.S.: Bp, NYp, NYsha, PIlevy, PROu. 10. US: Pu. 11. US: PHfk, PHhs, PIlevy, Wc. 12. US: NYfuld. 13. US: NYcu. 14. US: Bp, NYfuld, Wc. 15. D: MZfederhofer. 16. US: BU (another edition), PHf, PHhs, PIlevy, Wc. 17. US: CN, NYp (2 ex.), PIlevy, Wc. 18. US: Bp, NYp (2 ex.), PIlevy, PROu, Wc. 19. US: Pu. 20. GB: Lbl. Copy in Ars Fem coll. from GB: Lbl.
1–3. RISM A/I (J 654, 655, 656). 1–2. OCLC (9007772, 19011208). 1, 3. CPM, BUC. 4–6. NYp Spec. Coll. Shelf List, Sonneck, Tick, Cohen, NUC (under title). 7, 10. OCLC (20913770, 24608814). 7–11. Sonneck, Wolfe. 12–17. RISM A/I (JJ 656a, 656b, 656c, 656d, 656e). 18. RISM A/I (JJ 656f). Wolfe (25 American editions and arrangements; see Wolfe 4670–4695). 19. OCLC (24609586). 20. Letter (Ars Fem). Also at least 75 versions in CPM.

"Go, tuneful Bird." The words by Shenstone, the melody compos'd by Mrs. Jordan together with an Accompaniment for the Lute . . . London: Pub. for the author by J. Buckenger [179–?–1801].
voice/lute
GB: Lbl [H.1650.j.(2.)]. US: HA.
CPM, OCLC (19007678).

Jordan's Elixir of life, and cure for the spleen; or, a collection of all the songs sung by Mrs. Jordan, since her first appearance in London. With many other favourite songs, sung by her . . . Prefixed, authentic memoirs of Mrs. Jordan. London: s.n., [1789]. 68 pp. [Songs without music; many in collection were not composed by Mrs. Jordan.]
songs [music not given]
US: Bp, CA, NYcu, IO.
NUC (under title: NJ 0166356).

My father; a ballad, composed & sung by Mrs. Bland, with an accompaniment for the piano forte. London: Preston [181–?]. 3 pp.
voice/pf
US: NYp.
NUC (NJ 0163872).

The river queen, composed and sung by Mrs. Bland, with an accompaniment for the piano forte. London: 1801. 3 pp.
voice/pf
US: NYp.
NUC (NJ 0163873).

'Twas in the solemn midnight hour, composed and sung by Mrs. Bland, with an accompaniment for the piano forte. [London?]: 1801. 3 pp.
voice/pf
US: NYp.
NUC (NJ 0163874).

K

Kamermann, Mme

pub. c. 1783, Paris

*Deuxième pot-pourri sur le départ et la mort de M. Malbrough dialogué entre M. &
Mme Malbrough et son page arrangé pour le clavecin ou le fortepiano.* . . . Paris:
l'autheur/Melle Girard [1783]. 6 pp.

hpsch or pf

F: Pc (B.N.[D.11498]). Photocopy in C. Johnson collection.

RISM A/I (K 76), Paris Lib. Cat., letter (C. Johnson).

Kanzler, Josephine. See Flad (Fladt), Josephine von, née Kanzler (Giuseppa di Flad, nata Canzler)

Kauth, Maria Magdalena, née Graff

fl. 1780s, Berlin

*Danses des muses, consistant en 3. menuets, 3. angloises 1 & 3. allemandes à plusieurs
instruments.* Berlin: Johann Julius Hummel; Amsterdam: au grand magazin
de musique (#694), n.d. Keyboard arr. and parts.

kbd and orch versions

B: Bc (kbd arr.). D: Dl (10 parts), ROu (kbd arr.). SF: A (9 parts). Copy in
Ars Fem coll.

RISM A/I (K 209), Cohen, Eitner, letter (Ars Fem).

Das Gemälde der Natur, in Form eines Monodram. Musik und Text verfertigt von
. . . Berlin: s.n., 1789. Keyboard arr.

pf

D: B, SWl (2 ex.). Copy of D: B in Ars Fem coll.

RISM A/I (K 208), Cohen, Eitner, letter (Ars Fem).

3 Menuets pour clav. Berlin: Hummel, n.d.

kbd

B: Bc.

Eitner, Cohen.

Keller, Giovanna

pub. 1791, Vienna

Sonata per il clavicembalo o forte-piano. Vienna: F. A. Hoffmeister, 1791.

hpsch or pf

A: Wn.

RISM A/I (K 255).

Kerby, Caroline

pub. 1825–29, London and Philadelphia
A Rondo for the Pianoforte. London: [1825?].
pf
GB: Lbl [g.272.s.(23.)].
CPM.

The thornless rose. Philadelphia: R. H. Hobson, 1829. Text by S. Wild.
voice/pf
US: NYp.
Cohen, Block & Bates, Tick.

Kingston, Mary (Marielli, M., pseud.)

pub. c. 1805–35, London
The Ghost at Sea ("'Twas night"). Song. London: [1810?].
song
GB: Lbl [H.2832.o.(29.)].
CPM, Cohen, Stewart Green.

May day; a characteristic piece for Piano Forte. London: [1832]. Published under
pseud. of M. Marielli.
pf
GB: Lbl [h.118.(10.)].
CPM.

O Domine Deus. The prayer of Mary Queen of Scots . . . [quartet]. London:
[1835?].
Published under pseud. of M. Marielli.
voices (SATB)
GB: Lbl [H.2830.b.(4.)].
CPM.

Vocal music for the Young, a series of [6] original songs, duets, canons, glees,
etc. London: [1835?].
voices
GB: Lbl [H.2832.e.(11.)].
CPM, Cohen, Stewart Green.

When I was very, very young. A favorite song . . . with an accompaniment for
the harp or piano forte. London: L. Lavenu [c. 1805?]. 3 pp.
voice/harp or pf

GB: Lbl [H.1654.p.(6.)].
CPM, Cohen, Stewart Green.

Kochanowska (Kochanowskiéj), Franciszka (Françoise)
1787, Warsaw–1831, Warsaw
Kazimiérz Mnich [Kazimierz Mnich Śpiew Historyczny] ("Dobeze się Polsce za Chrobrego działo"). In: Julian Ursyn Niemcewicz, *Śpiewy historycznye* [Historic songs]. Warsaw: 1816, 1818. Texts by Niemcewicz.
voice/pf
F: Pn. PL: Kc, Wn, Wmickiewicz. Copies of the two editions in PL: Kc in Jackson coll.
Cohen, Sowinsky, letter (Poniatowska).

Kramer, Mme
late 18th cent.
[Work(s)] in: *VIIIe Recueil de petits airs de tout genre, entremelés d'ariettes choisies, avec accompagnements obligés de guitarre allemande ou cythre et de violon ou mandoline* . . . [arr.] par Mr. l'abbé Carpentier . . . Paris: l'auteur [1780].
voice/guit or zither and vln or mandolin
F: Pm, Psg.
RISM B/II (p. 330).

Krause, Ida
pub. c. 1800, Hamburg & Berlin
Acht Lieder mit Begleitung des Piano Forte . . . Ites Werk. Hamburg: Johann August Böhme.
voice/pf
B: Bc. D: SWl.
RISM A/I (K 1935), Eitner, Cohen.

Deutsche Gesänge mit Pfte. op. 3. Ed. Cranz. . . .
voice/pf
Old location, König. Hausbibl. im Schlosse zu Berlin (Eitner). Present location not confirmed.
Eitner.

Zwei Lieder mit Begleitung des Piano Forte. ("Liebe" & "Zum Frühlingsanfang"). Werke II. Berlin: F. S. Lischke (#886) [c. 1800].
voice/pf
B: Bc. US: Wc (M1621 K Case).
RISM A/I (K 1936), NUC (NK 0286544), Eitner, Cohen.

Krumpholtz, Anne-Marie, Mme, née Steckler

c. 1755, Metz–1813, London

A favorite Air of "Pray Goody" arranged for the Harp & Dedicated to Miss
Catherine Russell by Madame Krumpholz. London: Chappell, n.d.
harp
GB: Lbl [h.1480, h.(3.)]. Microfilm copy in Rempel coll.
CPM, letter (Rempel).

The favorite Air of "Robin Adair" arranged for the harp and Dedicated to Miss
Barbara Campbell by Madame Krumpholtz. London: J. Dale [1812?].
harp
GB: Lbl [H.1450.f.(11.)]. I: Nc. Microfilm of Lbl copy in Rempel coll.
RISM A/I (K 2926), CPM, MGG, NG (bio), Cohen, letter (Rempel).

A Favorite Piedmontois air with Variations by Dalvimare, Arranged & Dedicated
to Capt. Tookey, by Madame Krumpholz. London: James Platts [1810].
harp
GB: Lbl [h.1480.h.(3.)]. Microfilm copy in Rempel coll.
CPM, letter (Rempel).

"Lison dormoit" With an Introduction & Variations arranged for the Harp and dedi-
cated to Miss Metcalfe by Madame Krumpholtz. London: s.n. [1810?].
harp
GB: Lbl (h.184.b.(9.)]. Copy in bound volume of 19th cent. harp music in
Rempel coll.
CPM, Cohen, NG, letter (Rempel).

Krumpholtz, Fanny (married **Isaac Pittar,** afterwards pub. as **Mrs. Pittar**)

"Dedans mon petit Reduit?" 1. Air, Arranged with Variations for the
Harp & Dedicated to the Memory of the late celebrated Madame
Krumpholtz, by Her Daughter Madlle. [Fanny] Krumpholtz. London:
Rt. Birchall, n.d. 2. Air [English title "In my cottage"] arranged with variations for the harp by Madle. Krumpholtz. London: s.n. [1816].
harp or pf
1. GB: Lbl [h.1480]. Microfilm copy & copy in bound volume of 19th
cent. harp music in Rempel coll. 2. GB: Lbl [(h.116.(29.)].
Cohen, NG (in article Anne-Marie Krumpholtz, mother of Fanny
Krumpholtz).
1. CPM. 2. Letter (Rempel).

Fanny Krumpholtz's Manuscript Book of her own Compositions for the Harp. Ms., 1811. [20 pieces for harp. Contents page signed, "Fanny Krumpholtz now Mrs. Pittar."]
harp
GB: Lbl [Additional MS 49.288]. Microfilm copy in Rempel coll.
Letter (Rempel).

A Military divertimento for the Harp or Piano Forte dedicated by permission to the Rt. Honble. the Countess of Hardwicke, Composed by Mrs Pittar (ci devant) Madlle. Krumpholtz, l'ainée. London: published by the author [1817].
harp or pf
GB: Lbl [(h.116.(32.)]. Copy in bound volume of 19th cent. harp music in Rempel coll.
CPM, Cohen, NG (in article Anne-Marie Krumpholtz, mother of Fanny Krumpholtz), letter (Rempel).

A New March Composed for a Regiment of Bengal Sepoys, adapted for either a Military Band or Piano Forte By A Lady, F. K. [title page signed Fanny Krumpholtz]. London: published by the author [c. 1812, before her marriage to Isaac Pittar].
wind band or pf
GB: Lbl [(h.1480]. Microfilm copy in Rempel coll.
Letter (Rempel).

Krumpholtz, V. (Found in 1825 Royal Blue Book as **"Miss Krumpholtz"**)
pub. 1820s, London
Le Rantz des Vaches ou *Un Sovenir des Vallées Suisses,* arranged for the Harp, and Dedicated to The Lady Elizabeth Stuart by V. Krumpholtz. London: S. Chappell [c. 1826–36].
harp
GB: Lbl (h. 1480). Microfilm copy in Rempel coll.
Letter (Rempel).

Quadrille for the Harp Composed & Dedicated to Miss Eleanor Richards, by V. Krumpholtz. London: Birchall [before 1826].
harp
GB: Lbl (h. 1480). Microfilm copy in Rempel coll.
Letter (Rempel).

Kurakina (Kourakin), Natal'ya Ivanova, Princess

1766–1831

"Celui que plait le mieux." Romance. Accompt. par Gatayes. Paris: Boieldieu, [c. 1815].

Melody only by Kurakina
voice/lyre or guit
GB: Lbl [E.1717.o.(49.)].
CPM.

"Deh non partir mio dolce amore" & "La notte non riposo." Airs [Per canto e chitarra]. #33 in: *Journal d'airs italiens, française russes* [pour chant] *avec accompagnement de guitarre* [et pour deux guitarres] par I. B. Hainglaise. Année I. St. Petersburg: chez l'aut, et Gerstenberg et Dittmar, [1796], columns 66–67.

voice/guit
USSR: Lsc (M3 P–I/271(A–I)
Letter (USSR: Ml).

Duetto pour deux guitarres. #13[b] in: *Journal d'airs italiens, français et russes* [pour chant] *avec accompagnement de guitarre* [et pour deux guitarres] par I. B. Hainglaise. Année I. St. Petersburg: chez l'aut, et Gerstenberg et Dittmar [1796], column number 26–27.

2 guits
USSR: Lsc (M3 P–I/271(A–I).)
Letter (USSR: Ml).

Huit romances, composées et arrangées [pour le chant et] *la harpe* . . . contents: "Astre d'amour," "Je vais done quitter pour jamais," "Que faim avoir les hirondelles," "Viedras tu pas," "Quande nos jour," "Derobe ta lumière," "Rassembies de la nature," "Humble cabane de mon père." 1. St. Petersburg: Breitkopf, 1795. 2. Ms. copy, c. 1800

voice/harp
1. PL: LA. USSR: Lsc (M980–4/p.232). 2. DK: Km (R426).
1. RISM A/I (KK 1373 I,1), letter (USSR: Ml). 2. RISMdan.

Humble Cabane. Romance, pour le piano ou harpe. Paris: Chez Boieldieu [c. 1815]. 3 pp. [from *Huit romances,* see above].

voice/pf or harp
GB: Lbl [G.547.(2.)].
CPM.

Romance de Florian ("Je vais dono quitter pour jamais"). #13[a] in: *Journal d'airs italiens, français et russes* [pour chant] *avec accompagnement de guitarre* [et pour deux guitarres] par I. B. Hainglaise. Année I. St. Petersburg: chez l'aut, et Gerstenberg et Dittmar [1796], column number 26–27.
voice/guit
USSR: Lsc (M3 P–I/271(A–I).
Letter (USSR: Ml).

"T'amo tanto e tanto t'amo." Air [Per canto e chitarra]. #31 in: *Journal d'airs italiens, français et russes* [pour chant] *avec accompagnement de guitarre* [et pour deux guitarres] par I. B. Hainglaise. Année I. St. Petersburg: chez l'aut, et Gerstenberg et Dittmar [1796], columns 62–63.
voice/guit
USSR: Lsc (M3 P–I/271(A–I).
Letter (USSR: Ml).

Trois romances favorites avec accompagnement de forte-piano. St. Petersburg: Dalmas, n.d.
voice/pf
S: Skma.
RISM A/I (KK 1373 I,2).

L

L., Mme
[A song by Madame L.] In: *Les Amants françois* [play by Billardon de Sauvigny]. In: *Les Après soupers de la Société,* vol. III. [Paris: s.n., 1782].
song
GB: Lbl [Hirsch III.652.].
CPM, BUC.

L. P. D. L., Mme
pub. 1716, Paris
[Work(s)] in: *Recueil d'airs sérieux et à boire de différents auteurs pour l'année 1716.* Paris: J. B. C. Ballard, 1716.
song(s)
F: Pn. Other library holdings incomplete runs.
RISM B/II (p. 314).

La B . . . , (de), Mlle
pub. 1780, Paris
La Mère Abandonnée. Romance par Mr. Basile. [Paris]: Chés Camand [c. 1780].
song
GB: Lbl [B.362.a.(89.)].
BUC, CPM.

Labaillive, Mme
pub. 1780s?, Paris
"Ah! qu'une femme est à plaindre." Ariette [Paris: s.n., 1780?].
voice/kbd
GB: Lbl [B.362.a.(81.)].
RISM A/I (LL 2 I,1), CPM, BUC.

Lacerda, Bernarda Ferreira de (Perreira de Lacerda. Heroina.
Also literary works.)
1595–1644, Porto, Portugal
Cantadas. Ms.
voice(s)
E: Mp. Copy in Ars Fem coll.
Cohen, Letter (Ars Fem).

Soledades de Buçaco. Lisbon: [M. Rodrigues], 1634.
song(s)
US: CA, Cn. May be poetic text only.
Cohen, NUC (Ferriera . . . , NF 0102455).

Lackner, Mrs. de
pub. c. 1800?, London
Second set of six original German waltz's [*sic*], adapted for the piano forte.
London: E. Riley [1800?]. 4 pp.
pf
GB: Lbl [g.272.u.(7.)]. Copy in Ars Fem coll.
RISM A/I (L 150), CPM, BUC, letter (Ars Fem).

Lady, a (many anonymous composers)
pub. 1798, London
"Ah? could my sorrowful ditty." A favorite song written on Mr. Sheridan's
new play of *The Stranger.* Composed by a Lady. London: Printed for
W. Rolfe [1798].
voice/pf
GB: Lbl.
BUC.

pub. c. 1801–07?, eastern U.S.
Belisario ("Fortune how strangely thy gifts are awarded"). 1. New York:
[James Hewitt, 1801–07]. 2. [Date obolum, Belisario] ("O fortune . . .)
In: *The Baltimore Musical Miscellany,* II, p. 116–19. Baltimore, 1805. Melody
& text only. 3. [Date obolum . . .]. In: *The Nightingale,* pp. 165–67.
Portsmouth NH: Treadwell, 1804. Melody & text only.
1. voice/pf, 2–3. voice (unacc.)
1. US: Wc. 2. US: PROu, Wc, WOa. 3. US: Bp, Ba, BUg, Cn, CA,
NYcuh, NYfuld, NYp, PROu, PIlevy, SM, Wc, WOa.
1–3. Wolfe (5185, 5186, 433, 5187, 6534).

pub. 1797, London
"Bless'd be those sweetly shining eyes." Song. Music by a Lady. In: *Lady's
Magazine,* June 1797. [London]: 1797.
voice/pf
GB: Lbl.
BUC.

pub. c. 1796, Edinburgh
A collection of . . . marches, quick steps, airs &ce composed by a Lady.

Edinburgh: N. Steward & Co. [c. 1796]. 8 pp.
pf
EIRE: Dn. GB: En.
BUC.

pub. c. 1825, Baltimore
Colonel Wm. Steuart's march and quick step. Composed by a Lady. Baltimore:
John Cole [1825]. 2 pp.
pf
US: BAhs, Wc, WOa.
Wolfe (5188).

pub. c. 1797, London
Emma or the *Bough-pot Girl.* A favorite song composed by a Lady. London:
W. Hodsoll [c. 1797].
song
GB: Lbl.
BUC.

Fair the face of Orient day. A favorite song, composed by a Lady. London:
W. Hodsoll [c. 1797].
song
GB: Lbl.
BUC.

pub. c. 1759, Edinburgh
*A favorite march and quick step composed by a young Lady for the Edinr. Royal
Highland Volunteers.* Edinburgh: Gow and Shepherd [c. 1796].
pf
EIRE: Dn. GB: En.
BUC.

pub. 1801, Philadelphia
The forsaken nymph ("Ye tuneful warblers of the grove"). The words by a
young gentleman of this city. The music by an accomplished young lady.
In: *The Philadelphia Repository and Weekly Register,* I, #10, p. 5. Philadelphia:
1801.
voice/pf
US: For listing of the very numerous locations of this periodical see *Union
List of Serials.*
Wolfe (18, 6976).

pub. c. 1797, London
French Fraternity [song]. By a Lady, composed in honor of the . . . naval
victories, obtained by our three gallant admirals. [London]: T. Skillern,
for the Author [c. 1797]. 3 pp.
song
GB: Gu, Lbl, Ob.
BUC.

pub. c. 1800, New York
The Ghost of Crazy Jane ("The evening of a summers' day"). [Written and
composed by a Lady.] Arr. for flute or guitar. New York: J. &. M. Paff
[c . 1800–03]. 2 pp.
voice/pf with parts arr. for fl or guit
US: NYp [Early American Sheet Music, Am 1–V], Wc.
NYp Shelf List, Sonneck.

pub. c. 1745, Dublin and London
The Happy Lover. ("See Stella as your health returns.") [Song.] 1. Set by a
Lady [Dublin, c. 1745]. Separate sheet, fol. 52 of an unidentified collection. 2. The Happy Lover. [Song.] Set by a Lady [London: c. 1745].
voice/pf
1. EIRE: Dn. 2. GB: Lbl.
1–2. BUC.

pub. c. 1803–07, New York
"Haste soldiers, haste!" A favorite war song. Inscribed to Sir Ralph
Abercrombie. By a Lady. New York: J. & M. Paff [1803–07]. 3 pp.
voice/pf
US: ECstarr.
Wolfe (5189).

pub. 1796, London
How gay that air! Song . . . music by a Lady. In: *Lady's Magazine,* February
1796. [London]: 1796.
song
GB: Lbl.
BUC.

pub. c. 1797, London
I have found out a gift for my fair. A ballad [words by W. Shenstone] . . . The
music by a Lady. [London: s.n., c. 1797.]

song
GB: Lbl, Ob.
BUC.

pub. 1818–19, Philadelphia
Jerusalem ("Jerusalem, my happy home, how do I sigh for thee"). A Hymn.
Arranged for the organ. 1. Philadelphia: G. Willig [1818–19 or 182–?].
2. Baltimore: J. Carr, [1819?]. 4 pp.
2 solo voices / 3 part chorus / pf or org
1. US: NYp, PIlevy. 2. US: BUg, CHAhughes (lacks pp. 3–4), DM,
ECstarr, PIlevy, NYcuh, NYp.
1–2. Wolfe (5190, 5190A). 1. Tick. 2. OCLC (14251581).

pub. c. 1797, London
The Kiss. A favorite song sung by Master Braham at the Royalty Theatre.
The words by Mr. Vaughan. The music by a Lady. London: G. Smart
[1790]. 4 pp.
song
GB: Lbl.
BUC.

pub. c. 1824
LaFayette's welcome to Philadelphia. A new march with variations. Composed
by a young lady [2 editions]. Philadelphia: G. E. Blake [1824].
pf
US: AB, ECstarr, NYcuh, PHfk, PROu.
Wolfe (10103, 10104).

pub. c. 1800, Boston
The Little Sailor Boy ("The sea was calm, the sky serene"). Written by Mrs.
Rowson. The melody by a lady. Boston: von Hagen etc. [c. 1799 or 1800].
2 pp. With guitar arr.
voice / pf (also arr. for guit)
US: AB, Bp, PIlevy, NYp, PROu, Wc.
Sonneck.

pub. c. 1812, New York
Lochinvar ("O young Lochinvar is come out of the west"). From Scott's
Marmion. Composed by a young lady. 1. New York: A. T. Goodrich,
engraved by E. Riley [1812]. 2. [2 printings, reissued on same plates] New
York: Geib [1816–17].

voice/pf
1. US: CA, NYp, PROu. 2. CA, CHAhs, ECstarr, NYp.
1. US: NYp Shelf List. 1–2. Wolfe (10105, 10105A, 10105B).

pub. 1819, Philadelphia
"Love sheds no more his genial ray." A new song. By a Lady. In: *Lady's and Gentleman's Weekly Literary Museum and Musical Magazine,* IV,#12, p. 94. Philadelphia: Henry C. Lewis, 1819.
voice/pf
US: For listing of the very numerous locations of this periodical see *Union List of Serials.*
Wolfe (5191, 5200).

pub. c. 1790, London
The Match Girl ("Come buy of poor Mary good matches"), sung at most convivial societies. The words by T. H. The music by a Lady. 1. [London]: Fentum's Music Warehouse [c. 1790]. 2. Philadelphia: Carr and Co [1793].
voice/pf (2. with guit arr.)
1. GB: Lbl. 2. US: BUg, NYcuh, NYp, NYsha, SFbruning, WOa.
1. BUC. 2. Tick, Sonneck.

pub. 1798, London
Ode on the glorious victory gain'd over the French Fleet, off the mouth of the Nile, by Admiral Lord Nelson, on the 1st of August, 1798. The music . . . by a Lady. London: G. Smart [1798].
voice/pf
GB: Lbl, Ob.
BUC.

pub. between 1801 and 1810, London
Of the rose fair and young. Mrs. Jordan's favorite song in the popular comedy of *Hear Both Sides* written by Mr. Holcroft. The music by a Lady of Fashion. London: Clementi, Banger, Hyde, Collard & Davis [between 1801 & 1810]. 3 pp.
voice/pf
US: NH.
OCLC (19726822).

pub. 1827, Philadelphia
Oft in a Stilly Night, with Variations for the Piano Forte. Philadelphia: G. Willig, 1827.

pf
US: NYp.
Tick.

pub. 1797, London
On a lady weeping. [Song.] Words by Prior. Music by a Lady. In: *Lady's Magazine*, May 1797. [London]: 1797.
voice/pf
GB: Lbl.
BUC.

pub. c. 1793–96
Primroses. A Favorite song sung by Mrs. Pownal[l] with additions and alterations by a Lady. New York: J. Young [1793].
song
US: NYp [Early American Sheet Music, Am 1–V].
US: NYp Shelf List.

pub. 1785, Dublin
The Proofs of Passion, a favorite song, the words and music by a Lady. Preston: London [c. 1789]. 3 pp.
voice/pf
GB: Lbl.
BUC.

pub. 1785, Dublin
The Relenting Shepherdess. [Song.] The words by G. E. Howard Esp., the music by a Lady. Dublin: John Lee [c. 1785].
voice/pf
EIRE: Dn.
BUC.

pub. 1799, London
Rosa and Henry. The much admired song in the new comedy of *The Secret,* as sung by Mrs. Jordan, properly disposed of for the piano forte or harp, the music by a Lady of Fashion. [London]: Longman, Clementi & Co. [1799 or c. 1800]. 1 score and 2 parts. 4 pp.
voice/pf or harp, with parts for fl and guit
US: HA, NH.
OCLC (19727557, 19007643).

pub. c. 1786, Edinburgh
The Royal Edinburgh Cavalry march . . . by a Lady. Edinburgh: N. Stewart &
Co. [c. 1796]. 2 pp.
pf
GB: En.
BUC.

pub. 1797, London
"See, whilst thou weep'st." [Song]. Words by M. Prior. Music by a Lady.
In : *Lady's Magazine,* October, 1797. [London]: 1797.
voice/pf
GB: Lbl.
BUC.

pub. 1799, London
Sighs and tears reliev'd. A favorite song by a Lady. London: Broderip and
Wilkinson [c. 1799].
voice/pf
GB: Lbl, Ob.
BUC.

pub. c. 1800, London
Six ballads, with an accompaniment for the harp, the music by a Lady. [London]:
Printed for the Composer [c. 1800]. 13 pp. [GB: Lbl & Ob copies are
signed "B. S."]
voice/harp
GB: Cu, Lbl, Ob.
BUC.

pub. c. 1795, London
Six easy canzonets and three duets for the piano forte or harpsichord. Composed by
a Lady. London: Longman and Broderip, for the Authoress [c. 1795].
17 pp.
1–2 voices/pf or hpsch
GB: Gu, Lbl.
BUC.

pub. c. 1795, London
Songs and duetts composed by a Lady [Mrs. Woolf?]. London:
R. Birchall [c. 1795]. 27 pp.
1–2 voices/kbd

GB: Lam.
BUC.

pub. c. 1720, London
The South Sea Ballad. Set by a Lady. 1. [London, c. 1720]. 2. As: *Change Alley's so thin. The South Sea Ballad* [anony]. 3. *The second part of the South Sea Ballad.* Set by a Lady [London, c. 1721].
voice/pf
1. GB: Lam. 2. GB: Gm, Lbl. 3. GB: Lbl.
1–3. BUC.

pub. 18—?, London
Sympathy. A ballad, written & composed by a Lady, as sung at the vocal concerts by Mrs. Liston. [London]: Printed for the Author, [18—]. 3 pp.
voice/pf
US: HA.
OCLC (19728155).

pub. c. 1799, London
William and Mary. A favorite ballad, written to commemorate an . . . incident which happened on the embarkation of the 85 Regt August 10th 1799 at Ramsgate. The music by a Lady of Fashion. London: J. Dale [c. 1800].
voice/pf
GB: Ob.
BUC.

pub. c. 1796, Edinburgh
Wilt thou be my dearie. A favorite Scots song by Robt. Burns, the music adapted by a Lady. Edinburgh: J. Walker [c. 1796]. 2 pp.
voice/pf
GB: En.
BUC.

Lady (anonymous), of Baltimore
pub. c. 1824, Baltimore
Spanish rondo. Arranged for the piano forte . . . by a Lady of Baltimore. Baltimore: Willig [c. 1824].
pf
US: PHf.
Wolfe (5195).

Titus March. 1. [2 printings] Baltimore: J. Cole [1824?]. 2. Baltimore, G. Willig [1825?]. 3. New York: Dubois & Stodart [between 1827 and 1834]. 4. Boston: C. Bradlee [c. 1830]. 5. New York: S. T. Gordon [186–?]. *pf*
1. US: BAhs, CA, NYp, Wc, WOa. 2. US: BAhs, HA, NYp, WOa. 3. US: DM. 4. US: HA. 5. US: Pu.
1–3. Wolfe (5196, 5196A, 5197, 5198). 2–5. OCLC (18195429, 20469943, 18195434, 24347099). Tick.

Lady (anonymous), of Boston
pub. c. 1800, Boston?
"The fair Eliza's living grace." Addressed to Miss D. by a lady, both of Boston: In: [unidentified collection beginning with "A lesson"], pp. 5–6 [Boston: c. 1800].
voice/pf
US: PHhs.
Sonneck.

Lady (anonymous), of Charleston, S. C. (Wolfe identifies as **Murden, Mrs. Eliza Crawley,** d. between 1845 and 1851)
pub. 1814–15, Boston
United States Marine March. 1. Boston: Oliver Ditson [1814–15]. 2. Ms. copy, Jan. 15, 1856. 3. New York: S. T. Gordon [c.1860]. 4. Philadelphia: G. E. Blake [1814–15]. 5. Philadelphia: G. Willig [1815?]. 6. Baltimore: John Cole [1825?]. 7. New edition. Philadelphia: G. E. Blake [182–?]. 8. Anonymously, as unspecified instrumental quartet in open score, in: William Whiteley, *The Instrumental Preceptor,* pp. 44–45. Utica NY: Seward & Williams, 1816.
1–7. pf, 8. 4 wind instr. (cl, ob, fl, bsn?)
1. US: NYp. 2 & 3. US: HA. 4. US: BAhs, NYp, PHf, PIlevy, Wc. 5. CHAhs, NYcuh, NYp, PHfk, PIlevy, Wc, WOa. 6. US: BAhs, CHAhughes, NYcuh, NYp, PIlevy, PROu, R, RIhs, Wc, WGc. 7. CA. 8. AB, Bp, CA.
1–2. Tick, Sonneck. 2–3. OCLC (19007361, 18663578). 4–5. Wolfe (6360, 6361). 6–8. Wolfe (6362, 6363, 9885).

Lady, (E.?) (anonymous)
pub. 1825, New York
"And Ye Shall Walk in Silk Attire." [Text by Susanna Blamire.] The air [only] by a lady. Arranged by Henry R. Bishop. 1. Sung by Signorina Garcia . . . New York: Dubois & Stodart, 1825. 2. Sung by Miss M. Tree.

Baltimore: John Cole [1825?]. 3. Sung by Miss M. Tree. Baltimore: Geo. Willig [c. 1825]. 4. Philadelphia: John G. Klemm [c. 1825].
voice/pf
1. US: AB, CA, CAdriscoll, NYp, PHhs, PROu, WOa. 2. US: BAhs, CAdriscoll, NYp, PHfk, Wc. 3. US: CAdriscoll, ECstarr, NYcuh, NYp. 4. US: HA.
1–3. Wolfe (867, 868, 869), 4. OCLC (18852972). Tick.

Lady (anonymous), of Philadelphia

pub. 1793, Philadelphia
Asteria's fields. ("As o'er Asteria's fields I rove"). In: Moller & Capron's *Monthly numbers*, #3, pp. 21–22 [Philadelphia: s.n.,1793].
voice/pf
US: PHhs, Wc.
Sonneck.

pub. 1793, Philadelphia
"The Cheerful Spring Begins Today." [Song.] In: Moller & Capron's *Monthly numbers.* #1, p. 7. [Philadelphia: s.n., 1793].
voice/kbd
US: Wc.
Sonneck, Tick.

pub. c. 1824, Philadelphia
LaFayette's grand march. Composed by a lady of Philadelphia. Philadelphia: J. G. Klemm [1824?].
pf
US: NYp, PIlevy.
Wolfe (5199).

La Guerre (Laguerre, de La Guerre), Elisabeth-Claude, née Jacquet. See Jacquet de La Guerre, Elisabeth-Claude

Lamballe, Marie-Theresa-Louisa, Mme la Princesse de (Mary Theresa Louisa of Savoy Carignan, Princess de Lamballe)

1749–1792, Paris
Romance composée par Madame la Princesse de Lamballe, avec un rondeau de A. C. Furtado. Paris: Bouvin, 1791.
song
GB: Cu, Gu, Lbl [e.104.(7.)].
RISM A/I (L 355), CPM, Cohen.

Lambert, Mlle
pub. 1780, Paris
Le satyre et le Passant. Fable mise en vers par Mr de La Fontaine [Paris:
Camand, c. 1780?].
voice/kbd
GB: Lbl [B.362.e.(99.)].
RISM A/I (L 379), CPM, BUC.

**Lannoy de Clervaux, Clémentine-Joséphine-Françoise-Thérèse
de,** née **Comtesse de Looz-Corswarem**
1764, Schloß Gray–1820, Paris
Pièce a L'Eternel ("Dieu tout puissant") Pour la conservation des jours de
Sa Majesté Napoléon . . . composée le 25 8.bre, 1808 & Dédiée A Sa
Majesté L'Imperatrice Josephine . . . Pour quatre Voix, deux Violons, Alto,
Basse, Contre Basse, deux flutes, deux hautbois, deux corps [*sic,* for cor] et
un Basson. Ms. score, 1808.
SATB/2 vlns/vla/vlc/db/2fls/2 obs/2 hns/bsn
CH: AR [Mus. Ms. A 27 (Ms. 7464)].
RISM A/II (#10956).

"Plaisir d'aimer besoin d'un âme tendre." Romance. S.l.: s.n. [Berlin:
Hummel,1798].
song
D: LCH (without title page).
RISM A/I (L 611), Cohen, Eitner, MGG.

"Pour nous créer un cœur sensible." Romance. 1. s.l.: s.n., n.d. 2. arr. pour
piano forte ou harpe. Berlin: Johann Julius Hummel: Amsterdam, au
grand magazine de musique, aux adresses ordinaires, 1798.
1. song. 2. pf or harp
1. D: LCH (without title page) 2. NL: At.
1–2. RISM A/I (L 612, 613). MGG.

Quatriéme sonate (F) pour le piano forte avec accompagnement d'un violon et violoncelle
. . . œuvre IVme. Zürich: Alexandre. Parts.
pf/vln/vlc
I: Nc (pf only).
RISM A/I (L 615), Eitner.

Romances Pour Harpe ou Piano. Contents: "C'etait pour lui," "Dans le
printemps," "Jadis dans ma simple innocence," "Vous qui d'amour." Ms.

score, pp. 24–31.
voice/harp or pf
CH: AR [Mus. Ms. A 30 (Ms. 7523)].
RISM A/II (#11017).

Trois sonates pour le clavecin ou piano forte avec accompagnement d'un violon et violon-celle, op. 1. s.l., s.n. [Berlin: Hummel], 3 partbooks.
hpsch or pf/vln/vlc
CS: K (complete: kbd, vln, vlc). D: RH. Copy in D:Kf&m and UNikb.
RISM A/I (L 614), Frau & Musik, Frauenmusik, Cohen.

Larrivée, Agathe-Elisabeth-Henriette (married Borghese). See Borghese, Agathe-Elisabeth-Henriette, née Larrivée

Laschansky, Mme
late 18th cent.
Concerto à 5 [in B-flat for oboe and strings]. Ms. partbooks.
oboe/4-part string orch
D: SWl.
Haynes, Cohen.

Laugier, Mme
pub. 1780s, Paris
[Work(s)] in: *Etrennes de Polymnie. Recueil de chansons, romances, vaude-villes . . .* Paris: au bureau de la petite bibliothèque des théatres, Belin, 1785–89.
song(s)
D: LEm. F: Ma, Pcf, Pn, V. US: Wc.
RISM B/II (p. 168).

Le B. ne, S. R. Mad.me de
n.d.
[17 songs for voice and harp]. Ms.
voice/harp
CH: AR [Mus Ms A 27 (Ms. 7456)].
RISM A/II (#0010948).

Le Beau, Ernestine, Mlle
pub. 1820s, Paris
Contredanses variées pour le forte piano. Paris: chez Auguste LeDuc
[c. 1820–23].

pf
F: Pn (A.42.259). Photocopy in C. Johnson coll.
Letter (C. Johnson).

Le Brun (Lebrun), Franziska (Francesca) Dorothea, née Danzi
1756, Mannheim–1791, Berlin
Six sonatas [B-flat, E-flat, F, G, C, D] *for the harpsichord or piano forte with an accompaniment for a violin* [op. 1]. 1. London: James Blundell, for the author [c. 1778 or 1780]. 2. London: John Preston [c. 1785]. 3. London: J. Bland [c. 1785]. 4. *Six sonates . . .* œuvre lère. Paris: Sieber, 1781. 5. Berlin/Amsterdam: Hummel (#550) [c. 1783]. Titled as op. 1 by publisher, but same as *Six Sonatas,* op. II, see following entry].
hpsch or pf/vln
1. D: Mbs. GB: Lbl [Ch.1689.(1.)]. S: Skma. US: CHH, NYp. 2. GB: Ckc. S: Skma. US: CHH. 3. GB: Lbl [Ch.1480.o.(13.)]. 4. F: Pn [Vm12 34491 (lacks vln), Vm7 5366 (complete)] (microfilm, US: AA). 5. See op. 2. Copy in Ars Fem coll.
1–3. RISM A/I (L 1241–43). 1–2. BUC. 1, 3. CPM. 1. NUC (NL 0183969). 4. RISM A/I (L 1245–46), OCLC (micro. 23388204). 5. (RISM L 1244) see op. 2. MGG, Cohen, Hayes, Olivier, Cohen, letter (Ars Fem).

Six sonatas [D, B-flat, F, C, A, E-flat] for *the piano forte or harpsichord with an accompanyment* for a violin, op. II. 1. London: for the author, Longman, c.1780. Parts. 2. Six sonates . . . Mannheim, Götz (#98), [1784–85]. 3. Paris: Sieber, 1781. 4. As op. 1. Berlin/Amsterdam: Hummel (#550) [c. 1783]. 5. Worms: Kreitner.
hpsch or pf/vln
1. B: Bc. EIRE: Dn (incomplete). GB: Ckc, Cu, Lbl [h.1689.(2.)]. D: UNikb. US: NYp. 2. F: Pn [Vm7 5367]. US: R (lacks vln). USSR: Ml. 3. Unknown. 4. D: Dl (kbd/vln). US: PHu. 5. Location unknown. Copy in Ars Fem coll.
1–2. RISM A/I (L 1248–49, LL1249). 1. NUC (NL 0183970), Frauenmusik. 2. Paris Lib. Cat. 4. RISM A/I (L1244, as op. 1, LL1244), OCLC (14250857), NUC (NL0183971). MGG, Riemann, Hayes, letter (Ars Fem).

Sonata clavicembalo [B-flat major, apparently with violin]. Ms., c. 1780 [cembalo part only, vln missing].
hpsch/vln
D: RH (Ms 469).
RISM A/II (#82498).

Sonate pour le clavecin avec accompagnement du violon [B-flat major].
Ms., 1786 [cembalo part only, vln missing].
hpsch/vln
D: RH (Ms 470).
RISM A/II (#82499).

Trois sonatas [Nos. I, II, & III from op. 1] . . . Oeuvre 1. Offenbach:
André, 1783. 2. Mannheim: Götz, 1784/85. 3. Worms: Kreitner.
hpsch or pf/vln
1. D: Dl. PL: S. 2. location unknown. 3. location unknown. Copy in Ars
Fem coll.
RISM A/I (L 1247, LL1244), MGG, Cohen, Olivier, letter (Ars Fem).

Le Chantre, Mlle Elisabeth
b. circa 1752, fl. 1767–1770
"Trop souvent une belle." Ms., before 1800.
song
US: BE (Ms 775).
Letter (C. Johnson), Berkeley (#618, pp. 301–02).

Le Clere, Victoire, Mme
pub. 1800, London (French)
The virgin's first love. A favorite ariette, with an accompaniment for the harp
or piano forte and german flute . . . The melody by Madame V. Le Clere,
adapted to English words & the accompaniments by an eminent composer. London: Lewis Lavenu [c.1800].
Melody only by Le Clere
voice/harp or pf/fl
GB: Lbl [G.800.m.(37.)]
RISM A/I (L 1348), CPM, BUC, Cohen, Boenke

Le Jeune, Mlle
pub. before 1800, Paris
Recueil de romances et chansons . . . avec accompagnement de clavecin par Mlle Le
Jeune. Paris: auteur, Mlle Le Jeune (gravé par Mme Marie), n.d.
voice/hpsch
F: V.
RISM A/I (L 1671).

Le Noble, Madamoiselle
n.d.

14 Variations sur Les Folies d'Espagne [harpsichord].
hpsch
F: V. Copy in Ars Fem coll.
Letter (Ars Fem).

Le Descente de Mars. [harpsichord]
hpsch
F: V. Copy in Ars Fem coll.
Letter (Ars Fem).

Leonarda, Isabella

1620, Novara–1704, Novara
"Ah, Domine Jesu," " Sic ergo anima." 1. In: Gasparo Casati, *Il Terzo Libro de Sacri Concenti a 2. 3. e 4 voci,* op. 3. Venice: Bartolomeo Magni, 1640. 5 partbooks (SI, SII, A, B, bc). 2. In reprints of Casati, *Il Terzo Libro . . . ,* Venice: Magni, 1642. 3. Venice: Magni, 1644. 4. Antwerp: Madaléne Phalése & cohéritier, 1650. 5. Venice: Gardano, 1650. 6. Antwerp: Héretiers de Pierre Phalèse, 1668.
AT / org bc
1. B: Bc (SII). I: Bc, CO (SI A B Bc), Md, VCd (B). PL: WR (modern location not confirmed). 2. 1642: I: Bc. PL: WRu (SII inc.). 3. 1644: GB: Och. 4. 1650: I: ASc, Bc (SII A, B). 5. Location not known.
1. RISM B/I (1640[3]), Bohn. 2–4. RISM B/I (1642[2], 1644[2], 1650[3]), 1–6. Carter (lists additional reprints not in RISM). Cohen, MGG. NG (as Isabella Leonarda).

[op. 3] [18] *Sacri concenti à una, due, tré, et quattro voci . . .* Opera terza. Milan: Fratelli Camagni, 1670. 5 Partbooks (SATB org)
1 for 4 voices in various combinations / org bc / 1 with 2 vlns
GB: Lcm. Microfilm in US: CAi (3463.104.23.12).
RISM A/I (I 92), BUC, Eitner, NG (all under I as Isabella Leonarda). Carter, Cohen, MGG, letter (US: CAi).

[op. 4] *Messa, e salmi, concertati, & à capella con Istromenti ad libitum . . .* Opera quarta. Milan: Fratelli Camagni, 1674. 7 Partbooks (CATB, Vln 1 & 2, org bc). [1 Mass, 1 litany, 8 psalms, 1 Magnificat.]
SATB / 2 vlns / org bc in various combinations
CH: E (SA, org), Zz. D: BEU (SA). I: BGi (org). Microfilm of CH: Zz copy in US: CAi (3463.104.23.12).
RISM A/I (I 93), Eitner, NG (all under I as Isabella Leonarda). Carter, Cohen, MGG, letter (US: CAi)

[op. 6] [12] *Motteti a voce sola*, Parte con istromenti, e parte senza . . .
Opera sesta. Venice: stampa del Gardano, 1676. Score.
S/org bc; S/2 vlns/org bc; A/org bc; A/2 vlns/org bc; B/org bc; B/2 vlns/org bc
I: Bc (AA. 188). US: Wc. Microfilms in US: NYp, CAi (3463.104.23.12),
& Jackson coll.
*RISM A/I (I 94), NUC (micro. NI 0166420), Eitner, NG (all under I as Isabella
Leonarda). Carter, Cohen, MGG, letter (US: CAi).*

[op. 7] *Motteti a una, due, tre e quattro voci parte con istromenti e parte senza con le
litanie della Beata Vergine* . . . Opera settima. Bologna: Giacomo Monti,
1677. 5 Partbooks (CATB org bc) [12 motets and 1 litany].
1 for 4 voices/3 with 2 vlns/org bc., various combinations.
F: Pn (SAT org) [Vm1 1025]. I: COd (SA org), PS. Microfilm of I: PS
copy in US: CAi (3463.104.23.12).
*RISM A/I (I 95), Eitner, NG (all under I as Isabella Leonarda), Paris Lib. Cat.,
Carter, Cohen, MGG, letter (US:CAi).*

[op. 8] *Vespro a cappella della B.V. e motetti concertati* . . . opera VIII. Bologna:
Giacomo Monti, 1678. 5 Partbooks (CATB org bc).
8 for SATB/org; 1 for SAB/2 vlns/org; 2 for S/org
I: Bc (AA. 189), COd (ATB org). Microfilm of I: Bc copy in US: CAi
(3463.104.23.12).
*RISM A/I (I 96) Eitner, NG (all under I as Isabella Leonarda). Carter, Cohen,
MGG, letter from (US: CAi).*

[op. 10] *Motetti a quattro voci con le littanie della B.V.* . . . opera decima.
Milano: Fratelli Camagni alla Rosa. 1684. 5 Partbooks (CATB org bc)
[11 motets, 1 litany].
SATB/org bc
CH: DE (B), Zz (complete: SATB org). Microfilm of Zürich copy in US:
CAi (3463.104.23.2).
*RISM A/I (I 97), Eitner, NG (all under I as Isabella Leonarda). Carter, Cohen,
MGG, letter (US: CAi).*

[op. 11] [12] *Motetti a voce sola* . . . . opera XI. Bologna: Giacomo Monti,
1684. Score.
8 for S or T/org bc; 2 for A/org bc; 2 for B/org bc
I: Bc (AA. 190). Microfilm in US: CAi (3463.104.23.12).
*RISM A/I (I 98), Eitner, NG (all under I as Isabella Leonarda). Carter, Cohen,
MGG, letter (US: CAi).*

[op. 12] [14] *Motetti a voce sola* . . . . opera duodecima. Milan: Fratelli
Camagni, 1686. Score. 218 pp.
7 for S/org/bc; 3 for A/org bc; 4 for B/org bc
A: Wgm. GB: Lbl [E.1421]. Microfilm of Lbl copy in US: CAi
(3463.104.23.5).
*RISM A/I (I 99), NG, BUC, CPM, Eitner (all under I as Isabella Leonarda).
Carter, Cohen, MGG, letter (US: CAi).*

[op. 13] [12] *Motetti a una, due, e tre voci, con violini, e senza* . . . opera decima
terza. Bologna: Giacomo Monti, 1687. 6 Partbooks (CAB Vln I, Vln II,
org bc)
SAB/org bc (4 with 2 vlns) in various combinations
D: Mbs (org). F: Pn (complete: SAB, 2 vln, org) [Vm1 1026]. Microfilm of
F: Pn copy in US: CAi (3463.104.23.6).
*RISM A/I (I 100), Eitner, NG (all under I as Isabella Leonarda). Paris Lib. Cat.,
Carter, Cohen, MGG, letter (US: CAi).*

[op. 14] [10] *Motetti a voce sola,* . . . opera decima quarta. Bologna:
Giacomo Monti, 1687. Score.
6 for S or T/org bc; 2 for A/org bc; 2 for B/org bc
I: Bc (AA. 191). Microfilm in US: CAi (3463.104.23.11).
*RISM A/I (I 101), Eitner, NG (all under I as Isabella Leonarda). Carter, Cohen,
MGG, letter (US: CAi).*

[op. 15] [11] *Motetti a' voce sola* . . . opera decima quinta. Bologna: Pier-
Maria Monti, 1690. Score.
7 for S/org bc; 2 for A/org bc; 2 for B/org bc
I: Bc (AA. 192). Microfilm in US: CAi (3463.104.23.10).
*RISM A/I (I 102), Eitner, NG (all under I as Isabella Leonarda). Carter, Cohen,
MGG, letter (US: CAi).*

[op. 16] [12] *Sonate a 1, 2, 3, e 4 istromenti,* . . . opera decima sesta. Bologna:
Pier-Maria Monti, 1693. 4 partbooks (vln I, vln II, violone, org bc).
11 for 2 vlns/violone [vlc] and org bc; 1 for 1 vln/org bc
I: Bc (AA. 193). Copy in Jackson coll.
*RISM A/I (I 103), Eitner, NG (all under I as Isabella Leonarda). Carter, Cohen,
MGG.*

[op. 17] [12] *Motetti a voce sola* . . . opera decima settima. Bologna: Pier-
Maria Monti, 1695. Score.
8 for S/org bc; 2 for A/org bc; 2 for B/org bc

I: Bc (AA. 194). Microfilm in US: CAi (3463.104.23.9).
RISM A/I (I 104),Eitner, NG (all under I as Isabella Leonarda). Carter, Cohen, MGG, letter (US: CAi).

[op. 18] [3] *Messe A quattro voci concertate con Stromenti, & [3] Motetti à una, due e trè voci, pure con Stromenti . . .* opera decima ottava. Bologna: Pier-Maria Monti, 1696. 8 partbooks (CATB, vln I, vln II, violone or theorbo, org). *SATB/2 vlns/ org bc; S/2 vlns/org bc; SS/2 vlns/org bc; SAB/2 vlns/org bc* GB: Lcm. I: Bc (AA. 195). Microfilm of GB: Lcm copy in US: CAi (3463.104.23.14). Copy in Jackson coll. *RISM A/I (I 105), BUC, Eitner, NG (all under I as Isabella Leonarda). Carter, Cohen, MGG, letter (US: CAi).*

[op. 19] *Salmi concertati a 4. voci con strumenti . . .* opera decimanona. Bologna: Marino Silvani, 1698. 8 partbooks (CATB, vln I, vln II, violone or theorbo, org bc) [9 psalms, 1 magnificat, 1 canon for 3 T]. *7 for SATB; 1 for S; 1 for TTT; 1 for S or SATB; All 2 with vlns/bc* CH: Zz . D: OB. F: Pn [Vm1 1027]. I: Sac (org). Microfilm of CH: Zz copy in US: CAi (3463.104.23.12). *RISM A/I (I 106) Eitner, NG (all under I as Isabella Leonarda), Paris Lib. Cat., Carter, Cohen, MGG, letter (US: CAi).*

[op. 20] *Motetti à Voce sola, con Istromenti . . .* opera vigesima. Bologna: Marino Silvani, 1700. 5 partbooks (Parte che canta, vln I, vln II, bassetto, org bc) [13 motets, 1 litany]. *5 for S/2 vln/bc; 6 for A/2 vln/bc; 1 for A/org; 1 for B/2 vlns/bc; 2S (or 2T/org. (A,B ad lib.)* I: Bc (AA. 196). Microfilm in US: CAi (3463.104.23.12). *RISM A/I (I 107), Eitner, NG (all under I as Isabella Leonarda). Carter, Cohen, MGG, letter (US: CAi).*

Op. 1, 2, 5, 9. (missing)
Carter.

LePelletier, Madame
fl. 1810–1811, Baltimore
Air from the opera of The Sylphs. Arr. from F. H. Himmel. In: *Journal of Musick,* pt. 1, # 2, p. 9–12. Baltimore: Madame LePelletier, 1810.
voice/pf
US: Bp, BAhs, CA, NYcuh, NYp, PHf, PIlevy, Wc, WOa.
Wolfe (3856, 4696).

Boleros de l'opéra de Ponce de Leon ("Il faut garder votre savoir"). Arr. from
H. M. Berton. In: *Journal of Musick,* pt. 1, #3, p. 17–19. Baltimore:
Madame LePelletier, 1810.
voice/pf
US: Bp, BAhs, CA, NYcuh, NYp, PHf, PIlevy, Wc, WOa.
Wolfe (4696, 5344).

"Come tell me where the maid is found." words by T. Moore In: *Journal of
Musick,* pt. 1, #7, p. 46–48. Baltimore: Madame LePelletier, 1810.
voice/pf
US: Bp, BAhs, CA, NYcuh, NYp, PHf, PIlevy, Wc, WOa.
Wolfe (4696, 5344).

Fantasie sur un air Russe. Composèe pour le forte piano et dèdièe à Madame
Daschkoff, nèe Baronne de Preuzar, par Madame LePelletier. In: *Journal of
Musick,* pt. 2, #16–17, p. 108–19. Baltimore: Madame LePelletier, 1810.
pf
US: Bp, BAhs, CA, NYcuh, NYp, PHf, PIlevy, Wc, WOa.
Wolfe (4696, 5345).

Interlude of the opera Les Confidences. Composed by Nicolo Isouard. Arranged
for the piano forte by Madame LePelletier. In: *Journal of Musick,* pt. 1, #5,
pp. 28–31. Baltimore: Madame LePelletier, 1810.
pf
US: Bp, BAhs, CA, NYcuh, NYp, PHf, PIlevy, Wc, WOa.
Wolfe (4504, 4696).

Journal of Musick, composed of Italian, French, and English songs,
romances, and duetts, and of overtures, rondos, &c., for the piano forte.
[Several arrangements and compositions are identified as by Mme
LePelletier; others may be arr. by her.] Baltimore: Madame LePelletier, Pt.
I & II, 1810; Pt I, 1811.
1–2 voices/pf; pf solo
1810–I: US: Bp, BAhs, CA, NYcuh, NYp, PHf, PIlevy, Wc, WOa.
1810–II: US: BAhs, Bp, CA, PHf, PIlevy, NYcuh, Wc. 1811–I: US: BAhs,
NYp, Wc.
Wolfe (4696).

Overture and interlude of the opera Une Folie. Composed by Méhul. Arranged for
the piano forte by Madame LePelletier. In: *Journal of Musick,* pt. 1, #9–11,
pp. 58–71. Baltimore: Madame LePelletier,1810.

pf
US: Bp, BAhs, CA, NYcuh, NYp, PHf, PIlevy, Wc, WOa.
Wolfe (4749, 4696).

Overture to the opera L'Auberge de Bagnères. Composed by Catel. Arranged for the piano forte by Madame LePelletier. In: *Journal of Musick*, pt. 1, #1–2, pp. 2–8. Baltimore: Madame LePelletier,1810.
pf
US: Bp, BAhs, CA, NYcuh, NYp, PHf, PIlevy, Wc, WOa.
Wolfe (1715, 4696).

Overture to the opera La Romance. Composed by H. Berton & *Romance* de l'opera *La Romance* ("Du tendre amour—If in that breast so good so pure"). Arr. by Mrs. LePelletier, In: *Journal of Musick*, pt. 1, #25–26, p. 2–13; & pt. 1, #3, pp. 13–16. Baltimore: Madame LePelletier, 1811.
overture—pf; romance—voice/pf
US: Bp, BAhs, CA, NYcuh, NYp, PHf, PIlevy, Wc, WOa.
Wolfe (4696, 536, 539).

Le R . . . , Mlle
pub. 1770, Paris
"Cessez, charmante Iris." Air. [Paris]: Récoquiliée, 1770; *Mercure de France*, December, 1770.
song
GB: Lbl [298.e.1.].
BUC, CPM.

Le Vasseur, Mlle Rosalie
pub. 1770s–80s, Paris
Editor [and arranger?] of: *18è Recueil d'ariettes choisies arrangés pour le clavecin ou le forte-piano avec accompagnement d'un violon ad libitum . . . par Benaut . . .* Paris: l'auteur [1775–81]. 18th of 30 vol.
hpsch or pf/vln ad lib
B: Bc. F: AG, Pa, Pc, Pn. All holdings are incomplete runs.
RISM B/II (p. 317).

Levêque (Lèvesque), Louise, née Cuvelier [also literary works]
1708–1745, Paris
La bergère prudente. Paris: Cousineau (#247). Keyboard arr. [ascription questioned].
voice/pf [arr. of orch?]

CS: K.
RISM L 2177.

Lettres et chansons de Céphise et d'Uranie. Paris: Jean-Baptiste-Christophe
Ballard, 1731. Score, 87 pp. [songs for one voice or one voice and bass].
voice/bc [some without bass]
F: Pc [8o B.2166]. US: U, Wc (M 1619 A21 .85).
RISM A/I (L 2176), NUC (NL 0308722), Paris Lib. Cat.

Lévesque, Mlle (may be **Elisabeth de Haulteterre,** married name
Lévesque. See **Haulteterre, Elisabeth de**)

Levy, Sara, née Itzig (great-aunt of **Felix and Fanny Mendelssohn**)
1761–1854, lived in Berlin
[Songs.] Ms.?
songs
D: B? (at her death to Berlin Singakademie, then to the Preußische
Staatsbibliothek, modern location not confirmed).
Stewart Green, NG, MGG.

Licoschin, Catherine de
1780–1840
Polonaise in a-moll für Klavier. Wilhelmshaven: Heinrichshofen, n.d.
pf
D: UNikb.
Frauenmusik.

Liddiard, Anna
pub. 18th cent., Dublin
"Farewell thou last Bard of poor Erin, farewell." Dublin: I. Willis, n.d.
song
I: MOe (Mus. G. 205).
Estense.

Liebmann, Helene, née Riese
1796, Berlin–after 1819
Grande sonate [g] *pour le piano-forte* composée et dédiée à Monsieur
E. Ezechiel . . . par Helene Liebmann née Riese. œuv. 15. Leipzig: C. F.
Peters, bureau de musique, no. 1240/A Francfort sur le Mein, chez J. C.
Gayl. 20 pp.
pf

D: Kf&m, Mbs (4 Mus. pr. 16985, Beibd.4), UNikb.
RISM A/I (R 1410, as Riese), letter (D: Mbs), Frau & Musik, Frauenmusik, Cohen.

Grande sonate pour le piano-forte et violoncelle composée et dédiée à Monsieur Max Bohrer par Helene Liebmann née Riese. Oeuvre XI. Leipzig-Berlin: Bureau des arts et d'industrie, no. 553. 2 partbooks (19 & 4 pp.).
pf/vlc
D: B, Mbs (4 Mus.pr. 32790). Copy in Ars Fem coll.
RISM A/I (R 1409, Riese), letter (D: Mbs), Cohen, Pazdírek (as Riese, Liebmann H.), letter (Ars Fem).

Grande sonate pour le piano-forte . . . œuvre 3. Berlin: Bureau des arts et d'industrie, no. 105. Published as Helene Riese.
pf
A: Wkann.
RISM A/I (R 1408, as Riese), Cohen, Pazdírek (Riese, Liebmann H.).

Grande Trio pour le Pianoforte avec accompagnement de Violon et Basse composé et dédié à Monsieur Ferdinand Ries par Son Elève Helene Liebmann née Riese. Œuv. 13 [number provided by hand]. Leipzig: Bureau de Musique de C. F. Peters, Pl. #1217. 3 partbooks (19, 4, & 4 pp).
pf/vln/vlc
D: Mbs (4 Mus.pr. 55754).
Letter (D: Mbs), Cohen (but with another op. no.).

"Kennst du das Land." Lied von Göthe, aus *Wilhelm Meister . . .* op. 4.
1. Berlin: Kunst- und Industrie-Comptoir [1811]. Published as Helene Riese. 2. Ms., 19th century.
voice (S)/pf
1. D: DÜk, GB: Lbl [E. 253.b.(16.)]. US: NH (Music R43 4), NYp. 2. D: Hs (M C/292).
1. RISM A/I (R 1406, Riese), CPM, NUC (NL 0348024, NR 0273906), Cohen, Fétis (entries for Riese & Liebmann). 2. RISM A/II (#80180).

Sonate pour le Pianoforte avec un violon obligé, op. 14. Leipzig: C. F. Peters (#1238) [published as Liebmann, née Riese].
pf/vln
D: LEverlag Peters Archiv, probably now in LEm. Copy in Jackson coll. (supplied by Alan Pedigo, Booneville AR).
Cohen.

Sonate pour le Piano-Forte composée par Helene Riese, œuvre 1. Berlin: Bureau des arts et d'industrie. Published as Helene Riese. Ms. copy 1822, 6 pp.
pf
D: DO (Mus. Ms. 2568).
RISM A/II (#87621).

Sonate pour le piano-forte . . . œ. 2 [added by hand]. Berlin: Bureau des arts et d'industrie. Published as Helene Riese.
pf
A: Wkann.
RISM A/I (R 1407, Riese), Cohen, Pazdírek (Riese, Liebmann H.).

Variations de la romance favorite de La Petite Cendrillon (ou Aschenbrödel) pour le Piano-forte . . . dediées à Mademoiselle Nina de Belot. Vienna: Louis Maisch (plate #455) [c. 1815]. 5 pp.
pf
I: Ostiglia (Ediz. Musiche B-358). US: NYp. Copy of US: NYp in Ars Fem coll.
Ostiglia, NUC (NL 0348025. Cat. entry has E. [sic] Liebmann), letter (Ars Fem).

Lihu, Annette de
pub. 1812–17?, Paris
L'Orphéline. Romance [for two voices]. London: s.n. [1817?].
2 voices/pf
GB: Lbl [H.1675.(30.)]
CPM.

"Maman c'est bien dommage." Romance. London: s.n. [1815?].
voice/pf
GB: Lbl [G.806.c.(24.)].
CPM.

"Ni jamais, ni toujours." Romance, with an accompaniment for the piano forte. London: printed for the author [18—]. 5 pp. Bound with Westmorland, J. F. "Spirit of Bliss."
voice/pf
D: LÜh. US: CA.
RISM A/I (L 2417), NUC (NL 0362577).

Lihu, Annette de and Lihu, Victorine de
pub. 1812–17?, Paris

French Song ("Filles du hameau, laíssez voux condiure"), arr. for two voices by Mesdlles de Lihu. London: Printed for the Mesdlles de Lihu, [1812]. 3 pp.
2 voices / pf or harp
GB: Lbl [G.809.n.(6.)]. US: NYp.
CPM, NUC (NL 0362576).

Lihu, Victorine de
pub. 1812–17?, Paris
"Le troubadour" [by H. N. Gilles], arrangée par V. de Lihu. S.l.: s.n. [1817?].
2 voices / pf
GB: Lbl [H.1670.(15.)].
CPM.

Likoschin, Katherina (may be same as Licoshin, Catherine de)
n.d.
Six polonaises et six ecossaises composées pour le piano-forte. St. Petersburg: F. A. Dittmar, #1214, n.d.
pf
USSR: Mk.
RISM A/I (LL 2417 I, 1).

Lilien, Antoinette von, Baroness
pub. 1799, Vienna
IX. Variations pour le piano forte. Vienna: Joseph Eder, au magazin de musique, (#56) [1799].
pf
A:Wgm
CS: K. D: Mbs, Rp.
RISM A/I (L 2418, LL2418), Cohen.

VII. Variations pour le piano forte sur un thème dans le ballet d'Alcine . . . op. 2. Vienna: Joseph Eder, au magazin de musique (#12), n.d.
pf
A: Wgm. D: Rp
RISM A/I (LL 2419), Cohen.

VIII. Variations pour le piano forte sur la thème du trio "Pria ch'io limpegno" de l'opéra La molinara . . . œuvre 2. Vienna: Joseph Eder, au magazin de musique, (#57) [1799].

pf
A: Wgm. I: Nc.
RISM A/I (L 2421, LL 2418a), Cohen.

[10] *Variations pour le piano forte sur l'air "Rachelina," dans l'opéra La molinara*
. . . œuvre 2. Vienna: Joseph Eder, n.d.
pf
A: Wgm. CS: N. I: MOe (Mus. F. 635).
RISM A/I (L 2420, LL 2421), Estense.

X. *Variations pour le piano forte sur la cavatina "O caro Tonino," dans l'opéra Le geloise vilane* . . . op. 3. Vienna: Joseph Eder, au magazin de musique (#97) [1799].
pf
CS: K.
RISM A/I (L 2419).

Linwood, Mary [also known for poetry, prose, and needlework]
1755, Birmingham–1845, Leicester
David's First Victory, a sacred oratorio . . . with an accompaniment for the Organ or Pianoforte. Written [and] composed by Mary Linwood. London: Cramer, Addison & Beale [1840?]. 196 pp.
voices/org or pf
GB: Lbl [H.1069.]. US: Bp.
CPM, NUC (NL 0394183), Cohen.

The Kellerin ("I ponder on those happy hours") and [The White Wreath] ("Leave me to sorrow awhile"). [2 Ballads from unpublished Opera(s).] Nos. 1 & 2 in: *Operatic Fragments*. London: s.n. [1853].
voice/pf
GB: Lbl [H.2828.b.(9. & 10.)].
CPM, Cohen.

"Let us hence!" Canzonet . . . the subject from a rondo by W. Plachy. In: *The Harmonicon*, 1828 (vol. 6, pt. 2, pp. 101–05).
voice/pf
GB: Lbl [P.P.1947.].
CPM.

"Pretty Fairy!" Canzonet. 1. In: *The Harmonicon*, 1828 (vol. 6, pt. 2, pp. 45–49). 2. New York: Mesier [183–?]. 3. New York; Dubois & Stodart [c. 1830]. 4. In: *Musical Library*, Vol. 1. London: 1854. 5. In bound volume of 19th cent. harp music.
voice/pf [or harp]
1. GB: Lbl [P.P.1947.] 2. US: Bp. 3. US: NYp, Wc (M1. A13L). 4. US: Bp. 5. Rempel coll.
1. CPM, 2–4. NUC (NL 0394191–3), 5. letter (Rempel). Cohen.

The Sạbbath Bridal. A dialogue [song]. In: *The Harmonicon*, vol. 10, pt. 2, pp. 38–40. 1832.
voice/pf
GB: Lbl [P.P.1947.].
CPM.

Lobarczewska, Mme
n.d., pub. in Russia
Quatre polonoises [sic], deux ecossoises [sic], deux waltzes et deux quadrilles pour le clavecin ou fortepiano. St. Petersburg: F. A. Dittmar, #1009, n.d.
hpsch or pf
USSR: Mcm.
RISM A/I (LL2587 I,1).

Lolo, Mlle
pub. 1726, Paris
Work(s) in: *Meslanges de musique latine, françoise et italienne, divisez par saisons . . .* Paris: J. B. C. Ballard, 1726.
instruments not determined
F: Pc.
RISM B/II (p. 233).

Lolotte, Mlle (same as **Mlle Lolo?**)
early 18th cent., France
Work(s) in: *Meslanges de musique latine, françoise et italienne, divisez par saisons . . .* Paris: J. B. C. Ballard, 1726.
instruments not determined
F: Pc.
RISM B/II (p. 233).

Lombardini, Maddalena. See **Sirmen, Maddalena Laura,** née **Lombardini**

Louis, Marie-Emmanuelle, née **Bayon (Bajon)** (Often as **Bayon-Louis, Mme Victor,** or as Bajon)
1746, Marcel (Orne)–1825, Aubevoye, near Paris
Fleur d'épine, air from. Arr. by F. Petrini. In: *Journal de harp,* #10. Paris; chez l'auteur/chez la d[am]e Oger [c. 1779].
voice/harp
F: Pn.
Letter (C. Johnson).

Fleur d'épine, air from. "Au bord d'une onde pure." In: *Elite de Chansons et Ariettes décentes Avec Accompagnement de Basse continue.* Paris: Chez tous les M[archa]ds de musique.
voice/hpsch bc
F: Pn.
Letter (C. Johnson).

Fleur d'épine, air from. "Au bord d'une onde pure." In: *Sonates pour clavecin des divers auteurs* [voice & harpsichord]. Portuguese ms, from late 18th cent.
voice/hpsch bc
F: Pn [Vm7 4874].
Letter (C. Johnson).

Fleur d'épine, air from. "Au bord d'une onde pure" [listed as Le *Sommeil de Fleur d'Epine,* Opera Comique]. 1. In: M. Couarde de Narbonne, *Recueil d'Ariettes, avec accompagnement de Harpe.* Paris: chez l'Auteur/Cousineau [c. 1779]. 2. In: untitled French ms., c. 1780.
voice/harp
1. F: Pn. 2. F: Pn [Vm7 4823].
Letter (C. Johnson).

Fleur d'épine. Airs détachés. Paris: aux adresses ordinaires de musique (gravés par Huguet) [1776].
voice/kbd
F: Pa [Ars. M.734(1)], Pc (B.N. Y.522).
RISM A/I (B 1431, BB 1431) (Bayon-Louis), Paris Lib. Cat. Cohen (Louis), letter (C. Johnson).

Fleur d'épine, airs from. "A l'Amour tout est possible," "Au Bord d'une onde pure," "C'est l'Etat de notre Coeur," "Echo, echo que fleur d'Epine," "On ne doit compter," & "Quand on est tendre." In: *Extrait des airs françois de tous les opéras nouveaux . . .* Appropriés pour le chant ou la flûte avec la basse continue, #10. Amsterdam: La Haye, B. Hummel [c.1780].
voice or fl / bc
A: Wgm. B: Bc. CH: Bu, Zs. D: KIl, NE, LEm, Mbs, RU, WR. GB: Gu, Lbl, Lcm, Mp. NL: DHgm, DHk. S: Skma, Sm, VX. US: AA, Pu, Wc. All library holdings are incomplete runs.
RISM B/II (as Mme Louis, p. 170), letter (C. Johnson).

Fleur d'épine, airs from. "Au bord d'une onde pur" & "C'est l'etat de notre cœur." In: *Les Soirées espagnoles ou choix d'ariettes d'opéra comiques et autres avec accompagnement de guittare,* menuets et allemandes par Mr. Vidal . . . 37e & 39e feuilles. Paris: Boüin [1776].
voice / guit
CH: Zz (inc.). F: Pc (lacking pp. 121–24).
RISM B/II (Mme Louis, p. 359), letter (C. Johnson, dated 1782).

Fleur d'épine, airs from. "Au bord d'une onde pure," "A l'amour, tout est possible," & "Quand on est tendre." In: *IVe Recueil de douze ariettes avec accompagnement de clavecin ou forte piano.* Choisis de différents opéras comique arrangés par Valentin Roeser . . . Paris: Le Menuet [c. 1778–93].
voice / hpsch or pf
F: Pc. All other library holdings are incomplete runs.
RISM B/II (Mme Louis, p. 325), letter (C. Johnson).

Fleur d'épine, airs from. "Au bord d'une onde pure" & "On ne doit Compter d'exister." In: *12e &14e Recueil d'ariettes choisies arrangés pour le clavecin ou le forte-piano avec accompagnement 2 violons et la Basse chiffreé ad libitum . . .* par M. Benaut . . . Paris: l'auteur [c. 1778].
hpsch or pf/ 2 vlns ad lib
B: Bc. F: AG, Pa, Pc, Pn.
RISM B/II (Mme Louis, p. 317), letter (C. Johnson).

Fleur d'épine, airs from. In: *Journal hebdomadaire ou Recueil d'airs choisies dans les opera comiques melé de vaudeville, rondeaux . . . avec accompagnement de violon et basse chiffrée pour le clavecin,* XIV. Paris: chez M. De la Chevardière, 1777. Contents: "A l'Amour tout est possible," "Au bord d'une onde pure," "D'est l'etat de notre Cœur," "Je craindrai peu," "Je prétends déplacer," "Je tourne sans cesse," "Le calme renait," "Mes chers enfants," "On ne

doit compter d'éxister," "Quand l'himen," "Quand on est tendre."
voice / hpsch bc / vln
F: Pn.
Letter (C. Johnson).

Fleur d'épine, airs from. "Mes chers enfans soyez compatis dans la faim" &
"Quelle amante dans sa flamme." Ms.
songs
F: Pn [Vma ms. 967].
Letter (C. Johnson).

Fleur d'épine, airs from. Mss., 1776 [ms. for voice, violin, and continuo; ms.
for voice and keyboard].
voice / vln (for 1) / bc
F: Pn (Vma MS 967, ff. 11v–12r, 25v–26r).
Letter (C. Johnson).

Fleur d'épine, airs from. "On ne doit compter d'exister" & "A l'amour tout
est possible." In: *IIè. Recueil d'ariettes d'opéra et opéra comiqes arrangées pour une
voix et un violon ou pour deux violons* par Mr. Roeser . . . Paris: Le Menuet
Boyer [1777].
voice / 1 or 2 vlns
F: Pc.
RISM B/II (Mme Louis, p. 321), letter (C. Johnson).

Fleur d'épine, ariette from. "On ne doit compter d'exister." S.l.: s.n., 1777.
song
F: Pn [L.3192(2)].
Letter (C. Johnson).

Fleur d'épine, ariettes from. Paris, Mlle. Girard [c. 1779] [may be same as
Airs Détachés de Fleur d'épine, Paris: Aux Adresses ordinaires de musique,
c. 1776, and Paris: Houbant catalogue, 1779].
songs
F: V.
RISM A/I (B 1432, Bayon-Louis), Cohen (Louis), letter (C. Johnson).

Fleur d'épine. Comédie en deux actes, mêlée d'ariettes, representée pour la
première fois par les comédiens italiens ordinaires du Roi le 11 aoust
1776. 1. Paris: Chez le Sr. Huguet (imprimé par Bernard) [c.1776]. Score.
151 pp. 2. Paris: Houbaut, n.d. [libretto by C. H. Fusée de Voisenon].

stage work
1. D: Bds, HR, Mbs, WD (inc.). F: Pn (4 ex.) [Vm5 177], [H.954],
[Rés.F.367], [Rés.F.358]. GB: Lbl [H.506.]. US: Phu, Wc. 2. A: Wn,
D: WD (inc.).
1–2. RISM A/I (B 1428, 1429, BB 1428, 1429a, Bayon-Louis), 1. BUC,
CPM, OCLC (21933400), Paris Lib. Cat., Cohen, letter (C. Johnson).

Fleur d'épine. Ouverture . . . arrangé pour le clavecin ou le forte-piano avec
accompagnement d'un violon et violoncelle ad libitum par M. Benaut.
Paris: Houbaut/auteur/aux adresses ordinarires [1777].
hpsch or pf/vln & vlc ad lib
F: Pc (kbd, vlc), Pn (kbd) [L.5306 (19)], [Vm7 5843]. Photocopy in
collection of C. Johnson.
RISM A/I (B 1430, Bayon-Louis), Cohen, Meggett (Bayon, Mme. Louis), Paris
Lib. Cat., letter (C. Johnson), Hayes.

Recueil de chansons pour la harpe ou forte piano, mis en musique. Ms.
harp or pf
F: Pmeyer.
Letter (C. Johnson).

Six sonates pour le clavecin ou le piano forte dont trois avec accompagnement de violon
obligé . . . Œuvre I. Paris: auteur, aux adresses ordinaires; Lyon: Castaud
(gravée par Mlle Vendôme et le Sr. Moria) [c.1765 or1770]. Score. [GB:
Lbl copy inscribed "This Volume belongs to the Queen 1788".]
hpsch or pf/vln; hpsch or pf
F: Pa (Pmeyer). GB: Lbl [R.M.16.b.25.] Microfilm copy in US: CA.
RISM A/I (B 1433, Bayon-Louis), CPM, BUC, NUC Sup. (micro., NSB
0032854), Cohen, Meggett (Bayon), letter (C. Johnson), Hayes.

"Voici les lieux charmans ou mon âme ravie." As "Air de Me. Louis" in:
Recueil d'Airs choisis avec accompagnement de harpe. Paris: Mr. Naderman, n.d.
voice/harp
F: Pn.
Letter (C. Johnson).

Louisa Friderica (Luisa Friederike), Duchess of Mecklenburg-Schwerin, née von Württemberg
1722–1791
[Piece for pianoforte, C Major]. Ms. without title, composer's name supplied as Louisa Friderica von Mecklenburg-Schwerin, 18th cent.

pf
D: ROu (Mus. Saec. XVII 51 hoch 11).
RISM A/II (#42773), letter (Woods).

Lubi, Marianne

n.d., Austria
Leonardo und Blandine, ein Melodrama nach der Musik des Preussischen
Kapellmeisters *Rommermann* für das Piano Forte mit beygefügtem Texte
[arranged by Lubi]. S.l.: s.n., n.d.
voice/pf
H: Bn.
RISM A/I (LL 2893 I, 3).

Oestereichs Fama, Eine Kantate für's Klavier nach einer Musik des Herrn
Ritter v. Gluck [arranged by Lubi]. S.l.: s.n., n.d.
voice/pf
A: M. H: Bn.
RISM A/I (LL 2893 I, 4).

Zwölf Lieder fürs Klavier. S.l.: s.n., n.d.
voice/pf
A: M, Wgm.
RISM A/I (LL 2893 I, 1).

Zwölf neue deutsche Lieder fürs Klavier. S.l.: s.n., n.d.
voice/pf
A: M (2 ex.), Wgm. H: Bn.
RISM A/I (LL 2893 I, 2).

M

M., Comtesse de

pub. c. 1800, London

6 Romances pour une voix, avec Accompagnements de Forte Piano. London: Authoress [1800?]. 13 pp.

voice/pf

GB: Gm, Gu, Lbl [E.270.(19.)], Ob.

CPM, BUC.

M., Miss of O.

pub. c. 1800, Edinburgh & London

Lady Maria Parker's (now Lady Binning) Strathspey. Composed by Miss M. of O., to which is added four tunes, two of which are composed by Miss H. Baird of Saughton-Hall. Edinburgh: Gow & Shepherd; London: John Gow [1801?].

voice/pf

GB: Lbl [g.352.jj.(5.)].

CPM.

M . . . . . . , Mlle de

pub. 1731, Paris

[Work(s)] in: *Les Parodies nouvelles et les vaudevilles inconnus.* Livre second. Paris: J. B. C. Ballard, 1731.

song(s)

F: Pa, Pc (3 ex.), Pcf, Pn (2 ex.). GB: T. NL: DHk. US: Wc.

RISM B/II (p. 280).

M., Mme

pub. c. 1780, Paris

Sur le Mot Quatre. Chanson sur le nombre quatre. [Paroles] par Mr. H . . . , Musique de Mme M . . . . [Paris: s.n., 1780?].

song

GB: Lbl [B.362.b.(28.)].

CPM, BUC.

[Work(s)] in: *Les Plaisirs de la société.* Recueil d'ariettes choisies des meilleurs opéra, opéra-comiques et autres, arrangées pour le forte-piano ou le clavecin, avec un accompagnement de violon ad libitum . . . par Mr. Foignet. Paris: Le Menu, Boyer [1781]. 3 vol.

pf or hpsch/vln ad lib

D: Bds (only vol. 2), Bhm (only vol. 2), F: Pc, Pn. GB: Lbl (only vols.1–2).
RISM B/II (p. 288).

Mn . . . . . . , Mlle de

pub. 1711, French?
[Work(s)] in: *Recueil d'airs sérieux et à boire de différents autheurs . . .* Augmenté
considérablement . . . airs italiens et de cantates françoises. Amsterdam:
E. Roger, 1711.
song(s)
B: Bc, Lc. GB: Lbl (inc.), Lcm.
RISM B/II (p. 316).

M. et C. de G., Mmes

before 1800, France
Duo ("M'aimeras-tu toujours Silvie"). Musique et accompagnement par
Mmes M*** et C*** de G***. S.l., s.n.
2 voices/pf
CH: LAcu.
RISM A/I (IN 204).

Macdonald, Charlotte, Lady

pub. c. 1790, London
The pride of every grove [song]. Words by Prior. London: J. Bland [c. 1790].
Followed by an accompaniment for German flute or guitar.
voice/kbd/fl or guit
GB: Lbl [H.1653.a.(11.)].
RISM A/I (M 6), CPM, BUC.

Macdonald, Miss, of St. Martins

pub. c. 1800, Edinburgh
Sir John Sinclair's march. Edinburgh: Gow & Shepherd [c. 1800]. 2 pp.
pf
GB: En.
BUC.

Macintosh, Mary

pub. 18th cent., London
Six easy airs calculated for the voice and harpsichord or piano forte. [London]:
printed for the authoress [1785?].
voice/hpsch or pf
GB: Lbl (2 ex.) [G.296.(30.) & H.2831.h.(17.)]. Copy in Ars Fem coll.

RISM A/I (M 58, date 1785), CPM (date 1700), BUC (date c. 1790), Eitner, Cohen, letter (Ars Fem).

Macmullan, Mrs. (Mary Anne) [also literary works, spelling as Mrs. M'Mullan]
pub. 1817, London
Remembrances ("Mid the rose leaves") [song]. London: s.n. [1817].
song
GB: Lbl [H.1677.(9.)].
CPM.

Maddalena (Archduchess)
early 18th cent., German
Salve regina à Tenore solo con Org. e Violone. Ms. 3 partbooks.
voice (T)/org/violone [bc]
D: W.
Eitner.

Mancuso, Francesca
pub. 1615, Naples
[1 work] in: *Libro primo delle canzone villanesche a 3 voci* di D. Innocentio di Paula de Catanzaro. Napoli: G. G. Carlino. 1615. 3 partbooks. [18 works by di Paula, 4 by Fabio Mancuso, 1 by Francesca Mancuso.]
3 voices
B: Bc (SI SII only).
RISM B/I (1615 [19]), NG (mention of Francesca in entry on Fabio Mancuso).

Manners, Evelyn
pub. c. 1830, London
"I go where the aspens Quiver." Ballad. London: s.n. [1830?]
song
GB: Lbl [H.2835.b.(11.)].
CPM.

Love's Offering, or *Songs for Happy Hours.* [includes works by other composers]. London: Wybrow, 1831.
song
GB: Lbl [H.1653.r.(8.)].
CPM.

Mano, Mme
pub. c. 1730–40, Paris
[Work(s)] in: *Premier [-7è] Recueil de contredanses et la table par lettre alphabétique avec la basse continue et chiffrée.* Recueilly et mis en ordre par Mr. Le Clerc . . . Paris: Le Clerc [c. 1730–42].
instrument not specified/bc
F: Pc (lacking 4–5), Pn (7), V (1–3). US: LA (1), NYp (1–3).
RISM B/II (p. 324).

Mara, Gertrud Elisabeth, née **Schmelling (Schmeling)** (known as **La Mara**)
1749 or 1750, Kassel–1833, Reval, Estonia
"Ah che nel petto io sento." Adapted to Paisiello's "Nel cor piu." 1. [1791 or 1792]. 2. Another edition, c. 1795.
voice/harp
GB: Lbl, 1. [G. 199.(26.)]. 2. [H. 1654. kk.(12.)].
1–2. CPM, BUC (harp acc. attr. to J. Mazzinghi), Cohen, Eitner (attr. to J. Mazzinghi).

"Caro caffanno mio." Aria per soprano è cembalo. Ms., 11 pp. [Elizabeth Gertrude on ms. cover, Sigra Mara on ms. Written on two staves, with text between and treble cued notes over rests in top stave during interludes, possibly for flute.]
S/unfigured bc (orig. with fl.?)
US: Wc (M 1508 .A2M29). Copy in Jackson coll.
RISM A/I (M 374), Eitner, NG (bio), Cohen.

"High rolling seas that bear afar." A favorite air sung at Mr. Salomon's Concert . . . the words by P. Hoare . . . 1. London: author [1797]. Score. 6 pp. 2. Title as: *Hope No More* [same text]. [Recitative, air, and response.] 3. Arranged for piano by Chas. Gilfert. New York: John Paff [18—]. 3 pp.
1–2. voice/pf 3. pf
1. D: UNikb. GB: Gu, Lbl [D.392.(9.)]. 2. US: NYp, 1, 3. US: Wc (M 1613 .A2M34) (1. an autographed copy).
1. RISM A/I (M 374), CPM (date 1796), NUC (NM 0198592), BUC, Eitner, NG (bio), Frauenmusik. 2–3. Wolfe (5538), NUC (NM 0198593). Cohen.

"Say can you deny me." A favorite air . . . the words by P. Hoare. London: author [1798]. Score. 8 pp.
voice/orch (vln 1 & 2/b/2 bsns/2 fls/2 hns/hpsch)
D: UNikb. GB: Lbl [G.364.(34.)], Ob.
RISM A/I (M 375), CPM (date as 1796), BUC, Eitner, Frauenmusik, Cohen.

Marchal, T. S., Madame
pub. c. 1810, Paris
La Barcarolla, air Venitien varié pour la Harpe. Paris: [1810?].
harp
GB: Lbl [h.184.d.(21.)].
CPM.

Margerum, Mrs.
pub. c. 1805, London
Faithful Sue ("When Susan saw"). Ballad. London: s.n. [1805?].
song
GB: Lbl [H.2818.b.(25.)].
CPM.

Maria Antonia Walpurgis, Princess of Bavaria, Electress of Saxony
1724, Munich–1780, Dresden
[41 arias] Ms. Score and some parts.
voice / orch
D: Dlb (Mus. 3119–F–9, 10, 11 & 11a). [Score for all; parts for
3119–F–11 &11a only.]
Eitner (considers attribution doubtful), Cohen, letter (D: Dlb).

Il trionfo della fedeltà (Der Sieg der Treue). 1. Ein gesungenes Schäferspiel
von E. T. P. A. Dresden: Churfürst. Hofbuchdruckerey, 1767. [libretto
only]. 55 pp. [In slipcase with Italian libretto.] 2. [Italian libretto.] 63 pp.
Dresden: vedova Stössel e g. c. Krause [1754]
stage work (libretto only)
1–2. US: NYp.
1. NUC (NM 0217020). 2. NUC (NM 0217023).

Il Trionfo della Fedeltá. Dramma pastorale per musica [3 acts]. 1756. 1–3.
Ms. scores. Libretto by composer and Metastasio. [Music in part composed by J. A. Hasse, according to Sonneck and Loewenberg.] 4. [pub-
lished as] di E. T. P. A. [in 3 vol]. Leipzig: Johann Gottlob Immanuel
Breitkopf, 1756. Score. 100, 104, 79 pp.
stage work (opera)
1. D: Dlb (Mus. 3119–F–5–& 5a, with parts). 2. D: Mbs (1. 311, Eitner).
3. I: Nc (22.5.10). 4. A: Wgm, Wn. D: Dlb (Mus. 3119–F–501), Gs, Mbs,
LEm, LEu, Rtt, WIbh. F: Pa (Ars.[M.523]), Pc (B.N.[Rés.1974]). GB: Lbl
(3 ex.). I: Bc, Fc, Gi [B.2b 57/59 (c.1)], Mc, MOe (Mus E. 212), Rc. US:
AA, R, Wc. Copy in D: UNikb.

1. Letter (D: Dlb). 2. Eitner. 3. RISM A/II (#57358), Mellen (date as 1754). 4. RISM A/I (M 63), BUC, NG (bio), Cohen, Eitner, Mellen, NUC (NM 217024), letter (D: Dlb), Frauenmusik.

Il Trionfo della Fedeltà [excerpt]. "Al tempio al tempio andiamo." Ms. score
voice/kbd
D: Dlb (Mus. 3119–F–8).
Eitner, letter (D: Dlb).

Il Trionfo della Fedeltà [excerpt]. "Ne non adombro il vero." Ms. score.
voice/kbd
D: Dlb (Mus. 3119–F–7).
Eitner, letter (D: Dlb).

Il Trionfo della Fedeltà [excerpt], Overture from. In: *Raccolta delle megliore sinfonie di piu celebi compositori di nostro tempo, accomodate all' clavicembalo.* Leipzig: G. G. I. Breitkopf, 1761[–62], Vol. 2, pp. 1–6.
hpsch
B: Bc. D: B–MG, Dl, GOl, Kl. GB: Lbl. I: Rsc. NL: Uim. US: R.
RISM B/II (p. 298), BUC.

Il Trionfo della Fedeltà [excerpt], Overture from. #4 in: Kammel, Antonio. *Six Overtures in Eight Parts.* London: Welcker [1773].
orch
GB: Lbl [g.474.(7.)].
CPM, RISM B/II (as Princess Royal of Saxony, p. 278).

Il Trionfo della Fedeltá [excerpt]. "Si sperar tu sola." Aria di Clori. 1. [Ms.] Score. 2. In: *Journal Etranger,* Jan. 1756, Paris.
S/orch
1. D: Dlb (Mus. 3119–F–6). 2. GB: Lbl.
1. Letter (D: Dlb). 2. BUC.

Il Trionfo della Fedelta [excerpt]. Sinfonia [G major]. 10 part-books. Leipzig: Breitkopf, 1756. Ms. copy, c. 1770. [In another hand, Musica di Maria Antonia.]
orch (2 vlns/2 obs/2 fls/2 hns/2 vlas con basso)
D: Rtt (Maria Antonia 1).
RISM A/II (#61071), letter (D: Rtt), Eitner, Cohen (gives date as 1770).

Il Trionfo della Fedeltà [excerpts]. *Recueil d'airs à danser executés à Dresden.* Arr. by Adam. Leipzig: Breitkopf, 1756.
orch
B: Bc (Wagener coll.).
Eitner.

Intermezzi comiche à Sopr. e B. con strom. Ms.
voices (SB)/orch?
D: Dlb (apparently no longer extant, probably lost in WWII).
Eitner (attribution doubtful), Cohen, letter D: Dlb.

Meditationes. Lib. 1. 2. Meditationes Secondo lib. 1. 2. Prologus und Chorus. 1746. 4 vol. ms. score.
voices/orch?
D: Dlb (Mus. 3119–D–2).
Eitner, Cohen, letter (D: Dlb).

Motetti spirituali per la chiesa. Ms. score. 1730.
voices
D: Dlb (Mus. 3119–E–1).
Eitner, Cohen (1739), letter (D: Dlb).

Pastorale. Ms. score (1741).
voice(s)/orch?
D: DLb (Mus. 3119–D–1).
Eitner (attribution doubtful), Cohen, letter (D: Dlb).

"Prendi l'ultimo addio" song. 1. [For voice & kbd] Leipzig: Collection Litolff, n.d. 2. [For soprano, 2 violins, viola, and b.c.] s.l.: s.n.,1750.
voice/pf; S/2 vlns/vla/bc
1. D: UNikb. 2. D: Kf&m.
1. Frauenmusik. 2. Frau & Musik.

Talestri [excerpt]. Aria dell' Elettrice Vedova di Sassonia. Nell' opera di Talestri [for Tomiri, priestess of the Amazons]. Ms. [Bound with ms. collection of arias of d'Astorga, Pergolesi, Sacchini, and Martines (as Martinetz)]
S/string orch
US: Wc (M1528 A2 A86 Case).
Wc card cat.

Talestri, regina delle Amazoni. Dramma per musica di E. T. P. A. [in 3 vol].
Leipzig: Breitkopf, 1765. Score. 324 pp.
stage work
A: Wgm, Wn. D: Dlb (Mus. 3119–F–500), DO, Gs (also pr. libretto), Hs,
LEm, LEmi, LEu, Mbs, Mth, SWI (inc.), W, WIbh. F: Pn (4 ex.) (B.N.
(Rés.2414 (1–3)), L.10812 (1–3), [L.11188 (1–3), [D.7338), V. GB: Cfm
(incom.), Lbl (2 ex.). I: Nc, VEaf. S: Sm. US: R (2 ex., one incom.), Wc.
Copy in D: Kf&m.
RISM A/I (M 631), BUC, Eitner, letter (D: Dlb), Frau & Musik.

Maria Margherita
n.d., Portuguese?
Rondinella á cui rapita. Aria ded. a sua Maesta Ferdinando Secundo Re
di Portogallo. Poesia de Metastasio, Muzica di Maria Margherita. Ms.
voice/pf
US: Wc (M1621 .M Case, marked "from the Royal Coll., Lisbon, 1922").
US: Wc cat.

Maria Pawlowna (Paulowna), grand-duchess of Weimar (daughter of Tsar Paul I)
1786, Russia–1859, Weimar
"Muntre gärten lieb' ich mir." Trio with piano. Ms. [1834]. Text by
Goethe. [Basis for a 3 voice canon by J. N. Hummel, which is on p. 48 of
the same ms.]
3 voices/pf
GB: Lbl (Add ms. 32190, pp. 46–50).
Brit. Cat. Ms. (as Paulowna, Maria).

Marie-Adélaïde of Savoy, Duchess of Burgundy? (Mme la Dauphine)
1685, Turin–1712, Versailles
[Work(s)] in: *Les Parodies nouvelles et les vaudevilles inconnus.* Livre troisième.
Paris: J. B. C. Ballard, 1732. [Apparently published posthumously.]
song(s)
F: Pa, Pc (3 ex.), Pcf, Pn (2 ex.). GB: T. NL: DHk. US: Wc.
RISM B/II (p. 281, Mme la Dauphine).

[Work(s)] in: *Suite de danses pour les violons et haut-bois, qui se joüent . . . aux bals chaz le Roy. . . .* composez la plus grande partie par Philidor l'aîné . . . Livre premier. Paris: C. Ballard, 1699.
vlns/obs (with bc)

F: Pn.
RISM B/I (1699 [7]).

Marie Antoinette, Queen of France
1756, Vienna–1793, Paris
"Amour, fuis loin de moi" [with keyboard accompaniment in score]. 2 pp.
ms. Holograph.
voice/kbd
GB: Llb (Add. ms. 33966).
Brit. Cat. Ms.

"C'est mon ami." Melody is basis of many modern arrangements. Melody
also attributed to Prince Felix Youssaupoff. See modern editions.
song
Original source not known.

Marie-Therese-Louise of Savoy-Carignano. See Lamballe, Maria-Theresa-Louisa, Mme la Princesse de

Marielli, M. (pseud.). See Kingston, Mary

Marshall, Mrs. William
pub. c. 1830?, London & New York
The banished Pole, song founded on the within facts. Music and poetry written by Mrs. W. Marshall. New York: Dubois & Stodart [183–?]. 5 pp.
voice/pf
US: NYp, Wc (M1.A13M).
NUC (NM 0250420).

Woman's plighted love ("Oh! let me share"). Ballad. London: s.n. [1830?].
voice/pf
GB: Lbl [H.2832.b.(9.)].
CPM.

Martainville (Martinville), Caroline
pub. 1820s, Paris
Fantasie avec variations pour piano et violoncelle, ou violon. Op. 1 de Mme
Martainville et posthume de Duport. Paris: Carli [182–?]. Score for cello
and piano, partbooks for violin and for cello.
vlc (or vln)/pf

US: Bp.
NUC (NM 0253350).

Il reviendra demain matin. Romance. 1. Paris: Chez Carli [1828?]. 2. As
M.me Martinville. Ms., first decade, 19th cent. 2 pp.
voice/pf
1. GB: Lbl [G.561.c.(25.)]. 2. D: DO (Mus. Ms. 2516).
1. CPM. 2. RISM A/II (86667).

La Berceuse. Nocturne à deux voix. Paris: Chez Carli [1820?].
2 voices/pf
GB: Lbl [H.2262.b.(12.)].
CPM.

La Seine ("Rive enchantée"). Nocturne à deux voix. London: s.n. [1825?].
2 voices/pf
GB: Lbl [H.2835.(26.)].
CPM.

O! douce Hélène si tu voulais ("Mal que j'ignore"). Romance. Paris: s.n.
[1820?].
song
GB: Lbl [G.547.(24.)].
CPM.

Martin, Angelica, Mrs.
fl. 1818–1839?, New York
Faithful love ("Since honour bids my soldier go"). By Angelica Martin,
professor of music. Composed expressly for the *Ladie's* [sic] *Literary Cabinet.*
The words by a celebrated poet. *Ladie's Literary Cabinet*, I, #14, p. 110. New
York, 1820.
voice/pf/fl or vln acc.
See *Union List of Serials* for numerous US locations of this periodical.
Wolfe (5183, 5594).

Martinez (Martines), Marianna von [1 of 3 female members of
Accademia Filharmonia of Bologna]
1744, Vienna–1812, Vienna
"Ah rammenta o! bella Irene." Nella 14e cantata di Metastasio. [Da capo
aria] Ms. [Bound with ms. collection of arias of d'Astorga, Pergolesi,
Sacchini, and Maria Antonia Walpurgis.]

S/orch (2 hns/2 fls/2 vlns con sordini/vla/basso)
US: Wc (M1528 A2 A86 Case). Copy in Jackson coll.
US: Wc cat. (Sigra Marianna Martinetz).

Amor timido [cantata]. Ms.
voice (S)/instruments
A: Wgm (VI 17128 [Q3082]).
NG, Fremar, Eitner, Cohen, MGG.

Concerto in A per il Clavicembalo. Ms. score
hpsch/orch
A: Wgm (VII 12980 [Q16265]). Copy in D: UNikb.
Fremar, Eitner, Frauenmusik. (MGG lists only 2 concerti in A: Wgm; Cohen has 2 concerti).

Concerto in C per il Cembalo. Ms. score
hpsch/orch
A: Wgm (VII 12981 [Q16266]).
Fremar, Eitner. (MGG lists only 2 concerti in A: Wgm; Cohen has 2 concerti.)

Concerto in D per il Clavicembalo. Ms. score.
hpsch/orch
Copy in D: UNikb. Location of original not known.
Frauenmusik. (MGG lists only 2 concerti in A: Wgm; Cohen has 2 concerti).

Concerto per il Cembalo [in G Major] (1772). Autograph score.
hpsch/orch
A: Wgm.
Fremar, Eitner (partly score, partly partbooks), (MGG lists only 2 concerti in A: Wgm; Cohen has 2 concerti).

"Dixit Dominus," Psalm 109. Autograph ms. and copy, 1774.
choir/orch
D: Bds (autograph; RKZ B 15). I: Bc (ms.).
MGG, Fremar, Eitner, Cohen.

"Et vitam venturi." Ms.
4 voices (SATB) a cappella
I: Bc (ms.).
Fremar, Eitner, Cohen, MGG.

Il consiglio [cantata]. Autograph ms., 1778.
S/orch
D: Bds (Mus. ms. autogr. M. Martinez 5).
Fremar.

Il nido degli amori [cantata]. Ms.
S/orch
A: Wgm (III 3041 [Q899]).
Fremar.

Il primo amore [cantata]. Autograph ms., 1778.
S/orch
D: Bds (Mus. ms. autogr. M. Martinez 5).
Fremar.

"In exitu Israel," Psalm 113. 1. Autograph ms. 2. Ms. copy.
choir (SATB)/orch
1. A: Wn. (SA 67E82). 2. I: Fc (A552–54).
1–2. Fremar, MGG. Cohen.

Isacco figura del Redentore. Oratorium. Perf. Vienna, Kärtnertortheater, 1782. 1–4. Ms. scores. Text by Metastasio.
SSSTB solo/choir/orch
1. A: Wgm (III 8 [Q897]). 2. I: Baf (ms.). 3. D: B (Mus. ms. 13 680).
4. D: Bds. Copy in Jackson coll.
1–3. Fremar, Eitner, MGG. 4. NG. Cohen.

Kyrie a 4 voc. c. instrom. Autograph ms., score.
4 voices (SATB)/orch
I: Bc (ms.).
MGG, Eitner, Cohen.

La primerva [cantata]. Autograph ms.
Probably S/orch
Formerly in D: Bds. (Mus. ms. autogr. M. Martinez 4). Lost in WW II.
Fremar.

La tempestà. Autograph ms., 1778. Score. Text by Metastasio.
S/orch
A: Wn (SM 16569).
NG, MGG, Fremar, Eitner, Cohen.

Litania della B.V. Autograph ms., 1762.
choir / orch
A: Wgm.
Fremar, Cohen.

Litania della B. V. Autograph ms., 1775.
choir / orch
A: Wgm.
Fremar.

Litania "Lodate o giovani". Autograph ms.
choir / orch
A: Wgm.
Fremar.

Litaniae [G Major] de B. V.: da Canto, Alto, Tenore, Basso, Violini Due, Corni Due, Alto, Viola con Organo e Violonc:. 12 Ms. partbooks.
SATB / orch / org
CS: LIT (Sign. 651).
RISM A / II (#32532).

Mass in C Major [c.1760–1765], No. 1. Ms. score.
choir / orch
A: Wgm. D: LEt (in LEbh), Mbs. Copy in Jackson coll.
Fremar, Eitner, letter (A: Wgm), MGG, Cohen (as unspecified 3 Masses).

Mass No. 2 [1760]. Autograph ms, score.
choir / orch
A: Wgm.
Fremar, Eitner, Cohen (as unspecified 3 Masses).

Mass No. 3 [1761]. Autograph ms., score.
choir / orch
A: Wgm.
Fremar, Eitner, Cohen (as unspecified 3 Masses).

Mass No. 4 [1765]. Autograph ms., score.
choir / orch
A: Wgm.
Fremar, Eitner, Cohen (as unspecified 3 Masses).

"Miserere" ("Pietà signore"), Psalm 50. 1769. 1. Autograph ms. 2–6. Ms. score copies. Text, Italian translation by Saverio Mattei.
4 voices (SATB)/orch
1. A: Wgm. 2. I: BGc (Mayr C.5.38). 3. I: Bc (ms.). 4. I: Nc (22.4.16 (MGG), Mus. relig. 1193). 5. D: B (Grasnick collection). 6. I: Vlevi (CF.B.4).
1–5. Fremar, Eitner, MGG. 2. RISM A/II (#48365). 6. RISM A/II (#72116). Cohen.

"Miserere," Psalm 50. Autograph ms.
4 voices (SATB)/bc
A: Wn (SA 67E81).
Fremar, Eitner.

Occhietto furbetto [cantata]. Ms.
S/orch
I: OS (Mus. Musiche B3717).
Fremar.

Orgoglioso fiumicello [cantata]. Ms., 1786.
S/orch
A: Wst (MH 9331).
NG, MGG, Fremar, Cohen.

Overture in C. Autograph ms., 1770. Score.
orch
A: Wgm.
Eitner, Cohen, MGG, Cohen.

"Per pietà" [aria]. Autograph ms.
S/orch
D: Dlb (Mus. 1–f–82, 16–7).
Fremar.

Perchè compagne amate [cantata]. Autograph ms.
S/2 vlns/bc
I: Bc (ms.).
NG, MGG, Fremar, Eitner, Cohen.

"Quemadmodum desiderat cervus," Psalm 41. 1. Autograph ms., part-books. 2–4. Ms. scores. 5. "Come le limpide onde" Salmo XLI,

Quemadmodum . . . Ms. score, 89 pp. 6. Ms. score, 61 pp. Text, Italian translation by Saverio Mattei.
soli / choir / orch
1. A: Wn (SA 67E83). 2. I: Fc. 3. I: Nc (Mus.relig. 1191/1192). 4. I: Bc (ms., A552). 5. I: BGc (Mayr D.9.12.26). 6. D: MÜs (SANT Hs. 2521). *1–5. MGG, Fremar, Eitner. 5. RISM A/II (#48364). 6. RISM A/II (#75956). Cohen.*

"Regina coeli." Autograph ms., 1767.
8 voices / instruments
A: Wgm.
Fremar, Eitner, Cohen.

Salmo CXII [Psalm 112]. Ms.
choir (SATB) / orch
I: Fc (A553).
MGG, Fremar, Cohen.

Santa Elena al Calvario. Oratorio. Ms. score.
SATB soli / choir / orch
A: Wgm (III 1733 [Q898]). Copy in Jackson coll.
NG, Fremar, Eitner, MGG, Cohen.

"Se per tutti" [aria]. Autograph ms., 1769.
S / orch
D: Dlb (Mus. 1–f–82, 16–6).
MGG, Fremar.

Sinfonia in C. Autograph ms., 1770. Score.
orch
A: Wgm.
Fremar, MGG.

6 Motetten mit Instrumenten. Autograph ms., 1760–68.
voice (S) / orch
A: Wgm.
Fremar, Eitner, Cohen.

Sonata da Cembalo [G Major]. (1789) Ms.
hpsch [or pf]

D: Dlb (Mus. 3450–T–1).
Fremar (contains facs.).

Sonata in A Major for Cembalo. 1. Ms. 2. In: *Raccolta musicale contenente VI sonate per il cembalo solo d'altretanti celebri compositori italiani messi nell'ordine alfabetico co'loro nomi e titoli.* Nürnberg: J. U. Haffner, 1765 Vol. 5, #3.
hpsch [or pf]
1. D: B (Mus. ms. 13683). 2. D: LEm. GB: Lk [in Lbl].
1. Fremar. 2. RISM B/II (as M. A. Martines, p. 299), MGG.

Sonata in E Major for Cembalo. In: *Raccolta musicale contenente VI sonate per il cembalo solo d'altretanti celebri compositori italiani . . .* Nürnberg: J. U. Haffner, 1762, Vol. 4, #3.
hpsch [or pf]
D: LEm. GB: Lk (in Lbl).
Fremar, MGG.

[2 Arias] "Deh dammi un altro core" & "Tu vittime non vuoi." Ms., 1769. Score.
voice(S)/orch
D: B (Mus. ms. 13 681).
MGG, Fremar, Eitner, Cohen.

[2] Litania de B. M. V. Ms. [1760–65].
choir/orch
A: Wgm (I 1687, I 1689).
Fremar, Eitner, Cohen.

[2 Psalms]: "Cosi consolo almeno" (1769), "Ei sgombrera quel duolo" (1770). Ms. score. In Italian translation by Saverio Mattei.
4 voices (SATB)/orch
D: B (Mus. ms. 13 682).
Fremar, Eitner.

[24 Arias for voice and bc] Scelta d'arie, compiled 1767. Ms.
S (one for T)/orch
I: N-Feoli Cesare (33.3.27; 33.3.28).
MGG, Fremar, Cohen.

Mary, Queen of Scots (Mary Stuart)
1542, West Lothian–1587, Fotheringhay Castle

[2 songs] "Think on me" & "Las, en mon doux printemps."
voice/kbd
GB: Lbl. Copies in D: UNikb.
Frauenmusik.

Massarenghi (Mazzarenghi), Paola (Madonna da Parma)
c. 1585–?, Italy
Quando spiega l'insegn'al sommo padre. In: F.A. Gherardini, *Il primo libro de' madrigali à cinque voci* . . . Ferrara: Vittorio Baldini, 1686. 5 partbooks.
5 voices
I: Bc (A), MOe (all parts, but B inc.).
RISM B/I (1585 [24]), Eitner, Bowers & Tick, Cohen.

Mattei, Beatrice
fl. 1743, Italy
Il gefte [componimento drammatico]. Florence: s.n. 1743.
stage work
I: Rn (libretto only).
Cohen, Eitner.

Sonata per cembalo [b-flat major]. Ms. 5 pp.
hpsch
I: Gi(l) (SS.A.2.1. [G.8]).
Genova.

Meda, Bianca Maria
pub. 1691, fl. Pavia
Mottetti a 1. 2. 3. e 4. voci, con violini, e senza. Bologna: Pier Maria Monti, 1691. 6 partbooks (C, A + vln, T + vln, B, violone, org).
S/2 vlns; B/2 vlns; SB; SAB; SSB; SATB, all with org and violone bc
I: Bc (AA 282). Copies in Jackson coll. & Ars Fem coll.
RISM A/I (M 1695), Eitner, Bowers & Tick, Cohen, letter (Ars Fem).

Medici, Isabella de (di). See Orsini, Isabella de, née Medici, Duchess of Bracciano

Mellish, Miss
18th cent., English
"My Phillida adieu." 1. Dublin: Elizabeth Rhames. 2. Dublin: John & Edmund Lee. 3. London: Longman & Broderip [1795?]. 4. London:

Broderip & Wilkinson [1800?]. 5. Pub. as "anonymous." Dublin: Hime
[c. 1800]. 6. New York: J. Hewitt [18—], with part for clarinet added. 7. A
favorite ariette [with violin, arr. for voice and guitar printed on p. 4].
London: Longman & Broderip [c. 1795]. 4 pp. [#16 in volume with
binder's title: Songs, vol. 3]. 8. As: *Corydon's doleful knell* [same text]. In: *The
Philadelphia Repository and Weekly Register,* II, Mus. sup., #10. Philadelphia,
1801–02.
1–5., 8. voice/pf; 6. voice/pf/cl; 7. voice/pf/vln; voice/guit
1–2. EIRE: Dn (2 ex. of 1.). 3–4. GB: Lbl (2 ex.) [H.1771.x.(7.) &
[H.16001.e.(13.)], Lbl [H.2815.a.(9.)], Lbl [H.1653.n.(29.)]. 5. US: Wc
(M1.A11, v. 15, #24. Coll. of early Am. mus.) 6. US: NYp, Wc. 7. US:
NH. 8. See *Union List of Serials* for numerous locations of this periodical.
Copy in Ars Fem coll.
1–4. RISM A/I (M 2230, 2231, 2232, 2233). 3–4. CPM. 5. NUC (NM
04233562). 6. NUC (NM 04233562), Wolfe (5833). 7. OCLC (20913675).
8. Wolfe (6976). Cohen, letter (Ars Fem).

Melmouth, Mrs.
fl c. 1795
[1 song] in: Manuscript music book belonging to A. Bell, New York,
c. 1798 [a collection of marches, jigs, some tunes about the Duke of York,
soldiers, sailors and some love songs. One is attributed to Mrs. Melmouth
and one was sung by Mrs. Bannister].
song
US: WGw.
OCLC (14774482).

Menetou, Françoise-Charlotte de Senneterre (pub. as Mlle de Menetou)
1680–?
Airs de mademoiselle Menetou. 86 leaves of music, ms. (in 2–3 hands), not
before 1689. [Many items in this ms. are anonymous; some may be by
her. A ms. copy of her published *Airs sérieux à deux* is included and
identified. See *Airs sérieux à deux*).
songs
US: BE (Manuscript. 777, also microfilm).
OCLC (micro. 16975341), letter (C. Johnson).

Airs sérieux à deux. Paris: Christophe Ballard, 1691. Score.
2 voices/kbd

F. Pn. Copy in Ars Fem coll.
RISM A/I (M 2245), Cohen, letter (Ars Fem).

[4 Airs] in: *Recueil d'airs nouveaux, sérieux et à boire, de différent autheurs: a deux et trois parties.* Mis en ordre par Amedée Le Chevallier. Amsterdam: P. et J. Blaeu, 1691.
2–3 voices/kbd
GB: Ob.
RISM B/I (1691[3]), Cohen (as Airs sérieux), Gustafson.

Méon, Mlle
pub. 1780s, Paris
[Work(s)] in: *Etrennes de Polymnie. Recueil de chansons, romances, vaudevilles . . .* Paris: au bureau de la petite bibliothèque des théatres, Belin, 1785–89.
song(s)
D: B–MG, LEm. F: Ma, Pcf, Pn, V. US: Wc. All other library holdings incomplete runs.
RISM B/II (p. 168).

Merelle, Mlle
pub. c. 1800, London
Les folies d'Espagne. Avec de nouvelles variations pour la harpe. London: Broderip & Wilkinson [c. 1800]. 5 pp.
harp
GB: Lbl [h.118.(29.)], Ob. Copy in Ars Fem coll.
RISM A/I (M 2315), CPM, Eitner, Cohen, BUC, letter (Ars Fem).

New and complete instructions for the pedal harp in two books containing all the necessary rules with exercises, preludes . . . . London: . . . London: Broderip & Wilkinson, n.d.
harp (instruction)
D: LEmi. DK: Kk. GB: Cu, Lbl [g.301.(2.)], Ob. Copy in Ars Fem coll.
RISM A/I (M 2317), CPM, Eitner, letter (Ars Fem).

Petites piéces pour le harp. London: Broderip & Wilkinson [c.1800]. 9 pp.
harp
GB: Cu, Lbl [g.301.(14.)], Ob. Copy in Ars Fem coll.
RISM A/I (M 2316), CPM, Eitner, Cohen, BUC, letter (Ars Fem).

Merken (Mercken), Sophie
pub. c. 1798, Paris

Premier recueil de six romances . . . œuvre Ier. Paris: auteur [1798]. Score. 19 pp.
voice/kbd
F: Pn [Vm7 7631].
RISM A/I (M 2308), Paris Lib. Cat.

Metcalfe, Emily
pub. c. 1801, London
On Land Nelson ("Awake, awake") [song]. London: s.n. [1801].
song
GB: Lbl [H.2831.h.(18.)].
CPM.

The Siege of Alexandria [for pianoforte]. London: s.n. [1801].
pf
GB: Lbl [h.1480.p.(10.)].
CPM.

Spring. A favourite canzonet. London: Kaimtze & Hyatt [1801?].
song
GB: Lbl [H.2831.h.(19.)].
CPM.

Mezari, Maddalena. See Casulana de Mezari, Maddalena

Michon, Mlle
pub. c. 1750?, Paris
Amusemens de chambre avec basse continue et une sonnatte dans le goût italien et une suitte en duo pour vielle, musette et autres instrumens . . . second œuvre. Paris: auteur, Mme Boivin, Le Clerc (gravé par Mlle Fauchoux) [c. 1750]. Score. 18 pp.
vielle or musette or others/bc
F: Pn (2 ex.) [Vm7 6697] & [X636(2)].
RISM A/I (M 2708), Paris Lib. Cat., Eitner.

Divertissemens champêtres en quatre suittes avec la basse et deux dessus pour vielles, muzettes, fluttes et hautbois et autres instrumens . . . premier œuvre. Paris: auteur, Mme Boivin, Le Clerc [c. 1748]. Score. 23 pp.
2 vielles or musettes or fls or obs or other/bc
F: Pn (2 ex.) [Vm7 6696] & [X 636(1)].
RISM A/I (M 2707), Paris Lib. Cat., Eitner, Haynes.

Journaux &c. d'airs sérieux, d' airs bacchiques et de chansonnettes à deux et à trois parties, avec des seconds coupletz en diminution, le tout gravé au burin. Paris: G. de Luine [c. 1760]. Score. 18 pp.
2–3 voices/kbd (bc)
F: Pn [Vm7 615].
RISM A/I (M 2709), Paris Lib. Cat.

Milder, Jeanette Antonie (married Bürde)

1799, Huttleindorf (near Vienna)–?
Zwei Gedichte von Houwald und Goethe in Musik gesetzt. "Das Mädchen und der Todtenkopf" & "Das Heiden-Röslen." Berlin: s.m. [1830?].
voice/pf
GB: Lbl [E.253.(21.)].
CPM, Cohen (as Buerde).

Miles, Mrs. Jane Mary, née Guest. See Guest, Jane Mary

Millard, Virtue (Mrs. Philip Millard)

?–1840, pub. London
Alice Gray, a ballad. 1. London: A. Pettet [c. 1830]. 2. 2d ed. [c.1830].
3. 3d ed. [c. 1830]. 4. 4th ed. [c. 1830]. 5. 6th ed. [c. 1835]. 6. London:
C. Sheard, [1874] in: *Musical Banquet* (#3443). 7. New York: Bourne, 1828.
8. Boston: Bradlee, 182–?. 9. Baltimore: Geo. Willig [182–?]. 10. New
York: E. Riley [182–?]. 11. New York: Bourne depository of arts [183–].
12. Baltimore: John Cole [1830?]. 13. New York: Firth & Hall [after
1832?]. 14. Philadelphia: Blake [183–?]. 15. New York: Atwill's music
saloon [18—]. Arrangements: 16. Celebrated English ditty of olden time
with new symphony & accompaniment by R. Gaythorne, London:
W. Marshall [1878]. 17. . . . as a Part Song, arr. E. Land [1862]. 18. . . .
with an Introduction and Variations for the Piano Forte arr. P. Knapton
[1828?]. 19. . . . with easy variations, for the piano forte, arr. Thomas
Valentine [1833?].
1–15 voice/pf; 17. voices/pf; 18–19. pf
1–6. GB: Lbl [H.1980.n.(2.)], [H.1653.x.(12.)], [H.1653.h.(17.)], (2 ex. of
4.) [H. 1980.tt.(38.) & H.1601.n.(17.)], [G.805.g.(28.)], [H.2345]. 7. US:
NYp, NYlevy. 8. US: FWw, IO, Bp. 9. US: Cn, CHua, DM (M1 .A13M),
Wc (Ml.A13M.). 10. US: TU (M1621.M54 A45 1820). 11. US: Wc
(M1.A13M). 12. US: DM. 13. US: CHua, Cn. 14–15. US: Cn. 16–19.
GB: Lbl [H.1559.a.(14.)], [H.1559.a.(14.)], [g.232.d.(12.)], [h.60.uu.(19.)].
1–6. CPM (apparently 5th ed. is missing). 7. Tick. 8–10. OCLC (22259239,

7593504, 16187873). 8–15. NUC & Sup. (NM 0581683–8, NSM 0035944). 16–19. CPM. Cohen.

Ambition repentant: a Ballad, the words by Sir Gilbert Elliott. London: S. Chappell [1830]. 5 pp.
voice/pf
GB: Lbl [H.1676.(47.)].
CPM.

The Birks of Aberfeldy, a Ballad . . . The melody composed by Mrs. Philip Millard, the symphonies and accompaniments by P. Knapton. 1. London: A. Pettet [c.1830]. 5 pp. 2. Boston: Bradlee [1834–40].
Melody only by Millard
voice/pf
1. GB: Lbl [H.1601.m.(46.)]. 2. US: Cn.
1. *CPM. 2. NUC Sup. (NSM 0035945).*

Dinna forget! A ballad, the words by John Imlah. 1. London: S. Chappell [1831]. 5 pp. 2. Baltimore: J. Cole [183–?]. 3. Baltimore: G. Willig [c. 183–]. 4. New York: Dubois & Stodart [before 1834?].
voice/pf
1. GB: Lbl [H.1676.(43.)]. 2. US: Wc (M1.A13M). 3. US: DU. 4. US: CHua.
1. *CPM. 2–4. NUC (NM 0581689–91). Cohen.*

"Forget thee, my Susie!" 1. Song. In: *The Harmonicon,* vol. 9, pt. 2, pp. 133–35, 1831. 2. A Ballad [text] written [and music] composed by Mrs. P. Millard. London: S. Chappell [1832].
voice/pf
1–2. GB: Lbl. [P.P.1947., H.1676.(46.)].
1–2. CPM. Cohen.

Hame frae the wars. A ballad. London: s.n. [1835?].
voice/pf
GB: Lbl [G.806.f.(50.)].
CPM.

A happy new year! Ballad [text] written by John Imlah. London: S. Chappell [1831].
voice/pf
GB: Lbl [H.1676.(44.)].
CPM, Cohen.

I prithee give me back my heart. A ballad. (The words by Sir J. Suckling)
London: s.n. [1830?].
voice/pf
GB: Lbl [H.2830.g.(10.)].
CPM.

I'll ne'er forget that happy hour. A ballad. (The words by William L*** . . . .)
London: S. Chappell [1833]. 4 pp.
voice/pf
GB: Lbl [H.1676.(49.)].
CPM.

The Kiss on the Lips we love, a ballad. The words by John Imlah . . . the
melody by Mrs. Philip Millard . . . Arranged with a piano forte accompaniment, by Alfred Pettet. London: R. Cocks & Co., [1834]. 3 pp.
Melody only by Millard
voice/pf
GB: Lbl [H.1980.z.(10.)].
CPM.

The lament of the Scotch Fisherman's Widow; a Ballad. London: S. Chappell
[1832]. 3 pp.
voice/pf
GB: Lbl [H.1676.(45.)].
CPM, Cohen.

Love wakes and weeps. Serenade . . . the words by Sir Walter Scott. In: *The
Harmonicon,* vol. 10, pt. 2, pp. 196–97, 1832.
voice/pf
GB: Lbl [P.P.1947.].
CPM.

Lovely May . . . [song]. The poetry by W. Ball. London: B. Williams
[c.1855]. 5 pp.
voice/pf
GB: Lbl [G.1271.ii.(4.)].
CPM.

O Love is like the sunny ray. A ballad. London: s.n. [1830?].
voice/pf

GB: Lbl [H.2830.g.(9.)].
CPM.

Oh! she is the snowdrop fair. Ballad. London: S. Chappell [1834].
voice/pf
GB: Lbl [H.1676.(48.)].
CPM.

The Soldier's Return. A ballad. 1. London: s.n. [1830?]. 2. New York:
Dubois/Stodart [after 1828?].
voice/pf
1. GB: Lbl [2835.b.(16.)]. 2. US: CHu.
1. CPM. 2. NUC (NM 0581692). Cohen.

There is a land of pure delight. Sacred song. London: s.n. [1848].
voice/pf
GB: Lbl [H.1182.(16.)].
CPM.

Mitford, Eliza
pub. late 18th cent., London
Jack Latin. With variations. 1. [London]: J. Longman & Co. [c. 1800].
2. S.l., s.n., 1800. 3. [London, c. 1768?].
pf
1. GB: Cu. 2. GB: Lbl (2 ex.) [g.352.qq.(21.)] & [g.443.w.(8.)]. 3. GB: Lbl
[g.271, b.(3.)]. Copy in Ars Fem coll.
1–2. RISM A/I (M 2902, 2903), BUC. 2–3. CPM. Cohen, Letter (Ars Fem).

Montalembert, Marie-Joséphine de Comarieu, Marquise de
1750–1832
Six Sonatas for the Harpsichord or Piano Forte [g/E-flat, a/A, E-flat, g/G, d/D,
c/E-flat]. London: s.n., 1794.
hpsch or pf
F: Pn (A.44427). US: Wc. Photocopy of US: Wc in C. Johnson coll.
RISM A/I (M 3305), letter (C. Johnson).

Montgeroult, Hélène de Nervode, Countess of Charnay
1764, Lyon-1836, Florence
*Cours complet pour l'enseignement du forte piano conduisant progressivement des pre-
miers éléments aux plus grandes difficultés . . .* [3 vols.: vol. 1, 972 exercises; vol. 2,
70 études; vol. 3, 40 études and misc. pieces.] Paris: Pelicieu/Janet &

Cotelle (Marquerie frères) [1822 or 1825?].
instruction book (pf)
CH: Bu (67). F: Pn (3 ex. Vm8 s. 536, L.6590(1–3), & L.10.093(1–3). GB: Lbl [h.3760]. Microfilm of vol. 1–2 in US: BO; microfilm of vol. 1 of CH: Bu in C. Johnson coll.
Vol. 1–2, RISM A/I (M 3510, M 3511), CPM, OCLC (micro. 15268214), Eitner, Cohen, letter (C. Johnson), letter (Bogard).

Pièce pour le piano forte [E-flat] . . . œuvre 3. Paris: Melles Erard/Lyons: Chez Gernier [1804].
pf
F: Pn (Vm12 20977). Photocopy in C. Johnson coll.
Cohen (as Pièces), letter (C. Johnson).

Trois sonates [D, f, f#] *pour le piano forte* Composées Par Mme. de Mongéroult, œuvre 5. Paris: Mlles Erard/Den Haag: chez F. J. Weygand [1811?].
pf
F: Pn (Vm12 20978). Photocopy in C. Johnson coll.
Cohen, letter (C. Johnson).

Trois sonates [F, E-flat, f] *pour le forte-piano* . . . . op. 1. 1. Paris: au magasin du Conservatoire de musique/Troupenas [c. 1795]. 2. [3d sonata published separately as] Sonate für das Piano-Forte [f]. Berlin: F. S. Lischke (Pl.#861) [1793?].
pf
1. F: Pc (2 ex.) [D.8477(1)] & [Fol. Vm. 226(1)]. GB: Lbl [h.721.s.(14.)].
2. S: SKv. Photocopies of F: Pn and S: SKv in C. Johnson coll.
1–2. RISM A/I (M 3507, 3509), Eitner (date as 1800), letter (C. Johnson).
1. CPM. Cohen (sonata #3 as g minor).

Trois Sonates [g, C, a] *pour le forte-piano* [avec accompagnement de violon pour la 3e Sonate] . . . œuvre 2e. 1. Paris: Troupenas [c. 1807]. 2. Chez Janet et Cotelle/Au Magasin de Musique du Conservatoire Royal [c. 1825]. Parts. 38 pp.
pf/vln (only for Sonata #3)
1. F: Pc (pf, vln) [Vmg 6698 & D.8477(2)]. 2. GB: Lbl [h.61.s.(10.)]. Photocopy of F: Pc in C. Johnson coll.
1–2. RISM A/I (M 3508), letter (C. Johnson). 1. Paris Lib. Cat. 2. CPM. Cohen.

More, Isabella Theaker
pub. c. 1789, London
The walls of my prison. A favorite ballad. 1. London: G. Goulding [1789].
2. Philadelpia [1793–95]. 3. Dublin: John Lee. Piano, 2 staves, with interlinear text—at bottom of page a part for "Ger. Flute & Guitar." 4. In:
Young's vocal and instrumental musical miscellany, #5, p. 37. Philadlphia: 1795.
1–2. 4. voice/pf; 3. voice/pf/fl & [or] guit
1. GB: Lbl [G.377.(37.)]. 2. US: NYp. 3. US: MV [W–1368/C (bk)
A–286]. 4. PHu (Hopkinson coll.), Wc. Copy in Ars Fem coll.
*1. RISM A/I (M 3616), BUC (as c. 1785), CPM. 2. Tick. 3. NUC (NM
0763886). 4. Sonneck. Cohen, letter (Ars Fem).*

Morel, Virginie Du Verger, Baronne
1799–1870, French
Huit Etudes Mélodiques Pour Piano. Paris: Richault, 1857.
pf
F: Pn (2 ex.) (VmB s872, L. 6353).
Letter (C. Johnson).

2e Valse Brilliante Pour Piano. Paris: B. Richault [c. 1865].
pf
F: Pn (Vmg 6624).
Letter (C. Johnson).

Sonata pour piano avec accompagnement de violon [D] . . . Paris: l'auteur/Henri
Lemoine, n.d. 2 partbooks.
pf/vln
F: Pn (Vm15 4224). Photocopy in C. Johnson coll.
Cohen, Eitner (B.B.), letter (C. Johnson).

Variations Pour le Piano Forte sur l'Air de Don Juan ["Vedrai carino" by
Mozart], op. 2. Paris: chez l'Auteur et chez tous les Marchands de
Musique, n.d.
pf
F: Pn (2 ex.) (Vm15 21033).
Letter (C. Johnson).

Morgan, Lady Sydney, née Owenson
1783?, Dublin–1859, London
"Deep in love." The words & music composed & arranged by Miss
Owenson. 1. Dublin: S. Holden [c. 1892]. 4 pp. 2. New York: J. & M. Paff

[1807?].
voice/pf
1. US: NYp. 2. US: Wc (M1.A1M [M1621]).
1–2. NUC (0777269–70).

Friend of my soul. Poetry by Moore. Music by Miss Owenson.
[Philadelphia]: s.n. [c. 1812].
2 voices/pf
US: NH.
OCLC (20911609).

Twelve original Hibernian melodies, with English words, imitated and translated, from the "Works" of the ancient Irish bards, with an introductory
preface and dedication by Miss S. Owenson. Arr. for the pianoforte.
London: Preslon, n.d., 244 pp.
voice/pf
US: U.
NUC (0777371).

Mudie, Mme
pub. c. 1830, London
Piacque al cielo. Canzonetta [with accompaniment] for harp or pianoforte.
London: Preston [c. 1830]. 3 pp.
voice/harp or pf
GB: Lbl [H.1650.gg.(19.)].
CPM.

Müller, Elise
1782–?, pub. c. 1820, Leipzig
Sechs Gesänge mit Begleitung des Pianoforte in Musick gesetz . . . Leipzig: Bei
Griedr. Hofmeister [c. 1819/1820].
voice/pf
D: DÜk (cat. # 851).
Cohen (as Mueller), letter (D: DÜk).

Müller, Mad. (may be same as Müller, Elise)
pub. 1791, Vienna
Frühlingslieder & Winterlieder. In: *Liedersammlung für Kinder und Kinderfreunde am
Clavier.* Vienna: I. Alberti, 1791. 2 vols.
voice/pf

A: Wn (2 ex. of *Winterlieder*). US: NYp (*Frühlingslieder*), Wn (*Winterlieder*).
RISM B/II (p. 219).

Müllner-Gollenhofer (Müllner-Gallenhofer), Johannna (Josepha, Josephine)

1769, Vienna–?
[14 Lieder].
voice/pf
A: Wn, Wgm. Copy in Ars Fem coll.
Letter (Ars Fem)

Marche
harp
A: Wn, Wgm. Copy in Ars Fem coll.
Letter (Ars Fem)

Muratori, Angiola Teresa (married Scannabecchi, later married Moneta)

fl. 1689–1696, Bologna (also active as a painter)
Cristo morto. Oratorio, performed on Good Friday at the oratorio of the
Archconfraternity of S. Maria della Morte, 1696. Libretto by G. A.
Bergamori. Bologna: per gl'Eredi del Pissarri, 1696.
voices/orch
I: Bc. Printed libretto only.
Eitner, Sesini.

L'Esterre. Oratorio, performed on Palm Sunday at the Oratorio of
S. Filippo Neri, 1695. Libretto by G. A. Bergamori. Bologna: Pier-Maria
Monti, 1695.
voices/orch
I: Bc. Printed libretto only.
Eitner, Sesini.

Li Giochi di Sansone. Oratorio, performed at the Oratorio of S. Filippo Neri,
1694. Libretto by G. A. Bergamori. Bologna: per gl'Eredi del Pisarri,
1694.
voices/orch
I: Bc. Printed libretto only.
Eitner, Sesini.

Il Martirio di S. Colomba. Oratorio, performed at the Oratorio of S. Filippo
Neri, 1689. Libretto by G. A. Bergamori. Bologna: Pier-Maria Monti,
1689.
voices / orch
I:Bc. Printed libretto only.
Eitner, Sesini.

Murden, Eliza, née Crawly, Mrs. See Lady, of Charleston, S.C.

Murray, Hon. Miss
fl. c. 1800, Edinburgh and London
Pitthieveless castle. A favorite strathspey with four fashionable new dances for
the piano forte. Edinburgh: Robert Purdie, 1800. 2 pp.
pf
GB: Lbl [g.230.bb.(14.)]. Copy in Ars Fem coll.
RISM A/I (M 8200), CPM, letter (Ars Fem).

"Sei cheta O notte." Duettino. London: s.n. [1880?]. Text by Metastasio.
2 voices / pf
GB: Lbl [CH.1783.s.(48)].
CPM. [assigned date of 1880 must be an error]

Musigny, Mme de
pub. c. 1788–89, Paris
Six romances d'Estelle avec accompagnement de harpe ou piano-forte . . . [1er
recueil]. Paris: De Roullède [1788].. Keyboard arr. 9 pp.
voice / harp or pf
F: Pn [Vm7 7688 (1)]. Copy of one volume in Ars Fem coll.
RISM A/I (M 8212), Paris Lib. Cat., Cohen, Eitner, letter (Ars Fem).

Six romances d'Estelle avec accompagnement de harpe ou piano-forte . . . [2e recueil].
Paris: De Roullède [1789]. Keyboard arr. pp. 10–19.
voice / harp or pf
F: Pn [Vm7 7688(2)]. Copy of one volume in Ars Fem coll.
RISM A/I (M 8213), Paris Lib. Cat., Eitner, Cohen, letter (Ars Fem).

N . . . , Madame Théodore
pub. c. 1810, Paris
Un Jour dans le fond d'un bocage. Romance. [Paris: s.n., 1810?]
song
GB: Lbl [G. 548.(27.)].
CPM.

Nairne, Caroline, née **Oliphant, Baroness**
1766, Gask, Perthshire–1845, Gask
The Covenanter's Lament. Words and Music by Caroline, Baroness Nairne.
Harmonised by J. Yorkston. #14 in: *The Strathearn Collection of Part-Songs.*
Edinburgh: Paterson & Sons [1885–91].
Melody and texts only by Nairne.
voices
GB: Lbl [F.205].
CPM.

The land o' the leal, and other songs . . . London: W. Scott, n.d.
Texts only by Nairne?
songs
US: NH.
NUC (NN 0010162), Cohen.

Lays from Strathearn, arranged with symphonies and accompaniments for
the piano-forte by Finley Dun. 1. New ed. London: R. Addison [184–?].
2. Edinburgh: Paterson/ London: Hutchings & Romer, [185–?, first published 1846]. 3. Edinburgh: Paterson [c. 1860–1880?].
Melodies and text only by Nairne.
[Date of first edition unknown.]
voice/pf
1. GB: Ep. US: CA. 2. US: BAu. 3. US: LAu, NYp, WM.
1–3. NUC (NN 0010163–5), 1., 3. OCLC (22457676, 25057696;
14228468). Cohen.

Narbutowna (Narbuteruvey), Mlle Constance (Pany Konst.),
Countess (later **Mme Dembowska**)
pub. 1818, Warsaw
S. Żołkicwski Spiew historyczny ("Za szumnym Dnie strem na Cecor skim
błoniu gdzie"). In: Julian Ursyn Niemcewicz, *Śpiewy historycznye.* [Historic

songs.] Warsaw: 1818. Text by Niemcewicz.
voice/pf
F: Pn. PL: Kc, Wn, Wmickiewicz. Copy of PL: Kc in Jackson coll.
Sowinski, Cohen.

Nascinbeni, Maria Francesca (Modern ref. works spell as
Nascimbeni; spelling in original music is **Nascinbeni**)
b. 1657 or 1658?, Ancona
Canzoni e madrigali morali e spirituali a una, due, e tre voci. Ancona: Claudio
Percimineo, 1674. 4 partbooks (SSB/org).
S; SS; SSB; SSS/all with org bc
GB: Ob (complete: S I, S II, B, org). I: Bc (BB. 29), MAC, Rli (Musica
N. 2), Rv. Copies of I: Bc in US: CAi, Jackson coll., & Ars Fem coll.
*RISM A/I (N69), BUC, NG, Eitner, Bowers & Tick, Corsiniana, letters (US: CAi
& Ars Fem).*

"Sitientes venite" (Per il Santissimo Sacramento). pp. 60–65 in: Scipione
Lazarini, *Motetti à due, e tre voci* . . . Opera seconda. Ancona: Claudio
Percimineo, 1674. 4 partbooks (SSB/bc).
SS/bc
I: Bc (AA 173), Bsp, CEc (Bass only), Ls (A.158). Copy in Jackson coll.
*RISM B/I (1674 [1]), NG, Eitner, Cohen, Bowers & Tick, (MGG, as
"Francesco," in article on her teacher Lazzarini), Lucca.*

Newberry (Newbery), Miss
fl. 1790s, London?
Canzonets by a Lady. [London: c. 1795.] [The title page is ms., and according to ms. note, composer is "Miss Newbery, afterwards Mrs . . . "]
songs
GB: Lam.
RISM A/I (N 548), BUC.

A collection of country dances, and waltzen [sic]. For the violin, and bass: or
piano forte, composed by a young Lady. [London?: c. 1797.] [Ms. note on
the GB: Lam copy gives composer as "Miss Newberry."]
vln/b or pf
GB: Ckc, Lam.
RISM A/I (N 549), BUC.

Newton, Charlotte
pub. between 1823 and 1848, London

Auld Lang Syne. Arranged with Variations for the Harp and Dedicated to Miss Harriet Kerslake. London: Monro & May [between 1823 and 1848].
harp
In bound volume of 19th-century harp music in Rempel coll.
Letter (Rempel).

Niebelschitz, Anna von, née Zedlitzen

pub. 1601, Görlitz.
Zwey neue Geistliche Lieder . . . welche der . . . Gottseligen Frauen sehr lieb gewesen.
In Ihrer eigenen Weise zusingen. Oder im Thon: Durch Adams Fall ist gantz verterbt (in: *Christliche Leichpredigt . . .*). Görlitz: Johann Rhambau, 1601.
songs
D: Bds.
RISM A/I (N 682).

Noüailles, Mme de

pub. 1699, Paris
[Work(s)] in: *Suite de danses pour les violons et haut-bois, qui se joüent . . . aux bals chez le Roy . . . la plus grande partie par Philidor l'aîné . . . Livre premier.* Paris: C. Ballard. 1699.
vlns / obs
F: Pn.
RISM B/I (1699 [7]).

O

O'Brian, Mrs. Mary

fl. c. 1775, English?

The Temple of Virtue, composed c. 1775? [O'Brian may be the librettist rather than composer.]

stage work (burletta)

GB: Lbl (Ms. Add. 25927).

Mellen.

O'Moran, G[eorgina?], Mrs.

pub. c. 1809–15, London

The Emblem of Love ("A Rose was empearled"). Song, arr. by J. Wilkins. London: Clementi [1815?].

song

GB: Lbl [G.806.f.(84.)].

CPM.

Six ballads, with an accompaniment for the Piano Forte or Harp. London: Savory [1809].

voice/pf or harp

GB: Lbl (2 ex.) [H.1691.(49.) & R.M.13.f.28.].

CPM.

O'Moran, Georgina, (Mrs.?) (may be same as preceding)

pub. c. 1820, London

Song, in honor of Marquis Wellington ("Say what reward"). London: Mitchell's Musical Library [1820?]. 3 pp. Words by Sophia Rendall.

song

GB: Lbl [H.1625.n.(40.)].

CPM.

Ogle, Susannah

?, Durham–1825, Durham?

Service in E-flat [Anglican]. Responses to the commandments, Kyrie. Ms., c. 1800.

voices

GB: DRc [Music mss.].

Durham.

Olin, Elizabeth
1740–1828, Sweden
"En liten såland båck." Ariette af Hof Secreteraren Olins fru. Ms., 18th cent. 1 p.
voice
S: L (Saml. Kraus. 231). Copy in Ars Fem coll. as Lamento.
RISM A/II (#37305), Cohen, letter (Ars Fem).

Opie, Mrs. Amelia, née **Alderson** (**Alderson, Amelia.** Also literary works, as **Mrs. Opie**)
1769–1853
"If thou couldest know what it is to love" [song]. The words from Graham Hamilton [by Lady C. Lamb]. London: s.n. [1823].
voice/pf
GB: Lbl [H.1691.(50.)].
CPM.

Orsina, Lucrezia. See **Vizana, Lucretia Orsina**

Orsini (Orsina), Eleonora, Duchess of Segni
fl. 1560–80, Italian
"Per pianto la mia carne si distilla." [Canzona] In: Canzoni, Arie, . . . a voce sola ed a più voci con accompagnemento de Liuto. Compiled by Bottegari, 1573. Ms.
voice/lute
I: MOe (Mus. F. 311).
Cohen, Estense.

Orsini (Orsina), Isabella de, née **Medici, Duchess of Bracciano**
1542, Florence–1576
"Lieta vivo e contenta ." In: Canzoni, Arie, . . . a voce sola ed a più voci con accompagnemento de Liuto. Compiled by Bottegari, 1574–1602. Ms.
voice/lute
I: MOe (Mus. F. 311).
Eitner, Cohen, Estense, MGG (Medici family entry).

Örtel (Oertel), Mimi von
pub. 1778, Weimar
"Dein gedenk' ich." Andantino. In: *Der Teutsche Merkur vom Jahre 1778.* Wiemar: Wieland (ed.), 1778.
song

D: DÜk (cat. # 905).
Düsseldorf-Goethe.

Owen, Harriet Mary, née Browne
d. 1858
The Bell at sea. The words by Mrs. Hemans; the music by her sister. New York: J. L. Jewitt [18—?]. 3 pp.
voice/pf
US: TUua.
OCLC (22546611).

The captive knight: a ballad. The words by Mrs. Hemans; the music by her sister. New York: James Hewitt, [1832?]. 6 pp.
voice/pf
US: Pu.
OCLC (24599903).

The child's first grief: a duett. The words by Mrs. Hemans; the music composed & arranged for the piano forte by her sister. 1. New York: Dubois & Stodart [between 1824 and 1834]. 6 pp. 2. New York: Hall & Son [between 1848 and 1858]. 7 pp.
2 voices/pf
1–2. US: Pu.
1–2. OCLC (24995477, 25044321).

Evening song to the Virgin at sea: a duett ("Ave sanctissima, we lift our souls to thee"). The words by Mrs. Hemans; the music by her sister. 1. Boston: James Hewitt [c. 1827]. 3 pp. 2. with an additional verse written for this edition. Baltimore: John Cole [183–?]. 2 pp. 3. New York: Bourne [c. 1830]. 4. New York: Hall, [185–?]. [Bound with: *6 morceaux élégants sur des airs allemands favoris* . . . Mayence: Schott, [185–?]]. 5. Boston: Oliver Ditson [c. 1858]. 5 pp. 6. arr. [for guit] by F. Weiland. Boston: Ditson [c. 1858].
1–5. 2 voices/pf; 6. 2 voices/guit
1. US: TUua. 2. & 3. US: HA. 4. US: K. 5. & 6. US: HA.
1–6. OCLC (17697635, 17698341, 1769834, 11392486, 18063042, 18063042).

"I hear thee speak of a better land"; the words by Mrs. Hemans; the music by her sister; as sung by Mrs. Pomeroy, arr. by Robert Geo. Paige. New York: James Hewitt [c. 1836]. 3 pp.

voice/pf
US: HA, Pu.
OCLC (18511660).

The last wish, a ballad ("Bring me sweet flow'rs to shed"), written by Mrs. Hemans; the music by her sister. New York: Bourne [c. 1830]. 2 pp.
voice/pf
US: HA.
OCLC (17698118).

The messenger bird, a duet ("Thou art come from the spirit's land"). The poetry by Mrs. Hemans; the music by her sister. 1. New York: Dubois & Stodart [183–?]. 6 pp. 2. New York, Firth & Hall [c. 1832]. 3. Baltimore: Geo. Willig, jr., [184–?]. 4. Boston: Oliver Ditson [between 1844 and 1857].
2 voices/pf
1–2. US: HA. 3–4. US: Pu.
1–4. OCLC (17698157, 18663717, 25036074, 24512850).

The pilgrim fathers ("The breaking waves dash'd high"). Words by Mrs. Hemans; music by Mrs. [*sic*] Browne. 1. Baltimore: G. Willig, jr., [18—?]. 6 pp. 2. Boston: C. Bradlee [c. 1830]. 3. C. Badlee [c.184–?]. 4. New York: Firth, Hall & Pont [1846–47].
voice/pf
US: 1. TUua, 2. HA, 3. Wc. 4. Pu.
1–3. OCLC (22515042, 17698486, 23384168).

Tyrolese evening hymn; the words by Mrs. Hemans; music by her sister, Miss Browne. New York: Firth & Hall [c. 1835].
voice/pf
US: Pu.
OCLC (24600573).

Owenson, Miss. See **Morgan, Lady Sydney,** née **Owenson**

P

P., Mlle

pub. 1717, Paris
[Work(s)] in: *Recueil d'airs sérieux et à boire, de différents auteurs. Pour l'année 1717*. Paris: J. B. C. Ballard, 1717.
song(s)
F: Pn.
RISM B/II (p. 314).

P., Mlle de la

pub. 1700, Paris
[Work(s)] in: *Recueil d'airs sérieux et à boire, de différents auteurs. Pour l'année 1700*. Paris: C. Ballard, 1700.
song
F: Pc (2 ex.), Pn. Other library holdings incomplete.
RISM B/I (1700[2]).

Pacini, Euphrosine, Mlle

pub. c. 1810, Paris?
"Oh! che bella figurina." Cavatina, arrangée par E. Pacini [from G. Mosca] [1810?].
song
GB: Lbl [G. 557.(18.)].
CPM.

Paisible, Adélaïde-Félicité Mareschal (dite Melle)

pub. 1766, Paris
Premier Recueil d'ariettes choisies avec accompagnement de guitarre par Melle Paisible et de violon à volonté par M. son frère avec basse chiffrée. Paris: L'auteur, 1766. 32 pp.
voice/guit/vln ad lib/bc
F: Pn [A.35259].
RISM B/II (p. 318), Paris Lib. Cat.

Pannina, Marta

pub. 1706, Bologna
Il trionfo dell'amor santo espresso nella conquista del cuore della Signora Pannina Marta Pannini[,] da Cento . . . Canzonetta a due voci [S, B]. Bologna: "al insegna dell' Angelo Custode, per li Peri", 1706.
2 voices (SB)

I: PESd (one page).
RISM A/I (P 855).

Papavoine, Mme, née **Pellecier**

fl. 1754–70, Paris

La France sauvée, ou *La triomphe de la vertu.* Cantatille avec accompagnements.
Paris: auteur (imprimé par Tournelle), May 1757. Score.
voice/vln(s)/bc
F: Pn. Copy in Ars Fem coll.
RISM A/I (P 874), MGG (ascription considered doubtful), Cohen, letter (Ars Fem).

Le cabriolet. Cantatille à voix seule avec accompagnement de violons et
basse continue. Paris: auteur, Le Clerc, Bayard, Mlle Castagnery (gravé
par Mme Leclair), January 1756. Score. 10 pp.
voice/vlns/bc
F: Pn [Vmg. 5148]. Copy in Ars Fem coll.
*RISM A/I (P 873), Paris Lib. Cat., NG (entry on M. Papavoine), MGG, Cohen,
letter (Ars Fem).*

"Nous voici donc au jour de l'an." Étrennes (Chanson). In: *Mercure de
France,* January 1775, p. 105. Paris: s.n.,1755.
song
GB: Lbl [298.c.22.].
RISM A/I (P 875), CPM, BUC, MGG, Cohen.

Recueil d'airs choises de [Théâtre de] *l'Ambigu-comique,* mis en duo pour deux
violons . . . Oeuvre V. Paris: L'Auteur [c. 1770]. Parts.
2 vlns
GB: Ckc.
BUC, Cohen.

"Reviens, aimable Thémire." Chanson. Les parolles de Mlle B. . . . In:
Mercure de France, May 1761, p. 51. Paris: s.n. (gravée par Mme
Charpentier, imprimé par Tournelle), 1761.
song
GB: Lbl [297.d.29.]. Copy in Ars Fem coll.
RISM A/I (P 876), BUC, CPM, MGG, Cohen, letter (Ars Fem).

"Vous fuyez sans vouloir m'entendre." Chanson. Les parolles de Mlle B.
. . . In: *Mercure de France,* July 1756, p. 96. [Paris]: Tournelle, 1756.
song

GB: Lbl [297.d.2.]. Copy in Ars Fem coll.
RISM A/I (P 877), BUC, CPM, MGG, Cohen, letter (Ars Fem).

Paradis (Paradies), Maria Theresia von
1759, Vienna–1824, Vienna
"Auf Brüder, auf, geniesst des Lebens Wonne." [Only Johann Riedinger's text published] Vienna: Carl Gerold, 1813.
chorus
A: Wgm. Text only survives, music lost.
NG, Ullrich, Matsushita.

Auf die Damen, welche statt Gold, nun Leinwand für die verwundeten Krieger zupfen.
S.l. [Vienna, acc. to NG]: s.n., 1794.
S/pf
A: Wgm (II. 12809), Wst (MS. M. Inv. 39.212). CS: Pnm (MB 59 A 483).
Copy of A: Wgm in Ars Fem coll.
RISM A/I (P 907), NG, Eitner, letter (Ars Fem), Ullrich, Matsushita.

"Da eben seinen Lauf." Aria. Vienna: 1813. Ms. Also found in *Zwölf Lieder auf ihrer Reise*, see entry.
S/pf
A: Wgm (2 versions VI. 3757 & VI. 12810).
NG, Eitner, Ullrich, Matsushita.

Der Schulkandidat [ländliches Singspiel in 3 acts]. Perf. Vienna, 5 Dec. 1792. Libretto probably by Riedinger. Ms.
stage work
A: Llm (only musical portions survive; spoken texts are not extant).
NG, MGG, Ullrich, Matsushita.

Deutsches Monument Ludwigs des Unglücklichen [dedicated to Empress Maria Theresia]. 1. [Piano-vocal arrangement.] Vienna/Prague: von Schönfeld, 1793. 2. [Text vol.], Passau: Ambrosé, 1793. 3. [libretto only] Vienna: s.n.,1793. Text by J. Riedinger. 4. Ms. copies of orchestral parts, n.d.
voice/pf arr. (also ms. orchestral parts)
1. & 2. A: Sca (15434). 1. A: Wn (27.108), S. D: BNms, LEm. GB: Lbl [E.46.a.]. 3. US: MAu, PHu. 4. A: KR. Copy of A: Wn in Jackson coll.
1. RISM A/I (P 906), Ullrich, Matsushita, NG, Eitner, MGG (date incorrect as 1794), 2. BUC, CPM, 3. NUC (NP 0073906), 4. Matsushita.

Fantaise pour la piano-forte, dediée à sa chère petite ecoliere Nanette de Sprinz. July 26, 1811. Ms.
pf
A: Wn (SM 28.299). Copy in D: Kf&m.
Matsushita, Frau & Musik.

Fantaisie in G für das piano-forte. Vienna: Chemische Druckerei (#501), n.d.
pf
A: GÖ.
RISM A/I (P 908), Ullrich, Matsushita, NG, Meggett.

Geister Chor [C major]. [Composer's name supplied.] Ms.
choir/pf
A: RB (R 302).
RISM A/II (#33679).

Lenore. 1. Vienna: s.n., 1790. 48 pp. 2. ms. copy. Text by G. A. Bürger.
voice/pf
1. A: Wgm (VI. 3758). D: Bds. GB: Lbl [E.46]. 2. A: Wst (MH 199).
1. RISM A/I (P 905), BUC, CPM, NG, Eitner, MGG (incorrectly as Leonore), 1–2. Ullrich, Matsushita.

Lied auf die Blindheit des Frl. M. Th. v. Paradis ("Ich war ein kleines Würmchen"). In: *Wiener Musenalmanach.* Vienna: 1785, pp. 52–58. Text by G. K. Pfeffel.
voice/pf
A: Wn (620.155–A).
NG, MGG, Ullrich, Matsushita.

[Lieder]. Ms. In: Ein Sammelband von Liedern und Gesängen mit Klavier-Begleitung [1786?]. 210 pp.
1759, Vienna–1824, Vienna
S/pf
D:Dl (Ms. B910). Manuscript no longer in existence, may have been destroyed or misplaced during WWI or WWII.
Eitner, Ullrich, Matsushita.

Rinaldo und Alcina oder *Die Insel der Verführung.* [3 act opera] Text by Ludwig von Baczko. Königsberg: Hartung, 1794. Text only survives.
stage work

CS: Pu. US: Wc (Schatz collection #7770). Music lost, printed libretto only.
Ullrich, Matsushita, NG, MGG (date incorrect as 1797).

Sicilienne for violin and piano (also other combinations). [Arr., ed., and probably composed by Samuel Dushkin, Mainz: Schott, 1924. Falsely attributed to Paradis.]
vln or vlc/pf
Modern work, ascribed to Paradis. No original Paradis source.
Cohen, MGG, Briscoe (reprint), Matsushita.

[Sonata in E-flat, violin and piano]. 1795.
pf/vln
A: Wgm. Copy in Ars Fem coll.
Letter (Ars Fem).

Trauerkantate auf den Tod Leopold des Gütigen. Vienna: Koželuch, 1792. Text by Riedinger.
voice/pf
A: Wgm (according to NG, lost according to Matsushita).
NG, MGG, Matsushita.

2 sonatas [piano], 1793.
pf
A: Wgm. Copy in Ars Fem coll.
Letter (Ars Fem).

Zwölf Lieder auf ihrer Reise in Musik gesetzt. Leipzig: Johann Gottlob Immanuel Breitkopf, 1786. 35 pp.
voice/pf
A: Wn. D: BNms, Dl, HAu, LB, W. GB: Lbl [Hirsch III.975]. US: WA, BE. Copy of A: Wn in Jackson coll.
RISM A/I (P 904), BUC, CPM, NUC (NNP 0073906), OCLC (164354066), NG, Eitner, MGG, Ullrich, Matsushita.

Paradiser, Marianna von (Paradis, Maria Theresia von?)
[String Quartet in D Major] copyist's ms. 1795.
2 vlns/vla/vlc
A: Wn. Copy in Ars Fem coll.
Letter (Ars Fem).

[String Quartet in G Major]. Copyist's ms., 1829. [Title page as "Quintet." "5th part" is vla part transcribed for second cello to play if vla is lacking.]
2 vlns/vla/vlc
A: L. Copy in Ars Fem coll.
Letter (Ars Fem).

Park(e), Maria Hester, née **Reynolds** (according to NG & MGG née **Parke,** afterwards **Beardmore**)
1775, London–1822, London (NG, MGG)
A concerto, for the piano-forte or harpsichord . . . op. VI. London: Robert Birchal [*sic*], for the author [c.1795]. [Lbl copy uses name Maria Hester Park.]
2 pf or hpsch [no orch]
GB: Lbl (2 ex., one incomplete) [g.271, p.(5.) & g.543, u.(14.)]. Copies in C. Johnson coll. and Ars Fem coll.
RISM A/I (P 917), BUC, CPM (cat. as Reynolds), NG, Cohen, MGG, Meggett, letters (GB: Lbl, C. Johnson, Ars Fem).

A Divertimento for the Piano Forte. s.l.: s.n., n.d.
pf
GB: Lbl (2 ex.) [g.606.ii.(20.) & h.925.x.(3.)].
Letter (GB: Lbl).

"Go, tell Amynta." [Glee à 3]. Ms.
3 voices
GB: Lbl [Add. 31807, f.90b].
Letter (GB: Lbl).

"O dolce concento" ["Das klinget so herrlich" from *Die Zauberflöte*], the favorite air, composed by Mozart, with new variations [by Maria Hester Parke]. London: Goulding, De'Almaine, Potter [183–?].
voice/pf
US: NYp, Wc (M1619.S684, no. 53).
NUC (0097664).

A set of [6] *glees . . . with the dirge in Cymbeline* . . . op. 3. London: Birchall & Andrews, for the author [c. 1790]. Score. 18 pp.
3–4 voices
GB: GM, Lbl [E.207.c.(5.)]. US: Cn, Wc. Copy in Ars Fem coll.
RISM A/I (P 915), BUC, CPM (as Reynolds, afterward Park), NUC (NP 0097665), NG, MGG, Eitner, Cohen (but erroneously as piano work), letter (Ars Fem).

A sonata [C] *for the piano forte* . . . op. VII. London: Lewis Lavenu, for the author [c. 1796]. 11 pp.

pf

GB: Lbl [g.543..u.(15.)] [Lbl copy uses name form Maria Hester Park.] Copies in C. Johnson coll. and Ars Fem coll.

RISM A/I (P 918), BUC, CPM (as Reynolds), NG, Cohen, MGG, Meggett, letters (C. Johnson, Ars Fem).

Sonatas [C, B-flat, E-flat, G, D, F] *for the harpsichord or piano forte* [with vln], op. 1. [Brighton: Henry Davey], 1785. Score. 49 pp. [Dedicated to the Countess of Uxbridge.]

pf or hpsch/vln

GB: BA, Ckc, Lbl [h.74]. US: NYp, Wc (M219. R45486). Microfilm of Lbl copy in C. Johnson coll. (as Maria Hester Park(e)).

RISM A/I (R 1234), BUC, CPM (as Reynolds), letter (GB: Lbl), NUC (NR 0218174), Eitner, Meggett (as Reynolds), Cohen, letter (C. Johnson).

Three grand sonatas for the pianoforte, op. 1. 1. London: Longman & Broderip [c. 1790 or 1799]. 2. . . . *for the piano forte with additional keys:* op. 1ma. London: Broderip & Wilkinson [1799]. [This is probably the same as Miss M. F. Parke's *Three Grand Sonatas*, op. 1, see entry.]

pf

1. US: BE [as Maria Hester Parke. (M23 P367 op. 1 1799 Case X.)].
2. US: BE [as Maria Hester Parke, probably Parke, M. F., see entry.].
1. MGG (Parke, Maria Hester), NUC (as Maria Hester Parke) (NP 0097666).
2. OCLC (as Maria Hester Parke but probably M. F. Parke) (#21850765).

Three Sonatas [E-flat, F, C] for the harpsichord or piano forte . . . *opera 2.* London: Longman & Broderip, for the author [c. 1790].

hpsch or pf

GB: Lbl [F.65.o.(1.]. Microfilm copy in C. Johnson coll., as Maria Hester Park(e).

RISM A/I (R 1235), CPM (as Reynolds), Meggett (as Reynolds), letter (GB: Lbl), letter (C. Johnson).

Two grand sonatas for pianoforte and violin, op. 3. London: Lavenu, c. 1795.

pf/vln

GB: Lbl [f.65.o.(1.)].

CPM (as Reynolds), letter (GB: Lbl), Meggett (as n.d., n.p.), MGG, Cohen.

Two sonatas for the piano forte or harpsichord . . . op. IV. London: Longman & Broderip, for the author [c.1795]. [Lbl copy uses form Maria Hester Park.]
pf or hpsch
GB: Gu, Lbl [g.145.(9.)]. Copies of GB: Lbl copy in C. Johnson coll. and Ars Fem coll.
RISM A/I (P 916), BUC, CPM (as Reynolds, dated 1790), Eitner, Cohen, MGG, Meggett, letters (GB: Lbl, C. Johnson, Ars Fem).

2 sonatas for the piano forte [with violin accompaniment], op. 13. London: Birchall [c. 1801]. 15 pp. [Title page name, M. H. Park.]
pf/vln
GB: Lbl [g.421.u.(8.)].
CPM (as Reynolds, afterwards Park), letter (GB: Lbl), NG, Cohen.

Parke, M. F. Miss (identity problem. Sometimes identified as **Maria Hester Parke,** see entries above)
fl. 1787–c.1810, London
A Divertimento, and Military Rondo for the Piano Forte. London: Printed for Miss Parke [1807].
pf
GB: Lbl [h.60.1.(6.)].
CPM, letter (GB: Lbl).

"God of Slaughter, quit the field." Duet. London: s.n. [1806?]. [Lbl copy signed M. F. P.]
2 voices/pf
GB: Lbl [G.807.c.(46.)].
CPM, letter (GB: Lbl).

"I have often been told and began to believe" [song]. [London]: Longman & Broderip [1787].
voice/pf
GB: Lbl [H.1653.(40.)], Ob. US: AUS (as Miss Maria Hester Parke).
Copy in Ars Fem coll. (as Miss M. F. [Marie Hester] Parke).
RISM A/I (P 919), BUC, CPM, letter (GB: Lbl, as M. F. Park), OCLC (14761767, as Maria Hester Parke), Eitner (Miss M. Parke is identified as Maria Hester Parke), letter (Ars Fem).

Three grand sonatas for the piano forte with additional keys. op. Ima. London: Broderip & Wilkinson, for the author [1799]. 49 pp. [Lbl copy signed M. P.]
pf

GB: Lbl [g.145.(8.)], Ob. Copies of GB: Lbl copy in C. Johnson coll. and Ars Fem coll. (as Miss M. F. [Marie Hester] Parke).
RISM A/I (P 921, dated 1790), BUC, CPM, letter (GB: Lbl), NG, Eitner (Miss M. Parke is identified as Maria Hester Parke), Meggett (as Maria Hester Park(e)), letters (C. Johnson, Ars Fem).

Two Grand Sonatas, for the Piano Forte . . . and an accompaniment for the violin, ad libitum . . . op. 2. London: Author [1800]. Partbook (only piano part survives). 29 pp. [Lbl copies signed M. F. P.]
pf/vln ad lib
GB: Lbl (2 ex.) [h.60.1.(7.) & h.925.v.(4.)]. Microfilm of Lbl copy in C. Johnson coll.
CPM, letter (GB: Lbl), MGG, Meggett (as Maria Hester Park(e)),letter (C. Johnson).

Two Grand Sonatas for the Pianoforte . . . op. 2.
London: s.n. [1805?].
fl. 1787–c.1810, London
pf
GB: Lbl [g.271.g.(18.)].
CPM, letter (GB: Lbl), NG.

"What is beauty." A new duett. [London]: Lewis Lavenu [1810?]. [Lbl copy signed M. F. P.]
2 voices/pf
GB: Lbl [H.2831.a.(33.)]. US: NYcu. Copy in Ars Fem coll. Copy in Ars Fem coll. (as Miss M. F. [Marie Hester] Parke).
RISM A/I (P 920), CPM, letter (GB: Lbl), Eitner (Miss M. Parke is identified as Maria Hester Parke), letter (Ars Fem).

Parker, Mrs.
pub. c. 1800, Dublin
Malibran waltz. Boston: Prentiss, 1841. 3 pp. [May not be the same as Mrs. Parker].
pf
US: Bp, Wc (M1.A13A).
NUC (NP 0098262).

Mrs. Parker's much admired hornpipe [and] *Bangor Ferry.* A favorite Welsh dance. Dublin: Hime [c. 1800].
pf

GB: Lbl [H.1601.g.(104.)]. Copy in Ars Fem coll.
RISM A/I (P 933), BUC, CPM, Cohen, letter (Ars Fem).

Mrs. Parker's selection of Scotch tunes, strathspeys and reels for the piano-forte or harp-sichord. Dublin: Edmund Lee [c. 1800]. 14 pp.
pf or hpsch
GB: Ckc, DU (incomplete), En (incomplete), Lbl [g.352.mm.(14.)],
P (incomplete). Copy of GB: Lbl in Ars Fem coll.
RISM A/I (P 934), BUC, CPM, Cohen, letter (Ars Fem).

Pawlowna (Paulowna), Maria. See Maria Pawlowna (Paulowna), grand-duchess of Weimar

Paxton, Miss
pub. c. 1795, London?
Six easy Canzonets and three Duets for the Piano Forte or Harpsichord, composed by a Lady. S.l.: s.n. [1795].
voice/pf or hpsch; pf or hpsch (4 hand)
GB: Lbl [E.270.(16.)].
CPM.

Pean, Melle
pub. 1770s, Paris
Musique des chansons insérées dans l'article des poèsies traduites . . . In: Laus de Boissy (Louis de), *L'art d'aimer.* London/Paris: s.n., 1772, pp. 3–8.
songs
F: Pn (B.N. Imp [Y2 10809]).
Paris Lib. Cat.

[Work(s)] in: *La muse lyrique dédiée à Madame la Dauphine.* . . airs avec accompagnement de guitarre par Mr. Patouart fils. [Monthly] Paris: Julivet, 1770–1776.
Melody only by Pean
voice/guit
B: Bc. F: D (specific library not given in RISM), Pa, Pn, Psg. GB: Gm, Lbl.
NL: DHk. S: Skma. US: BR, Wc. All holdings are incomplete.
RISM B/II (Péan, p. 242).

[Work(s)] in: *Recueil de romances historiques, tendres et burlesques tant anciennes que modernes* . . . [Paris]: s.n., 1767–74.
song(s)

B: Bc, Lc. F: E, Pa (2 ex.), Pn (2 ex.), T, TLm. NL: DHk. S: Skma. US: ST.
Other library holdings are incomplete runs.
RISM B/II (Péan, p. 333).

[Work(s)] in: *Troisième Recueil d'airs en duo tirés des opéra de . . . Rameau, Rebel et Francoeur, et autres . . . pour les flutes, violons, pardessus de violes et dont la pluspart peuvent se jouer sur la vielle et la musette . . .* Paris: Bordet [1770].
2 fls, 2 vlns, 2 pardessus, or vielle and musette
F: Pc.
RISM B/II (Péan, p. 308).

Pélé, Mme D. S.
pub. 1780s, Paris
[Work(s)] in: *IIème Suite des plaisirs de la société.* Vè [-VIè] recueil . . . d'ariettes des meileurs opéra, opéra-comiques et autres, arrangées pour le
clavecin ou le forte-piano, avec un accompagnement de violon ad libitum
. . . par Foignet. Paris: Le Duc [1785].
hpsch or pf/vln ad lib
F: Pc, Pn (lacks V).
RISM B/II (Pélé, p. 376).

[Work(s)] in: *Les Plaisirs de la société.* Recueil d'ariettes choisies des meileurs
opéra, opéra-comiques et autres, arrangées pour le forte-piano ou le
clavecin, avec un accompagnement de violon ad libitum . . . par Mr.
Foignet. Paris: Le Menu, Boyer [1781]. 3 vol.
hpsch or pf/vln ad lib
F: Pc, Pn. Other library holdings are incomplete runs.
RISM B/II (p. 288).

Pellecier, Mlle. See Papavoine, Mme, née Pellecier

Pellegrini Celoni, Anna Maria
c.1780, Rome–1835
Grammatica o siano regole di ben cantare . . . op. 6. 1. Rome: P. Piale e Giul.
Ces. Martorelli, 1810. 56 pp. 2. 2d ed. Rome: Bourlié, 1817. German
Trans., issued in German and Italian. 3. Leipzig: Peters. 4. Another ed.
Leipzig: Breitkopf & Härtel.
instruction (voice)
1. GB: Lbl [F. 1692.o.]. I: Bc. 2. I: Bc (Kat. l, 323). 1., 3. (Eitner, B. B.
Dresd., present location not confirmed) 4. A: Wgm.
1. CPM, Eitner (his location for 1., 3. not confirmed), 1., 4. Cohen, 2. letter (I: Bc).

Metodo breve, e facile per conoscere il piantato della musica e sue diramazioni . . .
Accademica filarmonica del Liceo Bologna. Roma: de Romanis, 1823.
instruction
A: Wgm. D: Bds, Dlb. Modern locations not confirmed.
Eitner

Percy, the Honorable Anne Caroline Bertie (Mrs. Bertie Percy)
pub. 1830s–50?, London
"I wander'd forth a pilgrim lone." Song in: Lydia Kirkpatrick's Songbook:
A Collection of 109 English Songs and Hymns, p. 546–56. Ms.
song
US: BE.
Berkeley (pp. 213–17).

Pergolese, Eleonora Patrizia
fl. 1778, Italy?
"Ombra dilletta del caro figlio." Aria for contralto solo. Made for the use
of Antonio Vannuccini, 1778. Ms. score and parts.
A/2 vlns/2 obs/2 hns/vla/b (vlc)/db
I: Gi(l) [N.1.6.7.(sc.40)].
Genova.

Peruchona (Perucona), (Suor) Maria Xaveria (Saveria)
pub. 1675, Italy (b. Novara)
Sacri concerti de motetti a una, due, tre, e quattro voci, parte con violini, e parte senza
. . . opera prima. Milan: Francesco Vigone, 1675. 5 partbooks.
S/2 vlns; SS/2 vlns; SS; SB; SSB; SAT; SATB; SSAB; SSAT/all with org bc
I: Bc (BB 120). Microfilm in US: CAi (3682.755.14.1); Jackson coll., & Ars
Fem coll.
*RISM A/I (P 1498), Eitner, MGG (article on Vigone), letter (US: CAi), letter (Ars
Fem).*

Pfeffel, Karoline
pub. 1790s, Tübingen
"Auf einem Anger sass Erwin." From: *Mathilde, eine Schottische Novelle.* In:
Flora, *Teutschlands Töchtern* . . . Tübingen: Cotta, 1795, Vol. 2.
song
D: DÜk.
Düsseldorf-Goethe.

"Du holde Rose, treues Bild der Minne." In: Flora, *Teutschlands Töchtern* . . .
Tübingen: Cotta, 1797, Vol. 4.
song
D: DÜk (#916).
Düsseldorf-Goethe.

Grablied ("Wehmuthsvoll aus öder Ferne"). In: Flora, *Teutschlands Töchtern*
. . . Tübingen: Cotta, 1793, Vol. 4.
pub. 1790s, Tübingen
song
D: DÜk (#914).
Düsseldorf-Goethe.

Philarmonica, Mrs. (pseud.)
pub. 1715, London
Divertimenti da camera a due violini, violoncello o cimbalo. Parte seconda. London:
Richard Meares (Thomas Cross) [1715?]. Parts [bound together with
sonatas].
2 vlns/vlc or hpsch (bc)
GB: Ckc (incomplete), Lbl (complete: 4 parts, MUSIC. g. 1032, MUS.
MIC. 2601). Copies of GB: Lbl in Jackson coll. and Ars Fem coll.
RISM A/I (P 1766), BUC, CPM, Eitner, Cohen, letter (Ars Fem).

Sonate a due violini col violoncello obbligato e violone o cimbalo di Mrs. Philamonica
[pseud.] Parte prima. [6 Sonatas] London: Richard Meares (Thomas
Cross) [1715?]. Parts [cto. part-book labeled "organo"].
2 vlns/vlc/violone or hpsch [org] (bc)
GB: Ckc (incomplete), Lbl (complete: 4 parts. MUSIC. g. 1032, MUS.
MIC. 2601). Copies of GB: Lbl in Jackson coll. and Ars Fem coll.
RISM A/I (P 1766), BUC, CPM, Eitner, Cohen, letter (Ars Fem).

Philippine (Philippina) Charolotte, Duchess of Braunschweig
fl. mid-18th cent., Prussia and Braunschweig
Marsch [in E-flat for 2 oboes, trumpet, 2 bassoons]. Ms. [1751].
wind band
D: Bds.
Haynes, Cohen.

Pinel, Julie
fl. c. 1737, Paris
[dance]. Ms. [composer given as Pinelle].

unspecified instrument(s)
D: Kl (Pinelle. Ms. Kat. S. 65).
Eitner (not sure of identity of Pinel).

Nouveau recueil d'airs sérieux et à boire, à une et deux voix, de brunettes à 2 dessus, scène pastorale et cantatille avec accompagnement. Paris; author, Boivin, Le Clerc, 1737. Score.
1–2 voices/bc, 1 with 2 fls
F: Pn [Vm7 629]. Copy in Ars Fem coll.
RISM A/I (P 2384), Paris Lib. Cat., MGG (entry on Brunette), Eitner, Cohen, Tick & Bowers, letter (Ars Fem).

[1 piece for lute] Ms. [Identified with surname only. This piece may be by François Pinel, a lutenist (d. 1709).]
lute
F: Pc. [Ms. der Bibl. des C.P. (Kat. 485 of Weckerlin)].
Eitner (not sure of identity of Pinel).

Work in: *Suittes faciles pour 1 flute ou 1 violon & basse continue* de la composition de Messieurs du Fau, . . . Pinel [no first initial] . . . & autres.
Amsterdam: Estienne Roger [c. 1710].
fl or vln/bc
GB: Drc.
BUC (suggests Julie? Pinel), Eitner (not sure of identity of Pinel), RISM B/II (Pinel, p. 377).

Pinet, Mlle, la fille
pub. 1710, Paris
[Work(s)] in: *Recueil d'airs sérieux et à boire de différents auteurs pour l'année 1710.* Paris: C. Ballard, 1710.
song(s)
F: Mc (Mar., Apr., May), Pc (Jan., July–Aug., Oct.), Pn. NL: DHk (Jan.).
RISM B/II (p. 313).

Pinottini, Maria Teresa Agnesi. See Agnesi, Maria Teresa d'

Pio di Savoja, Isabella D., née Countess Scapinelli
c. 1768, Carpi–1809, Casinalbo, Modena
[3 ariette per canto e arpa . . .] "Placa gli sdegni tuoi," "Se lungi men'vo," & "Sei troppo vezzosa" [1775?]. Ms.
voice/harp

I: Moe (Mus. F. 945).
Cohen, Estense.

Piston, Julia, Mlle

pub. 1820s, London and Paris?
La Chapelle de l'amour [by A. Anson] arr. pour guitare ou lyre par Mlle
J. Piston. S.l.: s.n. [1821].
voice/guit or lyre
GB: Lbl [E.1717.p.(1.)].
CPM.

Les Folies du jour [by J. D. Doche] Accompt. de guitare par Mlle J. Piston.
In: *La Lyre du vaudeville,* année 1. nr. 10. S.l.: s.n. [1825].
voice/guit
GB: Lbl [E.1717.m.].
CPM.

"Tourment d'amour." Tyrolienne. London: s.n. [1825?].
song
GB: Lbl [H.2831.a.(41.)].
CPM.

Pitman, Mary Ann

pub. London, 1816
The Cottage Girl ("'Twas in a lonely Cottage dwelling"). A Ballad. Set to
Musick for the Voice and Piano Forte, with an Accompaniment for an
Harp and Violoncello. In: *The Ladies' Monthly Museum,* Feb. 1816.
voice/pf/harp/vlc
Rempel coll.
Letter (Rempel).

Pittar, Mrs. Isaac. Married name of **Krumpholtz, Fanny.** See entry

Plowden, Dorothea (Dorothy, Mrs. Francis Plowden)

pub. c. 1800, London
Virginia. A comic opera in three acts, as performed at the Theatre Royal
Drury Lane; the music entirely new. Composed by Mrs. Francis Plowden.
[Op.1.] 1. London: Clementi, Banger, Hyde, Collard & Davis, [1800?].
72 pp. [The overture and orchestral interludes arr. for pf; vocal pieces
with acc. of bass only.] 2. The overture and the whole of the music new;
the melodies composed by the author of the dialogue, and harmonized by

Dr. Arnold. London: Barker, 1800. [only libretto survives]
stage work
1. GB: Lbl (2 ex., the first with ms. additions) [H.147], [R.M.11.a.2.(4.)].
I: Rsc. US: NH, Su (missing pp. 47–50). 2. US: AA, AUS, BE, BLu, BU,
BUu, CHu, Cn, DM, FRE, LAuc, MSu, NH, O, Su, Wc.
1. RISM A/I (P 4960), CPM, NUC (NP 0426602). 2. NUC (NP 0426603).

Poirier, Mlle
pub. c. 1785, France
"Aimable et jeune enchanteresse." Romance avec accompagnement de
clavecin ou piano forte. S.l., s.n. [c.1785].
voice/hpsch or pf
GB: Lbl [B.362.n.(14.)].
RISM A/I (P 5004), CPM.

Pontcadeux, Floriande, Madlle
pub. 1809, London
An original air with variations for the Piano Forte. London: s.n. [1809].
pf
GB: Lbl [h.121.(26.)].
CPM.

Poole, Caroline
pub. c. 1800, London
The orphan that's wet with the rain. A favorite song. London: Lewis Lavenu
[179–? or 1800]. 3 pp.
voice/pf
GB: Lbl [H.2831.h.(23.)]. US: Wc (M1621.P). Copy of GB: Lbl in Ars
Fem coll.
*RISM A/I (P 5087), BUC, CPM, NUC (0478135), Eitner, Cohen, letter (Ars
Fem).*

The sequel to Crazy Jane. A favorite song. London: Lewis Lavenu [1800].
3 pp.
voice/pf
GB: Lbl [G.793.(12.)]. Copy in Ars Fem coll.
RISM A/I (P 5088), BUC, CPM, Eitner, Cohen, letter (Ars Fem).

Poole, Maria (married Dickons)
c. 1770, London–1833, English

Adeline. A favorite Air . . . with pedal harp or pianoforte. Dublin: Edmund
Lee [c.1795].
voice/pf or harp
GB: Lbl [G.426.cc.(14.)].
CPM.

"And say no." A favourite ballad. London: Longman & Broderip [1792].
4 pp.
voice/pf
GB: Gu, Lbl [G.360.(41.)]. Copy of GB: Lbl in Ars Fem coll.
*RISM A/I (P 5090), BUC, CPM (date 1788), Eitner (as Caroline), letter (Ars
Fem).*

Dear Le Verrou. A favourite ballad. London: Longman & Broderip
[c. 1792]. 3 pp.
voice/pf
GB: Gu, Lbl [G.360.(42.)]. Copy of GB: Lbl in Ars Fem coll.
RISM A/I (P 5091), BUC, CPM, Eitner (as Caroline), letter (Ars Fem).

Goodbye and How d'ye do ("One day Good bye"). Air. London: s.n. [1820?].
voice/pf or harp
GB: Lbl H.2830.f.(46.)].
CPM.

*Six canzonetts & a lullaby for the voice, with an accompaniment for the piano forte or
harp.* London: Longman & Broderip [c. 1794]. 33 pp.
voice/pf or harp
GB: Gu, Lbl [G.358.(8.)], Ob. Copy of GB: Lbl in Ars Fem coll.
*RISM A/I (P 5089), BUC, CPM (date 1797), Eitner (as Caroline), Cohen, letter
(Ars Fem).*

The wandering lamb. A favourite ballad sung repeatedly by Mr. Incledon . . .
London: author & Longman & Broderip [1795]. 4 pp.
voice/pf
GB: Gu, Lbl [G.367.(15.)], Ob. US: NH. Copy of GB: Lbl in Ars Fem
coll.
*RISM A/I (P 5092), BUC, CPM, OCLC (20913363), Eitner (as Caroline), letter
(Ars Fem).*

Then pr'y no more come to woo ("Ah think when you left, of all pleasure
bereft"). Composed & sung by Mrs. Dickons in the Comic opera of *Two*

Faces Under A Hood. Philadelphia: G. E. Blake [1803–13].
voice/pf
US: CHAhughes, NYcuh, NYp [Am.1–V], PIlevy.
US: NYp Shelf List, Wolfe (2528).

Porters, Miss
pub. c. 1830, London
Matilda's Grave. A sacred elegy. London: Printed for G. Shade [c. 1830].
song
GB: Lbl [H.1652.mm.(12.)].
CPM.

Potocką (Potockiéj, Potocka-Pilava), Laura (Laury)
pub. 1816, Warsaw
Władysław Łokietek ("Już noc swe czarne rozpostarła cienie"). In: Julian
Ursyn Niemcewicz, *Śpiewy historycznye* [historic songs]. Warsaw: 1816,
1818. Text by Niemcewicz.
voice/pf
F: Pn. PL: Kc, Wn, Wmickiewicz. Copies of 2 editions in PL: Kc in
Jackson coll.
Letter (Poniatowska), Sowinski, Cohen.

Pouillan, Augustine (Mlle Pouillard)
fl. 1782–87, France
"Je le tiens ce nid de fauvette." Ariette. In: *Choix de musique, dédié à S.A.S.
Monseigneur de duc regnant des Deux-Ponts* [bi-monthly]. ded. Deux-Ponts.
Paris: Sanson et Comp. (#22), 1784.
voice/kbd
B: Bc. D: B–MG, DS, HR, Mb (1784), ZW (1794). F: Pc, Pn. GB: Lbl.
RISM B/II (p.130), Eitner (under Choix de musique), letter (C. Johnson).

"Julie est sans desir." Ariette. In: *Choix de musique, dédié à S.A.S. Monseigneur
de duc regnant des Deux-Ponts* [bi-monthly]. ded. Deux-Ponts. Paris: Sanson et
Comp. (#27), 1784.
voice/kbd
B: Bc. D: B–MG, DS, HR, Mb. F: Pc, Pn. GB: Lbl.
*RISM B/II (p.130, Mlle Pouillard), Eitner (under Choix de musique), letter
(C. Johnson).*

"Suzon fermoit son cœur aux bergers." Ariette. In: *Choix de musique, dédié à
S.A.S. Monseigneur de duc regnant des Deux-Ponts* [bi-monthly]. ded. Deux-

Ponts. Paris: Sanson et Comp. No. 26, 1784.
voice/kbd
B: Bc. D: B–MG, DS, HR, Mb. F: Pc, Pn. GB: Lbl.
RISM B/II (p.130, Mlle Pouillard), Eitner (under Choix de musique), letter (C. Johnson).

Pownall, Mary Ann, née Wrighten

1751, England–1796, Boston
The favorite song of Teazing me so. London: Samuel, Ann & Peter Thompson, n.d.
voice/kbd
I: Rsc.
RISM A/I (W 2181, as Wrighten).

"I could not help laughing at that." A favourite ballad, composed and sung by Mrs. Wrighten . . . London: Samuel, Ann & Peter Thompson [1784]. 4 pp.
voice/kbd
GB: Gu, Lbl (2 ex.) [H.1653.(49.)] & [Mad. Soc. 21.(79.)].
RISM A/I (W 2178, as Wrighten), BUC, CPM.

Jemmy of the glen ("Where gently flows"). In: *Six songs for the harpsichord or piano forte,* composed by Mrs. Pownall and J. Hewitt. 1. New York: Hewitt & Pownall, 1794. [Separate prints.] 2. Philadelphia: Mathew Carey, 1794. 3. New York: J. C. Moller, n.d. 4. Baltimore: J. Carr, 1778. 5. In: *A collection of new & favorite songs.* Philadelphia: s.n. [c. 1800]. 6. #28 in: a collection of songs hand copied by Sarah Ann Foster, ca. 1800–10. Ms.
1–4. voice/hpsch or pf; 5–6. voice/pf
1. US: NYsha, Wc (3 ex.). 2. US: Wc. 3–4. US: NYp. 5. US: SFbruning. 6. US: DM (W.C.L. M780.88 M294A). Copy from US: Wc in Ars Fem coll.
1–2. RISM A/I (P 5298, P 5299). 3. NUC (NP 0534947). 4. Sonneck (date 1798), Tick. 5. Sonneck. 6. NUC (NP 0534948). Cohen, letter (Ars Fem).

"Kiss me now or never." A favourite ballad, written, composed, and sung by Mrs. Wrighten at Vauxhall Gardens. [London]: Longman & Broderip [c. 1785]. 4 pp.
voice/kbd
GB: Gu, Lbl [H.1653.(50.)]. US: AUS (M1621.3.W743 K57 1785).
RISM A/I (W 2179, as Wrighten), BUC, CPM, Sonneck, OCLC (17332131).
Kisses sue'd for ("Take oh take those lips away"). The words by Shakespear [*sic*] and music by Mrs. Pownall. New York: Printed for G. Gilbert, 1795.

[With added arr. for two Ger. flutes.]
voice/pf, also arr. for 2 fls
US: NYp [Am 1.v].
US: NYp Shelf List, Sonneck, Tick, Cohen.

Labyrinth of love ("Why oh why allmighty passion"), a favorite song by the
late Mrs. Pownall. New York: G. Gilfert [c. 1797]. 1 p. [on two staves with
interlinear words].
voice/pf
US: Cn, CAdriscoll.
NUC (NP 0534949), Sonneck.

Lavinia ("Why steals from my bosom the sigh"). 1. as #6 in: *Six Songs for the
Harpsichord or Piano Forte.* Philadelphia, Pownall and Hewitt [1794]. 2. In:
A collection of new & favorite songs. Philadelphia: s.n. [c. 1800].
voice/pf
1. US: NYp, NYsha. 2. US: SFbruning.
Tick, Sonneck.

*Mrs. Pownall's address, in behalf of the French musicians, delivered on her benefit con-
cert night . . . Philadelphia.* To which are added, Pastoral songs, written by
herself at an early period of life. Also the songs performed at the concerts.
Philadelphia: Story's office [1793]. 29 pp. [words only].
voice/hpsch or pf
US: NYp.
NUC (05344946), Cohen.

"No indeed not I." The melody composed by Mrs. Wrighten, set by Mr.
Hook. London: Thomas Skillern [179–?]. 2 pp.
Melody only by Wrighten
voice/kbd
US: Bp, PHu.
RISM A/I (W 2180, as Wrighten), NUC Sup. (NSP 0023018).

Six songs for the harpsichord or piano forte, composed by Mrs. Pownall and
J. Hewitt. Philadelphia: printed by Mrs. Pownall and J. Hewitt, sold at
Mathew Carey's store, 1794. [See also separate songs.]
voice/hpsch or pf
US: NYsha, Wc (3 ex.). Copy of US: Wc in Ars Fem coll.
Sonneck, Cohen, letter (Ars Fem).

The Straw Bonnet ("When faries [*sic*] are lighted by night's silver queen").
1. From: *Six Songs of Mrs. Pownall and J. Hewitt.* New York: Hewitt &
Pownall, 1794. 2. Separate issue from this collection, [1794]. 3. In: *A
collection of new & favorite songs.* Philadelphia: s.n. [c. 1800], pp. [98–99,
numbered] 13–14.
voice/pf
1. See *Six songs* . . . 2. US: NYp, NYsha. 3. US: SFbruning.
Sonneck, Tick.

"'Twas yes, kind Sir and I thank you too." A favourite Scotch ballad.
1. London: Samuel, Ann & Peter Thompson [c. 1785]. 3 pp. 2. As: "The
Ruddy morn blink'd o'er the Brae" [by Mrs. Wrighten]. Dublin: John &
Edmund Lee [c. 1790].
voice/kbd
1. GB: BA, DU, Gu, Lbl [H.1653.(51.)]. 2. GB: Gu, Lbl [H.1601.b.(56.)].
1–2. RISM A/I (W 2182, W 2183, both as Wrighten), BUC, CPM.

[Work(s), as Wrighten] in: *Thompson's miscellaneous collection of elegant duettinos,
consisting of great variety of songs, canzonets, marches [etc]* . . . *properly adapted for two
german flutes, hoboys, or violins* . . . Vol. I. London: Editors Warehouse [c. 1790].
2 fls, vlns, or obs
GB: Gm. S: L.
RISM B/II (p. 389).

Young Willy. A favourite Scots song written, composed & sung by Mrs.
Wrighten. London: Samuel, Ann & Peter Thompson [c. 1785]. 4 pp.
voice/kbd
GB: En, Lbl [G.808.f.(53.)]. I: Rsc.
RISM A/I (W 2184, as Wrighten), BUC, CPM.

Pratt, J., Miss
pub. 1802, London
Mutual Bliss. [Song.] Words & melody by Miss Pratt. Arr. for pianoforte
[accompaniment] by . . . J. Sanderson. London: E. Riley [1802].
Melody & text by Pratt
voice/pf
GB: Lbl [G.426.dd.(31.)], US: Wc (M1.A11,vol. 14, #3).
CPM, NUC (NP 0547673).

Prioli Morisina, Marieta
fl. 1665

Balletti et correnti a due violini, et violone, agionta la spineta. Venice: Francesco Magni detto Gardano, 1665. Partbooks [probably same as Sonata a 3. Bologna, 1665 in Eitner supl.].
2 vlns/violone/hpsch
I: Bc (vln I, spinetta; lacks vln II and violone). Copies in D: Kf&m and in Ars Fem coll.
RISM A/I (P 5475), NG (Priuli), Cohen, Eitner, letter (Ars Fem).

Provost, Mlle
pub. 1732, Paris
[Work(s)] in: *Les Parodies nouvelles et les vaudevilles inconnus.* Livre troisième. Paris: J. B. C. Ballard, 1732.
song(s)
F: Pa, Pc (3 ex.), Pcf, Pn (2 ex.). GB: T. NL: DHk. US: Wc.
RISM B/II (p. 281).

Quinciani (Quiciani), Lucia

pub. 1611, Venice

"Udite lagrimosi spirti." In: Marc' Antonio Negri, *Affetti amorosi* . . . libro seconda. Venice: Ricciardo Amadino, 1611. 1 vol. [solo monody]. *voice/bc*

B: Br. I: Gu.

RISM B/I: (1611[16]), Bowers & Tick.

R

R., E., a Lady

pub. c. 1806–20, London

Addison's hymn ("The Spacious Firmament") set to music for four voices by a lady, E. R. London: s.n. [1806].

SATB

GB: Lbl [H.1681.(1.)].

CPM.

Les Passetemps Quadrilles composed by a Lady [E. R.]. s.l.: s.n., [1820].

pf

GB: Lbl [h.127.(25.)].

CPM.

R. C., Mlle

pub. before 1800, Paris

Six Romances avec accompagnement de forte piano . . . Paris: "chez tous les marchands de musique" (gravées par Mlle Le Brun, écrit par Lefrançois), n.d. 10 pp.

voice/pf

F: Pn (incomplete, B.N. [Vm7 26118).

RISM A/I (IN 241), Paris Lib. Cat.

Randeles, Elizabeth

pub. 1824, London

A favorite Scotch air, with variations for harp . . . London: s.n., [1824]. [Moore adapted this air to his text "Oft in the Stilly night."]

harp

GB: Lbl [h.122.(3.)].

CPM.

Raschenau (Rasschenau), Marianna (Maria Anna) von

fl. 1690s–1703, Vienna

Il consiglio di Pallade [componimento per musica]. Vienna, 1697 [only libretto survives].

stage work

A: Wn. Printed libretto only.

Eitner.

Le sacre visioni di Santa Teresa [oratorio]. Vienna: 1703 [only libretto survives].
voices [soloists]/orch
A: Wn. Printed libretto only.
Eitner.

Ravissa, Mme, of Turin
b. Turin, pub. 1778, Paris
Six sonates pour le clavecin ou le forte piano, par Mme. Ravissa de Turin, maîtresse de clavecin et de chant italien, œuvre I. Paris: auteur, bureau du journal de musique, 1778.
hpsch or pf
A: Wn. Copies in D: Kf&m & UNikb.
RISM A/I (R 469), Cohen, Frau & Musik, Frauenmusik.

Ray, Mlle
Rondeau [for harpsichord and violin]. Piece #18 in: *Choix de musique, dédié à S.A.S. Monseigneur de duc regnant des Deux-Ponts* . . . Paris: Sanson, 1784.
hpsch/vln
B: Bc. D: B–MG, DS, HR, Mb (1784). F: Pc–Pn (Vm7 2417(1–2) & 4o Y.833). GB: Lbl. Photocopy of GB: Lbl in C. Johnson coll.
RISM B/II (p. 130), Eitner (under Choix de musique), letter (C. Johnson).

Sonata [violin and keyboard]. 1770.
vln/kbd
F: Pn. Copy in Ars Fem coll.
Letter (Ars Fem).

Reichardt, Bernadine Juliane, née Benda
1752, Potsdam–1783, Berlin
Daphne am Bach. Brunnenlied. S.l.
song
D: Bds (Eitner, modern location not confirmed).
Eitner, Cohen.

Das Mädchen bei dem Grabe ihrer Freundin ("Vier trübe Monde sind entflon").
In: *Blumenlese für Klavierliebhaber: Eine musikalische Wochenschrift,* Part I, #15.
Ed. Bossler. Speier: Hochf. Brandenb. Rath, 1782.
voice/pf
D: Bds, DÜk, F, Mbs, Rtt, SP, Tu, WRz. F: Pc. NL: DHgm. US: AA, U.
RISM B/II (p. 115)

Dora ("Ich hab, ich habe sie gesehen"). Ms. c. 1810. Text by
Sprickamann.
voice/pf
D: EU (Mh 37).
RISM A/II (#89186).

Duettino: Das Vögelein. Ms.
2 voices/kbd
D: Bds (Eitner, modern location not confirmed).
Eitner, Cohen.

"Ich nenne dich." Lied [composer's name as Benda]. Ms, c. 1790.
voice/pf
D: DGs (A202).
RISM A/II (#38721).

[Lieder] in: *Gedichte von Karoline Christiane Louise Rudolphi.* Erste Sammlung
heraus und mit Melodien begleitet von Johann Friedrich Reichardt [2d
ed.]. Wolfenbüttel: Schulbuchhandlung, 1785.
voice/kbd
B: Bc.
RISM B/II (p. 185), NG.

[Lieder] in: *Sammlung verschiedener Lieder von guten Dichtern und Tonkünstlern . . .*
Nürnberg: J. W. Schmidt, 1780–82. 4 vol.
voice/kbd
B: Bc. Other library holdings are incomplete.
RISM B/II (p. 348), NG (bio).

[17] *Lieder und* [2] *Claviersonaten.* Hamburg: Bohn, 1782.
voice/kbd; kbd
B: Bc. Copy in Ars Fem coll.
RISM A/I (R 987), NG, Eitner, Cohen, letter (Ars Fem).

[3 Lieder] in Parts 1 and 3 of: *Oden und Lieder von Klopstock, Stolberg, Claudius
und Hölty . . .* Johann Friedrich Reichardt. Berlin: J. Pauli, 1779, 1781.
voice/kbd
A: Wn. B: Bc. D: F, KIl, KNm, Mbs. GB: Lbl.
*RISM B/II (p. 270), BUC (with J. B. Reichardt), NG (1779), Eitner (1781),
Cohen (1781).*

Reichardt, Louise (Luise)

1779, Berlin–1826, Berlin

Choralbuch. Basel: C. F. Spittler [after 1826]. 66 pp. [named as composer in Foreword by anonymous editor; not named on title page]. Contains 140 chorales.

SATB

D: Mbs.

Eitner, Reich, MGG, Olivier.

Christliche, liebliche Lieder gesammlet und herausgegeben von Louise Reichardt. 1. Hamburg: A. Cranz [1827]. 2. 2d ed., Leipzig: F. Hofmeister [1836?].

2, 3, and 4 voices, a cappella

1. D: Mbs, SWl. GB: Lbl [E.724.n.(3.)]. 1. & 2. US: PHu. 2. USSR: KAu (formerly Kgl. & Uni.-Bibl. zu Königsberg).

1. CPM (dated c. 1820), 1–2. NUC (NR 0134189–90). Eitner, Cohen, Reich, MGG, Olivier.

Des Schäfers Klage von Louise Reicharde [*sic*]. #128 in Ms. collection, c. 1825. Text by Johann Wolfgang von Goethe.

voice/guit

D: EU (Mh 54).

RISM A/II (#89407).

Duette. Ms.

2 voices/pf

D: (B.B., Eit.) (Ms. 156 in K.) (modern location not confirmed).

Eitner.

[4 songs] in: *XII Deutsche Lieder von Johann Friedrich Reichardt und dessen Tochter Luise Reichardt*. Zerbst: C. C. Menzel [1800]. 31 pp.

Review: AmZ, 2 (April 1800), 474–75.

voice/pf

GB: Lbl [B.725.b].

BUC, CPM, Eitner, Reich.

Herzlich thut mich erfreuen (ms.?).

song

D: Bds (B.B., Eit.). USSR: KAu (formerly Kgl. & Uni-Bibl. zu Königsberg) (modern location not confirmed).

Eitner.

Hört wie die Wachtel. Ms.
voice/pf
USSR: KAu (formerly Kgl. & Uni.-Bibl. zu Königsberg) (Ms. Samlg. 401)
(modern location not confirmed).
Eitner.

Liebe. No. 99 in Ms, c. 1825.
voice/guit
D: EU (Mh 54).
RISM A/II (#89378).

Lied aus Ariels Offenbarungen ("Lilie, sieh' mich"). In: *Berlinische musikalische
Zeitung.* Jg. 2, Beilage 4., 1806. Also in: *XII Deutsche und italianische romantische
Gesaenge* . . . [1806].
voice/pf
GB: Lbl [Hirsch iv. 1131.(1.)].
CPM, Eitner.

Nach Sevilla wo die hohen Prachtgebäude. [Composer's name supplied.] No. 160
in Ms, c. 1825.
voice/guit
D: EU (Mh 54).
RISM A/II (#89439).

Sechs Deutsche Lieder für l Singstimme. Op. 6. Hamburg: Böhme, n.d.
voice/pf
D: Mbs. USSR: KAu (formerly Kgl. und Universitäts Bibl. zu
Königsberg).
Eitner, Cohen, Reich, Olivier.

Sechs Deutsche Lieder mit Begleitung des Pianoforte. . . . 6te Lieder Sammlung . . .
Hamburg: A. Cranz [1826]. 12 pp. [8te Sammlung, acc. to Whistling,
1826.]
Review, AmZ, 29 (August 1827), 542–44.
voice/pf
D: Mbs.
Eitner, Cohen (as op. 8), Reich, MGG, Olivier (as op. 8).

Sechs geistliche Lieder unserer besten Dichter . . . Hamburg: [Cranz],
Lithographirt bey Uckermann in Erfurt, 1823. Score (16 pp.) & 4 parts
(17–32 pp.)

4 voices (SSAA) / pf, figured bass
D: SWl, (B.B., Eit.), GB: Lbl [Hirsch III.1041.].
US: NH (Rare M 2004 .4 R34+).
CPM, NUC (NR 0134194), OCLC (20911752), Eitner, Cohen, Reich, MGG, Olivier.

Sechs Lieder von Novalis mit Begleitung des Piano-Forte . . . ihren geliebten
Schülerinnen zugeeignet . . . Viertes Werk. Hamburg: Joh. Aug. Böhme
[1819]. 11 pp.
voice / pf
D: Hs (MB/321).
Eitner, Cohen, Reich, MGG, Olivier.

Sei Canzoni di Metastasio coll Piano-Forte . . . dedicati alla sua cara Sorella
Sofia. Op. IV. Hamburg: alle Spese dell' Autore [1811]. 13 pp.
voice / pf
D: (B.B. Eit.). Unnamed private collector (see Reich).
Eitner, Reich, MGG, Olivier.

XII Deutsche und italiänische romantische Gesaenge mit Begleitung des Piano-Forte . . .
[für] Herzogin Mutter Anna Amalia von Sachsen Weimar und Eisenach.
Berlin: Realschul-Buchhandlung [1806]. 21 pp. [See also *Lied aus Ariels
Offenbarungen* (An den Frühling).]
voice / pf
Unnamed private collector (see Reich).
Eitner, Cohen, Reich, MGG, Olivier.

XII Gesaenge mit Begleitung des Fortepianos . . . ihrer jungen Freundin und
Schülerin Demlle Louise Sillem zugeeignet. Drittes Werkchen. 25 pp.
1. [Hamburg: Böhme, 1819]. 25 pp. 2. A later edition, Böhme,
c. 1839.
voice / pf
1. D: (B.B. Eit.). GB: Lbl[E.600.hh.(4.). USSR: KAu (formerly Kgl. &
Uni-Bibl. zu Königsberg). 2. D: Mbs.
CPM (dated c. 1815), Eitner, Cohen, Reich, Olivier.

Zwölf Gesänge mit Begleitung des Forte-Piano componirt und Ihrer geliebten
Schwester Friederika zugeeignet . . . 1. Hamburg: Johann August Böhme
[1811]. 16 pp. 2. *Zwölf Gesänge mit Begleitung der guitarre* . . . Breslau: C. G.
Förster [before 1819]. Issued in 6 fascicles, each with two songs [identical
with 1811 songs, but in different order].

1. voice/pf; 2. voice/guit
1. D: Hs, Mbs. USSR: KAu (formerly Kgl. & Uni-Bibl. Königsberg) (copy in D: Kf&m). 2. GB: Lbl [Hirsch III. 1040.].
Eitner, Cohen, Reich, MGG, CPM (dated 1820?), Olivier.

Reisner, Louise
pub. c. 1830, Paris
Thème varié très brillant pour l'Accordéon . . . Paris: s.n. [1830?].
accordion
GB: Lbl [h.3213.f.(10.)].
CPM.

Remusat, (P., Mme de)
pub. 1780s, Paris
[Work(s)] in: *Courier lyrique et amusant* ou *Passe-temps des toilettes par Mme. Dufrenoy* [bi-monthly]. [Paris: Knapen et fils], 1785–98.
undetermined
F: Pn. Other library holdings are incomplete runs.
RISM B/II (de Rémuzat, p. 147).

[Work(s)] in: *La muse lyrique dédiée à la Reine. Recueil d'airs avec accompagnement de guitarre par M. Patouart fils.* Paris: Baillon, [1777–89].
voice/guit
F: D, Pn. GB: Lbl. US: U, Wc. All library holdings are incomplete runs.
RISM B/II (Mme. P. de Rémuzat, p. 243).

Reynolds, Maria Hester (later Park(e)?) (identity problem; see also Park(e), Maria Hester)
pub. 1785–1790, Brighton/London
Sonatas [C, B-flat, E-flat, G, D, F] *for the harpsichord or piano forte* [with vln]. [Brighton: Henry Davey] 1785. Score. 49 pp. [Dedicated to the Countess of Uxbridge.]
hpsch or pf/vln
GB: BA, Ckc, Lbl [h.74]. US: NYp, Wc (M219. R45486). Copies of GB: Lbl in C. Johnson coll. (as Maria Hester Park(e) and Ars Fem coll. (as Reynolds).
RISM A/I (R 1234), BUC, CPM, NUC (NR 0218174), Eitner, Cohen, letters (GB: Lbl, C. Johnson, Ars Fem).

Three Sonatas [E-flat, F, C] *for the harpsichord or piano forte . . .* opera 2. London: Longman & Broderip, for the author [c. 1790].

hpsch or pf
GB: Lbl [F.65.o.(1.]. Copies in C. Johnson coll. (as Maria Hester Park(e)
and Ars Fem coll. (as Reynolds).
RISM A/I (R 1235), CPM, letters (GB: Lbl, C. Johnson, Ars Fem).

Ribouté, Mlle
pub. 1798, Paris
[Work(s)] in: *La Correspondance des dames ou journal des modes et des spectacles de
Paris . . . des accompagnemens sur le forte-piano des ariettes et romances nouvelles . . .*
Paris: Gide, 1798. 2 vol.
voice/pf
F: Pn.
RISM B/II (p. 147).

Ricci, Cesarina di Tingoli
fl. 1597, Tingoli
*Il primo libro de madrigali a cinque voci, con un dialogo a otto nouamente composti &
dati in luce . . .* l. Venice: Angelo Gardano, 1597. Partbooks. 2. Ms.
Intabulated in organ tablature. Dedicated from Monte Colombano to
Cardinal S. Giorgio.
1. 5, 8 voices; 2. org
1. B: Gu (ATB only) (Mus. Ms. 4480, #62, 78v–79v). 2. D: Mbs.
RISM A/I (R 1253), Cohen, NG, Göllner

Richards, Grace
pub. 1803–10, New England
Orphan nosegay girl ("Pray buy a nosegay cry'd a sweet child"). The words by
Mrs. Rowson. 1. 2 printings/Boston: G. Graupner [1803–06]. 2. In:
Oliver Shaw: *A Selection of progressive airs, songs &c,* p. 5. Dedham MA: H.
Mann, 1810.
voice/pf
1. US: Bp, CAdriscoll, NYp, PHhs, PROu, R, Wc, WOa. 2. US: BUg.
*Wolfe (7466, 7466A, 7467, 7986, identifies comp. from print of 1859 with identical
music "composed by Grace Richards").*

Riese, Helene. See **Liebmann, Helene** née **Riese**

Robertson, Mrs., of Ladykirk
pub. c. 1800–02, Edinburgh
*Miss Johnston of Huttonhall's reel, Berwickshire Vol. quick step, Rock and a wee pickle
tow, and Follow her over the border, with variations, &c.,* composed by Mrs.

Robertson of Ladykirk. Edinburgh: Gow & Shepherd [1801 or 1807]. 3 pp.
pf
GB: Lbl [g.352.k.(9.)]. US: Cn, NYp.
CPM, NUC (NR 0324014), Cohen.

The Ridicule, a reel (as a medley) by Mrs. Robertson [with: *The Countess of Dalhousie's strathy* by N. Gow, to which are added three favourite tunes (ascription not clear)]. Edinburgh: Gow & Shepherd [1800?].
pf
GB: Lbl [h.1480.a.(20.)].
RISM A/I (R 1794), BUC, CPM.

Robinson, Camilla, Lady
pub. 1797, London
The harmonic reveries of the cloister'd cell, for the harp and piano forte, with accompaniments. Overture, "Se potessi spiegar L'affanno," "Il Ti perdo mio cara," "Jupiter prete moi," "Un vielliard presd'une bergere," "Helas, helas quelle est notre folie," "Se il mio cor tu vedesti," Menuetto con variazioni. London: Longman & Broderip [178–? or 1797]. 19 pp.
harp / pf / other instruments and voice (#2–6)
GB: Lbl (acc. lacking) [E.601.11.(2.)]. US: BE (bound with Storace, Stephen, The favorite operas of *Mahmoud* & *The iron chest.* M1503 S72M3 Case X).
RISM A/I (R 1797), CPM, NUC (NR 03313379), OCLC (21861894).

Rochenard, Mme de la
pub. 1699, Paris
[Work(s)] in: *Suite de danses pour les violons et haut-bois, qui se jöuent . . . aux bals chez le Roy . . . la plus grande partie par Philidor l'aîné . . . Livre premier.* Paris: C. Ballard, 1699.
vlns / obs / other instruments?
F: Pn.
RISM B/I (1699 [7]).

Rodrigues, Maria Joachina
18th cent., Mexico
Musicos ruysenores: Cantata a duo al Nacimiento, alto, tenor, accompagñato al duo. Ms.
2 voices (AT) / bc or instruments
MEX: Min.
Stevenson, Cohen.

Roehn, Virginie

pub. c. 1830, Paris

Le Voyageur. Romance. Paris: s.n. [1830?]. Words by C. Viguier.

song

GB: Lbl [E.1717.(87.)].

CPM.

Rogers, J., Miss

pub. c. 1800, London?

The Silver Bow. A new favorite Song. [Together with a setting as a three-part glee.] [London?]: For the Author [1800?].

voice/pf; 3 voices

GB: Lbl [G.316.k.(52.)].

CPM.

Roland, Fanny

pub. 1797, Paris

Trois sonates [C, D, B-flat] *pour le fortepiano.* Œuvre Ier. Rennes: Citoyen Vve St-Marc/Paris: Fridzeri [1797]. 23 pp.

pf

F: Pn (Vm7 5600, Vm12 24645). Photocopy in C. Johnson coll.

Paris Lib. Cat., letter (C. Johnson).

Ronssecy, Madame de. See also under D., Madame

pub. c. 1800, London

Andante [from I. J. Pleyel, Sonata #2]. The variations by Mme. D. [Ronssecy?]. [1802?].

harp

GB: Lbl [H.2819.(40.)].

CPM.

Andante [from I. J. Pleyel, Symphony Concertante #1] *with variations for Harp,* the last 3 by Mde. de [Ronssecy] [1802].

harp

GB: Lbl [H.2819.(11.)].

CPM.

Andantino. The variations by Md. de Ronnsecy. London: S. Straight [1800?]. 3 pp.

harp

GB: Lbl [H.2819.(18.)].
RISM A/I (R 2456), BUC, CPM, Eitner, Cohen.

The Dirge in Cymbeline [by V. Rauzzini] adapted for the Harp or PianoForte by Mde de Ronssecy [1802].
harp or pf
GB: Lbl [H.2819.(9.)].
CPM.

Lullaby [from Stephen Storace] adapted for the harp, with variations . . . London: S. Straight [1800?]. 3 pp.
harp
GB: Lbl [H.2819.(6.)].
RISM A/I (R 2457), BUC, CPM, Eitner, Cohen.

Minuetto [by J. B. Krumpholtz . . .]; the variations by Mde. de Ronssecy. London: S. Straight [c. 1800].
harp
GB: Lbl [H.2819.(17.)].
RISM A/I (R 2461), CPM, Eitner, Cohen.

Scotch air. The variations by Mde. de Ronssecy. London: S. Straight [c. 1800]. 2 pp.
harp
GB: Lbl [H.2819.(16.)].
RISM A/I (R 2458), BUC, CPM, Eitner, Cohen.

Scotch tune. The variations by Mde. de Ronssecy. London: S. Straight [c. 1800]. 3 pp.
harp
GB: Lbl [H.2819.(15.)].
RISM A/I (R 2459), BUC, CPM, Eitner, Cohen.

Shepherds I have lost my love. A Scotch tune. The variations by Mde. de Ronssecy. London: S. Straight [c. 1800]. 4 pp.
harp
GB: Lbl [(H.2819.(3.)].
RISM A/I (R 2460), BUC, CPM, Eitner, Cohen.

Rossi, Camilla de, Romana

fl. early 18th cent., b. Rome

Cantata a 2. Canto et Alto. Fra Dori, e Fileno (Compositione Musicale). Ms. score.

SA / string orch

D: Dlb (formerly 2 copies [one as *Clori, e Fileno*, destroyed in WW II]) (Mus. 2382–L–1.). Copy in Jackson coll.

Eitner, Jackson, Cohen.

Il figliuol prodigo. Oratorium, 1709. Ms. score [libretto by composer, according to ms. score].

solo voices / orch / (strings)

A: Wn (Ms. 19122/23). Copy in Jackson coll.

Eitner, Jackson, Cohen.

Il sacrificio di Abramo. Oratorium, 1708. Ms. score. Libretto by Dario.

solo voices (SSAT) / orch (strings, lute, chalumeaux)

A: Wn [Ms. 17306 (ms. score), 406 745–B M (printed libretto)]. Copies in Jackson coll.

Eitner, Jackson, Cohen.

S. Alessio. Oratorium, 1710. Ms. score.

solo voices / orch (strings / lute / trs)

A: Wn (score and printed libretto) (Ms. 17307). Copies in Jackson coll.

Eitner, Jackson, Cohen.

Santa Beatrice d'Este. Oratorium, 1707. Ms. score and partial set of part-books. Libretto by Cardinal Pamphili.

solo voices (SAATB) / orch (strings, lute, 2 trs)

A: Wn (mus. & lib.) (Ms. 17312/13.), I: Bc (printed libretto of 1712 perf. in Perugia, 4406 745–B.M.). Copies in Jackson coll.

Eitner, Jackson, Cohen.

Rost, Emilie

fl. c. 1800, Germany

3 Lieder von W. Kritzinger für 1 Stimme mit Pfte. Erfurt: author, n.d.

voice / pf

D: Bds (B.B., Eitner, modern location not confirmed).

Eitner, Cohen.

Rusca, Claudia Francesca
pub. 1630, Milan
Sacri Concerti a 1. 2. 3. 4. e. 5. voci con Salmi e Canzoni francesi a 4. varii Motetti, Magnificat . . . Partbooks. Milan: 1630.
1–5 voices / bc
Formerly I: Ma. Destroyed in WW II, August 1943.
Eitner, Sartori, Cohen, letter (Milan, Biblioteca Ambrosiana, 7/29/1988).

S

S. T., Madame, élève de Pfeffinger
pub. c. 1800, Paris
Six chants de differens caractères avec accompagnement de piano . . . Paris: Auteur
(#2) [c. 1800]. 16 pp.
voice/pf
F: BO, Pn [Vm7 26195].
RISM A/I (IN 256), Paris Lib. Cat.

Sabatier, Madame
pub. c. 1820, Paris
Blanche Fleur, ou *Rose d'Amour* ("Toi pour qui seule"). Romance. Paris: s.n.
[1820?]. Words by M. E. Tressan.
song
GB: Lbl [G.548.(21.)].
CPM.

Saint-Simon, Mme. See Bawr, Alexandrine Sophie

Salmon, Fanny
pub. c. 1818, London
A first set of Quadrilles for the pianoforte or harp . . . (2d ed.). London: Clementi
[1818]. 5 pp.
pf or harp
GB: Lbl [h.925.z.(15.)].
CPM.

Sappho (pseud.)
pub. c. 1755, England
"Come all ye shepherds." S.l.: s.n., 1755.
song
GB: Lbl. Copy in Ars Fem coll.
Letter (Ars Fem).

"Long by an idle passion tost." S.l.: s.n., 1756.
song
GB: Lbl. Copy in Ars Fem coll.
Letter (Ars Fem).

Savage, Jane (married **R. Rolleston**)
fl. 1789–90, England
A favorite duett [C] *for two performers on one pianoforte or harpsichord,* opera VI.
London: Longman & Broderip, for the author, [c.1790]. 13 pp.
pf or hpsch (4 hand)
GB: Lam, Lbl [g.130.(10.)], Ob. Microfilm of Lbl copy in C. Johnson coll.
RISM A/I (S 1099), BUC, CPM (date1789), Eitner, NG (date1789), MGG (in entry on her father, William Savage), Meggett, Cohen, letter (C. Johnson).

God save the King. Adapted as a double lesson for the pianoforte. Opera 6th.
London: author [c. 1790]. 5 pp.
pf
GB: Ckc, Lbl [g.130.(12.)], Ob. Microfilm of GB: Lbl copy in C. Johnson coll.
RISM A/I (S 1101), BUC, CPM (date 1789), NG, MGG (in entry on her father, William Savage), Meggett, Cohen (error. as vocal), letter (C. Johnson).

Hail the woodman. A favorite song . . . opera V. London: Longman & Broderip, for the author [c. 1790]. 5 pp.
voice/kbd
GB: Gu, Lbl [H. 1653.(45.)]. Copy of GB: Lbl in Ars Fem coll.
RISM A/I (S 1098), BUC, CPM (date 1786), Eitner (without title), NG, MGG (in entry on her father, William Savage), Cohen, letter (Ars Fem).

Six easy lessons for the harpsichord or pianoforte . . . opera 2d. London: author [1783]. 21 pp.
hpsch or pf
GB: Lam. Copy in Ars Fem coll.
RISM A/I (S 1095), BUC, NG, MGG (in entry on her father, William Savage), Meggett, Cohen, letter (Ars Fem).

Six rondos [G, B-flat, C, G, F, B-flat] *for the harpsichord or pianoforte* . . . opera III. London: Longman & Broderip, for the author [c. 1783 or 1790]. 13 pp.
hpsch or pf
GB: Cu, Gu, Lam, Lbl [e.101.(7.)]. Copies of GB: Lbl in C. Johnson coll. and Ars Fem coll.
RISM A/I (S 1096), BUC, CPM (date 1786), Eitner, NG, MGG (in entry on her father, William Savage), Meggett, Cohen, letters (C. Johnson, Ars Fem).

Strephan [Stephan] *& Flavia*. A favorite cantata . . . opera IV. London: Longman & Broderip, for the author [c. 1790]. 9 pp.
voice/kbd
GB: Gu, Lam, Lbl [H.1653.(44.)]. Copy of GB: Lbl in Ars Fem coll.
RISM A/I (S 1097, as opera III), BUC, CPM (date 1786), Eitner (as cantata), NG, MGG (in entry on her father, William Savage), Cohen, letter (Ars Fem).

2 duetts, for voices . . . opera VII. London: Longman & Broderip, for the author [c. 1790]. 8 pp.
2 voices/kbd
GB: Gu, Lbl [G.354.(32.)].
RISM A/I (S 1100), BUC, CPM (date1789), Eitner, NG, MGG (in entry on her father, William Savage).

Schaden, Nanette von (Mme de Schaden)

pub. 1780s & 1790s, Speyer
Concert [B-flat] *pour le piano-forte avec l'accompagnement de deux violons, deux hautbois, cors de chasse, alte & basse* . . . par Mme de Schaden & Mr. Rosetti. Speyer: Bossler, 1791. 9 Partbooks.
pf/orch (2 vlns/vla/b/2 obs/2 hns)
D: B, Mbs.
RISM A/I (S 1232), Eitner, Cohen.

Concert [G] *pour le piano-forte avec l'accompagnement de deux violons, deux hautbois, cors de chasse, alte & basse* . . . par Mme de Schaden & Mr. Rosetti. Speyer: Bossler, n.d. 9 Partbooks. [According to Gerber, same as *2d Konzert*, Amsterdam: Schmidt.]
pf/orch (2 vlns/2 obs/2 hns/vla/b)
D: Dl, Mbs, RH. US: Wc.
RISM A/I (S 1233), Eitner, Gerber, Cohen.

[Work(s)] in: *Blumenlese für Klavierliebhaber, eine musikalische Wochenschrift.* Speyer: Rath Bossler, 1787. 2 vols.
pf
B: Bc (1). D: Bds (1), SP (1). NL: DHgm.
RISM B/II (p. 116).

Schauff, Marie

18th cent., Germany
Das Geheimniss und das Beständige, op. 3. Vienna: Diabelli & Co., n.d. Poem by Lenau.

voice/pf
USSR: KAu (formerly Kgl. & Uni.-Bibl. Königsberg, modern location not confirmed).
Eitner, Cohen.

SCH–L–N, Mademoiselle
pub. 1761–63, Berlin
2 Menuets. In: *Musikalisches Allerley von verschiedene Tonkünstlern,* pp. 119 & 149.
kbd (probably hpsch)
B: Bc (WQ 6313).
Letter (Alamire Music Publishers, Peer, Belgium).

Schröter, Corona Wilhelmine Elisabeth (Mlle Schröterin, Mslle. C. S***)
1751, Guben–1802, Ilmenau
[16] *Gesaenge mit Begleitung des Fortepiano* . . . Zweyte Sammlung. Weimar: "in Commission bey dem Industrie Comploir," 1794. 22 pp.
voice/pf
B: Bc. CH: BEsu. CS: K. D: Bds, Dl, DÜk, Ju, LEm, SWl, WRgs. GB: Lbl (2 ex.) [E.600.y.(17.)] & [Hirsch III.1083.]. US: R. Copy of B: Bc in Ars Fem coll.
RISM A/I (S 2148), BUC, CPM, Cohen, NG, Eitner, Friedländer-Goethe, Olivier, letter (Ars Fem).

An den Abendstern, nach einem Text von Matthisson für Singstimme und Klavier. s.l.: s.n.,1794.
voice/kbd
D: Kf&m, UNikb.
Frau & Musik, Olivier.

An die Nachtigall, für Singstimme und Begleitung. S.l.: s.n., 1794. [Text by Fr. Schmitt.]
voice/kbd
D: Kf&m, UNikb.
Frau & Musik, Olivier.

An Laura, für Singstimme und Begleitung. S.l.: s.n., 1786.
voice/kbd
D: Kf&m.
Frau & Musik, Olivier.

"Die ersten blümchen die ich fand." In: *Der Teutsche Merkur,* 1780, ed. Wieland. Weimar. [Name as Mselle C. S., supplied by D: DÜk as Corona Schröter.]
voice/pf
D: DÜk (cat. #1216).
Düsseldorf-Goethe.

Die Fischerin [incidental music for]. [1782.] Text by Goethe. Includes first setting of *Der Erlkönig.* Ms. piano score [orchestral score and parts lost].
stage work (Singspiel)
D: WRtl, WRdn. Copy of *Der Erlkönig* in D: Kf&m. Copy of ms. piano score in Randall coll.
Cohen, NG, Mellen, Olivier, Frau & Musik, MGG (in entry on Schröter family), letter (Randall).

Fünf und zwanzig Lieder. Weimar: "Annoch bey mir selbst, und in Commission in der Hoffmannischen Buchhandlung," 1786. 32 pp. Texts of Hölty, Miller, Goethe, etc.
voice/pf
D: DÜk, Kf&m, LEu, UNikb, WRz. GB: Lbl (2 ex.) [K.10.a.26. & Hirsch III.1082]. US: NYp. Copies in Jackson coll. & in Ars Fem coll.
RISM A/I (S 2149), BUC, CPM, Cohen, Eitner, MGG (entry on Schröter family), Frau & Musik, Olivier, letter (Ars Fem).

Jugendlied, nach einem Text von Johann Wolfgang von Goethe für Singstimme und Klavier. S.l.: s.n., 1775.
voice/kbd
D: Kf&m.
Frau & Musik, Olivier.

Lieder und Gesänge für Alt oder Baß mit Pianoforte. Ms.?
A or B voice/pf
D: Dlb (#8844. 4m, modern location not confirmed).
Eitner.

"O Mutter, guten Rat mir leiht," nach einem Text von Johann Wolfgang von Goethe für Singstimme und Klavier. s.l.: s.n.,1781.
voice/kbd
D: Kf&m (voice part only).
Frau & Musik.

"Quelle piume, bionde e nere" ("Diese Federn, weize und schwarze"),
trans. from Goethe. Canzonetta (Romana). S.l.: s.n., n.d. [Name as
Signor(a) C. S., supplied by D: DÜk as Corona Schröter.]
voice/pf
D: DÜk (cat. #1217).
Düsseldorf-Goethe.

Schuer Inseky, Princess
pub. 1775, London
[Work(s)] in: *A collection of minuets in which is that favourite one danced by
Madame Heinel at the Opera House in the Hay Market.* London: William Napier
[1775].
instruments not specified
GB: Ckc (incomplete), Lbl, Lcm.
RISM B/II (p. 67).

Schütze, Wilhelmine, née Henning
1787–1865, fl. in Weimar
Lebewohl ("So sprich's nur aus"). [Song] In: *Journal für Literatur, Kunst, Luxus
und Mode.* Hrsg. C. Bertuch. Weimar: Landes-Industrie-Comptoire, Bd.
39, 1824.
voice/pf
D: DÜk (#1250).
Düsseldorf-Goethe.

Scott, Isabella Mary (married Gibson). See Gibson, Isabella Mary, née Scott

Semphill, Lady
pub. c. 1780, Edinburgh
[Work(s)] in: *The Elements of music and of fingering the harpsichord, to which is
added a collection of airs and lessons for the harpsichord or piano-forte . . .* Ed. by
Anne Young. Edinburgh: Corri & Sutherland [c. 1780]. 65 pp. [See also
under Young, Anne.]
hpsch or pf
GB: Gu, P.
RISM B/II (p. 165).

Sessa, Claudia, Donna
fl. Milan, pub. 1613, Venice
"Vattene pur lasciva orechia humana" & "Occhi io vissi di voi." In:

D. Angelico Patto, *Canoro pianto di Maria Vergine sopra la faccia di Christo estinto . . . con un dialogo, et madrigale tramutati da l'istesso. . . .* Venice: B. Magni. 1613. 1 vol. score.
voice/bc (chitarone)
CS: Pu. I: Bc. Copy of I: Bc "Occhi io vissi di voi" in Ars Fem coll.
RISM B/I (1613 [3]), Eitner, Bowers & Tick, Cohen, letter (Ars Fem).

Sessi (Sessa), Marianne (Marianna) (married **Baron van Natorp** in 1795, after marriage **Sessi-Natorp**)
1771, Rome–1847, Vienna
[Song for 1 voice with keyboard accompaniment] Ms.?
voice/pf
A: Wgm.
Eitner, Cohen.

Sharp, Mary (Mrs. George)
pub. c. 1827, London
A Collection of original melodies with symphonies and accompaniments by Mrs. George Sharp . . . edited by J. Relfe. London: s.n. [1827].
songs
GB: Lbl [H.2818.e.(15.)].
CPM.

Sharpe, Miss
pub. 1780–90s, Edinburgh
[Work(s)] in: *A . . . collection of strathspey reels with a bass for the violoncello or harpsichord . . .* by Niel Gow at Dunkeld. Edinburgh: the author [1785–92] 3 vol.
treble instrument/vlc or hpsch
C: Tp. GB: Ep, Lbl. Holdings in other libraries incomplete.
RISM B/II (p. 76).

Sheredan, Mrs.
n.d.
"Thou art, O God!". S.l., s.n., n.d.
voice/pf
GB: En. Copy in Ars Fem coll.
Letter (Ars Fem).

Sherp, Miss
pub. 1790s, Edinburgh

[Work(s)] in: *A second selection of the most approved Highland strathspeys, country dances, English & French dances;* with a harpsichord & violoncello bass: by John Anderson. Edinburgh: J. Anderson [c. 1792].
treble instrument / hpsch / vlc
GB: En, Lbl.
RISM B / II (p. 103).

[Work(s)] in: *A second selection of the most approved Highland strathspeys, country dances, English & French dances;* with a harpsichord & violoncello bass: by John Anderson. Edinburgh: J. Anderson [c. 1795].
treble instrument / hpsch / vlc
GB: DU, Ep, Lbl.
RISM B / II (p. 103. Contents not identical with 1792 issue of same title).

Sicard, Mlle
pub. 1678–82, Paris
[1 Air] in: *Douzième livre d'airs sérieux et à boire, à 2. et 3. parties.* Par M. Sicard. Paris: C. Ballard, 1678. 3 partbooks. [1 by Mlle Sicard, the remainder by Jean Sicard. First publication in which Mlle Sicard appears.]
2 or 3 voices
B: Br (Dessus only). F: B, Pn (lacking B). GB: Lbl [A.274.a.(14.)] (3d part only).
RISM B / I (1678 [1]), CPM, NG (in entry on her father Jean Sicard).

[1 Air] in: *Quatorzième livre d'airs sérieux et à boire, à 2. et 3. parties.* Par M. Sicard. Paris: C. Ballard, 1680. 3 partbooks. [21 by Jean Sicard, 1 by Mlle Sicard.]
2 or 3 voices
B: Br (Dessus). F: Pn (lacking B).
RISM B / I (1680 [4]), NG (in entry on her father, Jean Sicard).

[1 Air] in: *Seizième livre d'airs sérieux et à boire à 2 et à 3 parties.* Par M. [Jean] Sicard. Paris: C. Ballard. 1682. 3 partbooks. [20 by Jean Sicard, 1 by Mlle Sicard.]
2 or 3 voices
B: Br (Dessus only). F: B (complete), Pn (lacking B).
RISM B / I (1682 [4]), NG (in entry on her father, Jean Sicard).

[3 Airs] in: *Treizième livre d'airs sérieux et à boire, à 2. et 3. parties.* Par M. Sicard. Paris: C. Ballard, 1679. 3 partbooks. [17 by Jean Sicard, 3 by Mlle Sicard.]

2 or 3 *voices*
B: Br (Dessus only). F: B, Pn (lacking B). GB: Lbl [A.274.a.(15.)] (3d part only).
RISM B/I (1679 [2]), CPM, NG (in entry on her father, Jean Sicard).

Sillery, Mme de. See **Genlis, Stéphanie-Félicité, Countess,** née **Ducrest de Saint-Aubin**

Silverparre, Sophie von
pub. 1812, Amsterdam & Leipzig
Lob der Jugend ("Glückliche Jugend, haben die Schmerzen") [Song.] In: *Die Schwestern auf Corcyra.* [A dramatic idyll by Amalie von Hellwig] Amsterdam & Leipzig: Kunst-und Industrie Comptoir, 1812.
voice/pf
D: DÜk (#1362).
Düsseldorf-Goethe.

Simons-Candeille, Julie. See **Candeille, Émilie-Julie**

Sirmen (Syrmen), Maddalena, née **Lombardini.** Often found as **Lombardini**
1745, Venice–1818, Venice. [RISM A/II gives dates as 1735–1785, but the above dates confirmed by Venetian baptismal records, death certificate, and will; see Berdes.]
Concerto [C major], Violino Principale, Violino Primo, Violino Secundo, Viola, Basso, Hoboe Primo, Hoboe Secundo, Corno Primo, Corno Secundo del Sigre Sÿrmein. Ms., 1870. 9 parts.
vln/orch
S: SK (25).
RISM A/II (#89755).

Concerto [B-flat major] a violino principale, violino primo et secundo, 2 flauti, viola et basso. Del Madame S. Ms., c. 1770. 6 parts [incomplete, flute 1 missing].
vln/orch
D: RH (Ms. 726).
RISM A/II (#82847).

[Concerto, violin & orchestra, B-flat major]. Ms., 9 parts, 18/19 cent., without title. [Vln princ, vlns 1 & 2, vla, db, fls 1 & 2, hns 1 & 2.]
vln/orch

YU: Dsmb (47/1357).
RISM A/II (#53158).

Due terzetti, un quartetto a strumenti da arco ed un Concerto a violino
obbligato con orchestra. Ms. score.
2 vlns/vlc; 2 vlns/vla/vlc; vln/orch
I: Bc (KK 126) (Composer's name as Syrmen Lombardini, Maddalena).
Letter (I: Bc).

Duetto II [B-flat major] Della Sig.ra Maddalena Laura Lombardini
Sirmen. Ms., 19th cent. 2 parts. [See also Six duetts . . .]
2 vlns
I: Rc (MS MUS 6093).
RISM A/II (#59618).

Duetto III [D major] Della Sig.ra Maddalena Sirmen. Ms., 19th cent.
2 parts. [See also Six duetts . . .]
2 vlns
I: Rc (MS MUS 6094).
RISM A/II (#59619).

Duetto IV [A major, for two violins] Della Sig.ra Maddalena Sÿrmen.
Ms., 19th cent. [See also Six duetts . . .]
2 vlns
I: Rc (MS MUS 6095).
RISM A/II (#59620).

Duetto V [E major] Della Sig.ra Maddalena Sirmen. Ms., 19th cent. 2
parts. [See also Six duetts . . .]
2 vlns
I: Rc (MS MUS 6096).
RISM A/II (#59621).

Duetto VI [E-flat major] Della Sig.ra Maddalena Sirmen. Ms., 19th cent.
2 parts. [See also Six duetts . . .]
2 vlns
I: Rc (MS MUS 6097).
RISM A/II (#59622).

Quartetto [B-flat major] della Sg.a Madalena Syrmen. Ms., 18th cent.,
4 parts.

2 vlns / vla / vlc
YU: Dsmb (47 / 1355).
RISM A / II (#53156).

Quartetto [B-flat major] della Sig.a Madalena Syrmen. Ms., 18th cent.,
4 parts.
2 vlns / vla / vlc
YU: Dsmb (47 / 1353).
RISM A / II (#53154).

Quartetto [E major] dela Sig.a Madalena Syrmen. Ms., 18th cent.,
4 parts.
2 vlns / vla / vlc
YU: Dsmb (47 / 1351).
RISM A / II (#53152).

Quartetto [E-flat major] della Sig.a Madalena Syrmen. Ms., 18th cent.,
4 parts.
2 vlns / vla / vlc
YU: Dsmb (47 / 1356).
RISM A / II (#53157).

Quartetto [f minor] della Sig.a Madalena Syrmen. Ms., 18th cent.,
4 parts.
2 vlns / vla / vlc
YU: Dsmb (47 / 1352).
RISM A / II (#53153).

Quartetto [g minor] dela Sig.a Madalena Syrmen. Ms., 18th cent.,
4 parts.
2 vlns / vla / vlc
YU: Dsmb (47 / 1354).
RISM A / II (#53155).

Sei Quartetti a violino I e II, viola e violoncello . . . composti da Lodovico e
Madelena Laura Syrmen. Opera III. [This piece jointly composed with
Ludovico Sirmen.] 1. Paris: Mme. Bérault [1769]. Parts. 2. As *Six
Quartettos for two violins, a tenor and bass* . . . by L. Syrmen and Lombardini.
London: W. Napier [c. 1775, 2d edition of 1.].
2 vlns / vla / vlc
1. B: Bc. F: Pn (vla. only) [B.N. Vm18 418]. GB: Ckc, Lbl, Mp. US: Wc

(M452.S627, op. 3. Case). 2. GB: Cu.
1–2. RISM B/II (M. L. Syrmen, p. 295). 1. BUC, CPM, NUC (NS 0584125), Paris Lib. Cat. (1771), Cohen, Eitner, NG, Olivier.

Sei Sonate per due Violini Soli [E-flat, D, B-flat, E, A, C]. Ms. [See also: Six duetts for two violins.]
2 vlns
I: Gi(l) (2 ex.) [N.1.6.6.(Sc.17)].
Genova.

[6 concerti] *A concerto, in seven parts,* composed by Madelena Laura Syrmen. Opera III. "There will be one concerto, pub. monthly, till the six are compleated; composed by the same author." London: William Napier, 1772. 8 part- books. [Same works as "Six concertos . . . op. 3," but without horns.]
vln/orch (2 vlns/vla/vlc/2 obs/bc)
US: AA (M 1040 .B29 C73, also microfilm copy).
Berdes, NUC (#0584126), OCLC (23631691, micro. 20036637).

[6 concerti] *Concerto* [B-flat] *à violino principale,* premier & second violon, alto & basse, hautbois et cors ad libitum, œuvre II. Paris: Borelly [between 1775 and 1777]. Parts [based on Napier print designated "opera III" (1773) and/or Hummel print designated "Oeuvre second" (1772)]
vln/orch
S: Skma (complete).
RISM A/I (S 3540), Berdes, Cohen, Olivier.

[6 concerti.] *Deuxième concerto* [E] *à violino principale,* premier et second violon, alto & basse, hautbois et cors ad libitum, œuvre III. Paris: Borelly (gravé par Mlle Hyver) [between 1775 and 1777]. Parts [based on Napier print "opera III" (1773) and/or Hummel print "Oeuvre second" (1772)].
vln/orch (2 vlns/vla/b; 2 obs/2 hns ad libitum)
S: Skma (complete). US: Wc.
RISM A/I (S 3541), Berdes.

[6 concerti.] *Six concertos* [B-flat, E, A, C, B-flat, C] *in nine parts . . .* opera III. London: William Napier, 1773. Parts. [See also "[6 concerti], A concerto in seven parts," for the same works without horns.]
vln/orch (2 vlns/vla/vlc/2 obs/2 hns/b)
B: Bc. E: Mn (only complete set of extant parts). GB: Lbl. I: Vc. US: Wc (incomplete: Concerto I & II also "in seven parts." M1012.S62 op.3).

Copy in Ars Fem coll.
Berdes, RISM A/I (S 3535), NUC (#0584130), Cohen, Eitner, NG, letter (Ars Fem).

[6 concerti] *Six concertos for the harpsichord or piano forte* [op. 3] . . . adapted for the harpsichord by Sigr. Giordani. 1. London: William Napier [1773]. 2. London: W. Napier [c. 1785]. 51 pp. 3. London: Longman & Broderip [1785]. Parts. 4. Ms. copies of keyboard reductions and transcriptions as keyboard concerti for Nos. I & III.
1., 3., 4. hpsch, 2 vlns, b; 2. hpsch or pf
1. GB: Ckc, Lbl (hpch, vln I, b) [R.M.17.c.4.(14.)]. I: Vc. US: NYp (hpch), Wc (hpch 3 ex. M1011.S64 op. 3.G5). 2. NYp. 3. GB: Lbl [h.73.]. Microfilm of Lbl copy in Calvert Johnson coll. 4. D: WRz (Mus IIIc:19, formerly in collection of Anna Amalia of Saxe-Weimar).
RISM A/I (S 3536, 3537 [arr. of RISM S 3535]), Berdes, BUC, CPM, NUC & Sup. (NS 0584129, NSS 0015754), letter (C. Johnson).

[6 concerti] *Trois concerts* [B-flat, E, A] *à violino principale, violino primo e secondo, alto et basse, hautbois et cornes de chasse ad libitum,* œuvre second.
1. Amsterdam: Johann Julius Hummel, No. 226 [by 1772] Parts. [Pirated from Napier, 1772–73.] 2. Ms. copies, 18th century, 8 parts.
vln/orch
1. B: Bc (complete). E: Mn (vln princ.). S: L, Skma. 2. S: L (Saml. Kraus 450). Copy in Ars Fem coll.
1. RISM A/I (S 3538), Berdes, Eitner, NG. 2. RISM A/II (#37595). Letter (Ars Fem).

[6 concerti] *Trois concerts* [C, B-flat, C] *à violino principale, violino primo e secondo, alto et basse, hautbois et cornes de chasse ad libitum,* œuvre troisième. Amsterdam: Johann Julius Hummel, No. 246 [by 1772]. Parts. [Pirated from Napier, 1772–73.]
vln/orch
B: Bc (complete). S: Skma, St (lacking vln princ, vln II), STr (lacking ob I, cor I). Copy of B: Bc in Ars Fem coll.
RISM A/I (S 3539), Berdes, Eitner, NG, letter (Ars Fem).

[6 concerti] *Troisième concerto* [A] *à violino principale, premier & second violon, alto & basse, hautbois et cors ad libitum,* œuvre IV. Paris: Borelly (gravé par Mlle Hyver). Parts [based on Napier's "opera III" (1773) and/or Hummel's "Oeuvre second" (1772)].
vln/orch/2 vlns, vla, b (2 obs, 2 hns ad libitum)

S: Skma (complete).
RISM A/I (S 3542), Berdes.

[6 concerti, ms. sources.] Concerto 1 in B-flat Major. 1. substitutes 2 flutes
for obs and hns of original. 2. as "Symphonie concertante' with written-
out cadenzas, labeled Concerto No. 4. 3. ms. 4. ms. 5. ms.
vln/orch
1. D: MÜu (Ms. 726, missing fl I). 2. I: Bc (Ms. KK. 126). 3. I: Gi(l)
(M.3b.24.25). 4. I: TRa (N.749/x.1.3.N.17, incomplete). 5. I: Vnm (Cod.
It. IV, 1524 [= 11472]).
Berdes, Olivier.

[6 concerti, ms. sources.] Concerto III in A Major. 1. Ms. 2. Two incomplete versions with separate title pages, ms.
vln/orch
1. B: Lc (77–2.M.I, solo part only). 2. I: OS (MS. Musiche B. 2795).
Berdes.

Six duetts [E-flat, D, B-flat, E, A, C] *for two violins.* 1. London: William
Napier, 1773. 2. *Six sonates à duex violons . . .* œuvre quatrieme. Den Haag:
Burchard Hummel. 3. *Sei duetti per due violini . . .* opera Va. Paris, Venier
(gravée par Richome), 1775. Parts. 4. William Napier [1778?].
5. Sei Duetti del Sigra. Syrmen. Ms., 2 parts [unspecified]. 6. Duetto
(I–VI) Compose Par Madame Sirmen. Ms., 1775. 7. VI Duetti da
Madame Sirmen opera IV. Ms., 1789. 2 parts.
2 vlns
1. E: Mn. GB: Lbl (3 ex.) [g.421.r.(12.)], [g.421.s.(7.)], & [h.2910.(5.)]. I:
Vc. US: Wc (2 ex.). 2. F: Pa (PMeyer). S: Skma. 3. F: Pc [K.6077]. 4.
Photocopy in US: NYp. 5. A: SEI (V 2708 I, II). 6. S: VX (Eklins saml.).
7. S: HÄ. Copy of 2. in Ars Fem coll., copy in D: Kf&m.
1–3. RISM A/I (S 3546, 3547, 3548. See also Sirmen, Ludovico). 1. BUC.
4. NUC (#4. NS 0584131). 5. RISM A/II (#26445. Last duet as c minor).
6. RISM A/II (158933). 7. RISM A/II (#86553). Cohen, Eitner, NG, Olivier,
letter (Ars Fem), Frau & Musik.

Six trios [F, C, D, A, G, f] *à deux violons et violoncello obligé . . .* œuvre première. 1. London: Welcker [c. 1770]. 2. Paris: Sieber; Lyon: Castaud, No.
153 [1771]. 3. Amsterdam: Johann Julius Hummel [c. 176–? or 1770].
4. Ms., 3 parts. 5. Trio (I–VI) Composée par Madame Lombard Sirmen.
Ms., 1779, 3 parts. 6. VI. Sonate da Madame Sirmen. Ms. 1789, 3 parts.
7. Six Sonates Par Mada.me Lombard Sirmen. Ms., 18th cent., 2 parts

(incomplete). 8. Six Trios a Deux violons et Violoncello obligato . . . Par Madame Lombardini Sirmen . . . Oeuvre Primiere, 1774. Ms, 1774, 3 parts.
2 vlns/vlc
1. B: Bc. E: Mn. F: Pc. GB: Cke (2 ex.), Lbl (2 ex.) [g.471] & [Hirsch.III.376], Mp. US: Wc. 2. B: Bc. F: Pc [K.6070 & 6076]. 3. S: Skma. SF: A. US: Wc. 4. US: NYp. 5. S: VX (Eklins saml.) 6. S: HÄ. 7. S: Sm (vln 1 missing). Copy in D: Kf&m. 8. S: L (Saml. Kraus 386). Copy of 5 Trios (F, D, A, G, f) in Ars Fem coll.
1–3. RISM A/I (S 3543, 3544, 3545. See also Sirmen, Ludovico), BUC. 3. NUC (NS 0584132). 4. NUC Sup. (NSS 0015755). 5. RISM A/II (#158934). 6. RISM A/II (#86552). 7. RISM A/II (#69565). 8. RISM A/II (#37596). Letter (Ars Fem), Frau & Musik, Cohen, Eitner, NG, Olivier.

Trii [*sic*] [C Major, for 2 violins and basso continuo. Two movements: Vivace, Minuetto]. Ms.
2 vlns/bc
I: Vc (old sig., 1421. n. inv. 27111, Torr. Ms. C. 33).
I: Vc Cat.

Trio Per Violini e Violoncello [A major] Dell Sig: Luigi Boccherini di Lucca [*sic*, work has been identified as by M. L. Syrmen]. Ms. 18th cent. 3 parts. [See also Six trios [F, C, D, A, G, f] à deux violons et violoncello obligé . . . œuvre première.]
2 vlns, vlc
S: Skma (W 3–R).
RISM A/II (#155453).

[Work(s)] in: *Journal d'ariettes, scènes et duo traduits, imités ou parodiés de l'italien.* Par Mr. D. C. amateur . . . Paris: De Roullède de La Chevardière. 1782–83
Instruments undetermined
B: Bc. D: HR, Mbs. F: AG, Pa, Pc. S: Skma. No library holds complete run.
RISM B/II (p. 206).

Skirving, W. (a lady)

n.d.
Miss Margt Hamilton's quickstep, for the pianoforte, guitar & german-flute . . . the whim, or Miss Agnes Graham's favourite, by a lady. Edinburgh: Muir Wood & Co. (G. Walker), n.d.

pf / guit / fl
GB: Lbl [g.934.cc.(4.)].
RISM A/I (S 3571), CPM.

Sleigh, Mrs.
pub. c. 1800, London
Come buy my sweet flowers. A new ballad, written and composed by Mrs.
Sleigh. London: Broderip & Wilkinson [c.1800]. 4 pp.
voice / pf
GB: Lbl [G.365.(13.)], Ob.
RISM A/I (S 3576), BUC, CPM (date 1802), Cohen

Sophie Elisabeth, Duchess of Braunschweig-Wölfenbüttel (Lüneburg), née Mecklenburg-Güstrow
1613, Güstrow–1676, Luchow
Christ fürstliches Davids-Harpfen-Spiel: zum Spiegel und Fürbild Himmel-flammender Andacht mit ihren Arien oder Singweisen hervorgegeben. 1. Nürnberg: Christoph
Gerhard, 1667. [60 Lieder.] 265 pp. 2. . . . im zweyten Druck her-
vorgegeben. Wolfenbüttel, Paul Weiss, 1670. [63 Lieder.] Texts by Anton
Ulrich von Braunschweig.
voice / bc
1. A: Wgm. CH: Zz. D: Cl, Gs, HR, LÜh, Mbs (Liturg. 1379z), PA, Rp,
SWl, W. NL: DHk. US: Cn, Hm. Copy of US: Cn in Ars Fem coll. 2. B:
Br. D: As, Bds (2 ex.), EU, Gs, GOl, HVk, HVl (2 ex.), Sl, W (7 ex.). DK:
Kk. US: NH.
*1. RISM A/I (S 3965), letter (D: Mbs), NG, MGG, Cohen, letter (Ars Fem). 2.
RISM A/I (S 3966), Eitner, NG.*

Die Triumphirende Liebe umgeben Mit den Sieghafften Tugenden Jn einem Ballet . . .
vorgestellet Am 12. Tagge des Weinmonats 1653 . . . Lüneburg: Johann
und Heinrich Stern, 1653. Parts.
SATB
D: CEbm, DS (SATB), HVl, Lr (incomplete), LO, Mth, W.
RISM A/I (S 3963).

[18 pieces] in: Schottelius, Justus Georg, *Neu erfundenes Freuden Spiel genandt
Friedens-Sieg . . . Zu Braunschweig im Jahr 1642 . . . vorgestellet . . .*
[Singspiel]. Wolfenbüttel: Conrad Bruno, 1648. Score.
stage work (solo voices / chorus / instruments)
D: W (W[444]). PL: WRu.
RISM A/I (S 3959), NG, MGG, Cohen, letter (Woods).

Glück dem Vermehrer der Wölpenstadt zieret. In: *Gloria et memoria natalitia.*
Wolfenbüttel: s.n. 1653.
voice / 3 instruments
D: W (2 ex.) (W [443]).
RISM A / I (S 3964).

Glückwünschende Freüdendarstellung . . . [Singspiel]. 1. Lüneburg: Johann und
Heinrich Stern, 1652. Score, 15 pp. 2. Wolfenbüttel: Johann und Heinrich
Stern, n.d. Score [5-pt sinfonia, 5 cto songs, chorus].
stage work (4 solo voices / chorus / 4 strings / bc)
1. D: SWl, W (3 ex.) (W [441, 442]). Photocopy in D: Mbs (8 Mus.pr.
6219). 2. D: Dl, W (3 ex.).
*RISM A / I (S 3961, 3962), letter (D: Mbs), NG, MGG, Cohen, DM Archiv,
letter (Woods).*

[114 chansons.] Autograph ms, begun at Güstrow, 1633.
voice / bc
D: W.
NG.

[Some songs by Sophie Elisabeth in a ms. of songs and sacred concerti.]
2 vols, 1647–55. Ms.
voice / bc
D: W.
NG.

Vinetum evangelicum. Evangelischer Weinberg. Gott zu Ehren und der Music
Liebhaber zu Wolgefallen . . . [texts by] Herzog August. Wolfenbüttel:
Johann und Heinrich Stern, 1651. [58 hymn melodies.]
voice / bc
D: Bds, Cl, Gs, HVl, LEm, LÜh, Nla, PRE, W (2 ex.).
RISM A / I (S 3960), NG (1651), Cohen (1647), MGG (1647).

Steemson, Miss

organist at Lancaster, c. 1780
A Dirge for Funerals. Ms., c. 1780.
org
GB: Lbl [Add.ms.37027 f.55b]. Transcription in C. Johnson coll.
Brit. Cat. Ms., letter (C. Johnson).

Stein, Nanette (Maria Anna) (married **Streicher.** Sometimes misspelled as **Nannette**)
1760, Augsburg–1833, Vienna
Klage über den frühen Tod der Jungfer Ursula Sabina Stage in Augsburg. Augsburg: Conrad Heinrich Stage, 1788.
song
D: LEm.
RISM A/I (S 5712), NG, Cohen, Eitner.

Stirling, Magdalene
pub. 1796, Edinburgh
Twelve tunes [Edinburgh]: s.n., 1796.
pf
GB: En, Lbl [g.149.(24.)], P. Copy in Ars Fem coll.
RISM A/I (S 6440), CPM, Cohen, letter (Ars Fem).

[Work(s)] in: *Part first [–fourth] of the complete repository of original Scots slow strathspeys and dances . . . for the harp, piano-forte, violin and violoncello . . .* by Niel Gow and son's . . . Edinburgh: Gow and Shepherd [1799-1817]. 4 vol.
harp/pf/vln/vlc
GB: DU, En, Ge, Gm, Lbl, Lcs, P. Holdings in other libraries are incomplete.
RISM B/II (Miss M. Stirling, p. 282).

Stockdale, Miss
pub. 1804, London & Dublin
Never from thee will I part. A Favorite song. London, Dublin: Goulding, Phipps, D'Almaine & Co. [1804]. 3 pp.
song
GB: Lbl [G.424.kk.(6.)].
CPM.

Strozzi, Barbara (Barbara Valle, Barbara di Santa Sofia)
1619, Venice–?1664 or later
Arie . . . opera ottava. Venice: Francesco Magni detto Gardano, 1664. Score.
voice(s)/bc
D: FUl. I: Baf, Bc (BB 422). Copies in D: Kf&m and Ars Fem coll.
RISM A/I (S 6989), Rosand, MGG, Frau & Musik, letter (Ars Fem).

Ariette a voce sola, opera sesta. Venice: Francesco Magni, 1657. Score.
voices/bc, includes 1 for 2 voices
I: Bc (BB. 367). Copies in US: WSwf and Ars Fem coll.
RISM A/I (S 6987), OCLC (micro. 11383577), Cohen, Eitner, NG, MGG, Rosand, letter (Ars Fem).

"Aure giacchè non posso . . . " cantata di Sopr. c. Bc. [from op. 8]. Ms. score.
S/bc
I: MOe (MS P).
NG, MGG, Eitner, Rosand.

Cantate, ariete a una, due, e tre voci . . . opera terza. Venice: stampa del Gardano, appresso Francesco Magni, 1654. Score. 58 pp.
1–3 voices/bc
GB: Lbl [K.7.g.4.(1.)]. Copies in US: U, WSwf and Ars Fem coll.
RISM A/I (S 6986), OCLC (micro. 9079920), BUC, CPM (dated 1651) Cohen, NG, MGG, Eitner, Rosand, letter (Ars Fem).

Cantate, ariette e duetti . . . opera seconda. Venice: Gardano, 1651. Score. 78 pp.
1–2 voices/bc
GB: Lbl (lacks title page) [K.7.g.4.(2.)]. I: Fn. Copies in US: WSwf and Ars Fem coll.
RISM A/I (S 6984), OCLC (micro. 11239469), BUC, CPM, Eitner, Cohen, NG, MGG, Rosand, letter (Ars Fem).

Diporti di Euterpe, overo cantate & ariette a voce sola . . . opera settima. Venice: Francesco Magni, 1659. Score. 169 pp.
S/unfigured b
GB: Gu. I: Bc (BB. 368) US: Wc (M1490.S82D5). Copies in US: CIu, WSwf and Ars Fem coll.
RISM A/I (S 6988), BUC, Rosand, OCLC (micro. 1302558), NUC (micro. NS 1012664–5), MGG, letter (Ars Fem).

Diporti d'Euterpe overo madrigali a due voci col basso. Ms. 1660. [Not the same music as Strozzi's opera settima.]
2 voices/bc
I: Vnm [Classe IV, codice 726 (10364)].
Rosand, NG (credits it to Strozzi as op. 8).

"Havete torto" [soprano] & "Un amante doglioso" [bass]. Ms.
voice (1 for S, 1 for B)/bc
D: Kl (ms. coll. of cantatas, fol. 34).
Eitner, MGG, Rosand.

Il primo libro de madrigali a due, tre, quattro, e cinque voci. Venice: Alessandro
Vincenti, 1644. Partbooks.
2–5 voices/bc
I: Bc (BB. 366), Fn. Copies in US: WSwf and Ars Fem coll.
*RISM A/I (S 6983), OCLC (micro. 11224437), Eitner, Cohen, NG, MGG,
Rosand, letter (Ars Fem).*

"Presso un ruscello algente" [soprano]. Ms.
voice (S)/bc
I: Vc (Coll. Correr II, #48).
Rosand.

"Quis dabit mihi" In: *Sacra corona, motetti a due, e trè voci di diversi eccellentissimi
autori moderni, novamente raccolti et dati in luce da Bartolomeo Marcesso . . .*
1. Venice: F. Magni, 1656. 2. Reprint. Antwerp: héritiers P. Phalèse, 1659.
4 partbooks.
3 voices (ATB)/bc
1. US: Wc. 2. B: Br (SI). GB: Och (lacking B).
RISM B/I (1656 [1], 1659 [2]), Bowers & Tick, Rosand.

"Rissolvetevi pensieri" and "Chi brama in amore." [from op. 6] 1. In: *Arie
a voce sola de diversi auttori raccolte da Francesco Tonalli . . .* Venice: Al. Vincent,
1656. 2. "Rissolvetevi pensieri" In: Songs with figured bass for harpsichord. Transcribed by Pietro Reggio for Monsieur Didie, London, 1681.
ms.
voice (S)/bc
1. GB: Lbl. 2. GB: Lbl [ms 59 (1681), fol. 31v or (Harley 1501)].
*RISM B/I (1656 [4], as B. Strozi), NG (as from op. 2 or 3), Bowers & Tick, Brit.
Cat. Ms., Rosand, MGG.*

Sacri musicali affetti. Libro Primo, Opera Quinta. Venice: Francesco Magni,
1655.
voice/bc
PL: WRu. Copies in US: WSwf and Ars Fem coll.
*RISM A/I (S 6985), OCLC (micro. 11484274), Rosand, Bohn, Eitner, NG,
MGG, Cohen, letter (Ars Fem).*

Suarda, Maria Virginia, Suora

pub. 1692, Venice. Nun at Bergamo

Balletti, correnti, minuetti [arranged into 11 suites]. Venice: Giuseppe Sala, 1692.

2 vlns/vlc/hpsch

I: Bc. Copy in Ars Fem coll.

Cohen, letter (Ars Fem).

Subligny, (Madam)

pub. c. 1700, London

"Come fill up ye bowl." A song in praise of punch [arranged] to ye tune of Mdm Sublignys minuet [London: s.n., c. 1700].

Melody only by Subligny

voice/kbd

GB: DRc, Mch. Copy of GB: DRc in Ars Fem coll.

RISM A/I (S 7099), BUC, Cohen, letter (Ars Fem).

Sully, Miss S[ally]

early 19th cent., Richmond, VA

Patriotic song ("Down the stream of time have glided") commemorative of opening the Union Hotel in the City of Richmond, Virga, on the Fourth of July, 1817 [text] by Leroy Anderson. Music by Miss S. Sully. New York: J. A. W. Geib, [1818–21]. 3 pp.

voice & chorus/pf

US: CAdriscoll.

Wolfe (9146, composer's name completed as the "Miss Sally Sully, professor of Music" in Richmond VA directory for 1856).

Szymanowska (Shimanovskaya), Maria Agata, née Wolowska (I. M. Pani Szymanowskiey, Szymanowskiéj)

1789, Warsaw–1831, St. Petersburg

The Cellarian Mazurka Waltzes . . . the choreography by T. Mason. London: T. Boosey & Co. [1844]. 7 pp.

pf

GB: Lbl [h.933.(36.)].

CPM.

Caprice sur la romance de Joconde ("Et l'on revient toujours") pour le pianoforte. 1. S.l.: author (Pl.#3067), s.d. 2. Leipzig: Breitkopf & Härtel, 1820. 7 pp.

pf

1. D: Mbs (in 2 Mus.pr. 3551). 2. US: WE.
Letter (D: Mbs), OCLC (16530160), NG, MGG, Meggett, Cohen.

Complainte d'un aveugle qui demandoit l'aumône au Jardin des plantes à Paris. Paris:
Hanry [182–?]. [Ed. with Moretti, L. 6 ariette, et al.]
voice/pf
US: CA.
NUC (NS 1127907).

[Compositions by] Marie Szymanowska. [S.l.]: author. 1 Vol. + 1 Heft au
Livrais. See individual works from D: Mbs (2 Mus.pr. 3551)
pf
D: Mbs (2 Mus.pr. 3551).
Letter (D: Mbs).

Cotillon, ou, *valse figurée pour le piano.* Paris: Hanry [1830?]. 7 pp.
pf
US: WE.
OCLC (16939112), NG, MGG, Meggett (publisher as Henry), Cohen.

Divertissement [B-flat major] *pour le pianoforte avec accompagnement de violon.*
1. S.l.: author (Pl.#3079), n.d. 2. Leipzig: Breitkopf & Härtel, 1820. 7 pp.
vln/pf
1. D: Mbs (in 2 Mus.pr. 3551). 2. PL: Kj. US: WE.
Letter (D: Mbs), OCLC (17998077), NG, MGG, Cohen.

Dix-huit danses de différent genre pour le piano-forte . . . Sixième livraison. 1. S.l.:
author (Pl. #3090), n.d. 2. St. Petersburg: Chez Dalmas [c. 1820]. 27 pp.
3. [Leipzig: Breitkopf & Härtel, 1820]. 27 pp.
pf
1. D: Mbs (in 2 Mus.pr. 3551). 2. GB: Lbl [h.1426.w.(3.)]. 3. US: WE.
1. Letter (D: Mbs). 2. CPM. 3. OCLC (17716767). NG, MGG, Meggett, Cohen.

Douze exercices: pour le piano-forte. Leipzig: Probst (Pl.#164b), s.d.
pf
D: Mbs (4 Mus.pr. 9366).
Letter (D: Mbs).

[Etude]. Vivace [d minor for piano]. Varsovie [autograph-remembrance
leaf]. June 16, 1819. 1 p. ms.
pf

D: DÜk (Cat. #1408).
Düsseldorf-Goethe.

Exercice pour le piano. In: *The Harmonicon,* vol. 4, pt. 2, pp. 252–53, 1826.
pf
GB: Lbl [P.P.1947.].
CPM.

Fanfara dwugolosowa [2 part fanfare].
2 hns/2 trs
PL: Kj.
NG, Cohen.

Fantaisie pour le pianoforte . . . Cinquième livraison. 1. S.l.: author (Pl.
#3093), n.d. 2. St. Petersburg: Chez Dalmas [c. 1820]. 12 pp. 3. Fantasie
[F] pour le pianoforte. Leipzig: Breitkopf & Härtel, 1820. 13 pp.
pf
1. D: Mbs (in 2 Mus.pr. 3551). 2. GB: Lbl [h.1426.w.(4.)]. 3. US: WE. One
edition is in PL: Wn (copy in D: Kf&m).
*1. Letter (D: Mbs). 2. CPM. 3. OCLC (17784297). Frau & Musik, NG, MGG,
Meggett, Cohen.*

*IV valses à trois mains pour le piano forte, composées et d´diées à Mlle la Ctesse Sophie
Plater pour le jour de sa fête.* Rotterdam: L. Plattner [18—].
pf (3 hands)
Formerly US: ERac. Since dissolution of this college in 1990, location of
the collection is not known.
NG, MGG, Glickman, Cohen.

Grande valse pour le pianoforte à quatre mains . . . Quatrième livraison. 1. S.l.:
author (Pl. #3072), s.d. 2. St. Petersburg: Chez Charles Lissner [c. 1820].
3. Leipzig: Breitkopf & Härtel, 1820. 9 pp.
pf (4 hands)
1. D: Mbs (in 2 Mus. pr. 3551). 2. GB: Lbl [h.1426.w.(5.)]. 3. US: WE.
1. Letter (D: Mbs). 2. CPM. 3. OCLC (1653038). MGG, NG, Cohen.

Jan Albrycht ("Już był Carogród i Krainę"), *Duma o Michale Glińskim*
("Wokropnych cieniach pieezarów podziemnych"), *Jadwiga Królowa Polska*
("Kiedy dni Piastów przecinał się wątek"). In: Julian Ursyn Niemcewicz,
Śpiewy historycznye [Historic songs]. Warsaw: 1816, 1818. Texts by
Niemcewicz.

voice/pf
F: Pn. PL: Kc, Wn, Wmickiewicz. Copies of both of the editions in PL: Kc
in Jackson coll.
Letter (Poniatowska), Sowinski, NG, MGG, Cohen.

Le départ, romance. [Words by Cervantes, trans. by Florian] 1. S.l.: author
(Pl. #3078), s.d. 2. Leipzig: Breitkopf & Härtel,1820. 7 pp.
voice/pf
1. D: Mbs (in 2 Mus. pr. 3551). 2. US: WE.
1. Letter (D: Mbs). 2. OCLC (16530492), NG, MGG, Cohen.

Le Murmure. Nocturne pour le piano. 1. Paris: Hanry [c. 1830]. 2. Leipzig:
Chez H. A. Probst [c. 1826]. 3. arr. for 3 hands by composer. St.
Petersburg: Schmitzdorff [1830?].
pf (also arr. for pf 3 hands)
1. GB: Lbl [h.60.f.(3.)], US: WE. 2. D: DÜk (cat # 1409). 3. US: WE.
1. CPM. 2. Düsseldorf-Goethe. 3. OCLC (17016010 & 17997605).

Menuett [E]. Ms.
pf
PL: Kj.
Meggett, MGG, Cohen.

Nocturne [B-flat]. 1. Ms. composed between 1828–31. 2. St. Petersburg:
1852, published posthumously.
pf
1. USSR: Lsc. 2. Location of original not known.
1–2. MGG. 2. NG. Cohen.

Polonaise sur l'air national favori du feu Prince Joseph Poniatowsky. 1. S.l.: author
(Pl.#3092), n.d. 2. Leipzig: Breitkopf,1820. 3 pp. 3. [May be same piece
pub. in *Musical Library. Instrumental Series III.* London: Charles Knight &
Co. between 1837–48, another printing 1843.]
pf
1. D: Mbs (in 2 Mus.pr. 3551). 2. location not known. 3. Copy in Rempel coll.
1. Letter (D: Mbs). 2. NG, Cohen. 3. Letter (Rempel).

Preludium [B-flat]. Ms.
pf
PL: Kj.
NG, MGG, Meggett (as Praeludium [E-flat]), Cohen.

Romance à Joséphine. Ms.
voice/pf
P: Kj.
NG, MGG, Cohen.

Romance de Monsieur le Prince Alexandre Galitzin, arr. pour le pianoforte et
dédiée à l'auteur par Mme. Marie Szymanowska . . . 1. S.l.: author
(Pl.#3091), n.d. 2. [Leipzig: Breitkopf & Härtel, 1820]. 7 pp.
pf
1. D: Mbs (in 2 Mus.pr.3551). 2. US: WE.
1. Letter (D: Mbs). 2. OCLC (17997929). NG, Cohen.

Sérénade pour le pianoforte avec accompagnement de violoncelle . . . Quatrième
livraison. 1. S.l.: author (Pl.#3077), n.d. 2. St. Petersburg: Chez Charles
Lissner [c.1820]. 3. Leipzig: Breitkopf & Härtel 1820. 4. S.l., s.n. [184–?].
vlc/pf
1. D: Mbs (in 2 Mus.pr. 3551). 2. GB: Lbl [h.1426.w.(5.)]. 3. PL: Kj. US:
WE. 4. US: Bp.
1. Letter (D: Mbs). 2. CPM. 3. OCLC (17780665). 4. NUC (NS 1127909).
NG, MGG, Cohen.

Six marches pour le pianoforte. 1. S.l.: author (Pl.#3071), n.d. 2. [Leipzig:
Breitkopf & Härtel,1820]. 13 pp.
pf
1. D: Mbs (in 2 Mus.pr. 3551). 2. US: WE.
1. Letter (D: Mbs). 2. OCLC (16530288). NG, MGG, Meggett, Cohen.

Six Minuets pour le pianoforte. 1. S.l.: author (Pl.#3094), n.d. 2. Leipzig:
Breitkopf & Härtel, 1820. 11 pp.
pf
1. D: Mbs (in 2 Mus.pr. 3551). 2. US: WE.
1. Letter (D: Mbs). 2. OCLC (17780665). NG, MGG, Meggett, Cohen.

Six Romances avec accompagnement de piano-forte . . . Deuxième livraison. 1. S.l.:
author (Pl.#3066), n.d. 2. St. Petersburg: Chez Charles Lissuer [c.1820].
14 pp. 3. [Leipzig: Breitkopf & Härtel,1820.] 14 pp. Texts by Shakespeare,
Saint-Onge, F. de Berni.
voice/pf
1. D: Mbs (in 2 Mus.pr. 3551). 2. GB: Lbl [H.1653.q.(17.)]. 3. US: WE.
1. Letter (D: Mbs). 2. CPM. 3. OCLC (16530120). NG, MGG, Cohen.

Spiewy historycznye [Historic songs]. Kazimierz Wielki [Casimir the Great] and Stefan Czarniecki. Ms., in Album-Autograph of Maria Szymanowska. Texts by Niemcewicz.
voice/pf
PL: Kj.
Letter (Poniatowska), NG, MGG, Cohen

Temat wariacji [theme for variations, b-flat]. Ms.
pf
PL: Kj.
NG, MGG, Meggett (as B Minor), Cohen

24 Mazurkas. 1. Leipzig: Breitkopf, 1826. 2. Collected and arranged for the pianoforte. London: [1830?].
pf
1. Location not known. 2. GB: Lbl [h.726.h.(34.)].
CPM, NG, MGG, Meggett, Cohen.

Valse [d]. Ms.
pf
PL: Kj.
NG, MGG, Meggett, Cohen.

Vingt exercices et préludes: pour le pianoforte. 1. S.l.: author (Pl. #3043), n.d. 2. [Leipzig: Breitkopf & Härtel, 1820]. 47 pp.
pf
1. D: Mbs (in 2 Mus.pr. 3551). 2. US: WE.
1. Letter (D: Mbs). 2. OCLC (16530067). MGG.

ↄ

T., Mlle de

pub. c. 1785, Paris

Un Baiser, ou la Rose. [Song, text by Mr Lieutaud, melody by Mlle de T.] Accmpt de guitarre par Mr Ducray. [Paris]: Chez les freres Savigny [c. 1785].

Melody only by Mlle de T.

voice / guit

GB: Lbl [B.362.f.(20.)].

BUC, CPM.

Tabary, Signora M . . . A . . . C . . . de

18th cent., Italy?

Numa Pompilio alla grotta d'Egeria. Intermezzo [c. 1800?]. Ms. score. [Orch of 2 flutes, 2 oboes, 2 clarinets, 2 horns, 2 trumpets, timpani, bassoon, and strings.]

stage work

D: Mbs (Mus. Mss. 3025., from Bibliothek-Herzogs Eugen von Leuchtenberg.). I: PAbs (27559–T–VI–17).

Letter (D: Mbs), Eitner, Parma BS, Cohen, Mellen.

Sesostri, opera seria in 2 atti. Ms. score, act I only.

stage work

D: Mbs (Mus. Mss. 3058, from Bibliothek-Herzogs Eugen von Leuchtenberg). I: PAbs (19603 4 N–V–11–12).

Letter (D: Mbs), Eitner, Parma BS, Cohen, Mellen.

Target, Madame Colonel (pseud.)

pub. 1821, Boston

"Tho' the day of my destiny's over." Words by Lord Byron. Music composed for the harp or piano forte by Madame Colonel Target. Boston: C. & E. W. Jackson [1821].

voice / pf or harp

US: NYp, PROu.

Wolfe (9207).

Tayler, F. E. (Mrs.)

pub. c. 1791, London

Twelve original contra dances. London: Preston & Son [c. 1791]. 12 pp.

pf

GB: Lbl [b.52.(4.)].
RISM A/I (T 295), BUC, CPM (1789).

Th., Mlle de

pub. late 18th cent., Paris
[Work(s)] in: *Almanach des grâces, étrennes érotiques-chantantes* . . . [annual].
Paris: Cailleau, 1786–94. 7 vol.
instruments undetermined
B: Bc. D: HR. F: AS, DO, Pa, Pn. S: Skma. All library holdings are
incomplete.
RISM B/II (p. 83, gives library siglum as F: As).

Thicknesse, Ann, née Ford. See Ford, Ann

Thiémé, Angélique, Mme

fl. c. 1790–19, France
Fantasie pour piano forte avec accompagnement de violon & basse obligés . . . œuvre
2. Paris: Chez Naderman (gravé par Mlle Aubert) [c. 1810–15]. Parts.
pf/vln/b (vlc)
F: Pn (2 ex. Vm17 918–919). I: PAc. Photocopy in C. Johnson coll.
RISM A/I (T 661), letter (C. Johnson).

*Premier recueil de romances, paroles de différents auteurs, avec accompagnement de forte
piano ou harpe.* Paris: chez tous les Marchand des Musique [c. 1790].
voice/pf or harp
F: Pn.
RISM A/I (T 659), letter (C. Johnson).

Romances et airs patriotiques avec accompagnement de forte piano . . . *terminé par l'air
de La montagne avec sept variations servant d'accompagnement au chant des couplets.*
Paris: Jean Henri Naderman; Rouen: [c. 1796].
voice/pf
F: Pn.
RISM A/I (T 660), letter (C. Johnson).

Thierry, Amalia

pub. c. 1805, Hamburg
Die Ideale. [Song with fortepiano]. Hamburg: Johann August Böhme
[1805?]. 11 pp. Text by F. Schiller.
voice/pf

GB: Lbl [Hirsch III.1125.].
CPM.

Würde der Frauen. In Musik gesetzt. Hamburg: "französische Musik-Handlung" (C. Lau), n.d.
voice/pf
D: Hmb.
RISM A/I (T 666).

Thürheim, Comtesse de
pub. 1791, Basel
Ariettes . . . dédiées à S. A. Madame la Princesse Bariatinskoy née Princesse de Holstein-Beck. Basel: Wilhelm Haas Sohn, 1791.
voice/pf
CS: K. D: Bhm.
RISM A/I (T 750).

Tibaldi, Rosa, née Tartaglini [1 of 3 female members of Accademica della Filarmonica of Bologna in 18th century]
?–1775, Bologna
"Lasciato il patrio nido." 1. In: 18 Duetti vor 2 Sopr. e Bc., No. 7. Ms. (dated Naples 1773–90). 2. In: Giuseppe Luigi Tibaldi, Duetti notturni. Ms. [G. L. Tibaldi was the husband of Rosa Tibaldi.]
SS/bc
1. I: Bc (Eitner). 2. D: Bds (Eitner, Ms 133).
Cohen, Eitner (under G. L. Tibaldi; also lists duet by Rosa Tibaldi), NG (under Giuseppe Tibaldi).

Tirinanzi, Nanette
pub. c. 1800, Regensburg
Huit Variations sur l'air "Quand l'amour naquit à Cythère." Regensburg: Keyser [1801]. 23 pp.
pf or hpsch
B: Bc. GB: Lbl (Hirsch III. 541). Copy in Ars Fem coll.
RISM A/I (T811), CPM, Eitner (Wagener collection), letter (Ars Fem).

Tomeoni, Mme (perhaps Irene Tomeoni)
?1763, Naples?–1830, Vienna
La Déclaration d'Amour. Barcarolle Venitienne à trois voix . . . Accomp. par Mr. Toméoni [Florido]. Paris: s.n. [1804?].[Tomeoni may have been her brother.]

3 voices / kbd
GB: Lbl [G.555.(30.)].
CPM.

Touch, Mrs.

pub. late 18th cent., Edinburgh
[Work(s)] in: *The Scots musical museum . . . of six hundred Scots songs with proper basses for the piano forte &c. . . .* the airs chiefly harmonized by S. Clarke.
Edinburgh: J. Johnson [1787–1803] 6 vol.
Probably melody only by Mrs. Touch
voice / pf
B: Bc. BR: Rn. C: SA. CH: Bu. EIR: Dn. GB: A, DU, En, Esl, Ge, Lbl, Lcm, Mp, P, WI. US: Cn, DE, HA, MI, Su, U, Wc, WI. Other holdings incomplete.
RISM B/II (p. 350).

Travanet (Travenet), B. de, Mme

pub. c. 1790–1800, Paris
Chanson patriotique ("Brave peuple quand tu flattais"). Air du Pauvre Jacques. 2 pp.
1. Paris: Frère [c. 1792]. 2. [Paris: Imbault, c. 1792].
voice / kbd
1–2. F: Pn 1 (B.N. [Vm7 16403]), (B.N. [Vmd 236 (33)]).
1–2. Paris Lib. Cat.

Couplets parodiés sur l'air Pauvre Jacques ("Pauvre peuple au mépris"). Paris: Frère [1795]. 2 pp.
voice / kbd
F: Pn (B.N. [Vm7 16450–16451]).
Paris Lib. Cat.

Le ramier. Paris: chez les marchands de musique, n.d.
voice / pf
F: V. Copy in Ars Fem coll.
RISM A/I (T 1094), letter (Ars Fem).

Le temps ("A voyager passant sa vie"). Paroles du Cn Segur cadet . . . Paris: Jean Henri Naderman (#577), [c. 1800]. 2 pp.
voice / pf
F: Pn (B.N. [Vma 100(8)], [Vm7 105827 (a–b)]). Copy in Ars Fem coll.
RISM A/I (T 1091), Paris Lib. Cat., letter (Ars Fem).

Premier [–Deuxième] *Recueil de romances et chansons av. acc. de fortep. ou de harpe.* Paroles et musique de la citoy. B. Travanet. Paris, chez les marchands de musique (Ier gravé par Michot, 2e gravé par Lohier) [c. 1798]. 11 pp.
voice/pf or harp
F: Pn (B.N. [Vmg 20473 (1–2)]).
Eitner, Paris Lib. Cat.

Romance ("Cruel amour je languis dans tes chaînes") . . . *accompt. de piano forte.* Paris: Jean Henri Naderman (#578) [c. 1800]. 2 pp.
voice/pf
F: Pn (2 ex.) (B.N. [Vm7 105826 (a–b)]). Copy in Ars Fem coll.
RISM A/I (T 1092), Paris Lib. Cat., letter (Ars Fem).

Romance de Malvina. Paris: Jean Henri Naderman (#565), n.d.
voice/pf
CH: Bchristen.
RISM A/I (T 1095).

Romance dédié au gros Louis cidevant Roi par Ladré ("Pauvre Sire, tu n'as plus de véto"). Air du Pauvre Jacques. 1. [Paris: Imbault, 1792]. 2 pp. 2. As "Pauvre Jacques." 1798? Ms. 3. As: Anony. "Pauvre Jaque quand je tois pres de toi—Pauvre Jaque when I was near to thee." New York/Philadelphia/Baltimore: B. & J. Carr [1796].
voice/kbd
1. F: Pn [B.N. [H2 158 (26)]. 2. US: PHf, PHu, Wc (M1.A11, vol. 26, no. 33). 3. US: NYp, NYsha, PHhs, PIlevy, Wmcdevitt, WOa. Copy of 1. F: Pn is in Ars Fem coll.
1. Paris Lib. Cat., letter (Ars Fem). 2. NUC (NT 0314359). 3. Sonneck.

Romance du Pauvre Jacques ("Pauvre Jacques quand j'étois près de toi") avec accompagne-ment de guittare. 1. [Paris]: les Godets frères. 2. as: *Pauvre Jaque* [*sic*]. In French and English. New York-Philadelphia: Benjamin Carr's musical repositories; Baltimore: Joseph Carr.
1. voice/guit; 2. voice/pf
1. F: Pn (B.N. [Vm Crlt 846 (233)]). 2. US: BAhs, CA, CHum, NYp (2 ex.), PHf, PHhs, PIlevy, WOa.
Paris Lib. Cat., RISM A/I (T 1093).

Tschiersky, Wilhelmine
pub. c. 1824, Mainz
Das kranke Landmädchen [song] . . . Guitarre Begleitung von C. Büttinger.

Mainz: B. Schott [1824?].
Melody only by Tschiersky
voice/guit
GB: Lbl [Hirsch M. 1300.(25.)].
CPM.

Das tanzlustige Mädchen [song]. . . . Guitarre Begleitung von C. Büttinger.
Mainz: B. Schott, [1824?].
Melody only by Tschiersky
voice/guit
GB: Lbl [Hirsch M. 1300.(26.)].
CPM.

Turner, Elizabeth
pub. 1750s–1780s, London
A collection of [19] *songs with symphonies and a thorough bass; with six lessons for the harpsichord.* 1. London: author [1756]. 32 + 42 pp. 2. [London]: The Author [1756?]. 32 pp. [Contains songs only. See also separate song titles.] [Some with unspecified instruments, some with flute.]
voice/bc (some with fl, some with other instruments)
1–2. GB: Ckc, Lbl (2 ex.) [H.1648.b.(4.)] & [G.424.uu.], Ob. 1. US: Cn (VM 1620 T945c). Copy of *6 Lessons* in C. Johnson coll.; of GB: Lbl in Ars Fem coll.
1–2. RISM A/I (T 1401), BUC, CPM. 1. NUC (NT 0393711). Cohen, letters (C. Johnson, Ars Fem).

"Drink to me only with thine eyes." Song (from: *A collection of* [19] *songs* . . . [No. 4]). In: *Lady's Magazine,* Dec. 1782. [London]: s.n., 1782.
voice/pf
GB: Lbl [P.P.5141]. US: PHu. Copy of GB: Lbl in Ars Fem coll.
RISM A/I (T 1405), BUC, CPM, letter (Ars Fem).

"Forgive, thou fairest of thy kind." To Celia. A new song. In: *The London Magazine,* Jan. 1750, p. 40.
song
GB: Lbl [157.1.12.]. US: SM. Copy of GB: Lbl in Ars Fem coll.
RISM A/I (T 1409), BUC, CPM, Cohen, letter (Ars Fem).

"The mind of bright Sukey's a jewel." A favourite song (from: *A collection of* [19] *songs* . . . [No. 19]). 1. In: *Lady's Magazine,* May 1783. [London]: s.n., 1783. 2. In: *The New Lady's Magazine,* vol. 3, pp. 200–02, 1788.

voice/pf
1. GB: Lbl [P.P.5141], US: PHu. Copy of GB: Lbl in Ars Fem. coll. 2. GB: Lbl [P.P.5141.b.].
1–2. RISM A/I (T 1408), BUC, CPM. Letter (Ars Fem).

"Not, Cloris, that I juster am." Song (from: *A collection of* [19] *songs . . .* [No. 3]). 1. In: *Lady's Magazine,* May 1784. [London: s.n. 1784]. 2. In: *Lady's Magazine,* 1796. Supplement.
voice/pf
1–2. GB: Lbl [P.P.5141]. US: PHu. 2. US: Pu. Copy of GB: Lbl in Ars Fem coll.
1–2. RISM A/I (T 1403, 1404). 1. BUC, CPM, letter (Ars Fem). 2. NUC (NT 0393712).

"Phyllis, with her enchanting voice." Song (from: *A collection of* [19] *songs . . .* [No. 6]). In: *Lady's Magazine,* Sept. 1795. [London]: s.n. 1795.
voice/pf
GB: Lbl [P.P.5141]. US: Pu, PHu. Copy in Ars Fem coll. (dated 1782).
RISM A/I (T 1406), BUC, CPM, NUC (NT 0393713), letter (Ars Fem).

"Say, curious painter, can thy art." Song (from: *A collection of* [19] *songs . . .* [No. 2]). In: *Lady's Magazine,* May 1788. London: s.n. 1788.
voice/pf
GB: Lbl [P.P.5141.]. US: PHu. Copy of GB: Lbl in Ars Fem coll.
RISM A/I (T 1402), BUC, CPM, letter (Ars Fem).

"Since my Chloe you ask." Song (from: *A collection of* [19] *songs . . .* [No. 8]). In: *Lady's Magazine,* January 1785. [London]: s.n. 1795.
voice/pf
GB: Lbl [P.P.5141.]. US: Pu. Copy of GB: Lbl in Ars Fem coll.
BUC, CPM, NUC (NT 0393714), letter (Ars Fem).

Twelve songs [actually 13] *with symphonies and a thorough bass for the harpsichord.* London: author [c. 1750]. 23 pp.
[#1, 2 with unspecified treble instruments and continuo, flute part on pp. 20–23].
voice/bc, 2 with treble instruments (fl)
GB: Ckc, Lam, Lbl [G.805.e.(4.)]. US: Cn (VM 1620 T 945a). Copy of US: Cn in Ars Fem coll.
RISM A/I (T 1400), BUC, CPM, NUC (NT 0393715), letter (Ars Fem).

Tytler, Mrs. Major

pub. c. 1796, Edinburgh

A collection of celebrated marches & quick steps for the pianoforte, flute, violin &c.
composed by . . . the Countess of Blacarras [*sic*], Mrs Major Tytler,
Muschett, Watlen &c. Edinburgh: J. Watlen [c. 1796].
pf/fl/vln etc.
GB: Gu.
BUC.

The Elgin Fencibles Grand March and Quick Steps. Set for the piano–forte,
violin, Ger. flute, clarionet . . . In: *A collection of celebrated Marches & Quick
Steps,* etc. [for Pianoforte] Edinburgh: J. Watlen [c. 1795].
pf/vln/fl/cl etc.
GB: Lbl [g.1780.q.(12.)].
CPM.

$\mathcal{V}$

V., Madame Elise
before 1800
Les Vétérans (Naguère en des tems de douleur), paroles de Mr. F. P.,
musique de Madme Elise V**. Paris: August Le Duc, n.d.
voice/pf or harp
CH: Bchristen.
RISM A/I (IN 267).

Valckiers, Josephine
n.d.
Quatre Romances avec Accompt. de Forte-Piano. Musique de Josephine Valckiers.
1er. Recueil. Paris: Aubert, n.d.
voice/pf
D: Rtt (Valckiers 1).
Letter (D: Rtt).

Valentine, Ann
c. 1762, Leicester–1842, Leicester
A Collect for the Sixth Sunday After Trinity. London/Dublin: Goulding,
D'Almaine, Potter & Co. [No title page. Publication information is transcription of drop title on p. 1. Bound together with other items of same
shelf number as part of a matched home library set belonging to Emma
Cope and Isaac Cope Fowke, Elmsthorpe, 1807–36. Words between staves
of keyboard part.]
voice/pf (or org.?)
US: BLl (M39.G47).
Mathiesen, letter (Lilly Library).

A favorite march & rondo for the Piano Forte. London: [1808].
pf
GB: Lbl [h.282.(1.)]. US: BLl (M25.D4 R4. Title page has autograph signature of composer).
CPM, Mathiesen, letter (Lilly Library).

A favorite slow Movement, And Rondo, for the Piano Forte. London/Dublin:
Goulding, D'Almaine, Potter & Co. [No title page. Publication information is transcription of drop title on p. 1. Bound together with other items
of same shelf number as part of a matched home library set belonging to
Emma Cope and Isaac Cope Fowke, Emsthorpe, 1807–36.]

pf
US: Bll (M39.G47).
Mathiesen, letter (Lilly Library).

The flight from Russia; a rondo for the piano-forte, with or without additional keys.
London: Goulding [181–]. 4 pp.
pf
US: Wc, BL1 (M39.G47, bound with other items of same shelf mark).
NUC (NV 0012638), Mathiesen.

Le Cheval De Course, A Favorite Divertimento for the Piano Forte.
London/Dublin: Goulding, D'Almaine, Potter & Co., n.d. [No title page.
Publication information is transcription of drop title on p. 1. Bound
together with other items of same shelf number as part of a matched home
library set belonging to Emma Cope and Isaac Cope Fowke, Elmsthorpe,
1807–36.]
pf
US: Bll (M39.G47).
Mathiesen letter. (Lilly Library).

Miss A. Valentine's sonatas [Violin part from Ten Sonatas], op. 1 [London:
1796?]. Parts.
pf or hspch/vln
US: Wc (vln only. M219.V155, op. 1).
*RISM A/I (V 37, part of V 35), NG (in John Valentine entry), NUC (NV
0012641), Mathiesen.*

Monny Musk [Scotch air], *arranged as a rondo for the piano-forte.* London:
Cahusac & sons, for the author [c. 1798]. 3 pp.
pf
GB: Lbl [g.140.(55.)]. US: Pu.
*RISM A/I (V 38), BUC, CPM, NUC (NV 0012639), NG (in John Valentine
entry), MGG (Robert Valentine family entry), Cohen.*

My Patie is a lover gay, an admired Scotch air, arranged as a rondo. London:
Goulding, D'Almaine, Potter & Co., n.d. 5 pp. (Bound with J. B. Cramer's
Instructions for the piano forte. London: s.n. [182–].)
pf
US: Bll (Lilly MT 225.08), and second copy bound separately.
NUC (NV 0012640), Mathiesen, letter. (Lilly Library).

Six sonatas [D, E-flat, F, A, D] *for the piano forte or harpsichord with an accompaniment for the violin or german-flute* . . . op. 1. London: Preston & son [c. 1795]. Parts. [Six of the *Ten sonatas* . . . , c. 1789, see following entry.]
pf or hpsch / vln or fl
GB: Lbl (pf, vln) [h.1613.t.(3.)]. Copy in Ars Fem coll.
RISM A / I (V 36, part of V35), CPM, NG (in John Valentine entry), letters (C. Johnson, Ars Fem).

Ten sonatas [D, E-flat, F, A, E-flat, G, B-flat, C, B-flat, E] *for the piano forte or harpsichord with an accompaniment for the violin or german-flute* . . . opera prima. London: printed for the author [by R. Wells, c. 1798]. Parts.
pf or hpsch / vln or fl
GB: Gu (incomplete), Lbl [g.161.f.(10.)], Ob (incomplete). US: NYp (pf only), Wc (vln only), BLl. Copies of GB: Lbl in C. Johnson coll. and Ars Fem coll.
RISM (V 35), BUC, CPM, NUC (NV 0012642), NG (John Valentine entry), MGG (Robert Valentine entry), Cohen, letters (C. Johnson, Ars Fem), Mathiesen, letter.(Lilly Library).

Three favorite waltzes composed & arranged for the piano-forte. London: William Maurice Cahusac, for the author [1805]. 3 pp.
pf / voice
GB: Lbl [h.282.(2.)]. US: Wsc. Copy of US: Wsc in Ars Fem coll, BLl (M1618.C3. Title page has autograph signature of composer).
RISM A / I (V 38), NUC (NV 0012643), CPM, letter (Ars Fem), Mathiesen.

Ye Gentlest Gales. Written by a Lady On the Death of Mr. Henry Kirk White. Composed & Arranged for the Piano Forte, by A. Valentine. London: Button, Whitaker, and Beadnell, n.d. [No title page. Publication information is transcription of drop title on p. 1. Bound together with other items of same shelf number as part of a matched home library set belonging to Emma Cope and Isaac Cope Fowke, Elmsthorpe, 1807–36.]
pf
US: BLl (M1503.H3 C7).
Mathiesen, letter (Lilly Library).

Valentine, Miss S[arah]

(after 1762, Leicester–fl. Leicester c. 1800–34)
The British March and Quick Step. Composed & arranged for the Piano Forte by Miss S. [or may be an ornate letter L.] Valentine. London/Dublin:

Goulding & Co., n.d. [Bound together with other items of same shelf number as part of a matched home library set belonging to Emma Cope and Isaac Cope Fowke, Elmsthorpe, 1807–36.]

pf

US: BLl (M39.G47).

Mathiesen, letter (Lilly Library).

Vannier, Mlle de

pub. c. 1762, Paris.

[Work(s)] in: *Récréations de Polimnie ou choix d'ariettes, monologues et airs tendres et légers avec accompagnment de violon, flûte, hautbois, pardessus de viole . . . aussi très bien à deux violons [etc] . . .* Paris, Leloup (de La Che-Vardière) [c. 1762]

8 vol.

voice/vln, fl, ob, or pardessus, etc.; also for 2 vlns, etc.

B: Bc (2, 8). CH: BEsu (3, 4). F: Pc (1), Pn (1). GB: Lbl (complete). US: Cn (incomplete).

RISM B/II (p. 299).

Viard, M[me de?]

pub. c. 1781, Paris

[Work(s)] in: *Recueil de romances, chansons et vaudeville arrangés pour la harpe . . .* Paris: Benaut [1781].

harp

F: Pc.

RISM B/II (M. de Viard, p. 333; considered same as Mme Viard in index).

[Work(s)] in: *Recueil de romances, chansons et vaudeville arrangés pour la guitarre, dédiés à la Reine par Tissier . . .* Paris: Benaut, n.d.

guit

F: Pc.

RISM B/II (p. 332).

Vidampierre, Comtesse de

pub. 1771–72, Paris

Le baiser. Ariette. In: *Mercure de France,* November 1772. Paris.

song

GB: Lbl [298.e.17]. Copy in Ars Fem coll.

BUC, CPM, Cohen, letter (Ars Fem).

Le regret. Ariette. In: *Mercure de France,* December 1772. Paris.

song

GB: Lbl [298.e.17]. Copy in Ars Fem coll.
BUC, CPM, Cohen, letter (Ars Fem).

L'heureuse securité [song]. In: *Mercure de France,* July 1771, and August 1772.
Paris.
song
GB: Lbl [298.e.6. & 298.e.15.]. Copy in Ars Fem coll.
BUC, CPM, Cohen, letter (Ars Fem).

Vielanda, Mengia, née Bisazia (Bisozia)
18th cent., Ticino, Switzerland
*Ovretta musicale chi consista in certas canzuns spirituales da diversa materia et in
diversas melodias, a glorificatiun dil Nom da Dieu.* Sun Componüdas da mia D.
Nezza Donna Mengia Vielanda nata Bisazia. 1. Scuol: J. N. Gadino,
1756). 2. Scuol: Jacob Nott. Gadina 1769.
Melodies only for 3 of 10 songs.
unacc. songs
1 & 2. US: I. 2. CH: Bu (kr VII122). GB: Lbl [885.d.27]. Photocopy of
CH: Bu. Copy in Jackson coll.
CPM, NUC (NV 0147224–5), Cohen.

Villard de Beaumesnil, Henriette. See Beaumesnil, Henriette-Adélaïde Villard de

Villeblanche, Mme de
d. before 1782 (at age 24), France
Quatre sonates [c, B-flat, C, D] *pour le piano-forte ou le clavecin.* Paris:
Desormery (gravées par Mme Brichet de St. Quentin) [after 1782]. 29 pp.
pf or hpsch
F: Pc (A.49173). Photocopy in C. Johnson coll.
RISM A/I (V1560), Paris Lib. Cat., letter (C. Johnson).

Vilm, Mlle de
pub. 1699, Paris
[2 airs] in: *Recueil d'airs sérieux et à boire de différents auteurs pour l'année 1699.*
Paris: C. Ballard, 1699.
songs
F: Pc, Pn.
RISM B/I (1699 [2]).

Virion, Mlle
fl. 1782, France
Sonate en simphonie [one movement]. In: Piesce [*sic*] de clavecin par
differens auteurs. Ms, 1782, copied by Ambroise Letendard, a student of
Balbastre.
hpsch
F: V (MS Mus 259).
Letter (C. Johnson).

Vizana, Lucretia Orsina (Vizani, Viziani, Vezzana, Lucrezia), Donna
c. 1593–1662. Active in Bologna.
[2 cantatas]. May be by this composer.
voice/bc
I: MOe (contained in Ms. group of 28 cantata volumes, under the name
Vezzani).
Eitner (as Vezzana, Lucrezia. Doubt about attribution of this item).

Componimenti musicali di Mottetti concertati à una et più voci. 1. Venice: Gardano,
1620 (but at end of Canto 1, dated 1623). 2. B. Magni, 1622. Note
"Dedic. Jesu Christo . . . 1 Dec. 1622, Bologna." 3 partbooks [S I, S II,
score].
SS/bc
PL: WRu (S I, score). I: Bc. (Kat. 2, 470 under Orsina). Copies of I: Bc in
US: WSwf and Ars Fem coll.
Bohn, Brenet, RISM A/I (V 2261), OCLC (micro.112484337), NG (as Orsina),
Bowers & Tick (as 1623), Eitner (2 entries, Vizana & Vezzana), letter (Ars Fem).

Volkonskaya (Volkonskaia), Zinaida (Zénéide) Alexandrovna, Princess (married to Prince Volkonsky)
1792, Turin–1862, Rome; Lived in St. Petersburg
Cantata à la mémoire d'Alexandre Premier. Carlsruhe: L. Geisendörfer [1865,
posthumous]. Score.
SSAATTBB/2 hns/2 vlas/2 vlcs
GB: Lbl (H.769.).
CPM, Cohen, letter (GB: Lbl).

Vuiet, Caroline. See Wuiet, Caroline

W

W., R. W., Miss
pub. c. 1820, London
The Rural Welcome to Box Hill ("Stranger whence so e'er you come"). [Glee]
London: s.n. [1820?].
voices
GB: Lbl [G.805.n.(31.)].
CPM.

Wainewright, Charlotte
pub. c. 1800, London
Three sonatas [B-flat, C, A] *for the harpsichord* . . . op. 1 London: author
[1800]. 19 pp.
hpsch
GB: Lbl [h.60.f.(1.)].
RISM A/I (W 62), CPM.

Wainewright (Wainwright), Harriet, née **Stewart**
c. 1780–c. 1840, England
A collection of songs, duetts, trios and chorus. Contents: "Crazy Jane," "Father
Dennis," "Conny bonny Kate of the West," "The season comes when first
we met," Rondo [Amiam o bella Iola], "To the snow drop," Hymn to
Hope, "The water King." London: s.n., c. 1810.
1–3 voices, chorus/pf
GB: Lbl [H.90.a.].
CPM, Eitner, Cohen, letter (GB: Lbl).

Comàla, a dramatic poem from Ossian. London. [Opera] perf. January
1792. [4 soloists, chorus of Bards (SSATB), 4 solo Bards (SSTB), & orch (2
fls/2 obs/bsn/2 hns/2 trs/timp/strings/hpsch)]. London: William Napier
for the Author [1803]. Score, 3 vols.
stage work
GB: Lbl (2 ex.) [H.90.] & [R.M.13.c.1.].
CPM (work spelled as Cornàla), Eitner, Cohen, letter (GB: Lbl).

Crazy Jane ("Why fair maid") [song]. London: s.n. [1822?].
voice/pf
GB: Lbl [H.2832.o.(73.)].
CPM.

Critical Remarks on the Art of Singing. London: Brown & Stratton, 1836.
instruction (voice)
GB: Lbl [797.dd.14].
CPM, letter (GB: Lbl), Cohen.

"Merrily, merrily passes the day" [glee for 3 voices and chorus]. London:
A Walker [1834].
voices/chorus
GB: Lbl [H.1683.(92.)].
CPM, Eitner, Cohen, letter (GB: Lbl).

"Oppression dies." Chorus on the taking of Seringapatam. London:
[1805]. Score. Text by Mason [orch: 2 fls/2 obs/bsn/2 hns/2
trs/strings/timp].
SATB/orch
GB: Lbl [I.345.].
CPM, letter (Lbl).

Walpurgis, Maria Antonia. See **Maria Antonia Walpurgis,
Princess of Bavaria, Electress of Saxony**

Walstein, Miss
pub. c. 1805, London
Forbear, fond youth, [song] . . . arranged with an accompaniment for the
Piano Forte by T. Cooke. London: [1805?].
Melody only by Walstein
voice/pf
GB: Lbl [H.1276.(7.)].
CPM.

Weichsell, Elizabeth. See **Billington, Elizabeth** née **Weichsell**

Weir, Mary (Maria), née **Brinckley (Brinkley) (Weir, Mrs. M.)**
1783–1840, New York
The Lord of the Castle; a favorite song composed and arr. for the piano forte
by Mrs. M. Weir. 1. New York: Author [182–?]. 2 pp. 2. New York: Firth
& Hall [c. 1832]. 2 pp. (#46 in a volume with binder's title, Music [col-
lected by] Mary J. S. Shorter.)
voice/pf
1. US: NYp, WOa. 2. US: DM.
1. Wolfe (9726). 2. NUC (NW 0163842). Cohen.

Westenholz, Elenore Sophia Maria, née **Fritscher**
1759, Neubrandenburg–1838, Ludwigslust
Das Glück der Liebe. #92 in ms., c. 1825. Text by Kosegarten.
voice/guit
D: EU (Mh 54).
RISM A/II (#89371).

Der Bund (text by Matthisson). [Song with soprano and string quartet.]
Ms. [Later appeared for voice and pf as #12 in: *Zwölf Deutsche Lieder mit Begleitung des Piano-Forte.*]
S/2 vlns/vla/b (vlc)
B: Bc.
Eitner, NG.

[11 Lieder]. Ms.
voice/pf
B: Bc.
Eitner, NG.

Gesänge [from *Wilhelm Tell*]. Leipzig: s.n., 1807 [attr. doubtful, NG].
voice/pf
D: SWl.
NG.

"Liebe, nur Liebe erwärmet das Herz" [Lied]. Ms. Oct. 16, 1811.
voice/pf
D: SWl.
NG, MGG.

[1 aria with obbligato fl]. Ms. c. 1800
voice/fl/orch
B: Bc.
Eitner, NG.

Rondo [B-flat] *pour le piano-forte* . . . œuvre 1. Berlin: Rudolph Werckmeister (#114), 1806.
pf
A: M, Wgm. B: Bc. CS: K. D: GOl. I: OS (Ediz. musiche. B-460).
RISM A/I (W 949), Eitner, NG, MGG, Cohen (as Rondo alla polacca), Ostiglia.

[Sonata for harpsichord or pf]. Ms.
hpsch or pf
D: SWl.
NG.

Sonate [F] *à quatre mains pour le piano-forte* . . . œuv. 3. Berlin: Rudolph
Werckmeister (#147), 1806.
pf (4 hands)
A: Wgm. B: Bc. D: GOl, SWl. Copy in Jackson coll.
RISM A/I (W 951), Eitner, NG.

Thème [A] *avec X* [actually XII variation] *pour le piano-forte* . . . œuvre II.
Berlin: Rudolph Werckmeister (#115), 1806.
pf
A: M, Wgm. B: Bc. D: GOl, Hs, WRtl. Copy in Jackson coll.
RISM A/I (W 950), Eitner, NG.

[2 Arias]. Ms. score.
voice/orch
B: Bc (Mss. 388/9).
Eitner, Cohen, NG.

[2 Choruses]. Ms. c. 1800
choir
B: Bc.
NG.

[2 sonatas for pf]. Ms.
pf
B: Bc.
Eitner, NG.

[2 Songs]. Ms. c. 1800.
voice/pf
B: Bc.
NG.

"Wie sie so sanft" [arr. of work by F. B. Beneken]. Ms., c. 1800.
4 voices (SATB)
B: Bc.
NG.

Zwölf Deutsche Lieder mit Begleitung des Piano-Forte . . . 4tes Werk. Berlin: Rudolph Werckmeister (No. 152), 1806.
voice/pf
B: Bc. D: GOl, WRtl. Copy in Jackson coll.
RISM A/I (W 952), Eitner, NG.

Weyrauch, Anna Julie von (Anne de Weyrauch)
6 danses pour le Pianoforte. Dresden: Weinholds Söhne, n.d. [May have been composed jointly with Sophie Auguste von Weyrauch.]
pf
Formerly D: Dlb. No longer extant.
Eitner, Cohen, letter (D: Dlb).

Weyrauch, Sophie Auguste von
fl. 1794, German
Differentes danses dont la dernière tirée de l'opéra De [sic] *Freischütz, pour le Pianoforte.* Dresden: Söhne [after 1821].
pf
Formerly D: Dlb. No longer extant.
Eitner, Cohen, letter (D: Dlb).

6 danses pour le Pianoforte. Dresden: Weinholds Söhne, n.d. [May have been composed jointly with Anna Julie von Weyrauch.]
pf
Formerly D: Dlb. No longer extant.
Eitner, Cohen, letter (D: Dlb).

Weyrauch, Sophie Auguste von & Weyrauch, Anne Julie von
fl. 1794, German
Nouvelles danses pour le Pianoforte, liv. II.
pf (4 hand & 3 hand)
D: Königl. Hausbibl. im Schlosse zu Berlin (Eitner). Modern location not confirmed.
Eitner, Cohen.

W[hite], E. C. C., Mrs.
pub. 1826, London
A Constitutional Portuguese Air; with Variations for the Piano Forte . . . London: s.n. [1826].
pf
GB: Lbl [h.125.(1.)].
CPM.

White, Maria (Mrs., of Leeds)
pub. c. 1820–40, London & York
The Favorite Irish Air, Savournah Deelish . . . with variations for the Piano forte.
London: For the Author by Mayhew [1823]. 9 pp.
pf
GB: Lbl [h.725.r.(24.)].
CPM.

The Favorite Scotch Air, We're a'noddin, the variations for the Piano forte
composed . . . by Mrs. White, of Leeds. 1. York: Knapton, White &
Knapton [c. 1820]. 2. [Reissue]. London: J. Alfred Novello [c. 1840].
pf
GB: Lbl 1. [h.726.d.(2.)], 2. (h.723.tt.(13.)].
CPM.

Wilbraham, Mrs.
pub. c. 1795, Westminster
A favourite anthem as performed in Westminster Abbey . . . Opera Ist. Anthem I
from the 108 Psalm: Andante "O God my heart is ready," Larghetto
"Awake my Lute and Harp," Vivace "For thy mercies are greater than the
Heavens." Westminster: Rock (#27) [c.1795].
*voice(S)/treble instrument in cues with voice part/bc (written out right hand in larghetto
section)*
GB: Lbl [G.423.(3.)]. Microfilm in Jackson coll.; copy in Ars Fem coll.
RISM A/I (W 1064), BUC, CPM (date 1785?), letter (Ars Fem).

Wilhelmine Sophie Friedericke, Margravine of Brandenburg-Culbach & Bayreuth, née Princess of Prussia
1709, Berlin–1758, Bayreuth
Argenore. [Opera, Trauer-Spiel.] Perf. 1740. Ms. score. Libretto by G. A.
Galletti.
stage work
D: ANs. Libretto at D: ERu (R. L. 57a).
Mellen.

Concerto à Cembalo obl. [3 movements, G minor]. Ms. score.
hpsch/fl/2 vlns/vla/vlc/b
D: W.
Eitner (as Friederike Wilhelmine Sophie, Markgräfin . . .), Cohen.

L'huomo [opera]. Resta teatrale per Musica e Balli composta in francese
. . . in versi italiani dal Sgr. Luiggi Stampiglia, Poeta della Corte. Ms.
Score and partbooks.
stage work
D: W (Ms. 65/66).
Eitner (as Friederike Wilhelmine Sophie, Markgräfin . . .), Cohen (6 arias from
L'huomo).

20 [Tyve] *lege for börn.* Let arrangrede for piano med tekst ved Wilhelmine.
Christiania (Oslo): C. Warmuth [18—]. 22 pp.
voice/pf
US: BO.
NUC (NNW 0307599).

Williams, Laetitia
pub. c. 1800–04, London
Allons danser sur la fougère. An old French air with variations . . . [for]
Pianoforte. London: E. Riley [c.1800].
pf
GB: Lbl [h.3870.bb.(3.)].
CPM.

The Question from Anacreon ("Behold the teeming earth") [song]. London:
s.n. [1802].
song
GB: Lbl [G.799.(23.)].
CPM.

The snow-drop [song]. London: s.n. [1804].
song
GB: Lbl [H.1688.(27.)].
CPM.

Willson, Mrs. Hill
pub. c. 1830, London
"There was once a golden Time." Ballad. London: I. Willis [1830?].
song
GB: Lbl [H.1654.x.(23.)].
CPM.

Withington, J., Miss

pub. c. 1828, Manchester

A new set of quadrilles for the Piano Forte or Harp. Manchester: s.n. [1828?].

pf or harp

GB: Lbl [h.125.(36.)].

CPM.

Woldersleben, Juliane Charlotte

fl. 1792, German

Die Umstimmung der Misstöne des widrigen Schiksals der leidenden Juliane Charlotte Woldersleben in XVI Gesängen am Piano Forte von ihr selbst in Music gesezt. s.l., s.n. [Gotha, 1792 (Eitner)].

voice/pf

CS: K. D: BNms, Mbs, RH. Copy of CS: K in Ars Fem coll.

RISM A/I (W 1773), Eitner, Cohen, letter (Ars Fem).

Wolf, [L.], née Mrasek, Mme

pub. 1804, VIenna

Thema avec Variations arangé pour Clavecin & Guitarre, dedie a Mme Jacobine de Schoeps. Vienna: T. Mollo (#1652) [1804].

pf/guit

A: Sca (#20678).

Salzburg.

Wolf, Maria Carolina, née Benda

1742, Potsdam–1820, Weimar?

An die Rose ("Herrlichste der "Frühlingesrosen"). In: *Der Teutsche Merkur,* 1779, ed. Wieland. Weimar: 1779.

voice/pf

D: DÜk (#1511).

Düsseldorf-Goethe, NG (Benda family).

Die Rose ("Rose, komm!") In: *Der Teutsche Merkur,* 1779, ed. Wieland. Weimar: 1779.

voice/pf

D: DÜk (#1512).

Düsseldorf-Goethe, NG (Benda family).

"Glänzender sinket die Sonne." Lied. In: *Der Teutsche Merkur,* 1785, ed. Wieland. Weimar: 1785.

voice/pf

D: DÜk.
Düsseldorf-Goethe, NG (Benda family).

Work[s] in: *Melodien zu dem Mildheimischen Liederbuche für das Clavier oder Pianoforte.* Neue vollständige Ausgabe. Gotha: in der Beckerschen Buchhandlung, 1817. [Printed on two staves, words between staves; neither index nor title page specify which of the over 700 songs are by Wolf.]
S/clavichord or pf
NL: At (205–H–30).
Cohen, NG (Benda family), letter (NL: At).

Wolff, Mrs.

pub. c. 1817, London
The Chieftan. A favorite air composed by Mrs. Wolff with variations for the pianoforte by J. Relfe. London: s.n., [1819?].
Melody only by Mrs. Wolff
pf
GB: Lbl [h.122.(7.)].
CPM.

Worgan, Mary

pub. c. 1745–50, London
The Constant Lover [song]. [London: s.n., c. 1745 or 1750?].
song
GB: Lbl [G.316.a.(58.)]. Copy in Ars Fem coll.
BUC, CPM, Cohen, letter (Ars Fem).

The Dying Nightingale. [London]: Printed for J. Simpson [c. 1745 or 1750?].
song
GB: Lbl [H.1994.b.(89.)]. Copy in Ars Fem coll.
BUC, CPM, Cohen, letter (Ars Fem).

The Power of Gold, a new song [London: s.n., c.1750?].
song
GB: Lbl [G.316.a.(57.)]. Copy in Ars Fem coll.
BUC, CPM, Cohen, letter (Ars Fem).

Worgan, (Mary?), Miss

pub. 1739, London
[Work(s)] in: *Calliope, or English harmony. A collection of the most celebrated English and Scots songs . . .* London: H. Roberts, 1739. 2 vols.

song(s)
GB: Ckc. US: BU, CAh. Other library holdings incomplete.
RISM B/II (p. 119).

Wrangel, Hedda

pub. 1828, Stockholm
Tre sanger utur Frithofs saga [3 songs from *Frithof's saga*] [Stockholm: s.n.,1828]. 7 pp.
songs
GB: Lbl [E.1601.dd.(5.)].
CPM.

Wrighten, Mrs. See Pownall, Mary Ann, née Wrighten

Wuiet (Wulet, Vuyet, Vuiet), Caroline (married Aufdiener or Auffdiener. Pseud. Donna Elidora)

1766, Ramboillet–1835, Paris
Finale [of first act] *De La Caravane* [from *Caire* of Grétry] . . . *arrangée pour le clavecin où le Forte-Piano avec Accompagnement de Violon* [par Melle Caroline Vuiet]. Paris: Mmes Le Menu & Boyer [1784]. Parts.
pf/vln
F: Pn (2 ex.) (Vm7 5815 & K.8387). Photocopy in C. Johnson coll.
Letter (C. Johnson).

Ouverture de l'Amore soldato [by Sacchini] . . . *arrangée pour le piano-forte avec un violon obligé* par Melle Caroline Vuiet. Paris: Mmes Le Menu & Boyer [1779 or 1786]. Parts.
pf/vln
F: Pc (K.8384). Photocopy in C. Johnson coll.
RISM A/I (V 2568, as Vuiet, Caroline), Paris Lib. Cat., letter (C. Johnson).

Ouverture de l'Heureux stratagême, opéra-comique [by Jadin] . . . *arrangée par l'auteur pour le piano-forte avec accompagnement de violon ad libitum.* Paris: Boyer/Mme Le Menu [1786]. Parts.
pf/vln ad lib
F: Pn (pf, vln) (as Vuiet, Caroline. Vm12 653). Photocopy in C. collection.
RISM A/I (V 2568, as Vuiet, Caroline), Paris Lib. Cat., letter (C. Johnson).

Ouverture du Mari indolent del Sig[no]*r Anfossi* . . . *arrangée pour le piano-forte avec un violon ad libitum* [par Melle Caroline Vuiet]. Paris: Mmes Le Menu & Boyer/Leduc, n.d. Parts.

pf/vln ad lib
F: Pn (Vm7 5842). Photocopy in C. Johnson coll.
Letter (C. Johnson).

Pot-pourri pour clavecin ou le forte Piano, op. 2. Paris: Boyer/Aux Adresse Ordinaire de Musique [1792].
hpsch or pf
F: Pn (Ac.p.306). Photocopy in C. Johnson collection.
RISM A/I (A 2852, Aufdiener), Cohen, letter (C. Johnson).

Rondeau de Giardini. In: *Journal de clavecin par les meilleurs maîtres*, 2me année, #8 (August 1783), pp. 62–63. Paris: LeDuc, 1783.
hpsch
F: Pn (Vm7 L.280).
RISM B/II (pp. 205–207), letter (C. Johnson).

[Work(s)] in: *Chansons nouvelles de M. de Piis* . . . dédiées à Monseigneur Comte d'Artois. Paris: Ph. D. Pierres, 1785.
song(s)
D: Cl. F: CH, Pn, V. US: NYp.
RISM B/II (Melle. Vuïet, p. 128).

[Work(s)] in: *Etrennes de Polymnie. Recueil de chansons, romances, vaudevilles* . . . Paris: au bureaude la petite bibliothèque des théatres, Belin, 1785–89.
5 vol.
song(s)
D: LEm. F: Ma, Pcf, Pn, V. US: Wc. Other library holdings are incomplete runs.
RISM B/II (C. Wuyet, p. 168).

Würtemberska (Würtemberskiéj, Würtemberskiey), Maria (Marie), née Czartoryska, Duchess

?, Poland–1854, Paris
Stefan Potocki Spiew historyczny ("Słuchajcie rycérze młodzi"). In: Julian Ursyn Niemczewicz, *Śpiewy historyczne*. Warsaw: 1816, 1818.
voice/pf
F: Pn. PL: Kc, Wn, Wmickiewicz. Copies of both of the editions in PL: Kc in Jackson coll.
Letter (Poniatowska), Sowinski, Cohen.

Wynyard, Mrs. Montagu
pub. c. 1816
A Favorite Waltz . . . by Mrs. M. Wynyard, arranged with variations for the Piano forte [by Charles Stokes]. S.l.: s.n. [1816].
pf
GB: Lbl [h.725.n.(6.)].
CPM.

$\mathcal{Y}$

Young, Anne (married **Gunn**)
pub. 1780–1810, Edinburgh
Elements of Music and of Fingering the Harpsichord, to which is added a collection of
airs & lessons for the harpsichord or piano-forte . . . and one or more minuets in each of
them . . . for the use of beginners. 1. Edinburgh: Muir Wood & Co., [c. 1810].
2. Edinburgh: Corri & Sutherland [c. 1780].
instruction with examples, hpsch or pf
1–2. GB: Lbl. 2. GB: Gu, P.
1–2. CPM (under composer's name and under title). 2. RISM B/II (p. 165).

Instructions for playing the musical games; invented by Anne Young. Edinburgh:
Printed by C. Stewart 1801 [bound with: Nelson, *A Poem,* 1814].
instruction
US: NH.
NUC (NY 0023890).

Zamoyska, Countess Sophie (Zofia), née Princess Czartoryska (Z. z X. C. Zamojskiéj, Zamoyskiey)

1779, Poland–1837, Florence

Jan Zamojski [Spiew o Janie Zamoyskimin]. In: Julian Ursyn Niemczewicz, *Śpiewy historyczne*. Warsaw: 1816, 1818.

voice/pf

D: Mbs. F: Pn. PL: Kc, Wn, Wmickiewicz. Copies of both of the editions in PL: Kc in Jackson coll.

Eitner, letter (Poniatowska), Sowinski, Cohen.

Zampieri, Elisabetta (Elizabetta)

b. Venice, fl. 1815

Variazioni per Forte-Piano dedicate a sua eccelenza Contessa Catterina de Bruce. Milan: Ricordi (#134), n.d. 11 pp.

pf

I: OS [Ediz. MUSICHE–C–537].

Ostiglia, Cohen.

Zepharovics, Teresa Maria

pub. c. 1795, Vienna

VI ariette italiane con accompagnemento di piano forte. Opera 1. Vienna: Giovanni Schäfer [c. 1795]. 10 pp.

voice/pf

GB: Lbl [E.724.k.(10.)].

CPM.

Zumsteeg, Emilie

1796, Stuttgart–1857, Stuttgart

Alpenlied [for male chorus]. #113 in: *Orpheus,* Band 3, pp. 56–57. Leipzig: [18—?].

male chorus

US: Bp (#113 in **M.1292.43.3).

NUC (NZ 0067135).

5 Lieder mit Begleitung des Guitarre in Musik gesetzt von Emilie Zumsteeg. Cologne/Bonn: Simrock (#1404), n.d.

voice/guit

D: Mbs (Mus. pr. 2/1054, xerokopie 2/1054a).

Letter (D: Mbs), MacAuslan.

Gut Nacht, fahr' wol. [Song with pianoforte, also with guitar.] Stuttgart:
G. A. Zumsteeg (#14), n.d. 3 pp. Text by von Chezy, German and
English.
voice/pf, also guit
D: Mbs (4 Mus.pr. 22585).
Letter (D: Mbs), NG (entry on J. R. Zumsteeg), Cohen.

Schillers "Lied an Emma." Musik von Emilie Zumsteeg. Ms., c. 1835.
3 voices
SF: A (Sammlung Clas Collan).
RISM A/II (#98362).

Ulrich in Exile [song]. Symphonies and accompaniments by J. J. Haite. Eng.
& Ger. London: Augener (Germania #76) [1889].
voice/pf
GB: Lbl [H.2128.].
CPM.

Appendix 1: Key to Collections Sigla, Terms, and Abbreviations

Collections Sigla

These abbreviations for libraries use the Répertoire International des Sources Musicales (RISM) sigla. Some additional libraries and collections have been given sigla which conform to the RISM system, with capital letters showing the city or town (in the spelling of its country) and the lowercase letters showing the library, institution, or collection. The assistance of the RISM office in Frankfurt has been invaluable in updating German library status, locations, and current sigla. For libraries that have merged or changed location, both the old and new locations are shown in this list wherever possible, although the references in the text are to the last known location. Private collections listed in Wolfe and Sonneck (see bibliography) or by RISM are shown with RISM or RISM-style sigla. Most private collections are not staffed for public access.

There are listings from some private working collections of currently active scholars, performers, and publishers. They are listed in a separate section at the end of this list and do not have sigla. They are not open to public use.

A: Austria

GÖ	Furth bei Göttweig, Benediktinerstift
K	Klagenfurt, Landesarchiv
KR	Kremsmünster, Benediktinerstift
L	Lilienfeld Zisterzienser-Stift, Musikarchiv und Bibliothek
M	Melk an der Donau, Benediktinerstift
RB	Reichersberg, Stift Reichersberg
Sca	Salzburg, Museum Carolino Augusteum
Sn	Salzburg, Nonnberg, Benediktiner-Frauenstift

SEI	Seitenstetten, Benediktinerstift
Wgm	Vienna, Gesellschaft der Musikfreunde
Wmg	Vienna, Pfarre, Maria am Gestade
Wn	Vienna, Österreichische Nationalbibliothek, Musiksammlung
Wst	Vienna, Stadtbibliothek, Musiksammlung

AUS: Australia

CNnl	Canberra, National Library of Australia
Sma	Sydney, Museum of Applied Arts & Sciences (See also Uma)
Uma	Ultimo, Museum of Applied Arts & Sciences

B: Belgium

Bc	Brussels, Conservatoire Royal de Musique
Br	Brussels, Bibliothéque Royale Albert Iᵉʳ/Koninklijke Bibliotheek Albert I
Gc	Ghent, Koninklijk Muziekconservatorium
Gu	Ghent, Bibliotheek van de Universiteit (Rijksuniversiteit, Centrale Bibliotheek)
Lc	Liège, Conservatoire Royal de Musique

BR: Brazil

Rn	Rio de Janeiro, Biblioteca Nacional

C: Canada

Lu	London, University of Western Ontario, Lawson Memorial Library
Qul	Quebec, Université Laval
SAu	Sackville, Mt. Allison University
Tp	Toronto, Toronto Public Library, Music Branch

CH: Switzerland

AR	Arenenberg, Napoleonmuseum
Bchristen	Basle, Werner Christen, *private collection* (RISM)
Bu	Basle, Öffentliche Bibliothek der Universität, Musiksammlung
BEsu	Berne, Stadt- und Universitätsbibliothek; Bürgerbibliothek
E	Einsiedeln, Benediktinerkloster
Fcl	Fribourg, Bibliothèque du Clergé
Gpu	Geneva, Bibliothèque Publique et Universitaire

LAc	Lausanne, Bibliothèque du Conservatoire de Musique
LAcu	Lausanne, Bibliothèque Cantonale et Universitaire
MO	Morges, Bibliothèque de la Ville
N	Neuchâtel, Bibliothèque de la Ville
Zs	Zurich, Bibliothek des Musikwissenschaftlichen Seminars der Universität
Zz	Zurich, Zentralbibliothek

CS: Czechoslovakia

(old boundaries)

Bm	Brno, Ústav Dějin Hudby Moravského Musea, Hubedněhistorické Odděleni
Bu	Brno, Státni Vědecká Knihovna, Universitni Knihovna
BER	Beroun, Okresni archiv v Beroune
K	Český Krumlov, Pracoviště Státniho Archivu Třeboň, Hudebni Sbírka; Krumlov, Zámecky hudebni archiv (Archives of the Chateau)
LIT	Litoměřice, Státni oblastní, archiv v Litomoricích
Pnm	Prague, Národni Muzeum, Hudebni Odděleni (Department of Music of the National Museum)
Pu	Prague, Státni Knihovna ČSSR, Universitni Knihovna

D: Germany

(Sigla for unified Germany as of March 1992)

As	Augsburg, Staats- und Stadtbibliothek (formerly Kreis- und Stadtbibliothek)
Au	Augsburg, Universitätsbibliothek (now has collection formerly at D: HR)
AAst	Aachen, Stadtbibliothe
AD	Adolfseck bei Fulda, Schloß Fasanerie, Bibliothek der Kurhessischen Hausstiftung
AN	Ansbach, Regierungsbibliothek (formerly Kgl. Schloßbibliothek, D: ANs)
ANs	See AN
B	Berlin, Staatsbibliothek Preußischer Kulturbesitz, Musikabteilung (with the collection from D: Bmfu [formerly D: Bmi] and also collections formerly in Marburg and Tübingen)
Bds	Berlin, Deutsche Staatsbibliothek, Musikabteilung (formerly Kgl. Bibliothek; Preußische Staatsbibliothek, Öffentliche Wissenschaftliche Bibliothek)

Bhm	Berlin, Staatliche Hochschule für Musik und Darstellende Kunst (formerly Kgl. Akademische Hochschule für Musik)
Bmfu	Berlin, Musikwissenschaftliches Institut der Freien Universität, Bibliothek (formerly Sektion Ästhetik und Kunstwissenschaften der Humboldt-Universität: D-brd: Bmi. Taken over by D: B, see entry above)
BE	Bad Berleburg (Wittgensteiner Land), Fürstlich Sayn-Wittgenstein-Berleburgsche Bibliothek
BFb	Burgsteinfurt, Fürstlich Bentheimsche Bibliothek (on loan to D: MÜu, see entry below)
BIR	Birstein über Wächtersbach, Fürst von Ysenburgisches Archiv und Schloßbibliothek
B-MG	Marburg, Westdeutsche Bibliothek (collection from the former Preußische Staatsbibliothek)
BNba	Bonn, Beethoven-Haus und Wissenschaftliches Beethoven-Archiv
BNms	Bonn, Musikwissenschaftliches Seminar der Universität
BNu	Bonn, Üniversitätsbibliothek
BOl	Bollstedt/Thüringia, Bibliothek
BÜ	Büdingen (Hessen), Fürstlich Ysenburg- und Büdingisches Archiv und Schloßbibliothek
Cl	Coburg, Landesbibliothek (with the collection from D: Cm, see entry below)
Cm	Coburg, Moritzkirche, Pfarrbibliothek (taken over by D: Cl, see entry above)
CEbm	Celle, Bomann-Museum
CO	Corvey, Fürstlich Ratiborsche Bibliothek
Dhm	Dresden, Hochschule für Musik Carl Maria von Weber (formerly Kgl. Konservatorium), Bibliothek
Dl	Dresden, Sächsische Landesbibliothek, Musikabteilung (former siglum, D: Dlb. With collections from D: Zi, D: Dkh, and much of the old collection of D: Dmb, D: Ell, and Löbau, whose former siglum was D: Dl)
Dlb	See Dl. [Entries in the *Guide* use the old form, D: Dlb]
DEl	Dessau, Stadtbibliothek (with Außenstelle Schloß Mosigkau; formerly Landesbibliothek Sachsen-Anhalt)
DEsa	Dessau, Stadtarchiv
DGs	Duisburg, Stadtbücherei
DO	Donaueschingen, Fürstlich Fürstenbergische Hofbibliothek, *private collection (RISM)*
DS	Darmstadt, Hessische Landes- und Hochschulbibliothek,

	Musikabteilung (formerly Großherzoglich Hessische Hofmusikbibliothek; Großherzoglich Hessissche Hof- und Landesbibliothek)
DÜfrauenmusik	Düsseldorf, Frauenmusikarchiv (now at D: UNikb, see entry below)
DÜk	Düsseldorf, Goethe-Museum (Anton-und-Katharina-Kippenberg-Stiftung)
EIl	Eisenach, Landeskirchenrat, Bibliothek (much of collection now at D: Dl, see entry above)
ERu	Erlangen, Universitätsbibliothek
EU	Eutin, Kreisbibliothek (formerly Großherzogliche Öffenliche Bibliothek; Eutiner Landesbibliothek)
F	Frankfurt am Main, Stadt- und Universitätsbibliothek, Musik- und Theaterabteilung (with the collection from D: Fsm, see entry below)
Fsm	Frankfurt am Main, Bibliothek für Neuere Sprachen und Musik (formerly Carl von Rothschildsche Öffentliche Bibliothek, now taken over by D: F, see entry above)
FRIts (FRI)	Friedberg im Hessen, Bibliothek des Theologischen Seminars der Evangelischen Kirche in Hessen und Nassau (old siglum D: FRI)
FUl	Fulda, Hessische Landesbibliothek
Gs	Göttingen, Niedersächsische Staats- und Universitätsbibliothek
GOl	Gotha, Forschungsbibliothek (formerly Landesbibliothek)
Hmb	Hamburg, Hamburger Öffentlichen Bücherhallen, Musikbibliothek
Hs	Hamburg, Staats- und Universitätsbibliothek Carl von Ossietzky, Musikabteilung
HAf	Halle an der Saale, Hauptbibliothek und Archiv der Franckesche Stiftungen (taken over by D: HAu, see entry below)
HAu	Halle an der Saale, Martin-Luther-Universität, Universität- und Landesbibliothek, Fachreferat Musik (with the collection from D: HAf, see entry above)
HEu	Heidelberg, Universitätsbibliothek
HR	Harburg über Donauwörth, Fürstlich Öttingen-Wallerstein'sche Bibliothek, Schloß Harburg (collection now in D: Au, see entry above)
HRD	Herdringen bei Arnsberg, Schloß Herdringen, Bibliotheca Fürstenbergiana (with some prints from D: PA)

HSk	Helmstedt, Kantorat St. Stephani, Bibliothek (taken over by D: W, see entry below)
HVk	Hanover, Arbeitsstelle für Gottesdienst und Kirchenmusik (formerly Kirchenmusikschule) der Evangelisch-Lutherischen Landeskirche Hannover
HVl	Hanover, Niedersächsische Landesbibliothek
HVs	Hanover, Stadtbibliothek
Ju	Jena, Friedrich-Schiller-Universität, Universitätsbibliothek
Kf&m	Kassel, Frau und Musik Internationaler Arbeitskreis e. V. Archiv
Kl	Kassel, Landesbibliothek und Murhardsche Bibliothek der Stadt Kassel
KA	Karlsruhe, Badische Landesbibliothek, Musikabteilung
KIl	Kiel, Schleswig-Holsteinische Landesbibliothek (with the collection from D: NM, see entry below)
KMr	Kamenz, Ratsbibliothek (now in the Stadtarchiv, D: KMs, see entry below)
KMs	Kamenz, Stadtarchiv
KNh	Cologne, Staatliche Hochschule für Musik (formerly Conservatorium der Musik, D: KNm), Bibliothek
KNmi	Cologne, Musikwissenschaftliches Institut der Universität
Lr	Lüneburg, Ratsbücherei und Stadtarchiv der Stadt Lüneburg, Musikabteilung
LCH	Lich (Kreis Giessen), Fürstlich Solms-Lich'sche Bibliothek, *private collection* (RISM)
LEb	Leipzig, Bach-Archiv (with the collection from LEt)
LEm	Leipzig, Musikbibliothek der Stadt Leipzig (Musikbibliothek Peters and various collections of the Leipziger Stadtbibliothek)
LEt	Leipzig, Thomasschule Bibliothek (taken over by Bach-Archiv, LEb, see entry above)
LO	Loccum über Wunstorf (Niedersachsen), Klosterbibliothek
LÜh	Lübeck, Bibliothek der Hansestadt Lübeck (formerly Stadtbibliothek der Freien und Hansestadt Lübeck), Musikabteilung
Mbs	Munich, Bayerische Staatsbibliothek (formerly Kgl. Hof- und Staatsbibliothek), Musikabteilung
Mm	Munich, Bibliothek St. Michael (formerly Michaelskirche, D: Mmk)
Mth	Munich, Theatermuseum der Clara-Ziegler-Stiftung, Bibliothek

MB	Marbach am Neckar, Schiller-Nationalmuseum, Deutsches Literaturearchiv, Musikaliensammlung
MÜms	Münster, Musikwissenschaftliches Seminar der WestfälischenWilhelms-Universität (with the collection from D: MÜs, now in D: MÜu)
MÜp	Münster, Diözesanbibliothek, Bischöfliches Priesterseminar und Santini-Sammlung (with the collection from D: MÜs)
MÜs	Münster, Santini-Sammlung (now in D: MÜp)
MÜu	Münster, Universitätsbibliothek (with the collection from D: MÜms)
MZfederhofer	Mainz, Prof. Dr. Hellmut Federhofer, *private collection* (RISM)
Ngm	Nuremberg, Germanisches National-Museum, Bibliothek
Nla	Nuremberg, Bibliothek beim Landeskirchlichen Archiv (with the collection from D: WE)
NEhz	Neuenstein (Kreis Öhringen, Baden-Württemberg), Hohenlohe-Zentralarchiv
NM	Neumünster (Schleswig-Holstein), Schleswig-Holsteinische Musiksammlung der Stadt Neumünster (collection now in D: KIl)
OF	Offenbach am Mainz, Verlagsarchiv André
PA	Paderborn, Erzbischöfliche Akademische Bibliothek (some single prints are now in collection of D: HRD)
PRE	Preetz, Predigerseminar der Evangelisch-Lutherischen Landeskirche Schleswig-Holsteins, Bibliothek
Rp	Regensburg, Bischöfliche Zentralbibliothek, Proske-Bibliothek
Rs	Regensburg, Staatliche Bibliothek (formerly Kreisbibliothek)
Rtt	Regensburg, Fürstlich Thurn und Taxis Hofbibliothek
RH	Rheda, Fürst zu Bentheim-Tecklenburgische Bibliothek (on loan to D: MÜu, see entry above)
ROu	Rostock, Wilhelm-Pieck-Universität, Universitätsbibliothek
Sl	Stuttgart, Württembergische Landesbibliothek (formerly Kgl. Hofbibliothek)
SAh	Saalfeld (Saale), Heimatmuseum
SPlb	Speyer, Pfälzische Landesbibliothek, Musikabteilung
SWl	Schwerin, Wissenshaftliche Allgemeinbibliothek (formerly Mecklenbürgische Landesbibliothek) (with the collection of D: SWs)
SWs	Schwerin, Stadt- und Bezirksbibliothek, Musikabteilung (collection now in D: SWl)
Tu	Tübingen, Eberhard-Karls-Universität, Universitätsbibliothek

UNikb	Unna, Internationale Komponistinnen-Bibliothek, affiliated with the Music Academy Detmold (formerly Frauenmusik Archiv, D: DÜfrauenmusik, merged with the private collection of Elke Masche Blankenburg)
W	Wolfenbüttel (Niedersachsen), Herzog-August-Bibliothek, Musikabteilungen (with the collection from D: HSk)
WE	Weiden (Oberpfalz), Pfannenstiel'sche Bibliothek, Evangelische-Lutherisches Pfarramt (taken over by D: Nla, see entry above)
WGp	Wittenberg, Evangelisches Predigerseminar, Bibliothek
WIbh	Wiesbaden, Breitkopf & Härtel, Verlagsarchiv
WINtj	Winhöring über Müldorf (Inn), Gräflich Toerring-Jettenbachsche Bibliothek
WRdn	Weimar, Deutsches Nationaltheater (formerly Großherzogliches Hoftheater), Archiv
WRgs	Weimar, Goethe-Schiller-Archiv
WRh	Weimar, Hochschule für Musik "Franz Liszt", Zweigbibliothek "Am Palais"
WRl	Weimar, Staatsarchiv (formerly Landeshauptarchiv)
WRtl	Weimar, Thüringische Landesbibliothek (formerly Großherzogliche Bibliothek), Musiksammlung (taken over by WRz)
WRz	Weimar, Zentralbibliothek der deutschen Klassik (with the collection from WRtl)
WÜu	Würzburg, Julius-Maximilians-Universität, Universitätsbibliothek
Z	Zwickau, Ratsschulbibliothek
ZI	Zittau, Stadt- und Kreisbibliothek "Christian-Weise-Bibliothek" (Exner collection from this library now in D: Dl, see entry above)
ZW	Zweibrücken (Rheinland-Pfalz), Bibliotheca Bipontina, Wissenschaftliche Bibliothek am Herzog-Wolfgang-Gymnasium

DK: Denmark

Kc	Copenhagen, Carl Claudius Musikhistoriske Samling
Kk	Copenhagen, Det Kongelige Bibliotek
Ku	Copenhagen, Universitetsbiblioteket 1. Afdeling
Kv	Copenhagen, Københavns Universitet, Musikvidenskabeligt Institut
Ou	Odense, Universitetsbibliotek

E: Spain

Mn	Madrid, Biblioteca Nacional
Mp	Madrid, Palacio Real (Royal Library)

EIRE: Ireland

Dn	Dublin, National Library and Museum of Ireland

F: France

AG	Agen, Archives Départementales de Lot-et-Garonne
AI	Albi, Bibliothèque Municipale
AM	Amiens, Bibliothèque Municipale
AS	Arras, Bibliothèque Municipale
B	Besançon, Bibliothèque Municipale
BO	Bordeaux, Bibliothèque Municipale
CF	Clermont-Ferrand, Bibliothèque Municipale et Universitaire, Section Centrale et Section Lettres
CH	Chantilly, Musée Condé
CN	Caen, Bibliothèque Municipale
D	Dijon, Bibliothèque du Conservatoire
DO	Dôle, Bibliothèque Municipale
Mc	Marseilles, Bibliothèque du Conservatoire de Musique et de Déclamation
Nm	Nantes, Bibliothèque Municipale
Pa	Paris, Bibliothèque de l'Arsenal
Pc	Paris, Conservatoire National de Musique (collection in F: Pn, see entry below)
Pcf	Paris, Comédie-Française Bibliothèque
Pi	Paris, Bibliothèque de l'Institut
Pm	Paris, Bibliothèque Mazarine
Pn	Paris, Bibliothèque Nationale
Po	Paris, Bibliothèque-Musée de l'Opéra
Ppo	Paris, Bibliothèque Polonaise de Paris (Biblioteka Polska)
Psg	Paris, Bibliothèque Sainte-Geneviève
R(m)	Rouen, Bibliothèque Municipale
RS	Rheims, Bibliothèque Municipale
Sim	Strasbourg, Institut de Musicologie de l'Université
Sn	Strasbourg, Bibliothèque Nationale et Universitaire
Tc (T)	Troyes, Bibliothèque Municipale
TLc	Toulouse, Bibliothèque du Conservatoire

TLm	Toulouse, Bibliothèque Municipale
V	Versailles, Bibliothèque Municipale
VN	Verdun, Bibliothèque Municipale

GB: Great Britain

A	Aberdeen, University Library, King's College
AB	Aberystwyth, National Library of Wales
Bp	Birmingham, Public Libraries
Bu	Birmingham, University of Birmingham, Barber Institute of Fine Arts
BA	Bath, Municipal Library
Ccc	Cambridge, Corpus Christi College
Cfm	Cambridge, Fitzwilliam Museum
Ckc	Cambridge, Rowe Music Library, King's College
Cpl	Cambridge, Pendlebury Library of Music
Cu	Cambridge, University Library
Cus	Cambridge, Cambridge Union Society
CDp	Cardiff, Public Libraries, Central Library
DRc	Durham, Cathedral
DU	Dundee, Public Libraries
En	Edinburgh, National Library of Scotland
Ep	Edinburgh, Public Library, Central Public Library
Er	Edinburgh, Reid Music Library of the University of Edinburgh
Es	Edinburgh, Signet Library (also found as GB: Esl)
Ge	Glasgow, Euing Music Library
Gm	Glasgow, Mitchell Library
Gtc	Glasgow, Trinity College
Gu	Glasgow, University Library
HAdolmetsch	Haslemere, Carl Dolmesch, *private collection* (RISM)
KNt	Knutsford, Tatton Park (National Trust)
Lam	London, Royal Academy of Music
Lbl	London, British Library (formerly British Museum, GB: Lbm)
Lcs	London, Vaughan Williams Memorial Library (Cecil Sharp Library)
Lgc	London, Gresham College (Guildhall Library)
Lk	London, King's Music Library (in GB: Lbl, see entry above)
LEp	Leeds, Public Library
LVp	Liverpool, Public Library

Mch	Manchester, Chetham's Library
Mp	Manchester, Central Public Library, Henry Watson Music Library
Ob	Oxford, Bodleian Library
Obharding	Oxford, Bodleian, Harding Collection
Och	Oxford, Christ Church
P	Perth, Sandeman Music Library
T	Tenbury, St. Michael's College
WI	Wigan, Public Library

H: Hungary

Ba	Budapest, Magyar Tudományos Akadémia Régi Könyvek Tára és Kézirattár
Bn	Budapest, Országos Széchényi Könyvtára
KE	Keszthely, Orzágos Széchényi Könyvtár Helikon Könyvtára (Helikon Kastélymüzeum)

I: Italy

Baf	Bologna, Accademia Filarmonica
Bc	Bologna, Civico Museo Bibliografico Musicale
Bl	Bologna, Conservatorio di Musica G. B. Martini
Bsp	Bologna, Basilica di S Petronio
BAn	Bari, Biblioteca Nazionale Sagarriga Visconti-Volpi
BGc	Bergamo, Biblioteca Civica Angelo Mai
BGi	Bergamo, Civico Istituto Musicale Gaetano Donizetti
CE	Cesena, (specific library not given in RISM B/II citation)
CEc	Cesena, Biblioteca Comunale Malatestiana
Fc	Florence, Conservatorio di Musica Luigi Cherubini
Fn	Florence, Biblioteca Nazionale Centrale
Gi(l)	Genoa, Conservatorio di Musica Nicolò Paganini
Ls	Lucca, Seminario Vescovile
Ma	Milan, Biblioteca Ambrosiana
Mc	Milan, Conservatorio de Musica Giuseppe Verdi
Mdemicheli	Milan, Demicheli, *private collection* (RISM)
MAC	Macerata, Biblioteca Comunale Mozzi-Bortgetti
MO(MOe)	Modena, Biblioteca Estense
N-Faoli	Naples, Feoli Cesare
Nc	Naples, Conservatorio di Musica S Pietro e Majella
N	Biblioteca Provinciale Francescana Naples, Convento S. Chiara (no microfilm or Xerox possible)

OS	Ostiglia, Fondazione Greggiati, Biblioteca Musicale; Biblioteca Comunale
PAbs	Parma, Biblioteca Suddetta
PAc	Parma, Conservatorio di Musica Arrigo Boito
PC	Piacenza, (specific library not given in RISM B/II citation)
PESd	Pesaro, Duomo
Raf	Rome, Accademia Filarmonica Romana
Rc	Rome, Biblioteca Casanatense
Rli	Rome, Accademia Nazionale dei Lincei e Corsiniana
Rsc	Rome, Conservatorio di Musica S Cecilia
Rvat	Rome, Biblioteca Apostolica Vaticana
Rvat(s)	Rome, Biblioteca Apostolica Vaticana, Sistine
TLP	Torre de Lago Puccini, Museo di Casa Puccini
TRa	Trent, Archivo di Stato
Vc	Venice, Conservatorio di Musica Benedetto Marcello
Vlevi	Venice, Fondazione Ugo Levy, *private collection* (RISM)
Vnm	Venice, Biblioteca Nazionale Marciana
VEaf	Verona, Accademia Filarmonica

M: Mexico

Min	Mexico City, Instituto Nacional de Bellas Artes

N: Norway

Ou	Oslo, Universitetsbiblioteket

NL: The Netherlands

Aomb	Amsterdam, Openbare Muziekbibliotheek
At	Amsterdam, Toonkunst Bibliotheek
Au	Amsterdam, Universiteitsbibliotheek
DHgm	The Hague, Gemeente Museum
DHk	The Hague, Koninklijke Bibliotheek
Lu	Leiden, Bibliotheek der Rijksuniversiteit
Uim	Utrecht, Instituut voor Muziekwetenschap der Rijksuniversiteit

NZ: New Zealand

Ap	Auckland, Public Library

P: Portugal

Ln	Lisbon, Biblioteca Nacional

PL: Poland

GD	Gdańsk, Bibliooteka Gdańska Polskiej Akademii Nauk
Kc	Kraków, Muzeum Narodowe, Biblioteka Czartoryskich
Kj	Kraków, Biblioteka Jagiellońska
LA	Lańcut, Muzeum
LZu	Lódz, Biblioteka Uniwersytecka
S	Szczecin (Stettin), Wojewódzka i Miyska Biblioteka Publiczna, Biblioteka Glówna im. St. Staszica
Wmickiewicz	Warsaw, A. Mickiewicz Museum
Wn	Warsaw, Biblioteka Narodowa (National Library)
WRu	Wroclaw, Biblioteka Uniwersytecka

S: Sweden

L	Lund, Universitetsbiblioteket
LI	Linköping, Stifts- och Landsbiblioteket
Sdt	Stockholm, Drottningholms Teatermuseum
Sk	Stockholm, Kungliga Biblioteket
Skma	Stockholm, Kungliga Musikaliska Akademiens Bibliotek
Sm	Stockholm, Musikmuseet
St	Stockholm, Kungliga Teaterns Biblioteket
SK (SKa)	Skara, Stifts- och Landsbiblioteket
STr (ST)	Strängnäs, Roggebiblioteket
Uu	Uppsala, Universitetsbiblioteket
VS	Växjö, Landsbiblioteket

SF: Finland

A	Turku [Åbo], Sibelius Museum Musikvetenskapliga Institutionen vid Åbo Akademi, Bibliotek & Arkiv (also as SF: T)
H	Helsinki, Yliopiston Kirjasto (Helsinki University Library) (also as SF: Hy)
T	Turku (see SF: A, see entry above)

US: United States of America

A	See entry AB below
AA	Ann Arbor, Mich., University of Michigan Music Library

AAclements	Ann Arbor, Mich., Clements, *private collection* (RISM)
AB	Albany, N.Y., New York State Library (some references as US: A)
AUS	Austin, Tex., University of Texas
Ba	Boston, Mass., Boston Athenaeum Library
Bh	Boston, Mass., Harvard Musical Association Library
Bhs	Boston, Mass., Massachusetts Historical Society
Bp	Boston, Mass., Public Library, Music Department
BAhs	Baltimore, Md., Maryland Historical Society
BAjh	Baltimore, Md., Johns Hopkins University Libraries
BE	Berkeley, Calif., University of California Libraries
BIu	University of Alabama at Birmingham
BER	Berea, Ohio, Ritter Library, Baldwin Wallace College
BIu	University of Alabama at Birmingham
BLl	Bloomington, Ind., Indiana University, Lilly Library
BLu	Bloomington, Ind., Indiana University, School of Music Library
BO	Boulder, Colo., University of Colorado Music Library
BU	Buffalo, N.Y., Buffalo and Erie County Public Library
BUg	Buffalo, N.Y., Buffalo and Erie County Public Library, Grosvenor Reference Division
Chs	Chicago, Ill., Chicago Historical Society Library
Cn	Chicago, Ill., Newberry Library
Cu	Chicago, Ill., University of Chicago Library
CA	Cambridge, Mass., Harvard University Music Libraries
CAa (CAahtl)	Cambridge, Mass., Andover-Harvard Theological Library
CAc	Cambridge, Mass., Harvard College Library
CAdriscoll	Cambridge, Mass., J. Francis Driscoll (deceased), *private collection* (Sonneck, Wolfe)
CAe	Cambridge, Mass., Eda Kuhn Loeb Music Library, Harvard University
CAh	Cambridge, Mass., Houghton Library, Harvard
CAi	Cambridge, Mass., Isham Memorial Library, Department of Music, Harvard
CH	Charlottesville, Va., University of Virginia Libraries
CHua	Charlottesville, Va., University of Virginia, Alderman Library
CHum	Charlottesville, Va., University of Virginia Music Library
CHAu	Charlotte, N.C., University of North Carolina at Charlotte Library
CHARhs	Charleston, S.C., South Carolina Historical Society
CHARhughes	Charleston, S.C., Josephine L. Hughes, *private collection* (Sonneck, Wolfe)

CHH	Chapel Hill, N.C., University of North Carolina Music Library
CIu	Cincinnati, Ohio, University of Cincinnati College-Conservatory of Music
CLp	Cleveland, Ohio, Public Library, Fine Arts Department
CLAc	Claremont, Calif., Claremont College
COu	Columbus, Ohio, Ohio State University Music Library
DE	Denver, Colo., Public Library, Art and Music Division
DM	Durham, N.C., Duke University Libraries
DN	Denton, Tex., North Texas State University Library
ECstarr	Eastchester, N.Y., Dr. Saul Starr, *private collection* (RISM)
ERac	Erie, Pa., Alliance College. No longer in existence. Current location of materials from this collection not known.
FA	Fayetteville, Ark., University of Arkansas Mullins Library, Special Collections
FWw	Fort Worth, Tex., Texas Wesleyan College Library
FRE	Fremont, Ohio, Hayes Library
G	Gainesville, Fla., University of Florida Library
Hm	Hartford, Conn., Case Memorial Library, Hartford Seminary Foundation
HA	Hanover, N.H., Dartmouth College, Baker Library
HP	Hyde Park, N.Y., Franklin D. Roosevelt Memorial Library, National Archives and Records Service, GSA
I	Ithaca, N.Y., Cornell University Library
IO	Iowa City, Iowa, University of Iowa Music Library
K	Kent State, Ohio, Kent State University Library
KIu	Kingston, R.I., University of Rhode Island
Lu	Lawrence, Kans., University of Kansas Libraries
LAu	Los Angeles, Calif., Walter H. Rubsamen Music Library, University of California at Los Angeles
LAuc	Los Angeles, Calif., William Andrews Clark Memorial Library, University of California at Los Angeles
LOu	Louisville, Ky., University of Louisville
MAu	Madison, Wisc., University of Wisconsin
MAN	Mankato State University, Mankato, Minn.
MI	Middletown, Conn., Wesleyan University, Olin Memorial Library
MID	Middlebury College, Middlebury, Vt.
MSu	Minneapolis, Minn., University of Minnesota Music Library
MV	Mount Vernon, Va., Mt. Vernon Ladies Association of the Union Collection
MOSu	Moscow, Idaho, University of Idaho

Nf	Northampton, Mass., Forbes Library
Nsc	Northampton, Mass., Smith College, Werner Josten Library
NH	New Haven, Conn., Yale University, School of Music Library
NYcu	New York, N.Y., Music Library, Columbia University
NYcuh	New York, N.Y., Music Library, Columbia University, Arthur Billings Hunt collection
NYfm	New York, N.Y., Grand Lodge of New York, F. & A. M. Library & Museum
NYfuld	New York, N.Y., James J. Fuld, *private collection* (RISM)
NYhs	New York, N.Y., New York Historical Society
NYlevy	New York, N.Y., Lester Levy, *private collection* (RISM)
NYp	New York, N.Y., New York Public Library at Lincoln Center
NYsha	New York, N.Y., Elliott Shapiro, *private collection* (Sonneck)
NYts	New York, N.Y., Union Theological Seminary Library
OB	Oberlin, Ohio, Oberlin College Conservatory of Music
Pu	Pittsburg, Pa., University of Pittsburgh, Theodore Finney Music Library
PHf	Philadelphia, Pa., Free Library of Philadelphia
PHfk	Philadelphia, Pa., Free Library of Philadelphia, Edward I. Keffer Collection
PHhs	Philadelphia, Pa., Historical Society of Pennsylvania
PHkm	Philadelphia, Pa., Lutheran Theological Seminary
PHlc	Philadelphia, Pa., Library Company of Philadelphia
PHps	Philadelphia, Pa., American Philosophical Society
PHtu	Philadelphia, Pa., Temple University
PHu	Philadelphia, Pa., University of Pennsylvania, Otto E. Albrecht Music Library
PIlevy	Pikesville, Md., Lester S. Levy, *private collection* (Sonneck, RISM)
PRts	Princeton, N.J., Speer Library, Princeton, Theological Seminary
PROu	Providence, R.I., Brown University Libraries
PROub	Providence, R.I., Brown University Libraries, John Carter Brown Library
R	Rochester, N.Y., University of Rochester, Eastman School of Music, Sibley Music Library
RIhs	Richmond, Va., Virginia Historical Society
Su	Seattle, Wash., University of Washington Music Library
SFbruning	San Francisco, Calif., Harry F. Bruning private collection (Sonneck)
SM	San Marino, Calif., Henry E. Huntington Library and Art Gallery

STu	Stanford, Calif., Stanford University, Memorial Music Library
SY	Syracuse, N.Y., University Music Library and George Arents Research Library
TUua	Tuscaloosa, Ala., University of Alabama
U	Urbana, Ill., University of Illinois Music Library
Wc	Washington, D.C., Library of Congress
Wmcdevitt	Washington, D.C., Josephine A. McDevitt and Edith A. Wright, *private collection* (Sonneck)
Ws	Washington, D.C., Folger Shakespeare Library
Wsc	Washington, D.C., Scottish Rite Masons, Supreme Council
WE	Wellesley, Mass., Wellesley College Library
WGc	Williamsburg, Va., William and Mary College
WGw	Williamsburg, Va., Colonial Williamsburg Research Department, historical collection
WI	Williamstown, Mass., Williams College, Chapin Library
WM	Waltham, Mass., Brendeis University Library, Music Library, Goldfarb Library
WOa	Worcester, Mass., American Antiquarian Society
WOh	Worcester, Mass., Holy Cross College
WSwf	Winston-Salem, N.C., Wake Forest University

USSR: formerly Union of Soviet Socialist Republics

(Locations use old RISM Sigla and show the name of the present country in the description)

KAu	Kaliningrad, Russia (formerly Königsberg, Prussia) Universitetskaya Biblioteka (formerly Kgl. & Uni.-Bibli., Königsberg)
Lsc	St. Petersburg, Russia (formerly Leningrad), Gosudarstvennaya Ordena Trudovovo Krasnovo Znameni Publichnaya Biblioteka imeni M. E. Saltïkova-Shcherina
Mcm	Moscow, Russia, Gosudarstvennyj central'nyj muzej muzykal'noj kul'tury im. M. I. Glinki
Mk	Moscow, Russia, Naučna a muzykal'naja biblioteka im. S. I. Taneeva, Gosudarstvennaja konservatorija im. P. I. Čajkovskogo
Ml	Moscow, Russia, Gosudarstvennaja biblioteka USSR im V. I. Lenina

YU: Yugoslavia

(old boundaries, locations, and sigla. Present status of materials unknown)
Dsmb   Dubrovnik, Franjevački Samostan Mala Braća
KLf   Klanjec, Franjevacki Samostan
Lu   Ljubljana, Narodne in Universitetne Knjižnica (National
                   and University Library)
NM   Novo Mesto, Knjižnica Frančiskanškega Samostana
Zha   Zagreb, Hrvatski Glazbeni Zavod

Some Private Working Collections of Scholars, Performers, and Publishers (not open to public)

Winnipeg, Canada, Ursula Rempel *private collection* (harp emphasis)
Cincinnati, Ohio, Annie Janeiro Randall *private collection* (Weimar emphasis)
Decatur, Ga., Calvert Johnson *private collection* (keyboard emphasis)
Fayetteville, Ark., Barbara Garvey Jackson *private collection* (basis for private research and ClarNan Editions publications; eventually to go to University of Arkansas Mullins Library, Special Collections)
Louisville, Ky., Ars Femina, *private collection* (basis for performances and publications of performing ensemble)

Reference Abbreviations

Bath Gillaspie, John. *The Catalogue of Music in the Bath Reference Library to 1985*. London: K. G. Saur, 1986.

Bates Bates, Carol Henry (later Neuls-Bates) "The Instrumental Music of Elisabeth-Claude Jacquet de la Guerre." Ph.D. diss., University of Michigan, 1978.

Bauldauf-Berdes Bauldauf-Berdes, Jane Louise. *Women Musicians of Venice: Musical Foundations, 1525–1855*. Oxford Monograph on Music. Oxford: Oxford University Press, Clarendon Press, 1993.

Berdes Berdes, Jane Louise Baldauf, ed. *Maddalena Laura Lombardini Sirmen, Three Violin Concertos. Recent Researches in the Music of the Classical Era*, vol. 38. Madison: A–R Editions, 1991.

Berkeley Emerson, John A. *Catalog of Pre-1900 Vocal Manuscripts in the Music Library of the University of California at Berkeley*. Berkeley: University of California Press [c. 1988].

Blechschmidt Blechschmidt, Eva Renate. *Die Amalien-Bibliothek: Musikbibliothek der Prinzessin Anna Amalia von Preußen (1623–1787). Historische Einordnung und Katalog mit Hinweisen auf die Schreiber der Handschriften*. Berliner Studien zur Musikwissenschaft #8. Berlin: Merseburger, 1965.

Block & Bates Block, Adrienne Fried, and Carol Neuls-Bates, eds. *Women in American Music: A Bibliography of Music and Literature.* Westport, Conn.: Greenwood Press, 1979.

Boenke Boenke, Heidi M., comp. *Flute Music by Women Composers: An Annotated Catalog.* Music Reference Collection, No. 16. New York/Westport, Conn./London: Greenwood Press, 1988.

Bohn Bohn, Emil. *Bibliographie der Musik-Druckwerke bis 1700 welche in der Stadtbibliothek, der Bibliothek des Academischen Instituts für Kirchenmusik, und der K. und Universitäts- Bibliothek zu Breslau aufbewahrtwerden.* Berlin: Albert Cohn, 1883. Reprint, Hildescheim: Olms, 1969.

Bonaventura Bonaventura, Arnaldo. "Le donne italiane e la musica," *Rivista Musicale Italiana,* XXXII/4 (1925): 519–34.

Bowers & Tick Bowers, Jane, and Judith Tick. *Women Making Music: The Western Art Tradition, 1150–1950.* Urbana: University of Illinois Press, 1986.

Borroff Borroff, Edith. *An Introduction to Elisabeth-Claude Jacquet de la Guerre,* Musicological Studies, vol. XII, Brooklyn N.Y.: Institute of Mediaeval Music, 1966.

Brenet Brenet, Michel [pseud. for Marie Bobillier]. "La musique dans les couvents de femmes," *La tribune de Saint-Gervais* (Bulletin Mensuel de la Schola Cantorum) IV (1898): 25, 58, 73.

Brit. Cat. Ms. *Catalogue of Music Manuscripts of the British Museum.* London: 1965.

BUC Schnapper, Edith B., ed. *British Union Catalogue of Early Music Printed Before the Year 1801: A record of the holdings of over one hundred libraries throughout the British Isles.* London: Butterworth's Scientific Publications, 1957.

Bullock Bullock, Helen Duprey. *My Head and My Heart: A Little History of Thomas Jefferson and Maria Cosway.* New York: Putnam, 1945.

Carruthers-Clement Carruthers-Clement, C. Ann. "The Madrigals and Motets of Vittoria/Raphaela Aleotti." Ph. D. diss., Kent State University (University Microfilms).

Carter Carter, Stewart Arlen. "The Music of Isabella Leonarda (1620–1704)." Ph. D. diss., Stanford University, 1981.

CarterAR Carter, Steward Arlen, ed. *Isabella Leonarda. Selected Compositions, Recent Researches in the Music of the Baroque,* vol. LIX. Madison: A–R Editions, 1988.

Citron Citron, Marcia J. "Corona Schröter: Singer, Composer, Actress." *Music & Letters* LXI (1980): 15–27.

Cohen Cohen, Aaron I. *International Encyclopedia of Women Composers,* 2d ed., 2 vols. New York/London: Books & Music USA, 1987.

Corsiniani *Roma. Biblioteca Corsiniani e dell'a Accademia Nazionale dei Lincei.*

Catalogo dei Fondi Musicali Chiti e Corsiniano. Milan: Istituto Editoriale Italiano, 1964.

CPM *Catalogue of Printed Music of the British Museum to 1980.* London: K. G. Saur, 1985.

Craw Craw, H. A. A. "Biography and Thematic Catalogue of the Works of J. L. Dussek (1760–1812)." Ph.D. diss., University of Southern California, 1964.

Cripe Cripe, Helen. *Thomas Jefferson and Music.* Charlottesville: University Press of Virginia, 1974.

De Jong De Jong, Carolyn (later Carolyn Britton). "The Life and Keyboard Works of Maria Theresia d'Agnesi." D.M.A. diss., University of Minnesota, 1979.

DM Archiv Heckmann, Harald, ed. *Deutches Musikgeschichtliches Archiv, Kassel. Mitteilungen und Katalogue der Filmsammlung,* Nr. 1. Kassel: Bärenreiter, 1955.

DTÖ Biber, H.F., *8 Violinsonaten,* edited by Guideo Adler, in *Denkmaler der Tonkunst in Österreich,* Jahrgang V/2. Vienna: Publiktionen der Gesellschaft zur Herausgabe der Denkmäler der Tonkunst in Osterriech, 1894.

D: UNikb Blankenburg, Elke Mascha, Mosei Boroda, and Robert Nemecek. *Katalog der Internationalen Komponistinnenbibliothek Unna: Noten/Literatur/Ton- und Bildträger.* Unna: Kulturamt der Stadt Unna, 1991.

Durham Crosby, Brian, comp. *Catalogue of Durham Cathedral Music Manuscripts,* Durham: Oxford Press for the Dean & Chapter of Durham, 1986.

Düsseldorf-Goethe Kippenberg, Anton. *Katalog der Sammlung Kippenberg [der Goethe-Museum, Düsseldorf].* Leipzig: Insel-Verlag, 1928.

Eitner Eitner, Robert. *Biographisch-bibliographisches Quellen-Lexikon der Musiker und Musikgelehrten der christlichen Zeitrechnung bis zur Mitte des neunzehnten Jahrhunderts.* Leipzig: 1900–1904; rev. 2d ed., Graz: Akademische Druck- und Verlagsanstalt, 1959–60, with supplement.

Estense *Catalogo delle opere musicali, città di Modena; Biblioteca Estense.* Bologna: Forni, 1923.

Fétis Fétis, F. J. *Biographie universelle des musiciens et bibliographie générale de la musique,* 2d ed. Paris: Firmin Didot Frères, 1866–1879.

Fontijn Fontijn, Claire A. "Antonia Bembo in Late 17th-Century France," unpublished paper, presented at the Festival of Women Composers, Indiana, Penn., March, 1993.

Frauenmusik Olivier, Antje. *Europäisches Frauenmusik Archiv: Komponistinnen: Eine Bestandsaufname.* Düsseldorf: Tokkata-Verlag für Frauenforschung, 1990.

Frau & Musik Oster, Martina, Christel Nies, & Roswitha Aulenkamp-Moeller. *Archiv Kassel: Noten 1990.* Frau und Musik Internationaler Arbeitskreis e. V., Schriftenreihe, Bd. 1. Kassel: Furore-Verlag, 1990 (with typed supplement).

Fremar Fremar, Karen Lynn. "The Life and Selected Works of Marianna Martines (1744–1812)." Ph.D. diss., University of Kansas, 1981 (University Microfilms).

Friedländer-Goethe Friedländer, Max. *Gedichte von Goethe in Compositionen seiner Zeitgenossen.* Weimar: Goethe-Gesellschaft, 1896–1916. Reprint. Hildescheim: Olms, 1975.

Friedländer-Lied Friedländer, Max. *Das Deutsche Lied.* Stuttgart: 1902. Reprint. Hildescheim: Olms, 1972.

Genova Pintacuda, S., ed. *Genova, Biblioteca dell'Istituto musicale N. Paganini: catalogo del fondo antico,* Bibliotheca musicae: collana di cataloghi e bibliographie, IV. Milan: 1966.

Gerber Gerber, Ernst Ludwig. *Historisch-biographishes Lexicon der Tonkünstler.* Leipzig: J. G. I. Breitkopf, 1790–92. Reprint, Graz: Akademische Druck, 1966, add. 1969.

GerberN Gerber, Ernst Ludwig. *Neues historisch-biographisches Lexikon der Tonkünstler.* Leipzig: A. Kühnel, 1812–14. Reprint, Graz: Akademische Druck, 1966, add. 1969.

Glickman Glickman, Sylvia, ed. *Maria Szymanowska: Music for Piano.* Bryn Mawr: Hildegard, 1991.

Göllner Gollner, Marie Louise, ed. *Bayerische Staatsbibliothek* [V/2]. *Katalog der musikhandschriften, Tabulaturen und Stimmbücher bis zur mitte des 17. Jahrhunderts.* Munich: Henle, 1979.

Gustafson Gustafson, Bruce. "The Music of Madame Brillon: A Unified Manuscript Collection from Benjamin Franklin's Circle," *Notes,* (March 1987): 522–543.

Hayes Hayes, Deborah. *Francesca LeBrun, Marie-Emmanuelle Bayon: Keyboard Sonatas.* Women Composers Series #23. N.Y.: Da Capo, 1990.

Haynes Haynes, Bruce. *Music for Oboe, 1650–1800: A Bibliography.* Berkeley: Fallen Leaf Press, Berkeley, Calif., 1985, 2d ed.,1992. Revision of *Music for Oboe to 1800* (interim edition), June 1982.

Huntington Backus, E. N., comp. *Catalogue of Music in the Huntington Library Printed Before 1801.* [San Marino, Calif.]: Huntington Library, 1949.

I: Vc Cat. Rossi, Franco. *I manoscritti del Fondo Torrefranco, Conservatorio Benedetto Marcello.* Florence: Olschki, 1986.

Jackson Jackson, Barbara Garvey. "Oratorios by Command of the Emperor: The Music of Camilla de Rossi," *Current Musicology,* XLII (1986): 7–19.

Johnson Johnson, Rose-Marie, comp. *Violin Music by Women Composers: A Bio-bibliographical Guide.* Music Reference Collection, No. 22. New York/Westport, Conn./London: Greenwood Press, 1989.

Kassel Archiv Heckmann, Harald, ed. *Deutches Musikgeschichtliches Archiv, Kassel,* Cat. nr. 3, bd, 3, nr. 3. Kassel: Bärenreiter, 1957.

Kerr Kerr, Jessica M. "Mary Harvey—the Lady Dering." *Music & Letters*, XXV/1 (January 1944): 23–33.

Komponistinnen Brand, Bettina, Martina Helmig, Barbara Kaiser, Birgit Salomon, and Adje Westerkamp, eds. *Komponistinnen in Berlin*. Berlin: Kulturelle Angelegenheiten der Hochschule der Künste Berlin, Sender Freies Berlin, Berliner Künstlerprogramm, 1987.

Königsberg Müller, Jos. *Die Musikalischen Schätze der Königlichen- und Universitätsbibliothek zu Königsbergin Preußen*. Bonn: Adolph Marcus, 1870. Reprint, Hildescheim/New York: Georg Olms, 1971.

Lucca *Lucca, Biblioteca dell Seminario*. Milan: Istituto Editoriale Italiano, 1965.

MacAuslan MacAuslan, Janna. *A Catalogue of Compositions for Guitar by Women Composers*. Portland, Ore.: Deer House Pub., n.d.

Mathiesen Mathiesen, Penelope. "Miss Valentine's Sonatas," *Continuo*, XVII/1 (February, 1993): 5–10.

Matsushita Matsushita, Hidemi. "The Musical Career and Compositions of Maria Theresia von Paradis (1759–1824)." Ph.D. diss., Brigham Young University, 1989. (University Microfilms).

Meggett Meggett, Joan M. *Keyboard Music by Women Composers: A Catalog and Bibliography*. Westport, Conn.: Greenwood Press, 1981.

Mellen Parsons, Charles H., comp. *The Mellen Opera Reference Index*. Lewiston, N.Y./Queenston, Ontario: The Edwin Mellen Press, 1986.

MGG Blume, Friedrich, ed. *Die Musik in Geschichte und Gegenwart*. 14 vols. Supplement, vols. 15–16. Register, vol. 17. Kassel: Bärenreiter, 1949–1968; suppl., 1973–1976; reg. 1986. Paperback edition, 1989.

Michaelskirche Herrmann-Schneider, Hildegard. *Die Musikhandschriften der St. Michaelskirche in München*. Kataloge Bayerischer Musiksammlungen, vol. 7. Munich: Henle, 1985.

NG Sadie, Stanley, ed. *The New Grove Dictionary of Music and Musicians*. 20 vols. London: Macmillan, 1980.

Northhampton Northhampton, Mass., Forbes Library. Card catalogue.

NTSU Lib. Cat. North Texas State University Library, Denton Tex. Card catalogue.

NUC (followed by identification number of work) *The National Union Catalog Pre-1956 Imprints* (and Supplement). Chicago, London: American Library Association, Mansell, 1967–1979. Suppl. 1980–.

OCLC (followed by identification number of work) OCLC International Library Computer Network.

Olivier Olivier, Antje, and Karin Weingartz-Perschel. *Komponistinnen von A–Z*. Düsseldorf: Tokkata-Verlag für Frauenforschung, 1988.

Ostiglia Sartori, Claudio, ed. *Biblioteca Musicae VII. Ostiglia. Biblioteca dell'*

Opera Pia Greggiati. Vol. I, Le Edizioni. Milan: Nuovo Istituto Editoriale Italiano, 1983.

Paris Lib. Cat. Lesure, François, ed. *Catalogue de la musique imprimée avant 1800 conservée dans les Bibliothèques Publiques de Paris.* Paris: Bibliothèque Nationale, 1981.

Parma Gasperini, Guido, and Nestore Pellicelli, comps. *Catalogo Generale della opere musicale, teoriche o pratiche, manoscritte o stampate, di autori vissuti sino al Primi Decenni del XIX Secolo Esistenti nelle Biblioteche e negli archivi d'Italia. Città di Parma.* Bologna: Forni, 1911.

ParmaBS *Catalogo Parma, Sezione Musicale della Biblioteca suddetta.*

Pazdírek Pazdírek, Franz (František), and Bohumil. *Universal-Handbuch der Musikliteratur.* Vienna: 1904–1910. Reprint, Hilversum: Frits Knuf, 1967.

Pescerelli Pescerelli, Beatrice. *I madrigali di Maddalena Casulana.* Florence: Olschki, 1979.

Regensburg Haberkamp, Gertraut. *Die Musikhandschriften der Fürst Thurn und Taxis Hofbibliothek Regensburg.* Munich: Henle, 1981.

Reich Reich, Nancy B. *Louise Reichardt: Songs.* Women Composers Series #7. New York: Da Capo, 1981.

Rempel Rempel, Ursula Mikulko. "A Critical Edition of British Library Additional Manuscript 49288: Fanny Krumpholtz's Manuscript Book of her Own Compositions for the Harp," M.A. thesis, University of California-Santa Barbara, 1979.

Riemann Riemann, Hugo. *Mannheimer Kammermusik des 18. Jahrhunderts,* II. Teil, vol. 28 (Jg. XVI), *Denkmäler der Tonkunst in Bayern.* Braunschweig: Litoloff, 1915, xl–xli.

RISM *Repertoire international des sources musicales.*

RISM A/I (followed by identification number of work) *Einzeldrucke vor 1800.* Kassel: Bärenreiter, 1971–. (Through XII, *Addenda e Corrigenda, G–L,* 1992.)

RISM A/II (followed by RISM number) Listings from the Zentralredaktion Databank, Frankfort, as processed to March 27, 1992.

RISM B/I (followed by year and number within year) *Recueils imprimés XVIe–XVIIe siécles: Liste chronologique.* Ed. François Lesure. Munich/Duisburg: Henle, 1960.

RISM B/II (followed by page number) *Recueils imprimés XVIIIe siécle* & Supplement. Ed. François Lesure. Munich/Duisburg: Henle, 1964. Supplement in *Notes,* xxviii (1971–1972): 397.

RISMdan *The Danish RISM Catalogue.* Ed. Nanna Schiødt. New York: Pendragon Press, 1977 [microfiche].

RISM-EICM *Écrits imprimés concernant la musique,* vols 1 & 2. Ed. François Lesure. Munich/Duisburg, G. Henle, 1971.

RISM-EK *Das Evangelisches Kirchenlied*. Ed. Konrad Ameln, Markus Jenny & Walther Lipphardt. Kassel/Basel/Tours/London: Bärenreiter, 1975.

Rollin Rollin, Monique and A. Souris, eds. *Oeuvres des Bocquet*. Paris: Editions du Centre Nationale de la Recherche Scientifique, 1972.

Rosand Rosand, Ellen. "Barbara Strozzi, *virtuosissima cantatrice*: "The Composer's Voice," *Journal of the American Musicological Society*, XXXI (1978): 241–81.

Salzburg Gassner, Joseph. *Die Musikaliensammlung im Salzburger Museum Carolino Augusteum*. Salzburg: [Museum],1962.

Scholes Scholes, Percy A. *The Great Dr. Burney*, vol. II. London: Oxford University Press, 1948.

Sesini Sesini, Ugo. *Catalogo della Biblioteca del Liceo Musicale di Bologna*, vol. 5. *Libretti d'opera in Musica*. Bologna: Cooperativa Typografica Azzoguidi, 1943.

Sonneck Sonneck, Oscar George Theodore. *A Bibliography of Early American Secular Music*. Revised and enlarged by William Treat Upton (first published 1905). Washington: Library of Congress, Music Division, 1945.

Sowinski Sowinski, Albert. *Les musiciens polonais et slaves: Dictionnaire biographique*. Paris: Libraire Adrien le Clere, 1857. Reprint, New York: Da Capo Press, 1971.

Stevenson Stevenson, R. *Renaissance and Baroque Musical Sources in the Americas*. Washington, D.C.: Organization of American States, 1970.

Stewart Green Stewart Green, Miriam. *Women Composers: A Checklist of Works for the Solo Voice*. Boston: G. K. Hall, 1980.

Tick Tick, Judith. *American Women Composers before 1870*. Ann Arbor: U.M.I. Research Press, 1983.

Ullrich Ullrich, Hermann. "Maria Theresia Paradis: Werkverzeichnis," *Beiträge zur Muzikwissenschaft*, V (1963): 117–54; "Nachtrag," VIII (1966): 253–55.

US: Wc Card cat. Library of Congress, Washington D.C. Card catalogue.

US: NYp Shelf List New York Public Library, Special Collections. Shelf list.

Wallon Wallon, Simone. "Les testaments d'Elisabeth Jacquet de la Guerre," *Revue de musicologie*, XL (December 1957): 206–14.

Winterfeld Winterfeld, Carl von. *Der evangelische Kirchengesang im siebzehnten Jahrhundert*. Leipzig: Breitkopf & Härtel, 1845.

Wolfe (followed by identifying number) Wolfe, Richard J. *Secular Music in America, 1801–1825: A Bibliography*. 3 vols. New York: The New York Public Library, Astor, Lenox and Tilden Foundations, 1964.

Wolfenbüttel *Katalogue der Herzog-August-Bibliothek Wolfenbüttel*. Die neue Reihe (Vol. 12 of *Musik alte Drucke bis etwa 1750*). Frankfurt am Main: Klostermann, 1967.

Wotquenne Wotquenne, Alfred. *Catalogue de la Bibliothèque du Conservatoire royal de musique de Bruxelles*. Brussels: Conservatoire royal de musique de Bruxelles, 1898–1912.

Wurzbach Wurzbach, Constant v. *Biographische Lexikon des Kaiserthums Österreich*. Vienna: Universitäts-Buchdr. von L. C. Zamarski, 1867. Reprint, N.Y.: Johnson, 1966.

Zahn Zahn, Johannes. *Die Melodien der deutschen evangelischen Kirchenlieder*. Gütersloh: 1889. Reprint, Hildescheim: Olms, 1963.

Terms, Abbreviations, and Performance Medium Designations

Instruments infrequently found in the works of women composers of the period covered, such as accordion, glass harmonica, viola da gamba, pardessus de viole, or violone are fully spelled out rather than abbreviated. Short instrument names such as harp or lute are also spelled out in full.

A	alto voice
acc.	accompaniment
ad lib	use of designated instrument optional
arr.	arranged, arrangement
B	bass voice
b	bass string instrument (usually cello) or bass line
bc	basso continuo
bsn	bassoon
C	cantus voice part (soprano)
c.	circa
cl	clarinet
clarino	clarino trumpet
copy	modern copy (such as microfilm, microfiche, photocopy, or ms. copy)
db	double bass
geb.	geboren; German indication of birth (maiden) name
ed.	edited, edition
ex	example (an original ms. or print held in a library or collection)
ff.	manuscript folios
fl	flute
fl picc	piccolo
guit	guitar
harp	harp
hn	horn

hpsch	harpsichord
inc	incomplete
instruction	pedagogical materials
kbd	keyboard, exact instrument not specified
lute	lute
mezzo-S	mezzo-soprano
n.d.	no date
née	French indication of birth (maiden) name. Used in this guide for all nationalities
ob	oboe
orch	orchestra
org	organ
pf	pianoforte
post.	posthumous
S	soprano voice
s.n.	sine nomine, without publisher's name
s.l.	sine locus, without place name
song	work for single voice, accompaniment not specified; sometimes melody only
stage work	opera or other stage work with music; instrumentation and number of singers not usually shown in this guide
str	stringed instrument or instruments
T	tenor voice
timp	timpani
trb	trombone
tr	trumpet
unacc.	unaccompanied
vla	viola
vlc	violoncello (cello)
vln	violin

Appendix 2: Composers for Whom No Surviving Music Has Been Located

$\mathcal{A}$

With Family Surname

Allegrante, Maddalena (fl. 1770–80s)
Angelini, Maria Victoria, Suor (Sister) (b. Rome, fl. 1670)
Aragona, Antonia of Naples (fl. 1545)
Archilei, Vittoria, née Concarini (1550–after 1618)
Archinta, Marguerite (c. 1520–?)
Auenheim, Marianne, née Aurnhammer [Auernhammer]
Augustenburg, Caroline Amelia (1792–1866). Consort of King Christian
  VIII of Denmark

Aristocratic, Religious, or Other Form of Name without Surname

Agata (fl. at the Pietà, Venice)
Amalia (Amalie) Juliane, Countess of Schwarzenberg (1637–1706)
Arcangela-Maria de Assunção (nun, b. Portugal, d. 1737)

$\mathcal{B}$

With Family Surname

Bachmann, Judith (late 18th cent., Vienese)
Baglioncella (Baglionella), Francesca (b. Perugia, 16th cent.)
Baroni, Eleanora (pseud. L'Adrianetta, 17th cent.)
Baroni-Basile, Adriana, née Basile (c. 1580–1640)
Barozzi-Beltrami, Eliza (18th cent.?)
Bartalotti, Signora (18th cent.)
Bassano, Mlle (17th cent.)

Baur, Constance Maude de (18th cent.)

Bayer, Karoline (1775, Vienna–1803, Vienna)

?Bel, Berthe . . . de (may be identical with Berthe (Biertha), née Offhuis, fl. 1775 in Liége)

Bergas, Marie (fl. 1720–1810)

Bernardi-Bellati, Eleonora (Lucca, 16th cent.)

Bertolajo-Cavaletti, Orsola (Ferrara, fl. 1611)

Birnie, Patie (Scotland, 1635–c. 1710)

Blewit, Gionata (Ireland, 1782–?)

Bolognese, Isabella (perhaps as Isabella, la Bolognese) (fl. 1645)

Borghi, Faustina (c. 1569)

Bovia, Laura (16th cent.)

Breinl, Anna (18th or 19th cent.?)

Broes, Mlle (b. Amsterdam,1791–d. Paris, ?)

Bruckenthal, Bertha von, Baronness (18th cent.)

C

With Family Surname

Cappello, Laura Beatrice (pub. in *La Ghirlanda della Contessa Angela Bianca Beccaria,* collected by Stefano Guazzi. Genoa: 1595)

Carafa, Livia (16th cent.)

Castro, Maria de (16th cent., Spanish, lived in Paris)

Cepparelli, Costanza, Suora (Sister) (17th cent.)

Clérembault, Mme (late 18th, early 19th cent., Paris)

Clifford, Anna (17th cent.)

Colonna, Vittoria (1490–1547)

Coltellani, Celeste (1764–1817)

Couperin, Louise (17th cent.)

Courmont, Countess von (Mme de Siesley) (18th cent.)

Aristocratic, Religious, or Other Form of Name without Surname

Caterina (niece of Willaert) (fl. 16th cent., surviving music?)

Constance of Austria, Queen of Poland (17th cent., surviving music?)

Cornelia la Morsia? (16th cent.)

D

With Family Surname

da Ponte, Vicenta (fl. at the Pietà, Venice)
Descarin, Sophie, and Caroline (18th cent., harpist-composers heard by Thomas Jefferson in Paris, 1789)
Deshayes, Thérèse, married Pouplinière (18th cent.)
Doni, Antonia (may be confused with Anton Doni, 18th cent.)
Dorn, Bertha (Frau Sobolewski) (fl. 1830s)
Dusckek, Josefina, née Hambacher (1754, Prague–1824, Prague)

Aristocratic, Religious, or Other Form of Name without Surname

Dorothea Sophia, Duchess of Parma (17th cent.)

E

With Family Surname

Enthaller, Sidonia (c. 1607–1676, Graz. Dominican nun, organist)
Escamilla, Manuela de (d. 1695. Spanish [Galician])
Esprit, Charlotte (pseud. of Fanny Krumpholtz, according to Cohen, but may be separate individual)
l'Etoile, Mme de (b. Rouen, fl. 1770s)

F

With Family Surname

Ferra, Susana (fl. 1545, Ferrara)
Ferrieres, Mme de (18th cent.)
Field, Miss A. (18th cent.)
Franceschini, Petronia (d. 1683, Bologna)
Fuggita, Lavinia (fl. 1670s–1680s, Venice. See Lavinia della Pietà)

G

With Family Surname

?Gehema, Virginia Renata von (owner of lute book, probably no compositions by her)

Gines, Teodora (Ma Teodora) (16th cent., black Dominican in Cuba)
Gonzaga, Margherita (15th cent.)
Gräfin (Grafe, Grafin), Sophia Regina (1770–1790). (See Sophia Regina, Gräfin, as this is probably a title rather than a surname)
Grunbaum, Theresa (1791–1876)
Guenin, Helene (b. 1791, Amiens)
Guidiccioni, Laura (18th cent.)

Aristocratic, Religious, or Other Form of Name without Surname

Geltruda (fl. at the Pietà, Venice)
Giulia (fl. at the Pietà, Venice)

H

With Family Surname

Hackett, Marie (Maria) (1783, London–1874)
Hague, Harriet (1793–1816)
Hatzlerin, Sister Clara (15th cent.)
Hohenholz, Sophie
Hoya, Katherina von (nun) (Cistercian convent at Wienhausen, near Celle, fl. 1420–70)
Hume, Agnes (Scotland, 17th cent.)

Aristocratic, Religious, or Other Form of Name without Surname

Helena (Venitiana) (c. 1545)

I

Aristocratic, Religious, or Other Form of Name without Surname

Isabella la Bolognese (fl. 1545)

J

With Family Surname

Jacobson, Henrietta (18th cent., Warsaw, all known works destroyed in 1939)

K

With Family Surname

Kercado (Cercado), Mlle le Senechal de (fl. 1805)

Kiernicka, Anna (18th cent., Poland)

Kingston, Marie Antoinette, Countess of Zedlitz (pseud. M. Marielli) (May be same as Mary Kingston)

Kirkpatrick, Lydia

Kohary, Marie, Countess, (1769–?)

Krähmer, Caroline, née Schleicher (Kraehmer, Karol Krahmer) (clarinet works known, but location unknown, 1794–1837 or 1850)

Kurzböck, Magdalene von (late 18th, early 19th cent.)

L

With Family Surnames

La Roche, Rosa (late 18th cent.)

Lebrun, Sophie, married Dülken (1781–after 1815)

Lerchenfeld, Marie von, Baroness (fl. 1842)

Leszczynska, Marie, Princess of Poland, later Queen of France (b. 1730)

Levi, Mme (gambist, especially on the Pardessus, b. Brittany, c. 1715, fl. Rouen.) Apparently not related to Levy, Sarah, née Itzig

Louvencourt, Mlle de (1680–1712)

Aristocratic, Religious, or Other Form of Name without Surname

Lavinia della Pietà (fl. at the Pietà, Venice, 1670s.)

M

With Family Surname

MacDonald, Miss, of St. Martins

MacLeod, Mary (fl. 1675–1705, principally literary works)

Maier, Katharine, née Schiati (fl. 1795–98)

Mancini, Elenora (16th cent.)

Mersanne, Maddalena (18th cent.?)

Mildmay, Lady (16th cent.)

Mizangere, Marquise de la (1693–1779)

Molza, Tarquinia, da Modena (16th cent.)

Mondonville, Mme, Anne-Jeanne, née Boucon (18th cent.)

Morsia, Cornelia la (16th cent. May be Cornelia la Morsia, with no surname)

Mosel, Catherine de, née Lambert (1789–1832)

Mozart, Maria Anna (Walburga Ignatia), married J. B. von Berchtold zu Sonnenburg (1751–1829, Salzburg). Nickname "Nannerl." Known to have composed works of which her brother Wolgang approved, but no extant works have been found.

Muratori, Angiola Teresa, married Scannabecchi, later married Moneta, fl. 1690s (no known surviving music, libretti only)

Aristocratic, Religious, or Other Form of Name without Surname

Maria Amalia, Duchess of Sachsen-Zeitz, née Brandenburg (first marriage von Mecklenburg-Gustrow) (1670–1739) (Ouvertüre for orchestra cited in Woods & Fürstenwald, location not known)

Maria Catharina Sophia, Countess of Hohenlohe und Gleichen (1680–1761)

Maria Charlotte Amalie (Amalia), Duchess of Saxe-Botha, Princess of Saxe-Meiningen (1751–?)

Maria Teresa Barbara de Bragança, Princess of Portugal, later Queen of Spain (1711–1758)

Maria Theresa, Empress of Austria (Hapsburg)

Michielina (fl. at the Pietà, Venice)

N

With Family Surname

Nicolay, Maria Antonia, née Cappas (Alsace, 1782–Aachen, 1855)

O

With Family Surname

Orsini, Teresa (fl. at the Pietà, Venice)

P

With Family Surname

Pachler-Koschak, Marie Leopoldine (1792, Graz–1855, Graz)

Palavigina, Ginevra and Barbara (fl. 1545)

Papara, Teodozja (b. 1797, Lvov–?, Polish)

Pignetelli, Mariana (16th cent.)
Pybus, Signora (ms. abschrift in Cambridge, dates unknown)

Q

With Family Surname

Quinault, Marie-Anne-Catherine (1695–1791)
Quinzana, Rosalba (Sister) (17th cent., related to or identical with Lucia?)

R

With Family Surname

Raschenau (Rasschenau), Marianna (Maria Anna) von (fl. 1690s, music lost,
    only libretti for her oratorios survive)
Richmond, (Heiress) (fl. c. 1705)
Ridderstolpe, Caroline Johanna Louisa, Countess, née Kolbe (b. 1793–?)
Rossi, Pasqua (fl. at the Incurabile, Venice)
Ruffin, Fräuline (d. 1526)
Rusca, Claudia Francesca (fl. 1620, all known work destroyed August 1943)
Rutherford, Ellen

S

With Family Surname

?Sarret, Mlle de (ms. at Chateau de Coussergues, compiler or owner of key-
    board book, probably not a composer, 18th cent.)
Schwartz, Regina Gertrud (b.1690, Greifswald?–?, poet and musician, text
    only survives of Festspiel for King Carl XII of Sweden, 1707)
Siefert, Justina (fl. 1645)
Sinibaldi, Anna di (court of Maximilian III, Castillo Sinibaldi?)
Strinascchi (Strina Sacchi), Regina (married Schlick) (violinist, may not have
    composed, 1764, Ostiglia–1839, Dresden)
Sczuka-Jezierkska (18th cent.)

Aristocratic, Religious, or Other Form of Name without Surname

Sanza (Santa, Samartina) (fl. at the Pietà, Venice)
Sophia Charlotte (mistress of Friedrich the Great) (c. 1732–?)
Sophia Regina, Gräfin (pub. 1716, Leipzig)

$\mathcal{T}$

With Family Surname

Tarroni, Antonia (Renaissance)
Théis, Mme de (pub. 1786–94)
Thicknesse, Miss (18th cent., gambist)
?Thierry, Marguerite (wife of Alexander Thierry [Thiéry]) (17th cent.,
    owner or compiler of keyboard book, may not have been a composer)
Tondeur, Wilhelmine (c. 1797–1838)
Tranetinna?

$\mathcal{V}$

With Family Surname

Varisi, Giulia (16th cent.)
Velthemin, Charlotte (1830s, apparently not the same as Velthemin, Frau
    C . . . E . . .)
Venier de Petrus, Teresa (18th cent.)
Verger, Maria (b. Dresden, fl. at the Pietà, Venice)
Villers, Mlle Clémence de (pub. 1770s)

Aristocratic, Religious, or Other Form of Name without Surname

Victoria Maria Louisa, Duchess of Kent (1786–1861)

$\mathcal{W}$

With Family Surname

Waldenburg, Eveline von (pub. 1813, Berlin; may have been wife of Prince
    August of Prussia)
Wallaert, Caterina (niece of Willaert?). See Caterina

Aristocratic, Religious, or Other Form of Name without Surname

Wilhelmine, Caroline of Ansbach, later Caroline, Queen of England
    (1683–1737)
Wilhelmine, Baroness of Trosche und Rosenwehrt (fl. 1800)

Appendix 3: Male Composers Who Have Been Misidentified as Females

There are several listings in works such as Cohen's *International Encyclopedia of Women Composers* of "women composers" who were in fact males. Freia Hoffmann relates a fascinating tale of gender misidentification with a one-hundred-and-fifty-year history.[1] She quotes the Berlin music critic Ludwig Rellstab who, misled by a typographical error on the title page of a volume of fugues by the Benedictine church musician Pater Marian Stecher, gave a scathing review in the Berlin *Allgemeinen Musikalischen Zeitung* (1825) to a supposed woman composer who had the temerity to write fugues. It is a wonderful example of prejudicial stereotyping. Ironically, the error has turned up in several reference works of the twentieth century in which the compilers were indeed delighted to have found a woman from that period who had written some quite good fugues. In the interest of preventing errors of either kind, a list of male composers who appear in Cohen as women composers is provided here. In most cases the errors originated earlier and may be traced through his bibliographic references, but almost everyone who has ever been thought to have been a woman has ended up in Cohen.

Anonia La Greca, detto Fardiola. Listed in Eitner and Gerber, this "anonymous Greek [gender uncertain], known as Fardiola" became Greca, Antonia La (Fardiola) in Cohen.

D'Astorga, Emanuele Gioacchino Cesare Rincon (family name Rincon d'Astorga), Baron. Listed in Cohen as Emmanuelle d'Astorga. The confusion may be complicated by the name of his wife (Emanuela Guzzardi) who is not known to have been a composer (NG, MGG).

Bariona, Madelka Simone. In Cohen. Identified by D: Mbs as male.

1. Freia Hoffmann, "Einleitung: Die Orgelkomponistin Mariane Stecher," *Instrument und Körper: Die musizierende Frau in der bürgerlichen Kultur*, Frankfurt am Main/Leipzig, 1991, pp. 16–21.

Clerambault, N. (1676–1749). In Cohen. Probably confused with Louis-Nicolas Clérambault who had those dates and who composed the works listed.

Geertsom, Jan van. In Cohen as Joanne van Geertsom. Work listed was composed by Jan van Geertson. See NG, MGG.

Molinaro, Simone. Listed in Cohen. See Eitner, MGG, NG for biography.

Pattarini, Giovan Maria. In Cohen as Maria Pattarina. "Song" in Cohen's works list is an instrumental "Canzon a tre" for cornetti or viols by Giovan Maria Pattarini. Correction supplied by letter from D: Rp.

Santini, Giuseppe Maria. Listed in Cohen as Maria Santini.

Stecher, Marian (or Mariano). Misidentified by Rellstab because of typographical error on a title page which changed the spelling of Marian or Mariano to "Mariane" in the second edition of his *VIII Fugen für die Orgel oder Klavier*. His life as a Benedictine monk is well documented, and biographies appear in the eighteenth and nineteenth centuries in Gerber and Fétis. Subsequently, the feminine spelling has turned up in various twentieth-century reference works as Marianne, the correct spelling for a female name but incorrect for this composer.

Taroni (Tarroni), Antonio. Held title as a Canon at S. Barbara in Mantua. In Cohen as Antonia Tarroni. See Eitner, MGG, Fétis, and NG.

Toesca (Tasca, Tosca, Toesca, Toéschi). Listed by Eitner without given name, gender not indicated. The concerto Eitner lists (which appears to be the one referred to in Cohen) is in the Sächsische Landesbibliothek in Dresden but is by Alessandro Toéschi. Name appears in Cohen as Tasca (Tosca), Mme.

Zamparelli, Dionisio. In Cohen as Dionisia Zamparelli. In Eitner and Schmid, and corrected by letter from I: M.

Appendix 4: Family Relationships between Composers within the Guide

Aleotti
Raffaela Aleotti, Vittoria Aleotti, may have been sisters or may have been two names for the same person

Aurnhammer (Auernhammer)
Josepha Barbara Aurnhammer
Marianne Auenheim, née Aurnhammer (no music found), daughter of Josepha Barbara

Barthélemon
Maria Barthélemon, née Young
Cecilia Maria Barthélemon (accent mark sometimes dropped in this generation), daughter of Maria Barthélemon

Benda
2 sisters
Wolf, Maria Carolina, née Benda
Juliane Bernadine Reichardt, née Benda
Luise Reichardt, daughter of Juliane Reichardt

Brentano
Bettina von Arnim, née Brentano, may be related to Josepha Brentano

Browne-Kemble family
3 sisters
Mrs. Robert Arkwright, née Kemble
Felicia Hemans, née Browne
Harriet Mary Owen, née Browne

Burney
Cecilia Burney, niece of the novelist Fanny Burney (no music known), and granddaughter of Charles Burney

Caccini
2 sisters, daughters of Giulio Caccini
Francesca Caccini, married Signorini
Settimia Caccini, married Ghivizzani

Czartoryska
Izabela Czartoryska, née Elizabeth Fleming
Sophie Zamoyska, née Czartoryska, sister-in-law of Izabela Czartoryska
Maria Würtemberska (Württemberg), née Czartoryska

Dibdin
Mary Ann Dibdin, daughter or step-daughter of the Mrs. Charles Dibdin
who composed. (There were two Mrs. Charles Dibdins, but apparently
only one wrote music.)

Dussek
Sophia Dussek, née Corri, wife of Jan Ladislav Dussek
Olivia Dussek, married Buckley, daughter of Sophia Dussek
Katerina Veronika Anna Rosalia Dussek, married Cianchettini; sister of Jan
Ladislv Dussek and sister-in-law of Sophia Dussek
Veronika Elizabeth (Clelia) Cianchettini, daughter of Katerina Rosalia
Cianchettini

Hohenzollern
Sisters of Frederick the Great
Anna Amalia, Princess of Prussia
Philippine Charlotte, Duchess of Braunschweig, née Princess of Prussia
Wilhelmine Sophie Friedericke, Margravine of Brandenburg-Culbach and
of Bayreuth, née Princess of Prussia
Anna Amalia, Duchess of Saxe-Weimar, daughter of Wilhelmine Sophie
Relationship unknown: Pauline von Hohenzollern, fl. c. 1800

Jordan (professional name)
Dorothea Jordan (birth name Bland, later Mrs. Ford, professionally Mrs.
Jordan)
Mrs. Frances Alsop. Daughter
Maria Theresa Bland, née Romanzi. Sister-in-law

Krumpholtz
Anne-Marie Krumpholtz, née Steckler
Fanny Krumpholtz (married Pittar). Daughter of Anne-Marie Krumpholtz
V. Krumpholtz. Probably younger sister of Fanny Krumpholtz and daughter
of Anne-Marie Krumpholtz

Lihu
2 sisters
Annette de Lihu
Victorine de Lihu

Valentine
2 sisters
Ann Valentine
Sarah Valentine

Weyrauch
2 sisters
Sophie Auguste Weyrauch
Annie Julia Weyrauch

Marie Antoinette, Queen of France
Daughter of Maria Theresa, Empress of Austria (probably composed but
   no music known)

Appendix 5: Modern Editions, Arrangements, and Facsimile Reprints

Agnesi, Maria Teresa
Harpsichord Concerto in F Major (1740). For 2 violins, cello, and harpsichord. Louisville, Ky.: Ars Femina (EAF 35-12).

Agostino, Corona
Beati omnes. From: Asola: *Sacra omnium . . .* , 1592. In: D. Fouse, "The sacred music of Giovanni Matteo Asola." Ph. D. diss., University of North Carolina.

Ahlefeldt, Elisabeth
Telemak pa Calypsos, Suite from (1792). String ensemble. Louisville, Ky.: Ars Femina (EAF 35-12).

Aleotti, Raffaela
"Angelus ad pastores ait" (SSATB a cappella) from: *Sacrae cantiones.* Ann Carruthers-Clement, ed. In: *Nine Centuries of Music by Women* (series). New York: Broude Bros., 1983. OCLC (11644571).

"Ascendens Christus in altum" (SATTB a cappella) from: *Sacrae cantiones.* Ann Carruthers-Clement, ed. In: *Nine Centuries of Music by Women* (series). New York: Broude Bros., 1983. OCLC (11644484).

"Facta est cum angelo" (SAATB a cappella) from: *Sacrae cantiones.* Ann Carruthers-Clement, ed. In: *Nine Centuries of Music by Women* (series). New York: Broude Bros., 1983. OCLC (11644610).

Sacrae cantiones quinque, septem, octo, & decem vocibus . . . liber primus (Venice: Amadino, 1593). Ann Carruthers-Clement, ed. Complete works of Vittoria and Raffaela Aleotti. New York: Broude Bros., forthcoming.

Aleotti, Vittoria

"Baciai per haver vita" (SATB a cappella) from: *Ghirlanda de madrigali*. Ann Carruthers-Clement, ed. In: *Nine Centuries of Music by Women* (series). New York: Broude Bros., 1983. OCLC (11646414).

"Di pallide viole." From: *Giardino de musici* . . . 1591. In: Ann Carruthers-Clement, ed. *Complete works of Vittoria and Raffaela Aleotti*. New York: Broude Bros., forthcoming.

Ghirlanda de madrigali a quatro voci (Venice: Vincenti, 1593). In: Ann Carruthers-Clement, ed. *Complete works of Vittoria and Raffaela Aleotti*. New York: Broude Bros., forthcoming.

"Hor che la vaga Aurora" (SATB a cappella) from: *Ghirlanda de madrigali*. Ann Carruthers-Clement, ed. In: *Nine Centuries of Music by Women* (series). New York: Broude Bros., 1983. OCLC (11648521).

Madrigals from: *Ghirlanda de madrigali*. In: Helen Kim Abbott, "Eight Madrigals by Vittoria Aleotti, 1593: An Introduction and Edition," M. M. thesis, University of Arkansas-Fayetteville, 1982.

Madrigals from: *Ghirlanda de madrigali*. Lana R. Walter, ed. (transcription and commentary). Microfilm, 1984. OCLC (18245258).

"T'amo mia vita" from: *Ghirlanda de madrigali*. P. G. Pistone, ed. *Raccolta di Musiche Corali Antiche e Moderne*. Turin: Paravia, 1941. 49 pp.

Aleotti, Vittoria/Raffaela

Ann Carruthers-Clement. "The Madrigals and Motets of Vittoria/ Raphaela Aleotti." Ph.D. diss., Kent State University, 1982. University Microfilms, 1982. OCLC (20775337).

Anna Amalia, Duchess of Saxe-Weimar

"Auf dem Land und in der Stadt" from *Erwin und Elmire*. In: *Goethe in Lied: Kompositionen seiner Zeitgenossen für Singstimme und Klavier*. Kassel: Bärenreiter, 1949 (pp. 3–4).

Das Veilchen. In: Max Friedlaender, ed. *Gedichte von Goethe in Compositionen seiner Zeitgenossen*. Schriften der Goethe-Gesellschaft, vol. 11 & 31. Weimar: 1896 and 1916. (Ex. in US: Wc (M1503 .A59E6).)

Divertimento [clarinet, viola, cello, piano]. Ed. by Beyer. Score and Parts. Winterthur, Switzerland: Amadeus, 1993. [Composer incorrectly identified as Anna Amalia of Prussia.]

Erwin und Elmire. Ein Schauspiel mit Gesang von Goethe . . . (ms., 1776). Max Friedlaender, ed. Leipzig: C. F. W. Siegel (R. Linnemann), 1921. 178 pp., with facsimile title page of 1776. [examples in GB: Lbl (2 ex.)] [G. 6563. & Hirsch M. 667.], US: Wc (M1503 .A59E6). See OCLC (21803070, 18717587) for 8 other U.S. locations.

Erwin und Elmire (excerpts) (ms., 1776). *Jahrmarktsfest zu Plundersweilern.* Max Hermann, ed. *Entstehungs-und Bühnen Geschichte.* Berlin: Weidmann, 1900. (Ex. in GB: Lbl.)

[Lieder & Duette]. "Auf dem Land und in der Stadt," "Sie scheinen zu spielen," "& Sieh mich, Heil'ger, wie ich bin" In: Max Friedländer, ed. *Gedichte von Goethe in Compositionen seiner Zeitgenossen.* Weimar: Verlage der Goethe-Gesellschaft, 1916. Reprint, Hildescheim: Olms, 1975.

Anna Amalia, Princess of Prussia

Allegro für zwei Violinen und basso continuo. In: G. Ph. Kirnberger, *Die Kunst des reinen Satzes,* vol. 2, p. 89. Reprint, Hildesheim: 1968.

An den Schöpfer (July 14, 1780). Facsimile in: *Hohenzollern-Jahrbuch:* 1910.

Der Tod Jesu, chorale from. "Du Dessen Augen flossen" In a publication of 1910. Formerly in D: Bds (Mus. 0.11349, but lost since 1945).

Der Tod Jesu (excerpts) [original never completed]. In: G. Ph. Kirnberger, *Die Kunst des reinen Satzes,* vol. 1, p. 226, Vol. 2, 75. Reprint, Hildesheim: 1968.

Der Tod Jesu [original never completed]. Text by Carl Wilhelm Ramler. Für gem. Chor, Streichorch. u. Orgel od. Harm. Carl Hirsch, ed. Hameln: H. Oppenheimer (VN 777), n.d. (Ex. in D: Bds (63770), UNikb.)

4 Regiments-märsche (arranged for string orchestra). Gustav Lenzewski, ed. and arr. Berlin: Vieweg, 1927/28, in series: Musikschätze d. Vergangenheit. Reprint, 1989.

Kriegslied ("Auf! tapfre Krieger"). Schlachtgesang (text by Rammler). Gustav Lenzewski, ed. 4 versions, all from Berlin: A. Stahl: 1. for 1 voice and piano [1915]. 2. for school-choir. Score [1916]. 3. for men's choir [1916]. 4. for mixed choir [1916] (examples in D: Bds (1. 0.48083 2. 0.48105 3. 0.49257 4. 0.49289).) [Location of original not known.]

Sonate B-Dur für Altblockflöte und Cembalo (transcription of the F major flute sonata for recorder). Gundrun E. Quer, ed., continuo realization by Winfried Michel. Winterthur: Amadeus, 1988. OCLC (22224602, 21720176).

Sonate [F major] *für Flöte (Violine) und Cembalo.* Gustav Lenzewski, ed. Berlin/Lichterfelde: Vieweg [1918] (in series: *Musikschätze d. Vergangenheit*). Reprint: Munich: Chr. Friedrich Vieweg, 1975 (C. F. Peters agency in USA and Canada). Also reprinted in Briscoe. OCLC (Berlin 2016468, 5200953; Munich, 2687436).

Sonata [F major] *for flute,* first movement (Adagio). Reprinted from Gustav Lenzewski, ed., Munich: Chr. Friedrich Vieweg, on pp. 84–87, in: *Historical Anthology of Music by Women.* James R. Briscoe, ed. Bloomington: Indiana University Press, 1987.

Trio [D major] *für zwei Violinen und Baß (Violoncello und Kontrabaß) mit Cembalo (Klavier).* Gustav Lenzewski, ed. Berlin/Lichterfelde: Vieweg [1918] (in series: *Musikschätze d. Vergangenheit*). Reprint, 1989 (example of 1989 reprint in D: UNikb). OCLC (20166463, 21839373, 4347249).

Anna Sophie, Landgravine of Hesse-Darmstadt (Anna von Mecklenburg)

[Lieder]. In: Ch. W. Stromberger, ed. *Der Landgrafin Anna Sophie von Hesse-Darmstadt, Aebtissin von Quedlinburg, Leben und Lieder.* Halle: J. Fricke, 1856. (Ex. in US: Cu, PHkm.)

Anna von Köln (Anna of Cologne)

Blarr, O. G. *Vier Cantus aus ihrem Liederbuch.* Organ arrangements of four tunes from: *Liederbuch der Anna von Köln.* S.l.: s.n., n.d. (Ex. in D: Kf&m.)

Liederbuch der Anna von Köln (um 1500). In: Walter Salmen and Johannes Koepp, eds. *Denkmäler rheinischer Musik,* bd. 4. Düsseldorf: L. Schwarm, 1954. (Ex. in US: I, NYp, PRs, CA, CHH, AA, BO, LAuc.)

Arnim, Bettina von, née Brentano

Lied des Schülers aus *Isabella von Ägypten*. Erzählung von Achim von Arnim (1839). Tübingen: 1976.

Lied des Schülers. In: Achim von Arnim, *Isabella von Ägypten: Kaiser Karl des Fünften erste Jugendliebe. Gesamtausgabe,* vol. 1.

"O schaudre nicht." In: Max Friedländer, ed. *Goethes Gedichte in Kompositionen von Zeitgenossen.* Weimar: Verlag der Goethe-Gesellschaft, 1896.

Romanze für Singstimme und Klavier. In: Achim von Arnim, *Armut, Reichtum, Schuld und Buße der Gräfin Dolores. Gesamtausgabe,* vol. 8 & 9.

[10 songs for voice and piano]. In: Max Friedländer, ed. *Sämtliche Werke,* vol. 4. Berlin: Propyläen, 1920. Contents: "Mondenschein schläfert ein," "Aus Faust," "Ein Stern der Lieb," "Vom Nachem getragen" [duet], "Lied des Schülers," "Romanze," "Vision des Heiligen Johannes," "Hafis," "Wanderers Nachtlied," "Suleika."

Assandra, Caterina

Ave verum corpus and *Ego flos campi.* In: *Organ Music by Women before 1800.* Calvert Johnson, ed. Pullman, Wash.: Vivace, 1993.

"Duo Seraphim." From: *Motetti a dua, & tre voci,* op. 2 (1609). In: *Two Sacred Works for Three Treble Voices* by Caterina Assandra, Pavese and Maria Francesca Nascinbeni d'Ancona. Barbara Garvey Jackson, ed. Fayetteville, Ark: ClarNan Editions (CN12), 1990.

"Jubilate Deo." for soprano, bass, and keyboard. From: *Motetti a dua, & tre voci,* op. 2 (1609). (Ex. in D: Kf&m.)

Auenbrugg (d'Auenbrugg, Auenbrugger), Marianna von

Sonata in E-flat Major, Rondo Allegro from. In: Barbara Harbach, ed. *Women Composers for the Harpsichord.* Bryn Mawr: Elkan-Vogel (a subsidiary of Theodore Presser), 1986. Name as d'Auenbrugg.

Sonata in E-flat Major, Rondo Allegro from. In: *Women Composers.* "At the Piano" (series). Alfred Publishing Co., 1990. Name as von Auenbrugger.

Sonata per il clavicembalo o forte piano [in E-flat major, 1787]. Sylvia Glickman, ed. Bryn Mawr: Hildegard, 1990. Name as D'Auenbrugg.

Aurnhammer, Josepha Barbara von
Sechs Variationen über ein ungarisches Thema [piano]. Rosario Marciano, ed. Kassel: Furore Edition (fue 118), 1988.

Badalla, Rosa Giacinta
Camillo Tellier (1697). Cantata for baritone, 2 trumpets, organ/violoncello. Louisville, Ky.: Ars Femina (EAF 35–23), n.d.

Barthélemon, Cecilia Maria
[4] *Accompanied Keyboard Sonatas for the Piano forte or Harpischord, with violin, violin and cello, and flute and cello.* Calvert Johnson, ed. Fayetteville, Ark.: ClarNan, 1993.

Beatrice, Princess (19th cent.)
[Work] in: Neil Fairbairn & Clive Unger-Hamilton. *Royal Collection: an historical album of music composed exclusively by members of the Royal Family of Great Britain and Ireland.* Borough Green, Kent: Novello, 1977.

Bigot de Morogues, Marie, née Kiéné
Sonata [in B-flat major for piano], op. 1. In: *Historical Women Composers for the Piano: Marie Bigot.* Calvert Johnson, ed. Pullman, Wash.: Vivace, 1992.

Suite d'etudes. In: *Historical Women Composers for the Piano: Marie Bigot.* Calvert Johnson, ed. Pullman, Wash.: Vivace, 1992.

Bocquet, Ann Marguerite (or Ann and Marguerite)
Monique Rollin and A. Souris, eds. *Oeuvres des Bocquet* [lute]. Paris: Editions du Centre Nationale de la Recherche Scientifique, 1972.

Boleyn, Anne
"O deathe, rock me asleepe." 1. In: Neil Fairbairn & Clive Unger-Hamilton, *Royal Collection: an historical album of music composed exclusively by members of the Royal Family of Great Britain and Ireland.* Borough Green, Kent: Novello, 1977. 2. Reprinted in: James Briscoe, ed. *Historical Anthology of Music by Women*, with an introduction by Edith Borroff. Bloomington: Indiana University Press, 1987, pp. 14–17. 3. "O Death rock me asleep" for voice, guitar, or keyboard. London: Boosey & Hawkes (#7544). [1912].

Bon, Anna (di Venezia)
6 Cembalosonaten (1757) [facsimile ed.]. Traude Kloft, ed. Düsseldorf: Edition Donna, 1991.

Six Divertimenti Op. III for 2 Flutes and Basso Continuo. Sally Fortino, ed. Bryn Mawr: Hildegard, 1993.

VI sonate da Camera per il Flauto Traversiere e Violoncello o Cembalo (1756). Barbara Garvey Jackson, ed. Fayetteville, Ark: ClarNan Editions (CN 11), 1989.

VI sonate da Camera per il Flauto Traversiere e Violoncello o Cembalo (1756) [facsimile ed.]. Florence: Scelte, 1988.

Bourges, Clementine de (married to de Peyrat)

Da bei rami (1583). In: J. Bonfils, ed. (registration, G. Litaize & J. Bonfils). *Clém. de Bourges et N. de La Grotte, Oeuvres complètes. Fantasies.* Paris: Editions musicales de la Schola Cantorum et de la Procure géneral de Musique [1960]. L. Organiste liturgique. #29, #30. (Ex. in GB: Lbl). OCLC (19652210).

Brillon de Jouy, Anne-Louise

Marche des Insurgentes, arranged for brass quintet. Daniel Nightingale, ed. and arr. Bryn Mawr: Hildegard, 1992.

2d Duo de Harpe et piano, sol mineur. Barbara Jackson, ed. Fayetteville, Ark.: ClarNan, 1993.

Caccini, Francesca

"Aure volanti" [SSA, 3 flutes, and bc]. In: Carolyn Raney, ed. *Nine Centuries of Women in Music* (series). New York: Broude Bros., 1977.

"Dove io credea le mie speranze vere" (1621). Aria à 1 voce (Soprano col basso continuo). In: Luigi Torchi, ed. and arr. *L'Arte Musicale in Italia: Secolo XVII.* Vol. 5, pp. 212–13. Milan: 1898–1907; reprint, Milan: Ricordi, 1968.

Il primo libro delle musiche a una e due voci di Francesca Caccini ne' Signorini [sic] [facsimile ed.].In: Gary Tomlinson, *Italian Secular Song: 1606–1636,* vol. 1 (Florence). New York / London: Garland, 1986.

La Liberazione di Ruggiero dall'Isola d'Alcina (1625). *Aria of the Shepherd.* Reprinted from Smith College Archives edition, Doris Silbert, ed. in: James R. Briscoe, ed. *Historical Anthology of Music by Women.* Bloomington: Indiana University Press, 1987, pp. 34–38.

La Liberazione di Ruggiero dall'Isola d'Alcina (1625) [chorus]. In: Edouard Deldeves, ed. *Fondation de l'opéra en France*, pp. 15–17. Paris: [1859]. (Ex. in US: Bp (#6 in **M. 356. 11).)

La Liberazione di Ruggiero dall'Isola d'Alcina (1625), excerpt. "Chi nel fior." Aria Syreny z opery "Wybawienie Ruggiera z wyspy Alcyny." Score and parts (for S, 2 vln, vlc, harp, & hpsch). Szweykowski, Zygmuntx Kazimierz Sikorski, and Tadeusz Ochlewski, eds. and arr. In series: *Florilegium musicae antiquae*, #33. Kraków: Polskie wydawnictwo muzyczne, 1969 (example in GB: Lbl [G.1302]).

La Liberazione di Ruggiero dall'Isola d'Alcina (1625) (excerpts). In: H. Goldschmidt, ed. *Studien zur Geschichte der italienischen Oper.* Anhang C [Leipzig, 1901] (example in GB: Lbl [2268.c.4.]).

La Liberazione di Ruggiero dall'Isola d'Alcina (1625). *Lied eines Hirten* and *Ritornell für Singstimme und Klavier* (*Aria of the Shepherd*). In: Ludwig Landshoff, ed. *Alte Meister des Bel Canto,* 5 vols. Leipzig: Peters (#9689), 1912–1927.

La Liberazione di Ruggiero dall'Isola d'Alcina. A balletto (1625). Doris Silbert, ed. Northhampton: Smith College Music Archives, VII, 1947. Score, 141 pp. (examples in GB: Lbl [G. 1241.]. US: Bp, BAT, BE, COu, Cn, Madison WI, PHu, Nsc, Wc).

"Laudate Dominum" & "Maria, dolce Maria" from *Il Primo Libro.* In: James R. Briscoe, ed. *Historical Anthology of Music by Women.* Edited with an introduction by Carolyn Raney. Bloomington: Indiana University Press, 1987, pp. 22–34.

"O che nuovo stupor." Aria voor (mezzo-) sopraan, viool (fluit, blockfluit hebe) en basso continuo. In: *Een versameling liederen en aria's met obligato instru-mentem,* #17. Amsterdam: Brockmens en Van Poppel, 19— (examples in US: PHu-Music (ML 784.89 C118) and D: UNikb).

[vocal works]. In: Arnaldo Bonaventura, ed. *Arie di Francesca Caccini e Barbara Strozzi.* Rome: 1930.

[1 song] from ms. I: Bc (Q49). In: Robert Maria Haas. *Die Musik des Barocks, Handbuch der Musikwissenschaft.* Potsdam: 1928, p. 49.

Casson, Margaret

The Cuckoo (c.1790). 1. #20 of a series titled: *Cyclopedia of Music.* Misc. series of Songs. London [1856]. 2. Reissued, London: Blackwell [c. 1860]. 3. Misidentified as by F. Giardini. *Musical Bouquet* #3370, London: [1874]. 4. Arr. by A. Moffat in Staff and Sol-fa notations, in: *Songs in Unison,* No. 2. London, Glasgow: Bayley & Ferguson [1910]. 5. Arr. by Alec Rowley as 2 pt. song for trebles, *Ashdown Vocal Duets,* No. 261. London: Edwin Ashdown [1954]. (Examples listed in CPM. 1. GB: Lbl [H.2342]. 2. GB: [H.1601.k.k.(2.)]. 3. GB: Lbl [H.2345]. 4. GB: Lbl [E.811]. 5. GB: Lbl [E.1601.].)

Casulana (Casolana), Maddalena

Pescerelli, Beatrice. *I madrigali di Maddalena Casulana.* Florence: Olschki, 1979.

Madrigal VI. "Morte—Che vôi?—Te chiamo." Reprinted from: Beatrice Pescerelli, *I madrigali di Maddalena Casulana.* In: James R. Briscoe, ed. *Historical Anthology of Music by Women.* Edited with introduction by Beatrice Pescerelli. Bloomington: Indiana University Press, 1987, pp.18–21.

Charlotte Augusta, Consort of Leopold Prince of Saxe-Coburg

[Work] in: Robert Huish, *Memoirs of her late Royal Highness Charlotte Augusta.* Includes a facsimile of a piece of music composed by her Royal Highness, between pp. 178–79. [London]: 1818 (example in GB: Lbl [6j10.i.9.(1.)]).

Charrière, Isabella, née van Tuyll (Sophie de Charriére, the Belle van Zuylen)

Flothuis, Marius. *Musical works composities van Belle van Zuylen.* Amsterdam: Donemus, 1983. 3 volumes. OCLC (13292666).

Clèry, Mme de, née Duvergé

Trois sonates [C, E-flat, B-flat] *pour la harpe ou piano-forte avec accompagnement de violon . . . œuvre Ier* (1785). Barbara Garvey Jackson, ed. Fayetteville, Ark.: ClarNan Editions (CN9), 1988.

Colbran, Isabella

"Sempre piu t'amo" for voice and piano. In: *Women Composers.* s. l.: Hers Publishing, 1988.

Craven, Elizabeth, née **Berkeley,** later **Margravine of Anspach (Ansbach)**
"O Mistress mine." A favorite madrigal, the words from Shakespear . . . (1795). In: *Cyclopedia of Music. Miscellaneous Series of Songs,* #356. London: c.1856 (example in GB: Lbl [H.2342]).

Danzi, Maria Margarethe, née **Marchand (Marchend)**
Sonate für Violine und Klavier, op. 1, nr. 1 [E-flat major]. From op. 1, *Trois sonates pour le piano forte avec violon obligé* . . . œuvre I. (München: Macario Falter (#77), 1799). Robert Münster, ed. *Varie musiche di Baviera,* vol. 1. Giebing: Emil Katzbichler, 1967. OCLC (72533717, 21452677)

Demars, Helene
Les Avantages du Buveur (1737). Cantata for soprano, violin, cello, and harpsichord. Louisville, Ky.: Ars Femina (EAF 35–21).

Dering, Lady Mary, née **Harvey**
"And This is All? What, One Poor Kiss" (1655). In: *Musica Britannica, English Songs, 1625–1660,* Ian Spink, ed., vol. 33, p. 172. London: Stainer & Bell, 1971.

Devonshire, Georgiana (Spencer) Cavendish, Duchess of
"I have a silent sorrow here" (1798). 1. In: *Cyclopedia of Music. Select Songs. Ladies' Series,* #13. London: s.n. [1858]. 2. London: s.n. [1866]. 3. In: *Musical Bouquet* (#3296). London: s.n. [1874] (examples in 1. GB: Lbl [H.2342.b.]. 2. GB: Lbl [H.1275.a.(13.)]. 3. GB: Lbl [H.2345]).

Dilcaro (Del Caro), Signora
Madame Del Caro's Celebrated Hornpipe (1785). For 2 violins, cello, trumpet, organ, and timpani. Louisville, Ky.: Ars Femina (EAF 35–11).

Droste-Hülshoff, Annette Elizabeth von
Karl Gustav Fellerer, ed. *Lieder und Gesänge für Singstimme und Klavier.* Rüschhaus-Bücher, Heft 5. Münster/Westphalen: Aschendorff, 1954; 2d ed. 1966 (examples in D: UNikb and US: AA, NYp). 2d ed. OCLC (10177366).

Droste-Hülshoff, Annette Elizabeth von
Armin Kansteiner, ed. *Annette von Droste-Hülshoff, historisch-kritische Ausgabe, Musikalien.* Tübingen: Niemeyer, 1986.

Christoph Schlüter, ed. [24] *Lieder mit Pianoforte-Begleitung* [with *2 Lieder ohne Worte*]. Münster: Adolph Russells Verlag, 1877 (examples in D: UNikb, US: BLu, CA).

Duchambge, Pauline

"A mon ange gardien," "La blanchisseuse de fin," "Cancione amorosa," "Les cloches du couvent," "La sincère." In: *Anthology of Songs*. (Also includes Viardot-Garcia, Vieu, Puget). Susan C. Cook and Judy S. Tsou (introduction). *Women Composers Series*, vol. 22. New York: Da Capo Press, 1988. OCLC (12918131).

Dussek, Sophia Giustina, née Corri

Sonata for harp, op. 2, no. 3. In: *Sonatas for harp by Sophia Corri and Johann L. Dussek*. Nicanor Zabaleta, ed. Mainz: B. Schott's Söhne/New York: Associated Music Publishers, 1954. OCLC (23259251).

Duval, Louise

Suite from Les Genies (1736). String ensemble, harpsichord. Louisville, Ky.: Ars Femina (EAF 35–05), n.d.

Edelmann (Edelman), Madamoiselle

Rondeau for Violoncello & Piano (1750). Louisville, Ky.: Ars Femina (EAF 35–05), n.d.

[1 sonata] in: *Trois Sonates pour le Clavecin ou Piano-Forte, composés par Mademoiselle Edelman, Monsieur Dardondau & Monsieur Pin*. Leipzig, C. G. Hilscher, 1787. R. Raspé, ed. #3, *Series IV:* Series in Collaboration with the Brussels Royal Conservatory of Music. Peer, Belgium: Alamire, 1992.

Edgeworth, Elisabeth (17th cent.)

Livre de clavecin. Thesaurus Musicus #9. Peer, Belgium: Alamire, 1993. Facsimile.

Flad, Josephine von

Missa in g-moll für 6 Singstimmen und Orgel. Score. Munich: Max Hieber (MH 7015), [1989].

Gambarini, Elisabeth de

"Honors, riches, marriage, blessing." Song. In: *A Collection of Uncommon and Rare Pieces of Shakespeare Music*. (Example in US: Wc [M 1619.5 .S52Al Case].)

Aria ("Lover, Go and Calm Thy Sighs"), *Gavotta Variations on the Foregoing Song, Giga.* From: op. 2. *Lessons for the Harpsichord* . . . (1748). In: Barbara Harbach, ed. *Eighteenth Century Women Composers for the Harpsichord or Piano,* vol. 1. Pullman, Wash.: Vivace Press, 1992.

Minuet, Tambourin, and Allegro (from op. 2. *Lessons for the Harpsichord,* 1748). In: Barbara Harbach, ed. *Women Composers for the Harpsichord.* Bryn Mawr, Pa.: Elkan-Vogel (a subsidiary of Theodore Presser), 1986.

Genlis, Stéphanie-Félicité, Countess, née Ducrest de Saint-Aubin
Nouvelle méthode pour apprendre à jouer de la harpe en moins de 6 mois de leçons . . . Paris: Mme Duhan 1802, 1811. Geneva: Minkoff, 1974. [Facsimile reprint.]

Gibson, Isabella Mary, née Scott
Loch na Garr, arranged as a four-part song. In: *Paterson's Part Music,* #15. J. Bogue, ed. [London]: Paterson, Sons & Co. [1890?]. (Example in GB: Lbl [F.1686.].)

Lochnagarr. [Song.] James Masterton, arr. Glasgow: James S. Kerr, 1971.

Gracia Baptista (nun)
Conditor alme [for organ]. From: Luis Venegas de Henestrosa, *Libro de cipra nueva.* Alcalá de Henares: 1557. In: *Monumentos de la música española,* vol. 2, *La musica en la corte de Carlos V.* 1Higini Anglès, ed. Madrid: 1944. 2d. ed. revised, Barcelona: 1965. 2. In: *Organ Music by Women before 1800.* Calvert Johnson, ed. Pullman, Wash.: Vivace, 1993.

Grazianini, Catterina Benedetta
"Consolati che il petto" from *S. Geminiano Vescous e Protettore di Modena (1705)* [A, ob, vln, bc]. In: *Arias from Oratorios by Women Composers of the Eighteenth Century,* vol. 1. Barbara Garvey Jackson, ed. Fayetteville, Ark.: ClarNan Editions (CN6), 1986.

"Il ancor ti resta in petto" [tenor] from *S. Teresia* and "A veder si raro oggetto" [soprano] from *S. Gemigniano Vescous e Protettore di Modena (1705)* [voice, vlc obligato, bc]. In: *Arias from Oratorios by Women Composers of the Eighteenth Century,* vol. 3. Barbara Garvey Jackson, ed. Fayetteville, Ark.: ClarNan Editions (CN14), 1990.

Grimani, Maria Margareta

Closing chorus ("Ogni Colle") to *La Visitazione* [1713]. Chorus SAB, string ensemble, harpsichord. Louisville, Ky.: Ars Femina (EAF 35–09), n.d.

"L'esser fida" [S, ob, bc] & "A un core innocente" [A, vln, vla, bc]. From: *La decollazione di S. Giovanni Battista* (1715). In: *Arias from Oratorios by Women Composers of the Eighteenth Century*, vol. 1. Barbara Garvey Jackson, ed. Fayetteville, Ark.: ClarNan Editions (CN6), 1986.

Sinfonia, from *Pallade e Marte* (1713). Introduction by Barbara Garvey Jackson. Facsimile from manuscript in A: Wn (Mus.Hs.17.1741) in: James R. Briscoe, ed. *Historical Anthology of Music by Women*. Bloomington: Indiana University Press, 1987, pp. 77–83.

Sinfonia to La Decollazione [1715]. String ensemble, harpsichord. Louisville, Ky.: Ars Femina (EAF 35–03), n.d.

Sinfonia to La Visitazione [1713]. String ensemble, harpsichord. Louisville, Ky.: Ars Femina (EAF 35–02), n.d.

Sinfonia to Pallade et Marte [1713]. String ensemble, harpsichord. Louisville, Ky.: Ars Femina (EAF 35–04), n.d.

Guest, Jane Mary (married Miles)

The bonnie wee wife. Song. In: *Musical Bouquet*, #3453. London, [1874] (example in GB: Lbl [H.2345.]).

Gunn, Anne, née Young

Instructions for playing the Musical Games. Edinburgh, 1801. [Facsimile edition.] C. Stewart, 1948 (?). [See MGG, entry on John Gunn.]

Hoijer, Anna Ovena

Two Old Dutch Carols (Christmas/Epiphany). [Arr. from Annae Ovenae Hoijers *Geistliche und weltliche poemata*, 1650.] Chorus SATB, continuo. Louisville, Ky.: Ars Femina (EAF 35–22), n.d.

Hortense (Eugénie de Beauharnais), Queen of Holland

Album Artistique de la Reine Hortense. Paris: Heugel [1860?]. (Example in GB: Lbl [1754.b.20.].)

A child of mercy [words?], by E. Whittaker. [Tunes by Queen Hortense?]. London: s.n., 1855. (Example in GB: Lbl [H.1756.(45.)].)

Livre d'art de la reine Hortense. Une visite à Augsbourg, espuisse biographique. Letters, dessins, musique [12 songs]. Additional title page reads "Album artistique de la reine Hortense." Paris: Heugel [1860?]. (Example in GB: Lbl [Hirsch m. 8846.].)

Partant pour la Syrie. Also found under: "The romance of Dunois," "Dunois the young and debonair," "It was Dunois," etc., and in various instrumental and vocal arrangements. GB: Lbl lists over 75 arrangements listed from 1810 to 1900 in addition to many publications which give the composer as "anonymous."

Recueil de romances. Twelve series, each of which contains twelve songs. Paris: s.n. [1856?]. (Example in GB: Lbl [H.1932.].)

Jacquet de La Guerre, Elisabeth

Carol Henry Bates. "The Instrumental Music of Elizabeth Claude Jacquet de la Guerre." Ph.D. diss., Indiana University, 1978 [edition of all the instrumental music, with biography and commentary].

Cantates françoises [livre 1] (1708). David Tunley, ed. *The Eighteenth Century French Cantata.* 3 vols. [with cantatas by André Campra]. New York: Garland, 1990. [Facsimile reprint.] OCLC (21909166).

Cantates françoises [livre 2] (1712). David Tunley, ed. *The Eighteenth Century French Cantata.* 3 vols. [with cantatas by J. B. Morin]. New York: Garland, 1990. [Facsimile reprint.] OCLC (22117932)

Cephale et Procris. Excerpt from Act II, scene I (1694) [S/flute/bc]. Paul Brunold, ed. Les Remparts, Monaco/Paris: Éditions de l'Oiseau-lyre, 1938. (Ex. in US: Wc (M 1508).) OCLC (16158767, 5347344).

Deux cantates pour soprano avec accompagnement de violons: Le passage de la Mer Rouge; Samson. Geneva: Minkoff. [Facsimile reprint.]

Deux sonates pour violon seul (1707) *avec viola de gambe obligée et basse continuo.* Renée Viollier, ed. Reproduced from copyist's ms., with realized figured bass. Société des émissions de radio-Genève [195-?]. (Ex. in US: NYp.) NUC (NL 0033363).

Jéphte (1711) [cantata]. In: Borroff, Edith. *An Introduction to Elisabeth-Claude Jacquet de la Guerre.* Brooklyn, N.Y.: Institute of Medieval Music, 1966, pp. 67–86.

Loure, aus der opera Cephale et Procris, für Oboe und Continuo. In: *Das Musikwerk, Der Tanz,* vol. 27. Cologne: Arno Volk Verlag.

Pièces de Clavecin [premier livre, 1687]. Carol Henry Bates, ed. Paris: Heugel (Le Pupitre #66), 1986.

Pièces de Clavecin qui peuvent se Jouer sur le Viollon . . . (1707). Paul Brunold (1938), ed., rev. Thurston Dart (1965). Les Remparts, Monaco: Éditions de l'Oiseau-lyre, by J. B. Hanson, 1965. [1707 dances in new order, lacking Sarabande et Gigue.] OCLC (2439230).

Raccomodement comique de Pierrot et de Nicole. Carolyn Raney, ed. In: *Nine Centuries of Music by Women* (series). New York: Broude Bros., 1978.

Rondeau [g minor]. In: Eva Rieger and Käte Walter, eds. *Frauen komponieren: 22 Klavierstücke.* Mainz: B. Schott's Söhne, 1985, p. 14.

Sarabande et gigue. From: *Pièces de clavecin qui peuvent se Jouer sur le Viollon . . .* 1707). In: Paul Brunold. *Les Maîtres français du clavecin des XVIIe et XVIIIe siècles.* Paris: Sénart, 1921. (Ex. in US: Wc (M2 .M19).) OCLC (20386582).

Semelé (c. 1715) [cantata]. In: James Briscoe, ed. *Historical Anthology of Music by Women.* Susan Erickson and Robert Bloch, eds. Continuo realization by Robert Bloch. Bloomington: University of Indiana Press, 1987.

Sonata No. 1 in g for 2 Violins (Oboes / Flutes) and Basso Continuo. [From the 4 trio sonatas in ms. in F: Pn.] Robert P. Block, ed. *Music for Chamber Ensemble* (N.M. 243). London: Nova Music Ltd., 1985. OCLC (15281131, 14222118).

Sonate No. 3 [A major], first movement. Pp. 15–17 in: Eva Rieger and Käte Walter, eds. *Frauen komponieren: 22 Klavierstücke.* Mainz: B. Schott's Söhne, 1985.

Sonata, violin & continuo, No. 2 in D Major (1707) [vln, bc]. Edith Borroff, ed. Pittsburgh: University of Pittsburgh Press, 1961. [Also ms. version, 1966.]

[Works in an Italian 17th cent. keyboard anthology.] Rome, Biblioteca del Conservatorio di Musica Santa Cecilia, MS A/400. Vol. 13, *Italian Anthologies.* Compiled by Alexander Silbiger. *Seventeenth century Keyboard Music* (series). New York/London: Garland Press, c. 1990. [Facsimile.]

"La Flamande" and "Chaconne" from *Piéces de Clavecin* [1707]. Reprinted from Thurston Dart, Editions de l'Oiseau Lyre, in: James R. Briscoe, ed. *Historical Anthology of Music by Women.* Introduction by Susan Erickson. Bloomington: Indiana University Press, 1987, pp. 57–65.

Kauth, Maria Graff
Danses des Muses (1780). String ensemble. Louisville, Ky.: Ars Femina (EAF 35–13).

La Pierre, Mlle
Pièces de Clavecin (1680). Geneva: Minkoff, 1983. [Facsimile.]

Lady (anonymous)
Lesson VI in D Major. From: *Six Lessons for Harpsichord.* In: Barbara Harbach, ed. *Eighteenth Century Women Composers for the Harpsichord or Piano,* Vol. 1. Pullman, Wash.: Vivace Press, 1992.

Le Brun, Franziska, née Danzi
Grazioso und Allegro für ein Melodieinstrument und Gitarre. In: *Leichte Duette.* Frankfurt: Zimmermann, 1986.

Six sonates [B-flat, E-flat, F, G, C, D] *pour clavecin ou forte piano avec accompagnement d'un violon. Oeuvre II (1780).* In: Deborah Hayes, ed. (introduction). *Keyboard Sonatas by Francesca LeBrun and Marie-Emmanuelle Bayon,* Women Composers Series, vol. 23. New York: Da Capo Press, 1990. OCLC (19911204, 23024766). Recording OCLC (9300250, 9352825).

2 Rondos für ein Melodieinstrument und Gitarre. In: *Musik der engl. Klassik.* Frankfurt: Zimmermann, 1987.

Leonarda, Isabella
Kyrie & Crucifixus from *Messa Prima from op. 18.* Reprinted from ClarNan Editions, 1st ed. in: James R. Briscoe, ed. *Historical Anthology of Music by Women.* Edited with introduction by Barbara Garvey Jackson. Bloomington: Indiana University Press, 1987, pp. 39–53.

Kyrie, from Messa concertata, op. 4, no. 1; "Volo Jesum," op. 3, no. 6; "Ad arma, o spiritus," op. 13, no. 3; "Paremus nos, fideles," op. 13, no. 1; *Sonata prima* (2 vlns/bc) and *Sonata duodecima* (1 vln/org bc), op. 16; "Care plage, cari ardores," op. 17, no. 9; and "Beatus vir," op. 19, no. 4. In: Stewart Carter, ed. *Isabella Leonarda. Selected Compositions. Recent Researches in the Music of the Baroque Era,* Vol. 59. Madison: A–R Editions, 1988.

Messa Prima from Op. 18, a 4 voci (SATB) con violini (1696). Barbara Garvey Jackson, ed. Fayetteville, Ark.: ClarNan Editions (CN1, CN1:2ed). 1st ed. 1981, 2d ed. 1988.

Motetti a voce sola, Op. 11 (Bologna, 1684), Op. 12 (Bologna, 1686), Op. 14 (Bologna, 1687), Op. 15 (Bologna, 1690), Op 17 (Bologna, 1695). Vol. 4, *Novara* (Pt. 1 & 2). In: Anne Schnoebelen, ed. *Solo Motets from the Seventeenth Century.* New York/London: Garland Press, c. 1990. [Facsimile.]

Quam dulcis es, from op. 13, (1687). Solo motet for soprano, 2 vlns, organ/cello (bc). Barbara Garvey Jackson, ed. Fayetteville, Ark.: ClarNan Editions (CN2),1984.

Sonata Duodecima from Op. 16 (1696), for violin and continuo. Barbara Garvey Jackson, ed. *Baroque Chamber Music Series,* no. 16. Toronto: Dovehouse Editions, 1983.

"Ave Regina Caelorum," for SAT soli, mixed chorus (SATB), and continuo. Stewart Carter, ed. In: *Nine Centuries of Music by Women* (series). New York: Broude Bros., 1980.

Stewart Carter. "The Music of Isabella Leonarda (1620–1704)." Includes: "Ah Domine Jesu" (Casati collection), and examples from op. 2, 6, 8, 10, 11, 13, 16, 17, 18, 19. Stanford University, Ph.D. diss., 1981.

Liebmann, Hélène, née Riese

Grande sonate [b-flat major] *pour le piano-forte et violoncelle . . .* œuvre XI. (1806 [*sic*]). Nona Pyron, ed. Grancino Editions, 1982. OCLC (12915383).

Lied von Göthe aus Wilhelm Meister, op. 4.
("Kennst du das Land"). In: *Lieder by Women Composers of the Classic Era,* Vol. 1. Barbara Garvey Jackson, ed. Fayetteville, Ark.: ClarNan Editions (CN7), 1987.

Louis, Marie-Emmanuelle, née Bayon (Bajon)
Sonatas for keyboard by Marie-Emmanuelle Bayon (1769). In: *Keyboard Sonatas by Francesca LeBrun and Marie-Emmanuelle Bayon.* Deborah Hayes, ed. (introduction). In: *Women Composers Series,* vol. 23. New York: Da Capo Press, 1990. OCLC (19911204, 23024766).

Maria Antonia Walpurgis
Il Trionfo della fedeltà (1755) [selections]. 1. Sinfonia (Ouverture) zur oper ill Trionfo della fedeltà. 2. Marsch. 3. Scene aus *Talestri.* 4. Arie aus *Talestri.* In: Schmid, Otto, ed. *Musik am Sächsischen Hofe,* vol. 3. [Leipzig: Breitkopf & Härtel, 1919.] (OP, ex. in US: BE and Wc (M2 .M92).) OCLC (16453501).

"Prendi l'ultimo addio." [Aria for soprano, string quartet and continuo.] Score and 4 parts. Amsterdam: Broekmans & Van Poppel, 1977. OCLC (11524654).

Sinfonia from The Queen of the Amazons (1762). Strings, 2 oboes, 2 horns. Louisville, Ky.: Ars Femina (EAF 35–01), n.d.

Marie Antoinette, Queen of France
"C'est mon ami." Air composed by the queen Marie Antoinette, arranged for the pianoforte by A. Polinski. London: s.n. [1875]. (Ex. in GB: Lbl [h.1494.s.(49.)].)

"C'est mon ami." Arr. by J. B. Wekerlin as: 1. *Evening* ("Hushed in silence") [song]. London [1872]. (Ex. in GB: Lbl [H. 2764.(7.)].)
2. "Hail, Evening bright." [Trio]. # 48 in: *Popular . . . Choruses for Ladies' Voices* [1879]. (Ex. in GB: Lbl [E.308.f.].) 3. Wekerlin & D. Freer, arr. as: "If you go to Yonder Village." #24 in *Classical and Standard Songs.* London: J. Williams, 1929. (Ex. in GB: Lbl [G.1173.].)

"C'est mon ami." Arr. by Maurice Pesse. Paris: Editions C. H. Bigolet, 1928. (Ex. in US: NYp.)

"C'est mon ami" as: *Marie Antoinette's Song.* For Three-part Female Chorus. Arr. by M. Andrews and M. Jacobson. New York: C. Fischer, 1934. (Ex. in GB: Lbl [F.638.f.(40.)].)

"C'est mon ami." In: *Der Freund . . . Lied für eine Singstimme mit Piano.* Arr. by M. Sembrich. Berlin: Ries & Erler [1886]. (Ex. in GB: Lbl [H.2836.v.(53.)].)

"C'est mon ami" In: Quinto E. Maganini, *The Royal Ladies*. 1. *Fête champetre, on the tune "C'est mon ami" by Marie Antoinette*. 1939. (Ex. in GB: Lbl [f.244.s.(4.)].)

"C'est mon ami" *The favorite Song of Marie Antoinette*. Arr. from the French Air by L. B. Crist. 1915. (Ex. in GB: Lbl [H.1846.k.(53.)].)

Chanson ("On dit que le plus fier c'est moi"). Ms.?, copyright 1934. Melody attri. to Marie Antoinette, arr. by Myron Jacobson; Eng. vers. by A. M. Fischer. (in US: PL). NUC (NM 0219430).

Martinez, Marianne von

Allegro from the Sonata in E Major [harpsichord or piano]. In: Barbara Harbach, ed. *Women Composers for the Harpsichord*. Bryn Mawr: Elkan-Vogel, 1986.

Sonata [A major for piano], first movement. Reprinted from E. Pauer, ed., *Alte Meister, Sammlung wertvoller Klavierstücke des 17. und 18. Jahrhunderts* (#60), Breitkopf & Härtel [1868–85] in: *Historical Anthology of Music by Women*, with introduction by Karin Pendle. James R. Briscoe, ed. Bloomington: Indiana University Press, 1987, pp. 88–93.

Sonate A-dur, Sonate E-dur. In: E. Pauer, ed. *Alte Meister, Sammlung wertvoller Klavierstücke des 17. und 18. Jahrhunderts* (#60). Leipzig: Breitkopf & Härtel [1868–85]. [A Major Sonata reprinted in Briscoe.] (Ex. in A: Wg, Wn (MS 7062). US: NYp, U.

Sonata in A Major. In: Barbara Harbach, ed. *Eighteenth Century Women Composers for the Harpsichord or Piano,* Vol. 2. Pullman, Wash.: Vivace Press, 1992.

Sonata No. 3 [A Major], first movement. In: Rieger, Eva & Walter, Käte, eds. Pp. 15–17. *Frauen komponieren: 22 Klavierstücke*. Mainz: B. Schott's Söhne, 1985.

Sonate E-Dur, Sonate A-Dur. Die Cembalo Musik der Maria Anna Martinez, Traud Kloft, ed. Düsseldorf: Edition Donna, 1989. OCLC (23267027, 22549020).

Three Sonatas (E major, A major and G major). Shirley Bean, ed. Bryn Mawr: Hildegard Pub. Co., 1992.

Mattei, Beatrice

Sonata per Cembalo [B-flat major]. In: *Manoscritti della biblioteca del Conservatorio musicale Nicolò Paganini di Genova.* Genoa: Edizioni della Polifonica Genovese dei Madrigalisti [c. 1975]. [Facsimile of Ms.] (Ex. in GB: Lbl (f.246.x.(4.).) OCLC (6645841).

Meda, Bianca Maria

Cari Musici (1691). Solo motet for soprano, 2 violins, continuo. Louisville, Ky.: Ars Femina (EAF 35–08), n.d.

Montgeroult, Hélène de Nervode, Countess of Charnay

Etude de vélocité pour le piano (No. 53. *22me Etude de main droite, pour en accroître la vitesse*) from: Isidore Philipp, ed. *Cours Complete pour l'Enseignment du Forte Piano . . .* (vol. 2, pp. 150–53). Panthéon des pianistes, #1615. Paris/Brussels: Henry Lemoine, 1929. (Ex. in F: Pn [4o Vm8 s110(16)].)

Trois sonates pour le piano forte . . . œuvre 5. (1811). Geneva: Minkoff, 1983. Facsimile of example in F: Pn. OCLC (13590512).

Nairne, Carolina, née Oliphant, Baroness

Songs by the baroness Nairne. Edinburgh: O. Schulze, 1902. (Ex. in US: NH.) NUC Sup. (NSN 0001142).

[Songs]. In: Rev. Charles Rogers, ed. *Life and songs of the Baroness Nairne, with a memoir and poems of Caroline Oliphant the younger.* Edinburgh: J. Grant, 1886. (Ex. in US: Bp, PRu). NUC Sup. (NSN 0001141).

Paradis, Maria Theresia von

"Da eben seinen Lauf vollbracht" from: *Zwölf Lieder auf ihrer Reise in Musik Gesetzt (1784–86).* In: Barbara Garvey Jackson, ed. *Lieder by Women Composers of the Classic Era,* vol. 1. Fayetteville, Ark.: ClarNan Editions (CN7), 1987.

Lenore, ballad for voice & piano (1789). Hidemi Matsushita, ed. Fayetteville, Ark.: ClarNan Editions (CN10), 1989.

Morgenlied eines armen Mannes. From: *Zwölf Lieder auf ihrer Reise in Musik Gesetzt (1784–86).* In: *Denkmäler der Tonkunst in Österreich,* vol. 54. *Das Wiener Lied von 1778 bis Mozarts Tod.* Irene Schlaffenberg, music ed. Vienna: Universal-Edition, (1920), pp. 99–100.

Morgenlied eines armen Mannes. Reprinted from: *Das Wiener Lied von 1778 bis Mozarts Tod. Denkmäler der Tonkunst in Österreich,* vol. 54. Vienna: Universal-Edition, (1920), in: James R. Briscoe, ed. *Historical Anthology of Music by Women.* Introduction by Karin Pendle. Bloomington: Indiana University Press, 1987, pp. 94–98.

Overture to Der Schulkandidat. Hidemi Matsushita, ed. Score and parts. Fayetteville, Ark.: ClarNan Editions (CN16), 1992.

String Quartet in D Major [c. 1795]. Score and parts. Chamber Series #35–06. Louisville, Ky.: Ars Femina, 1991.

Zwölf Lieder auf ihrer Reise in Musik Gesetzt (1784–86). Hidemi Matsushita, ed. *Lieder* by *Women Composers of the Classic Era,* vol. 2. Fayetteville, Ark.: ClarNan Editions (CN8), 1987.

Paradis, Maria Theresia von [attributed to]
Sicilienne (in versions for violin or cello and piano, and for piano alone) "arranged" by Samuel Dushkin [attr. to Paradis; listed as ed. & arr., but probably composer]. 1. Mainz: B. Schott's Söhne (BSS 32924), c. 1924, 1931, 1981. 2. Violin version reprinted in: James R. Briscoe, ed. *Historical Anthology of Music by Women.* Introduction by Karin Pendle. Bloomington: Indiana University Press, 1987, pp. 99–100. 3. Cello version. Budapest: Editio Musica (Z.13 524), 1989.

Park, Maria Hester
Concerto in E-flat Major for Piano or Harpischord (with string parts). Barbara Harbach, ed. Pullman, Wash.: Vivace, 1993.

Sonata for the Piano Forte in C Major, Opus VII [c. 1795]. In: Barbara Harbach, ed. *Eighteenth Century Women Composers for the Harpsichord or Piano,* vol. 2. Pullman, Wash.: Vivace Press, 1992.

Sonata in F Major. From: op. 4. In: Barbara Harbach, ed. *Eighteenth Century Women Composers for the Harpsichord or Piano,* vol. 1. Pullman, Wash.: Vivace Press, 1992.

Reichardt, Louise (Luise)
[42] *Songs* [reprinted from 8 published song collections]. Nancy Reich, ed. (selection and introduction). *Women Composers Series,* vol. 7. New York: Da Capo Press, 1981.

Ausgewählte Lieder. Daphne am Bach, Heimweh, Vaters Klage, Hier liegt ein Spielmann begraben, Poesia, Durch die bunten Rosenhecken, Notturno, Canzone, Wohl dem Mann, Ruhe, Süßliebchen, Das Mädchen am Ufer, An Maria, Unruhiger Schlaf, Hymnen an die Nacht. In: Gerty Rheinhardt, ed. (introduction) *Musikalische Stundenbücher.* Munich: Drei Masken Verlag, 1922. (Ex. in GB: Lbl [Hirsch M. 172], US: Wc (M2.M93) and D: Kf&m.) OCLC (12309846).

[*Das Mädchen am Ufer* ("Es singt ein Vöglein").] 1. Hark! yonder bird . . . Song. [Wrongly attributed to C. M. F. von Weber.] [Orig. in: Reichardt, *Sechs Deutsche Lieder* . . .] [London: 1869]. (Ex. in GB: Lbl [H.2760.(21.)]). 2. "There sings a wild bird." Song. [Orig. in: *Sechs Deutsche Lieder* . . .] London: [1864]. (Ex. in GB: Lbl [H.1773.a.(1.)].)

[*Heimweh,* also known as *Hoffnung* ("Wenn die Rosen blühen").] "In the Time of Roses." [Orig. in: *Sechs Deutsche Lieder* . . .] Arr. for 3-part Chorus or Trio by W. Stickles. New York: Chappell-Harms, 1933. (Ex. in GB: Lbl [F.217.f.(12.)].)

[*Heimweh,* also known as *Hoffnung* ("Wenn die Rosen blühen").] *In the Time of Roses.* [Orig. in: *Sechs Deutsche Lieder* . . .] Arr. for 3-part Chorus by Hazel Gertrude Kinscella. Boston: Boston Music Co. [1939]. (Ex. in GB: Lbl [F.217.l.(17.)].)

[*Heimweh,* also known as *Hoffnung* ("Wenn die Rosen blühen").] *In the Time of Roses.* Concert transcription for violin and piano. [Orig. in: *Sechs Deutsche Lieder* . . .] #2 in: Louis Persinger, arr. *Concert Transcriptions for violin and piano* (series). New York: C. Fischer [1916 or 1917]. (Ex. in GB: Lbl [h.1612.ii.(12.)] & US: PHci & Salem, U of Oregon.)

[*Heimweh,* also known as *Hoffnung* ("Wenn die Rosen blühen").] "When the Roses bloom." Song. [Orig. in: *Sechs Deutsche Lieder* . . .] 1. C. Deis, arr. New York: G. Schirmer, 1934. 2. New York: G. Schirmer [19—?]. 3. Boston: B. F. Wood, n.d. 4. N[ew] Y[ork]: Jack Snyder, 1924. (Ex. in 1. GB: Lbl [F. 1275.nn.(30.).] 2. US: BIu, ST, MID. OCLC (11368687, 19800201). 3. US: LAu, ST, M. OCLC (19800188, 14954665). 4. US: MAN. OCLC (20120666).

[*Heimweh,* also known as *Hoffnung* ("Wenn die Rosen blühen").] "When the Roses bloom." [Orig. in: *Sechs Deutsche Lieder* . . .] Arr. for SSAA by J. Adamson. Toronto: Anglo-Canadian Publishers Assn., 1917. (Ex. in GB: Lbl [F.1623.e.(27.)].)

[*Heimweh,* also known as *Hoffnung* ("Wenn die Rosen blühen")]. "Wondrous is the Story." Sacred Song. Words by Rev. Harry Leland Martin. [Orig. in: *Sechs Deutsche Lieder . . .*] Arr. with symphonies & accompaniments by D'Auvergne Barnard. Boston: B. F. Wood, 1914. (Ex. in (GB: Lbl [G.517.dd.(38.)]. & US: HA.)

Kriegslied des Mays / XII Gesänge. Munich: Drei Masken Verlag / Hamburg: Böhme, 1922 (reprint of 1819).

[Lieder.] Contents: "Der Schnitter Tod," "Der Spinnerin Nachtlied," "Ich wollt' ein Sträußlein binden," "Wassersnoth." Leipzig: Peters (#5503), n.d.

Liederschatz [3 Lieder für Gesang und Klavier]. "Ich wollt ein Stäusslein binden," "Der Spinnerin Nachtlied," "Der Schnitter Tod." Leipzig: Peters, n.d. (Ex. in D: UNikb.)

Nach Sevilla! Leipzig: Peters (#7390), n.d.

[*Nach Sevilla.*] *To Sevilla, to Sevilla;* serenade to Ross, adapted by C. P. C. Boston: Geo. P. Reed, 1844. (Ex. in US: Wc (M1. A13R).)

Six geistliche Lieder for women's voices with basso continuo. Contents: *Dem Herrn, Buss-Lied, Morgenlied, Fürbitte für Sterbende, Weihnachtslied, Tiefe Andacht.* German and English texts. Carolyn Raney, ed. In: *Nine Centuries of Music by Women* (series). New York: Broude Bros., 1979.

Rossi, Camilla de (Romana)

Dori e Fileno. Cantata for soprano, alto, & string orchestra. Barbara Garvey Jackson, ed. Fayetteville, Ark.: ClarNan Editions (CN3), 1984.

Il Sacrifizio di Abramo (1708). Oratorio for SSAT soloists and orchestra (strings, lute, chalumeaux). Barbara Garvey Jackson, ed. Fayetteville, Ark.: ClarNan Editions (CN4), 1984.

"Quanto, quanto mi consola" [SA/bc] from *S. Beatrice d'Este,* "Strali, fulmini, tempeste, procelle" [S/strings] from *Il Sacrifizio di Abramo,* "Cielo, pietoso Cielo" [S/vln/strings] from *S. Alessio.* In: Barbara Garvey Jackson, ed. *Arias from Oratorios by Women Composers of the Eighteenth Century,* vol. 1. Fayetteville, Ark.: ClarNan Editions (CN6), 1986.

"Rompe il morso" [T/strings/vlc/bc], "Lascia, o Figlio, il tuo dolore" [T/vlc/bc] from *Il Figliuo Prodigo* and "Sono il fast, e la bellezza" from *S. Beatrice d'Este* [A/vlc/bc]. In: Barbara Garvey Jackson, ed. *Arias from oratorios by Women Composers of the Eighteenth Century*, vol. 3, Fayetteville, Ark.: ClarNan Editions (CN14), 1990.

S. Beatrice d'Este (1707). Oratorio for SSATB soloists and orchestra (strs, lute, concertante vlc, 2 trs). Barbara Garvey Jackson, ed. Fayetteville, Ark.: ClarNan Editions (CN5), 1986.

"Sonori concenti" [T/2 trs/strings] from *S. Alessio* and "Qui dove il pò . . . Poiche parmi di sentire" [B/2 trs/strings] from *S. Beatrice d'Este*. In: Barbara Garvey Jackson, ed. *Arias from Oratorios by Women Composers of the Eighteenth Century*, vol. 2, Fayetteville, Ark.: ClarNan Editions (CN13), 1990.

Sarret, Mlle de (de Coussergues) (owner or compiler)
Recueil de pièces choisies de plusieurs auteurs apartenant à Mlle. de Sarret (1765). Christopher Hainsworth, ed. (introduction). Facsimile of ms. in Bibliothèque du Château de Coussergues. Béziers: Société de musicologie de Languedoc, 1985. (17702991).

Recueil de pièces choisies de plusieurs auteurs apartenant à Mlle. de Sarret (c. 1765) [3 pieces from]. Béziers: Société de musicologie de Languedoc, 1980, 2d ed.1982. OCLC (15368876, 2d ed. 17709316).

SCH–L–N, Mademoiselle
2 Menuets. In: *Musikalische Allerley von verschiedenen Tonkunstlern*, pp. 119 & 149. G. Haenen, Introduction to facsimile edition. Peer, Belgium: Alamire Music Publishers, 1992. [Facsimile ed.]

Schale, Mademoiselle
Menuet für Klavier. In: *Deutsche Klaviermusik des 17. und 18. Jahrhunderts*, vol. 8. Berlin: Vieweg (#2064), n.d.

Schröter, Corona
[5 Lieder.] From: *Fünf und zwanzig Lieder* (1786). In: Max Friedländer, ed. *Das deutsche Lied.* Weimar, 1902.

"Die Wachtel" & "Das Mädchen am Ufer." From: *Fünf und Zwanzig Lieder (1786).* In: Barbara Garvey Jackson, ed. *Lieder by Women Composers of the Classic Era*, vol. 1. Fayetteville, Ark.: ClarNan Editions (CN7), 1987.

Der Erlkönig, "Liedchen der Sehnsuch, and "Der suße Schlaf" from: *Die Fischerin* (1782). Text by Goethe. In: Max Friedländer, ed. *Das deutsche Lied.* Weimar, 1902.

Fünf Volkslieder componirt von Corona Schröter. Das Grabmal der Corona Schroeter in Ilmenau von H. Burkhardt. Max Friedländer, ed. and composer of piano accompaniments. Ilmenau/Wiemar: Putze & Hölte, 1902.

Fünf und zwanzig Lieder. Im Musik gesezt, von Corona Schröter (Weimar, 1786). Leopold Schmidt, commentary. Leipzig: Insel-Verlag, 1907. [Facsimile ed.] NUC (NS 0285793).

Jugendlied [1775], *Der Erlkönig* [1786], and "Mutter, guten Rat mir leiht" [from *Die Fischerin,* 1782]. In: Max Friedländer, ed. [16]. *Gesaenge mit Begleitung des Fortepiano (1794). Gedichte von Goethe in Compositionen seiner Zeitgenossen.* Weimar: Goethe-Gesellschaft, 1896–1910.

Sirmen, Maddalena Laura, née Lombardini

Adagio für Streichorchester, Blasinstrumente und Klavier ad lib. [from Lombardini-Sirmen]. In: *Kleine Sinfonieschule. Sammlung leichter Stücke von Meistern des 18. Jahrhunderts.* Berlin/Lichterfelde: Robert Lienau, 1941.

Maddalena Laura Lombardini Sirmen. Three Violin Concertos. Recent Researches in the Music of the Classical Era, vol. 38. Jane L. Berdes, ed. (Cadenzas by Robert E. Seletsky). Madison: A–R Editions, 1991. Contents: Concertos, violin, orchestra, op. 3 (1773). [No. 1 in B–flat major, No. 3 in A major, No. 5 in B-flat major.]

Due terzetti per 2 violini e violoncello obbligato [by Laura Maddalena Lombardini]. Padua: G. Zanibon, 1983. OCLC (22360120).

(6) *Sonates pour deux violons,* Op. 4 (1770). Louisville, Ky.: Ars Femina (EAF 35–15–20). Name as Maddalena Lombardini.

String Quartet in E Major. Louisville, Ky.: Ars Femina (EAF 35–25). Name as Maddalena Lombardini.

Sophie Elisabeth, Duchess of Braunschweig-Wolfenbüttel, née Mecklenburg-Güstrow

Christ-Fürstliches Davids-Harfen-Spiel: "Herder du mich nebst andern ausersehen," "Mein Seelenbräutigam," "Mein Gott nun hab' ich dir verheissen," "Das höchste Gut darin mein Sinn," "Wie bin ich doch so sehr betrübet" (excerpts). 1667. In: Carl Georg von Winterfeld, ed. *Der evangelische Kirchengesang*, vol. 2. Leipzig: 1845, reprint 1966.

Christ-Fürstliches Davids-Harpfen-Spiel [39 songs from]. In: Johannes Zahn, ed. *Die Melodien der deutschen evangelischen Kirchenlieder.* Gütersloh: 1894. Reprint 1963.

Glückwünschende Freüdendarstellung . . . [facsimile pages from] [Singspiel]. In: MGG, XIV, pls. 43–44. [Facsimile excerpts.]

Himmlische Lieder und Christ-Fürstliches Davids-Harpfen-Spiel. [Text by Anton Ulrich, Herzog von Braunschweig und Lüneburg.] Blake Lee Spahr, introduction. New York: Johnson Reprint Corp., 1969. OCLC (10320461).[Facsimile]

Neuerfundenes Freuden-Spiel genandt Friedens-Sieg (1648) [excerpts]. In: M. Schneider, "Ein Braunschweiger Freudenspiel aus dem Jahre 1648," Musik und Bild: Festschrift Max Seiffert. Kassel: 1938, p. 87.

Christ-Fürstliches Davids-Harpfen-Spiel [excerpt]. In: B. L. Spahr, *Classics in German Literature and Philosophy.* New York/London: 1969. [Facsimile.]

Steemson, Miss

A Dirge for Funerals. In: *Organ Music by Women before 1800.* Calvert Johnson, ed. Pullman, Wash.: Vivace, 1993.

Strozzi, Barbara

"Amor dormiglione." from *Arie e Ariette.* In: *Italian Airs and Songs,* vol. 1 Text in Italian and English. Boston: Oliver Ditson, 1923. (Ex. in D: UNikb.)

"Amor dormiglione," "La crudele," "Costume de grandi" in: *Arie italiene dal XIII al SVIII secolo.* Milan: Zerboni. (Ex. in D: UNikb.)

"Amore è bandito" from: *Ariette a voce sola . . .* op. 6 (1657). In: *Airen und Kanzonetten des 17./18. Jahrhunderts.* Kassel: Bärenreiter. (Ex. in D: UNikb.)

"Amore è bandito" from: *Ariette a voce sola . . .* op. 6 (1657). In: *Eleganti canzoni ed arie italiane del secolo XVII; saggi antichi ed inediti della musica vocale italiana raccolti,* #13. Milan: Ricordi, n.d. (Ex. in D: UNikb.) OCLC (23259251).

Arie, op. 8 (1664). *Antiquae musicae italicae: Monumenta Veneta,* vol. 2. Bologna: Università degli Studi di Bologna, 1970. [Facsimile reprint] OCLC (15507593).

"Chiamata a nuovi amori" in: *Antiche gemme italiene.* Milan: Ricordi, n.d. (Ex. in D: UNikb.)

"Con le belle non ci vuol fretta." From: *Il Primo Libro de' Madrigali* (1644) [SATB/bc]. Carolyn Raney, ed. In: *Nine Centuries of Music by Women* (series). New York: Broude Bros., 1978. OCLC (4581683).

"Consiglio amoroso." From: *Il Primo de' Madrigali* (1644) [SAB]. Carolyn Raney, ed. In: *Nine Centuries of Music by Women* (series). New York: Broude Bros., 1978. OCLC (4581700).

Diporti di Euterpe, overo Cantate e Ariette a Voce Sola. Opera Settima. Venezia, 1659. Archivum musicum. Cantata barocca, vol. 3. Piero Mioli, introduction. Florence: Studio per edizioni scelte, 1980. Facsimile. OCLC 21805464.

[56 works]. *Barbara Strozzi* (1619–1664), *The Italian Cantata in the Seventeenth Century,* vol. 5, Ellen Rosand, ed. New York & London: Garland, 1986. Facsimile. OCLC (12917976).

"Lagrime miei" from: *Diporti di Euterpe* . . . op. 7. In: Carol MacClintock, ed. *The Solo Song, 1580–1730: a Norton Music Anthology.* New York: Norton, 1973.

"Lagrime miei" from: *Diporti di Euterpe* . . . op. 7. In: J. Racek, *Stilprobleme der italienische Monodie.* Prague: 1965.

"Non c'e più fede," "Ciamata a nuovi amori," "Soccorrete, luci avare" from: *Ariette a voce sola,* op. 6. Bologna: Editore F. Bongiovanni, n.d. [early 1900s]. (Ex. in D: UNikb.)

[1 aria] from: *Arie a voce sola,* op. 9. In: F. Vatielli, ed. *Antiche cantate d'amore.* Bologna: 1907–20.

Sacri musicali affetti. Libro Primo, Opera Quinta. Ellen Rosand, introduction. Da Capo *Women Composers Series,* #21. New York: Da Capo Press, 1988. [Facsimile.] OCLC 16092241.

"Soccorrete, luci avare" & "Spesso per entro al petto" In: *Arie et Arietti*. Copenhagen: Hansen, 1949.

"Spesso per entro al petto" from: *Cantate, ariette e duetti*, op. 2. In: K. Jeppesen, ed. *La Flora*, vol. 2. Copenhagen/Frankfurt: Hansen, 1949. (Ex. in D: UNikb.)

[vocal works]. In: Arnaldo Bonaventura, ed. *Ariette di Francesca Caccini e Barbara Strozzi*. Rome: 1930.

Stuart, Mary (Queen of Scots)
Las! En mon doux printemps. Arranged for voice and piano. (Ex. in D: Kf&m.)

Think on me. Arranged for voice and piano by Richard D. Row. (Ex. in D: Kf&m.)

Szmanowska, Maria Agata
Contradance in A flat major, Menuet in E major, Polonez in F minor, Etude in F Major, Etude in D Minor, Etude in C Major, [4] Valses for Three Hands. In: Sylvia Glickman, ed. *Maria Szymanowska: Music for Piano*. Bryn Mawr, Pa.: Hildegard, 1991.

[5 dances for piano.] *Piéc tánców na fortepian* [Cinq danses pour piano]. Regina Smendzianka, ed. Kracow: Polskie Wydawnictowo Muzyczna [1975]. OCLC (82112224)

Nocturne, B-flat. Kracow: Polskie Wydawnictwo Muzyczne, [1970]. OCLC (5000175).

[Nocturne, B-flat]. Le Murmure. Nocturne pour le piano. [Based on] 1. Paris: Hanry [c. 1830]. 2. Leipzig: Chez H. A. Probst [c. 1826]. Kracow: Polskie Wydawnictwo Muzyczne, 1977. OCLC (5813478). Reprinted in Briscoe and *Frauen componieren*.

Nocturn [B-flat major]. In: Eva Rieger and Käte Walter eds. *Frauen komponieren: 22 Klavierstücke*. Mainz: B. Schott's Söhne, 1985, pp. 18–23.

Nocturne [B-flat major for piano]. Reprinted from *Polskie Wydawnictwo Muzyczne*. In: James R. Briscoe, ed. *Historical Anthology of Music by Women*. Introduction by Nancy Fierro, CSJ. Bloomington: Indiana University Press, 1987, pp. 101–108.

Nokturn . . . Nocturne. [for pianoforte]. A facsimile of the first edition. 1. In: Lucyi Rucinskiei, ed. *Album muzyczne na fortepian.* St. Petersburg, 1852. (Ex. in GB: Lbl [7901.p.53.].) 2. Also in a Russian ed. by I. F. Belza, 1956.

Nokturn B-Dur na fortepian [B-flat major for piano]. Warsaw: Polskie Wydawnictwo Muzyczne, n.d.

Serenade [violoncello and piano, c major, arrangement]. Krakow: Polskie Wydawnictwo Muzyczne [c. 1982]. OCLC (12385025).

25 Mazurkas. [Set of 24 mazurkas, and one from earlier set of dances.] Irena Poniatowska, ed. Bryn Mawr: Hildegard, 1992–93.

[2 Nocturnes for piano.] *Dva noktiurna; lia fortepiano.* Igor Belza, ed. Moscow: Gos. muzykl'noe izzd-vo, 1962. OCLC (23710992).

Wybór kompozycji / Marii Szymanowskiej (album of piano music: Maria Szymanowska). Kracow: Polskie Wydawnictowo Muzyczna, 1953. In: Jozef Mirscy, Wladyslaw Hordynski Maria, and Jana Hoffmana, eds. *Maria Szymanowska: 1789–1831;* album; materialy biograficzne; stambuchy; wybor kmopozycji. Music on pp. 109–58. Contents: *7 Etiuada* (Etudes), *Le Murmure, Menuet in E, Polonez in F* (Polonaise), *Switezianka.* (Ex. in D: Mbs (Mus.th. 5128mb), GB: Lbl [E.1856], US: BLu , U.) OCLC (18311637).

Thiery, Marguerite (owner or compiler)
J. Bonfils, restorer. *Le Livre d'orgue de Marguerite Thiery: anonyme français du 17. siècle.* Paris, Editions musicales de la Schola cantorum et de la Procure générale de musique [196–]. OCLC (6220790).

Trolle, Christiana Charlotte Amalie (compiler and/or owner?)
Das Klavierbuch der Christiana Charlotte Amalie Trolle (1702). Neumünster: Waltholtz, 1974.

Turner, Elizabeth
[Lesson No. 1, 3, 5] In: *Four Harpsichord Pieces.* Edited by Richard Graves for pianoforte. London: A. Weekes [1948]. 7 pp. (Ex. in GB: Lbl [g. 1126.1.(11.)].)

Six Lessons for Harpischord and Piano. Barbara Harbach, ed. Pullman, Wash.: Vivace, 1993.

Victoria, Duchess of Kent (19th cent.)
[Work] in: Neil Fairbairn and Clive Unger-Hamilton, eds. *Royal Collection: an historical album of music composed exclusively by members of the Royal Family of Great Britain and Ireland.* Borough Green, Kent: Novello, 1977.

Villeblanche, Mme de
Four Sonatas for Piano or Harpischord. Calvert Johnson, ed. Pullman, Wash.: Vivace, 1993.

Westenholz, Elenore Sophia Maria, née **Fritscher**
Die Erscheinung & *Der Bund. Sie an ihn.* From: *Zwölf Deutsche Lieder mit Begleitung des Piano-Forte,* Op. 4. In: Barbara Garvey Jackson, ed. *Lieder by women composers of the classic era,* vol. 1. Fayetteville, Ark.: ClarNan Editions (CN7), 1987.

Wilhelmine, Margravine of Bayreuth (consort of **Friedrich, Margrave** of Bayreuth)
Argenore: Trauer-Spiel. [Orig.: Bayreuth: Johann Schirmer, 1740.] Laber-Verlag, 1983. [Facsimile.] (Ex. in D: UNikb.) OCLC (4844711).

Cavatina für Sopran und Streicher. Leipzig: C. F. Kahnt (#5383) (photocopy in D: UNikb).

Cembalo-Konzert, für Cembalo solo, Flöte und Streichquintette, g-moll. Willy Spilling, ed. (enriched and provided with cadenzas by Spilling). Munich: Leuckart, 1959. (Ex. in UNikb.) OCLC (4844711).

Straus, Joseph N.
Music by Women for Study and Analysis. Englewood Cliffs, N. J.: Prentice Hall, 1993.

Bibliography

A. Catalogues and Bibliographies

Backus, E. N., comp. *Catalogue of Music in the Huntington Library Printed before 1801*. San Marino, Calif.: Huntington Library, 1949.

Bittman, Inge, comp. *Catalogue of Gieddes Music Collection in the Royal Library of Copenhagen*. Denmark: Edition Egtved, 1976.

Blankenburg, Elke Mascha, Mosei Boroda, and Robert Nemecek. *Katalog der Internationalen Komponistinnenbibliothek Unna: Noten / Literatur / Ton-und Bildträger*. Unna: Kulturamt der Stadt Unna, 1991.

Blechschmidt, Eva Renate. *Die Amalien-Bibliothek: Musikbibliothek der Prinzessin Anna Amalia von Preußen (1623–1787). Historische Einordnung und Katalog mit Hinweisen auf die Schreiber der Handschriften*. Berliner Studien zur Musikwissenschaft #8. Berlin: Merseburger, 1965.

Boenke, Heidi M., comp. *Flute Music by Women Composers: An Annotated Catalog*. Music Reference Collection, No. 16. New York/Westport, Conn./London: Greenwood Press, 1988.

Bohn, Emil. *Bibliographie der Musik-Druckwerke bis 1700 welche in der Stadtbibliothek, der Bibliothek des Academischen Instituts für Kirchenmusik, und der K. und Universitäts-Bibliothek zu Breslau aufbewahrtwerden*. Berlin: Albert Cohn, 1883. Reprint, Hildescheim: Olms, 1969.

Catalogo delle opere musicali, città di Modena; Biblioteca Estense. Bologna: Forni, 1923.

Catalogo Parma, Sezione Musicale della Biblioteca suddetta.

Catalogue Bayerischer Musiksammlungen, vol. 8. Munich: Henle, 1987.

Catalogue of Music Manuscripts of the British Museum. London: 1965.

Catalogue of Printed Music of the British Museum to 1980. London: K. G. Saur, 1985.

Crosby, Brian, comp. *Catalogue of Durham Cathedral Music Manuscripts*. Durham: Oxford Press for the Dean and Chapter of Durham, 1986.

Eitner, Robert, and Kade, eds. *Katalog des Musik-Sammlung der Kgl. Öffentlicher Bibliothek zu Dresden im japanische Palais.* Leipzig: Breitkopf & Härtel, 1890.

Emerson, John A. *Catalog of Pre-1900 Vocal Manuscripts in the Music Library of the University of California at Berkeley.* Berkeley: University of California Press, c. 1988.

Fenlon, Iain. *Catalogue of the Printed Music and Music Manuscripts before 1801 in the Music Library of the University of Birmingham Barber Institute of Fine Arts.* London: Mansell, 1976.

Forbes Library. Northhampton, Mass., Card catalogue.

Gasperini, Guido, and Nestore Pellicelli, comps. *Catalogo Generale della opere musicale, teoriche o pratiche, manoscritte o stampate, di autori vissuti sino al Primi Decenni del XIX Secolo Esistenti nelle Biblioteche e negli archivi d'Italia. Città di Parma.* Bologna: Forni, 1911.

Gassner, Joseph. *Die Musikaliensammlung im Salzburger Museum Carolino Augusteum.* Salzburg: [Museum], 1962.

Gillaspie, John. *The Catalogue of Music in the Bath Reference Library to 1985.* London: K. G. Saur, 1986.

Gmeinwieser, Siegfried. *Die Musikhandschriften in der Theatinerkirche St. Kajetan in Munich.* Munich: Henle, 1979.

Göllner, Marie Louise, ed. *Bayerische Staatsbibliothek* [V/2]. *Katalog der Musikhandschriften, Tabulaturen und Stimmbücher bis zur mitte des 17. Jahrhunderts.* Munich: Henle, 1979.

Grun, Rita von der, ed. *Venus Weltklang. Musikfrauen, Frauenmusik.* Berlin: Elefanten Press, c. 1983.

Gustafson, Bruce, and David Fuller. *A Catalogue of French Harpsichord Music, 1699–1780.* Oxford: Clarendon Press, 1990.

Haberkamp, Gertraut. *Die Musikhandschriften der Benediktiner-Abtei Ottobeuren.* Kataloge Bayerischer Musiksammlungen, vol. 12. Munich: Henle, 1986.

———. *Die Musikhandschriften der Fürst Thurn und Taxis Hofbibliothek Regensburg.* Munich: Henle, 1981.

Haynes, Bruce. *Music for Oboe, 1650–1800: a Bibliography.* Berkeley, Calif.: Fallen Leaf Press, 1985; 2d ed.,1992. Revision of *Music for Oboe to 1800* (interim ed.), June 1982.

Heckmann, Harald, ed. *Deutches Musikgeschichtliches Archiv, Kassel. Mitteilungen und Kataloge der Filmsammlung,* No. 1. Kassel: Bärenreiter, 1955.

———. *Deutches Musikgeschichtliches Archiv, Kassel,* Cat. no. 3, vol. 3, no. 3. Kassel: Bärenreiter, 1957.

Heinrich, Adel, comp. *Organ and Harpsichord Music by Women Composers: An Annotated Catalog.* Westport, Conn.: Greenwood Press, 1991.

Herrmann-Schneider, Hildegard. *Die Musikhandschriften der St. Michaelskirche in München.* Kataloge Bayerischer Musiksammlungen, vol. 7. Munich: Henle, 1985.

Johnson, Rose-Marie, comp. *Violin Music by Women Composers: A Bio-biblio-graphical Guide*. Music Reference Collection, no. 22. New York/Westport, Conn./London: Greenwood Press, 1989.

Katalogue der Herzog-August-Bibliothek Wolfenbüttel. Die neue Reihe (vol. 12 of *Musik alte Drucke bis etwa 1750*). Frankfurt am Main: Klostermann, 1967.

Kippenberg, Anton. *Katalog der Sammlung Kippenberg [der Goethe-Museum, Düsseldorf]*. 2d ed. Leipzig: Insel Verlag,1928.

Lesure, François, ed. *Catalogue de la musique imprimée avant 1800 conservée dans les Bibliothèques Publiques de Paris*. Paris: Bibliothèque Nationale, 1981.

Library of Congress, Washington D.C. Card catalogue.

Lucca, Biblioteca dell Seminario. Milan: Istituto Editoriale Italiano, 1965.

MacAuslan, Janna. *A Catalogue of Compositions for Guitar by Women Composers*. Portland, Oreg.: Deer House Pub., n.d.

Meggett, Joan M. *Keyboard Music by Women Composers: A Catalog and Bibliography*. Westport, Conn.: Greenwood Press, 1981.

Müller, Jos. *Die Musikalischen Schätze der Königlichen-und Universitätsbibliothek zu Königsbergin Preußen*. Bonn: Adolph Marcus, 1870. Reprint, Hildescheim/New York: Georg Olms, 1971.

The National Union Catalog Pre-1956 Imprints (and Supplement). Chicago/London: American Library Association, Mansell, 1967–1979. Sup. 1980– .

New York Public Library, Special Collections. Shelf list.

North Texas State University Library, Denton, Tex. Card catalogue.

OCLC International Library Computer Network.

Olivier, Antje. *Europäisches Frauenmusik Archiv: Komponistinnen: Eine Bestandsaufname*. Düsseldorf: Tokkata-Verlag für Frauenforschung, 1990.

Oster, Martina, Christel Nies, and Roswitha Aulenkamp-Moeller. *Archiv Kassel: Noten 1990*. Frau und Musik Internationaler Arbeitskreis e. V., Schriftenreihe, vol. 1. Kassel: Furore-Verlag, 1990 (with typed supplement).

Pintacuda, S., ed. *Genova, Biblioteca dell'Istituto musicale N. Paganini: catalogo del fondo antico*, Bibliotheca musicae: collana di cataloghi e bibliographie, IV. Milan: 1966.

Pohlmann, Ernst. *Laute, Theorbe, Chitarrone: Die Lauten-Instrumente, ihre Musik und Literatur von 1500 bis zur Gegenwart*. 2d ed. Lilienthal/Bremen: Editions Eres, 1972.

[RISM] *Repertoire international des sources musicales. Einzeldrucke vor 1800*. Kassel: Bärenreiter, 1971–. (Through XII, Addenda G–L, 1992.)

The Danish RISM Catalogue. Ed. Nanna Schiødt. . . New York: Pendragon Press, 1977 [microfiche].

Das Evangelisches Kirchenlied. Ed. Konrad Ameln, Markus Jenny, and Walther Lipphardt. Kassel/Basel/Tours/London: Bärenreiter, 1975.

Écrits imprimés concernant la musique, vols. 1 & 2. Ed. François Lesure. Munich/Duisburg, G. Henle, 1971.

Listings from the Zentralredaktion Databank, Frankfurt, as processed to March 27, 1992.

Recueils imprimés XVIIIe siécle & Supplement. Ed. François Lesure. Munich/Duisburg: Henle, 1964. Supplement in Notes, xxviii (1971–72, 397). (Through XII, Addenda G–L, 1992.)

Recueils imprimés XVIe–XVIIe siécles: Liste chronologique. Ed. François Lesure. Munich/Duisburg: Henle, 1960.

Roma. *Biblioteca Corsiniani e dell'a Accademia Nazionale dei Lincei. Catalogo dei Fondi Musicali Chiti e Corsiniano.* Milan: Istituto Editoriale Italiano, 1964.

Rossi, Franco. *I manoscritti del Fondo Torrefranca, Conservatorio Benedetto Marcello.* Florence: Olschki, 1986.

Sartori, Claudio. *Bibliografia della musica strumentale italiana stampata in Italia fino al 1700.* Florence: Olschki, 1952.

———, ed. *Biblioteca Musicae VII. Ostiglia. Biblioteca dell' Opera Pia Greggiati.* vol. 1, Le Edizioni. Milan: Nuovo Istituto Editoriale Italiano, 1983.

Schnapper, Edith B., ed. *British Union Catalogue of Early Music Printed before the Year 1801: A record of the holdings of over one hundred libraries throughout the British Isles.* London: Butterworth's Scientific Publications, 1957.

Sesini, Ugo. *Catalogo della Biblioteca del Liceo Musicale di Bologna,* vol. 5. Libretti d'opera in Musica Bologna. Cooperativa Tipographica Azzoguidi, 1943.

Sonneck, Oscar George Theodore. *A Bibliography of Early American Secular Music.* Revised and enlarged by William Treat Upton (first published 1905). Washington: Library of Congress, Music Division, 1945.

Stevenson, R. *Renaissance and Baroque Musical Sources in the Americas.* Washington, D.C.: Organization of American States, 1970.

Stewart Green, Miriam. *Women Composers: A Checklist of Works for the Solo Voice.* Boston: G. K. Hall, 1980.

Wolfe, Richard J. *Secular Music in America, 1801–1825: A Bibliography.* 3 vols. New York: The New York Public Library, Astor, Lenox and Tilden Foundations, 1964.

Wotquenne, Alfred. *Catalogue de la Bibliothèque du Conservatoire royal de musique de Bruxelles.* Brussels: Conservatoire Royal de Musique de Bruxelles, 1898–1912.

B. Encyclopedias and Dictionaries

Blume, Friedrich, ed. *Die Musik in Geschichte und Gegenwart.* 14 vols. Supplement, vols. 15–16. Register, vol. 17. Kassel: Bärenreiter, 1949–68; Sup., 1973–76; Reg. 1986. Taschenbuchausgabe, 1989.

Browne, J. D., and S. S. Stratton. *British Musical Biography: A Dictionary of*

Musical Artists, Authors, and Composers Born in Britain and Its Colonies.
Birmingham: Stratton, 1897. Reprint, New York: Da Capo Press,
1971.

Cohen, Aaron I. *International Encyclopedia of Women Composers*, 2d ed., 2 vols.
New York/London: Books & Music USA, 1987.

Eitner, Robert. *Biographisch-bibliographisches Quellen-Lexikon der Musiker und
Musikgelehrten der christlichen Zeitrechnung bis zur Mitte des neunzehnten
Jahrhunderts.* Leipzig: 1900–04; rev. 2d ed., Graz: Akademische Druck-und
Verlagsanstalt, 1959–60, with supplement.

Fétis, F. J. *Biographie universelle des musiciens et bibliographie générale de la musique,*
2d ed. Paris: Firmin Didot Frères, 1866–79.

Gerber, Ernst Ludwig. *Historisch-biographishes Lexicon der Tonkünstler.* Leipzig: J.
G. I. Breitkopf, 1790–92. Reprint, Graz: Akademische Druck, 1966, add.
1969.

———. *Neues historisch-biographisches Lexikon der Tonkünstler.* Leipzig: A. Kühnel,
1812–14. Reprint, Graz: Akademische Druck, 1966, add. 1969.

Olivier, Antje, and Karin Weingartz-Perschel. *Komponistinnen von A–Z.*
Düsseldorf: Tokkata-Verlag für Frauenforschung, 1988.

Parsons, Charles H., comp. *The Mellen Opera Reference Index.* Lewiston,
N.Y./Queenston, Ont.: The Edwin Mellen Press, 1986.

Pazdírek, Franz (František), and Bohumil. *Universal-Handbuch der
Musikliteratur.* Vienna, 1904–10. Reprint, Hilversum: Frits Knuf, 1967.

Sadie, Stanley, ed. *The New Grove Dictionary of Music and Musicians.* 20 vols.
London: Macmillan, 1980.

Sowinski, Albert. *Les musiciens polonais et slaves: Dictionnaire biographique.* Paris:
Libraire Adrien le Clere, 1957. Reprint, New York: Da Capo Press, 1971.

Wurzbach, Constant von. *Biographische Lexikon des Kaiserthums Österreich.*
Vienna: Universitäts-Buchdr. von L. C. Zamarski, 1867. Reprint, New
York: Johnson, 1966.

C. Other Sources

Bates, Carol Henry (later Neuls-Bates). "The Instrumental Music of
Elisabeth-Claude Jacquet de la Guerre." Ph.D. diss., University of
Michigan, 1978.

Baldauf-Berdes, Jane Louise. *Women Musicians of Venice: Musical Foundations,
1525–1855.* Oxford Monograph on Music. Oxford: Oxford University
Press, Clarendon Press, 1993.

Berdes, Jane Louise Baldauf. "Musical Life at the Four Ospedali Grandi of
Venice." D. Phil. diss., Oxford, 1989.

——, ed. *Maddalena Laura Lombardini Sirmen, Three Violin Concertos. Recent Researches in the Music of the Classical Era*, vol. 38. Madison: A–R Editions, 1991.

Block, Adrienne Fried and Carol Neuls-Bates, eds. *Women in American Music: A Bibliography of Music and Literature*. Westport, Conn.: Greenwood Press, 1979.

Bonaventura, Arnaldo. "Le donne italiane e la musica," *Rivista Musicale Italiana*, 32/4 (1925): 519–534.

Borroff, Edith. *An Introduction to Elisabeth-Claude Jacquet de la Guerre*, Musicological Studies, vol. 12, Brooklyn, N.Y.: Institute of Mediaeval Music, 1966.

Bowers, Jane, and Judith Tick. *Women Making Music: The Western Art Tradition, 1150–1950*. Urbana: University of Illinois Press, 1986.

Brand, Bettina, Martina Helmig, Barbara Kaiser, Birgit Salomon, and Adje Westerkamp, eds. *Komponistinnen in Berlin*. Berlin: Kulturelle Angelegenheiten der Hochschule der Künste Berlin, Sender Freies Berlin, Berliner Künstlerprogramm, 1987.

Brenet, Michel [pseud. for Marie Bobillier]. "La musique dans les couvents de femmes," *La tribune de Saint-Gervais* (Bulletin Mensuel de la Schola Cantorum), 4 (1898), 25, 58, 73.

Britton, Carolyn. See De Jong, Carolyn.

Carruthers-Clement, C. Ann. "The Madrigals and Motets of Vittoria/Raphaela Aleotti." Ph. D. diss., Kent State University (University Microfilms), 1982.

Carter, Stewart Arlen. "The Music of Isabella Leonarda (1620–1704)." Ph. D. diss., Stanford University, 1981.

——, ed. *Isabella Leonarda. Selected Compositions, Recent Researches in the Music of the Baroque*, vol. 59. Madison: A–R Editions, 1988.

Citron, Marcia J. "Corona Schröter: Singer, Composer, Actress." *Music & Letters* 61 (1980): 15–27.

Craw, H. A. "A Biography and Thematic Catalogue of the Works of J. L. Dussek (1760–1812)." Ph.D. diss., University of Southern California, 1964. (Cited in editor's note of Zingel, which see).

Cripe, Helen. *Thomas Jefferson and Music*. Charlottesville: University Press of Virginia, 1974.

De Jong, Carolyn (later Carolyn Britton). "The Life and Keyboard Works of Maria Theresia d'Agnesi." D.M.A. diss., University of Minnesota, 1979.

Fontijn, Claire Anne. "Antonia Bembo: *Les goûts réunis*. Royal Patronage and the Role of the Woman Musician during the Reign of the Sun-King." Ph.D. diss. in progress, Duke University, Durham, N. C.

Fremar, Karen Lynn. "The Life and Selected Works of Marianna Martines (1744–1812)." Ph.D. diss., University of Kansas, Lawrence, Kans., 1981 (University Microfilms).

Friedländer, Max. *Das deutsche Lied*. Stuttgart: 1902. Reprint, Hildescheim: Olms, 1972.

——. *Gedichte von Goethe in Compositionen seiner Zeitgenossen*. Weimar: Goethe-Gesellschaft, 1896–1916. Reprint, Hildescheim: Olms, 1975.

Glickman, Sylvia, ed. *Maria Szymanowska: Music for Piano*. Bryn Mawr: Hildegard, 1991.

Gustafson, Bruce. *French Harpsichord Music of the 17th Century*. Ann Arbor: University Microfilms, 1977.

Gustafson, Bruce, and David Fuller. *A Catalogue of French Harpsichord Music, 1699–1780*. Oxford: Clarendon Press, 1990.

Hayes, Deborah. *Francesca LeBrun, Marie-Emmanuelle Bayon: Keyboard Sonatas*. Women Composers Series #23. New York: Da Capo, 1990.

Hoffmann, Freia. *Instrument und Körper: Die musizierende Frau in der bürgerlichen Kultur*. (insel taschenbuch 1274) Frankfurt am Main/Leipzig: Insel Verlag, 1991.

Jackson, Barbara Garvey. "Oratorios by Command of the Emperor: The Music of Camilla de Rossi," *Current Musicology*, 42 (1986): 7–19.

Kerr, Jessica M. "Mary Harvey—the Lady Dering," *Music & Letters*, 25/1 (Jan. 1944): 23–33.

Krille, Annemarie. *Beiträge zur Geschichte der Musikerziehung und Musikübung der deutschen Frau (von 1750 bis 1820)*. Berlin: Triltsch & Huther, 1938.

Laini, Marinella. "Antonia Bembo: Una Compositrice Veneziana alla Corte di Luigi XIV," paper delivered at the conference "Donne Musiciste dalle Corti del Rinascimento alle Scene Teatrali del '700," October 1988, Ferrara.

La Laurencie, Lionel de. "Benjamin Franklin and the Claveciniste Brillon de Jouy," Translated by Theodore Baker. *The Musical Quarterly*, 9 (1923): 345–359.

Mallio, Michele. *Elogio storico della Signora Maria Rosa Coccia, Romana, Maestra pubblica di capella, academica filarmonica di Bologna e tre i Forte di Roma*. Rome: Cannetti, 1780.

Mathiesen, Penelope. "Miss Valentine's Sonatas," *Continuo*, 17/1 (February 1993): 5–10.

Matsushita, Hidemi. "The Musical Career and Compositions of Maria Theresia von Paradis (1759–1824)." Ph.D. diss., Brigham Young University, 1989. (University Microfilms).

Pescerelli, Beatrice. *I madrigali di Maddalena Casulana*. Florence: Olschki, 1979.

Randall, Annie Janeiro. "A Contextual Study of Music and Drama in Weimar 1774–1782: A Social-Historical Perspective." Ph.D. diss., in progress, University of Cincinnati College-Conservatory of Music.

Reich, Nancy B. *Louise Reichardt: Songs*. Women Composers Series #7. New York: Da Capo, 1981.

Rempel, Ursula Mikulko. "A Critical Edition of British Library Additional Manuscript 49288: Fanny Krumpholtz's Manuscript Book of Her Own Compositions for the Harp," M.A. thesis, University of California-Santa Barbara, 1979.

Riemann, Hugo. *Mannheimer Kammermusik des 18. Jahrhunderts*, II. Teil, v. 28 (Jg. XVI), *Denkmäler der Tonkunst in Bayern*. Braunschweig: Litoloff, 1915, pp. xl–xli.

Rollin, Monique, and A. Souris, eds. *Oeuvres des Bocquet*. Paris: Editions du Centre Nationale de la Recherche Scientifique, 1972.

Rosand, Ellen. "Barbara Strozzi, *virtuosissima cantatrice*: The Composer's Voice," *Journal of the American Musicological Society*, 31 (1978): 241–81.

Scholes, Percy A. *The Great Dr. Burney*, vol. 2. London: Oxford University Press.

Tick, Judith. *American Women Composers before 1870*. Ann Arbor: U.M.I. Research Press, 1983.

Ullrich, Hermann. "Maria Theresia Paradis: Werkverzeichnis," *Beiträge zur Muzikwissenschaft*, 5 (1963): 117–54; "Nachtrag," 8 (1966): 253–55.

Wallon, Simone. "Les testaments d'Elisabeth Jacquet de la Guerre," *Revue de musicologie*, 40 (December 1957): 206–14.

Weissweiler, Eva. *Komponistinnen aus 500 Jahren: Eine Kultur-und Wirkungsgeschichte in Biographien und Werkbeispielen*. Frankfurt: Fischer Taschenbuch Verlag, 1981.

Willier, Stephan A. "The Present Location of Libraries Listed in Robert Eitner's *Biographisch-bibliographisches Quellen-Lexikon*," *Fontis* 28/3 (1981): 220–39.

Winterfeld, Carl von. *Der evangelische Kirchengesang im siebzehnten Jahrhundert*. Leipzig: Breitkopf & Härtel, 1845.

Woods, Jean M. "'Angestellte Freude über den längst gewünschten Frieden': Ein Festspiel der Regina Gertrud Schwart auf König Karl XII. von Schweden (1707)," *Wolfenbütteler Barock-Nachrichten* 12 (1985): 106–11.

—, and Maria Fürstenwald. *Women of the German-Speaking Lands in Learning, Literature and the Arts during the 17th and early 18th Centuries: A Lexikon*. Stuttgart: J. B. Metzlersche Verlagsbuchhandlung, 1984.

Zahn, Johannes. *Die Melodien der deutschen evangelischen Kirchenlieder*. Gütersloh: 1894. Reprint, Hidescheim: Olms, 1963.

Zingel, Hans Joachim. *Harp Music in the Nineteenth Century*. Mark Palkovic, trans. & ed. Bloomington: Indiana University Press, 1992. (Originally published as *Harfenmusik im 19. Jahrhundert*. Wilhelmshaven: Heinrichshofen, 1976).

Index by Medium of Performance

Vocal Music

Song (for 1 voice, accompaniment instrument or instruments not determined, some unaccompanied)

A.v.K.
Abrams
Anastasia, Schwartzburg
Anley
Anna Amalia, Weimar
Anna Sophie, Hesse-Darmstadt
Anna, Köln
Augusta Sophia, Great Britain
Aurore
B., Mlle
B . . . d . . . , Mlle
Bataille
Beaumesnil
Bianchi
Biber
Billeh
Blangini
Boleyn
Bouvardisnka
Boyd
Buttier
C . . . , Mlle de
C . . . T, Mme de
Cabanes
Candeille
Caroline, of Litchfield
Caron
Carr
Carter
Carver
Casson, M.
Catalani
Clark of Tetbury, Mrs.
Clarke, E.
Cléry
Coco
Collier
Coultart
Crouch
Czartoryska
D . . . , Mlle
D . . . et
Dall
Dashkova
Dawson
Demar
Denis
Dibdin, M. A.
Duva[al]
E[bdon]
Evance
F., Mlle de
Ferrier
Flint
Foote
Ford
G . . . D, Mme
Gattie
Gaudin

Georgon
Gibson
Gingant
Goguo
Gouy
Grètry
Guedon de Presles
Haden
Harrison, A. M.
Helv . . . ,
Hemery
Hérault
Herville
Hoijer
Horne
Horsley
Hutz
Jacquet de la Guerre
Jordan
Kingston
L., Mme
La B . . . (de), Mlle
Le R . . . , Mlle
L. P. D. L., Mme
Lacerda
Lady, a (several anonymous composers)
Lamballe
Lannoy de Clervaux
Laugier
Le Chantre
Levêque
Levy
Liddiard
Louis
M . . . , Mlle de
M., Mme
Mn . . . , Mlle de
Macmullan
Manners
Margerum
Marie-Adelaïde, Savoy
Marie Antoinette, France
Martainville
Melmouth
Menetou
Méon
Metcalfe
N . . . , Mme Théodor
Nairne

Newberry
Niebelschitz
O'Moran
Olin
Örtel
P., Mlle
P., Mlle de la
Pacini
Papavoine
Pean
Percy
Pfeffel
Pinet
Piston
Porters
Provost
Reichardt, B. J.
Reichardt, L.
Roehn
Sabatier
Sappho (pseud.)
Sharp
Stein
Stockdale
Turner
Vidampierre
Vielanda
Vilm
Williams
Willson
Worgan, M.
Worgan, Miss
Wrangel
Wuiet

1 voice, unaccompanied (includes chant)

Anna, Köln
Caroline, of Litchfield
Carter
E[bdon]
Echenfeld
Guedon de Presles
Hoijer
Hortense, Holland
Jacquet de la Guerre
Levêque

1 voice with basso continuo

Amalia Catarina, Erbach
Anna Amalia, Prussia
Badalla
Bembo
Buttier (S/bc)
Caccini, F. (includes lute bc)
Caccini, S. (S/unfigured bc)
Campana
Coccia (S/org bc; A/org bc)
Cozzolani
Giusta
Guedon de Presles
Horatio (S/bc)
Jacquet de la Guerre
Lady, a (anonymous)
Leonarda (S/org bc; A/org bc; T/org bc; B/org bc)
Levêque
Louis
Maddalena (T/org/violone bc)
Nascinbeni (S/org bc)
Pinel
Quinciani
Rusca
Sessa (lute bc)
Sophie Elisabeth
Strozzi
Turner
Vielanda
Vizana

1 voice with basso continuo and instrument(s)
Added instruments and some voice ranges specified.

Alessandra (vln)
Anonymous nun of S. Clare
Badalla (B/2 trs)
Cozzolani (S/2 vlns)
Dupré (unspecified treble instrument)
Gambarini (fl)
Grétry (fl or vln)
Guedon de Presles (fl)
Jacquet de la Guerre (1 or 2 vlns [other treble instrument(s) possible])
Leonarda (S/2 vlns; A/2 vlns/; T/2 vlns; B/2 vlns. All with org bc)

Louis (S/vln)
Mara (S/fl?)
Martinez (2 vlns)
Meda (S/2 vlns/org bc; B/2 vlns/org bc)
Paisible (guit/vln ad lib)
Papavoine (vln)
Turner (fl; unspecified treble instrument)
Wilbraham (unspecified treble)

1 voice and written-out piano or harpsichord
(some for unspecified keyboard). Instrument of
accompaniment shown.

Abrams (pf)
Alexandre (kbd)
Alsop (pf)
Anley (pf)
Anna Amalia, Weimar (pf)
Arkwright (pf)
Arnim (pf)
Atkinson (kbd)
Aubigny (pf)
Aurelia (kbd)
B., Mme de (pf or harp)
B******, Mrs. (pf)
B., Pauline (pf)
Bachmann (kbd)
Bannister (pf)
Banti (pf)
Barthelemon, C. (pf; hpsch)
Barthélemon, M. (kbd)
Bartolozzi (pf)
Bawr (pf or harp)
Bazin (pf or hpsch)
Beaucé (pf)
Beaucourt (pf)
Beaumesnil (kbd)
Beydale (pf)
Blackwood (pf)
Bland, M. (pf)
Bonaparte (pf)
Bonwick (pf; opt. guitar/fl)
Brandenstein (kbd)
Brandes (pf)
Breitenbauch (pf)
Brentano (pf)
Bresson (pf)

Breynton (pf)
Briggs (pf)
Brillon de Jouy (pf)
Brühl (hpsch)
Bryan (pf)
Bühler (pf)
Bürde (pf)
Burney (pf)
Campbell, A. (pf or harp)
Campet de Saujon (pf)
Candeille (pf or harp)
Cantelo (pf, hpsch, or harp)
Casson, M. (pf or harp)
Catalani (pf or harp)
Catley (pf)
Chamberger (pf)
Chambers (pf)
Charriére (hpsch or pf)
Chodkiewicz (pf)
Cianchettini (pf)
Clarkson (pf)
Cléry (pf or harp)
Colbran (pf or harp)
Cramer (pf)
Craven (pf)
Crouch (pf or harp)
Cumberland (pf or harp)
Darion (pf or harp)
Dauvergne de Beauvais (pf)
Davis (pf)
Dawson (kbd)
Demars (pf or harp)
Dering (kbd)
Devonshire (kbd, probably pf)
Dibdin, M. A. (pf)
Dibdin, Mrs. C. (pf)
Droste-Hülshoff (pf)
Duchambge (pf)
Duchange (pf)
Dussek, S. (pf or guit)
Edwards (pf)
Eichner (pf)
Elizabeth, England (pf)
Ellis (pf)
Essex (pf; pf or harp)
Fitz-Gerald (pf)
Fowler (pf)
G. C. (pf)
Gail (pf)

Galli (kbd)
Gambarini (pf; hpsch)
Gardel (pf or harp)
Gatehouse (pf)
Gattie (pf)
Gay (pf)
Georgeon (pf)
Geraldini (pf or harp)
Gibson (pf; pf or harp)
Gobau d'Hovorst (pf)
Gore (pf)
Gougelet (hpsch)
Guest (pf)
Gyllenhaal (pf)
Hague (pf)
Hardin (kbd)
Harrison, E. (pf or harp)
Haulteterre (hpsch or harp)
Hemans (pf)
Hime (pf or harp)
Hinckesman (pf)
Hodges (pf)
Hoffmann, J. (pf)
Hohenlohe (pf)
Hohenzollern (pf)
Hortense, Holland (pf)
Hunter, A. (pf)
Hutchinson (pf)
Jervis (pf)
Johnson (pf)
Jordan (pf)
Kerby (pf)
Kingston (pf or harp)
Kochanowska (pf)
Krause (pf)
Kurakina (pf)
Labaillive (kbd)
Lady, a (several anonymous composers)
   (pf; hpsch)
Lady (E.?) (pf)
Lady of Boston (pf)
Lady of Philadelphia (pf)
Lambert (kbd)
Lannoy de Clervaux (pf or harp)
Le Jeune (hpsch)
LePelletier (pf)
Levêque (pf)
Liebmann (pf)
Lihu, A. (pf)

Linwood (pf; pf or harp)
Louis (kbd)
Lubi (pf)
M., Comtessa de (pf)
M., Miss of O. (pf)
Macintosh (hpsch or pf)
Mara (pf)
Maria Antonia Walpurgis (kbd)
Maria Margherita (pf)
Marie Antoinette, France (kbd)
Marshall (pf)
Martainville (pf)
Mary, Scotland (kbd)
Mellish (pf)
Merken (kbd)
Milder (pf)
Millard (pf)
More (pf)
Morgan (pf)
Mudie (pf or harp)
Müller, E. (pf)
Müller, M. (pf)
Mullner-Gollenhofer (pf)
Musigny (pf or harp)
Nairne (pf)
Narbutowna (pf)
O'Moran (pf or harp)
Opie (pf)
Owen (pf)
Paradis (pf)
Park(Parke) (pf)
Parke, M. F. (pf)
Paxton (pf or hpsch)
Poirier (pf or hpsch)
Poole, C. (pf)
Poole, M. (pf or harp)
Potocka (pf)
Pouillan (kbd)
Pownall (kbd)
Pratt (pf)
R.C. (pf)
Rebouté (pf)
Reichardt, B. J. (pf)
Reichardt, L. (pf)
Richards (pf)
Rogers (pf)
Rost (pf)
S. T. (pf)
Savage (kbd)

Schauff (pf)
Schröter (pf; kbd)
Schütze (pf)
Sessi (pf)
Sheredan (pf)
Silverparre (pf)
Sleigh (pf)
Subligny (kbd)
Szymanowska (pf)
Target (pf or harp)
Thiémé (pf or harp, pf)
Thierry (pf)
Thürheim (pf)
Touch (pf)
Travanet (kbd)
Turner (pf)
V., Mme Elise (pf or harp)
Valckiers (pf)
Valentine, A.
Wainewright, H. (pf)
Walstein (pf)
Weir (pf)
Westenholz (pf)
Wilhelmine Sophie Fredericka (pf)
Woldersleben (pf)
Wolf, M. C. (pf)
Wolf, M.C. (?) (clavichord or pf)
Würtemberska (pf)
Zamoyska (pf)
Zepharovics (pf)
Zumsteeg (pf)

1 voice with guitar (some with additional instruments, as shown in items).

Bonneuil
Bonwick (pf with optional guit/fl)
Candeille (pf/ ob/ guit; pf or guit; guit)
Casson, M. (pf and/or harp with
    optional guit/ fl)
Cherbourg
Delorme
Devonshire (kbd/guit)
Dussek, S.
Gail
Genty
Georgeon
Golovyna

Gore
Gougelet
Grétry
Hardin (fl/vln/and/or guit & hpsch)
Hortense, Holland
Kramer
Kurakina
Lady, a (several anonymous composers)
Louis
Macdonald, C. (kbd with fl/guit)
Mellish
More (pf with fl and/or guit)
Owen (2 voices/guit)
Paisible (guit/vln ad lib/bc)
Pean
Piston
Reichardt, L.
Remusat
T., Mlle de
Travanet
Tschiersky
Westenholz
Zumsteeg

1 voice and lute (including theorbo or chitarone.
Some with additional instruments)

Bryan (lute or pf or harp)
Caccini, F. (lute bc)
Dering, (lute/viola da gamba)
Jordan (lute, pf, or hpsch)
Orsini, E. (lute bc)
Orsini, I. (lute bc)
Sessa (lute bc)

1 voice with 1 instrument and keyboard.
Instruments and some specific voice ranges shown.

Abrams (vln/pf; fl/pf)
Ahlefeld (kbd/fl)
Beaumesnil (pf/vln)
Bonwick (pf/optional guit or fl)
Brillon de Jouy (pf/hn)
Casson, M. (pf or harp/fl or guit)
Catalani (pf/fl)
Charriére (hpsch/vln ad lib)
Devonshire (fl/kbd; fl or guit/kbd)

Gail (pf/fl)
Lady, a (pf or hpsch/fl or guit)
Le Clere (pf or harp/fl)
Louis (hpsch bc/vln)
Macdonald, C. (kbd/fl or guit)
Maria Antonia Walpurgis (S/strings or
 kbd)
Martin (pf/vln or fl)
Mellish (pf/cl; pf/vln or guit)
More (pf/fl or guit)
Paisible (guit/vln ad lib/bc)
Pownall (pf/fl)

1, 2, or 3 voices and harp, some with alternate
instruments of accompaniment

Abrams (1–3 voices with harp or pf)
Agnesi
B., Mme de
Bawr (harp or pf)
Bryan (pf, harp, or lute)
Campbell, A. (harp or pf)
Campbell, C.
Campet
Candeille (harp or pf with1–3 voices)
Cantelo (harp, hpsch or pf)
Casson, M. (harp or pf)
Catalani (pf or harp)
Cléry (harp; pf or harp)
Colbran (harp or pf)
Cosway (1–2 voices with harp)
Cramer
Crouch (harp or pf)
Cumberland (harp or pf)
Darion (harp or pf)
Demars (harp or pf)
Devonshire (2 voices with harp or kbd)
Dussek, S.
Gail (1–2 voices with harp)
Gardel (harp or pf)
Georgeon (harp or pf)
Geraldini (harp or pf)
Gibson (harp or pf)
Harrison, E. (harp or pf)
Haulteterre (harp or hpsch)
Hime (harp or pf)
Hortense, Holland (pf, harp or guit)
Hunter, A. (harp or pf)

Jordan (harp or pf)
Kingston (harp or pf)
Kurakina
Lady, a (several anonymous composers)
Lannoy de Clervaux (harp or pf)
Le B. ne S. R., Mme de
Lihu, A. & V. (2 voices with pf or harp)
Linwood (harp or pf)
Louis
Mara
Mudie (harp or pf)
Musigny (harp or pf)
O'Moran (harp or pf)
Pio di Savoja
Pitman (harp/ pf/ vlc)
Poole, M. (harp or pf)
Robinson (harp/pf/other instruments)
Target (harp or pf)
Thiémé (harp or pf)
Travanet (harp or pf)
V., Mme Elise (harp or pf)

*1 voice with basso continuo and 1 other
instrument*

Gambarini (fl/bc)
Grétry (vln/bc)
Guedon de Presles (fl/bc)
Turner (fl/ bc; unspecified treble instru-
    ment/bc)

*1 voice with more than 2 instruments (includes
orchestra)*
Some specific voice ranges given

Anonymous nun of S. Clare (S/ 5
    strings/bc [org]; A/5 strings/bc [org]))
Agnesi (5 strings; various other instru-
    ments; orch)
Ahlefelt (S/2 vlns/2 hns/b)
Anna Amalia, Weimar (Mezzo-S/ orch)
Badalla (B/ 2 trs/org bc)
Barthélemon, M. (S or T/vln/pf or
    string quartet)
Boetzelaer (orch)
Bonita
Brandes (orch)

Candeille (2 vlns or fls/bc)
Charriére (2 vlns/hpsch; fl vln/hpsch;
    vln ad lib/hpsch)
Demars (various instruments)
Devonshire
Eberlin (S/2 vlns/2 hns/org bc; S/2
    vlns/org bc)
Galli (S/vln/vla/db)
Maria Antonia Walpurgis (orch;
    S/strings)
Mara (orch)
Martinez (S/orch; T/orch)
Papavoine (vlns/bc)
Paradis (S/orch)
Pergolese (A/2 vlns/2 obs/2
    hns/vla/vlc/db)
Peruchona (S/2 vlns/org bc)
Pinel (2 fls/bc)
Pitman (pf/harp/vlc)
Sophie Elisabeth (3 instruments)
Vannier (vln, fl, ob, or pardessus de viole)
Westenholz (string quartet; fl/orch; orch)

2 voices, unaccompanied
Some specific voice ranges given

Anna Amalia, Prussia
Cesis
Devonshire
Guedon de Presles (SS; B/vln)
Jacquet de la Guerre
Kingston
Pannina (SB)
Reichardt, L.
Sicard

*2 voices with basso continuo; some with other
instruments*
Some specific voice ranges given

Anna Amalia, Prussia
Anonymous nun of S. Clare (AA/4
    strings/org bc)
Assandra (SB/org bc;
    SB/vln/violone/org bc)
Bembo (SB/vln/bc)
Caccini, F. (SB)

Calegari
Campana
Cozzolani (SS/ bc)
Jacquet de la Guerre (including some
    with vln/bc)
Leonarda (SS/2 vlns ad lib/org bc;
    SS/org bc; SA/org bc; SB/org bc;
    AA/org bc; TT/org bc; TB/ org bc;
    AT/org bc)
Meda (SB/org bc)
Michon
Nascinbeni (SS/org bc)
Peruchona (SS/2 vlns/org bc; SS/org
    bc; SB/org bc)
Pinel
Rodrigues (AT/bc?)
Rusca
Strozzi
Tibaldi (SS)
Vizana (SS)

2 voices with written out accompaniment
(instruments of accompaniment indicated)
Some specific voice ranges given

Abrams (pf; harp or pf)
Amalia, M. F. A. (orch)
Anna Amalia, Prussia (SA/strings/bc)
Anna Amalia, Weimar
Arnim (pf)
Bonita
Brandes (SS/strings)
Brillon de Jouy (strings)
Brühl (fl/guit/pf/vlc)
Candeille (pf or harp)
Catalani (ST/pf)
Cosway (SS/harp)
Craven (kbd)
Delieu (guit)
Devonshire (kbd or harp)
Duchambge (pf)
Elizabeth, Saxe-Weimar (hpsch)
Flad (hpsch or pf)
G., M. & C. (pf)
Gail (pf or harp; ST/hpsch)
Galli (TT/kbd)
Gattie (pf)

Guest (pf)
Hinckesman (pf)
Hunter, A. (pf)
Jervis (pf)
Lady, a (several anonymous composers)
    (pf or hpschd)
LePelletier (pf)
Lihu, A. (pf)
Lihu, A. & V. (pf or harp)
Lihu, V. (pf)
M. et C. de G., Mmes (pf)
Maria Antonia Walpurgis (SB/orch)
Martainville (pf)
Menetou (kbd)
Morgan (pf)
Murray (pf)
Owen (pf)
Parke, M. F. (pf)
Reichardt, B. J. (pf)
Reichardt, L. (pf)
Rossi (SA/string orch)
Savage (kbd)
Wainewright, H. (pf)

3 voices, unaccompanied

Abrams (3 male voices)
Campana
Casson, E.
Casulana
Hodges
Kingston
Leonarda (TTT in canon)
Mancuso
Park(e)
Reichardt, L.
Rogers
Sicard
Zumsteeg

3 voices with accompaniment (instrument of
accompaniment and some specific voice ranges
indicated)

Abrams (pf)
Assandra (SSB; SAT;SSn/org bc)

Bembo (3 voices/bc)
Candeille (pf or harp)
Cozzolani (SSB/bc)
Gail (pf or guit)
Hortense, Holland (pf)
Leonarda (SAB/org bc; SS or TA/B ad
    lib/org bc)
Maria Pawlowna (pf)
Menetou (kbd)
Michon (kbd)
Nascinbeni (SSB/ org bc; SSS/org bc)
Peruchona (SSB/org bc; SAT/org bc)
Strozzi (bc)
Tomeoni (kbd)
Wainewright, H. (pf)

*3 voices with accompaniment of more than one
instrument (includes orchestra). Some voice
ranges given. (Some may be performed chorally)*

Ahlefeldt (SSB/orch [originally—only
    pf reduction survives])
Anonymous nun of S. Clare (ATB/2
    vlns/bc[org])
Barthélemon, C. (SAB/2 vlns/org)
Cazati (2 vlns/bc)
Meda (SAB/org bc; SSB/org bc)

*More than 3 voices, unaccompanied
(some may be performed chorally)*

Agostino (5 voices)
Aleotti, R. (4-10 voices)
Aleotti, V. (4 and 5 voices)
Anna Maria, Prussia (5 voices)
Anna Maria, Sachsen (5 voices)
Assandra (8 voices)
Calegari (unaccompanied?)
Casulana (3, 4, and 5 voices)
Cesis (4, 5, 6, 8, and 12 voices)
Flad (4 voices)
Gail (4 voices)
Guest (4 voices)
Hinckesman (4 voices)
Kingston (4 voices, SATB)
Martinez (SATB)

Massarenghi (5 voices)
Nairne
Ogle
Park(e) (4 voices)
Reichardt, L. (4 voices, SATB)
Ricci (5 & 8 voices)
W., R. W., Miss
Westenholz (4 voices, SATB)

*More than 3 voices, with keyboard or instru-
mental accompaniment
(some may be performed chorally)*

Calegari (6 voices/instruments)
Coccia (SATB/org bc)
Cozzolani (SAAT/bc; SSAT/bc; &
    SSSTT/bc; SSTT/ 2 vlns/ bc; 8
    voices/bc)
Gail (pf, guit, or harp)
Galli
Leonarda (SATB/2 vlns [some pieces
    ad lib]/org bc. Theorbo somtimes
    continuo instrument with org)
Martinez (8 voices/instruments)
Meda (SATB/org bc)
Peruchona (SATB; SSAT; SSAB/ org bc)
Reichardt, L. (SSAA/pf bc)
Rusca (4 & 5 voices/bc)
Strozzi (4 & 5 voices/bc)

*Choir (sacred) or chorus (secular), unaccompa-
nied or with instruments*

Amalia, M. F. A. (sketches for choir in
    keyboard score with text underlaid)
Anna Amalia, Prussia (SATB/orch;
    SATB/org; SATB, unaccompanied)
Anna Amalia, Weimar (4 voices/orch)
Barthélemon, M. (S solo/SS/treble uni-
    son choir/org; SS/unison choir/org;
    S solo/SS/SAB choir/org)
Bembo (4 voices/instruments/bc; SSB
    soli/choir/strings/bc; SSB/2 vlns/bc;
    SSATB/2 vlns/bc)
Biber (SSATTB)
Boetzelaer (chorus/ orch)

Clarke, J. (choir/ organ or pf)
Coccia (SS soli/SSAATTBB choir/org
  bc; SATB soli/choir/orch; SATB)
Flad (choir unaccompanied; choir with
  instruments)
Gattie
Lannoy de Clervaux (SATB/orch)
Leonarda (SATB/2 vlns/org bc;
  SATB/org bc. Theorbo sometimes
  continuo instrument with org)
Maria Antonia Walpurgis
Martinez (SATB/orch; SATB unac-
  companied; SATB/bc)
Paradis (choir/pf)
Peruchona (SATB; SSAB; SSAT/org bc)
R., E. (SATB)
Sophie Elisabeth (SATB)
Sully (solo/chorus/pf)
Wainewright, H. (chorus/pf;
  SATB/orch; 3 soli/chorus)
Westenholz (choir)
Zumsteeg (male chorus)

**Large vocal works, usually with
orchestra (includes some works
for which only libretto survives)**

Oratorios and long cantatas

Anna Amalia, Prussia (incomplete work)
  (SATB/orch)
Coccia (SSAT soli/orch; 4 voices
  solo/orch)
Grazianini (SSAB soli/orch; SATB
  soli/orch)
Grimani (SSATB soli/orch; SSAB
  soli/orch)
Lady, a (2 soli/chorus/pf or org)
Linwood (choir/ org or pf)
Martinez (SSSTB soli/ SATB choir/
  orch; SATB soli/SATB choir/orch)
Muratori (voices/orch [libretto only])
Raschenau (voices/orch [libretto only])
Rossi (SAATB solo/ orch; SSAT/orch;
  SA solo/ string orch)
Volkonskaya (chorus SSAATTBB/2
  vlas/2 vlcs/2 hns

*Stage works (voice ranges and instrumentation
  not given)*

Agnesi
Ahlefeldt
Amalia, M. F. A.
Anna Amalia, Weimar
Aubert
Bawr [libretto only]
Beaumesnil
Bembo
Boyd [libretto only]
Caccini, F.
Candeille
Charriér
Craven [libretto only]
Devisme
Dezéde
Dubois [libretto only]
Gail
Grétry
Grimani
Jacquet de la Guerre
Louis
Maria Antonia Walpurgis
Mattei [libretto only]
O'Brian
Paradis
Plowden [libretto only]
Raschenau [libretto only]
Schröter
Sophie Elisabeth
Tabary
Wainewright, H.
Wilhelmine Sophie Fredericke (hpsch)

Keyboard, harp, guitar, lute

Accordion

Reisner

*Guitar (1 or more guitars. See also voice and
guitar)*

Cherbourg (2 guits)
Fedele

Ford
Frotta
Galli (2 guits, 2 fls, or 2 vlns)
Grétry
Hardin (fl, vln, guit or hpsch)
Kurakina (2 guits)
Skirving (guit, pf, or fl)
Viard
Wolf, [L.] (pf/ guit)

Harp (1 or 2 harps. Also includes works desig-
nated "harp or harpsichord" or "harp or
pianoforte")

Baur
Bertrand
Bonnay (harp or pf)
Brillon de Jouy (harp/ pf)
Bryan (harp or pf)
Bury
Bussi
Campbell, C. (harp; harp or hpsch)
Campet de Saujon (harp/ pf)
Catalani
Cléry
Cosway (2 harps)
Crouch (harp or pf)
D., Madam
Delaval, Mme
Demars (harp or pf)
Dibdin, M. A.
Dubonnet (harp or pf)
Dufresnoy (harp or pf/ 2 hns ad lib;
    harp/ vln ad lib)
Dumur (harp or pf)
Dussek, S. (harp; harp or pf)
Essex (harp or pf)
Gail
Gannal (harp; 2 harps)
Gautherot
Genlis
Gobau d'Hovorst (harp or pf)
Grétry
Hinckesman
Hoffmann, J. (harp/pf or 2 harps)
Hoffman, J. A. (harp or pf)
Jackson
Krumpholtz, A.

Krumpholtz, F. (harp; harp or pf)
Krumpholtz, V.
Lannoy de Clervaux (harp or pf)
Louis (harp or pf)
Marchal
Merelle
Müllner-Gollenhofer
Newton
Randeles
Ronssecy
Salmon (harp or pf)
Viard
Withington (pf or harp)

Harpsichord (includes works designated "harpsi-
chord or pianoforte" or "harpsichord or harp")

Agnesi
Auenbrugg
Aurnhammer
Barthélemon, C. (pf or hpsch)
Benaut
Billington
Bon
Brillon de Jouy
Campbell, C. (hpsch or harp)
Candeille (hpsch or pf)
Charriére (hpsch or pf)
Diede (hpsch or pf)
Edelman (hpsch)
Gambarini
Gautherot
Gouglet (hpsch or pf)
Grétry
Gunn
Hagen (pf or hpsch)
Hardin
Jacobson
Jacquet de la Guerre
Kamermann (hpsch or pf)
Keller (hpsch or pf)
Le Noble
Lobarczewska (hpsch or pf)
Louis (hpsch or pf)
Maria Antonia Walpurgis
Martinez (hpsch or pf)
Mattei
Montalembert (hpsch or pf)

Park(e) (hpsch or pf)
Parker (hpsch or pf)
Ravissa (hpsch or pf)
Reichart, B. J. (Clavier—could be
  hpsch, pf or clavichord)
Reynolds (hpsch or pf)
Savage (hpsch or pf)
SCH-L-N (hpsch or pf)
Semphill (hpsch or pf)
Sirmen (hpsch or pf)
Tirinanzi (hpsch or pf)
Villeblanche (hpsch or pf)
Virion
Wainewright, C.
Westenholz (hpsch or pf)
Wuiet (hpsch or pf; hpsch)
Young

Lute (See also voice and lute.)

Bocquet
Bryan
Pinel

Organ

Agnesi
Anna Amalia , Prussia
Assandra
Bourges
Gambarini (organ concerto)
Gracia Baptista
Ricci
Steemson

Piano (includes clavichord and undesignated kbd. Also includes works designated "harp or piano" or "piano or harpsichord")

Abrams
Agnesi (pf or hpsch)
Anna Amalia, Prussia (kbd)
Anna Amalia, Weimar
Anonymous, of Limerick
Auenbrugg
Aurnhammer

B., C. (kbd)
B., Countess of
B., Dems. (clavichord or pf)
B., Madam Elsie
Bachmann
Bamberger
Barthélemon, C. (pf or hpsch)
Bartolozzi
Bauer, C.
Bauer, K.
Beaucé
Benaut
Berthe (kbd)
Bigot de Morogues
Billington
Bland, M.
Bonnay (pf or harp)
Borghese
Bouchardy
Brandes
Brillon de Jouy
Bryan (pf or harp)
Burney
Butler
C., Elisabeth
C. B., Miss
Campbell, M.
Campet de Saujon
Candeille (pf or hpsch)
Caroline de Saxe (kbd)
Casson, M.
Catalani
Charriére (pf or hpsch)
Christie
Cibbini
Clark, C.
Clarkson
Coventry
Crouch (pf or harp)
Cuboni
Dahmen
Delaval, C.
Demars (pf or harp)
Demilliere
Dennett
Desfossez
Desmaisons
Diede (pf or hpsch)
Dilcaro

Young
Zampieri

Piano, 3 or 4 hands

Dussek, K. (4 hands)
Dussek, S. (4 hands)
Festetits (4 hands)
Hoffmann, J. (4 hands)
Hortense, Holland (4 hands)
Paxton (4 hands)
Savage (pf or hpsch, 4 hands)
Szymanowska (3 hands; 4 hands)
Westenholz (4 hands)
Weyrauch, S & A. (3 hands; 4 hands)

2 or more keyboard instruments

Brillon de Jouy (2 hpschs; hpsch/pf; 2
  pfs/hpsch; 3 hpschs)
Candeille (2 pfs)
Cibbini (2 pfs/vlc)
Gobau d'Hovorst (2 pfs)
Park(e) (2 pfs or 2 hpschs)

Piano and harp

Brillon de Jouy
Campet de Saujon
Cosway (harp/hpsch, pf, or organ)
Delaval, Mme (2 hns ad lib)
Dussek, K.
Dussek, O.
Dussek, S.
Gannal
Hoffmann, J. (pf/harp or 2 harps)
Jordan
Robinson (with voice and other instru-
  ments)

Instruction

*(Many instruction books also contain music by
the author)*

Aubigny (voice)
Bawr (music history)
Ford (glass harmonica; guit)
Gannal (harp)
Genlis (harp)
Gougelet (hpsch)
Gunn (hpsch; music theory)
Hullmandel (musical game)
Merelle (harp)
Montgeroult (pf)
Pellegrini Celoni (voice)
Wainewright, H. (voice)
Young (hpscd or pf; musical games)

Instrumental Music, Strings

*1 violin and basso continuo (instrument for bc
indicated only when specifically other than harpsichord. Includes works designated "violin or
flute")*

Gambarini (vln or fl)
Jacquet de la Guerre (hpsch or vln/b[c];
  (vln/viola da gamba/org or hpsch bc)
Leonarda (org bc)
Newberry (pf/b)
Pinel (vln or fl)
Sharpe (unspecified treble instrument,
  probably vln or fl/hpsch/vlc bc)
Sherp (unspecified treble instrument,
  probably vln or fl/hpsch/vlc bc)

*1 violin with written-out keyboard or harp
(includes parts designated as "violin or flute"
or as "violin ad lib")*

Ager (hpsch/vln or fl)
Argenville (hpsch)
Aurnhammer (hpsch)
Barthélemon, C. (pf or hpsch)
Barthélemon, M. (pf or hpsch)
Biro (pf)
Brandenstein (hpsch)
Brillon de Jouy (pf)
Candielle (pf or hpsch)
Cantello (fl or vln/kbd)
Cléry (harp or pf)

D. C., Mme (pf)
Danzi (pf)
Delaval, Mme (hp or pf;
    harp/vln/vla/vlc)
Demars (harp)
Dilcaro (pf)
Dubonnet (harp or pf)
Dufresnoy (harp)
Dussek, S. (fl or vln/harp; vln or fl/pf or
    hpsch)
Edelmann (hpsch)
Essex (pf)
Freystater (hpsch)
Guest (fl or vln/ hpsch or pf)
Hoffman, J. A. (harp or pf)
Le Brun (pf or hpsch)
Le Vasseur (hpsch or pf/ vln ad lib)
Liebmann (pf)
Louis (hpsch or pf)
M., Mme (pf or hpsch/ vln ad lib)
Martainville (vlc or vln/ pf)
Martin (pf/vln or flute)
Montgeroult (pf)
Morel (pf)
Murray (pf)
Paradis (pf)
Park(e) (pf or hpsch)
Parke, M. F. (pf)
Pélé (pf or hpsch)
Ray (hpsch)
Reynolds (pf or hpsch)
Szymanowska (pf)
Valentine, A. (pf or hpsch; vln or fl/pf
    or hpsch)
Wuiet (pf)

1 violoncello and piano(s)

Cibbini (2 pfs)
Edelmann
Liebmann
Martainville (vlc or vln)
Szymanowska

2 instruments without keyboard

Anna Amalia, Prussia (vln/vla)

Beaumesnil (2 vlns or 2 vlcs or 2 cls)
Gail (2 vlns)
Galli (2 vlns, 2 fls or 2 guits)
Grétry (2 vlns or 2 vlcs)
Louis (2 vlns or voice/vln)
Papavoine (2 vlns)
Pean (2 fls or 2 vlns or 2 pardessus de
    viole or vielle and musette)
Pownall (2 fls or 2 obs or 2 vlns)
Sirmen (2 vlns)
Vannier (2 vlns or other instruments)

2 violins with basso continuo

Anna Amalia, Prussia
Blangini
Dufresne
Gambarini
Leonarda
Philarmonica (pseud.) (vlc or bc)
Prioli Morisina (with violone/hpsch)
Sirmen

*2 violins with basso continuo and at least partly
independent bass part (bass instrument indicated)*

Jacquet de la Guerre (viola da gamba)
Philarmonica (pseud.) (vlc and bc)

*2 strings and written-out keyboard (including
some ad lib parts and parts designated "violin
or flute")*

Brillon de Jouy (vln/vlc/pf)
Bussi (2 vlns/hpscd or pf)
Candeille (vln/vlc/pf)
Desfossez (vln/vlc ad lib/pf)
Dussek, K. (vln/vlc/pf)
Dussek, S. (vln/vlc/pf or harp)
Forrest (vln/vlc/pf or hpsch)
Lannoy de Clervaux (vln/vlc/pf or
    hpsch)
Liebmann (vln/ vlc/ pf)
Louis (2 vlns/hpsch or pf; vln/vlc/pf or
    hpsch)

Sirmen (2 vlns/hpsch/b)
Thiémé (vln/b(vlc)/pf)

String trio or string quartet with no keyboard

Dufresne (2 vlns/b [vlc])
Paradiser (Paradis?) (2 vlns/vla/vlc)
Sirmen (2 vlns/vlc; 2 vlns/vla/vlc)
String ensemble with keyboard

Barthélemon, C. (vln or fl/pf or hpsch/vlc)
Barthélemon, M. (pf/strings)
Brillon de Jouy (2 vlns/b [vlc]/hpsch)
Jacquet de la Guerre (2 vlns/viola da gamba [or vlc]/bc)
Stirling (pf/harp/vln/vlc)
Suarda (2 vln/vlc/hpsch)

Winds (see also orchestra, wind band, large vocal works)

Works including 1 or 2 flutes with keyboard (sometimes with other instruments)

Abrams (voice/pf/fl)
Ager (hpsch/vln or fl)
Ahlefeldt (voice/kbd/fl)
Anna Amalia, Prussia (fl/bc)
Balcarres (pf/vln/fl/other instruments)
Barthélemon, C. (pf or hpsch/vln or fl/vlc)
Blondel (7 instruments including flute)
Bon (fl/bc or vlc; 2 fls/bc)
Brillon de Jouy (pf/fl)
Candeille (voice/2 vlns or fls/bc)
Cantelo (fl or vln/ kbd)
Casson, M. (voice/pf or harp/fl and/or guit)
Catalani (voice/fl/pf)
Charriére (voice/fl/vln/hpsch)
Devonshire (2 hns/2 fls/ob/2 vlns/vla/pf)
Dussek, K. (fl/pf)
Dussek, S. (vln or fl/pf or hpsch)
Galli (2 fls or 2 guits/bc)

Gambarini (voice/fl/bc; fl or vln/hpsch)
Guedon de Presles (voice/fl/bc)
Guest (fl or vln/hpsch or pf)
Hardin (fl/vln/guit/hpsch)
Hinckesman (pf/fl ad lib)
Hortense, Holland (pf or harp/fl)
Hunter, H. (fl/pf)
Lady, a (voice/fl or guit/pf)
LeClere (voice/fl/ pf or harp)
Louis (fl/bc)
Macdonald (voice/kbd/fl or guit)
Martin (voice/pf/fl or vln)
Michon (2 fls, 2 obs, 2 vielles or 2 musettes/bc)
More (voice/pf/fl or guit)
Pean (2 fls, 2 vlns, 2 pardessus de viole, or vielle & musette)
Pinel (voice/2 fl/bc; fl or vln/bc)
Pownall (2 fl)
Skirving (fl/guit/pf)
Turner (voice/fl/bc)
Tytler (vln/fl/pf/and other instrument[s])
Valentine (fl or vln/pf or hpsch)
Vannier (vln/fl/ ob/pardessus de viole)
Westenholz (voice/fl/orch)

Works including clarinet (does not include orchestral works)

Anna Amalia, Weimar (pf/cl/vla/vlc)
Beaumesnil (2 vlns or 2 vlcs or 2 cls)
Dilcaro (2 cls)
Rossi (chalumeaux, in oratorio)
Tytler (cl/pf/vln/fl/and/or other instruments)

Works including oboe (does not include orchestral works)

Blondel (7 instruments including ob and bsn)
Chaistaignerais (ob/vln/bc?)
Devonshire (2 hns/2 fls/ob/2vlns/vla/pf)
Jacquet de la Guerre (ob/bc)
Laschansky (ob/orch)
Maria-Adelaïde, Savoy (obs/vlns/bc)

Michon (2 obs, 2 fls, 2 vielles, or 2 musettes/bc)
Noüailles (vlns/obs)
Pergolese (A/2 vlns/2 obs/2 hns/vla/vlc/db)
Pownall (2 obs)
Rochenard (vlns/obs/and other unspecified instruments)
Vannier (vln/fl/ob/pardessus de viole)

Works including trumpets and/or horns (does not include orchestral works)

Ahlefelt (S/2 vlns/2 hns/b)
Badalla (B/2 trs/org bc)
Brillon de Jouy (voice/hn/pf)
Delaval, Mme (pf/harp/2 hns ad lib)
Devonshire (2 hns/2 fls/ob/2vlns/vla/pf)
Dilcaro (2 hns/timpani)
Dufresnoy (pf or harp/ 2 hns ad lib)
Eberlin (S/2 vlns/2 hns/org bc)
Pergolese (A/2 vlns/2 obs/2 hns/vla/vlc/db)
Rossi (in oratorios)
Szymanowska (2 trs/2 hns)

Instrumentation undetermined or unspecified

Sketches

Amalia, M. F. A.
Anna Amalia, Prussia
Flad

Undetermined or unspecified

Ahlefeld
Ahlström
Anna Amalia, Prussia
Audini
Aurnhammer
Baird
Balcarres
Blondel (7 instruments, some unspecified)
Breitenbauch

Dilcaro
Genlis
Grétry
Johnson, L. (unspecified instrument/vlc or hpsch)
Lolo
Lolotte
Mano (instrument/bc)
Pinel
Remusat
Schuer Inseky
Sharpe (unspecified treble instrument, probably vln or fl/hpsch/vlc bc)
Sherp (unspecified treble instrument, probably vln or fl/hpsch/vlc bc)
Th., Mlle de

Large instrumental ensembles

Wind band

Anna Amalia, Prussia
D., Madam
Edwards
Krumpholtz, F.
Lady, of Charleston
Phillippine Charlotte

Orchestra (See also large vocal works which often include purely orchestral overtures, dances, and other pieces.)

Ahlefeldt
Anna Amalia, Weimar
Brandes (orch)
Brillon de Jouy
Duval, L.
Kauth
Maria Antonia Walpurgis
Martinez

Concerti and other extended works for solo instrument iand orchestra (solo instrument indicated)

Agnesi (kbd; hpsch)
Anna Amalia, Weimar (hpsch)

Candeille (pf or hpsch)
Cécile (pf)
Gambarini (org)
Laschansky (ob)
Martinez (hpsch)

Park(e) (2 pfs or 2 hpschs with no orch)
Schaden (pf)
Sirmen (vln)
Wilhelmine Sophie Fredericke (hpsch)